Somerset: *An Architectural History*

PAUL BAKER TOUART

Maryland Historical Trust
Somerset County Historical Trust, Incorporated

Somerset: *An Architectural History*

PAUL BAKER TOUART

December 1998

Paul B Touart

A cooperative project of

Maryland Historical Trust
Division of Historical and Cultural Programs
Department of Housing and Community Development
45 Calvert Street, Annapolis, Maryland 21401
and
Somerset County Historical Trust, Incorporated
Route 3, Box 331, Princess Anne, Maryland 21853

ISBN 1-878399-00-4 *(hardback)* ISBN 1-878399-06-3 *(paperback)*
Library of Congress Catalog Number: 89-622-651

This project has been administered through the Maryland Department of Housing and Community Development (DHCD) by the Maryland Historical Trust, an agency partially funded by the National Park Service, U.S. Department of the Interior. Content, opinions and conclusions expressed do not necessarily reflect the views and policies of the Department of the Interior.

This book was set in a digitized version of Janson, a typeface designed in the seventeenth century by Nicholas Kis.

Design by Whitney·Edwards Design, Easton, Maryland
Art Director: Charlene Whitney Edwards
Art Assistants: Elaine Brockley, Barbara Christopher and Annie Loweree
Printing by Collins Lithographing, Incorporated, Baltimore, Maryland

Title page illustration, Cottage Hall farm, c. 1900, courtesy of John Fitzgerald.

Contents

Preface

Since the late nineteenth century, travelers passing through the Eastern Shore have often remarked on the distinctive qualities of Somerset County architecture. The interest of scholars, county residents, and the general public is still increasing as people continue to discover one of the most diverse collections of eighteenth and nineteenth century buildings in Maryland. In addition to the county's architectural prominence, historians have acknowledged the pivotal role Somerset County played during the settlement of Maryland.

Unfortunately, little has been written to document or explain the county's valuable architectural legacy. Discouraging as well is the lack of a comprehensive history that explains in detail the overall development of Somerset County.

The Reverend Clayton Torrence holds the distinction as Somerset County's first historian. In his well-researched book, *Old Somerset on the Eastern Shore of Maryland*, published in 1935, Torrence began the task of chronicling the county's history. With countless hours of detailed research, he established a careful time line of early Somerset events, specializing in the settlement history of the region. As the Episcopal minister of St. Andrew's Church in Princess Anne, he focused special attention on the religious history of early Somerset as well as on important genealogical information. Torrence established high standards of research and analysis that have stood later historians and general readers in good stead.

Regrettably Torrence did not continue his writing, and no one has attempted a comprehensive county history since. Good work has been done on specific subjects, such as the history of Crisfield and its vicinity by Colonel Woodrow T. Wilson and the voluminous record research and transcription of Ruth T. Dryden. In his meticulous plotting of land survey boundaries, Harry L. Benson accomplished a herculean feat that has contributed greatly to knowledge of land ownership in Somerset County. More recent notable works include John R. Wennersten's *The Oyster Wars of Chesapeake Bay*. Probably most significant during the past decade is the work accomplished through the St. Mary's City Commission. This state agency has sponsored research on the impermanent architecture of the seventeenth century coupled with investigation into domestic life in the Chesapeake region during the seventeenth and eighteenth centuries.

No one, however, has undertaken the complex task of drawing together a comprehensive county history, and this volume is not intended to fill that void. Rather, the objective is to bring to print one of the least known collections of eighteenth and nineteenth century buildings in Maryland. Beyond the purely documentary intentions of the book is a broader interest in interpreting the buildings as they relate to the historic themes that have shaped Chesapeake and Eastern Shore life.

In an effort to place county buildings in perspective, a brief social and economic history of Somerset County has been assembled to accompany the building chronology. With the discussion organized in specific time periods, a clear developmental sequence emerges that details over three centuries of county history and architecture. Concerted efforts have been made to free this manuscript of mistakes; nonetheless, errors are inevitable in a project of this scope. Apologies are extended in these cases.

The publication of this architectural history has been the long-awaited desire of the Maryland Historical Trust and the Somerset County Historical Trust, Inc., who hope that its readers will gain a stronger awareness of Somerset architecture and history. The inventory process is part of a larger effort by the Maryland Historical Trust to catalog and register the state's architectural and archeological sites, so that Maryland's heritage may be better protected for future generations. The properties illustrated within this volume are largely in private hands and respect to personal property must be maintained.

This book is the result of many years of collaborative effort between the Maryland Historical Trust, an agency of the Maryland Department of Housing and Community Development, and the Somerset County Historical Trust, Inc., a non-profit preservation committee that has overseen the application of federal and state grant monies. Those at the Maryland Trust who have been directly involved in the administration of the project include J. Rodney Little, Mark R. Edwards, Rita Brunner, Ray Disney, and Miriam Hensley. Also, Pamela Caldwell, Amy Dorbin, Ron Andrews, Peter Kurtze, and more recently Kathy Lopez and Tom Lutz have provided assistance with contractual obligations and have attended to the various tasks necessary for the successful completion of yearly schedules.

A book of this scope incurs many debts along the way beyond its financial and contractual operations. Many long and rewarding hours have been spent mulling over various aspects of Somerset County history and architecture. Tom

Davidson, Richard Hughes, and especially Orlando Ridout V have contributed generous amounts of their time and expertise to the chapters. In addition, Edward Chappell, Willie Graham, John Bernard, and Jeff Bostetter of the Colonial Williamsburg Architectural Research Department along with Orlando Ridout V and Nancy Kurtz of the Maryland Historical Trust have contributed in various ways to the high quality of the line drawings contained within these pages. As editor, Pamela James Blumgart deserves special recognition for her long hours of work and dedication to crafting the best book possible from a rough manuscript.

In Somerset County hundreds of local residents have been generous with their time and knowledge of local history. The amount of detailed architectural information contained within these pages is a true testimony to the number of cooperative property owners who afforded me access to the most remote and private spaces of their homes.

Local support was provided by a number of county groups and individuals who deserve particular recognition. The Somerset County Arts Council has been extremely supportive with successive grants that have funded artistically related portions of the book. Perhaps the most significant volunteer aspect of this seemingly endless project was the intensive land records and genealogy research largely supplied through the untiring efforts of Meredith Johnson and Joseph Shores. Their charitable natures and strong interest in accurate family histories and property chains resulted in a wealth of intimate detail not found in another book of this kind.

Also instrumental in the research effort were Kent Griffith and Michael and Kathy Day. Kent, a local railroad historian, provided indepth insight into the rail history of the Eastern Shore and unselfishly shared his wealth of transcribed period accounts. The high quality of the image reproductions is largely due to the work of Michael and Kathy Day of the Image Preservation Company, whose standards of excellence in photography are unmatched on the Shore. In addition, Randy Stadler deserves credit for introducing me to the computer technology that expedited the writing stages of this expansive tome. Lastly, the Somerset County commissioners are recognized for the office and secretarial assistance they provided.

Despite this array of diverse cooperation, the past six years of research and writing would not have begun without the foresight and stamina of the Somerset County Historical Trust, Inc. The committee has been chaired during this period by Gale H. Yerges, whose professionalism and drive have inspired loyalty and utmost commitment to the production of this book. During the period of survey and publication the committee has included, Mark C. Adams, Freedom Ainsworth, Atwood Barwick, Mr. and Mrs. Thomas Bennett, John C. Bond, Mrs. Omar Carey, Charles C. Chervenie, Mrs. Robert Creed, E. McMaster Duer, Mr. and Mrs. Robert W. Erickson, George B. Fitzgerald, Fred T. Ford, Jr., Mrs. Ralph French, Thomas S. George, Jr., David Germanowski, Mrs. B. K. Haffner, Mrs. John D. Haffner, Elizabeth W. Hall, Mrs. Edison L. Hawkins, Mrs. Gerry Harrington, John Jeffries, Wilmer O. Lankford, Mrs. Thomas Larsen, Charles Massey, Mrs. Harry Miller, Mrs. Stephen Monick, Mrs. William Morsell, Jr., Mrs. Thomas Nicholson, Mr. and Mrs. Charles Nittel, James G. Oglesby, Mrs. Elmo Powell, Mrs. William H. Ruark, Richard P. Smith, Mrs. Reed Taylor, Mrs. Joan Terry, Mrs. Paul V. Twining, Jr., Mrs. William G. Vessey, and Wayne Winebrenner. Those not on the committee but who have offered financial support or volunteer assistance are remembered in the donors' list in the back of the book.

It is impossible to recognize everyone in these acknowledgments, but I would lastly like to thank my friends in Somerset County for patiently listening to the neverending ordeal of producing this book and, especially, my parents, Robert Louis and Lois Rogers Touart, for their consistent and everpresent support of my interest in architectural history.

Paul Baker Touart
Westover, Maryland
June 1989

An Architectural History of Somerset County, Maryland

CHAPTER I,
"Their houses are built like our Arbors"
Richard B. Hughes

When the land that is now Somerset County was first inhabited by man approximately 12,000 years ago, the landscape bore little resemblance to the scene that greeted the first European settlers. Massive ice sheets, then in retreat from their furthest southern advance into present-day New York, Pennsylvania, and New Jersey, profoundly influenced the geography of the region. Evidence from Virginia, New Jersey, and North Carolina indicates that by 12,500 B.C. the larger region had gradually changed from treeless tundra to a mixed environment of grasslands and open coniferous forests of spruce, pine, and fir.[1] The climate was cold with high levels of precipitation. Wildlife in the region included giant sloth, mastodon, mammoth, caribou, moose, bison, and musk ox.[2] A gradual warming took place during the Paleo-Indian period (10,000 B.C.-7500 B.C.); nonetheless, the presence of a cold-tolerant species of spruce along the Pocomoke River as late as 7000 B.C. indicates a cold climate persisted for a very long time.

Perhaps the greatest effect on the landscape came from the dramatically low sea levels. A vast amount of free water on the earth's surface was locked up in the snow and great glaciers formed in the last Ice Age. This frozen water had

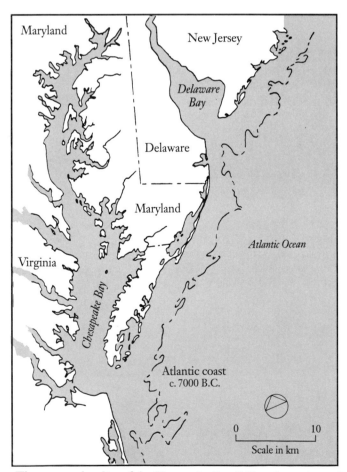
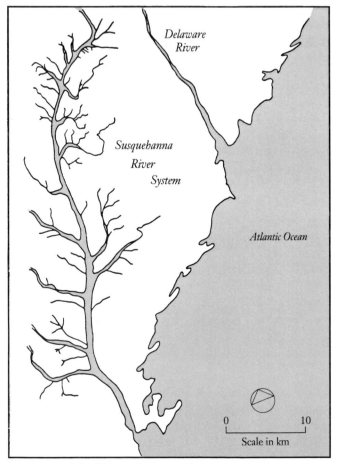

The current shoreline of the Chesapeake Bay (left) and a conjectural reconstruction of the Chesapeake region shoreline c. 7000 B.C. (right) (Steve Wilke and Gail Thompson, Prehistoric Archeological Resources in the Maryland Coastal Zone, *Maryland Department of Natural Resources, 1977).*

Indians fishing as depicted by Theodore de Bry after watercolors by John White, c. 1585 (courtesy of the British Museum and Dover Publications, Inc. from A briefe and true report of the new found land of Virginia, Thomas Harriot, *1972).*

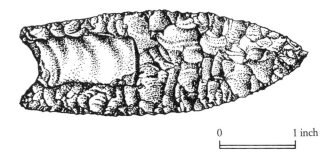

A characteristic Paleo-Indian fluted projectile point from Maryland's Eastern Shore, Nancy Kurtz.

never melted, drastically decreasing the amount of liquid water in the rivers, bays, seas, and oceans. At the height of the Ice Age, the sea level was approximately 130 meters (427 feet) below its present height.[3] This dramatically low sea level meant the Chesapeake Bay did not exist. Where the bay lies today was dry land, broken only by the wide valley of the Susquehanna River. The Susquehanna ran south-southeast until it emptied into the Atlantic Ocean from a shoreline that lay 50 to 100 miles east of its present location.

Archeological evidence indicates man first entered the area at the end of the last Ice Age, around 10,000 B.C. In Somerset County the only traces that remain of these Paleo-Indian groups are isolated finds of the characteristic fluted projectile or "arrow" points they made from stone. No camps or occupation sites have been found, and the environmental changes that have occurred since this first habitation make it likely most Paleo-Indian sites lie beneath the waters of the Chesapeake and its tributaries. That these submerged lands were once the high and dry homeland of these early people is clearly demonstrated by the frequency with which watermen dredging for oysters bring up Paleo-Indian fluted points.

It has traditionally been postulated that Paleo-Indian groups lived primarily by hunting the large game animals in the region. This theory may be correct for the earliest part of the period, but as the climate warmed the inhabitants appear to have adopted a more diversified subsistence strategy. The snow and ice melted and the sea level rose, leading to changes in vegetation and wildlife. In response, the people began to exploit a wider range of food resources, although hunting probably remained their primary source of food.

Little is known about their social organization, but the Paleo-Indians who inhabited the region probably lived in flexible, band-level social groups much like present-day hunter-gatherers. These bands would have been nomadic, moving throughout the year to exploit seasonally available foods or other resources such as the stone they used to make tools. The concentration of Paleo-Indian artifact finds in areas where high quality stone was available as cobble or other deposits suggests such sources may have become the focal point of Paleo-Indian settlement patterns.[4]

Reconstruction of a European late Paleolithic period Magdalenian tent from Pincevin, France. The mobile Magdalenian hunters of Europe lived in easily portable structures that were probably very similiar to the dwellings of Somerset County's Paleo-Indian people (courtesy of Hamlyn Publishing Group Limited, The Pictorial Encyclopedia of The Evolution of Man, *J. Jelinek, 1975*).

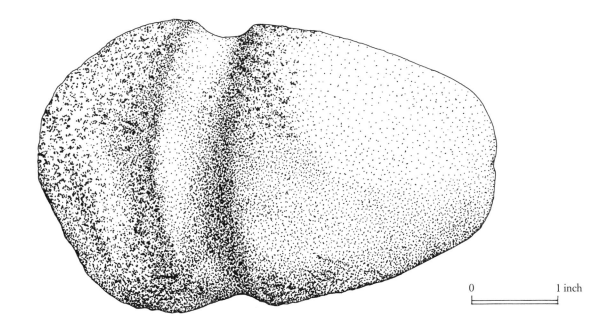

0   1 inch

An Archaic period ground and polished stone axe, Nancy Kurtz.

Although no traces remain, it seems likely the dwellings of these nomadic people were constructed with a wood or bone framework and covered with hides or other materials such as woven mats. These structures would have been easy to erect and take down, an essential feature for the frequent moves their lifestyle required.

By 6500 B.C., the gradual warming of the climate begun in the Paleo-Indian period had resulted in a landscape markedly different from the one the earliest Paleo-Indian settlers encountered. The mixed grassland and open coniferous forest had been replaced by a forested environment very similar to that which greeted the first European explorers. The Chesapeake Bay was formed as low-lying land was flooded by the rising sea level. A modern continental climate with marked seasonal variations in temperature and precipitation prevailed. As forests spread and swamps and marshes formed, rich animal and vegetable food resources appeared. The vegetation and animal communities during the Archaic period (7500 B.C.-1200 B.C.) were similar to those on the lower Eastern Shore today, although they had very different patterns of distribution and association.

In response to this vastly different environment, human groups developed totally new lifeways, which are reflected in the archeological record. New tool kits appeared, with much more variety in type than those seen in the Paleo-Indian period. For the first time, stone tools fashioned by grinding and polishing appeared alongside tools made with the earlier, flaking technology. The new ground stone tools included axes, gouges, grinding stones, and plant processing tools developed to exploit the resources of the changed environment.[5]

A greater number of archeological sites is noted on the lower Eastern Shore during the early to middle part of the Archaic period, possibly indicating an increased population in the area.[6] These inhabitants focused increasingly on seasonal use of resources in response to the more dramatic variations in the climate. When an abundance of seasonal foods was available locally, they lived in large camps that probably housed bands of families.[7] When resources near the base camp were depleted or declined with the change of seasons, the bands split into smaller groups and moved to areas with food resources sufficient to support their reduced numbers. These smaller groups, probably individual families or related family groups, ventured out on short-term forays to hunt or gather foods. When the food supply again increased in the vicinity of the base camp, the smaller groups returned to the larger social unit. This flexible lifestyle allowed people to adjust to the variation in food resources during the year and to respond to declining food yields caused by overharvesting or other factors.

By the middle of the Archaic period, the inhabitants were making stone tools from exotic materials unavailable locally, suggesting the development of increasingly widespread contact with distant groups.[8] Whether this contact was direct, involving travel, or whether the exotic stones were traded from group to group over long distances is unclear. It is clear, however, that middle Archaic peoples in the Somerset region were making a significant number of their stone tools out of materials whose nearest source was western Maryland, Pennsylvania, or beyond. This growing preference for non-local materials suggests the development of an increasingly complex society by 4000 B.C.

Around 3000 B.C. the climate of the lower Eastern Shore became warmer and drier than it had been during the previous 2,000 years. This change in climate, particularly the decrease in precipitation, had a clear effect on the distribution of animal and plant communities in the area. The oak and pine forests probably expanded, and swamp areas along rivers such as the Pocomoke became established. Changes in human society seem to reflect this environmental shift. Most importantly, the archeological record shows people were becoming less nomadic and more sedentary in their lifestyle. Larger groups were settling in larger base camps and staying in them much longer. Although smaller groups still went out to obtain

Semi-subterranean pit house, Poplar Thicket site, 7S-G22 (courtesy of the Delaware Division of Historical and Cultural Affairs).

resources away from the main camp, most people stayed in one place most of the time.

The main base camp was now located in an area very different from the camps of the early Archaic period people. The increasingly warm, dry conditions undoubtedly made it advantageous to settle near a dependable source of fresh water. Accordingly, the new, larger camps tended to be situated along large watercourses, often near highly productive estuaries.[9]

The rise in sea level gradually slowed, and more stable river, estuarine, and marsh habitats formed, providing new food sources such as oysters, waterfowl, and fish that seasonally ascended the rivers to spawn. Not surprisingly, Archaic period camps have been discovered in areas suited to the exploitation of these food resources. Shellfish, particularly oysters, became such an important food that large heaps or middens of discarded oyster shells were created. Surviving shell middens are often many feet thick and cover thousands of square feet. Shelltown in lower Somerset County owes its name to one such remnant of the past.

The first physical evidence of houses on the Eastern

Shore and in Delaware dates from this later portion of the Archaic period. Semi-subterranean pit houses and associated pit features used for food storage have been excavated in Delaware and in Cecil County, Maryland. This type of house consisted of a large oval pit approximately three meters (ten feet) or more in maximum diameter, which was dug into the ground to a depth of up to 110 centimeters (three and a half feet). The walls of the pit were normally vertical with a flat, hard-packed dirt floor. One excavated house had a stone fire hearth in the center of the floor. Around the perimeter of the pit archeologists have found postmolds—dark circular stains in the earth where posts standing in holes had rotted away. These features indicate where the posts or poles that made up the house structure once stood.[11]

It is not clear why houses were constructed in this manner, but it is likely the pit house provided a more weathertight and comfortable dwelling than one located directly on the ground surface. The labor required to build these houses as well as their semi-permanent form emphasizes the increasingly sedentary lifestyle that had arisen by this time.

Evidence that the people in the region had contact with

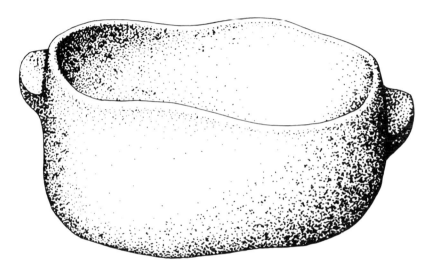

A characteristic Archaic period carved soapstone vessel with lug handles, Nancy Kurtz (after a steatite cooking kettle in The New England Indians, *by C. Keith Wilbur, published in 1978 by Globe Pequot Press).*

outside groups, largely through trade and exchange of new materials, continues into the late Archaic period. At that time, the exchange of exotic materials appears to have intensified, accompanied by the development of a distinctive social stratification. Finds of large caches or hordes of exotic raw materials such as the stone rhyolite from western Maryland and Pennsylvania indicate access to these materials was controlled, most probably by special high status groups.[12] Why these groups were formed is unclear, but an apparent growth in population combined with a more restricted, sedentary lifestyle probably encouraged social stratification as a means of regulating access to scarce resources. Over the next 2,000 years, this stratified social structure evolved into the complex system of chiefdoms, tribes, and allied confederacies encountered by Europeans when they first came face to face with the native people of the region.

By the beginning of the Woodland period (1200 B.C.-A.D. 1600), the people on the lower Shore were inhabiting a landscape virtually identical to that noted by the earliest European explorers. Vast hardwood forests, stable coastal marshlands, and interior swamps provided a rich abundance of game

such as deer, turkey, rabbit, waterfowl, and shellfish as well as a vast diversity of plant foods.

During the initial portion of the Woodland period, ceramic vessels made of fired clay and tempering material made their first appearance. In general, the earliest ceramic vessels exhibit the flat-bottomed shape with lug handles characteristic of earlier, late Archaic period vessels carved from soapstone. The influence of the earlier technology is further evident in the use of crushed soapstone as the tempering agent in some of the earliest ceramic vessels. Interestingly, however, this pottery apparently was not the first ceramic to be made on the lower Eastern Shore.[13] A different type, named after the Somerset County locale of Dames Quarter, used a crushed black stone as the tempering agent. This Dames Quarter ware seems to appear slightly later than the soapstone-tempered ceramics noted elsewhere. The apparent lack of soapstone-tempered ceramics at sites in the vicinity of Somerset County suggests a conservative continuation of non-ceramic Archaic period technologies.

Like the ceramic shapes, early Woodland period settlement patterns show an apparent continuation of late Archaic

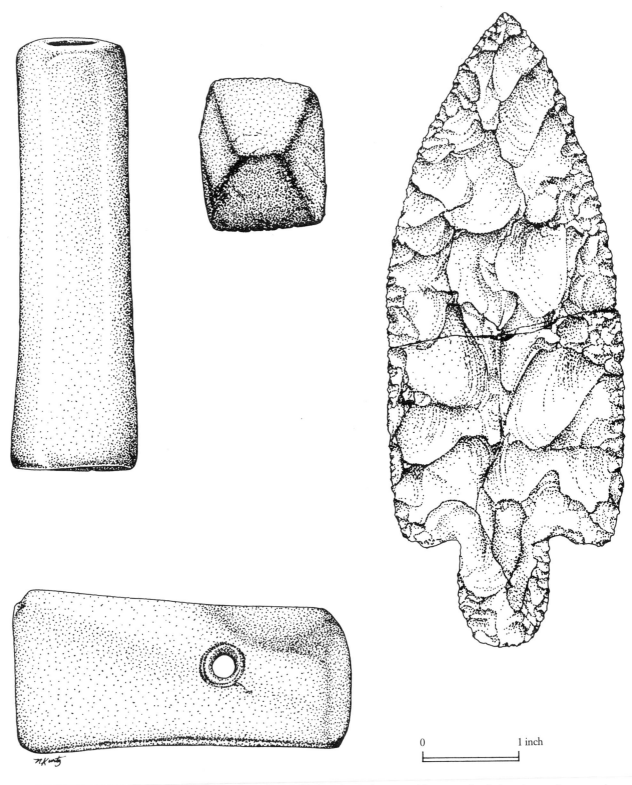

0   1 inch

Characteristic Adena artifacts, including a chipped stone blade, a hematite pyramid, a carved tubular pipe, and a ground and polished gorget (from the West River Adena site, Anne Arundel County, Maryland), Nancy Kurtz.

period adaptations. Large base camps with smaller outlying camps and resource procurement areas continue to appear in the archeological record. However, an apparent increase in the number of storage pits at the base camps suggests the lifestyle became more focused on settlement in large, fixed camps.

Changes in social organization and the long distance trade of exotic goods also continued to evolve from trends first noted during the later part of the Archaic period. One of the most dramatic manifestations of the complexity of prehistoric life-ways on the lower Eastern Shore was the appearance of traditions and goods associated with the Adena culture, based far to the west in present-day Ohio. The Adena culture was marked by elaborate burial customs in which certain members of the society were buried with rich offerings of ceremonial goods such as copper beads, tubular pipes, gorgets (probable personal ornaments made of polished stone), and elaborate chipped stone blades.

Early Woodland period sites showing Adena characteristics have been found at a number of places on the Eastern Shore and in Delaware and at one site in Anne Arundel County on Maryland's western shore. The Nassawango burial site, excavated in Worcester County, Somerset's neighbor, contained copper artifacts made of metal from the Great Lakes region and tubular pipes of Ohio fireclay.[14]

Interestingly, these Adena cultural manifestations apparently did not occur anywhere between these locations in the Chesapeake area and the tribe's Ohio homeland. The reasons for this are not known, but immigration of actual Adena groups is considered unlikely. Rather, it seems probable that ideas as well as goods were transferred through the obviously elaborate exchange network. Other aspects of the material and social order of the native Chesapeake and Delaware peoples show a direct connection to the earlier inhabitants of the region from at least the Archaic period. The presence of ceremonial burial sites indicates continued development of the stratified social structure that apparently had arisen in the later phase of the Archaic period.

Archeological evidence suggests that settlement, subsistence, and social patterns remained relatively stable until approximately A.D. 1000. At that time, multiple changes occurred that indicate far-reaching alterations in the lifestyle of the prehistoric inhabitants of Delaware and the Eastern Shore. Exotic materials disappear from the archeological record, showing a clear breakdown in the trade networks. Elsewhere along the Atlantic seaboard, settlement shifted to rich river bottom lands. This change was probably due to the appearance and growing importance of agriculture as a source of food. Rich floodplain soils would have been best suited to the planting and growth of domesticated plants such as corn, beans, and squash, which first appeared around this time.

On the lower Eastern Shore as in much of the middle Atlantic region, archeological evidence indicates wild food resources were heavily used in conjunction with the new agricultural crops.[15] The surplus food produced by farming was a cause of the increasingly sedentary lifestyle. However, the main focus of subsistence probably still revolved around hunting and gathering rather than full-time farming.

Archeologists have equated differing types of ceramics and their varying forms of decoration with different social groups and traditions.[16] The archeological record of the late Woodland period reveals that distinct groups with varying technological and social traits inhabited Delaware and the Chesapeake region. This increasing cultural diversity probably led to the variety of peoples noted by the first European explorers.

On the lower Eastern Shore at this time, the shell-tempered ceramics known as Townsend ware predominated. On portions of the western shore archeological sites exhibit a profusion of Potomac Creek ware, which is a differently decorated ceramic tempered with sand or crushed quartz. Potomac Creek ware occurs at sites in Somerset County, but it is always far less abundant than Townsend ware. It is likely the Townsend ceramic-making people were the indigenous inhabitants of the area, but they clearly had some contact with the Potomac Creek peoples to the west.

Archeological investigations of Potomac Creek sites in the Shenandoah and Potomac river valleys have provided evidence of large villages surrounded by wooden stockades made of posts set upright in the ground. These stockaded villages often included large pits containing human burials. Trash deposits with remains of small mammals, fish, shellfish, and agricultural crops such as corn and squash show a subsistence pattern that included both farming and hunting-gathering, much like that noted on the lower Eastern Shore. Remnants of similar palisaded villages have been found on the Eastern Shore of Maryland.[17] The presence of stockades around late Woodland villages may indicate the appearance of increasing competition among native American groups, competition that

An artist's reconstruction of typical Algonquian circular and rectangular structures (courtesy of C. A. Weslager).

gave rise to hostilities and warfare. The reasons for this development are unclear, but increasing population, competition for resources, and social diversity are likely factors.

When the native American peoples of the Eastern Shore and Delaware first came into contact with Europeans is also unclear. As early as 1524 Giovanni da Verrazano had landed on the east coast of North America at a place he called "Arcadia." This spot was probably on the coast of Delaware or Maryland, perhaps in present-day Worcester County. Unfortunately, Verrazano's explorations produced little or no specific information about the area. Only in 1608 with the exploratory voyage of Captain John Smith did precise descriptions of the region and its inhabitants become available. Smith explored many rivers and inlets and later prepared detailed maps of much of the Chesapeake Bay region using information gathered during his 1608 voyage.

Regrettably, Smith's observations were far less detailed for the area of present-day Somerset County than for other locations, such as the Potomac and Patuxent rivers. However, it is known that European contact with the native people of the lower Eastern Shore did not result in the immediate and total disruption of the cultural pattern seen during the later part of the Woodland period.[18] Initial contact primarily came through trade rather than European settlement. Increased competition among native groups for control of this trade probably affected native American settlement patterns and may have led to increasing hostility among the diverse cultural groups. The people of the Eastern Shore belonged to the Algonquian-speaking group, which inhabited most of the lands bordering the Chesapeake. To the north lived fierce Iroquois groups, primarily the Susquehannocks, who raided south into Algonquian territory, although they never reached as far as present-day Somerset County.

Seventeenth century records give vivid descriptions and drawings of Algonquian life along the eastern seaboard. Captain John Smith described houses in the midst of gardens of 20 to 200 acres and villages containing from 2 to 200 houses. These dwellings took two basic forms, either circular structures up to 25 feet in diameter or rectangular structures about 12 feet in width and anywhere from 20 to 100 feet in length. Wrote Smith,

Their houses are built like our Arbors, of small young springs bowed and tyed, and so close covered with Mats, or the barkes of trees very handsomely, that notwithstanding either winde, raine, or weather, they are as warme as stooves, but very smoaky, yet at the toppe of the house there is a hole made for the smoake to goe into right over the fire.[19]

The poles were set in the ground a few feet apart around the perimeter, and their tops were bent over and tied together with bark, fibrous roots, or hide strips. Rectangular houses had ends formed by upright poles. The bark or reed mats that covered the framework could be rolled up to admit light and air in the warmer months. Windows did not appear until later, when they were adopted as a result of European influence. A palisade wall often enclosed the main villages. In 1585 Thomas Harriot described an Algonquian village in North Carolina as houses

covered and enclosed some with matts, and some with the barcks of trees. All compassed about with small poles stuck thick together instead of a wall.[20]

Food was obtained by a combination of cultivation, hunting, fishing, and gathering, as it had been for centuries. Smith

The Algonquian village of Secota as depicted by Theodore de Bry after watercolors of John White, c. 1585 (courtesy of the British Museum and Dover Publications, Inc.).

Indians in body paint as depicted by Theodore de Bry after watercolors of John White, c. 1585 (courtesy of the British Museum and Dover Publications, Inc.).

wrote that in Virginia, "for neere 3 parts of the yeare, they naturally affordeth from hand to mouth...."[21] This comment suggests cultivated foods provided little more than one-third of total food production. John White's drawings of Indians hunting and fishing have left a vivid picture of these activities in Algonquian life.

Overall, the records left by early European explorers present a picture of an intensely vital and diverse native culture at the time of first European contact. The native Americans were a people of varied culture, vast skill, and far-reaching knowledge concerning the world they lived in. Unfortunately, they were also a people doomed to all but disappear from their land within a few decades. The reasons for this disappearance are numerous. Disease, warfare, forest clearance, and migration all contributed to their decline and eventually their almost total absence from the historical record.

The colonial Maryland government recognized four major Indian groups on the lower Eastern Shore—the Nanticokes, Pocomokes, Choptanks, and Assateagues. Of these, the Pocomokes were the principal group in what is today Somerset County. The Pocomoke Indians were first described by Captain John Smith, who had encountered them during his 1608 voyage of exploration. Smith recorded that the

people at first with great fury seemed to assault us, yet at last with song and daunces and much mirth became very tractable.[22]

He also noted they were smaller in stature than Indians living to the south on the Eastern Shore of Virginia and that they spoke a different dialect.

Closely affiliated with the Pocomokes were at least three

other groups known as the Annemessex, Manokin, and Monie, who lived immediately to the north along the waterways that now bear their names.[23] Throughout the first half of the seventeenth century, all the Indians in the region were subjected to increasing pressure from the growing numbers of European settlers seeking to settle and farm the land. The Pocomoke in particular were savagely harassed by Colonel Edmund Scarburgh, who lived on the Virginia portion of the lower Eastern Shore. In *Captains and Mariners of Early Maryland*, Raphael Semmes describes an attack Scarburgh led against the Pocomoke:

> *In order to have some excuse for his campaign against these Indians, Colonel Scarburgh had a rumor spread about that the Pocomokes were planning to massacre the whites. After he collected a troop of well armed and experienced Indian fighters, the Virginia colonel set out to "capture or kill the King of Pocomoke, the leading spirit of the supposed conspiracy." The hiding place of the Indians was soon located. The order to charge was given. Some of the terrified savages were shot down in the first onslaught; others were slashed to death with "the sabres and long hunting knives" of the troopers. Many were taken prisoners. Two of the captives, whom Scarburgh considered ringleaders, were "bound neck and heels with a chain."[24]*

Subject to depredations such as this, the Pocomoke, Manokin, and Annemessex Indians abandoned their land and moved to the east. There they joined another group known as the Assateagues, who were living in a village called Askiminikansen, located in present-day Worcester County.[25]

Twelve Indian towns on the lower Eastern Shore are mentioned in surviving colonial records. Of these, the seven known as Queponqua, Askiminikansen, Parrahockon, Cottinghams Creek, Tundotanke, Puckamee, and Great Monie fell within the boundaries of colonial Somerset County, which included present-day Worcester and Wicomico counties.[26] These towns were the outgrowth of increasing European demand for land and the Indians' resultant complaints to the colonial government. In response to these complaints, the government set aside tracts of land for the exclusive use of the Indians. Some of these towns, which were similar to modern reservations, were quite large. Askiminikansen, the home of the Pocomokes and the Assateagues, comprised 5,000 acres; Queponqua encompassed 3,000 acres; and Parrahockon 2,000 acres. However, continuous encroachment by Europeans throughout the seventeenth and eighteenth centuries resulted in the steady shrinking of all these Indian towns.

The last reference to the Pocomoke Indians as a separate people occurred in May 1686. At that time, the Emperor of the Assateague mentioned the Pocomokes in a petition to the colonial Council of Maryland as one of the eight groups under his authority.[27] Continuing encroachment by European settlers caused most of the groups living under the emperor's rule to move north into present-day Delaware. By 1742 this group had disappeared from the historical record, and by 1770 all reference to Indian towns on the Eastern Shore of Maryland ceases.[28] 🌳

CHAPTER II, 1608-1700
"With Fruitfull and Delightsome Land"

Laced with navigable rivers and situated between the Atlantic Ocean and Chesapeake Bay, the lower Eastern Shore of Maryland figured prominently in the early history of the Chesapeake region. For more than a century before the settlement of Somerset County, the area was described by explorers and traversed by trappers and Indian traders. The Maryland proprietors viewed early settlement and development of the lower Shore as principal achievements in an effort to strengthen provincial boundaries against encroachment from adjacent colonial governments. For the settlers, the region provided the opportunity to engage in a lucrative though volatile European tobacco market in a virgin and religiously tolerant territory.

Little more than a quarter century after Christopher Columbus's voyage to the New World, European explorers were skirting Chesapeake Bay in hopes of discovering a water passage to the East Indies. Giovanni da Verrazano, a Florentine sailing under the French flag in 1524, is known to have reached the peninsula lying between the bay and the Atlantic. He landed on the ocean side and crossed to the bay side, later reporting he had seen the Western Ocean. Shortly afterwards, Lucas d'Allyon of Spain entered the Chesapeake with identical dreams of reaching the Spice Islands by sailing westward. In 1603 Bartholomew Gilbert landed on the tip of the peninsula in an effort to establish a settlement under the authority of James I, the first Stuart king of England. Gilbert's party was attacked by Indians, and Gilbert and one companion were killed.[1]

Although these early explorers reached the Chesapeake, it was not until John Smith's voyages of 1607-1608 that detailed exploration and observations were made of the country surrounding the Bay. Smith described the region:

Within is a country that may have the prerogative over the most pleasant places of Europe, Asia, Africa, or America, knowne, for large and pleasant navigable rivers: heaven and earth never agreed better to frame a place for mans habitation...were it fully manured and inhabited by industrious people. Here are mountaines, hils, plaines, valleyes, rivers and brookes all running most pleasantly into a faire Bay compassed but for the mouth with fruitfull and delightsome land.[2]

Smith explored the western and northern Chesapeake in

some detail, but he did not venture far inland on the Eastern Shore. His expedition did find itself off the coast of Somerset County looking for water at one point, and he wrote of the region that

the Land [is] but low, yet it may prove very commodious, because it is but a ridge of land betwixt the Bay and the maine Ocean. Finding this Easterne shore, [to be] shallow broken Isles, and for most part without fresh water...so broad is the bay here, we could scarce perceive the great high clifts on the other side....[3]

Captain Smith's voyage in 1608, the settlement of Jamestown the year before, and the publication of Smith's map in 1612 marked the beginning of a half century of trade and exploration in what later became Somerset County. Traders and trappers made forays along the waterways of the region during the 1620s and 1630s. One reference to this travel is in a deposition John Westlock submitted to the Somerset Court in 1670. Then ninety years old, Westlock referred to "the pointe of the forke where I traded...fifty years agoe...."[4]

Also in the second decade of the seventeenth century, George Calvert (circa 1580-1632), Baron Baltimore and friend to Charles I, was negotiating a royal charter for a colony on Chesapeake Bay. Issued in June 1632 to Cecilius Calvert, the Second Lord Baltimore, the provincial charter of Maryland included lands roughly bounded by the thirty-eighth and fortieth degree north latitudes.[5] This vast, unsettled region was fixed between the Virginia colony to the south and early Dutch and later Quaker settlements to the east and north. Despite royal signatures on the Calvert charter, disagreements over the exact boundaries between neighboring colonies instigated armed and verbal disputes that lasted until the nineteenth century.

The earliest and best remembered conflict over the authority of the Calvert charter involved William Claiborne, who founded a trading colony on Kent Island in 1631 under the auspices of William Cloberry and Company, an English mercantile firm. Claiborne was given the right to trade with the Indians in the Chesapeake region, and as a result, established a trading post on the southern tip of Kent Island. As might be expected, Claiborne violently opposed the Calvert charter, for it infringed on his claim to the Kent Island settlement.

John Smith, Virginia, *1608 (courtesy of the Maryland State Archives, Huntingfield Map Collection, MdHR G 1399-101).*

Claiborne's refusal to acknowledge Cecilius Calvert's proprietary right to the developed land on Kent Island eventually resulted in armed conflict at the mouth of the Pocomoke River. On April 23, 1635, Claiborne's armed wherry *Cockatrice* clashed with two Maryland vessels, *St. Helen* and *St. Margaret*. The *Cockatrice* surrendered, but two weeks later another engagement evidently ended in Claiborne's favor. Nevertheless, royal opinion in London sided with Calvert sovereignty over Kent Island.[6]

Meanwhile, Leonard Calvert, first provincial governor and representative for his brother Cecilius, supervised the founding of St. Mary's City in 1634.[7] During the following decades, the vast province was slowly divided into counties, beginning with St. Mary's in 1637 and followed by Kent County by 1642 and several Western Shore counties during the 1650s.[8]

Prior to 1660, no colonial settlements had been established on the lower Eastern Shore. However, in March of that year, the General Assembly of the Virginia colony passed a law forbidding the expression of the Quaker faith.[9] Whatever political or military reasons there may have been for this, the prohibitive Virginia policy enhanced settlement of the border territories between Maryland and Virginia.

In direct response to a petition from Virginia Quakers asking permission to relocate in the Maryland province, Governor Philip Calvert penned a proclamation on November 6, 1661:

...takeing into Consideracion the peticion of divers persons...now or late Inhabitants of Northampton County otherwise called Accomack in Virginia who are desirous to transplant themselves and familyes into this Province And for the more speedy and Effectuall prosecucion of his said Lordships Comand to me to see that parte of this Province next adjoyneing to the County aforesaid peopled and for the ease and benefitt of all such persons whoe shall transplant themselves into this Province from Accomack aforesaid I have nominated constituted and impowred...Coll Edmund Scarburgh Randall Revell and John Elzey Gent or any two of them being within this Province to grant warrants for land....[10]

Settlements were established during the following six months, first at Annemessex and shortly after at Manokin.

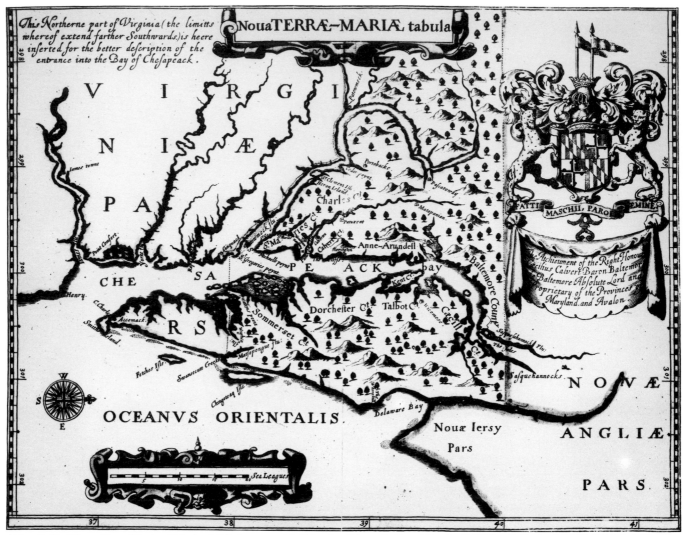

John Ogilby, Noua Terra Mariae Tabula, *1671 (courtesy of the Maryland State Archives, Huntingfield Map Collection MdHR G 1399-187).*

The Annemessex settlement, chiefly consisting of Quaker followers, was located south of the Great Annemessex River and northeast of Coulbourne's Creek. By March 1662 the Manokin settlement is thought to have been firmly rooted along the Manokin River and Back Creek.[11] This settlement immediately became the seat of the Eastern Shore commissioners. A liberal provincial land policy ensured fifty acres for every person transported, "upon such Condicions & tearmes as are Expressed in his Lordships condicon of plantacion now remayning upon Record regulated according to his lordships Declaracion of the 22th September 1658...."[12]

On May 2, 1662, Randall Revell, as a commissioner of the Eastern Shore, reported to the Provincial Council on the extent of settlement in Manokin and Annemessex:

...there weare now at this present seated there fifty tithable psons viz at Monokin and Anamessicks a place distant som fower miles from Monokin. that thy had made an agreement with their neighbour Indians viz: the

Emperor of Nanticoke. which they desired mought be by the Governor and Councell confirmed, which is as followeth. viz that the Emperor and his Jndians weare to have for every plantation six match coates to bee payd by them that seates such plantations. That they weare to bringe in all runaways for which they weare to receave a matchcoate p pole for every runaway delivered. that they should not Kill nor murther any the English, neither should any English murther any of theirs.[13]

Clearly, then, by 1662 settlers had established a foothold along the Annemessex and Manokin rivers in what was firmly believed to be the province of Maryland. Nonetheless, Colonel Edmund Scarburgh (also Scarborough), surveyor-general and treasurer of his Majesty for Virginia, attempted to claim the new settlements as part of the Virginia colony. At the same time, he instigated the formation of Accomac County, Virginia, which was divided from Northampton County in March 1662. Complaints from Northampton accusing Scarburgh, the commissioner for Accomac, of taking advantage of the situation "to our great detriment and Loss" foreshadowed the complaints Maryland settlers would soon have with him.[14]

In his effort to claim additional acreage for Accomac County, the irascible Scarburgh disagreed with the location of the northern boundary between Maryland and Virginia. His principal argument centered on the exact location of "Watkin's Point," which he insisted headed the Wicomico River rather than the Pocomoke River. On John Smith's map of 1612, the Pocomoke is labeled "River Wighco." Colonel Scarburgh interpreted "Wighco" as the Wicomico, which justified moving the Maryland-Virginia line thirty miles north of its original location.[15]

Without authorization from officials at Jamestown, Scarburgh undertook to demand obedience to the king and payment for their lands from the residents of Manokin and Annemessex. Early in 1663 he wrote to Randall Revell, then head of the settlement, claiming the territory for Virginia. In February of that year, Scarburgh arrested John Elzey, another early Somerset leader, while he was conducting business in Accomac. Scarburgh served Elzey with a letter demanding his obedience to the king and payment for the "right of land and gov'mt" in Manokin.[16]

Elzey responded to Scarburgh's epistle with another letter, and as a result Scarburgh freed him. Nevertheless, when Elzey returned to Manokin, he drafted an eloquent letter to Henry Sewall, a member of the Provincial Council of Maryland. His hope was to secure help, including defense, from Lord Baltimore:

> ...Now J beseech your honor that you will with what speed you can, urge his Lordship to consider our Condicion, how Wee lye betweene Sylla & Charibdis, not knowing how to gett out of this Labarinth. J could not understand but that hee doth intend to come up with a Competent Company to force us, who are not in a Capacity to defend our selves against the Pagans, who doe grow very insolent, & tells us Wee are Lyars, & that our greate Men care not for us, because that none of them comes to us.[17]

In response to Elzey's plea, the Council drafted a letter to Sir William Berkeley, governor of Virginia, on April 8, 1663, requesting a commission to establish the location of "Watkin's Point" according to Lord Baltimore's charter for Maryland. Five months passed before the Virginia Assembly convened on September 10, 1663, and established "An Act Concerning the Bounds of this Colony on the Eastern Shore." The legislation concluded that

> the same place of Wattkins point to be the northside of Wicomocoe river, on the Eastern shore, and neere unto and on the south side of the streight limbe opposite to Potuxent river,...within which bounds his majesties subjects that are now seated are hereby comanded to yeild due obedience at their perill,....[18]

The legislation went further to engage Colonel Edmund Scarburgh, John Catlett, and Richard Lawrence as representatives of the Virginia colony to meet with Lord Baltimore's lieutenants or deputies concerning the boundary controversy. In the meantime, however, Scarburgh was authorized to demand submission from those inhabitants living south of "Watkin's Point."[19]

Scarburgh interpreted this authorization in his own fashion, and during October 1663 descended on the settlements at Annemessex and Manokin, located in his words "on ye Eastern Shoare of Virginia." Accompanied by Colonel Stringer, "foure of ye Commission & about fourty horsemen," Colonel Scarburgh confronted first the Quaker men at Annemessex and then the settlers at Manokin.[20] After receiving hostile replies to his demands from the Quakers, Scarburgh left for the Manokin settlement where he was received in a cautious but more cordial manner. Since the Manokin settlers were fearful of reprisals from the local Indians, they welcomed the protection Scarburgh's forces afforded.[21] Indeed, the Manokin settlers' fears were well founded since a war had been fought with the Assateague Indians in northern Accomac County in 1659.[22]

By now the boundary question needed to be resolved. It was clear that Colonel Scarburgh had overstepped his authority, and Governor Calvert organized a commission consisting of Philip Calvert, chancellor of the Province, and Jerome White, surveyor-general, to represent Maryland interests in establishing the rightful location of "Watkins Point."[23] Finally, in June 1668, more than five years after Scarburgh first attempted to secure the Annemessex-Manokin settlements for Virginia, Philip Calvert and Edmund

Scarburgh, as surveyor-general of Virginia, were appointed by their respective governments to settle the boundary question. On June 25, 1668, the two men signed articles of agreement that guaranteed title to settlers holding land in the disputed territory. In the same document, confirmation of the site of Watkin's Point at the head of the Pocomoke River was secured, and a boundary line was run from there to the Atlantic Ocean.[24]

The political controversies and boundary disputes that beset Somerset County early in its history did not hamper the granting of land patents on the lower Eastern Shore. From 1661 to 1665 close to 80,000 acres were surveyed, almost 10 percent of the entire land mass of the region.[25] Settlement was located principally along the Pocomoke, Great Annemessex, Manokin, Wicomico, and Nanticoke rivers as well as Marumsco, Monie, and Back creeks.

In consequence of such extensive settlement, on August 22, 1666, Cecilius Calvert, Lord Baltimore, proclaimed that

> *wee for the ease & benifitt of the people of this our pvince & for the Speedy & more exact Administracon of Justice have erected & doe by theis pnts erect all that Tract of land within this our province of Maryland bounded on the South with a line drawne from Wattkins point (being the North point of that bay into which the River Wighco formerly called Wighcocomoco afterwards Pocomoke & now Wighcocomoco againe doth fall exclusively) to the Ocean on the East. Nantecoke river on the North & the Sound of Chesipiake bay on the West into a County by the name of Sommersett County in honour to our Deare Sister the lady Mary Somersett....*[26]

By the first month of the following year, court was held at Thomas Poole's house in Manokin, where the county commissioners met to consider several important topics. Chief among these was the decision that "A Tract of Land in ye most Conveniente place for the whole Countie be taken up for ye Counties use & a house to be builded thereupon." In addition, the commissioners described "The high way for ye Countie of Sommersett": "from ye Landing place upon Capt. Goyeders Land in Pocomoke river to Morumsco Dambs neare ye house of Robert Hignett." From Robert Hignett's, the highway continued "downe to ye head of Thomas Prices Creeke to ye head of William Colebornes

Creeke And from ye head of Will Colbornes Creeke to Wattkins point." In the center of the county, the highway connected "ye Dambs yet lyeth by Robert Hignetts to ye Lower Dambs yet lyeth at ye head of Anamessick river from thence to ye Lower Dambs yet lyeth at ye head of ye back Creeke of Manonoakin river And from thence to ye head of Manonoakin river & from thence to the head of Wiccocomoco Creeke." At the meeting, the commissioners also divided the county politically into five hundreds: Pocomoke, Annemessex, Manokin, Great and Little Monie, and Wicomico.[27] The term "hundred" is an old English word, but its exact meaning remains clouded.[28]

A site for the courthouse was not agreed upon for quite some time, and it was only the prodding of the governor that forced a decision. The courthouse was built in 1675, but little is known about its location and less about its appearance. In any case, by 1683 the Somerset Court was in need of other accommodations, and in November of that year Henry Smith was retained to finish the new courthouse for 12,000 pounds of tobacco. The court directed Smith

> *to Finish or Cause to be finished the Court house well plankt above as also bilowe with good & Substantiall sleepers in both the Lower roomes the upper roomes to be devided into Two the outermost Doores of ye house with hinges Locks and keyes staires Glass windowes Carpenters Joyners & Turners worke, Barr Seates for Justices pinacles Tables & all other necessaries to ye Compleating of ye Said Court house.*[29]

In 1688 William Venables, a joiner, contracted with the court for additional work. Under this agreement, he was to "Cover the Court house and to remove the staires that now are & make a new Staire case in the next Corner & to remove the particon further in,...." The Somerset Court also commissioned Venables to craft "a Table for the Justices as alsoe to make aseate for the Justices with a greate chaire in the Middle and apenell over head the said Chairs with [Lord Baltimore's] Coate of Arms to be Carvd in the same & abarr with a Table & asiate for the Clerk...."[30]

Originally built on a tract of land known as "Webley," the courthouse was relocated in 1694 to a site on Dividing Creek considered by some to be a more central location as the county developed along the Atlantic coast. At the Dividing

Augustine Herrman, Virginia and Maryland, *1670 (courtesy of the Geography and Map Division, Library of Congress).*

Creek site, the court desired a fifty by twenty-foot frame courthouse with a brick gable end and a "Chimney below and above to be underpind with brick." The court remained at Dividing Creek until 1742, when it was moved for the final time to Princess Anne.[31]

Within two years of the formation of Somerset County, the provincial council and governor, on June 8, 1668, appointed certain locations as "ports of entry." Restricting entry of goods from overseas to these sites gave the proprietor better control of the colony's trade. In Somerset County a site referred to as "Deepe point att Randall Revell's" was designated the port of entry, and in October 1668 Randall and Katherine Revell conveyed twenty acres, "a parcel of land called Sommerton," to the Lord Proprietor for a county port. The site of this town is generally thought to be near the Clifton plantation house at the end of Revell's Neck. Although a plat has not surfaced for the early town, "Sommerton" or "Somerset Town" was indicated on Augustine Herrman's map drawn in 1670.[32]

In an effort to enhance control of trade and encourage additional town development, the General Assembly passed "An act for Advancement of trade" in November 1683. The act clearly defined the Assembly's desire to establish local inspection sites for all goods, imported as well as "Tobaccos goods wares & Merchandizes of the growth Produccon or manufacture of this Province." The inspection sites in Somerset County included the following:

> ...in Wiccocomico River on the South side on the Land next above the Land of the Orphants of Charles Bollard & on the Land on the North side of Windford [Mudford] Creeke, (vizt) Smiths & Glannills Land & on Horseys Land in Annimessex & on Morgans Land formerly called Barrowes towards the head of Pokamoake, & on the Land betweene Mr Jenkins Plantacon & Mr Howards Plantacon on the North side Pokamoake....[33]

The lands belonging to the orphans of Charles Ballard, located on the south side of the Wicomico, evidently never developed into a port, while the town on the Smith and Glanville land survived until the early eighteenth century. Also lasting until the eighteenth century was Annemessex Town, situated on the Horsey family tract known as "Coulbourn." The last two sites, both on the Pocomoke River, have not faded into obscurity. The village established at the headwaters of the river was named Snow Hill, and the land between the Jenkins and Howard plantations was set aside for Rehoboth Town, named for Colonel William Stevens's extensive estate. Snow Hill became the seat of local government when Worcester County was divided from Somerset in 1742, while Rehoboth developed into a modest-sized river village with a tobacco warehouse and prominent Presbyterian and Anglican churches.

By the late seventeenth century, the lower Eastern Shore agricultural society ranged from wealthy to medium-sized planters to smaller freeholders, white and black. Owning smaller tracts or lots were various craftsmen, tradesmen, ministers, and storekeepers. Indentured servants and slaves were left to the lowest rung of county society. This rough class structure, however, was not strict, and movement upward depended largely on hard work, perseverance, and good luck. Women, on the other hand, were relatively scarce until the last decades of the seventeenth century, when sex ratios began to even.[34]

The planters who occupied the highest level of Chesapeake society during the seventeenth and eighteenth centuries took advantage of all available opportunities. Known to historians as merchant-planters, these men usually owned large, riverside agricultural estates along with the servants or slave labor force to operate them. They participated in the lucrative tobacco agriculture of the period, but it is clear they diversified relatively early, marketing excess grains, cured pork, and livestock as well as native stands of timber and lumber products. They shipped their own products to British ports, but handled their neighbors' export crops and raw materials as well. In exchange for these exported products, they brought home manufactured European goods, which they sold to local residents. Much of this exchange was conducted on a credit basis due to the scarcity of gold or silver currency.

Epitomizing the wealth and status of Somerset merchant-planters of the seventeenth century was Colonel Francis Jenkins (also spelled Jenckins), perhaps the richest man of his day living on the lower Eastern Shore. At his death, his estate, probated on June 27, 1710, was valued at the then extraordinary sum of £4,006.[35] Jenkins first appeared in local records in the 1670s as a member of the Commission of the Peace for Somerset as well as one of His Lordship's Justices.[36]

Between 1683 and 1688 Jenkins served as high sheriff of Somerset, and by 1697 he was chief justice of the county. During the same period he was elected a member of the Provincial Court, and a year later a contemporary recommended him for the provincial council as "a man of the best sence and Estate &c in Somerset County, who hath born[e] all offices there...." Jenkins continued to serve on the council until his death.[37]

Through his first marriage to the widow Lucy Weedon in April 1672, Francis Jenkins assumed control of the 400-acre Weedon plantation on the west side of the Pocomoke River just south of the village of Rebobeth. Not much is known about his second wife, Rozanna, but his marriage to Mary King, daughter of Major Robert King I of Kingsland, united two of the most prominent estates in Somerset County during the late seventeenth and early eighteenth centuries.

Jenkins purchased the Pocomoke River plantation, which was then called "Mary's Lott," from William Weedon in 1700.[38] Somerset land records between 1682 and 1710 reveal that Francis Jenkins bought and sold over 7,200 acres adjacent to the Pocomoke River as well as acreage near St. Martin's and along Rewastico Creek.[39]

The best indication of Francis Jenkins's exceptional prominence, however, is the room-by-room inventory Ephraim Wilson and Samuel Worthington prepared following his death.[40] Francis and Mary's house was exceptionally large and well-furnished for their day, and in addition they retained and apparently used a second, earlier house on the home plantation. Stores and outbuildings are also detailed on the inventory, along with the trading goods and farm implements they contained. (See Chapter III for a detailed discussion of these buildings and their contents.)

Jenkins's mercantile interests in Britain and the West Indies are clearly evident in the amounts of saleable merchandise inventoried. Packed in one store was "A Cargo of European Goods came since ye Colonel deceased from Bristol," valued at £450, and "A Parcel of Linnen and Woolen, Iron Work and Salt and Haberdashery and Rum and Molasses," worth £168. The rum, molasses, and salt were common imports from Jamaica and other Caribbean islands.

In addition to the overseas imports, the plantation was littered with domestic manufactures and the implements for producing them. Twenty-two slaves of differing ages wielded axes, a harrow, a plow, and hoes in the planting and tending of tobacco and grains. Two large grindstones undoubtedly milled various grains for market, and large or small wheeled carts carried produce to a waiting pinnace or shallop for loading. Stored in cask were 132,847 1/2 pounds of tobacco valued at £330.1.0.

Jenkins's resources did not end with his home plantation, however. Located on the Pocomoke River estate and three tenant farms was an extensive amount of livestock, including 129 cattle, seventy sheep, sixty male and female pigs of varying age, and three horses. Other miscellaneous saleable items of local origin included 1,200 feet of cypress plank, a parcel of empty tobacco casks, seventeen hides, and four skins.

One of the last items in the inventory is "A List of Money Debts" valued at £1,348, over one-third of Jenkins's entire estate.

By capitalizing on all the social, political, and economic opportunities available to him, Francis Jenkins amassed what amounted to several fortunes in seventeenth century Somerset County. But further, as reflected in the list of debts in his inventory, is the pivotal role Jenkins and others like him played in the daily lives of countless less advantaged county residents. These merchant-planters extended credit, provided otherwise unobtainable product markets, and offered finished manufactures normally out of reach, thereby enriching the lives of their neighbors.

Only a few Eastern Shore contemporaries could match the position Jenkins achieved in Somerset County during the seventeenth century; in fact, most of the population operated with far less. Perhaps more representative of average wealth and status for the period is Edward Day, whose estate was inventoried on May 17, 1699, and valued at £147.10.3. More than three-quarters of Day's moveable estate consisted of his investments in servants, slaves, and livestock. A negro man and woman valued together at £50 comprised over one-third of his probated worth.[41]

Where Edward Day lived is not known, for he owned several tracts of land, including "Days Beginning," surveyed in 1688 for 295 acres, and "Coxe's Discovery," laid out for 745 acres in the same year.[42] His marriage to Jane Walker in April 1681 is recorded in Somerset County records, as are his positions as a justice of the peace in 1687 and a commissioner to carry out the provisions of the Act for the Advancement of Trade.[43]

Although Day served in at least two official positions and patented more than 1,000 acres, the room-by-room inventory prepared at his death indicates the house he and his family shared was a modest one. It was a single story, hall plan dwelling with a single chamber on the second floor. Also located on the property were an "old house" and a detached kitchen.

Other seventeenth century inhabitants of Somerset County included a small group of free black planters, who had arrived with the initial settlers. Anthony and Mary Johnson, along with their negro slave John Casor, emigrated from Northampton County in 1665 with scores of other, white settlers. At that time, those who sponsored immigrants to Maryland were paid by the head, so many acres per settler. The Johnsons arrived in the colony as headrights for Randall Revell and Ann Toft, two wealthy landowners who patented over 2,000 acres between the Manokin River and Back Creek (on the peninsula now known as Revell's Neck).[44]

In 1666 Anthony Johnson purchased a twenty-year leasehold on a 300-acre tract from Stephen Horsey. Johnson named the tract on the south side of Wicomico Creek "Tonies Vinyard."[45] Shortly afterward Johnson died, but in 1670 his wife, Mary, renegotiated the lease for ninety-nine years.[46] In her will, written in 1672, she directed that her sons, John and Richard, would inherit the small Wicomico Creek plantation.[47] By holding title to property, the Johnsons and their children could plan and hope to improve their status in the plantation society as it developed on the lower Eastern Shore. However, as slavery became established in the late seventeenth and early eighteenth centuries, these expectations were dimmed. Free blacks, who never constituted a large part of the population, retained their freedom but with restrictions that prevented their rise in society.

In an attempt to insulate themselves somewhat from the volatile nature of the tobacco economy, Somerset planters and yeoman farmers in general engaged in a diversified agriculture that centered on tobacco production but also included market products in wheat, corn, and livestock. Seemingly limitless stands of virgin timber supplied additional exports highly valued in England and the West Indies. Home manufacture of cloth, leather, and other crafts contributed to the diversity of local production.

Many Somerset residents, however, did not participate in the market agriculture of the period. Instead they may have grown a variety of subsistence foodstuffs and worked as skilled laborers. Included in this group was Samuel Lennon, whose estate, probated on October 10, 1705, was valued at only £3.10.0.[48] The items listed in his inventory reveal that Lennon earned his living as a joiner and owned little more than the tools of his trade, a few clothes, and a minimum of household furnishings. Part of his worth was evaluated at 1,390 pounds of tobacco, outstanding debts from six different accounts. The absence of Lennon's name in the Somerset County land records suggests he leased or rented the land where he lived.

Samuel Lennon did not die with a large or even a comfortable estate. He earned his way in Somerset County, perhaps working through long years of service as an indentured servant before achieving the status of a freeman. Indentured servants, those immigrants who arrived in the Chesapeake region with their passage paid by others, were obligated by contract to work for their benefactors until their period of service had expired, often six to seven years. Research has shown that the servants who arrived during the seventeenth century were predominantly middle class yeoman farmers and trained craftsmen. Opportunities to own virgin soil in a religiously tolerant territory were unavailable in their own land, and these individuals saw a chance to advance in the freer atmosphere of a developing colony.[49] Most such bonded servants came to Somerset County from the British Isles.

In addition to indentured servants, planters who could afford it purchased slaves imported from the Caribbean and Africa. Although large numbers of slaves were not imported into the region until the eighteenth century, planters at the close of the seventeenth century looked increasingly to permanent investments in slave labor as lessened opportunity stemmed the tide of indentured servants.

Although the cultivation and export of tobacco shaped the lives of most planters, their families, and their servants, religious meetings were an important and integral part of life in Somerset County during the seventeenth century. As promulgated by Maryland proprietary policy, the colony was to be a haven for members of various religious persuasions. Among the first on the lower Eastern Shore to take advantage of this freedom were the beleaguered Quakers of Northampton and Accomac counties. After the Virginia Assembly passed its restrictive policy of 1660, William Coulbourne is recorded in Virginia records with fines of £100 sterling for entertaining Quakers. In addition, Thomas Leatherbury, Henry White, Ambrose Dixon, and Levin Denwood were brought before county magistrates for "breach of law concerning Quakers."[50]

Upon arrival in Maryland, the former Virginia Quakers held meetings in their homes or in barns if the groups were very large. George Fox (1624-1691), English founder of the Society of Friends, visited the newly settled Quakers on the lower Shore in 1672. He entered in his journal,

> *wee passed 8 milles to a captains house who is a Justices whose name is [William] Colleburne where wee hade service & on the 19th wee pased aboute 9 milles among frinds & on the 20th day wee had a very pressious & ag[l]orious meeting at the Justices house before mentioned & there was many people of account & the Judge of that Country & Captaine & hee yet was the late high shirive & the head secretary....& there was 4 new England men masters of shipps and marchants...*[51]

Regular meetings were also held at the home of Ambrose Dixon, who volunteered land for the first Annemessex meeting house, erected prior to 1687. It is thought this building survived until the turn of the eighteenth century, when meetings were again held in private houses. A second Quaker meeting, sited between Great Monie Creek and the Wicomico River, was evidently organized by 1679 when reports from the monthly meeting at "Munny" were received on the Western Shore. A third group of Quakers formed the Bogerternorton Meeting during the late seventeenth century at the headwaters of the Pocomoke River. This group was visited by Thomas Chalkley, a Quaker missionary, in 1698.[52]

During the same period, Presbyterian congregations were formed along the Pocomoke and Manokin rivers. In 1680 Colonel William Stevens, a prominent merchant-planter and state official, petitioned the Presbytery of Laggan in northern Ireland for a minister of the Presbyterian faith to serve the needs of the lower Eastern Shore. Within the next five years, Reverend Francis Makemie along with reverends William Traile, Samuel Davis, and Thomas Wilson arrived in Somerset County.[53]

Although Francis Makemie visited the various colonial congregations in an effort to strengthen Presbyterianism on a regional scope, he settled permanently in Accomac County, Virginia. William Traile served the Rehobeth congregation in its early years, and Thomas Wilson ministered to the Presbyterians living near the Manokin River. Samuel Davis is credited with founding the Snow Hill church.[54] Not much is known about the earliest church buildings, but seventeenth century church architecture on the lower Eastern Shore was probably similar to this description recorded in the summer of 1697: the "Dissenters...hath a house...at Nearokin [Manokin] about 30 feet long [a] plain country building...."[55]

Leaving behind the religiously tolerant policies of the Lords Baltimore, the 1680s brought permanent changes to the spiritual life of the colony. After England's Protestant Revolution (also known as the Glorious Revolution) of 1688-1689 and the abdication of James II, a group in Maryland known as the Associators assumed control of the proprietary government. William and Mary, newly seated on the English throne, supported these rebels and replaced Lord Baltimore's proprietary rule with a Protestant government. The first royal governor was Lionel Copley, who arrived in the colony in 1692.[56]

Included in the new government's early legislation was "An Act for the Service of Almighty God and the Establishment of the Protestant Religion in the Province."[57] As a result, Maryland was divided into parishes, with four in Somerset County: Coventry, Somerset, Snow Hill, and Stepney. The act provided for the support of the Church, its rectors, and its buildings through a comprehensive tax of forty pounds of tobacco per person regardless of religious belief. In the following decade early churches were erected in Rehobeth for Coventry Parish and on the "Almodington" estate of Arnold Elzey for Somerset Parish.

As evidenced by the political and religious machinations of the seventeenth century, a secure and strife-free life in Lord Baltimore's colony was by no means guaranteed. Complicating life on a local level were disease and high mortality rates. Fluctuating market prices for tobacco and other export products made incomes uncertain at best. Nonetheless, by the end of the century plantations and settlements were well rooted along several rivers, the seat of local government was established in a central location on Dividing Creek, and various religious denominations served the spiritual needs of settlers in a new land. 🌳

CHAPTER III, 1660-1700

"To Sawe a Good Suffitiont Frame"

The architecture of seventeenth century Somerset County has not survived to modern times. Recent architectural fieldwork and historical research have not identified any structures that date from the settlement period. The available historical records and most recent research in Somerset County agree with the current theory that seventeenth century building traditions relied largely on impermanent, earth-fast frame construction practices that, at best, lasted a few generations.[1]

During the first few decades of settlement, the new inhabitants of the lower Eastern Shore focused their energies on converting virgin land into productive plantations. Building impressive, long-lasting brick or frame houses was not an immediate or even available choice for most early settlers. From all accounts, the bulk of seventeenth century domestic architecture consisted of single story frame dwellings with one- or two-room plans. Even these modest structures were erected with a close accounting of time, materials, and expense.

Although impermanent foundation systems jeopardized the long-term survival of most early domestic buildings, research indicates some seventeenth century public and domestic architecture in Somerset County was professionally erected in the best traditions of English vernacular architecture. Carpenters and joiners, as well as the necessary building materials, were available during the earliest years of the county's settlement. With these resources either in the area or a short distance away in Accomac and Northampton counties, Virginia, the harsh difficulties of the early period were somewhat mitigated in Somerset County. In fact, close economic and social relationships among family members and friends in Somerset County and on the Virginia Shore have been an integral and significant element in the history of the region.

When they arrived in Somerset County during the 1660s, the first settlers erected makeshift shelters until more substantial accommodations could be assembled. Those emigrants from nearby Northampton and Accomac counties would have had the luxury of time in which to plan and only a short distance over land or water to travel. They probably brought with them canvas tents or tools for building a temporary lean-to or hut of saplings and natural cover. The wealthier emigrants might have used their greater resources to hire carpenters who could fashion the parts necessary for

a rudimentary house before they left Virginia. These materials would then have been transported to Somerset County by ship.

No documents have surfaced to detail what settlers built in Somerset County during their first months, and only fragmentary records survive for what followed. From the few period sources, it appears Somerset planters were no different from their contemporaries throughout the Chesapeake region: Most individuals financed economically dimensioned frame houses with one- or two-room plans and the outbuildings needed for a fledgling plantation. Quickly assembled, these early braced frame structures were built with earthfast or hole-set posts that provided structural support for the house. In Somerset County the high watertable would not have allowed a normal four- to five-foot post-hole depth in many places. In these cases, the framing members may have been set in shallower holes or perhaps built directly on the ground.

The braced frame skeleton of this early house type provided the framework to which riven clapboards were traditionally nailed or pegged. Clapboards—riven boards four to five feet long—were laid horizontally with the end of one clapboard meeting the end of the next board. The ends of each board were fashioned with a feathered edge to achieve a weathertight sheathing. In addition to enclosing the exterior walls, closely nailed clapboards gave rigidity to the frame, reducing the need for expensive mortise and tenon joinery. Clapboards were also used to partition rooms and cover the roof.

Oak and cypress were the indigenous woods that naturally split to form clapboards, and the durable nature of cypress clapboards made them especially attractive as a local export product. A contemporary record documents that John Anderson, a sawyer, was bound to John West in 1671 for "fifteene hundred good sufficient well rived Claboards & also to Deliver ye said West as aforesaid his shalops full load of good Cypress quarters fitt to make good covering Claboard of five foot four inches long."[2]

If clapboards were scarce, or too costly, local grasses could be used for roof covering. A 1683 judicial court reference documents an agreement between William Thomas and Richard Harris to supply enough buildings to cure the tobacco crop that year. If other buildings were required, Harris was contracted to "hyre a thatcher and pay for Cutting

Conjectural drawing of an early, 15 x 12, one-room frame house with catted chimney, c. 1688, Paul Touart and Nancy Kurtz.

of Sedge and nailes to naile the lafthes upon the rafters."[3]

Most houses were fitted with some sort of chimney. Brick was available for the affluent, but records of the period indicate that in its absence a "welsh" or timber chimney was erected. A timber chimney stack traditionally consisted of four corner posts set into the ground with short, horizontal timbers fitted between them and daubed with mud. Because of the rather dangerous nature of wooden chimneys, care was taken to ensure their safety. A revealing Somerset court case, reviewed in 1676, illustrates the expense of a timber chimney. In this record, construction of a welsh chimney was valued at 200 pounds of tobacco, while the assembly of a thirty-foot dwelling was valued at 1,400 pounds of tobacco and six days of planing plank was compensated with 240 pounds of tobacco.[4]

Impermanent settlement period houses were not expected to last beyond ten to fifteen years, and when possible planters replaced them with more substantial structures.[5] In 1688 Captain William Whittington, a prominent Somerset landholder, merchant, and officer, financed a well-built dwelling. He contracted John Swain "to Sawe a good Suffitiont frame for a house," a description of which was recorded in county judicial proceedings:

> *forty foot long over getted of each side one foot without the plates the house below the plates twenty foot wide the stoods & rafters three & four inches thick in the flatt sides of them the studdes eight foot longe Rafters eighteen foot*

& halfe Longe the Couplings for every rafter nine foot long three & four inches thick on the flatt sides with braies of convenient lenght & thickness plates forty foot long six & Seaven inches on the flatt sides the Joise to be five & six inches on the flatt sides the ground sells Six & Seaven Inches likewise & the false plates for each side four & five inches on the flatt sides....[6]

This description outlines the basic elements of a single story timber frame house, a type of dwelling erected throughout the Chesapeake region and known by contemporaries as the "Virginia house."[7] The eight-foot studs were topped by a main plate on which a layer of joists or tie beams was placed. The "false plates" were laid across the outer ends of the tie beams to carry the eighteen-and-a-half foot rafters, which rendered a fifty-five degree roof pitch. The rafter pairs were stabilized by collars, called couplings in the description.

The signals that Captain Whittington desired a better built, more permanent type of dwelling than many constructed at the time lie in the size of the building's dimensions and the fact that it rested on a heavy timber sill instead of hole-set posts. The contracted agreement, supported by the Somerset Court, ensured that Whittington's house would be no smaller than forty by twenty feet, which was undoubtedly more than twice the size of most of its contemporaries. This space probably allowed Captain Whittington two rooms on the first floor instead of one.

The mention of "ground sells" in the description points

to heavy timber sills that supported the structural frame and, unlike hole-set posts, protected the framing members from insect and water damage. To provide additional protection, the sills were sometimes elevated off the ground by timber or masonry piers.

An alternative construction method for the "Virginia house" combined brick gable ends and frame front and back walls. This combination of materials appears to have been a thrifty method of employing brick to enhance the structure's safety and permanence. Brick chimneys and fireplaces were clearly safer to use and maintain, and a brick foundation was an obvious deterrent to moisture and rot.

The earliest reference to a brick-ended structure in Somerset County appears in the court records referring to construction of the Dividing Creek courthouse in 1694. Francis Jenkins and William Whittington were charged with

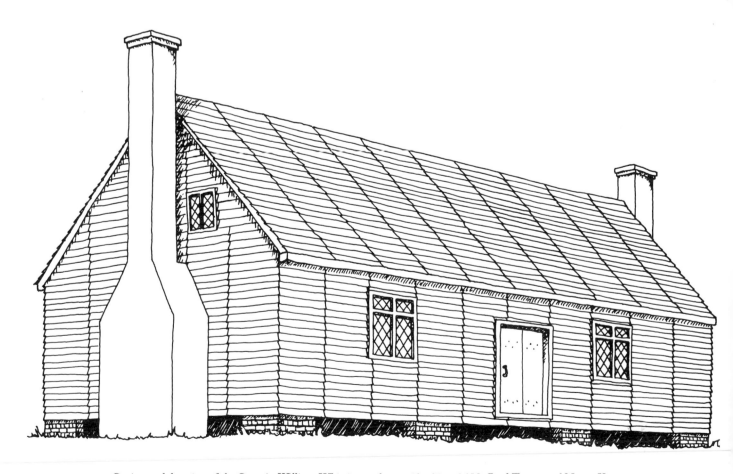

Conjectural drawing of the Captain William Whittington house, 40 x 20, c. 1688, Paul Touart and Nancy Kurtz.

purchasing a tract of land not exceeding 200 acres and erecting a 50 by 20 foot courthouse with at least one gable end of brick.[8] During the following century, brick gable end construction became widely used in Somerset County as well as on the Eastern Shore of Virginia.[9] Pear Valley, one of the earliest buildings to survive on Virginia's Shore, has a brick gable end dominated by a massive exterior brick chimney and three frame walls.[10]

The Powell-Benston house, built around 1700, stood near Rehobeth until the mid-1960s. The brick-ended frame dwelling was the closest example of a settlement period house to survive in Somerset County until modern times. Like Pear Valley, the original one-room plan dwelling had three frame walls and a brick gable end decorated with glazed headers. According to reports taken when the earliest section was dismantled for the Museum of Early Southern Decorative

Powell-Benston house, destroyed, photograph c.1964 (courtesy of the Museum of Early Southern Decorative Arts, Winston-Salem, N.C.).

Arts in Winston-Salem, North Carolina, the one-room plan house had been enlarged with a two-room, brick-ended addition later in the eighteenth century.[11]

Early features that distinguished the seventeenth century part of the Powell-Benston house included an extremely steep roof pitch, exposed and decorated framing members, and small gable end windows originally fitted with casements. The one-room plan house was served by a six-foot wide fireplace framed with a wide bolection molding and exhibiting a small arched niche in each side of the firebox. To the right of the fireplace was a winder stair and to the left a paneled closet door.

With its superior construction and finish, the Powell-Benston house clearly belonged to the upper range of expensively built houses dating to the period around 1700. Yet the original hall plan dwelling encompassed no more than 360 square feet on the first floor. Accordingly, the variety of major and minor daily activities of a prominent planter and his family were accomplished within the confines of a single room. The second floor, lighted by small gable end

Powell-Benston house, hearth wall, photograph c. 1964 (courtesy of the Museum of Early Southern Decorative Arts, Winston-Salem, N.C.).

windows, provided additional sleeping and storage space.

As a survivor of the type, the Powell-Benston house offered a rare opportunity to examine an early Somerset County dwelling. Also unusual is a handful of room-by-room inventories taken during the fourth quarter of the seventeenth century. Probably not too different from the one-room plan Powell-Benston house was the dwelling of Edward Day. As delineated in the 1699 inventory of his estate, the house included a single room on each floor.[12]

The variety of furnishings in the "hall" reflected the different public and private activities that took place in the single first floor room of the house. Assessed were a "Feather Bed and Bedstid," one rug, a hammock, a bolster, a pillow, and a pair of sheets, as well as "curtains and Vallens." The other furniture in the hall included one small table and carpet, a "Wainscot Chest," three old leather chairs and four "white chairs," another small table, and a small trunk. On the wall were two hanging tin candlesticks.

Like the Powell-Benston house, the Day house had a hall closet. Stored in it were various dishes and eating utensils, including "50 lbs. of Good Pewter, 17½ lbs. of old Broken Pewter, 2½ dozen Pewter Plates, 7 sauce dishes, 2 pewter salts, 2 Brass candlesticks, one Brass Chafing Dish, 1 old warming pan, 1 old Silver Cup and one old silver tankard." Evidently Edward Day and his family ate in the hall, while sleeping quarters were split between the hall and the chamber above. Upstairs was another feather bed along with a "Truckle Bedstid" that fit underneath. A "Standing Bedstid" and "one old flock bed" were upstairs as well. Four chairs completed the furnishings in the room. Also stored upstairs was "1 Long Gun."

Standing nearby was an "old house" and a detached kitchen. This one-room house was furnished with a small feather bed, one wainscot chest, and five chairs. The kitchen held an assortment of cooking implements along with a "hand mill," "2 Woolen wheels," "2 old Flax Wheels," a parcel of nails, one old crosscut saw, and two old whip saws.

Larger and more complex than the Day house were the hall/parlor plan structures inventoried during the same period. These dwellings closely follow the description of a "Virginia house." Included in this group is the property of Andrew Jones, located along the Wicomico River.[13] In 1684, when his possessions were inventoried, Jones's house included five principal rooms—the hall, parlor, hall chamber,

parlor chamber, and porch chamber. This disposition suggests a single story, rectangular house with a projecting porch tower, which would have given the dwelling a T shape.

The first floor of the Jones house was divided into two rooms, which served as the principal living spaces of the house. The front door normally provided direct access into the hall, whereas access to the parlor was usually limited to an interior doorway. The hall continued to serve as a largely public room used for everyday activities; the parlor was often smaller and reserved for more private family functions. Corresponding rooms on the second floor were the hall chamber and the parlor chamber. The tower may or may not have been enclosed on the first floor, while its second floor—the porch chamber—provided additional storage or sleeping space. Also listed in the inventory was a kitchen, which most likely stood to the side or behind the house.

The room-by-room appraisal of Andrew Jones's belongings allows a rare glimpse of the seventeenth century room furnishings and function of a moderately well-to-do planter. The hall contained a predictable mixture of domestic furniture, including a table, two wainscot chairs, two chests, and an old couch. The hall also served as storage space for a variety of carpenters' tools, two iron casement windows, locks, hinges, and a pintel.

In contrast, the parlor was evidently used for formal entertaining, storage of valuable goods, and sleeping. Along with ten leather chairs, one wainscot chest, and a wainscot cupboard, the parlor contained the most expensive bed in the house. Valued at £7, the bed was fitted with a bolster, pillows, and a feather mattress. Unlike any of the other beds in the inventory, it was dressed with "Curtains and Vallons."

The most elaborately furnished room upstairs was the parlor chamber, which contained a less expensive bedstead and mattress as well as seventeen leather chairs. Along with some linen goods, the contents of the room included a wainscot chest, a trunk, and a bushel of beans. The hall chamber was less elaborately appointed with a chest, two beds, and a keg with some feathers. The sparsest room was the porch chamber with a bed and mattress, two leather chairs, two broken chairs, and one old barrel.

The detached kitchen contained "asundry kitchen utensils," three beds, and four old guns. The beds were probably used by the four slaves and three indentured servants also listed in this part of the inventory. The slaves and servants,

Conjectural drawing of the Francis Jenkins house, c.1690, Paul Touart and Nancy Kurtz.

assessed at £164.7.1, comprised nearly one-third of the entire value of Jones's estate.

Similar hall/parlor houses with porch towers were found on the property of John Evans in 1686 and Colonel David Browne in 1697.[14] Outstanding among the late seventeenth century properties in Somerset County, however, was that of Colonel Francis Jenkins, introduced earlier as the epitome of the merchant-planter. According to his inventory, probated in 1710, two dwellings were located on his Pocomoke River plantation—Francis and his wife Mary's eight-room residence and an "old" six-room dwelling, perhaps the Weedon house.[15]

Like the Andrew Jones house inventoried in 1684, the main Jenkins house contained a "Hall" and "Parlour" on the first floor and a "Parlour Chamber" and "Porch Chamber" on the second floor. A rare sophistication for the period was the elaborately inventoried "Dining Room," evidently also on the second floor. With the absence of a hall chamber in the room disposition, it appears the dining room was located next to the parlor chamber. Each of the four principal rooms was

inventoried with a variety of andirons, brass dogs, fire shovels, tongs, and fenders and/or bellows. The third level of rooms— the "Chamber over the Dining Room," the "Chamber over the Parlour Chamber," and the "Chamber over the Porch Chamber"—had no fireplace equipment. This fact supports the assumption that a large central chimney, not uncommon for the period, served fireplaces in the four principal rooms of the house.

Francis Jenkins furnished his house with an abundance of expensive furniture. The most public room, the hall, had eighteen newly fashionable Russian leather chairs and a Russian leather couch, along with "1 Large Oval 3 square Tables and a large Looking Glass." Relating to his public offices and ceremonial duties, Jenkins owned "3 Halberts a Leading Staff, 2 Standard Staves & 3 maps" and "2 Drums and 2 Sets of Damask Silk Colours," all of which he probably displayed proudly.

In fashion similar to the Andrew Jones house, the Jenkins parlor was used for a variety of private and formal public activities. An expensive bed, dresser, and looking glass were accompanied by ten chairs, four maps, two punch bowls, and two "Sillabub Pots." Along with several smaller items, Jenkins had £474 of "Ready Cash in Gold and Silver" stored in the parlor, a relative fortune in itself to many Chesapeake planters of his day.

The parlor chamber was the most expensively fitted bedroom, with a large bed and furniture valued at £19, along with a smaller bed, "1/2 Doz: Turky work Chairs," and "a small Table with other fancies." Three more maps, a looking glass, a crimson silk damask cloth, and two pairs of muslin hangings further distinguished the room.

Despite the obvious extravagance with which the Jenkinses furnished these three rooms , they saved the second floor dining room for their most ostentatious statement of worldly sophistication. Francis Jenkins's penchant for charts and maps must have been satisfied while dining for he displayed one map "of ye Celestial and Terestial Globe and of London" and three maps of the quarters of the world. Alongside he hung "4 Small Draughts of Pauls Monument Exchange" and "2 large Heads of K[ing] Wm and Q[ueen] Mary in frames." Furniture inventoried in the room included two dozen cane chairs, one chest of drawers, one large oval table, a carpet, and a large looking glass with a silk cloth. The most expensive item mentioned was a cupboard filled with £80 worth of silver plate. Unlike any of the other rooms, the windows were dressed with calico hangings.

Evidently standing only a short distance from the Jenkins house was the old Weedon house, also a T-shaped structure, which seems to have had six rooms. The room disposition was similar to that of the Andrew Jones house with the exception of a "Study" in place of the hall. In addition to fully furnished rooms, the house was apparently used to store large amounts of linens, including 6 3/4 yards of fine damask. For some reason many of Colonel Jenkins's personal belongings, including clothing, boots and spurs, saddle and bridle, pistols and holster, and a "Silver Rapier," were located in the parlor of this house.

Aside from the two houses, the plantation consisted of Francis Jenkins's store building; another "old Store," perhaps the one used by James Weedon; a kitchen; a milk house; and probably other agricultural buildings that went unmentioned.

Although Francis Jenkins and his family occupied an extravagantly furnished eight-room house five or six times larger than the houses most Chesapeake planters could afford, there is no indication that its construction guaranteed long-term survival. Jenkins's wealth and resources may have afforded a few permanent features such as a brick chimney and a brick foundation, but in all likelihood the house continued the impermanent frame traditions of the seventeenth century with clapboard sheathing over a lightly framed skeleton. With over two-thirds of his £4,006 estate invested in slaves, tobacco, livestock, vessels, imported manufactures, and outstanding debts, it appears Jenkins fully understood the source of his wealth. Building impressive and long-lasting brick or frame houses was left to future generations.

Indeed, in the seventeenth and early eighteenth centuries brick was relatively scarce and expensive. It was used only sparingly, even in the construction of the Dividing Creek courthouse in 1694. Colonel William Stevens, Francis Jenkins's neighbor, tried to finance the construction of "a brick house" in 1674, only to be frustrated by his builders. John Lenham had agreed to erect the brick dwelling according to the dimensions, manner, and form detailed in specifications held by Lawrence Gere. Evidently Gere would not share these with Lenham, and the latter erected a larger house than agreed.[16] More detailed information about the appearance of the brick house was not included in the court deposition, and the Stevens house is not known to have survived to modern times.

Over the course of the late seventeenth century, the face of Somerset County changed from a virgin wilderness to a region of major and minor plantations where men and women engaged in the difficult pursuit of turning a profit or of merely subsisting in a new land. Testimony to the immigrants' efforts, frustrations, mistakes, and successes are clearly visible in the written record. However valuable this evidence is in determining what seventeenth century life was like on the lower Eastern Shore, it must be remembered that these references are extremely fragmentary and heavily biased toward the upper end of early Somerset society. The lives and living conditions of the less well-off did not often enter the written record in their own time, and it is only recently that historians have been interested in gleaning information about people at this level of society. It can only be surmised that a large number of seventeenth century Somerset residents occupied smaller, meaner dwellings that went unrecorded before time and decay erased them from the landscape. 🌳

CHAPTER IV, 1700-1775
Tobacco, Corn, and Wheat

Although economic circumstances during the settlement period attracted immigration and investment on the Eastern Shore, by the turn of the eighteenth century Atlantic trade routes were disrupted by war and the tobacco economy was suffering from overproduction and falling prices. King William's War began in 1689 and continued for eight years, and Queen Anne's War lasted from 1702 until 1713.[1] These two conflicts pitted British armies against French forces in close to twenty years of battle.

The warfare stymied attempts to expand England's commercial empire, particularly the reexport of tobacco.[2] Transportation networks between England and the Chesapeake became tenuous as French privateers seized cargo ships, and market prices were pushed higher as England levied more duties on imported tobacco. In consequence, the tobacco market stagnated. This situation, combined with an increased population and decreased opportunities for new settlers, virtually ended immigration of indentured servants. To augment the evaporating servant system, planters on the lower Eastern Shore were increasingly forced to invest in expensive, imported slave labor.

As grim as the economic picture was for Chesapeake planters, brighter prospects and permanent social change were close at hand. Conflict between Britain and France ended by 1713, and as early as 1717 the Atlantic trade was expanding to include markets in Ireland, Northern Europe, and, especially, France.[3] In fact, the French government supported a tobacco monopoly that financed the purchase of a large share of the Chesapeake crop and then resold it in other European markets.[4]

During the relatively peaceful period between Queen Anne's War and the American Revolution, the tobacco trade slowly increased in value each year.[5] Despite short recessions, modest increases in prices encouraged continued production. As a result of the brighter economic outlook, average wealth generally increased through the middle years of the eighteenth century, enabling some lower Eastern Shore planters to engage in more ambitious building programs. The result was a class of plantation architecture that has survived to modern times.

While the growth and export of tobacco dominated Maryland's agriculture through the seventeenth and early eighteenth centuries, an unexpectedly complex agriculture characterized Somerset County before the Revolution.[6] At that time, the county was basically divided into three areas economically, which correspond roughly to the present-day boundaries of Somerset, Worcester, and Wicomico counties.

The area that is now Somerset County—comprising essentially Monie, Manokin, Pocomoke, and Annemessex hundreds—outstripped the other two regions in accumulated wealth and influence throughout the colonial period. Planters in this region continued to grow tobacco during the depressed period from the 1680s to the 1730s.[7] However, by the early to mid-eighteenth century they were also growing corn and wheat for export and shipping flour, pork, livestock, and lumber. This mixed agriculture proved extremely lucrative during a period when these commodities were highly valued in Europe and the West Indies.

In contrast, most planters living in the northern hundreds along the Wicomico and Nanticoke rivers, now Wicomico County, concentrated on planting corn when they turned away from a focus on tobacco during the 1740s.[8] The planters living along the Atlantic coast, away from the navigable sections of the Pocomoke River, experienced yet another variation of the colonial economy. There, neither corn nor tobacco were grown in sufficient quantities to generate cash surpluses. Rather, planters along the ocean side, in what later became Worcester County, appear to have profited from valuable stands of cypress and yellow pine and related lumber products or to have invested in the manufacture of cloth or shoes.[9]

The differences in agriculture and export trade in each section of eighteenth century Somerset County appear to be mirrored by contrasting patterns in rebuilding. Planters who maintained significant levels of both tobacco and grain production—and who probably exported lumber, pork, and livestock as well—were able to undertake the construction of impressive brick or frame plantation houses as early as the 1730s and 1740s. On the other hand, those planters who readjusted their priorities to rely solely on grain production in lieu of tobacco behaved more like their counterparts in nearby grain-producing regions in northeastern Maryland and northern Delaware. Major rebuilding in these areas did not occur until the late eighteenth and early nineteenth centuries.[10]

Concurrent with the fluctuations in agriculture and the economy during the early to middle eighteenth century were shifts in the social structure of the Chesapeake region. On

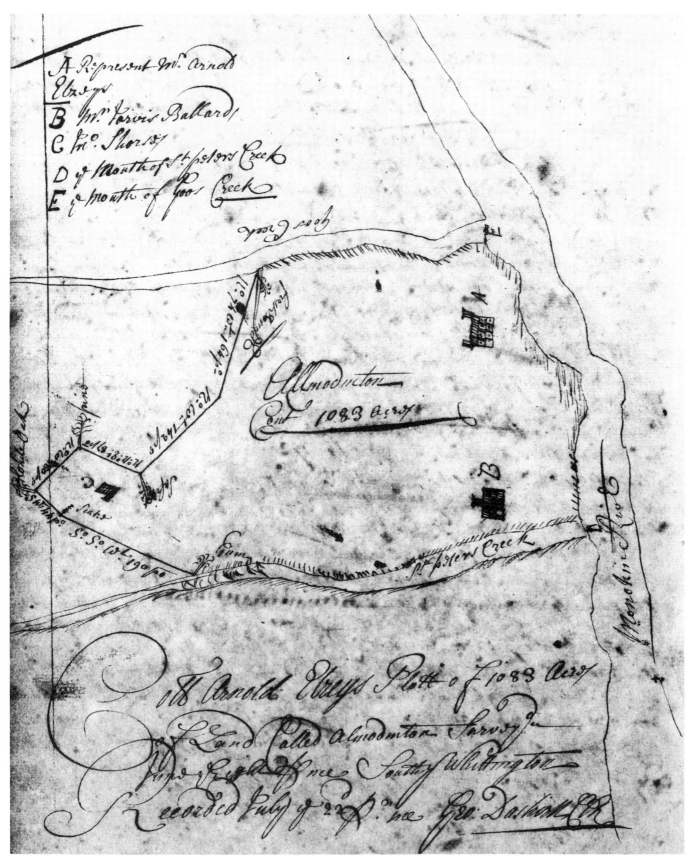

"Allmodinton" plat, Somerset County Land Commissions 1717-1721 (MdHR 9172; 1/45/5/7), p.78, 8 June 1720, (courtesy of the Maryland State Archives).

one hand, an increased colonial population evened out the unbalanced sex ratio characteristic of seventeenth century society. On the other, the decreased pressure to tame a virgin wilderness allowed Somerset County's inhabitants to devote more time and expense to developing plantations, large or small, and the families needed to protect accumulated wealth and status. Privileged second and third generation descendants of early settlers amassed considerable property, often secured through strategic marriages and business partnerships. By the mid to late eighteenth century, the gentry and middle class in the Chesapeake had created a close-knit network of upper class society through intermarriage and friendship. Individuals from this group seized control of key state and local public offices and shaped life on the Eastern Shore well into the nineteenth century.

Changing at the same time as the rest of society was the servant system on the lower Shore. As the Somerset population expanded after 1700, land and opportunity for indentured servants decreased. Planters turned increasingly to more permanent investments in slaves imported from Africa and the Caribbean. During the early eighteenth century restrictive laws and slave codes were passed to manage the ever-expanding population of slaves in the Chesapeake. These laws robbed blacks of all freedoms they had possessed during the seventeenth century, and slavery became institutionalized and irrevocable.

As the eighteenth century progressed and local agriculture and small-scale industry diversified, opportunities broadened for medium-sized planters, yeoman farmers, merchants, and artisans in the Chesapeake region. Somerset County probate inventories reveal a steady increase in the number of evaluated estates containing tools associated with carpentry, blacksmithing, shoemaking, tanning, and cloth production during the second and third quarters of the eighteenth century.[11] This enhanced local and regional economy meant less advantaged county residents could operate more independently, without relying so strongly on the wealthy merchant-planters for their product markets, finished goods, and sources of cash.

The same trends that encouraged a stable, more diversified county society also promoted the development of towns on the lower Shore and the eventual stabilization of the county seat. Artisans, merchants, ministers—in essence the skilled segment of the county population—provided services for the planter society rather than acquiring expansive river-front estates. Modest-sized town lots provided sufficient land on which to build a house and operate a business, many times accomplished with the same structure.

During the early 1730s two groups of Somerset residents petitioned the Maryland Assembly for the erection of towns at the head of the Manokin and Wicomico rivers. In March 1733 the Assembly proceedings record this petition:

Whereas, several Inhabitants of Somerset County, have, by their Petition to this General Assembly, set forth, That there is a very convenient Place for a Town, near the Head of Monokin River, on the South Side thereof, by the Bridge, on a Tract of Land now in Possession of David Brown,...Be it therefore Enacted, by the Right Honourable the Lord Proprietary, by and with the Advice and Consent of the Upper and Lower Houses of Assembly, and the Authority of the same, That Col. Levin Gale, Capt. George Dashiels, Major Robert King, Capt. Henry Ballard, and Mr. George Gale, or any Three of them, shall

Somerset County map of the five early hundreds, Paul Touart and Nancy Kurtz.

be, and are hereby appointed Commissioners for Somerset County aforesaid; and are hereby authorized and impowered, as well to agree for the Buying and Purchasing Twenty Five Acres of Land out of the Tract aforesaid,...as lies most convenient to the Water, as for Surveying and Laying out the same, in the most convenient Manner, into Thirty equal Lots, to be erected into a Town.[12]

In honor of the twenty-four year old daughter of King George II, the new village was named Princess Anne Town.[13] The twenty-five acres of David Brown's "Beckford" tract were subsequently laid out into thirty lots on a grid plan. Principal access was provided by the north-south road, originally named Bridge Street, which crossed the Manokin River. Front Street ran along the low land on the south bank of the river, and the major east-west intersections with Bridge Street were Broad and Prince William streets. The periphery of the town was bordered by narrow alleys—Back Alley on the east (now Beechwood Street), Low Alley on the west (now Beckford Street), and Upper Alley on the south (now Washington Street).[14]

In hope of ensuring the town's development, the legislation included a clause requiring anyone who purchased a town lot to "build upon such Lot or Lots, within Eighteen Months, an House, with one Brick Chimney, that shall cover Four Hundred square Feet,...." A second act, enacted by the Assembly at their session in April-May 1736, provided for moving the county jail to Princess Anne.[15]

Another petition, initiated and passed in 1732, allowed for a town at the head of the Wicomico River, then in Somerset as well. Fifteen acres were to be purchased in the fork of the river "at the Landing commonly now called Handy's, or Carr's Landing." The town was later renamed Salisbury.[16]

By the 1740s it was clear settlement on the lower Eastern Shore had increased sufficiently to warrant two counties instead of one. The three largest towns were located far apart, and the county courthouse, on a fourth site at Dividing Creek, was an inconvenient distance from all of them. In 1742 the General Assembly of Maryland passed "An Act to divide Somerset County, and to erect a new County on the Sea-board Side, by the name of Worcester." The legislation stated that

after the Tenth Day of December next, the Bounds of Somerset County shall contain as followeth: Beginning at Watkins's Point, and thence running up Pocomoke-Bay to the Mouth of Pocomoke-River, up and with the said River to the Mouth of Dividing-Creek; thence up the Westermost Side of the said Creek and main Branch to the Bridges called Denstone's Bridges, and from thence West to the main Road called Parahawkin-Road; thence up and with the said Road to John Caldwell senior's Saw-Mill, thence up and with the said Road, over Cox's Branch, to Broad-Creek Bridge, and down the said Branch and Creek into Nanticoke-River; thence down the said River with Dorchester County, to the Mouth thereof, and from thence, including all the Islands formerly deemed to be in Somerset County, to the Beginning called Watkins's Point;....[17]

This act also designated Snow Hill the county seat of Worcester and Princess Anne the new county seat of Somerset. During the fall of the following year, the northeast corner lot bordering Bridge and Broad streets and extending eastward to Back Alley was officially purchased for "Erecting and building a Court house and prison upon in Somerset County...."[18] The Broad Street lot was evidently the site of the county jail built in 1736. Construction of the first courthouse was completed for the June court of 1747.[19]

As the century reached its midpoint, the Eastern Shore entered what is popularly considered the region's "golden age." The most prominent planters during the third quarter of the eighteenth century are well-known for the elaborate Georgian-style dwellings they erected as symbols of their wealth and power. In addition, the period was marked by the successful establishment of a private school in Somerset County, which achieved a fine reputation throughout the Chesapeake.

Begun in 1767 as Somerset Academy and later known as Washington Academy, the school was first located on the lands of Samuel Wilson, a Princeton-educated lawyer and one of the wealthiest planters on the lower Shore. A contemporary description of the academy, published in the *Virginia Gazette* on February 23, 1769, described the school leaders as "a number of public spirited Gentlemen, of different denominations" who were motivated by "deep conviction of the great importance of learning both to church and state generously united to encourage it upon such a Catholic plan as might render it beneficial to persons of all denominations."[20]

The first school building, "a genteel commodious house, sixty-two feet in length and twenty in breadth" accommodated forty students at £17 each annually. Instruction was provided in English grammar, orthography, Latin and Greek, geography, "logick," navigation and surveying, debating, and oratory. Three early instructors, also educated at Princeton, were Luther Martin, Hugh Henry Brackenridge, and Philip Freneau.[21] The quality of education drew students not only from Somerset County but from the entire Eastern Shore.

The author of the *Virginia Gazette* article was so impressed with the academy that he wrote,

Though a foreigner, and unconnected with the colony, yet as a citizen of the world, and a common friend of literature; I cannot but rejoice that such a useful institution is erected, especially in that part of the country, which is so remote from colleges, and so much needs the genial rays of science. May friends and benefactors be daily rising up to patronize, encourage, and support it, and may it inspire and stimulate other Gentlemen in the southern colonies to enlarge the commonwealth of learning, the following of which is so necessary to the preservation of liberty and the prosperity of church and state.[22]

Rehoboth Presbyterian Church, photograph, c. 1900 (courtesy of Mrs. Merton Yerger).

Manokin Presbyterian Church, photograph c. 1870 (courtesy of William Marshall Scott).

Alongside advances in the education of Eastern Shore gentry, the various religious denominations financed major improvements in their facilities during the pre-Revolutionary period. The Rehoboth Presbyterian congregation is credited with erecting the extant single story brick church as early as 1706. During construction, the siting of the "dissenters" church within a half mile of the existing Coventry Parish church was contested by the local Anglican clergy. After two years of litigation, the Somerset Court entered into the proceedings, "This day (Vizt) the 10th day of June Ano Dom 1708 Ordered yet ye New Meeting house built by Protestant dessenters at Rehoboth Town in Somerset County in ye Province of Maryland be & is hereby appointed to be a house & place for ye Publick Worship of Allmighty God...."[23]

During the late seventeenth century, the Presbyterians had erected what must have been a frame meeting house several miles north on the Manokin River. But by the 1760s contemporary reports indicate the "Meeting House was decayed in almost every part, and not worth repairing and that it is too small to contain people that often attend."[24] The opinion of the Session, one of the ruling bodies of the Presbyterian church, was submitted during December 1764. Shortly afterwards the congregation proceeded to "build a new [meeting house] of brick 50' x 40' in the clear 16 feet from the water table to the plate...."[25] As originally designed, the rectangular, Flemish bond brick church was highlighted with glazed headers on the principal elevations, and two large arched doors pierced the south wall on either side of a central

arched window. The interior was distinguished by a raised pulpit on the north wall opposite the entrances. Boxed pews and a gallery provided congregational seating.

The Anglican congregations in Somerset and Coventry parishes expanded enough during the seventeenth and early eighteenth centuries to warrant the construction of chapels of ease a distance from the parent churches. With the main church of Coventry Parish situated in Rehobeth,[26] parishioners living along the Annemessex rivers were too remote to participate easily in Sunday worship services. Thus, services were held as early as 1726 at a chapel of ease known initially as Annemessex Chapel, near the head of Coulbourne's Creek.[27]

By 1762 the first chapel building at Coulbourne's Creek had evidently reached such a dilapidated state that 62,400 pounds of tobacco were levied to purchase two acres of land and finance the construction of a second building. In 1760 Stephen Horsey and Michael Holland had transferred to the vestry of Coventry Parish a parcel of land "Beginning at a marked Cedar Stake being the bounder of a Tract of Land called Pomferet near the Westermost Corner of the new Chappell..., two acres being to Include the ground whereon the said New Chappell now stands."[28]

During the pre-Revolutionary War period, the principal Monie congregation was relocated and two chapels of ease were erected in Somerset Parish. Sometime after 1708 the early riverside church on the Almodington plantation was abandoned. Tradition holds that in 1710 a new church was

St Andrew's Episcopal Church, southwest elevation.

built farther inland near the head of the Little Monie Creek, and this building stood until the late nineteenth century.[29] The first chapel of ease, known as King's Mill Chapel, was built in 1723 at the head of King's Creek. It served Somerset Parish until 1767.[30] At that time it was clear to the congregation that the chapel was inconveniently sited, too small, and in dire need of repair or replacement. The Somerset Parish vestry decided to petition the General Assembly for a levy to finance the purchase of lots in Princess Anne Town and to construct a new chapel. For £28 Robert Geddes transferred Lots 27 and 28 bordering New Market Street and Low and Upper alleys to Hamilton Bell, rector; Jesse King, William Waller, John Jones (Goose Creek), Revell Horsey, Isaiah Tillman, and Andrew Francis Cheney, vestrymen; and William Fountain and John McGraw, wardens.[31]

The vestry minutes of Somerset Parish record in detail the dimensions and finish of the new chapel. When it was finally completed in 1773, the Flemish bond brick building was probably the most expensive church raised within the parish and the most elaborate structure yet erected in the town limits of Princess Anne. Levin Ballard was awarded the contract to build the church for £800 in the manner designated by the vestry:

> *The...Vestry Agreed on a plan for a New Chapel to be Built in Princess Anne Town in Manner and form following, Viz To be Sixty feet In Length and Forty feet in Wedth in the clear. Exclusive of an Arch or Simey Circle for the Communion Table or Chancel, the Walls to be Twenty feet High Between the Surface of the Earth and the Wall plates, the walls to be three Bricks and ahalf thick as high as the Water Table which is to be Two Feet and ahalf High*

from the Earth, and from that to the Wall Plates Two Bricks and a half Thick with three Girders A Cross, A Gallery A Cross the West End Ten feet Wide the front part of the Gallery to be plain winscutt. with four Rows of Seats In the above Gallery, Four Windows In Each Side, Each Window to Contain forty Eight Panes of Glass the Glass to be Eight Inches by Ten, Exclusive of an Arch over Each Window, a Small Window at the Back of the pulpit to Contain fifteen Panes of Glass Eight Inches by Ten, two Windows In the Arch or Simey Circle for the Chancel, Each Window to Contain Thirty two Panes of Glass, Exclusive of an Arch over Each Window, one Small Window in the End over the Gallery to Contain fifteen Panes of Glass Eight Inches by Ten, Two Large Arch folding pannell, Doors, in the West End, the floor to be Laid with toyl and raised, a foot from the Surface of the Earth, and the whole Chapel to be Sealed over Head with plank Three Quarters of an Inch thick, and to be Covered with Green Cypress Shingles Inch Thick, and three shingles to Cover a foot, the Shingles to be put on with Ten penny Nails, the Insides of the Wall to be Well Plastered and White Washed up to the Sealing, and the Wall of the Simmy Circle to be Carried up as High as the other wall and the Simmy Circle So to be made at the North and South alleys of the Said Chapel Shall Lead Into it, a Door about three feet wide In the North Sides, at the West End of the Said Chapel With Brick Stepts to Lead Into the Gallery to the Stairs, and Also Build a Belfry to the said Chapel Provided Two Workmen Can Compleat the Same in Twenty four Hours

Otherwise be paid for the time over and Above In Proportion for the said Work.[32]

Work on the basic structure continued for two years, and it was not until May 1770 that specifications were submitted to detail the interior woodwork: Fifty-three pews were required, each three feet ten inches high, and a railing of the same height was to enclose the chancel. The chancel banisters, upper rails, and doors were to be fashioned from walnut. Construction of the new chapel lasted until 1773, and in September of that year the vestry allotted the pews.[33]

In many ways, the first three quarters of the eighteenth century were an especially prosperous period in Eastern Shore history. Diversification in agriculture, expansion of a trade economy with Europe and the Caribbean, and increases in craft manufacture broadened economic opportunities on several levels of Somerset society. Domestic life in general made significant strides, with stabilization of the native population and family structure and improvements in housing, churches, and schools. For the blacks in Somerset society, however, these decades saw the end of economic opportunity for the already small free black community and the institutionalization of an oppressive slave system.

The large strides in quality of life many in Somerset County experienced were soon to be seriously threatened. The ever-widening political and economic differences between England and her colonies resulted in the outbreak of war in 1776, jeopardizing trading ties and the connections that had led to much of the region's economic success. ❧

CHAPTER V, 1700-1775
Halls, Parlors, and Courts

For many Somerset planters in the early and mid-eighteenth century, profits earned through the mixed agriculture and trade economy financed the rebuilding or replacement of seventeenth century housing. In contrast to houses common in the preceding century, these new brick and frame dwellings were erected with more permanent building practices, including brick foundations. In addition, changes in social habits during the eighteenth century demanded more complex floor plans that could provide family privacy and room specialization. Finely crafted paneled interiors enhanced domestic life and offered elaborate settings for private as well as public functions. Professional masons, carpenters, joiners, and related craftsmen engaged in the construction of an impressive class of plantation architecture. These buildings not only have survived to modern times in

remarkable repair, but the standards of design and craftsmanship they set have lasted with them.

While the significance of these early houses is readily apparent, the bias inherent in their survival distorts the modern view of pre-Revolutionary War building in Somerset County. These houses are best understood as the cream of domestic architecture from the period and in no manner representative of the average dwelling. Indeed, it is only because of their superior construction and finish with above-average materials that they have survived.

Architectural trends during the early to middle eighteenth century are evident both in the extant collection of buildings and in surviving court records of the time. The data suggests the era saw a distinct increase in the frequency of masonry construction as well as a wider variation in floor

Makepeace, photograph c. 1900 (courtesy of the Maryland Historical Trust).

Salisbury, southwest elevation.

plans than previously thought. Thirty-five Orphans Court evaluations recorded in Somerset County between 1739 and 1759 show that half the frame or log houses had at least one brick chimney. The four brick houses assessed for the court between 1749 and 1755 averaged over 830 square feet on the ground floor, nearly twice the floor space of more modest dwellings.[1]

Whether brick was employed in erecting walls, foundations, or chimneys, its mere presence in a house provided for a more stable existence. Brick clay was often excavated close to the building site, and the thousands of bricks necessary to build a house were fired on the site. Contrary to popular belief, brick was not a valuable commodity imported from England in quantities sufficient to erect many buildings. However, contemporary records do show some small shipments of brick for ballast.[2] As lime is not a natural resource on the lower Eastern Shore, colonists used oyster shell mortar, which rendered a hard, long-lasting binder for brick walls.

The oldest extant houses in Somerset County are a small group of story-and-a-half, one- or two-room brick dwellings estimated to date from the first half of the eighteenth century. These houses share several early construction practices, including Flemish bond brick walls; tilted false plates in the roof; a large common room or "hall" with a generous cooking fireplace; and decorated, exposed joists.

Thought to be one of the oldest in this group is a story-and-a-half brick dwelling known since about 1800 as Salisbury.[3] Situated on the north bank of the Great Annemessex River, this Flemish bond brick house was obviously erected in two stages: The back hall, a remnant of the origi-

Salisbury, chamfered floor joist with lamb's-tongue stop.

nal one-room house, is believed to date from around 1700. The present kitchen, which originally was two rooms, appears to have been an early to mid-eighteenth century addition that gave the house a three-room plan common to the period. Remaining in the back hall is a series of exposed, heavy second floor joists of pine finished with chamfered edges that terminate near the wall surface with a lamb's-tongue stop. An identical floor joist was reused under the house as a sill around 1880, when the old brick house was reduced in size and a two-story frame addition was attached.

The roof construction of the earlier part of the house is similar to that in other contemporary dwellings. Originally, the eaves of the house were exposed, and the common rafters were carried by a tilted false plate system not unlike the framing practice detailed in the 1688 house description discussed in Chapter III. An interesting survival is the sawn board roof fastened with wrought-iron nails located over the back hall.

Beauchamp house, northwest elevation.

Beauchamp house, hall paneling.

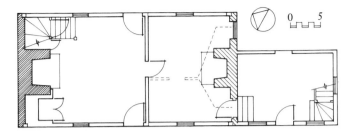

Beauchamp house, floor plan, Cary Carson, Paul Touart and Nancy Kurtz.

Beauchamp house, north gable end diaper pattern.

A nearby dwelling that follows a similar developmental pattern is the Beauchamp house, which stands southeast of Westover at the head of the Annemessex River. Initially built around 1710-1730 as a story-and-a-half, one-room plan frame dwelling with a brick gable end, the house was expanded later in the eighteenth century with a two-room, brick-ended addition.

The north gable end of the original house exhibits the most sophisticated glazed header diaper pattern surviving in Somerset County. Glazed bricks were often used in more expensive dwellings as decorative highlights in Flemish bond walls. The gray-blue glaze of the headers enhances the checkerboard brick pattern created by the Flemish bond. The diaper pattern, found on four surviving Somerset houses,

is an elaborate masonry technique whereby intersecting diagonal rows of glazed headers are laid to create a decorative effect.

Inside the early room of the Beauchamp house, the ceiling is distinguished by a series of exposed second floor joists finished with a cyma-curve corner molding. Reflective of the mid-eighteenth century is the fully paneled north end of the main room. This finely crafted raised panel wall incorporates a built-in cupboard with glazed upper doors in the northwest corner and a winder stair with closet in the opposite corner. The small bricked-in windows in the gable end and the style of the paneling suggest the one-room interior remained unfinished for a time, perhaps only covered with a coat of whitewash. The paneling appears to have been inserted during the mid-eighteenth century.

The Beauchamp house was enlarged in the same manner as the Powell-Benston house, cited in Chapter III, and Salisbury—two rooms built to one side of the hall. The resulting three-room plan allowed for more private space on the first floor. Originally heated by separate fireplaces, the new rooms were probably furnished as a first floor chamber and perhaps a dining room, a feature that became more prevalent as the century continued.

An unfinished interior like that at the Beauchamp house was not uncommon in houses of the colonial period. Other surviving dwellings as well as contemporary descriptions indicate owners often financed the finishing of a house much later than its initial construction. However, there were probably other reasons for unfinished interiors as well. In some cases where houses appear to have been half-finished, it may have been because the owner died, rather than deferred the expense of finishing. For example, when Revel Horsey was orphaned, his father left him a 100-acre parcel of land on Revells Neck improved by

one Dwelling house about twenty feet in Length and Sixteen feet wide one plank floor below none above nor any Stairs nor is the said house Lathed nor filled in....[4]

The Somerset County Orphans Court records offer another example of a seemingly unfinished dwelling, on William Turpin's land, recorded in 1734: "a Large house with a Brick Chimney in the midst Two Rooms below Staires and a porch but no Rooms above...." The remainder of the de-

Williams Green, east elevation.

Williams Green, hall paneling, Michael Harrison Day—photographer.

Sudler's Conclusion, east elevation.

Sudler's Conclusion, transverse section A-A₁

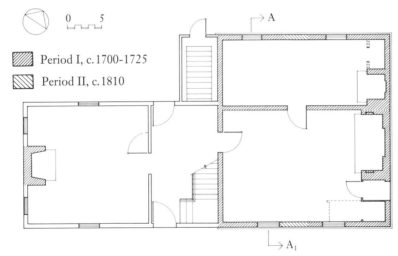

Period I, c.1700-1725

Period II, c.1810

Sudler's Conclusion, first floor plan (courtesy of the Historic American Buildings Survey, Library of Congress).

scription, however, indicates the age of the house and suggests that sometimes interiors were never finished: "the Covering…much Decayed and rotten as also the Lower part of the frame much Decayed being Very Old…."[5]

Perhaps the most illustrative example of an interior finished at a later date is the early eighteenth century Flemish bond brick house commonly known as Williams Green or Williams Conquest. Thomas Williams is credited with the construction of the hall/parlor Flemish bond brick house around 1733, but the interior evidently remained unfinished for a number of years. Williams did not finance the installation of the raised paneling until the late 1740s or 1750s.[6] This delay in finishing was revealed by the discovery of plastered wall surfaces with accumulations of dirt under the paneling. It was not normal practice to plaster surfaces intended to be covered with woodwork unless those walls were left unfinished for a period of years.

Williams Green is also interesting for its demonstration of another way a three-room plan could be achieved. At the same time the woodwork was installed, the old parlor or first floor chamber was divided into two rooms with individual fireplaces, creating a floor plan not unlike that of the Powell-Benston and Beauchamp houses. This division of space provided for a dining area adjacent to the detached kitchen, which was located immediately east of the house.

The most elaborate woodwork at Williams Green is found in the expansive hall, where a wide bolection molding frames a six-foot fireplace. Three diamond panels framed by short fluted pilasters highlight the overmantel. It has been suggested these panels might have contained hatchments hung to commemorate the family's ancestry. A complex crown molding tops the expertly paneled wall. Fixed in the northwest corner is a winder stair and closet, and a four-panel door in the northeast corner opens into another storage space. The two smaller rooms created from the parlor are finished in a similar fashion, with paneled overmantels. Beaded second floor joists distinguish each of the rooms.

Sudler's Conclusion is another Flemish bond brick house

evidently erected during the first decades of the eighteenth century. Its brick walls rise from a molded water table and are pierced by segmental-arched window and door openings. The east end wall is marked by a sawtooth belt course, a feature shared by only two other county houses, the Beauchamp house and Makepeace. Tilted false plates concealed within the boxed cornices support the common rafter roof system.

On the first floor a brick partition divides the large south room or hall from a narrow north room, which was probably originally fitted as a first floor chamber. The principal room of Sudler's Conclusion has ten-foot ceilings with exposed ovolo-molded ceiling joists and a large cooking fireplace on the east wall. The raised paneling that once distinguished the fireplace wall was removed some time ago.

As reflected in these early dwellings, the second quarter of the eighteenth century witnessed an increase in the number of expertly executed Georgian exteriors and interiors. Records survive of one man's quest for such a dwelling. In 1740 Christopher Dominick Jackson, a surgeon, hired John McCuddy, a local carpenter, for many rudimentary woodworking jobs associated with Jackson's shop and house. In part, McCuddy charged Jackson for stair construction at £1.16; "To winscotting your Hall" at £9; and "To cornising your house and cupboard" at £1.5. Wainscoting the hall, or installing paneling, was by far the most expensive item on the list of tasks performed.[7]

The construction of these well-built and finely finished dwellings marked more than the flowering of a fine school of local carpentry. More important, these buildings satisfied the

Arlington, southwest elevation.

Hayward's Lott, east elevation.

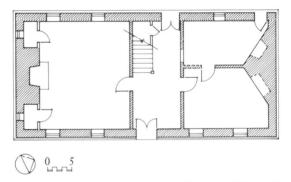

Hayward's Lott floor plan, Paul Touart, Paul Sigrist, and Nancy Kurtz.

desire of Somerset planters to establish permanent seats of residence where they could display their accumulated wealth and hold public and private gatherings in settings comparable to those of their English contemporaries.

During the quarter century preceding the Revolution, this desire for better built, more ostentatious dwellings developed on more than one level. At that time, a group of planters in Somerset County financed the construction of brick plantation houses that outdistanced all other dwellings known to have stood on the lower Shore at that time. These pretentious houses were assembled with more sophisticated exterior features and more formal floor plans than those that had gone before. Most significant, a center hall or passage allowed for entrance into a public rather than a private space, controlling access into more intimate rooms. Finely paneled parlors with built-in cupboards provided elaborate backdrops for formal entertaining as well as daily activities.

Standing on the south shore of Back Creek is Arlington,

a mid-eighteenth century dwelling reflecting these new interests. The two-story, five-bay Flemish bond brick house boasts expensive masonry details such as glazed brick checkerboard patterns and rubbed brick finishes highlighting door and windows. In addition, the front corners of the building and the south belt course are constructed of decorative rubbed brick.

Inside the house, the floor plan follows a straightforward center hall plan with a large room to either side of a wide passage. The turned baluster stair survives in the passage, but the formal mid-eighteenth century paneling has been removed from both first floor rooms.

This center passage, single-pile (one room deep) floor plan was modified by other wealthy planters to suit even more specialized needs. Hayward's Lott, not far from the Pocomoke River, was also built during the 1750s with similar attention to extravagant brickwork. This two-and-a-half story Flemish bond brick dwelling is enhanced with glazed brick checkerboard patterns, rubbed brick arches, and an unconventionally molded water table. It was the centerpiece of an extensive plantation complex maintained by the Hayward family until the twentieth century. The center passage floor plan at Hayward's Lott is slightly more complicated than that at Arlington. The large parlor south of the hall extends the full depth of the house, while to the north are two smaller rooms, each fitted with a corner fireplace. The mid-eighteenth century paneling was removed from Hayward's Lott during the early to mid-nineteenth century.

Yet another variation on the center hall, single-pile house is provided by Almodington, located on the north shore of the Manokin River. Also estimated to date from the

Almodington parlor paneling, (courtesy of the Metropolitan Museum of Art, Rogers Fund, 1918, 18.99.1).

Almodington, south elevation, photograph c. 1967 (courtesy of the Maryland Historical Trust).

1750s, this two-story, five-bay Flemish bond brick house measures 55'4" across by 24'6" deep. As with the other houses in this group, Almodington is distinguished by a carefully executed checkerboard pattern of glazed headers. A simple water table and belt course continue around all four sides, and rubbed brick detailing decorates the window openings. Stretching across the base of the roof is a plastered cove cornice, a rare period feature surviving on only three other houses in Somerset County (Arlington, Panther's Den, and Cherry Grove).

The front door of Almodington opens into a spacious center passage. A dogleg stair is embellished with turned balusters, a decorated stringer, and a molded handrail that terminates at its base in a spiral. Located to the west of the passage is the most formal room, the parlor, originally fitted with the most extravagant Georgian paneling known in a Somerset County dwelling. The nearly square 19' by 21' room had floor-to-ceiling raised paneling, and the fireplace wall was embellished with built-in shell-backed cupboards on each side of a paneled overmantel flanked with fluted pilasters. The Federal-style mantel was added at a later date. The mid-eighteenth century woodwork in the room was so highly prized it was removed in the early twentieth century and installed in the Metropolitan Museum of Art as a backdrop for the museum's Chippendale furniture collection.

To the east of the center passage is a smaller room, probably used for dining. Although not as richly detailed as the parlor, the room had a chimney breast and window reveals covered with raised paneling. A floor-to-ceiling raised panel partition separates the dining room from a narrow passage along the north wall. Connecting the hall and a door in the east gable end, this period passage evidently was used to get from the dining room to an exterior door near the kitchen.

In contrast to the center passage tradition in large plantation houses is Waterloo, estimated to date from the late 1740s or early 1750s. Henry Waggaman, one of the wealthiest planters in central Somerset County during the mid-eighteenth century, chose a different orientation for his impressive dwelling: The entrance was placed in a bold pedimented gable, which then served as the principal elevation. Although he employed decorative conventions similar to those in the houses just described, including glazed checkerboard and diaper patterns in Flemish bond brick walls, Waggaman chose to highlight the three most visible corners of his house with decorative quoins. The cornice, enhanced with rows of modillions, trims the perimeter of the steeply pitched roof.

The four-room plan at Waterloo provided Waggaman and his family with more opportunity for room specialization on the first floor. Located in the southwest corner is the stair hall, which survives with an elaborately fashioned, four-flight, twisted baluster stair. The raised panel wainscoting in the hall continues up the stairwell. North of the hall is the parlor, the largest first floor space, and to the east of the hall and parlor are two smaller rooms, one of which probably served as a dining room. All of the rooms except the hall have corner fireplaces and have been stripped of their mid-eighteenth century woodwork.

Relatively few Somerset County residents aspired to such ostentatious architectural statements as a Waterloo or an Almodington. Nonetheless, other planters during the period financed similarly planned dwellings, albeit on a smaller scale.

Prominent among the smaller dwellings dating to the pre-Revolutionary War period is the Waddy house, historically known as the Jarvis Ballard house. A glazed brick checkerboard pattern enhances the north wall. Like Almodington and Arlington, this facade has door and window openings capped with segmental arches of alternating glazed bricks. The squarish, story-and-a-half structure follows the four-room disposition with a triple-run turned baluster stair

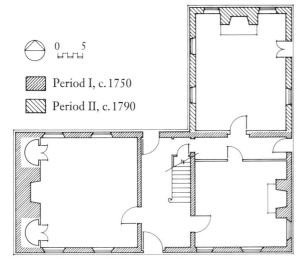

0   5

Period I, c. 1750

Period II, c. 1790

Almodington floor plan, Paul Touart, Bobbie Stadler, and Nancy Kurtz.

Waterloo, south elevation.

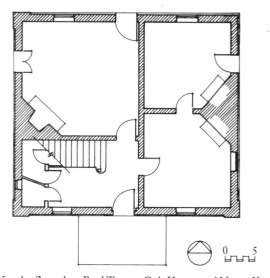

Waterloo floor plan, Paul Touart, Gale Yerges, and Nancy Kurtz.

in the southeast corner of the stair hall. Corner fireplaces provide heat for the three first floor rooms, and raised paneling with fluted pilasters marks the parlor interior.

A similarly early four-room plan brick dwelling with a less conventional architectural history is The Reward, sited along the north shore of Pocomoke Sound near the entrance to the Pocomoke River. The Reward is unique in Maryland as the only surviving house to incorporate diamond-shaped chimney stacks, a feature more common to seventeenth century English architecture.[8]

Another unusual feature at The Reward was the original jerkinhead roof, a rare roof shape employed almost exclusively as a Georgian style feature. Framing evidence visible in the roof near the end walls indicates the old jerkinhead was altered to a plain gable around the turn of the twentieth century. Aside from the series of originally exposed beaded

joists and the corner locations of the three fireplaces, the interior woodwork dates from an 1826 remodeling.

Also an upper range plantation dwelling on a smaller scale is Harrington, a two-story, four-room plan frame house judged to have been erected for Thomas Holbrook some time after he purchased the property in the 1740s. The house follows an elaborate four-room plan similar to that at Waterloo and the Waddy house, and the first floor interiors are fitted with fine period woodwork. A turned baluster stair and raised panel wainscoting remain in the hall, while the parlor exhibits fluted pilasters on each side of a raised panel fireplace wall. The parlor is also finished with exposed, beaded joists and paneled wainscoting.

In contrast to other Maryland counties, Somerset can boast a remarkable survival of houses from the pre-Revolutionary era. However, these dwellings were erected for the wealthiest segment of county society and do not reflect how the majority of people lived. The balance of the Somerset population occupied much smaller, less substantial structures that disappeared because of fire, decay, or everyday use. Probably more typical of a common dwelling of the time is the house evaluated on the property of Charles Woolford in April 1753. The officials of the county Orphans Court described the structure as

> *One Small dwelling house twenty feet Long and Sixteen feet wide Covered with Oak Clapboards and weather-boarded with pine plank with one Small Sash window with plank floor above and below Stairs, plastered below Staires and Sealed with pine Plank above Staires with a Brick Seller under the afd house with one out Side Brick Chimney....*[9]

Woolford's house most likely contained one room on

each floor with a corner stair to one side of the fireplace. Evidently the house contained only one window, and the second floor may or may not have had a separate fireplace. The most unusual feature was the continuous brick foundation, which enclosed the cellar and provided a substantial means of support for the frame structure. In most cases the officials of the court did not bother to mention the understructure of a house, so it is assumed the brick cellar improved the value of the dwelling and contrasted with other houses, which were supported by brick or timber piers, earthfast posts, or nothing at all.

Not all dwellings in Somerset County were built of brick or frame. By the mid-eighteenth century large numbers of hewn, sawn, and round log houses populated the countryside. In 1757 Thomas Gibbons inherited a

Dwelling house twenty foot Square hewed Loggs Weatherboarded with Pine Boards and Double covered with Oak boards Plank flored above & Below and Not Plastered and One bricked chimney...[10]

Smaller and meaner yet was the improvement on the property of orphan Joseph Dashiell, situated on the Wicomico River. On this land in 1752 was "one Small house fifteen feet Long and Twelve feet wide Built with Round poles."[11]

Large or small, brick, frame, or log, these plantation houses were not intended to stand alone as so many of the surviving ones do today. Accompanying the house were any number of support buildings that served the domestic and agricultural needs of the plantation. Sadly, no surviving outbuilding in Somerset County can be dated before the

Waddy house, northwest elevation.

Revolution, although the existence of such structures is well documented.

Subscribers for the Somerset County Orphans Court recorded an especially extensive array of outbuildings on April 12, 1749, at the estate of Colonel George Dashiell.[12] Immediately surrounding the 52' by 22' brick house were one 16' by 15' "fraimed Kitchen…weatherbarded with plank and Shingled with Cyprus Shingles with an out side brick Chimney the Sides fild in with brick with Shelves and Dressers Convenient for a Kitching"; another frame building measuring 40' by 20' with "one End weatherbarded up with plank with a Brick Chimney to it for a weaving and Spining hous the other End open on one side and one End for a prise hous"; "one fraimed hous 12 by 12 foot with a Shed on one

Side"; "one fraimed hous 15 by 10 with A shed on one side"; a brick milkhouse, 12' by 10'; and "one brick oven and hous over it Covered with Clabbords." Probably standing farther from the main house were two barns, one fully floored; two corn houses, one of sawn logs and one of round logs; a 10' by 5' frame office; a 45' by 20' quarter with a brick chimney; a 16' by 14' "Round Pold" smith's shop; a 24' by 11' log stable; a 10' by 10' "sawd log" hen house; and an 11' by 11' schoolhouse of round poles with a brick chimney.

Aside from the buildings, most plantations included bearing fruit trees and paled gardens. The Dashiell plantation had apple, pear, plum, peach, and cherry trees, in addition to a fruit tree nursery and a 140' by 120' fenced garden that probably contained vegetables and herbs. Surrounding much of the

Harrington, south elevation.

The Reward, photograph c. 1910 (courtesy of Mrs. William S. Morsell, Jr.).

plantation was a fence erected to discourage predators from ravaging the vulnerable crops.

Colonel Dashiell's domestic and agricultural complex was significantly larger and more complicated than most eighteenth century plantations, and it is clear he must have had a large slave or servant labor force to operate it. By the 1740s planters in Somerset County and Maryland in general had shifted from purchasing bonded or indentured servants to investing in slaves imported from Africa and the West Indies. This switch was caused by the dearth of indentured servants coming to the Chesapeake region after 1700, when the opportunities in land and freedom offered their predecessors were no longer available. Planters, unable to operate without help, increasingly invested in slaves. In Somerset County few planters could afford more than a dozen slaves, and most operated with only a few.

From all accounts and references, slave housing in the pre-Revolutionary period went the way of most wooden buildings erected close to the ground without much protection from insects, moisture, and fire. The absence of any surviving examples speaks of the impermanent nature of the slave quarters built during this period.

Other than four walls, a roof, and a fireplace, slave houses were built with few amenities. Dirt floors and windowless rooms were not uncommon. Probably typical was the "old Log'd quarter" with "wooden chimney" found on the property of James Coventon in 1749.[13] Some slaves slept above the kitchen as suggested in the assessment of Andrew Jones's prop-

erty in 1684, but on William Turpin's farm in 1734 a different arrangement was described: "Kitchen and Quarter Under one Roof with a Brick Chimney in the Midst."[14] Multi-family structures were sometimes erected on the larger plantations. One example is the 45' by 20' frame quarter on Colonel George Dashiell's Wicomico Creek plantation. This structure had a brick chimney, which was undoubtedly centered to serve two separate 20' by 20' rooms. In general, slave housing was erected cheaply to fill an immediate need and was not expected to endure much beyond the lives of its occupants.

Despite some revealing references to more common types of plantation improvements, many issues concerning the poor and enslaved in the eighteenth century are left unclear. Even for the middle to upper classes, for which representative dwellings survive, the architectural and documentary evidence amounts to no more than a small fragment of the whole picture. Nevertheless, it appears there was a distinct trend in Somerset County from 1700 to 1775 for those who could afford improvements to build more permanent, more sophisticated residences as money and time allowed. These new building patterns reflect the social and economic realignment that took place in the Chesapeake region at the time. The stability caused by the switch from transient cash crop agriculture to a broader-based local and regional agrarian economy allowed major and medium-sized planters both to develop elaborate seats of residence where they could display their acquired wealth and status and, in turn, to bequeath the property to the next generation. ❧

CHAPTER VI, 1775-1850
The Revolution and the New Republic

The seventy-five years from the start of the Revolutionary War to the mid-nineteenth century pose interesting contrasts and developments in the history of Maryland's lower Eastern Shore. The region managed to endure eight years of conflict without a major campaign fought on its shore, but Somerset and Worcester counties suffered a more insidious fate as ardent Toryism and invading enemy warships penetrated undefended shorelines. Marauding picaroons raided defenseless plantation owners, stealthily maneuvering their small boats through the familiar bays, rivers, creeks, and guts of the lower Shore.

In spite of these difficulties, the plantation economy of the region remained relatively healthy through the war years and eventually broadened as transportation networks increased between Norfolk and Baltimore. Agriculture experienced long overdue reform, and by the end of the period plantation owners had abandoned tobacco and shifted their attention to lucrative cash crops in corn, wheat, potatoes, and other foodstuffs.

During the early months of the Revolution, it was clear to British commanders that the Chesapeake would play a key role in determining the result of the war, and it was their firm desire to control bay waters as soon as possible. By mid-summer 1775 British forces had seized the fishing villages on Tangier and Smith islands, after which the islands served as a midway station for the Tories operating between mainland Somerset and enemy ships offshore.[1]

Strong Tory sentiments on the peninsula were well-known in Annapolis, and Samuel Chase, as a member of the Maryland Council on Safety, commented on them while addressing the Continental Congress: "Tories have been gathering in Sussex, Worcester, and Somerset counties for several days. They have 250 men collected at Parker's Mill nine miles from Salisbury with intention to seise the Magazine and destroy the property of the Whiggs."[2] With its isolated and undefended location, Somerset County proved especially popular as a haven for Tory activists, deserters, and refugees.[3] In particular, many residents in the environs of Somers Cove were widely recognized as sympathetic to the English cause.

Indeed, the vulnerable condition of the undefended Eastern Shore caused many to worry for their plantations as well as for their lives. Luther Martin, Maryland's first attorney general, resided near Princess Anne when he commented in 1777, "There was a period of considerable duration throughout which, not only myself but many others, did not lay down one night in our beds without the hazard of waking on board a British armed ship, or in the other world."[4]

Conditions worsened as the war continued, and little defense was directed to the Eastern Shore. Colonel Joseph Dashiell, Worcester commander under Governor Thomas Sim Lee, tried to convey to the governor the urgency of the situation in 1780. He wrote, "Enemy boats are twenty miles up our river burning our vessels...plundering houses...afraid people will rebel...From all appearances we are in a worse situation than we have been in this war."[5]

Thomas Seon Sudler of Sudler's Conclusion recorded specific details surrounding the plundering of his own property. Late in the night of February 6, 1781, or early the following morning, "British Barges and Neighbors" entered his Back Creek plantation while Sudler was visiting Captain Nehemiah King. Upon Sudler's return he found countless items missing, which he carefully entered in his diary. Among the goods stolen were "1 negroe girl named Sarah about 16 years old, 100 gallon of Brandy, 2 large silver ladles, 1 dozen large tablespoons, 1 silver Tea Tongues, £55 in hard money, 2300 dollars in certificates" and "several hundred weight of Bacon and Beef." Sudler also mentioned that "John Price and James Clarkes vessels assisted to plunder me" and that he was never compensated.[6]

So desperate had the situation become by the early 1780s that twenty-six Somerset countians drafted a letter to the Maryland Council of Safety in a plea for help:

> *The defenseless situation of the rivers and the much exposed inhabitants in this part of the state loudly calls for assistance. The numberless depredations committed with impunity by picaroons and the Prospect of Continuance of such Outrages clearly point out the immediate Necessity of adopting some effective measures to check their progress.*[7]

The crimes of Tory villains like Joseph Wheland, Jr., who terrorized much of the Chesapeake, received high visibility, and the plundering of plantations evidently continued until the end of the war. A solution to the problem was prevented by the clandestine nature of the thefts, the high number of Tory sympathizers in the region, and the meagerness of the local militia's equipment. Nonetheless, many yeomen and small Somerset planters were able to maintain a

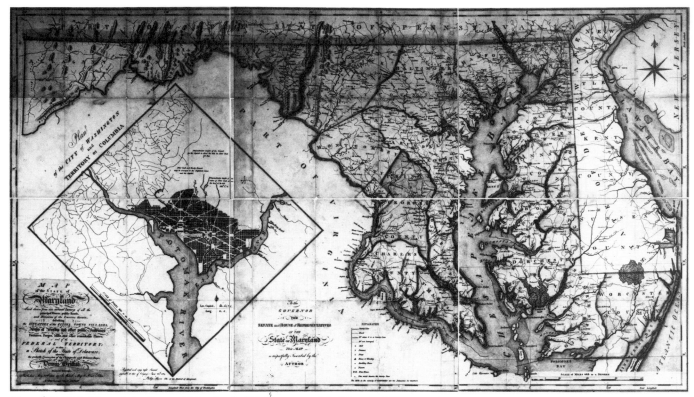

Dennis Griffith, Map of the State of Maryland, *1794 (courtesy of the Maryland Historical Society)*.

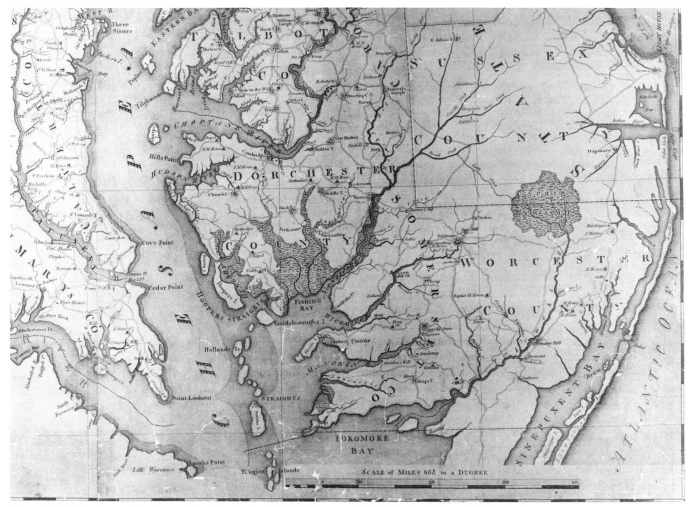

Dennis Griffith, Map of the State Maryland, *detail, 1794 (courtesy of the Maryland Historical Society)*.

strong loyalist philosophy without violent actions against their neighbors.

Better known among the Eastern Shore events surrounding the Revolution was the "Battle of the Barges." On November 30, 1782, British barges were spotted entering Kedges Straits north of Tangier Island. In close pursuit was the Maryland barge *Protector* and four other colonial vessels, the *Defence*, the *Fearnaught*, the *Flying Fish*, and the *Terrible*.[8] With its eighteen-pound guns, the *Protector* appeared at first to overwhelm the three British warships. When two ammunition chests exploded on board, however, the conflict was turned in favor of the British. With the principal colonial vessel ablaze and clearly in trouble, the other Maryland boats retreated to Virginia waters. The *Protector* was eventually boarded, and Captain Zedekiah Walley was killed in defense of his ship.[9]

Although the lower Eastern Shore remained largely undefended through eight years of conflict and fractious politics instigated countless crimes against personal property, the agricultural and minor industrial economy remained stable throughout the period. Planters continued to grow a mixture of tobacco, corn, and wheat in addition to other grasses and livestock. During the war, Henry Jackson and George Dashiell are recorded at different times as sources of desperately needed meat for starving colonial troops. On September 22, 1780, Henry Jackson of Beckford sent 2,744 pounds of bacon and nineteen barrels of pork to Head of Elk (later Elkton) by wagon in order to evade enemy boats. Likewise, George Dashiell drove 100 cattle to the head of the bay,[10] where Colonel Henry Hollingsworth served as deputy quartermaster general of the Eastern Shore.[11]

Following the Revolution, the primary focus of agriculture on the lower Eastern Shore began to shift. Tobacco, planted for over 100 years as the principal cash crop, declined in production through the last quarter of the eighteenth century. It was not until the second quarter of the nineteenth century, however, that tobacco was completely replaced with lucrative harvests of wheat, corn, oats, and potatoes.

Littleton Dennis Teackle, considered one of the most influential men of his time, set down a detailed description of Somerset agriculture around the turn of the century. In an effort to establish trade with the Liverpool firm of Barclay and Salkeld and Co., Teackle wrote an introductory letter in February 1806:

Somerset is accounted one of the wealthiest Counties of Maryland, its exports are estimated at half a million dollars p. annum, the crop of tobacco is about two thousand hogsheads—its situation however being low and quite levil, is consequently subject to injury from the water in wet seasons—which particularly effected the Agricultural Interest during 1802 and 1803 but more especially during 1804 when great importations were actually required to supply the necessities of its inhabitants....The several prices affixed are such as are paid here and at which they would be delivered on Wicomico, in which a ship of 1000 tons may load. There are two Rivers of that name, Wicomico in Somerset County on the Eastern Shore of Maryland one or two days sail from Norfolk is herein alluded to. Besides lumber this county abounds in many substantial articles of export such as wheat, corn, oats, peas, beans, tobacco, pork, and oak bark. The amount of exports are estimated at $500,000.[12]

The shift away from dependence on tobacco was a slow one, and individual Somerset planters realigned their agricultural pursuits when they saw fit. Thomas S. Sudler relied heavily on his tobacco crop through the early nineteenth century and even wagered with his farmhand Nace on the size of his harvest in 1800. Nace bet his owner one dollar against a new pair of shoes that the yield would be upwards of 8,000 pounds. That year the harvest reached 8,069 pounds, and Nace evidently won the bet. On March 19, 1802, Sudler delivered seven hogsheads for inspection at Maddox's warehouse on Back Creek. His final tally for that year was 10,780 pounds.[13]

By 1840, however, tobacco fields had virtually disappeared from the Eastern Shore landscape. Crop statistics entered in the agricultural schedule of the 1840 census reveal that Eastern Shore planters were focusing their efforts on raising large numbers of cattle, sheep, swine, and poultry and significant amounts of various grains. Somerset planters maintained competitive levels of production with other Eastern Shore counties by harvesting 428,102 bushels of Indian corn; 125,697 bushels of oats; and 36,778 bushels of wheat. In addition, the 52,000-pound potato harvest in 1840 exceeded that of any other Eastern Shore county, and the value of Somerset lumber products and home manufactures remained high.[14]

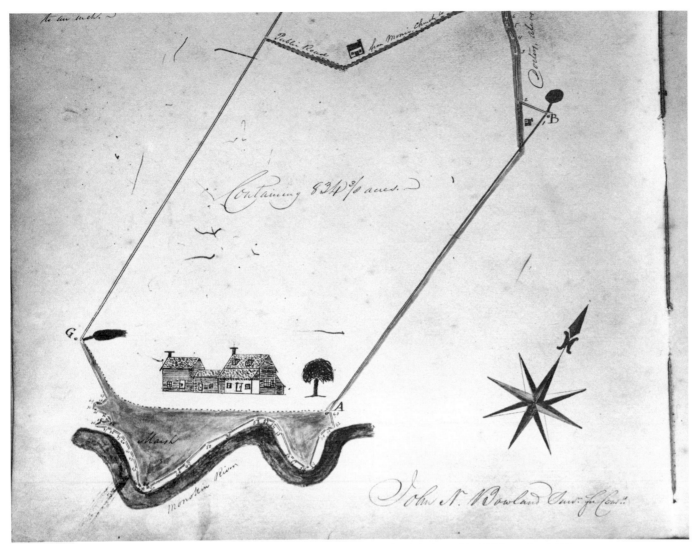

"Brownstone" plat, Somerset County Judicial Records LH #1 (MdHR 13,169; 1/48/4/15), p.158, 30 November 1840 (courtesy of the Maryland State Archives).

More insight into the economy of the period is gained from a letter written on September 20, 1841, by Levin Handy, then clerk of court for Somerset County. Handy described the agriculture and trade on the lower Shore at the time for David Ridgely, a former state librarian who was compiling a "geographical description" of Maryland:

The inhabitants of Somerset along the Bay and Sound side and on our rivers depend chiefly on boating between our rivers the Great and Little Annamessex, Monokin, Wicomico all within the limits of Somerset County as well as such part of the Nanticoke and Pocomoke rivers as is within said limits, to Richmond, Norfolk, Alexandria, Washington, George Town, Baltimore, Philadelphia, and New York—and the articles of trafic are corn, wheat, oats—Timber, wood, staves, oysters, Terrapins, Fish—Sweet Potatoes, Melons—In the Interior the pursuits of the people are chiefly agricultural consisting in the growing of Wheat, Corn, and Oats, the two latter being the more regular and successful products….[15]

The level of production recorded in 1840 was not reached without some effort, however. Planters such as James

Wilson of "Brownstone" plantation left accounts of their efforts to attack the pervasive problem of poor soil husbandry. A century of overuse and neglect had rendered many Somerset fields infertile. In former years the solution had been to clear additional land, but by the Revolution this practice was no longer practical. Keeping in step with other progressive agriculturalists, Wilson rotated his crops as early as 1773.[16] On October 16 of that year, he wrote in his farm account books that the rye was sown in the tobacco ground. In the next two days another half bushel of rye was planted, the rye fields were harrowed, and the corn fields were plowed. On October 20, the last of his tobacco was cut. The next day wheat was sowed in the same fields. In addition to tobacco, corn, wheat, and rye, Wilson grew smaller amounts of peas and oats. Fifteen years later, in 1788, he recorded his attempts to experiment with alternative planting patterns for his tobacco crop as well as enriching the tobacco hills with animal manure.[17]

James Wilson was by no means alone in his desire to better the quality of his plantation. Nevertheless, he was one of only a few Eastern Shore planters in the late eighteenth century to take heed of current essays on soil husbandry and apply what he learned. Agricultural reform eventually gained momentum, however, and by the first decade of the nineteenth century it was not uncommon for guardians of orphaned children to include new farming procedures in official estate evaluations. For example, in 1819 the Orphans Court stipulated that the renter on the lands of Levin Waters and Arnold E. Waters was "allowed to cultivate one third part of the ground in indian corn annually (except the manured lots), in regular rotation, beginning with the one that has been longest out of corn, and in like manner to the next,…." The Waterses' guardians also detailed that "the ditches on or around the part to be tended is to be cleansed each year,…."[18]

Ditches, in fact, had been an integral part of the Somerset landscape since the seventeenth century because of the high water table in the region and the frequent need to drain fields of standing water. Ditches also served as boundary markers between adjacent properties and as a source of water transportation during high tides.

During the second quarter of the nineteenth century, rotating crops among three or four fields and enriching soils with marl, lime, animal manure, or imported South American guano became common practices. The natural absence of abundant lime and marl deposits on the lower Eastern Shore was remarked by David Ridgely. An alternate solution was available, however, as he explained in his description of Somerset County:

> No fossil deposits answering as marl have been found in this County, but a material almost as valuable occurs,* abundantly in various places, constituting those accumulations of oyster shells, believed to have been made on the site of ancient Indian Settlements. These shellbanks occur on the Nanticoke, at the mouth of Wetipquin Creek, on the Wicomico, on the Manokin, and at several other places. It is the principal agricultural resource of the County and by a proper application of it the lands may be made to double their produce.
>
> *It has been recently stated that marl has been found of good quality in this county.[19]

Broad impressions of the agricultural landscape of Somerset County in the late eighteenth century are best garnered from a close analysis of the federal tax assessment levied in 1798. The tax assessors were required to list the size of a property, the name or names of the tracts, and the name of the owner, along with the number of slaves and types of improvements found on the property.[20] A look at this tax record for six of the Somerset hundreds reveals the general pattern of land ownership on the lower Eastern Shore around 1800.

The northern, central, and southern parts of Somerset County are represented by Wicomico, Monie, Dividing Creek, Pocomoke, and Great and Little Annemessex hundreds. Of the 568 plantations listed in these six hundreds, 375, or well over half, were medium-sized estates of 100 to 500 acres. There were 112 property owners, or a little less than 20 percent, who possessed fewer than 100 acres. The richest planters, those owning over 500 acres, comprised little more than one percent of the estates reviewed. Slightly more wealthy planters resided in Monie and Great Annemessex hundreds, while the largest numbers of small yeoman farmers were located in Pocomoke and Little Annemessex hundreds.[21] Although significant numbers of working plantations were present by the end of the eighteenth century, this development was widely dispersed over the county and vast amounts of acreage remained in virgin wilderness.

The plantation agriculture of the period depended on a slave labor force, and by 1790 the number of slaves had reached more than 7,000 out of a total county population of 15,610.[22] Although slave labor was widely used, acquiring and maintaining slaves were expensive propositions. A few planters, such as Nehemiah King, held scores of slaves. According to the 1798 assessment, King owned seventy-four to run his property of several thousand acres.[23] More average slave ownership in Monie, Manokin, and Great Annemessex hundreds ranged between seven and ten slaves per planter. Still fewer slaves were held on the average by the yeoman planters who made their homes in the southern hundreds along Dividing Creek and the Pocomoke and Little Annemessex rivers.[24]

The Federal Assessment of 1798 is also helpful in establishing the range of plantation dwellings valued at $100 or more. These structures varied in size and construction from single story, one-room log or frame houses to palatial two-and-a-half story brick mansions with formal passages and finely finished rooms. Standing out as the most expensive dwelling in the assessment is Beverly, finished in 1796 for Nehemiah King. Measuring sixty feet across and forty-two feet deep, the Flemish bond brick house was designed with more elaborate finishes than most dwellings of its day.

Monie, Manokin, and Great Annemessex hundreds, which had harbored the wealthiest planters before the Revolution, maintained that status through the post-Revolutionary era. These three hundreds had the largest percentage of dwellings of more than 1,000 square feet, and plantation owners there had financed the construction of more brick houses than anywhere else in Somerset County.[25]

Few Somerset planters were able to afford such grand architectural spaces, however, and most landowners erected far less commodious accommodations. In the seven hundreds analyzed, over half the property owners in each occupied houses ranging in size between 500 and 1,000 square feet. Most common were single story frame structures of square or rectangular proportions with one, two, or perhaps three rooms on the first floor.

During the half century following the 1798 tax assessment, profits from valuable grain harvests marketed in south-ern Europe and the West Indies made it possible for more planters to rework or rebuild family residences. As a result, some lower Eastern Shore planters financed the construction of an impressive group of Federal and Greek Revival style dwellings, which furthered the rebuilding begun before the Revolution.

The tax records show that by 1798 Princess Anne had emerged as a modest-sized courthouse town centrally sited in the agrarian landscape of Somerset County. In addition to the services of the county court, the town provided the agricultural community with the basic needs of rural living. Eight stores stocked a variety of local and imported provisions, while two blacksmiths catered to the needs of horse and carriage transportation. One doctor and one tailor worked in town, both operating shops on a lot jointly owned by Levin Gale and Alexander Stewart. Zadock Long and John Bloodsworth owned taverns on Lots 15 and 23, respectively.[26] Each

Beverly, northeast elevation, photograph c. 1930 (courtesy of the Maryland Historical Society).

"Plat of Princess Anne Town," Somerset County Land Records N (MdHR 40, 125-4; 1/45/1/37), p.43, April 1801 (courtesy of the Maryland State Archives).

tavern keeper supplied billiard tables for patron entertainment, and occasional plays and dances were held on their premises. In his diary, Thomas S. Sudler recalled an event on Tuesday, August 13, 1799, when actors performed in Princess Anne and "A Woman dances in hornpipe."[27] A few years later, on February 22, 1805, a ball was held in Princess Anne.[28]

In 1798 Princess Anne included twenty-three assessed dwellings ranging from the smallest single story, 16' by 16' structures to the impressive houses owned by William Done and Dr. Arnold Elzey. Done's residence, on Lot 22 facing Bridge Street (now Somerset Avenue), measured 42' across and 30' deep and rose two stories. Elzey's dwelling of similar size, known as the Colgan house, still stands on part of Lot 3 facing Bridge Street near the Manokin River.[29]

The 1798 tax assessment shows that the average house in Princess Anne at that time was a one-and-a-half story dwelling with about 900 square feet on the first floor. The half story was probably lighted by dormer windows. Houses were largely of frame construction, covered with beaded, plain, or flush weatherboards and heated by interior or exterior brick end chimneys. Standing behind most houses were groups of frame or log outbuildings, including kitchens, smokehouses, stables, milk houses, carriage houses, necessaries, and lumber houses. The only buildings erected entirely of brick were the Presbyterian and Episcopal churches.

Commercial activity in Somerset County during the late eighteenth century was centered in Princess Anne, near the site of the courthouse on the northeast corner of Bridge and Broad streets. Stores, warehouses, tanyards, and shops stood on both sides of the river, but contrary to popular tradition large trade ships did not enter the upper reaches of the Manokin. Around 1800 Littleton Dennis Teackle indicated the Wicomico River was the best waterway for ships of 1,000 tons burden. Forty years later Levin Handy, clerk of Somerset Court, reflected on the restrictive nature of the Manokin waterway:

> The Town Princess Anne is situated at the head of Manokin River, about twenty miles from its mouth, is equidistant as to the most Northern & most Southern limits of Somerset County....The Town is pleasantly situated—laid out with broad, airy & rectangular streets....By reason of a mudflat extending about two miles the Manokin River is not navigable for large sized Bay Craft or larger vessels nearer than 12 miles from the Town and all the produce taken to or goods & freight brought from the vessels trading on this river are conveyed by means of scows and flat boats. Between the Mud spoken of and the town, the water is sufficiently deep to admit the approach of vessels of 50 tons within 1½ miles from the Town.[30]

Even though the mudflats in the Manokin restricted trade and probably contributed to Princess Anne's eventual stagnation, the first half of the nineteenth century saw a period of growth and development that changed the face of the eighteenth century county seat. By 1850 the town had exceeded its original boundaries and a number of prominent dwellings stood on its perimeter.

The prosperity of the early nineteenth century encouraged many town residents to build finely crafted brick or frame houses. In fact, owning both a town property and a country estate was not an unusual practice for the wealthier segments of society. At the east end of Prince William Street, Dr. Matthias Jones and his wife, Milcah Gale Wilson Jones, financed the construction of East Glen in 1803. The gable-front frame house followed the prevailing regional taste in Federal design with an elaborate fanlighted entrance and an intricately carved cornice of paired modillion blocks.[31] In the vicinity of Westover, the Joneses operated a 540-acre plantation known as Cedar Hill on land Milcah Gale Wilson had

William Geddes house (Tunstall Cottage), northeast elevation.

Teackle Mansion, east elevation, photograph c. 1900, E.I. Brown—photographer (courtesy of William Marshall Scott).

inherited from her father, Samuel Wilson.[32]

At the opposite end of Prince William Street, Littleton Dennis Teackle laid out an impressive ten-acre estate on part of the Beckford lands, beginning in 1802.[33] The centerpiece of Teackle's property was his five-part brick mansion, erected in stages between 1802 and 1820. Containing over two dozen rooms as well as an inside bath, the Federal style brick dwelling represented the extreme height in domestic comforts of the time.

It was also during this period that Teackle presided over the early Bank of Somerset and the Steam Company of Princess Anne. The bank was chartered in 1813,[34] and its directors erected a two-story brick building on Lot 16 on the northwest corner of Prince William and Bridge streets.[35] The bank opened with $200,000 in assets secured through the United States government, but by 1816 unstable financial conditions resulting from the War of 1812 were straining its resources. In 1820 the bank was forced to close its doors.[36]

Teackle put his innovative ideas to work in other areas of the local economy as well. In a region increasingly dependent on grain harvests, the local mills powered by water and wind could not meet the demand for flour processing. Teackle planned to build a mill that would address the problems of convenience and reliability. In 1815 he leased a three-acre parcel to the "Steam Company of Princess Ann" along the Manokin River near the present Deal Island Road bridge.[37] To make the mill more productive, it was constructed to take advantage of contemporary technology in steam-generated power, avoiding the problem of dependence on wind or tide.

The mill burned in 1818[38] and the property was sold, but the mill was rebuilt and operated by various proprietors until the late 1840s.

Not only were steam mills and banks erected in Princess Anne during the early nineteenth century, but the number of dwellings tripled between 1798 and 1840. A new brick courthouse was erected in 1832-33 to replace the eighteenth century building, which had burned in 1831.[39] The two-story Flemish bond brick courthouse followed the preference for gable-front buildings initiated in Princess Anne by Littleton Dennis Teackle.

No one commented on the size and character of Princess Anne during this period better than Levin Handy. In an 1841 letter to David Ridgely, he observed,

> *The Public buildings consist of a Court house—a large building adjoining it in which are the Clerk's and Register's offices and a county prison. The places of religious worship are a Presbyterian, an Episcopal, and a Methodist Episcopal Church. These buildings are all erected of brick and are quite capacious...There are about 70 dwelling houses and nearly an equal number of buildings consisting of offices, stores, shops, and other buildings...The number of inhabitants of the Town is I think correctly stated on the last census at 630. There has been a Small increase since 1830, but this has been a good deal diminished by the removal of several families to the south.*[40]

Until the early nineteenth century, regional and long dis-

62

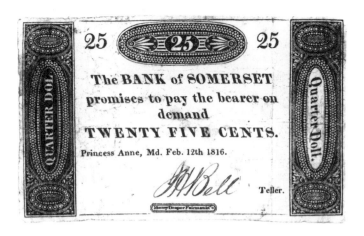

Bank of Somerset bank notes, 1816 (courtesy of the Somerset County Historical Society).

Somerset County courthouse and the former Bank of Somerset, c. 1900, E.I. Brown—photographer (courtesy of Robert Withey).

Coventry Parish Church, northwest elevation, photograph c. 1915 (courtesy of Rehoboth Presbyterian Church).

tance travel had centered on the navigable waterways that linked Somerset County residents with their neighbors and, more importantly, with vital markets in Richmond, Norfolk, Washington, Georgetown, Baltimore, Philadelphia, and New York, as well as Europe and the Caribbean. Steamboat traffic, beginning in the 1830s, reinforced the network of water travel that connected the Shore to distant markets.

Dependable land travel developed more slowly on the peninsula. The wide, deep rivers that sponsored shipping and early commerce impeded convenient land travel across the Eastern Shore. The road conditions were marginal at best, and numerous private ferries slowed personal travel considerably. Despite these problems, stagecoach service between Princess Anne and Baltimore or Philadelphia was offered as early as 1835.[41] A two-day schedule began in Princess Anne on Monday, Wednesday, and Friday mornings at 5:00 A.M., with advertised arrival at Milford, Delaware, at 5:00 P.M. the same day. The next day, patrons were delivered to the New Castle and Frenchtown Railroad by which they could journey to Philadelphia or Baltimore. Travel rates were levied at five cents per mile with forty pounds of baggage.

With more ambitious plans in mind to enhance transportation and trade on the Shore, a handful of influential leaders developed the Eastern Shore Rail Road Company, chartered in 1833. The plan was to stretch a rail line from Somers Cove up the Shore to the New Castle and Frenchtown Railroad, which had opened the year before to connect the Delaware Bay with the Chesapeake. In support of this plan, the Maryland legislature passed a million dollar bond issue to encourage private subscribers.[42] Littleton Dennis Teackle, then serving in the Maryland House of Delegates, wrote to Thomas R. Joynes, Esquire, of Accomac County, in hopes of finding support for a connecting line to the Eastern Shore of Virginia through Worcester County.[43]

By August 1838 notices in the *Herald*, a Princess Anne paper, advised contractors that clearing work had begun in Somerset and Cecil counties at each end of the line.[44] Despite these early efforts, the project suffered from the Panic of 1837 and related economic problems. Money tightened throughout the state, and subscribers failed to honor their pledges. By 1840 it was clear the railroad was not going to materialize, and the charter for the Eastern Shore Rail Road Company was revoked.[45]

As businessmen on the lower Shore attempted to broaden the transportation networks of the region, Episcopal ministers worked to expand their congregations in competition with the rising tide of Methodism. Following the Revolution, the Anglican Church experienced widespread dissension as a well-known defender of English sentiments during the war. Nevertheless, Coventry Parish, perhaps in an effort to attract new parishioners to a strong and healthy congregation, financed the construction of the most elaborate church yet erected on the Eastern Shore.

The new brick church was raised in Rehobeth at the site of an earlier building; in fact, the bricks from the old church were sold at fifteen pence per thousand.[46] An advertisement for a builder was entered into the vestry minutes in July 1784, and by the following March a contract for construction of the brickwork with "Ruff Door frames and Window frames" had been awarded to Isaac Marshall at £700.[47] More than a year later, the vestry agreed to ask Major Thomas Bruff and Captain George Waters to prepare a "draft" of the church, and during the June 1786 meeting it was decided that Elijah Braughton would craft thirty-one window frames at £3.9.[48] Construction apparently lagged over the next year, and by July 1787 the parishioners were asked again to devise a method for completing the unfinished church.[49] Vestry minutes indicate the building was finally occupied in 1792, close to ten years after the project began.

During the first half of the nineteenth century, the Episcopalians relocated Annemessex Chapel twice and erected St. Mark's Chapel on the northern fringe of Coventry Parish. In 1818 a new frame chapel at Annemessex was built on the lands of Benjamin Coulbourne in the vicinity of present-day Marion.[50] Thirty years later, shifts in development and population instigated the relocation of this chapel once again. With materials from the 1818 building, the congregation financed the construction of a wholly new type of chapel several miles away. Keeping in step with recently published designs for rural church architecture, the frame building was erected in Gothic Revival taste with board and batten siding and pointed arch doors and windows. The new chapel was consecrated in 1848 as St. Paul's Protestant Episcopal Church.[51]

More in line with the prevailing church architecture of the 1840s is St. Mark's Church, built around 1846 near Kingston in Coventry Parish.[52] Standing on the former site of a Methodist church, St. Mark's reflects the unassuming and modest proportions of rural meeting houses commonly erected before the Civil War. The rectangular, gable-front church is covered with plain weatherboards and lighted by standard nine-over-nine sash windows.

In 1845 Wicomico Parish was carved out of Somerset Parish to serve the Episcopalians of Hungary Neck. Vestry minutes state the early meetings of Grace Protestant Episcopal Church were held at the "Witch Bridge School," beginning on April 12, 1845. A month later a building committee was established to erect the Greek Revival style church that stands there today.[53] Finished in 1847, the classical, temple-front frame church was designed with Gothic Revival pointed arch doors and windows, a rather unconventional mixture of mid-nineteenth century styles.

While the Episcopal Church reorganized, relocated, and rebuilt their churches after the Revolution, Methodism swept the peninsula under the teachings of the English theologians John and Charles Wesley. In 1781 the Methodists established the Somerset Circuit, and in April of that year Freeborn Garrettson, an early Methodist minister, visited the lower Shore. To his apparent surprise, he found small groups already gathering in various parts of the county. Methodist meetings are thought to have been held on Deal Island before 1782. Miles Chapel, later St. Peter's, and Curtis Chapel near Westover are thought to have begun services at about the same time.[54]

In addition to individual churches, Methodist meetings were held in private homes through the late eighteenth century. John Gale, a prominent planter living on Gale's Creek, claimed an exemption on the 1798 tax list for a 36' by 24' frame house "situated in the woods...." The exemption was honored since the house was donated along with one

St. Paul's Episcopal Church, north elevation.

St. Mark's Episcopal Church, southwest elevation.

Joshua Thomas log canoe, taken from The Parson of the Islands *by Adam Wallace, 1861.*

acre to the Methodist Society, and Gale could continue the exemption as long as "they shall make use of it as a preaching house."[55]

Methodist congregations developed throughout Somerset County after the turn of the nineteenth century. Churches were established at Oriole around 1810 and at Princess Anne in 1817. At Rehobeth the Frogeye church was started around 1830, and the nearby Quindocqua congregation was holding meetings in 1820. A fifth group, in the vicinity of Upper Fairmount, started a church in 1842.[56]

Best remembered, however, is the ministry of Reverend Joshua Thomas, known as the "Parson of the Islands." Thomas was born on August 30, 1776.[57] During his seventy-seven years he sailed in his log canoe, "The Methodist," to minister to congregations on Tangier, Smith, and Deal islands and other meetings throughout Somerset County.[58] In 1850 a new Greek Revival frame church was erected at "Park's Grove" on Deal Island where Reverend Thomas delivered his final sermon. At his death in 1853, he was buried under a large table marker at the south corner of the new building.[59]

Improvements in education were among the most noted and longest lasting of the contributions to the quality of Somerset life in the post-Revolutionary era. In 1797 the trustees of the Washington Academy met to discuss the consequences of the fire that had recently destroyed the thirty-year-old institution. Instead of closing the academy, the group

Grace Episcopal Church, interior.

Old Washington Academy, photograph c.1900,
E.I. Brown—photographer (courtesy of Robert Withey)

Joshua Thomas Chapel, taken from The Parson of the Islands *by Adam Wallace, 1861.*

organized a committee to procure a new piece of ground.[60] On January 28, 1801, a resolution was passed to have the land of Whittington King laid off for the school, and on the same day the committee called for 250,000 bricks.[61] James Wilson was contracted as brick supplier, and Cyrus Sharp was hired to execute the brickwork. Isaac Gibbons was retained to complete the carpentry.[62]

When the new academy was finished, the two-and-a-half story, nine-bay brick structure must have been an impressive landmark on the flat Somerset terrain. Not only did a raised foundation give the building added height, but four narrow brick chimneys and an octagonal cupola towered over the large hip roof. Washington Academy continued to serve Somerset County as an enviable private institution until the end of the nineteenth century.

Much less is known about Eden Academy, formerly located at the headwaters of the Wicomico Creek about five miles north of Princess Anne. Perhaps in the wake of the reconstruction of the Washington Academy in 1803 and the resulting competition for students, the lands of Eden Academy were offered for sale in 1805. The Talbot County newspaper known as the *Eastern Shore Intelligencer* advertised the following:

> *…all the land and tenements belonging to Eden School, and formerly vested in the Visitors of the said School, containing as expressed in the conveyance for the same, one*

> *hundred and sixty nine acres more or less. The said lands are pleasantly situated on the headwaters of Wicomico creek, about five miles from Princess Ann, contiguous to navigable water, and are well accepted to the cultivation of wheat, corn, and tobacco, with a sufficient proportion of timbered land for the use of the plantation.*[63]

Aside from the Washington and Eden academies, the scope of antebellum education in Somerset County is somewhat vague. Small frame schoolhouses were apparently located on private plantations or situated in a community for the general welfare of neighborhood children. Local tradition suggests an 1839 date for the establishment of a schoolhouse on the Fairmount peninsula, formerly known as "Potato Neck,"[64] and the 1804 Orphans Court evaluation of Nehemiah King's property indicates a schoolhouse was included among the numerous outbuildings on his plantation.[65]

As the nineteenth century neared its midpoint, residents of Somerset County and of the lower Eastern Shore in general had experienced some turbulent years. On the whole, though, improved transportation, enhanced agricultural yields, a fine institution of advanced education, and a relatively stable agrarian society suggested that prosperity would not fade. However, the security of the Eastern Shore plantation culture and its established trade economy was tied to sizable investments in slave labor, an issue that would soon embroil the nation in a bitter four-year struggle. 🌲

CHAPTER VII, 1775-1850
Building in the Best Traditions

The vibrant agricultural and minor industrial economy of the post-Revolutionary period engendered a flowering of Somerset County architecture. Profits realized from lucrative cash crops in tobacco and timber, and later corn and wheat, encouraged the construction of one of the finest collections of late Georgian, Federal, and Greek Revival style dwellings in Maryland. At the same time, a distinctive stepped or "telescope" form of house emerged across the Eastern Shore as a preferred method of conveniently joining the main house and the once separate domestic services.

The refinements of Eastern Shore architecture that characterized the post-Revolutionary era clearly began during the second and third quarters of the eighteenth century, but were interrupted by eight years of war. As tensions subsided between England and her former colonies, planters on several economic levels returned their thoughts to improving their estates. These improvements often took the form of replacing houses and outbuildings that no longer served the changing needs of their owners.

The craftsmen's skills employed in the construction of mid-eighteenth century houses such as Almodington and Arlington were drawn on once more to construct a new generation of late Georgian and Federal style dwellings that demanded a broader repertoire from the builder's expertise. Not only were these new houses sometimes larger and more complex in plan, but craftsmen were required to install projecting bays; decorative plasterwork; and intricately carved stairs, mantels, and cornices in an effort to imitate the designs shown in English style books circulating during the period. The published designs, which pointed to standards of taste current in England, were often used as guides rather than copied exactly.

These pattern books provided builders with exact drawings of fashionable house designs and the details of their construction. Among the most influential volumes were various editions of the sixteenth century treatises written by Andrea Palladio (1518-1580), whose work dominated English taste through much of the eighteenth century. The first translation of Palladio's *Four Books of Architecture* was edited by Isaac Ware and published in London in 1738.[1] Other books carrying similar influence were James Gibbs's *A Book of Architecture, Containing Designs of Buildings and Ornaments* (1728); Robert Morris's *Select Architecture* (1755); and William Salmon's *Palladio Londinensis*, first printed in 1734.[2] During the late eighteenth century the brothers Robert and James Adam, Scottish-trained architects, promoted neoclassical taste in architecture, furniture, and interior design. Widely followed in England, Europe, and America, their designs were published first in *Works in Architecture* in 1773.[3]

Obviously influenced by published drawings of Palladian designs, Thomas King financed the construction of Kingston Hall between 1780 and 1783, despite the Revolution.[4] The two-story Flemish bond brick dwelling is a symmetrical three-bay structure that displays the earliest known local use of a projecting pavilion capped by a decorative pediment, an academic architectural feature not common to vernacular traditions.

Inside Kingston Hall, the room disposition follows a four-room plan not unlike that at Waterloo. Three of the four unequal-sized rooms are fitted with a fireplace, and the decorated stair rises in the northeast corner of the "entry." The Georgian style, turned baluster stair and the floor-to-ceiling raised paneling in the parlor comprise the most significant original woodwork in the house. The bold cyma curves in the stair brackets; the heavily raised paneling; and the complex cornice, chair rail, and baseboard moldings reflect the robust qualities of Georgian design.

As the eighteenth century reached its last decade, a prominent group of Somerset planters shared ambitious desires to replace old and, in some cases, worn out family houses

Kingston Hall, south elevation.

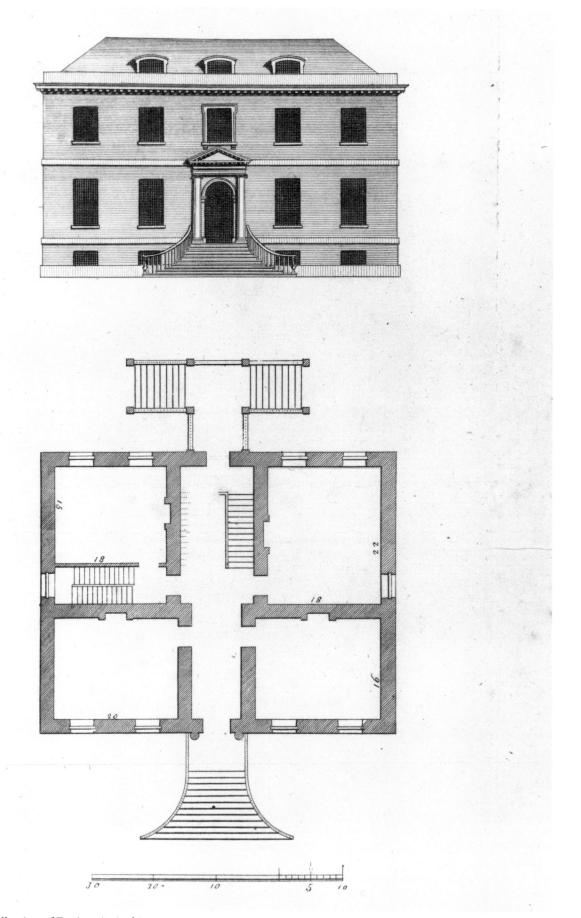

Abraham Swan, A Collection of Designs in Architecture, *Vol. I, London, 1757, Plate XI, "A Design for a House of four Rooms upon a Floor, with two stair-cases. The best room is 22 feet by 18." (courtesy of the Winterthur Library Printed Book and Periodical Collection).*

Tudor Hall, southwest elevation.

with dwellings crafted in the best traditions of the period. Whether conceived completely in brick or in frame with a continuous brick foundation and brick chimneys, these are the first houses in Somerset County to survive in large numbers until modern times. This group of plantation dwellings is also known for interiors lavishly fitted with superior woodwork and plaster decoration that combine Georgian and popular neoclassical designs of the Federal period. The five houses that best illustrate these trends show interesting similarities suggesting the same craftsman's touch. At the same time, clear contrasts between the structures reveal a parallel interest in creating distinctive personal spaces suited to individual needs and aspirations.

The Palladian inspiration for the exterior elevations of Tudor Hall and Liberty Hall, both on the Great Annemessex River, is much more subtle than at Kingston Hall. Constructed circa 1790, Tudor Hall is a two-and-a-half story, three-bay frame dwelling with strictly symmetrical front and rear eleva-

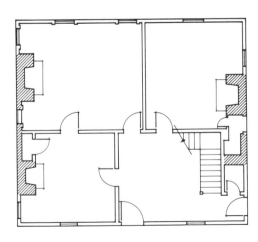

Tudor Hall floor plan, Paul Touart, Gale Yerges, Bobbie Stadler, Kennard Gochnour, and Nancy Kurtz.

70

Tudor Hall, second floor stair.

tions. Slender, corbeled cap chimneys frame the gable ends. The house is raised on a high Flemish bond brick foundation with expansive brick fire walls on each gable end. Its other two walls are sheathed with beaded weatherboards. Highlighting the front and rear cornices are rows of bold modillions with carved flowers embellishing the soffit between each pair of blocks. Inside, the first floor is divided into four rooms, three of which open off a spacious stair hall. The squarish hall is distinguished by a quarter-turn stair with a decorated stringer of carved flowers. Raised panel wainscoting and a modillioned cornice trim the plaster walls. Three raised panel doors framed by crossetted surrounds open into the adjacent rooms.

The most elaborate finishes at Tudor Hall were reserved for the parlor, which is the largest room. An exceedingly high style Federal mantel covered with complex gougework patterns and carvings dominates the projecting chimney breast on the west wall. The mantel's center tablet is embellished with a carved basket of flowers. Trimming the perimeter of the room are raised panel wainscoting and a highly decorative modillion cornice with a base rope molding. Robust crossetted surrounds frame the four windows and two doors. Overall, the parlor at Tudor Hall is unsurpassed in decorative treatment by any extant Somerset County dwelling of the late eighteenth century.

Nearby, on the north branch of the Great Annemessex, is Liberty Hall, a two-story frame house built in 1795. Although of smaller dimensions than Tudor Hall, Liberty Hall shows similar attention to expensive woodwork. The four-room plan house is fitted with bold late Georgian and Federal style woodwork not unlike that found at Tudor Hall. Similar finishes and molding profiles suggest the same master craftsmen executed both dwellings.

The parlor, the largest room, is finished in a manner similar to the Tudor Hall parlor, with raised panel wainscoting, crossetted surrounds, and a large Federal style mantel.

Liberty Hall, dining room mantel.

Liberty Hall, northwest elevation.

Liberty Hall, stringer decoration.

Stretching around the perimeter of the room is a dentiled cornice. Fitted into the narrow passage behind the parlor is the stair, with a scroll-decorated stringer and raised panel wainscoting. The S-shaped scroll was a common embellishment for the stair and appears in period pattern books.

Most reflective of the earlier Georgian style, however, is the southwest room of Liberty Hall, now used for formal dining. The corner fireplace wall is distinguished by a well-proportioned mantel with a decorated frieze terminated with scroll-shaped ends. The complex molded shelf casts deep shadows typical of the Baroque profiles of Georgian woodwork.

Without question, Workington and Beverly epitomized the height in architectural achievement for the period ending the eighteenth century. As originally constructed, both houses carried refinements of plan and detail not lavished on any other dwelling known to stand at the time. In different ways each design reflected the strong influence of English and American prototypes. Unfortunately, Workington burned in 1922 and Beverly was gutted by fire during the 1930s. Although great effort was taken to restore Beverly, the original late eighteenth century woodwork was not duplicated.

In 1793 Henry and Elizabeth Wilson Jackson contracted the best skilled masons, carpenters, and related craftsmen to build Workington. The two-and-a-half story, five-bay Flemish bond brick house once stood on the south bank of Back Creek. The principal facade, a strictly symmetrical elevation, was marked by a projecting two-story pavilion with an arched, fanlighted entrance and a full-size Palladian window above. The pediment that capped the pavilion was trimmed with a modillioned cornice and pierced by a lunette window. Flanking the pediment were two gabled dormers.

Inside the double front door, a wide and elaborately finished center passage provided access to the adjacent rooms as well as to the four-flight stair in the northeast corner of the house. The L-shaped passage at Workington agreed with the period trend to create an unobstructed space in the center of large, double-pile dwellings.[5] Stretching the full depth of the house and fitted with the most expensive carpentry, the passage

Workington, passage door, photograph c. 1918, Robert Hughes & Company—photographer (courtesy of Mrs. Charles Wainwright).

Workington, stair, photograph c. 1918, Robert Hughes & Co.—photographer (courtesy of Mrs. Charles Wainwright).

was elevated in the hierarchy of rooms as a convenient space for entertaining and relaxing during the hotter months of the year.[6] The Workington passage was distinguished by raised panel wainscoting and two archways that visually divided the space. Each archway consisted of paired Ionic columns supporting fully articulated entablatures under segmental, raised panel soffits. The passage doors leading to the parlor and dining room were framed with crossetted surrounds topped by robust consoles, a cushion frieze, and a richly decorated cornice. No expense was spared in finishing the passage or the stair.

The decorated stair rose four flights to the finished attic. The staircase was fitted with raised panel wainscoting, ramped and molded handrails, turned balusters, and intricately scrolled stringer brackets. As in many contemporary and later dwellings, the stair was built against a window and a handrail stretched between the window reveals. Placing the stair against a window allowed for consistent symmetry on the exterior, a naturally lighted staircase, and an unobstructed passage.

Paralleling the richly decorated passage and stair were the parlor and dining room, located in the southeast and southwest corners of the first floor, respectively. Distinct similarities in the finishes of these rooms and the finishes of Tudor Hall and Liberty Hall suggest the same master craftsmen executed the

woodwork. A prominent Federal style mantel was fixed on the projecting chimney breast in the parlor. Like the parlor mantel at Tudor Hall, the pilasters were fluted and the end blocks executed in an intricate gougework pattern. Carved on the center tablet was a basket of flowers, also found at Tudor Hall. The Workington mantel was further embellished with intersecting carved ellipses that highlighted the intermediate inset panels. Along with the raised panel wainscoting, the rectangular room was fitted with an elaborate modillioned cornice complicated with rope, egg-and-dart, and dentil rows. The large, sixteen-over-twelve sash windows were framed by crossetted surrounds with scrolled base moldings. Interior raised panel shutters were built into the window reveals.

The dining room, located across from the parlor, had a corner fireplace accented by a mantel similar to the dining room mantel at Liberty Hall. A crossetted surround was topped by a scrolled frieze with raised diamond panels and gouged flutes. The room was embellished further with raised panel wainscoting and a richly decorated cornice.

Beverly, finished on the south side of King's Creek in 1796, was planned on the same scale as Workington but with a slightly different exterior appearance. The two-and-a-half story Flemish bond brick dwelling has a three-sided, two-story pavilion that incorporates the formal entrance as well as

Workington, southeast elevation, photograph c. 1918, Robert Hughes & Co.—photographer (courtesy of Mrs. Charles Wainwright).

Workington, first floor hall, photograph c. 1918, Robert Hughes & Co.—photographer (courtesy of Mrs. Charles Wainwright).

William Adams house, southwest elevation, photograph c. 1890 (courtesy of Edward L. Fowler).

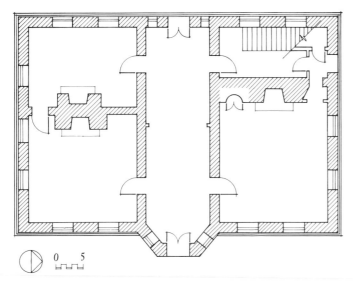

Beverly plan, Paul Touart, Gale Yerges, and Nancy Kurtz.

an arched window on the second floor. Twin chimneys rise from the core of the house and pierce the gable-on-hip roof.

Inside Beverly, the floor plan is essentially the same as that of Workington, with a center passage extending the full depth of the house and a four-flight stair rising in a separate room in the northwest corner. The interior finishes, however, were executed in the prevailing neoclassical taste. Intricately carved mantels, gougework decorated chair rail, and flat panel wainscoting were combined with highly decorative plastered cornices.

A late eighteenth century house finished with the same high standards as Workington and Tudor Hall but with a different appearance was erected for William Adams, Jr. around 1790 on the south side of Wicomico Creek. Sadly, this dwelling fell into disrepair during the twentieth century and was demolished. Unlike Workington and Beverly, the two-story, four-bay brick house was designed closer to the ground and without the formal symmetry and central focus of a prominent entrance. Instead, a two-story portico stretched across the entire front. A curious anomaly of this portico was that the west gable end of the house, complete with water table and belt course, extended to shelter the west end of the porch. Furthermore, the multipane sash windows that lighted the house also pierced the curtain wall to provide air and light to the porch space.

Similar to other Somerset houses of the last decade of the eighteenth century, the interiors of William Adams's house were finished in high craftsman tradition with raised panel wainscoting, crossetted door and window surrounds, and late Georgian style mantels. The interiors of the Adams house were also distinguished by some of the most elaborate plaster decoration known for the time in Somerset County. A bold plaster cove cornice and a large center medallion embellished with a trailing garland motif trimmed the parlor ceiling.

These five brick and frame dwellings form the upper range of late eighteenth century plantation accommodations and in no manner represent the average house. More common for the period, though still upper end, were story-and-a-half frame dwellings such as the glebe house erected on the lands of Somerset Parish in 1784 for the use of the minister. The squarish house, built with a Flemish bond brick

Glebe house, southeast elevation.

south wall and three frame walls, followed a variation of the four-room plan with a stair hall in the northeast corner and two large rooms to the south heated by corner fireplaces. A fourth room, located behind the stair, was left without a direct source of heat. The interior was fitted with raised panel fireplace walls and a turned baluster stair with a raised panel soffit.

Simpler yet were single story frame houses of one or two rooms like that found on the J. B. Green farm near Hudson's Corner. Assessed in 1798 under the ownership of Evans Willing, the one-room house measured 20' by 16' with a ten-foot shed across the back. The two rooms are finished with exposed, beaded ceiling joists, and a winder stair is located in the southeast corner of the main room.

Few of these small houses have survived to the present as they usually were modified or replaced. One example is the late eighteenth century hall/parlor frame house that now serves as a wing of the nineteenth century dwelling on the Brittingham farm near Cokesbury. The story-and-a-half weatherboarded dwelling was originally built with brick gable ends, which were removed when the house was reworked in the late nineteenth century.

As the eighteenth century turned to the nineteenth, Somerset planters and merchants continued to enjoy the benefits of sustained profits from the agrarian economy of the Eastern Shore. The burgeoning population centers around Baltimore and Philadelphia and poor harvests in southern Europe enhanced demand for the ever-increasing harvests of local grain and produce. This booming economy enabled more Somerset residents to support local craftsmen, who constructed large and small brick and frame dwellings throughout the first half of the nineteenth century.

The houses that mark this period followed many of the traditions established during the eighteenth century. A tenacious hold on familiar plans and conservative interior finishes characterized a large part of Eastern Shore building. Nonetheless, improvements in room disposition and the introduction of new styles significantly altered the architecture of Somerset County. These changes included imported materials from afar and design assistance from trained architects for those who could afford it.

Outstanding among the early nineteenth century dwellings of Somerset County is Beckford, evidently erected around 1803 for John Dennis, who served six terms in the United States Congress. The two-story, five-room plan brick

Beckford, southeast elevation.

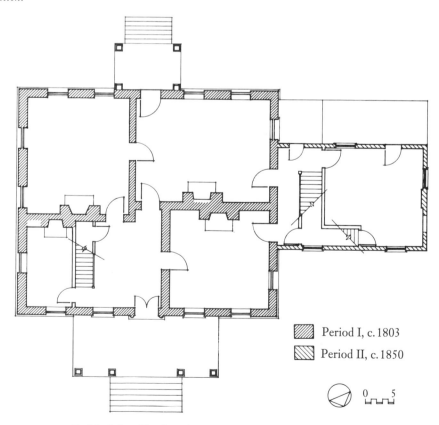

Period I, c. 1803

Period II, c. 1850

0 ___ 5

Beckford plan, Freedom Ainsworth, Paul Touart, and Nancy Kurtz.

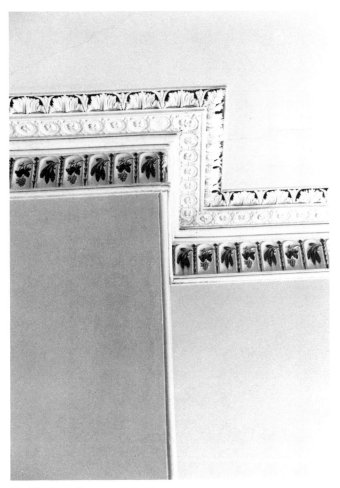

Beckford, southwest room cornice.

Beckford, northwest room mantel.

house stands prominently on the western edge of Princess Anne. Five bays across by three bays deep, the Flemish bond brick house is covered with a gable-on-hip roof through which tall, slender chimneys protrude. The sheer size of the house hints at Georgian style proportion formulas, but gone are the robust moldings and deep shadows well-known in Baroque woodwork. Instead, both the exterior and interior are finished in a more restrained manner with finely detailed and attenuated features that speak clearly of neoclassicism and the Federal style.

Rigidly symmetrical, the principal elevation has a center entrance framed by reeded pilasters and flanked by pairs of nine-over-six sash windows topped by stone jack arches with projecting keystones. The stone was imported, probably from upland Virginia. Instead of a belt course, a series of rectangular, inset plaster panels decorates the wall surface between the first and second floor windows. Similar plaster panels remain on two contemporary houses, the Teackle Mansion and Waters River. Highlighting the perimeter of the roof is a wooden cornice of paired blocks, a feature repeated at the Teackle Mansion and East Glen.

Inside Beckford, the first floor follows a slightly different floor plan with three rooms across the front of the house and two large rooms beyond. Centrally located in front is the spacious entrance hall, which contains a delicate staircase rising in two flights to the second floor. Atypical of the period, its slender, square balusters are set on an angle to support a ramped handrail. Matching the main railing is a half-rail fixed in the adjacent plaster wall.

Immediately left of the stair at Beckford is a small, heated office and to the right is the dining room. The two large rooms in back are fitted with the most expensive Federal woodwork and molded plaster decorations. The southwest room is distinguished by a large plaster medallion of classical motifs, while the cornice is decorated with molded grapes and tobacco leaves. Classically inspired urns and swags embellish the mantel in the northwest room, called the great room. This mantel would have been imported as well, perhaps from Robert Wellford's Philadelphia-based firm, which produced composition ornaments between 1801 and 1839.[7] Like that in the southwest room, the ceiling in the great room is embellished with a molded plaster cornice.

Also early in the nineteenth century, Littleton Dennis Teackle assembled the largest and most ambitiously planned estate dwelling yet erected in Somerset County. Teackle began by purchasing a ten-acre parcel of the Beckford lands in May 1802.[8] Shortly afterwards he financed the construction of the center block of his five-part house.

Following precedents established at Waterloo, at Wye House in Talbot County, and in Palladian-inspired pattern books, Teackle erected a temple or gable-front center block resting on a raised foundation. The first period of construction also included two bays of each flanking hyphen[9] and a number of outbuildings scattered around the estate. Marking

Teackle Mansion, parlor wall with mirrored windows, Michael Harrison Day—photographer.

Teackle Mansion parlor, Michael Harrison Day—photographer.

Teackle Mansion, east elevation, Michael Harrison Day—photographer.

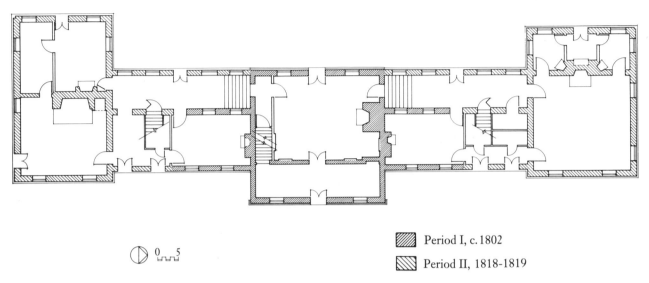

Period I, c. 1802

Period II, 1818-1819

Teackle Mansion floor plan, Paul Touart and Nancy Kurtz.

the entrance to the property on the edge of Princess Anne was a pair of two-story, gable-front frame tenements for housing domestic servants.

Perhaps more than any other antebellum dwelling in Somerset County, the center block of the Teackle Mansion displays the sophistication and experience of a trained architect. The temple-front, Flemish bond house was built with a variety of unusual features not used in the county before or after the construction of this house. Highlighting the wall surface between the first and second floor openings are three molded panels with classical urns and grape-laden vines. These designs were lifted from period style books available during the early nineteenth century. The pediment above is pierced by a round window, and the cornice is trimmed with rows of distinctive paired modillion blocks.

Sophisticated, academic architectural features are found on the interior as well. Inside the double door entrance is a transverse hall, behind which the parlor is located. Fixed along the south wall in the hall is an enclosed stair embellished with a classical plaster arch. A recessed niche was included at the north end of the room to balance the stair recess. The parlor also exhibits a forced symmetry. The fireplace wall was designed with two arched niches; the west recess contains a working door that leads to a passage, while the east recess is fitted with a matching false door. Another false door is located on the south wall of the parlor to balance the door to the south hyphen. One of the most unusual features in the room is the pair of mirrored windows on the east wall, which is an interior partition. Fitted with a molded surround, the six-

over-six sash windows are located on each side of the double-door parlor entrance. Their mirrored panes reflect light and brighten an otherwise dark room.

Despite its impressive beginnings, the five-part house did not reach its full size until late in the summer of 1819.[10] In June 1818 Teackle's wife, Elizabeth, wrote to her sister Anne Eyre of Northampton County, Virginia. Evidently pleased with the prospect of the additions, Elizabeth penned,

We are going on with our building with little or no bustle of a disagreeable nature—The walls are raised one story already—It will be I hope a capital improvement to our house & I want much to see you and Mr. E[yre] that you may suggest any idea that you may think an additional advantage or convenience....[11]

The Teackles' enlarged brick house, now encompassing over two dozen rooms—including an interior marble-laid bath and underground cistern—was so overwhelming in contrast to most of its contemporaries that it prompted this commentary in a letter from Eleanor Gilliss Waters of Beechwood around 1818:

I have been all through Lord Littleton's Palace even to the kitchen and it is more like the old castles which we read of in novels than anything else—vaulted passages, arched doorways and private staircases. Adjoining her ladyship's lodging room are two dressing closets one for each of them, a fireplace in each and between the closets is laid with marble and a very large marble bath; above her room is Elizabeth's with a large dressing closet and a library adjoining it. Elizabeth's room is to be papered with pink with the figure of Flora, very apropos as you recollect Mr. Robertson styled her Flora in the Acrostia. The kitchen is the most convenient place I ever saw and it may be kept as neat as a drawing room. There are places made under the bottom shelf to put the pots and ovens and every other utensil of that kind. There is a large store room adjoining the kitchen with shelves and drawers on every side. There is also a Patent steam machine for cooking and the hearth all around this steam machine is paved with marble. His library is very stylish also, the Housekeeper's apartments

are as large as your house. It is really a curiousity or it was to me. I should be lost directly. It is not near completed.[12]

Following Teackle's lead, gable-front frame and brick buildings were erected in town as well as in rural settings for the next forty years. While a variety of room arrangements were used, many houses repeated some version of the transverse hall plan with finishes executed in Federal and Greek Revival taste. In most instances the transverse hall was laid out on a generous scale with doors located at each end to provide ample air circulation, suggesting the hall was used as a principal living space during the hotter months of the year. Prominent among the Princess Anne examples of this house

William Johnston house, northwest elevation.

type are the Sarah Martin Done house, raised in 1823; the William W. Johnston house, built in 1834; and the old Episcopal parsonage, erected around 1816. The second county courthouse, finished in 1833, was also built with a temple-front orientation.

Elmwood, built by Arnold Elzey Jones around 1820, is perhaps the best known of Somerset's Federal gable-front plantation houses. The two-and-a-half story Flemish bond brick house stands on the north shore of the Manokin River in the vicinity of Oriole. A symmetrical three-bay elevation is highlighted by wooden jack arches with projecting keystones over each door and window, not unlike those at the Teackle Mansion. The pediment, however, is pierced by a pair of quarter-round lights. The interiors have survived largely unaltered with fine examples of Federal and Greek Revival finishes. The spacious transverse hall, which opens into two rooms behind, is fitted with a delicate Federal style stair in the north end that rises four flights as it passes adjacent windows.

Another gable-front house exhibiting fine traditional craftsmanship is the William Costen house, erected in 1829 on the level terrain east of Dividing Creek between Wellington and Cokesbury. Oriented to the entrance lane, the three-bay pedimented elevation is highlighted by a modillion cornice with an arched and drilled fascia. A center double door covered by a Tuscan-columned porch opens into a wide transverse hall with an open-string Federal stair rising in the south end. Located west of the hall are two rooms of nearly equal size fitted with flat panel wainscoting and corner fireplaces.

Although the transverse hall plan remained popular until the 1840s, some Somerset County residents adhered to more traditional plans introduced during the mid-eighteenth century. Many planters and town residents chose the four-room or side passage/double-pile floor plans common to the eighteenth century. Keeping in step with current taste, however, these early nineteenth century brick and frame houses were fitted with well-executed Federal woodwork.

Waters River, a four-room plan house located on the north shore of the Great Annemessex River, is a well-built, two-story Flemish bond brick dwelling constructed around 1813. Raised on an elevated foundation, the three-bay house is marked by symmetrical elevations highlighted by inset plaster panels. Slender brick chimneys rise from each gable end. Inside, a quarter-turn Federal stair is fixed in the northeast corner of the entrance hall, and three rooms of unequal size are finished with period woodwork.

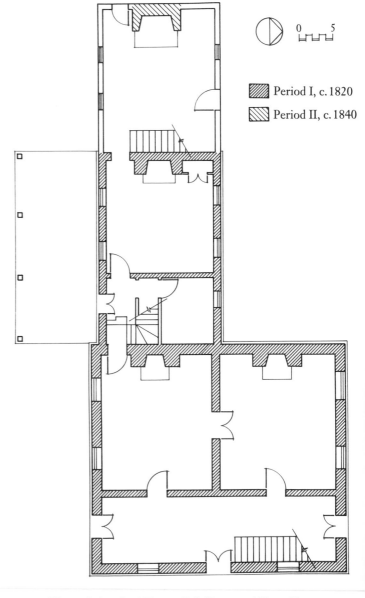

0   5

▨ Period I, c. 1820
▧ Period II, c. 1840

Elmwood plan, Paul Touart, Gale Yerges, and Nancy Kurtz.

Elmwood, northeast elevation, photograph c. 1890 (courtesy of George Fitzgerald).

Waters River, southeast elevation, photograph c. 1900 (collection of the Britton family).

Built around 1830 with a similar floor plan is the Samuel Miles house, a two-story, weatherboarded frame dwelling located east of Princess Anne and west of Dividing Creek. The exterior of the three-bay frame house is arranged in the same manner as Waters River with a center entrance and evenly spaced flanking windows. Rather surprising is the delicately abstract treatment of the front cornice. The boxed cornice is trimmed with bed and crown moldings as well as a drilled decoration under the soffit. The minimal drilled and gouged design takes the form of classical swags. The four-room first floor is treated in a standard manner for the period and region with a corner stair hall and three adjacent rooms each fitted with flat panel wainscoting and period mantels.

Perhaps the most architecturally sophisticated small house known for the period in Somerset County was built for William Costen as his first residence on the family plantation. After his father's death in 1806, Costen, then twenty-seven, evidently contracted craftsmen to erect a two-story, one-room plan frame house. He occupied this well-crafted dwelling for the next twenty-three years, before building a larger house on the same property in 1829.

Outstanding in its architectural finish, the small two-bay frame dwelling was distinguished by a classically framed entrance with an arched fanlight and a dentiled pediment. The front and rear cornices were embellished with delicately tapered modillions, and the front cornice was further enhanced by a decorated fascia of alternating six-point stars and vertical gouge marks. Following in the same tradition of superior craftsmanship, the first floor interior was masterfully finished with an elaborate gougework mantel, flat panel wainscoting, and a tightly winding corner stair.

Concurrent with the construction of Georgian, Federal, and Greek Revival style buildings on the post-Revolutionary Eastern Shore landscape is the development of what has been known as the stepped or "telescope" house—"big house, little house, colonnade, and kitchen." A variety of reasons, ranging from enlarged families to increased wealth, has been offered to explain this regional building form. But, while extra money and the need for more space doubtless affected whether additions were built, the underlying reasons for the development of this house form were linked to a broader movement that began during the third quarter of the eighteenth century and enhanced the function and use of the domestic services of vernacular plantation houses.

Until the middle years of the eighteenth century, a typical plantation was probably not unlike the property of Isaac Windsor, son of Lazarus Windsor, which was assessed in 1749 while Isaac was under a guardian's care. On the property were

One good dwelling house weather borded with pine plank and Double Covered with Oak Clapboards tite with two Dormon windows Shingled and two brick Chimneys plank

Samuel Miles house cornice, south elevation.

Samuel Miles house, south elevation.

Costen house, north and west elevations, Orlando Ridout V, Paul Touart, and Nancy Kurtz.

Costen house cornice, south elevation.

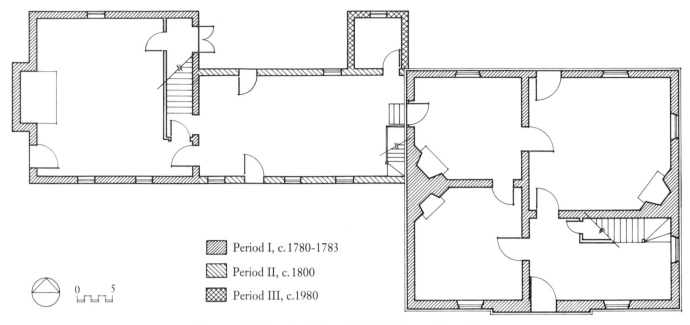

Period I, c. 1780-1783

Period II, c. 1800

Period III, c. 1980

0   5

Kingston Hall plan, Paul Touart, Bobbie Stadler, and Nancy Kurtz.

The Reward, northeast elevation.

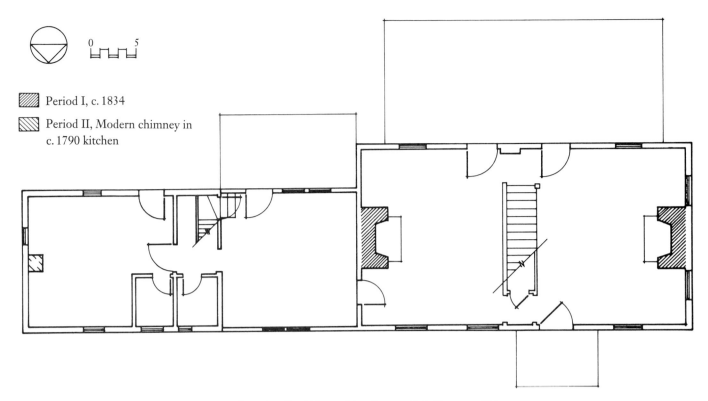

Lankford house floor plan, Paul Touart, Tom George, Gale Yerges, and Nancy Kurtz.

floors Above and below Stares and plastered one Log'd house wooden Chimney Covered with Oak Clapboards in good Repaire one Small Log'd house Covered with pine Clap Boards put on with wood pins one Small Log'd Corn house Covered with Clapboards put on with wood pins one old tobacco house Covered with pine plank old and ready to fall down three old Log'd houses Very Rotten and Crasy one Log'd Chitchen wooden Chimney Covered with Clapboards old and Crasy one Corn house hewed Logs Covered with pine plank in good repair....[13]

The description indicates this plantation included a story-and-a-half frame house surrounded by a variety of log and frame outbuildings that served the family as well as the farm. The log kitchen stood separately to the side or a short distance behind the house.

By the third and fourth quarters of the eighteenth century, this separate arrangement of house and kitchen had begun to change and service sections were increasingly included within the scope of the main house. One solution to improving the domestic spaces of the dwelling complex was the insertion of an open or enclosed passage—the colonnade or hyphen—between the house and kitchen to provide a protected walkway and additional storage space. This convention was by no means new, but earlier attached service wings had largely been a luxury enjoyed by the very wealthy.

Three houses that illustrate how various colonnades were introduced into an existing dwelling include Kingston Hall, The Reward, and Tudor Hall. Around 1800, some twenty years after the initial construction of Kingston Hall, brick walls were erected between the dining room door and the two-story kitchen. Not only did this single story structure

provide protected passage but it undoubtedly doubled as storage and additional work space.

A second extant colonnade is found at The Reward, the mid-eighteenth century brick dwelling on Williams Point. The house was evidently reworked during the 1790s and included in the improvements was the addition of a brick-ended frame kitchen. Inscribed in the kitchen chimney is the date April 18, 1794. In 1798 the federal tax assessors described the house with "a covered way from the said kitchen to the dwelling house of wood."[14]

Although the colonnade has not survived at Tudor Hall, its construction and history are documented through tax assessments and photographs. From the 1798 tax assessment and physical evidence at the site, it is clear the main house and the two-story brick kitchen were initially planned as separate structures with an open space of about twenty feet between them. Around 1820 a single story frame colonnade was built to join the two-story brick kitchen to the frame house. This change provided sheltered access to the front hall as well as to the cellar. At the same time, a second stair was built against the north wall of the colonnade. This flight led to a small passage cut through the exterior brick fire wall to reach the dining room.

Many eighteenth century houses were evidently refitted to include a colonnade or hyphen that joined them to a nearby kitchen, and with the turn of the nineteenth century, the stepped profiles of rural as well as town dwellings were well-known across the Eastern Shore. By the late 1820s owners as well as builders began to visualize substantial additions and even whole houses in various stepped forms.

When Henry and Nancy Lankford took possession of her father's plantation on Marumsco Creek in 1834, the couple

Lankford house, north elevation.

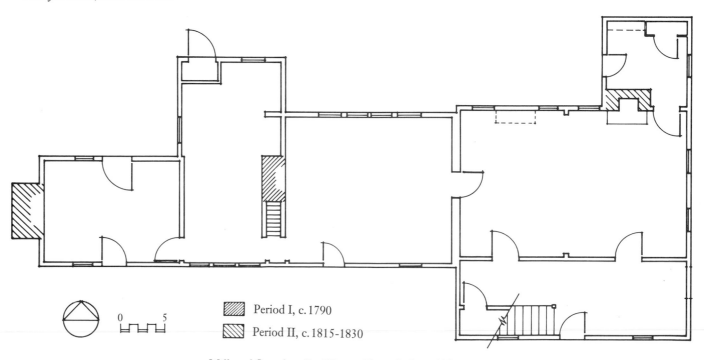

Period I, c. 1790

Period II, c. 1815-1830

Millwood floor plan, Paul Touart, Yvette Ogle, and Nancy Kurtz.

initiated a building program that replaced the old eighteenth century brick-ended dwelling. Whether the main house was torn down or had burned is not certain, but included in the plan was a decision to reuse the story-and-a-half, 20' by 16' frame kitchen. The Lankfords must have visualized their house with the popular stepped profile for they added a colonnade between the old kitchen and the new two-story, four-bay main house. In addition, the west wall of the kitchen and the old kitchen stair were rebuilt when the colonnade was assembled. The stair was reoriented so it opened from inside the colonnade instead of from the kitchen.

Alexander Jones and his wife, Elizabeth, also chose the stepped house form when they began to rework the late eighteenth century story-and-a-half house on "Manning's Resolution." Unlike the Lankfords, the Joneses used the existing house as a center structure and enlarged the dwelling to each side. To the east, the couple erected a two-story, gable-front main block with a transverse hall and two rooms behind. To the west of the old house, they built an open colonnade (now enclosed) and a story-and-a-half, one-room kitchen.

The stepped house form had achieved such unanimous acceptance by the 1830s that whole houses were eventually conceived with the distinctive profile. One of the most prominent examples is Linden Hill, built in 1835-1836 for James and Nelly Ker Stewart. Perched on a high rise on the northern perimeter of Princess Anne, the two-story, weatherboarded frame house consists of three parts. In this case, a two-story colonnade joins a four-room plan main block and a two-story kitchen. Architectural evidence and Stewart family tradition agree that the three-part house was erected in a single period.

Linden Hill, southwest elevation.

Uniform beaded weatherboards sheath the entire house, and a mixture of Federal and Greek Revival features distinguish the various rooms.

The William Nelson homestead, erected about the same time as Linden Hill, is another three-part frame house that assumed its stepped appearance in a single building program. The roof structure indicates none of the sections ever stood independently of the others, and all three sections were assembled with mature cut nails. On the exterior, uniform finish features such as the distinctive cornice end boards, impressed with five-point stars, also indicate a single period of construction. The interior finishes of the house form an almost unbelievable mixture of Georgian, Federal, and even Greek Revival styles and suggest some of the woodwork may have been reused from an earlier house.

While significant architectural developments were changing the appearance and function of some plantation houses, the shapes and construction of the attendant outbuildings remained relatively constant through the mid-nineteenth century. Pre-industrial storage practices and domestic processes were not altered significantly until the second half of the nineteenth century, when distinct changes affected the types of support buildings accompanying the house and farm.

The tobacco barn that evidently served Somerset planters through much of the eighteenth and early nineteenth centuries is represented by several structures surviving in the county.

William Nelson homestead, southwest elevation.

William Nelson homestead cornice, south elevation.

On the Ballard farm near Manokin, a gable-front frame barn of braced mortise-and-tenon construction is divided into three sections consisting of sheds on each side of a central space. Structural evidence found in this barn, as well as in three others of similar age, indicates poles of tobacco leaves were hung in tiers from three levels of collar beams in the upper structure of the barn. Temporary tier poles were probably assembled in the lower part of the barn for curing. The side sheds may have been used for stripping the tobacco leaves from the stalks or for packing the cured tobacco into hogsheads. In the Sudler's Conclusion barn, at least, there is evidence the side sheds were used for hanging tobacco as well. Features that tie three of the four barns together include wrought-nail construction and slightly tilted false plates. The Ballard barn retains sections of original beaded weatherboarding still fastened with wrought-iron nails.

As planters began to shift their agricultural focus away from tobacco during the early nineteenth century, many tobacco houses were refitted as granaries. With the introduction of interior board walls, tobacco houses at Sudler's Conclusion and the Thomas Sudler farm were converted around 1825. The Thomas Sudler barn was also refitted with a second floor loft and a slatted corn crib in the northern shed.

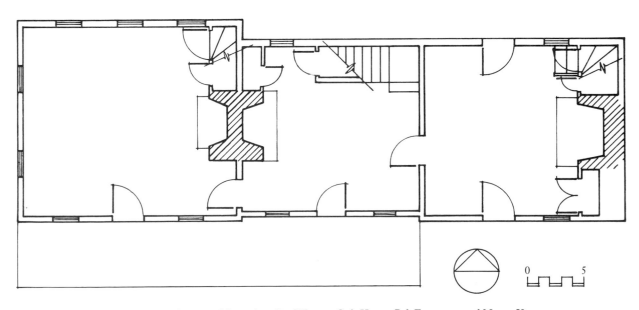

William Nelson homestead floor plan, Paul Touart, Gale Yerges, Bob Ferguson, and Nancy Kurtz.

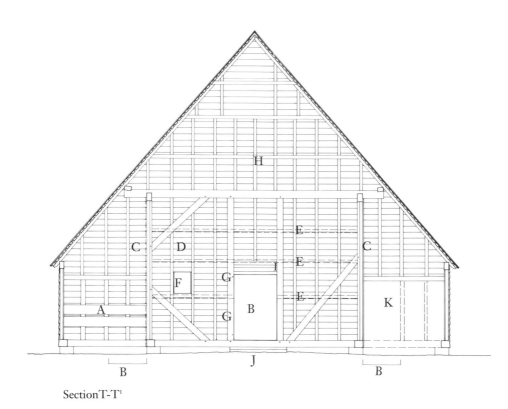

A Second-period (early twentieth century) sheathing for stall.
B Original door locations.
C Originally the outer face of both interior walls were sheathed.
D Studs coped to receive original weatherboards.
E Original ledger locations.
F Second-Period window.
G Holes for strap hinge pintles.
H Original strut lapped and nailed to collar.
I Upper header indicates height of original door.
J Long original brick pier survives below door.
K Wall cut out for vehicle access.

SCALE; ³/₈"= 1'-0"

0 1 3   6   12 feet

0 1   8 meters

Section T-T¹

Ballard farm tobacco house, Edward Chappell, Willie Graham, John Bernard, and Nancy Kurtz
(courtesy of the Colonial Williamsburg Architectural Research Department).

Ballard farm tobacco house, west elevation.

Although sometimes incorporated into other buildings, corn cribs were more often erected as freestanding log or frame structures. Usually rectangular in shape, they ranged in size from 15' to 20' long by 5' to 8' wide. The early nineteenth century corn crib standing at Cottage Hall farm fell within these dimensions before it was enlarged during the late nineteenth century. The early Cottage Hall example is a single story braced frame crib that rests on a foundation of brick piers and is sheathed with horizontal boards. Larger corn cribs were also built on some Somerset County farms in the late eighteenth and early nineteenth centuries. Period tax records indicate more extensive plantations warranted great

tunnel-like structures measuring 40' long by 10' deep.[15]

Tobacco barns, granaries, and corn cribs comprised the key storage facilities of post-Revolutionary War agriculture, but a host of other buildings unrepresented by extant examples contributed to the operation of a plantation. Stables, chicken houses, cider houses, carriage houses, blacksmith shops, wood houses, slave quarters, tenant houses, and even schoolhouses added to the small village appearance many plantations acquired.

Even though no documented slave dwellings have survived in Somerset County, the 1798 federal tax assessment provides the dimensions of various structures built to house

Cottage Hall farm corn cribs, southwest elevation.

95

Sudler farm slave house, location unknown (Lord family collection).

slaves. In these tax lists it is evident a variety of different buildings were erected, ranging from single cell, twelve foot square frame or log structures to multiple family single story structures built with frame, log, or occasionally brick walls. Long rectangular structures, many of which measured thirty feet across by sixteen feet deep, were undoubtedly divided into two cells with a center chimney that served both rooms. Floors, windows, and other amenities were probably the exception rather than the norm. Unusual in the assessment were brick quarters and the two-story slave dwelling on the lands of Elizabeth Wilson Jackson.[16]

Situated close to the main house were any number of domestic outbuildings. Most important among these were the smokehouse and milk house, where domestic supplies of meat and milk were processed and stored. Representative of the typical smokehouse are the squarish log structures found

Cottage Hall farm smokehouse, south elevation.

Teackle Mansion smokehouse, south elevation.

on the Cottage Hall farm and at Liberty Hall (moved from the Thomas Sudler farm). At both sites, sawn log planks fitted with dovetailed corners are sheathed with closely set vertical boards and covered by a gable roof. Inside the Thomas Sudler smokehouse a loose board floor was laid over a small brick pavement. When meat was smoked the floor was removed and a smoldering fire started on the pavement. After the smoking, the floor was put back to keep pests away from the newly prepared meat.

With a high percentage of pork in the Eastern Shore diet, the smokehouse was a common sight on most rural and town properties. The largest and most elaborate smokehouse to survive stands behind the Teackle Mansion. This 15' 4" square frame structure was built on a continuous brick foundation with a small brick chimney and had closely set studding to discourage theft. In the absence of a smokehouse, the

attics of kitchens or other outbuildings were sometimes used to prepare smoked meats.

Often located near the smokehouse was the dairy, where domestic supplies of milk were stored. Frame dairies, such as the one at Cottage Hall farm, were erected with movable louvered vents that provided air circulation when needed. Inside, shelving was fitted around the perimeter of the room for large, earthenware jugs in which milk or butter was stored. To take advantage of the cooling properties of thick masonry walls, some dairies were constructed of brick with a milk well along one wall. Spoilage could be prevented by placing the thick-walled crocks in the cool water in the well. In other cases the floor of the dairy was dug well below the surrounding ground level so the insulating nature of the earth would help preserve the dairy products.

Prior to the mid-nineteenth century, the smokehouse and

B Original window locations; that at front left retains evidence of square bars set vertically.
H Fascia originally wrought nailed to joists.

A Original window locations.
E Second -period doorway.
I Wrought nailed tapered and unbeaded rakeboard.
J Original weatherboards, random width on sides and rear, relatively uniform on front.

0 1 2 _____ 8 feet

0 1 _____ 3 meters

SCALE: ¹/₂"= 1'-0"

Ballard farm dairy, Edward Chappell, Willie Graham, John Bernard, and Nancy Kurtz
(courtesy of the Colonial Williamsburg Architectural Research Department).

Cottage Hall kitchen, southeast elevation.

Kingston Hall icehouse, north elevation.

dairy were often accompanied by a detached kitchen. The two-story frame kitchen on Cottage Hall farm stands near Sudler's Creek thirty yards west of the house. The two-bay, one-room plan kitchen was built with a large cooking fireplace and a corner stair on the first floor. Sudler family tradition relates the second floor was occupied by domestic slaves.

A rare sophistication during the post-Revolutionary period was a constant supply of ice. Only a few plantations or estate dwellings had such a luxury. The sole surviving icehouse in Somerset County is a circular brick structure at Kingston Hall. Probably erected during the early nineteenth century, the conical-roofed brick structure was built into a small knoll west of the house. A circular shaft descends approximately twenty-five feet, forming a cavernous storage room. Icehouses were also found at Brentwood and at the Teackle Mansion. Elizabeth Teackle commented on the newly erected brick ice-house (now gone) in a letter to her daughter Elizabeth dated August 10, 1818:

> *The Ice House is begun, indeed almost finished (the brickwork). It will be a great advantage being so near the kitchen. If you remember the place, it is just in the middle of those locusts, within the lot, which leads to the quarter.*

> *We have plenty of Ice this summer—but the Ice House we now use is much farther off, and Mr. Jesse takes his time to go and come. As the new one is fixed I can have every thing put in it, even the wine for dinner if I choose. It is made on an improved plan of your Uncle Eyre's....*[17]

The introduction of more convenient domestic services, often connected to the dwelling, was only part of the significant development in Eastern Shore architecture in the half century before the Civil War. Profits realized from the sale of market supplies of tobacco, corn, wheat, timber, livestock, and other products enabled planters and town residents alike to rebuild once again. With its combination of familiar and novel ideas in house design and interior finish, the continued rebuilding of plantations and town residences slowly changed the nature of the Somerset County landscape.

Buildings from this period survive in greater numbers than those from the eighteenth century. In particular, the survivors include some houses that belonged to county residents with middle incomes. Less well-built structures, however—whether houses or outbuildings—still have not survived in any quantity, making an understanding of living conditions for slaves and the poorer inhabitants difficult. ❧

CHAPTER VIII, 1850-1900
The Civil War and Industrial Somerset

As the nineteenth century passed its midpoint, the Eastern Shore entered a distinct period of economic, social, and political change that reshaped the agrarian and minor industrial society of Somerset County. The decade of the 1850s held much promise for the lower Eastern Shore, but this progress was frustrated when differing political, economic, and social philosophies held by Northern and Southern states embroiled the nation in four years of war. Somerset County residents, along with many others on the Eastern Shore, harbored thoughts of secession, especially in hopes of protecting investments in slave labor essential to the health of plantation agriculture. However, opinions were divided throughout the state and county, and many sided with Northern abolitionists. Although the Eastern Shore did not experience any battles during the conflict, the region was considered strategic for federal control because of its proximity to Virginia and the advantages of a newly built railroad and telegraph line.

The years preceding the Civil War were prosperous for the county, state, and nation. Sustained profits from lucrative agrarian trade encouraged continued confidence in the plantation agriculture that had served Somerset County since the seventeenth century. In addition, major agriculture-related industries developed in the county during the period. Growing populations on the Shore as well as in the nearby urban centers of Baltimore, Philadelphia, and New York increased demand for the foodstuffs, timber, and local manufactures long a part of the Somerset economy. That farmers could take advantage of the market for perishable foodstuffs was due both to the newly introduced technology of preserving fruits, vegetables, and oysters for shipping and to the erection of a railroad connecting the county to major urban areas.

Although the lower Eastern Shore did not assume an industrial lead as northern Maryland did, census statistics from 1850 reveal major commitments to agriculture-related industries. Thirty-eight saw and grist mills powered by wind, water, and steam operated in the county. According to the census, eight millers still depended on the vagaries of the wind to turn sails, while six mills were operated by reliable steam-generated power, which had been introduced thirty-five years earlier by Littleton Dennis Teackle. For the most part, however, both saw and grist mills were powered by water.

The census also shows six boat builders active in Somerset County, along with five blacksmiths, one tinsmith, two carriage makers, two tanners, six shoemakers, one hatter, and a single baker.[1] Many farmers and other residents performed these same tasks at home, as well as producing saleable goods whose manufacture went unrecorded by the census takers.

Perhaps the most significant event affecting Somerset County in the 1850s was the second attempt to provide rail service to the isolated peninsula. Instead of traversing the Eastern Shore, the new route involved a connection with the Delaware Railroad, in hopes of eventually joining New York, Philadelphia, and Norfolk. Construction began in 1854, and by August 1855 tracks had been laid between New Castle and Middletown, Delaware. Four years later, on December 20, 1859, the tracks finally reached the Delaware-Maryland state line.[2] The railroad received much local support, as shown in an 1858 engineer's report submitted by E. Q. Sewell, Jr., then superintendent of the Delaware Railroad:

> *It is due to all concerned to state, that it was by subscription among individuals (chiefly in Wilmington and Laurel, Delaware, Salisbury and Princess Anne, Maryland, and their vicinities) that the expense of the Survey from Seaford to the Annemessic, and of this report, was provided for.*[3]

Indeed, a railroad connecting major urban centers would cure an age-old problem experienced in Princess Anne because of the restrictive nature of shipping on the Manokin River.

The subscribers' money was not ill-spent, for a rail line connecting Salisbury to the completed Delaware track was finished in time for a maiden voyage on the Fourth of July, 1860.[4] However, plans to stretch the line to Tangier Sound were obstructed when Confederate forces captured Fort Sumter in April 1861, signaling the start of four years of internal war.

Maryland was a border state, and its population was divided on war issues. An essentially Southern plantation economy and society characterized life on the Western and Eastern shores, while Piedmont Maryland fell more in line with the industrial, anti-slavery focus of the Northern states. With strong connections to Virginia and trade agreements in the South, Somerset County and the lower Eastern Shore in general aligned largely with the Southern cause.

To President Lincoln and his generals, Maryland's role in the war was of utmost concern as the nation's capital was located between Virginia and Maryland and three major rail-

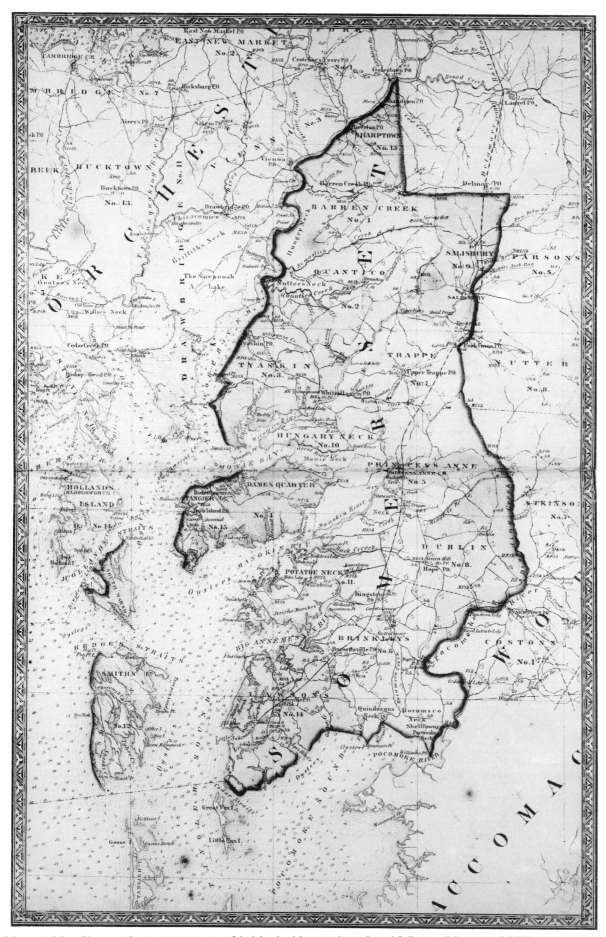

Martenet's Map of Somerset County, 1866 (courtesy of the Maryland State Archives) Special Collections (Maps) 286 (MdHR 1427: 005/1/2).

roads converged in Baltimore en route to Washington. Union General John A. Dix wrote to General George B. McClellan in August 1861 stating that Eastern Shore secessionists were becoming more organized and friends of the Union were demanding arms and federal troops for protection. In an effort to control an immense traffic in contraband to the South, federal troops were stationed at Fort Upton in Salisbury near the terminus of the newly built Delaware/Maryland railroad.[5]

In another letter, dated October 7, 1861, General Dix asked General McClellan about steamboats or tugs that would draw no more than five feet to "go up the rivers and enter the numberless inlets and bays on the Eastern Shore…breaking up…the meetings which are held…in hostility to the Government."[6] A month later 4,500 federal troops under the command of General Henry H. Lockwood assembled in Salisbury, Pocomoke City, and Snow Hill to prepare for an invasion of Accomac and Northampton counties.[7]

During the war years the Republican party soundly controlled the Maryland legislature, and some Democratic senators from the lower Eastern Shore were viewed with suspicion as Southern sympathizers. After his election in 1864, Senator Levin Littleton Waters of Somerset County (1828-1900) was suspected of collaboration with his brother-in-law, General Arnold Elzey, a prominent Confederate officer. Waters was also connected with an incident involving the raising of a Confederate flag outside his newspaper office in Princess Anne. With orders from General Lewis Wallace's headquarters in Baltimore, General Lockwood arrested the newly elected senator and imprisoned him, first in Baltimore and later at Fort Hamilton at Hampton Roads, Virginia. After an appeal was made to President Lincoln, Waters was exonerated of all charges. He eventually returned to the Maryland legislature.[8]

While many Eastern Shore Democrats adhered to Southern politics, United States Congressman John Woodland Crisfield, seated in a special election in 1861, supported President Lincoln's war effort with a strong pro-Union philosophy. It was Crisfield's hope that a long and destructive war could be averted. In the early years of the conflict, he worked for a restoration of peace as well as fair compensation for loyal Southern slaveholders. However, an agreement between President Lincoln and the slaveholding congressman was never realized. In 1863 Lincoln issued the Emancipation Proclamation, which freed slaves in the rebellious states. Although it did not free slaves in the border states, the proclamation did signal an end to slavery in Maryland.[9] In a constitutional convention held the following year, slaves were officially freed in Maryland on November 1, 1864.[10]

On the heels of General Lee's surrender at Appomattox Courthouse in April 1865, Somerset County was involved in yet another controversy with distinct opposing factions. During a constitutional convention held in Annapolis in the spring of 1867 to consider several war issues, Thomas J. Rider, a Quantico lawyer, and J. Hopkins Tarr of Worcester County presented plans to create a third county on the lower Eastern Shore. In addition to increasing Democratic representation in the legislature, Rider and Tarr argued the new county was needed to serve the residents in the northern end of Somerset County and the western precincts of Worcester County. They also pointed out that Salisbury was a quickly growing trading center and demanded road and wharf improvements that politicians in Princess Anne would not approve.[11] Lastly, the boundary line separating Somerset and Worcester counties, known as Division Street, divided Salisbury, creating a split tax and voting structure unsuitable for cohesive town development. After a lengthy debate, a committee created to consider the issue forwarded a recommendation for approval of the new county. Article XIII of the constitutional convention included a few stipulations: first, that the consent of the majority of legal voters residing within the proposed limits was required, and second, that 400 square miles was a minimum size for any new county. Wicomico County was officially created on October 5, 1867.[12]

Despite Somerset County's reduced size, the 1860s brought an infusion of newfound vitality. Expanding product markets in nearby urban centers and a larger Eastern Shore population increased demand for the agricultural products grown and harvested by lower Shore farmers. In addition, the ability to preserve vegetables and fruits commercially opened an entirely new industry that would dominate Shore agriculture through the turn of the century. Most significant to the regional economy, however, was the completion of the railroad to Somers Cove. Because of its importance to Delaware as well as Maryland, the *Smyrna Times* announced the railroad's completion on August 29, 1866:

The Delaware Railroad is now completed to the Annamessex. The wharf at that place is being built and a new steamer for that line to be run between Annamessic and

City of Norfolk at the Crisfield wharf, photograph c. 1867 (courtesy of H. Graham Wood).

View of railroad at Crisfield, stereoview c. 1867 (courtesy of Michael Luby).

Norfolk will be finished in about two weeks. When opened this line will afford passengers traveling to the Southern States a shorter and quicker route than via Baltimore, saving about 100 miles in distance and about five hours time.[13]

The railroad also carried local freight and produce.

By 1860 Somerset agriculture had broadened to include a wider range of foodstuffs, livestock, and home manufactures. In that year Somerset County farmers produced the largest sweet potato harvest on the Eastern Shore—about 76,442 bushels. During the second half of the century, Somerset farmers directed most of their attention to harvesting large amounts of wheat, corn, oats, peas, and beans, as well as Irish and sweet potatoes. Somerset County farmers and their wives were also busy tending and selling garden produce valued at $6,416 and making 104,729 pounds of butter, also high levels in contrast to nearby counties. Along with these crops and products, Somerset farmers managed large numbers of cattle, sheep, and, especially, swine.[14]

Those farmers who maintained extensive agricultural holdings after the Civil War depended on their former slaves as a labor source. Considered tenants or sharecroppers, land-less blacks and their families often worked the same fields they had tended as slaves. Modest payment was arranged in terms of part of the yearly harvest or in lieu of rent for a house on the property.

Beginning in the 1860s and 70s county farmers joined the ranks of other Eastern Shore landowners in growing toma-toes as well as peaches and strawberries for an expanding pro-duce market. By 1879 the strawberry fields were so extensive around Marion and Westover that a writer for *Harper's Weekly* commented:

> *About sixteen miles north of Crisfield stands a way-side railway station called Westover. The transient traveller might be surprised by the number of freight-cars standing along the switch at this apparently unpromising country station, but quiet as it looks, unbusinesslike as it might appear to him, it is in reality one of the busiest points along the road, for Westover is one of the chief centres of berry (especially of strawberry) culture of all the fruit-producing peninsula. In the early morning a different sight presents itself at the quiet station. Large vans piled high with crates of berries, shouting of teamsters, cracking of whips, he-hawing of mules, combine in a babel of noises ever in-creasing as cart after cart rumbles up to the station in a cloud of dust not unlike a miniature thunder-storm....*
>
> *The berry yield of 1878 was a particularly light one in this region owing to a sudden spell of chilly weather that somewhat stunted the fruit, preventing it from attaining its full degree of size and lusciousness; but even in that season 500,000 baskets of strawberries were shipped from this point alone in the short period during which this fruit flourishes.[15]*

As the century continued, Marion and its vicinity became as well known as Westover for large shipments of strawberries.

Although canning produce for export began as early as the late 1850s near Dover, Delaware,[16] fruit and vegetables were not processed and shipped in bulk quantities from Somerset County until the early 1870s. The earliest documented venture to market canned local produce was Hamblin, Baker & Co., which was also shipping oysters by 1871.[17] On the south shore of the Manokin River, not far from the site of the old Maddox tobacco warehouse, the firm erected a small village of buildings

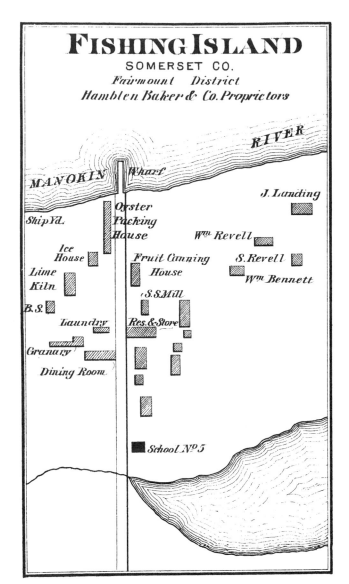

Fishing Island from the Lake, Griffing, and Stevenson atlas, 1877 (courtesy of the Somerset County Historical Society).

known as Fishing Island to capitalize on many of the business ventures under way at the time. In the Lake, Griffing, and Stevenson atlas of Somerset County, published in 1877, the firm ran this advertisement:

> *HAMBLIN, BAKER & CO., are prepared to furnish Fresh Oysters by the barrel, gallon, or can. Hermetically sealed Oysters, Peaches, & c., at the lowest rates. All orders addressed to us at Westover P.O., Somerset County, Md., will receive prompt attention.[18]*

Fruit and oyster packing houses at Fishing Island were sited near the wharf along with a steam sawmill, a lime kiln, a blacksmith shop, and a granary. Lime was produced by burn-ing the discarded oyster shells, while the sawmill processed rich stands of timber for local and regional trade. The granary

John Branford and crew, photograph c. 1900 (courtesy of Margaret Miles).

held farmers' crops until shipment. Also located along the river was a shipyard where John Branford, a Finnish immigrant, supervised the construction of some of the finest baycraft of the late nineteenth century. Filling out the balance of the complex were several dwellings, a schoolhouse, a store, a dining room, and a laundry.

Hamblin, Baker & Co.'s operation on Fishing Island was an exceptionally large and complex enterprise for the period. A small, private, self-sufficient community financed by outside capital, the firm undoubtedly hired local labor to process and can the produce. The large population of freed slaves in Somerset County probably comprised a large part of the work force during the 1870s. Other firms packaging local produce during the same period were Miles, Avery, & Co., also established on the Fairmount peninsula, and H. H. Dashiell of Princess Anne.[19]

Although the canning houses provided desperately needed new jobs and investment for the county's post-war economy, the oyster-packing industry on Tangier Sound always overshadowed the Somerset fruit and vegetable canneries.[20] As early as the second quarter of the nineteenth century, the oyster industry had begun growing steadily in the Chesapeake region as Yankee traders sought to supplant the exhausted beds off the New England coast. The industry burgeoned during the third quarter of the century, and Somers Cove expanded in a few short decades, becoming a nationally recognized export center for bay oysters and other seafoods.[21] By the summer of 1866 the small fishing village was joined to the string of nearby urban areas with a spur line of the Eastern Shore Railroad. To honor the spur's chief promoter, Somers Cove was renamed for John Woodland Crisfield, a prominent Princess Anne attorney, U.S. congressman, and president of the Eastern Shore Railroad.

Bayard Taylor, writing for *Harper's New Monthly Maga-*

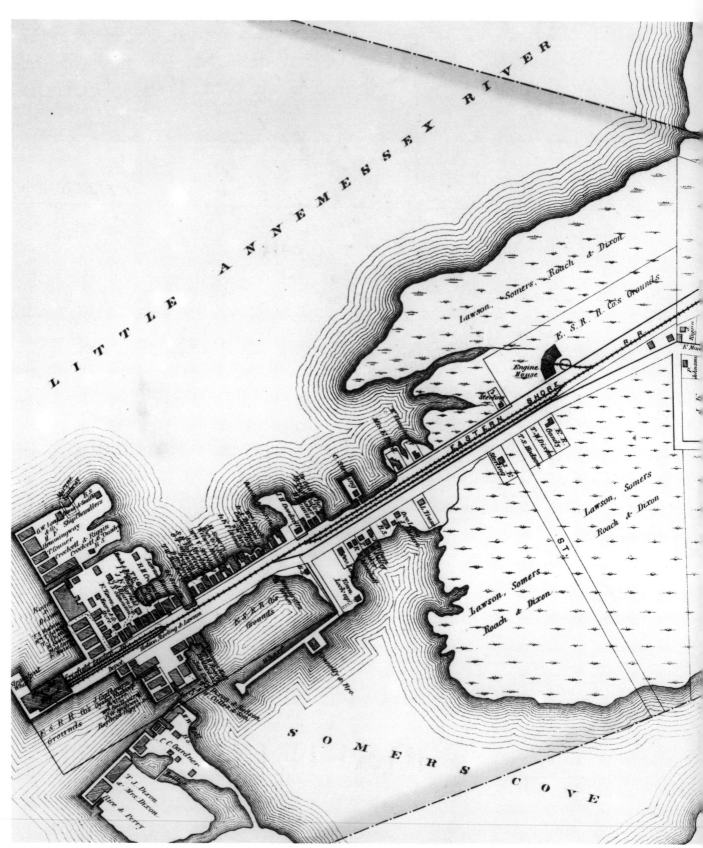

Crisfield from the Lake, Griffing, and Stevenson atlas, 1877 (courtesy of the Somerset County Historical Society).

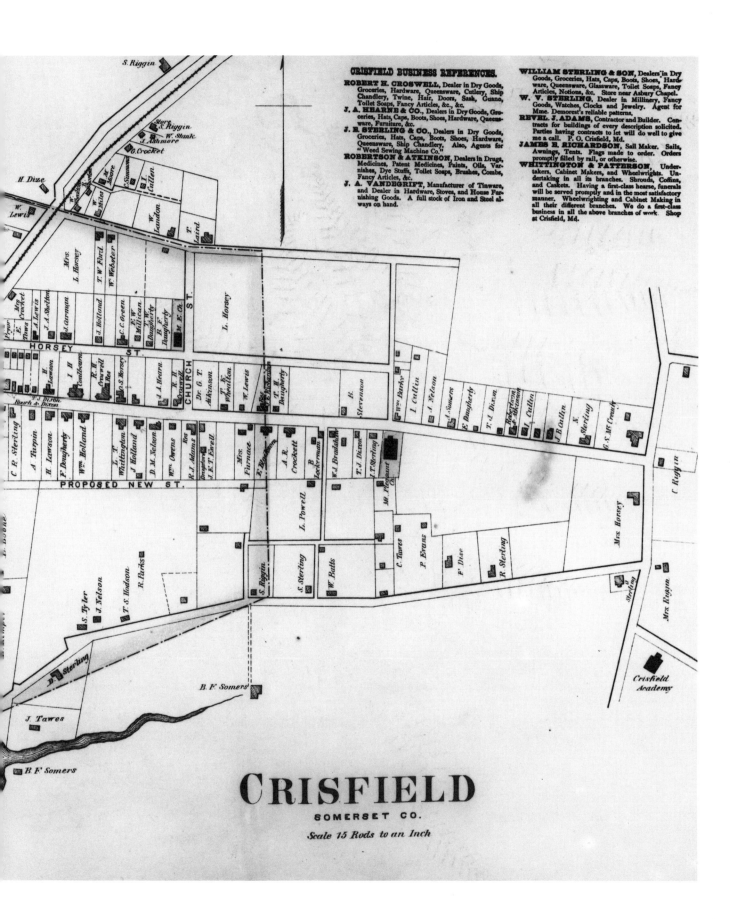

CRISFIELD BUSINESS REFERENCES.

ROBERT H. CROSWELL, Dealer in Dry Goods, Groceries, Hardware, Queensware, Cutlery, Ship Chandlery, Twine, Hair, Doors, Sash, Guano, Toilet Soaps, Fancy Articles, &c., &c.

J. A. HEARNE & CO., Dealers in Dry Goods, Groceries, Hats, Caps, Boots, Shoes, Hardware, Queensware, Furniture, &c.

J. R. STERLING & CO., Dealers in Dry Goods, Groceries, Hats, Caps, Boots, Shoes, Hardware, Queensware, Ship Chandlery. Also, Agents for "Weed Sewing Machine Co."

ROBERTSON & ATKINSON, Dealers in Drugs, Medicines, Patent Medicines, Paints, Oils, Varnishes, Dye Stuffs, Toilet Soaps, Brushes, Combs, Fancy Articles, &c.

J. A. VANDEGRIFT, Manufacturer of Tinware, and Dealer in Hardware, Stoves, and House Furnishing Goods. A full stock of Iron and Steel always on hand.

WILLIAM STERLING & SON, Dealers in Dry Goods, Groceries, Hats, Caps, Boots, Shoes, Hardware, Queensware, Glassware, Toilet Soaps, Fancy Articles, Notions, &c. Store near Asbury Chapel.

W. V. STERLING, Dealer in Millinery, Fancy Goods, Watches, Clocks and Jewelry. Agent for Mme. Demorest's reliable patterns.

REVEL J. ADAMS, Contractor and Builder. Contracts for buildings of every description solicited. Parties having contracts to let will do well to give me a call. P. O. Crisfield, Md.

JAMES H. RICHARDSON, Sail Maker. Sails, Awnings, Tents, Flags made to order. Orders promptly filled by rail, or otherwise.

WHITTINGTON & PATTERSON, Undertakers, Cabinet Makers, and Wheelwrights. Undertaking in all its branches. Shrouds, Coffins, and Caskets. Having a first-class hearse, funerals will be served promptly and in the most satisfactory manner. Wheelwrighting and Cabinet Making in all their different branches. We do a first-class business in all the above branches of work. Shop at Crisfield, Md.

CRISFIELD

SOMERSET CO.

Scale 15 Rods to an Inch

zine, traversed the peninsula during the summer of 1874 and published his impressions of the trip. His description of Crisfield provides a clear image of the bustling town it had become:

> *I went to bed on leaving Berlin, and slept soundly until awakened by the incessant noise of rolling barrels. We were upon the pier at Crisfield, and three steamers beside us were taking on their freight. My companions were, in addition, tormented by mosquitoes; so we all arose early and looked about us. The bay here is part of Tangier Sound, divided by three islands from the main body of the Chesapeake. Crisfield, which is a new place, built on a foundation of oyster shells, is the terminus of the road, one hundred and thirty-five miles south of Wilmington and eighty-five miles north of Norfolk. The three steamers left during our stay—one for the latter city, one for the Accomac shore, and one for Wilmington by sea. The small population lives by fishing and by opening oysters during season. Last year's exportation of oysters, if I remember rightly, was about nine thousand tons. The water fairly swarms with fish and crabs, and the marshes around are a paradise for the sportsman.[22]*

As the population of Crisfield increased, so did its land area. Discarded oyster shells were dumped into the marsh to create firm ground for extensive development. In order to acquire deep water moorage for large vessels, the wharf and freight depot were located well beyond the mainland, and the area on each side of the track was filled with oyster shells to create building lots. By 1877, less than a dozen years after the first locomotive had arrived, more than 200 structures lined the new streets of Crisfield, making it Somerset County's fastest growing town. The harbor, punctuated with piers and choked with workboats, steamers, and schooners, carried on the largest oyster trade in the state. As a result, Crisfield boomed with the rapid construction of oyster-packing houses, commercial structures, and quickly erected housing for workers, businessmen, ship captains, and the affluent owners of the packing plants.

The rapidly growing town supported six full-time carpenter-builders and an equal number of ship carpenters, according to the 1871 *Maryland State Gazette*.[23] By 1884, Henry Hall had recorded more than 1,400 fishing vessels in Crisfield, although half of them were log canoes not large enough to register at the customs house. Also in his *Report on the Shipbuilding Industry*, Hall stated that about 175 oyster boats were fashioned on the lower Shore yearly and that there were twenty marine railways. Hall credited the large supply of boats to professional builders, but he also discovered a surprising number were assembled by private builders or watermen themselves, often in their own backyards.[24] The steamboats that regularly serviced the port of Crisfield were considered by many to be the workhorses of Chesapeake Bay transportation. Made elsewhere, they shuttled between the Eastern Shore, Wilmington, Baltimore, and Norfolk until the early twentieth century.

Another impression of Crisfield during its expansion appeared in *Harper's Weekly* in 1879:

> *A town of oysters built on oyster shells. Such is Crisfield. A man buys a building lot at the bottom of the harbor and then purchases oyster shells to raise it above high-water mark. Crisfield stands, as it were, up to its knee in water of a little harbor that cuts jaw-like into the end of a small peninsula formed by the Annamassec River on the north and the Pocomoke Sound on the south.*
>
> *A general whiteness illumines the streets of Crisfield, a crisp rattle of loose shells sounds under the tread of the pedestrian, a salt breeze blows from the beautiful waters of Tangier Sound, tainted, alas! by a slight odor of defunct oysters. Oysters, oysters, everywhere in barrels, boxes, in cans, in buckets in the shell and out…Along [the railroad] and in the side streets collect the houses, all of frame, varying in architecture from the cottage to the negro shanty. Along the waters edge are a number of large barnlike buildings—the oyster packing houses.[25]*

The get-rich-quick philosophy that pervaded Crisfield during the peak years of the oyster harvests exacerbated century-old rivalries between Virginia and Maryland watermen. Severe competition for oyster beds as well as the harshness of winter work on the bay instigated barroom brawls, oyster-knife stabbings, and even gun battles between warring oystermen on open water. The attendant lawlessness in Crisfield, which was largely confined to the area around the waterfront, gave the town a reputation not unlike that of the rough mining towns in the West.[26]

Reasons for the extreme animosity between Virginia and

Aerial photograph of Crisfield, c. 1890, C. C. Ward—photographer (courtesy of the Historic American Buildings Survey, Library of Congress).

Maryland watermen were not limited to territorial oyster beds in Pocomoke Sound. Differences in harvesting techniques between hand tongers and unscrupulous oyster dredgers also provoked hostilities, which often led to armed conflicts. While many oyster dredgers respected established laws for harvesting, others assumed a piratical nature and raided protected waters at night, chasing tongers from their beds and scrambling for as many oysters as possible. Their thoughts lay only with the handsome profits to be made before the supply was exhausted.[27]

With hopes of protecting the oyster beds used by independent tongers and keeping general peace on the Chesapeake, the Maryland General Assembly created the "Oyster Navy" in 1868.[28] Led first by Captain Hunter Davidson from Kent Island, the meager force was expanded a few years later with Captain James Clements from Baltimore and Captain Robert H. McCready of Somerset County.[29] By the early 1870s conditions had reached such a hostile state that police boats were regularly stationed on the Manokin River and Somerset County had financed its own force to maintain a vigil at the mouth of the Wicomico.[30]

Heightening the difficulties between watermen of the lower Chesapeake was the question of the exact boundary between Maryland and Virginia waters. A decreasing supply

of the lucrative bay delicacy significantly increased the value of the richest oyster bars in the Chesapeake, principally located in Tangier and Pocomoke sounds. Since the two sounds separated the two states, Maryland and Virginia watermen hotly contested their rights to work what each group considered their time-honored territory.

After several years of verbal and armed dispute, the state legislatures finally reached an agreement. As determined by the Jenkins-Black Award of 1877, the line was stretched between the low water mark on the south shore of the Potomac River to Smith's Point at the southern end of Smith Island, and then to Watkins Point on the north shore of the Pocomoke.[31]

The lucrative trade in oysters and fish, wildfowl, crabs, and terrapin, as well as the canning and boat-building industries, kept Crisfield one of the fastest growing cities in Maryland during the late nineteenth century. A commercial profile of the town published by the *Maryland State Gazette* in 1871 gives an impression of daily life. To supply the everyday needs of Crisfield's diverse populace, no less than fifteen merchants advertised their businesses, and eight hotels, saloons, and boarding houses provided rooms and entertainment. In an effort to accommodate his cross-section of customers, the Gazette reported, Robert H. Croswell offered a variety of

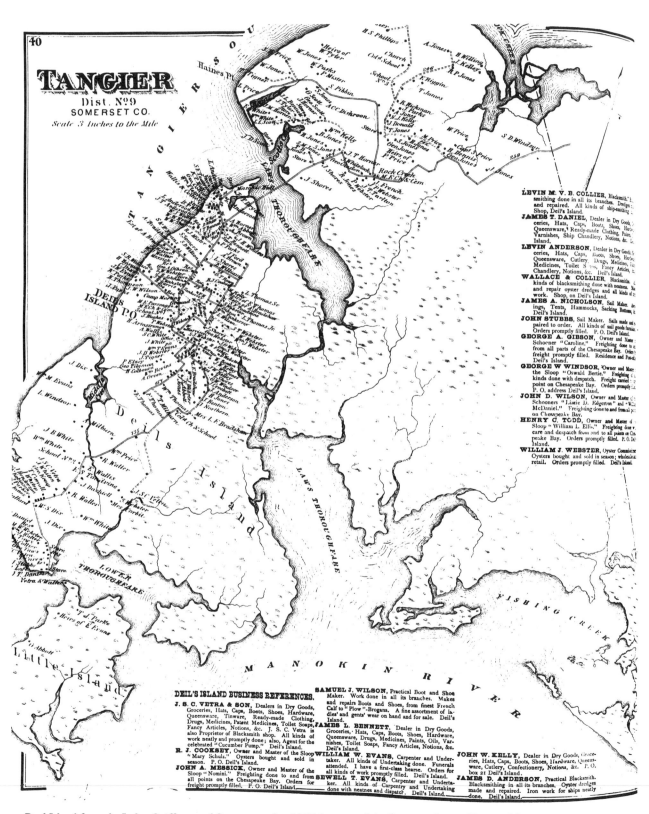

Deal Island from the Lake, Griffing, and Stevenson atlas, 1877 (courtesy of the Somerset County Historical Society).

items to outfit the body, a boat, or perhaps a boudoir. Not to forget his practical agrarian patrons, Croswell carried hardware, queensware, cutlery, hair, doors, sash, and guano. Additional commercial listings in the *Maryland Gazette* article included four oyster packers—A. R. Crockett, N. Dixon, C. C. Gardener, and T. H. Goodsell; one physician; two blacksmiths; one barber; one minister; and five shoemakers.[32]

By the end of the century Crisfield was the largest town in Somerset County, with a bulging population of 2,600. The *Maryland Gazetteer* of 1891-92 described the bayfront town:

> *Crisfield is an important town…located on the Little Annemessex River and N.Y., Phila., and Norfolk RR, in the extreme southern part of Somerset County, 19 miles south of Princess Anne [courthouse]. A regular line of*

> *steamers connects it with Baltimore. Crisfield is incorporated and contains 5 churches, good public schools, 2 hotels, and supports a weekly newspaper, the Leader. Oyster packing and fishing are the principal industries here. In the winter a number of firms are actively engaged in packing oysters and in the summer in catching and shipping crabs, fish, & c. The manufacturing products include fertilizers, fish oil, and ships.*[33]

Concurrent with the explosive growth in Crisfield was the expansion of smaller water-oriented communities along Somerset's extensive shoreline. During the third quarter of the nineteenth century, Deal Island grew into a sizable bay-oriented community of 1,000 residents.[34] It was reached by a ferry that crossed Laws Thoroughfare until a wooden bridge

Deal Island wharf, photograph c. 1910 (courtesy of Thurston's Studio).

Aerial view of Princess Anne looking north, photograph c. 1890, E.I. Brown—photographer (courtesy of Robert Withey).

was erected around 1870. Adam Wallace, biographer of the Reverend Joshua Thomas, wrote a description of the island in 1861:

> Deal's, (or as they were formerly called Devil's) Islands, are two in number, and are situated to the N.E. of Tangier, near the main, and not between the Sound and the Bay...
>
> The larger one, (on which there is a good sized Methodist Church, and where camp meetings have been held most of the years since 1828,) is about three miles in length, by one in width. It is a very productive soil, suitable for almost any species of grain, fruit, or vegetables. An immense quantity of sweet potatoes is raised there, as also a large yield of corn, and some excellent wheat.
>
> But the population, (numbering nearly one thousand,) like that on the smaller islands, has to depend more on the water than on land for support.[35]

The fourth quarter of the nineteenth century brought

additional growth, and when the century closed Deal Island had become the second largest community in Somerset County. Boasting a population of 1,500 residents, the islands were served by five general stores, two blacksmiths, a gristmill, a sail loft, and a veterinary surgeon.[36] By the turn of the century a hotel and store complex operated by Captain Levin Anderson stood at the north end of the island near the quarter-mile long steamboat wharf.

Unlike Crisfield and Deal Island, Princess Anne was not located near open navigable water and so had no direct connection with steamboat traffic. However, the arrival of the Eastern Shore Railroad by March 1866 gave the small courthouse town new commercial vitality.[37] By the time the Lake, Griffing, and Stevenson atlas was published in 1877, the Manokin Flour Mill, operated by Rudolph S. Cohn, and the fruit canning operation of H.H. Dashiell were located near the track.[38] Through the second half of the nineteenth century additional town lots were created, extending the town to the north, south, and west. The old Teackle estate was divided

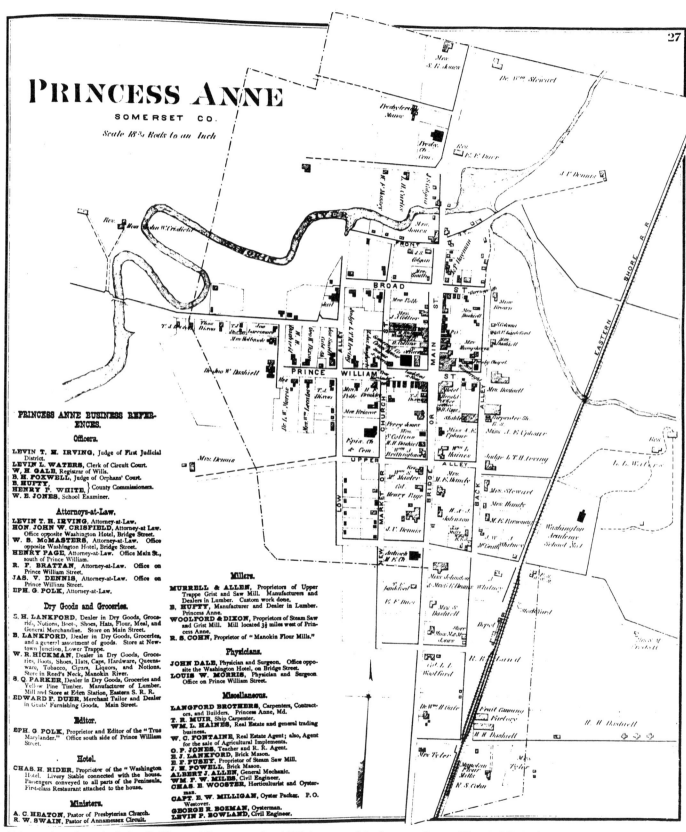

PRINCESS ANNE
SOMERSET CO.
Scale 18¾ Rods to an Inch

27

PRINCESS ANNE BUSINESS REFERENCES.

Officers.

LEVIN T. H. IRVING, Judge of First Judicial District.
LEVIN L. WATERS, Clerk of Circuit Court.
W. H. GALE, Registrar of Wills.
B. H. FOXWELL, Judge of Orphans' Court.
B. HUFTY,
HENRY F. WHITE, } County Commissioners.
W. B. JONES, School Examiner.

Attorneys-at-Law.

LEVIN T. H. IRVING, Attorney-at-Law.
HON. JOHN W. CRISFIELD, Attorney-at Law. Office opposite Washington Hotel, Bridge Street.
W. S. McMASTERS, Attorney-at-Law. Office opposite Washington Hotel, Bridge Street.
HENRY PAGE, Attorney-at-Law. Office Main St., south of Prince William.
R. F. BRATTAN, Attorney-at-Law. Office on Prince William Street.
JAS. V. DENNIS, Attorney-at-Law. Office on Prince William Street.
EPH. G. POLK, Attorney-at-Law.

Dry Goods and Groceries.

S. H. LANKFORD, Dealer in Dry Goods, Groceries, Notions, Boots, Shoes, Hats, Flour, Meal, and General Merchandise. Store on Main Street.
B. LANKFORD, Dealer in Dry Goods, Groceries, and a general assortment of goods. Store at Newtown Junction, Lower Trappe.
W. R. HICKMAN, Dealer in Dry Goods, Groceries, Boots, Shoes, Hats, Caps, Hardware, Queensware, Tobacco, Cigars, Liquors, and Notions. Store in Reed's Neck, Manokin River.
S. Q. PARKER, Dealer in Dry Goods, Groceries and Yellow Pine Timber. Manufacturer of Lumber. Mill and Store at Eden Station, Eastern S. R. R.
EDWARD F. DUER, Merchant Tailor and Dealer in Gents' Furnishing Goods. Main Street.

Editor.

EPH. G. POLK, Proprietor and Editor of the "True Marylander." Office south side of Prince William Street.

Hotel.

CHAS. H. RIDER, Proprietor of the "Washington Hotel. Livery Stable connected with the house. Passengers conveyed to all parts of the Peninsula. First-class Restaurant attached to the house.

Ministers.

A. C. HEATON, Pastor of Presbyterian Church.
R. W. SWAIN, Pastor of Annamessex Circuit.

Millers.

MURRELL & ALLEN, Proprietors of Upper Trappe Grist and Saw Mill. Manufacturers and Dealers in Lumber. Custom work done.
B. HUFTY, Manufacturer and Dealer in Lumber. Princess Anne.
WOOLFORD & DIXON, Proprietors of Steam Saw and Grist Mill. Mill located 3½ miles west of Princess Anne.
R. S. COHN, Proprietor of "Manokin Flour Mills."

Physicians.

JOHN DALE, Physician and Surgeon. Office opposite the Washington Hotel, on Bridge Street.
LOUIS W. MORRIS, Physician and Surgeon. Office on Prince William Street.

Miscellaneous.

LANGFORD BROTHERS, Carpenters, Contractors, and Builders. Princess Anne, Md.
T. R. MUIR, Ship Carpenter.
WM. L. HAINES, Real Estate and general trading business.
W. C. FONTAINE, Real Estate Agent; also, Agent for the sale of Agricultural Implements.
O. F. JONES, Teacher and R. R. Agent.
E. J. LANKFORD, Brick Mason.
B. F. PUSEY, Proprietor of Steam Saw Mill.
J. E. POWELL, Brick Mason.
ALBERT J. ALLEN, General Mechanic.
WM. F. W. MILES, Civil Engineer.
CHAS. E. WOOSTER, Horticulturist and Oysterman.
CAPT. B. W. MILLIGAN, Oyster Packer. P. O. Westover.
GEORGE R. BOEMAN, Oysterman.
LEVIN F. ROWLAND, Civil Engineer.

Princess Anne from the Lake, Griffing and Stevenson atlas, 1877 (courtesy of the Somerset County Historical Society).

during the early 1850s, and part of the Beckford tract was partitioned into building lots in 1884.[39] By the end of the century the population of Princess Anne had reached 1,000. At the time, the town boasted two canning factories; three churches; a bank; a large new public school; a hotel; two weekly newspapers, *The Marylander* and the *Somerset Herald*; and over 150 structures lining the town streets.[40]

Inland Somerset was not without its villages, which grew up along the roadside to service the agricultural communities that surrounded them. Upper Fairmount, situated on the highest ground between the Manokin and Great Annemessex rivers, had begun to develop along the peninsula road as early as the second quarter of the nineteenth century. This growth

included Maddox's Church, a Greek Revival style structure that formerly stood in the center of the village. Although a few dwellings in Upper Fairmount date from the antebellum period, including the Hall house and the western half of the Robert Jones house, major construction did not occur until the second half of the century.

The Lake, Griffing, and Stevenson atlas documents Upper Fairmount's size in 1877 with over fifteen dwellings, two general stores, a boot and shoe store, two physician's offices, and new Methodist churches for the white and black congregations. The old Greek Revival church was evidently used as the town hall during the 1870s, after the white congregation had erected a new structure. This old church building later

"Scene at Upper Fairmount," photograph c. 1910 (courtesy of Thurston's Studio).

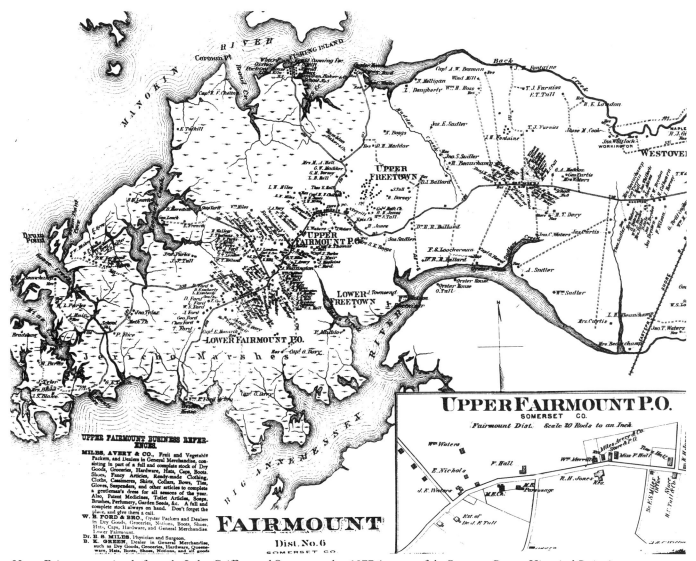

Upper Fairmount peninsula from the Lake, Griffing and Stevenson atlas, 1877 (courtesy of the Somerset County Historical Society).

housed one of the principal stores in the town, Miles, Avery and Co., which placed this advertisement in the business directory of the atlas:

> *MILES, AVERY AND CO., Fruit and Vegetable Packers, and Dealers in General Merchandise, consisting in part of a full and complete stock of Dry Goods, Groceries, Hardware, Hats, Caps, Boots, Shoes, Fancy Articles, Ready-made Clothing, Cloths, Cassimeres, Shirts, Collars, Bows, Ties, Gloves, Suspenders, and other articles to complete a gentlemen's dress for all seasons of the year. Also, Patent Medicines, Toilet Articles, Soaps, Brushes, Perfumery, Garden Seeds, &c. A full and complete stock always at hand. Don't forget the place and give them a call.*[41]

Two small black communities on the periphery of Upper Fairmount, first developed during antebellum years as Upper and Lower Freetown, expanded between 1865 and 1877. In

the latter year, Upper Freetown included over two dozen frame structures, while Lower Freetown was composed of about a dozen buildings. Later in the century the two towns were renamed Upper Hill and Lower Hill. The residents in each village sponsored the construction of a Methodist church.

At the tip of the Fairmount peninsula, small groups of watermen's houses were erected during the early to mid-nineteenth century on the spits of high ground between Tangier Sound and the Jericho marshes. Eventually known as Frenchtown and Rumbley, these two communities were served by a Methodist church and a school, both sited along the road connecting the two villages. An adjacent island known as "Hazards" was also occupied until the turn of the century, when several dwellings, such as the Ovid French house, were partially dismantled and floated to new sites as the community consolidated into two distinct villages.[42]

Farther off the Somerset mainland, three watermen's villages expanded on Smith Island during the same period.

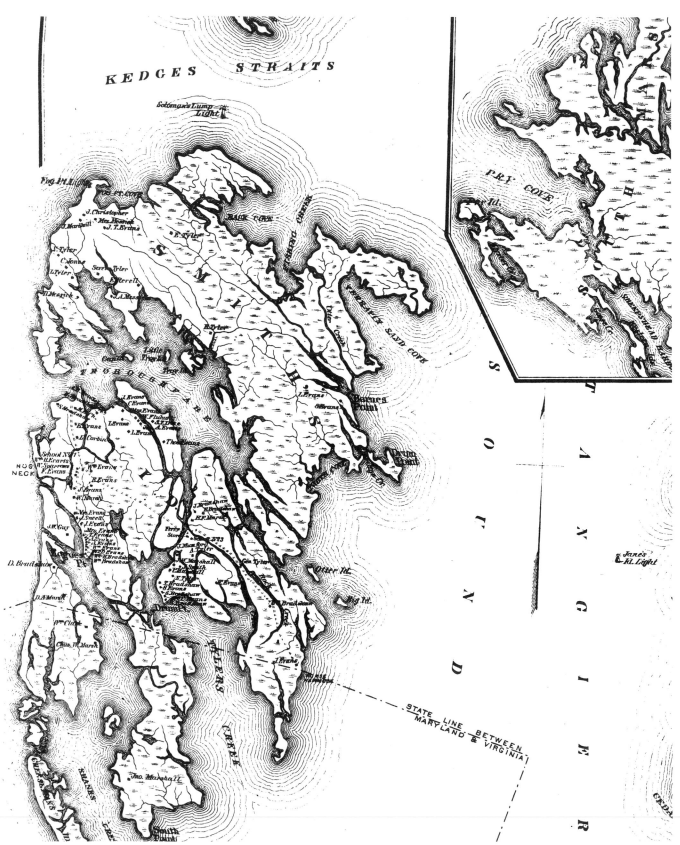

Smith Island from the Lake, Griffing, and Stevenson atlas, 1877 (courtesy of the Somerset County Historical Society).

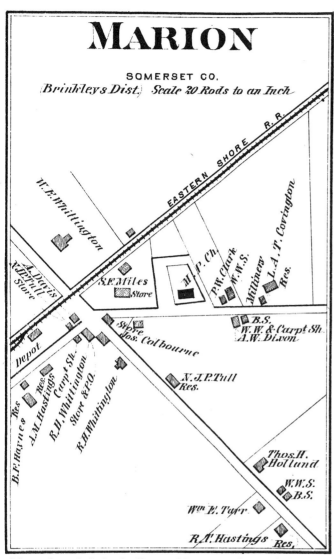

Marion from the Lake, Griffing, and Stevenson atlas, 1877 (courtesy of the Somerset County Historical Society).

Named after Henry Smith, the original patentee of "Pitchcroft," the largest tract, the island was inhabited through much of the seventeenth and eighteenth centuries. Nevertheless, tax records and maps suggest the villages of Ewell, Tylerton, and Rhodes Point were not officially established until the nineteenth century. Rhodes Point, formerly "Rogues Point," developed along Shanks Creek at the southwest tip of the island and by 1877 included a score of frame houses and a school.[43] By the same time the village on the north end of the island, later named Ewell, included a Methodist Episcopal church and a dozen frame dwellings largely owned by the Bradshaw and Evans families. Tylerton was located on a detached part of the island group reached during the 1870s by a ferry that crossed Tyler Creek.

In northern Somerset County the village of Mt. Vernon developed along the only road that stretched across Hungary Neck between the Wicomico River and Great Monie Creek.

In contrast to the cohesive nature of Upper Fairmount, the several dozen dwellings and three stores that defined Mt. Vernon during the late nineteenth century were dispersed over a two-mile stretch of county road.

Towns sprang up throughout the county along the Eastern Shore Railroad line, which reached Somers Cove in 1866. Stations, some of which developed into villages, included Eden, Loretto, Westover, Kingston, Marion, and Hopewell.

Marion, located in the center of a thriving agricultural region in southern Somerset County, grew into one of the largest villages during the second half of the nineteenth century. In exchange for donating the railroad right-of-way through his land, John C. Horsey named the depot village after his daughter. The large rural population surrounding Marion ensured the expansion of the small crossroads village into a prominent, service-oriented town for the local agrarian economy. By 1877 Marion boasted a handful of craft-related workshops, including two carpenter shops, two blacksmith shops, and two wagon shops. At each corner of the crossroads was a general store, and east of the intersection were the blacksmith shops and a Methodist Protestant church. The 1877 atlas shows these commercial and religious structures accompanied by at least ten dwellings.[44] Marion experienced its greatest expansion during the late nineteenth and early twentieth centuries; this residential development occurred largely to the south and west of the town.

During the same period, the Worcester and Somerset Railroad Company was established to extend a rail line from Kings Creek to Newtown, later Pocomoke City. By May 1872 the *Salisbury Advertiser* repeated an article first printed in the *Somerset Herald* describing the new route:

> *The stations on the Worcester & Somerset Railroad (now in course of construction) have been named as follows: The point where the Eastern Shore Railroad and the W&S Railroad forms a junction at King's Creek, is called Newtown Jct., the next station is situated where the county road crosses the Railroad near Green Hill, this is called Dublin; next is on the John Lankford farm, three miles from Newtown, this is called Costen's; the next is at the terminus, Newtown. The Rails were laid up to Costen's station on Wednesday, leaving a balance of three miles to be laid.*[45]

The railroad ended at the northern edge of the Pocomoke

River. Despite much speculation about extending a line across the river and southward into Virginia soon afterwards, construction of the railroad through Accomac and Northampton counties was not accomplished until October 25, 1884, after the Eastern Shore Railroad was purchased by the newly formed New York, Philadelphia, and Norfolk Railroad Company.[46]

Just as the landscape of the Eastern Shore was marked by pivotal developments during the postbellum years, religion in Somerset County underwent its own changes. Methodism continued to grow and expand, while the Episcopalians and Presbyterians tried to consolidate and maintain their congregations.

St. Andrew's Episcopal Church, northeast elevation, photograph c. 1900, E.I. Brown—photographer (courtesy of William Marshall Scott).

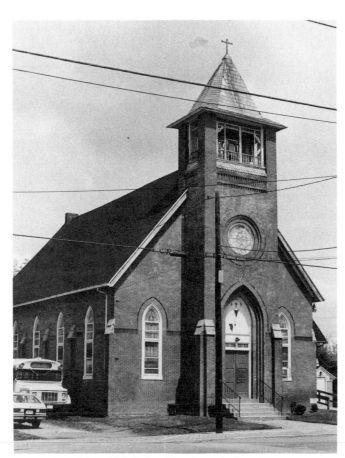

Metropolitan United Methodist Church, south elevation.

All Saints Church at Monie, southeast elevation, photograph c. 1900, E.I. Brown—photographer (courtesy of Robert Withey).

Facing dwindling attendance, the Episcopalians of Coventry Parish considered reducing the size of the eighteenth century church at Rehobeth in order to decrease maintenance costs. Finally, though, the Rehobeth vestry decided to abandon the structure and merge with the congregation at St. Paul's near Tull's Corner.[47]

The churches in Somerset Parish also experienced considerable change. Monie Church was reconsecrated in 1845 as All Saints Church, but it was destroyed in a windstorm on July 31, 1879. Two years later, a simple, rectangular, Gothic Revival frame church was erected on the same site and consecrated by the Right Reverend Henry Champlin Lay, bishop of Easton.[48]

By the mid-nineteenth century St. Andrew's Church in Princess Anne was considered the principal Somerset Parish congregation. Throughout the second half of the century various modifications were made to the Flemish bond brick church, beginning with the construction of the corner bell tower in 1859.[49] Six years later, in 1865, the original boxed pews and old altar furnishings were replaced and a center aisle plan created. Later in the century, the congregation financed the most radical changes, executed between 1892 and 1897. Following drawings and specifications submitted by William Holsey Wood, an architect from Newark, New Jersey, the entire church was extensively reworked. The failing west gable end was rebuilt, the hammer beam truss

Manokin Presbyterian Church, south elevation, photograph c. 1900, E.I.Brown—photographer (courtesy of William Marshall Scott).

roof of Georgia pine was erected, the chancel was remodeled, and the spire was raised. The firm of Thomas W. Slemons and Albert W. Lankford of Wicomico County was contracted for the work.[50]

Likewise, the Manokin Presbyterian Church underwent considerable alteration when the 1765 Flemish bond brick church was reworked after the Civil War. In 1872 the pair of entrances in the south wall were bricked up and the main entrance was reoriented to the east gable end. At the same time, the roof was raised and brackets were added. Inside, the eighteenth century box pews were removed to allow for center and side aisles. In 1888 a three-story entrance and bell tower was raised against the east gable end. Finally, in 1892, a small addition was attached to the west end to accommodate a larger altar.

While Presbyterians and Episcopalians were improving their churches, the Methodists were holding popular revival meetings across the county, encouraging the formation of many new congregations. Rigid moral codes that forcefully condemned licentious behavior appealed to strict Victorian sensibilities and attracted many rural and town residents.

Members of the black community were especially drawn

Eliza F. Smith Home for Girls, Princess Anne Academy, photograph c. 1895 (courtesy of the Image Preservation Company).

Third Washington Academy, photograph c. 1900, E.I. Brown—photographer (courtesy of William Marshall Scott).

to Methodism with its antislavery philosophy and the founding of the Delaware Conference of Colored Methodists in 1864. Perhaps the best known of the black Methodist congregations in Somerset County is the Metropolitan United Methodist Church of Princess Anne, formed in 1866 as the Wesley Chapel. In 1884 the congregation purchased the lot where the Somerset County jail once stood and by 1886 had erected an impressive Gothic Revival brick church.

Alongside efforts to encourage black congregations during the post-Civil War years, the Methodist Church raised money to create schools to educate the black population in the South. In the Chesapeake region, the Delaware Conference of the Methodist Episcopal Church and the Centenary Biblical Institute of Baltimore shared an interest in establishing a black-oriented school for advanced learning on the Eastern Shore.[53] Through the influence of Joseph Robert Waters, a Fairmount-born black minister, and John Alfred Banum Wilson, a white Methodist minister who served the Metropolitan Church during the early 1880s, Princess Anne was chosen as the site for the school.[54] Wilson purchased part of the old "Olney" plantation in June 1886 and two months later transferred title to the Centenary Biblical Institute for $2,000.[55] By using the old plantation house on the property for classrooms, the school was able to open that fall with thirty-seven students.[56]

Formally known in its early years as the Delaware Conference Academy, the school was popularly referred to as the Princess Anne Academy. Through the Morrill Act of 1890, it qualified for state and federal monies, but in spite of government assistance the academy faced difficult years and an uncertain future.[57]

Under the leadership of its first president, Benjamin Oliver Bird, the school expanded its holdings in 1890 with the purchase of a 103-acre tract that comprised the balance of the "Olney" estate. By the end of the century, enrollment had reached ninety-three and two frame dormitories and an industrial arts building augmented the old plantation house.[58] The early curriculum of the school focused on the liberal arts and social sciences. Later in the nineteenth century, however, the classes were broadened to include more practical training in carpentry, blacksmithing, agriculture, tailoring, and shoe-making for male students and dressmaking, cooking, and hand and machine stitching for the girls.[59]

As the Methodists were struggling to keep the Princess Anne Academy solvent during the 1880s and 1890s, the trustees of the Washington Academy were also wrestling with the future of their 123-year-old institution. Several factors contributed to thoughts of abandoning the building on King's Creek, not the least of which was the poor repair of the 1802 brick structure. John W. Crisfield, president of the board of trustees, submitted his comments concerning the school on November 21, 1890:

> *...it is represented that the academy building in Princess Anne is very much out of repair and is otherwise inconvenient and unsuitable for the purposes for which it is devoted; and large expenses will be required to put it in even tolerable order....*[60]

Although eighty-one students attended class at the old academy during the 1890 school year, plans were under way by April 1891 to merge the school with the Somerset school system and to erect a new building in Princess Anne over the summer.[61] On May 26, 1891, the trustees of the Washington Academy and the Somerset County school commissioners entered into the following agreement:

> *Whereas it has become necessary for the proper and efficient management of the public schools in Princess Anne*

Fairmount Academy, south elevation.

town,…to erect a new school building in which can be acco-modated, with comfort and convenience, both the High School and the primary schools of the said town…begin-ning the same during the ensuing summer, a building of agreeable and tasteful architecture, of sufficient dimensions and properly adapted, and conveniently arranged for the use as a public high school, with accomodations also for a primary school, to cost whatever may be necessary, not less in any event than $5000.[62]

True to the agreement, during the summer of 1891 a large brick school was built in the popular Romanesque Revival style on the eastern fringe of Princess Anne next to the Beech-wood estate.

Around 1865, on a less ambitious scale, the Fairmount Academy evidently replaced its schoolhouse, which had occu-pied the site since the late 1830s. The expanding population on the Fairmount peninsula during the third quarter of the nineteenth century led the school's trustees to erect a two-story, hip-roofed frame structure trimmed with bracketed eaves and corner pilasters.

Similar in size and date to the new Fairmount school was the Crisfield Academy, which formerly stood along Asbury Avenue. Built in 1876 the two-story, four-bay by four-bay frame school was distinguished by a pyramidal-roofed bell tower. In addition, the modified hip roof and front pediment were trimmed with brackets. The Crisfield Academy served the bay-front town well into the twentieth century.[63]

These four academies were by no means typical of educa-tion facilities erected in the county during the second half of the nineteenth century. More common were the single story, one-room frame schoolhouses built shortly after the Civil

War. One of the few surviving examples is the Quinton schoolhouse, which formerly stood next to the Quinton Methodist Episcopal Church near the old Costen railroad station. The plain, weatherboard frame school is decorated with Gothic-arched gable end vents and wooden rooftop finials. When the schoolhouse was abandoned, the structure was moved to a nearby farm.

The construction of small schoolhouses throughout the county improved the chances that a rudimentary education would reach a larger portion of the Somerset County population. Indeed, in some ways life improved for many in the county during the second half of the nineteenth century. With the construction of the railroad to Princess Anne and Crisfield, economic opportunities broadened as new businesses emerged alongside established firms. Inventions and new technologies infused the county with the economic strength to repair the financial destruction provoked by a divisive civil war. For the black population, low wages and poor economic prospects were offset by enjoyment of daily freedoms that had long seemed unobtainable. Small communities, often centered around a newly formed church, provided former slaves with the opportunity to run their own lives. ♣

Quinton schoolhouse, north elevation.

CHAPTER IX, 1850-1900

Machine Age Building

Just as new technologies altered the social and economic nature of the Eastern Shore, they also made the second half of the nineteenth century a period of distinct architectural change. New construction techniques utilizing mass-produced materials were applied to the execution of a range of newly introduced, nationally popular styles that influenced the domestic, religious, and commercial architecture of Somerset County. In spite of these new trends, county residents' strong conservatism coupled with modest building aspirations encouraged the continued use and adaptation of long-standing traditions in vernacular house design.

Prior to mid-century, construction relied heavily on age-old hand craftsmanship to hew timbers, burn brick, and split shingles. Inside the house, carpenters and joiners fashioned hand-built stairs, doors, windows, and mantels, while plasterers smoothed rough and finish layers of plaster over hand-split lath. In a few rare instances, materials were imported from afar, but for the most part building on the Eastern Shore was limited to well-known skills handed down from one generation to the next. Changing style preferences altered exterior and interior house finishes, but the building forms remained largely those used through two centuries of craftsmanship.

The arrival of the Industrial Revolution altered the entire building process. By no means was hand craftsmanship re-

Andrew Jackson Downing, Design VIII, Suburban Cottage, Figure 33, The Architecture of Country Houses, *1853.*

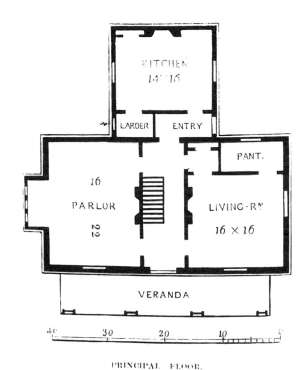

PRINCIPAL FLOOR.

Andrew Jackson Downing, Design VIII, Suburban Cottage, Figure 34,
The Architecture of Country Houses, 1853.

placed, but the manufacture of windows, doors, mantels, and moldings and the availability of commercially burned brick and precut, sized lumber considerably expedited the building process. Shipped by steamboat or rail car, these materials were easily obtained by local carpenters constructing houses and churches as well as a new generation of agricultural, industrial, and commercial buildings. At the same time, scores of construction and design manuals were published in the United States and Great Britain. These volumes disseminated popular house plans and revival designs, including the Italianate, Gothic Revival, and Queen Anne, to carpenter-builders across the nation.

Although a broader variety of plans and styles was available by the mid-nineteenth century, Eastern Shore residents most often showed conservative architectural tastes. Many people adopted a popular style for architectural trim but adhered to a familiar house plan. Only a few Somerset residents were adventurous enough to build a house wholly in one of the new styles.

Perhaps the most instructive place to contrast the variety of mid-to-late nineteenth century house types in Somerset County is Princess Anne, where something is known about a specific craftsman who practiced carpentry and house building. Seth D. Venables (1821-1897), who had married Susan Jones on February 15, 1849, was listed in the 1850 U.S. census as a house carpenter.[1] Lamentably, Venables's working career is largely undocumented; however, he is recorded in the Somerset County commissioners' minutes of August 10, 1858, as the craftsman hired to complete repairs on the courthouse.[2] His name also appears on deeds associated with several residents of Princess Anne who financed the construction of houses in the 1850s. Evidently, in lieu of cash payment, Venables's skills were sometimes compensated by the transfer or temporary mortgage of personal property.[3] After his death in 1897, Venables was buried in the Antioch Methodist Church cemetery in Princess Anne.[4]

Attributed to Seth Venables is the William Lecates house, also known as the Fontaine-Fitzgerald house, one of the first structures to be built on the lots created from the old Teackle estate. The two-story, three-bay center passage frame dwelling repeats a vernacular house type used in the county since the mid-eighteenth century. What distinguishes the Lecates house from earlier examples and indicates its date is the consistent mid-nineteenth century Greek Revival woodwork. The most notable exterior feature is the two-story pedimented porch supported by square, paneled columns. Sidelighted doorways on each floor of the porch are framed by wide, paneled surrounds, and original handrails survive on the second floor.

The interior of the Lecates house, with its Greek Revival finishes, is as well-preserved as the exterior. Highlighting the center stair hall is a peculiar rustication of the wall surface below the stringer. Carefully executed rectangular blocks were substituted for the plaster surface that would normally have finished the triangular space. A technique found in at least three other houses in Princess Anne, this treatment appears to have been a distinctive signature of Seth Venables's work. Although Venables would have hand-crafted the individualistic rustication, many elements of the Lecates house were ready-made. The six-over-six sash windows, louvered shutters, four-panel doors, turned newel post and balusters, and post-and-lintel mantels, as well as other features, were undoubtedly manufactured elsewhere and delivered to the Prince

William Lecates house (Fontaine-Fitzgerald house), northeast elevation.

William Street address for Venables to use in constructing the house.

Another example of Venables's workmanship is the house that stands at 14 Mansion Street, which he built circa 1853 for himself and his wife. As in the William Lecates house, Venables followed a long-used vernacular house form, in this case, the side hall/parlor plan. The overt stylistic features of the weatherboarded exterior are relatively few, but the bracketed hood over the four-panel front door is a distinctive feature for the mid-nineteenth century. Inside, the house is finished with a mixture of late Federal and Greek Revival woodwork. Instead of the robustly turned newel and balusters of the Lecates house, Venables probably crafted the delicate Federal style stair railing of heart pine to save the expense of a more costly manufactured stair. The balance of the house is plainly finished with mid-nineteenth century Greek Revival woodwork.

Alongside these traditional vernacular house forms with their Greek Revival features are several dwellings that follow the temple- or gable-front design popularized fifty years earlier by Littleton Dennis Teackle. Characterized as Greek Revival when they were built are the Judge Levin T. H. Irving house on the northeast corner of Prince William Street and Beckford Avenue and the Joseph B. Brinkley house, located on the northeast corner of South Somerset and Railroad avenues. Erected during the 1850s, probably by Seth Venables, the houses follow the side hall/double-pile plan, and both exteriors are trimmed with corner pilasters. The interiors

William Lecates house (Fontaine-Fitzgerald house), stair.

Seth D. Venables house, east elevation.

Levin T. H. Irving house (Somerset Parish rectory), south elevation.

Francis Barnes house, photograph c. 1900 (courtesy of Wilmer O. Lankford).

of the houses were executed in similar taste, with bold mid-nineteenth century Greek Revival mantels, turned baluster stairs, and four-panel doors. The Judge Irving house also exhibits the unusual stair rustication.

Yet another mixture of late Federal and Greek Revival features brought together to finish a traditional side hall/double-pile plan house is found at the Rufus Parsons house across the street from the Teackle Mansion. Built in 1858 for Rufus and Charlotte Parsons, the two-story, three-bay frame dwelling is trimmed with paneled pilasters at each corner. A classically inspired entrance frames the front door, while late Federal style corner block surrounds distinguish the six-over-six sash windows. Unlike the previously cited examples, the Parsons house rests on a high brick foundation and is covered by a low-pitched, nearly flat roof. The interiors have survived largely intact, with Greek Revival finishes. Most notable are the marble mantels that distinguish the first floor fireplaces. Obviously not of local origin, they were shipped to Princess Anne, probably from Baltimore.

In contrast to these Federal and Greek Revival inspired

houses is the Francis Barnes house. Around 1854 Francis Barnes financed the construction of an impressive two-story, three-bay frame dwelling that falls most comfortably into the Italianate style. Built on Lot 2 of the old Teackle estate, the center passage house rests on a raised brick foundation and is trimmed with a bracketed eave. A bracketed porch stretches across the front.

More than any other house of its period in Princess Anne, the Francis Barnes house was planned and assembled with imported features finer than most houses of its day. Outstanding are the silver-plated hinges and hinge covers, gold-decorated china door and shutter knobs, interior shutters, and factory-made mantels, doors, and stair fittings. The parlor mantel was executed in marble.

The Francis Barnes house is the closest example in Somerset County of what Andrew Jackson Downing, a prominent mid-nineteenth century architectural essayist, labeled the Italianate style. Downing described this style in his book *The Architecture of Country Houses*, published in New York in 1853:

Dennis-Dashiell house, destroyed, photograph c. 1967, northeast elevation.

Rufus Parsons house (JOSH house), southeast elevation.

There is a strong and growing partiality among us for the Italian style. Originally adapted to the manifestation of social life, in a climate almost the counterpart of that of the Middle and Southern portions of our country—at least so far as relates to eight months of the year, it is made to conform exactly to our tastes and habits, with perhaps, less alteration than any other style. Its broad roofs, ample verandas and arcades, are especially agreeable in our summers of dazzling sunshine, and though not so truly Northern as other modes that permit a high roof, still it has much to render it a favorite in the Middle and Western sections of our Union.[5]

Even more reflective of the exuberant Italianate style was the Dennis-Dashiell house, which formerly stood on South Somerset Avenue next to the post office in Princess Anne. The three-story, five-bay frame house, built around 1867, was highlighted by an undulating bracketed roof and a decorated front porch. The house was torn down in the early 1970s. In spite of these two examples, the Italianate style was little used in Somerset County and never expressed in its most elaborate form.

Another mid-nineteenth century revival design unusual in Somerset County was the Second Empire style, characterized by the consistent use of the mansard roof. French architect François Mansart (1598-1666) first popularized the steeply pitched roof shape and associated monumental building forms. His designs were widely revived in France during the mid-nineteenth century, and the style was copied and adapted in the United States. As with the Italianate style, Somerset County residents did not widely embrace this foreign-influenced design. In Princess Anne the Levin Woolford house displays the steeply pitched mansard roof shape, but in every other way the side hall/double-pile dwelling is a reflection of local traditions. Built for Washington and Caroline Miles around 1853 by Seth Venables, the three-bay frame house is another in the group of contemporary dwellings in which Venables used his distinctive ashlar-style blocks under the stair.

A later example that evokes the blockish monumentality usually associated with the Second Empire style is the Noah Webster homeplace, tucked away on Deal Island. Built around 1883 the five-bay frame house follows a traditional center hall/double-pile plan, but both the main house and the rear service wing are covered with mansard-style roofs pierced with pointed arch dormers. Evidently the carpenters struggled with building a mansard roof on Deal Island during the 1880s, for the upper hip-roofed section is much steeper and more apparent from the ground than it would normally have been. Enhancing the front of the house is a turned post porch embellished with delicate sawn and spindle decoration.

Stemming from a different architectural tradition, the Gothic Revival style found expression in Somerset County as

Woolford house, northwest elevation.

St. John's United Methodist Church, Deal Island, southwest elevation.

early as the 1840s with the construction of St. Paul's Episcopal Church near Tull's Corner in 1848. Without many exceptions, the Somerset County churches erected during the second half of the nineteenth century followed the Gothic Revival style in some manner. Examples range from the highly elaborate Mt. Pleasant Methodist Protestant Church in Crisfield, built in 1892, to the simpler interpretation at the Metropolitan United Methodist Church, erected in 1886 for the black Methodist congregation in Princess Anne. Both brick churches are distinguished by entrance bell towers, Gothic-arched windows, and decorative brickwork. Repeating a familiar Gothic formula for a church is St. John's United Methodist Church on Deal Island, built in 1879. The tall center nave, illuminated by pointed-arch gable end and clerestory windows, is flanked by shed-roofed side aisles. Rising on the northwest corner is an elaborate entrance and bell tower

Noah Webster homeplace, east elevation.

Francis Barnes farmhouse, destroyed, northeast elevation.

with pinnacles topped by an octagonal spire.

Only a few houses in Somerset County were designed with strong references to the Gothic style, and the Francis Barnes farmhouse, which formerly stood near the Green Hill crossroads, was the closest example. The T-shaped house was built around 1880 on an old side hall/parlor plan that was extended to the rear with a two-story, two-room plan service wing. But in contrast to the traditional nature of its floor plan, the frame dwelling was encrusted with elaborate sawn bargeboards, wooden peak finials, and turned post porches and had Gothic-arched attic windows. Inside, the house had a curving stair in the side hall and floor-to-ceiling, pocket-type windows in the parlor.

Of all the popular styles, the Queen Anne had perhaps the greatest influence on the late nineteenth century domestic architecture of Somerset County. Known for its asymmetrical forms and eclectic use of decorative features, the style dictated the adoption of room dispositions unfamiliar in the pre-Civil War building vocabulary of the county. Towers; wraparound porches; textured wall surfaces; and tall, multifaceted chimneys contributed to an exuberant architectural display.

The most extensive collection of Queen Anne style houses in Somerset County lines the streets of Crisfield, where profits from the oyster and seafood trade sponsored the construction of several prominent examples. Recently restored on Main Street, the Pauline Crockett house best exemplifies the intricate variety of textures, shapes, and patterns in wood and brick typical of the style. Built during the boom years of the oyster harvests by Abednego Riggin Crockett, a prominent oyster packer and merchant, the two-and-a-half story house outdistances contemporary Somerset County dwellings in the variety of its decorative finishes. Family tradition relates that A. R. Crockett, after seeing a similar house in Denver, Colorado, had the Queen Anne style dwelling duplicated in Crisfield between 1880 and 1890. Distinguished by its irregular, steeply pitched slate roof, the Crockett house is sheathed with a combination of narrow weatherboards, decorative shingles, and elaborate woodwork. Rising from the east side is a Frank Furness-style brick chimney, with a heavily corbeled cap and a multifaceted shaft.[6] The interior is divided into an asymmetrical plan with four principal rooms that open off a central stair hall. All of the rooms are fitted with an abundance of superior late nineteenth century woodwork, including highly decorative mantels with mirrored overmantels and tiled hearths.

In Princess Anne the Hinman Funeral Home, historically known as the Joshua Miles house, is the most prominent example of the Queen Anne style. Distinguished by a three-story polygonal tower covered with a bell-shaped roof, the large, squarish main block is surrounded by a Tuscan-columned porch, a classically inspired feature that reflects the variety of design origins and eclecticism of the style. A photograph of the house taken shortly after the turn of the century captures the various shingle patterns that highlighted the tower as well as the different gables and dormers. Skirting the top

Pauline Crockett house, north elevation.

Joshua Miles house, photograph c. 1900, E.I. Brown—photographer (courtesy of Robert Withey).

of the pyramidal shaped roof was a railing with ball finials atop each support post.

The Charles H. Hayman house, built in 1898 on the south side of Prince William Street, also falls under the Queen Anne label, although the three-bay, double-pile frame dwelling has a more classical than Victorian appearance. The large, two-and-a-half story frame house, designed with a basically symmetrical facade, has a recessed entrance that boasts slender colonettes on either side. Stretching across the first floor is a Tuscan-columned porch trimmed with a rooftop balustrade. In contrast to these classically derived features, Gothic-arched window panes fill the second floor center window sash as well as the large, rooftop gabled dormer. As at the Hinman Funeral Home, the crest of the modified pyramidal roof was trimmed with a balustrade that matched the first floor porch railing. The interior of the Hayman house displays a rich variety of period woodwork that combines columned Victorian mantels and classical moldings.

Popular Queen Anne style houses were not limited to Princess Anne and Crisfield, for a number of significant examples were erected on county farms. The old Whittington farmhouse south of St. Paul's Episcopal Church survived until the mid-1980s. The house consisted of a Queen Anne style dwelling that had been added to an older single story house, which then served as the kitchen wing. Built around 1890 the asymmetrically designed addition included bracketed eaves, paneled pilasters, a two-story bay window to the south side, and a decorated front porch. Fish-scale shingles covered two gables, and pointed arch windows illuminated the attic.

As demonstrated by the Whittington farmhouse, rural as well as town residents kept in step with more modern tastes by building additions that radically changed their houses. Such considerations evidently crossed the mind of Robert W. Adams when he purchased a 100-acre farm south of Princess Anne from James Teackle Dennis in 1897.[7] At that time the farm contained a two-story frame house dating from the second and third quarters of the nineteenth century. Shortly after his purchase, Adams began reworking the farmhouse in current Victorian taste. The changes included attaching a side hall/parlor section to the north and erecting a double galleried porch across the new five-bay west facade. When the roof was rebuilt to cover both sections, a cross gable was placed at its center to provide a more symmetrical design. Period trim was limited to simple porch brackets, fish-scale

shingles in the eaves, and a decorative sawn ornament in the peak of the gable.

What Robert Adams strived to achieve with additions, many Somerset county farm families built in one period, although on a much smaller scale. The cross-gabled farmhouse, usually following a center hall, single-pile plan, was built repeatedly across Somerset County and the entire Shore during the fourth quarter of the nineteenth century. Numerous examples are found along the streets of Princess Anne and Crisfield and populating the watermen's villages of Ewell, Tylerton, and Rhodes Point on Smith Island. Planned with a center hall and a room to each side, most of the examples extend to the back with a one- or two-story service wing.

Attached kitchen wings were not a new idea in Somerset County, but before mid-century they were more often than not connected to the house with a hyphen or colonnade. Joining the service wing directly to the house brought the kitchen closer to the main dwelling, which provided a more efficient use of space and materials. In addition, the attached wing made the second floor of the kitchen accessible from the main house, whereas the use of a hyphen left that room isolated.

As early as 1853 Andrew Jackson Downing noted the trend to reorient the service sections of the house:

Though the kitchen is sometimes placed in the basement, in the Middle States, yet the practice is giving way to the more rational and convenient mode of putting it on the

Charles H. Hayman house, northeast elevation.

Scott farmhouse, destroyed, photograph c. 1910 (courtesy of William Marshall Scott).

Adams farmhouse, west elevation.

Old Whittington farmhouse, destroyed, west elevation.

Captain Leonard S. Tawes house, south elevation.

In Somerset County the hyphenated service wing remained a popular architectural form until the end of the century. In addition, many houses included a semidetached summer kitchen to provide a cooler place in which to cook during the hot summer months. The Leonard S. Tawes house in Crisfield, reworked during the 1880s, exhibits both a semidetached summer kitchen and a winter kitchen. Incorporated in the two-story rear service wing is a dining room and the winter kitchen. Attached to the south side of the service wing is a single story, one-room plan summer kitchen, which was originally attached to the main house by an open breezeway.

In spite of the wide variety of new styles and floor plans from which Somerset County residents could choose in the second half of the nineteenth century, a decidedly conservative streak runs through the domestic architecture of the period. Countless residents, especially those living in rural regions, adhered to long-established building patterns, bending little to current shifts in house design. An example of this adherence to tradition is the Isabella White house, built on Deal Island during the third quarter of the nineteenth century. The conservative nature of this traditional design is reflected in the floor plan as well as the severely plain exterior of the two-story, side hall/double-pile frame house. Decoration was limited to paneled corner pilasters and a heavily molded four-panel front door. Attached to the back of the house is a single story hyphen, which connects the house and the story-and-a-half kitchen.

Although conservative county residents adhered to long-standing ideas of how to plan and build a house, most incorporated innovative ideas to improve the domestic workings of the household. Perhaps the most significant development during the second half of the nineteenth century was the widespread production and use of iron stoves for cooking and heating. The iron stove allowed safer, more controlled cooking; no longer was it critical to separate the cooking processes in a detached building for safety reasons.

Planned with the kitchen were other conveniences such as a nearby well, a pantry, or perhaps a laundry. As more and more domestic services were incorporated into the main house, the need for a group of specialized outbuildings faded. Nevertheless, the dairy, smokehouse, and privy remained important through the end of the nineteenth century.

Improvements in the construction of dairies added to their cooling qualities. The mid-nineteenth century dairy surviving at Cottage Hall farm was built with foot-thick brick walls covered by a large, overhanging pyramidal roof, which shades the exterior walls. To take advantage of the cooling qualities of the surrounding earth, the interior floor surface was excavated below ground level and a milk well fixed along the east wall. To give the dairy a stylish appearance, decorative sawn fascias were applied to the perimeter of the roof.

Although most dairies were not constructed with brick walls, other examples reflect solutions to peculiar problems. In the low-lying watermen's communities, it was not uncommon to build the dairy on stilts to avoid damaging high tides. The most interesting example of this type is found in

Isabella White house, northwest elevation.

Cottage Hall farm brick dairy, southeast elevation.

Frenchtown, relocated in the past few years to the yard of the Ovid French house. Not only was this dairy built on stilts, but the mortise-and-tenon frame was covered by a gable roof with an extended front eave that shaded the interior from a southern exposure. Paired louvered vents were fitted into three sides. Inside, two layers of beaded shelving provided space to store dairy products. In a fashion similar to the Cottage Hall farm dairy, the eaves of the Frenchtown structure were trimmed with decorative Victorian fascias and bargeboards.

Although smokehouses were continually used through the end of the nineteenth century, their construction did not significantly change during that period. The small gable-roofed smokehouses common to the post-Civil War era were lightly framed structures sheathed with vertical siding or horizontal weatherboards. The small frame smokehouse on the Adams farm south of Princess Anne was provided with a brick firebox in the center of the dirt floor.

Few privies have survived on Somerset County farms since indoor plumbing outdated their use, but standing on the Cottage Hall farm is a late nineteenth century example

Frenchtown stilted dairy, southeast elevation.

138

Cottage Hall farm privy, southwest elevation.

Cottage Hall farm barn, south elevation.

with weatherboard siding, a board door, and a gable roof. Unlike most examples, this privy was built with a two-over-two sash window hung with louvered shutters. Inside, narrow board sheathing covers the walls, and seats were built at two different levels.

The more utilitarian farm structures changed slowly in Somerset County until a realignment in agriculture during the mid-nineteenth century required new types of storage buildings. A continued emphasis on grain production required accommodations not just for livestock, but for increased amounts of hay, wheat, and corn as well. As a result, a new type of barn, quite different from the tobacco house, began to appear on lower Shore farms after the Civil War.

The board-and-batten frame barn at Cottage Hall, a representative example of the new hay and horse barn, has two principal levels. The gable end faces forward, and the ground floor is divided into aisles and stalls. A longitudinal aisle that stretches from the front wall to the rear section of the barn divides rows of horse stalls, while a transverse passage in back allowed for wagons to pass through and unload hay intended for long-term storage on the upper level. A moveable hayfork fixed in a track in the peak of the

roof facilitated the placement of hay in the spacious upper level. This bi-level arrangement provided a convenient method for feeding animals stalled below. To maximize the amount of storage space on the upper floor, the front wall of the loft of this barn projects over the stalls and is supported by cantilevered joists. The projecting section, known as the forebay, also shelters the animal stalls below. Despite its presence here, the forebay is a relatively rare feature on existing Somerset County barns.

Granaries retained their basic form through the post-Civil War years, although in some cases they were decorated with stylish Victorian trim. The granary on the Francis Barnes farm, which formerly stood near the Green Hill crossroads, had a three-part plan similar to antebellum examples. The center section was fitted with smooth board walls and bins for safely storing the wheat crop, and sheds to each side incorporated corn cribs or wagon bays. County farmers also commonly refitted unused tobacco houses as granaries by inserting a mid-level floor and flush board walls.

Corn cribs remained essentially unchanged in basic shape, although shifting construction technologies rendered subtle differences in siding and roof structure. Two generations of

Francis Barnes farm granary, destroyed, south elevation.

Francis Barnes farm corn cribs, south elevation.

corn cribs on the Cottage Hall farm, connected by a gabled roof, offer an interesting contrast between the corn cribs built before and after the Civil War. With its vertical siding and extended eaves, the Victorian corn crib appears quite different from its antebellum neighbor, which has horizontal siding and flush gable ends. The extended eaves of the later crib provided space for a dovecote. On the old Francis Barnes tenant farm near the Green Hill crossroads, a fancy pair of corn cribs was enriched with sawn bargeboards, turned pendants, and wooden peak finials. These expressive cribs were eventually moved to Talbot County.

An additional building on post-Civil War farms was the tenant house, which was occupied into the twentieth century by hired farmhands or freed blacks and their families. Often sited along a lane or boundary line, the tenant house was a modest one- or two-story frame dwelling with few amenities. The distinctive row of tenant houses along Beckford Avenue in Princess Anne was evidently built during the 1870s to

house the freed slaves from the adjacent Beckford farm. The two-story, one-room plan frame houses were built with a single story, one-room plan wing and an interior brick chimney that provided flues for stoves to heat the rooms. Similarly modest dwellings were erected on many Somerset County farms.

Farmers were not the only ones adding different types of buildings to the Somerset County landscape in the antebellum era; the agriculture-related industries that developed after the Civil War required specific types of buildings, as well. Largely utilitarian in nature, warehouses for the canning companies were unremarkable gable-roofed structures sheathed with vertical or horizontal board walls. Inside, assembly lines processed fruit and vegetables or perhaps made packing boxes or cans in which to ship the produce.

Cannery owners also provided rudimentary housing for workers, which amounted to little more than quickly erected frame shelters enclosed with a roof, frame walls, and one or

Beckford Avenue tenant houses, west elevation.

Permanent residents of the houses at W. T. Handy's packing house, July 1940, Farm Securities Administration, Jack Delano—photographer (courtesy of the Library of Congress).

Tomato wrappers at work in the Kings Creek Canning Company, July 1940, Farm Securities Administration, Jack Delano—photographer (courtesy of the Library of Congress).

two windows. In a few cases multiple family housing on more than one level afforded minimal accommodations.

Similarly, the oyster-packing industry was housed in large, quickly built barn-like buildings situated along the shoreline for easy access to oyster-laden workboats. Initially constructed without much consideration for safety, these early frame oyster-packing houses were either torn down or burned, especially in Crisfield, where several fires devastated the town during the late nineteenth century. Housing for the oyster company workers was erected by various firms, and a few examples survive in Crisfield along Chesapeake Avenue, where identical, modestly sized frame houses stand in a row.

Industrial sites near deep water were highly advantageous as were locations near the recently erected Eastern Shore Railroad. Industrial and commercial buildings appeared along the railroad shortly after its completion in 1866. The last surviving steam flour mill in Somerset County was erected near

the track at Westover by William Mahew Ruark in 1876. The original three-story center section was enlarged shortly afterwards by a three-story storage bin on its west end. Attached to the northeast corner was a single story office, which was later obscured by a large, shed-roofed addition.

Also new to the Somerset County landscape were the specialized buildings demanded by the railroad companies. Passenger and freight stations and attendant support buildings hugged the track at each whistle stop, village, or town. The early railroad stations, by no means impressive buildings, were nevertheless well-designed single story structures of frame construction. Usually covered by a broad roof with generous overhanging eaves, they offered shelter from the weather. Sheathed with weatherboards, decorative shingles, or board-and-batten siding, the exterior often carried a contrasting color scheme. The siding bordered on olive drab, while the trim was picked out in brown, and the window sash

Ruark-Ritzel mill, northeast elevation, photograph c. 1900 (courtesy of Lucille Ritzel).

Westover passenger station, south elevation.

were painted a rich brick red. Usually divided into at least two rooms, the interior had walls and ceiling covered with narrow, tongue-and-groove beaded boards.

Only a few nineteenth century stations have survived on the lower Eastern Shore. The Westover passenger station, evidently erected around 1884, when the Eastern Shore Railroad was purchased by the New York, Philadelphia, and Norfolk line, still stands in the vicinity of Westover along Maryland Route 361. Jennings R. Richards, the last ticket agent to work in the station, preserved the building by moving it behind his house. In May 1987 the station was relocated once more on the north side of the Westover-Fairmount Road. The cross-shaped frame building is sheathed in weatherboards and covered by a gable roof with corresponding cross gables centered on each side. Each gable boasts a small colored glass window. The roof is not as broad as those on some stations, but the eaves are underpinned with distinctive C-shaped brackets.

The utilitarian aspect of nineteenth century railroad and mill architecture was also a principal consideration in the design and construction of stores and other commercial buildings. Usually built without much pretension, town and village commercial buildings followed long-standing vernacular traditions. One or two stories in elevation, a typical village store included a main display and sales room with secondary storage rooms or perhaps modest living quarters for the storekeeper.

The old Green Hill store, built around 1870, was owned by Francis Barnes during the third quarter of the nineteenth century. Standing at the rural crossroads south of Westover, the story-and-a-half rectangular structure was embellished with stylish Victorian trim limited to the eaves. Through the double front door was a large public room fitted with smooth board walls. The shelving and counters have been removed. The secondary front entrance provides access to a small hall, which contains a winder stair to the partitioned second floor.

Somerset Avenue looking south, Princess Anne, photograph c. 1903, E.I. Brown—photographer (courtesy of William Marshall Scott).

Green Hill store, southwest elevation.

Small pocket windows on a second floor interior partition parallel similar features in Barnes's own dwelling and his tenant farmhouse.

Standing in Upper Fairmount is Cecil Ford's store, one of the last nineteenth century stores remaining in active use in Somerset County. The two-story, gable-front frame structure was erected next to the old Methodist church during the last decades of the century. Although the Greek Revival church has been lost, the shingled store building has served the residents of Upper Fairmount for over 100 years. The second floor has been used for various purposes, and at one time it housed the local movie theater. Attached to the side of the plain rectangular main building is a separate shop used in the past as a millinery. A few gravestones directly west of the store attest to the site of the church.

Significant among the nineteenth century commercial buildings in Somerset County because of their distinct refer-

Old Bank of Somerset, photograph c. 1967, west elevation.

John W. Crisfield law office, southwest elevation.

ences to a particular style are the John W. Crisfield law office and the old Mutual Fire Insurance Company building, both in Princess Anne. The Crisfield law office, standing across the street from the Washington Hotel, was initially erected around 1847-1848 as a store for town merchant Littleton Long. The two-story, three-bay frame structure is distinguished by its pedimented front, which links it to Long's house as well as to the other temple-front buildings in town. The building was sold to Crisfield in 1859.

The two-story brick office erected around 1884 by the Mutual Fire Insurance Company of Somerset and Worcester Counties borrowed design inspiration from the Romanesque Revival style. Distinctive features include the rounded arches with corbeled brick window heads. The second floor opening creatively incorporates a pair of Gothic-arched lancet windows. The eave is highlighted by distinctive brick corbeling, also typical of Romanesque Revival buildings. Although built by the insurance company, the building has been better known as the old Bank of Somerset, which rented the first floor space after its formation in 1889.

As the nineteenth century came to a close, nationally popular styles and manufactured building parts increasingly affected long-standing architectural traditions on the lower Eastern Shore. County residents were gently pushed to rethink the familiar order of daily life, and many rebuilt or remodeled their dwellings with some concern for the fashion of the day. So pervasive were the changes in construction and taste that many congregations, some merchants, and a few companies planned and styled their buildings in the most modern taste. Notwithstanding these external and internal influences, numerous county residents, for whatever reasons, stood by the familiar, time-tested order that had long served their parents and grandparents. ❦

CHAPTER X, 1900-1987
Modern Times

Not unlike the early historic periods of Somerset County's past, the twentieth century is characterized by contrasting social, economic, and political events that have shaped county development. With the turn of the century, Somerset County entered a period of significant growth and change that signaled long-lasting improvements in the quality of life on the lower Eastern Shore.

By 1910 the county population had peaked, and the economy consisted of diverse agricultural and seafood-related interests.[1] An expanded agriculture combined with the support of farm-related organizations such as the Grange and the Somerset Farm Loan Association helped modify the personal risks of independent farmers. At the same time, rural and town electrification, improved road transportation, and reliable train and steamboat networks significantly expanded what county residents considered the basic requirements for living.

Despite the optimism garnered from such progressive improvements during the first quarter of the century, the stock market failure in 1929 and the ensuing depression led to difficult times for Somerset County. Broad-based industrial investments failed to develop, and the population steadily dropped as a significant migration of county residents took

New courthouse of 1904-1905, photograph c. 1905 (courtesy of William Marshall Scott).

Loading goods on a train at Westover, July 1940, Farm Securities Administration , Jack Delano—photographer, (courtesy of the Library of Congress).

place between 1930 and 1970. The lower Shore as a whole wrestled with strained racial tensions as segregation was increasingly challenged nationwide. Despite these difficulties, Somerset County and the lower Eastern Shore have entered the last quarter of the twentieth century with increasing outside interest, an expanding population, and stable agriculture- and seafood-related industries, as well as prospects for further investment.

The years surrounding the turn of the century were full of promise for many residents of Somerset County. Between 1870 and 1910 the county population rose by more than 8,000 residents to 26,455, a level that has not been exceeded since.[2] A vibrant county agriculture included cultivation of wheat, corn, and other grasses as well as vegetables (especially potatoes and tomatoes) and fruit (primarily strawberries). These crops proved extremely profitable during the early twentieth century. Between 1900 and 1930, nearly 100 local canneries and packing companies were started. Many of these operated for only a few years, but others, like Long Brothers, Inc. and the Somerset Packing Company, have remained in business.[3]

Several organized groups were formed around 1900 to support local agricultural interests. One of the earliest associations was the Somerset Grange, started in 1910 and formally known as the Patrons of Husbandry.[4] The Grange was a national organization, and its principal goal was to improve market conditions for farmers.

In Somerset County a cooperative was established in an effort to supply farmers with fertilizer and new farm implements. In addition, the Tomato Growers Association was founded in 1917, and three years later the Somerset Agricultural Association began holding demonstrations of new tractor developments. Also in 1917 the first Agricultural Show opened in the courthouse with fifty exhibits of potatoes and thirty of corn.[5]

The growth and shipment of strawberries continued to expand after the turn of the century as considerable profit was realized in the distant markets of Baltimore, Washington, Philadelphia, and New York. In 1915 alone 637 refrigerator cars of strawberries were shipped from Marion, Westover, and Princess Anne, containing an average of 7,800 quarts per car. While the pickers were reported to have earned $120,260 for their efforts, the growers, averaging eight cents per quart, reaped close to $400,000.[6] Such was the interest in establishing the best market price for the delicate red fruit that a strawberry auction was established, first at Marion in 1911 and then at Princess Anne in 1920.[7]

The county agricultural agent of the period, H. S. Lippincott, recommended that farmers rotate their crops for best results and broaden their farming activities.[8] In particular, he suggested they diversify by building poultry houses and hog houses and starting dairy herds. Before 1920 chickens were largely raised for their eggs, and P. E. Twining near Princess Anne was well-known in the region for egg production.[9] Beginning in the mid-1920s, some farmers turned to growing broiler chickens, modeling their ventures on D. W. Steel's plant in Ocean View, Delaware.[10] While hog production and raising cattle had long been a part of Somerset agriculture, dairy farming on a large scale was relatively new. To expedite the processing of local milk, the Princess Anne Cooling Station and the Princess Anne Creamery were opened in 1926.[11]

In addition to raising livestock, Somerset County farmers experimented with other national agricultural trends. Although soybeans were not extensively grown before the Depression, government subsidies and the need for soybean oil during World War II greatly increased the incentives to raise the versatile legume. Soybeans have been a familiar sight on the Somerset landscape ever since.

While agricultural pursuits were thriving in the early twentieth century, the oyster industry fell into a steady decline

Crab floats at Crisfield, A. Aubrey Bodine—photographer, 1947 (courtesy of the Mariners' Museum, Newport News, Virginia).

Bank of Somerset, postcard c. 1910 (courtesy of Mrs. Merton Yerger).

after the prosperous decades of the 1880s and 1890s. By 1884 the Maryland oyster harvest had reached a staggering 15 million bushels, but only twenty-six years later it had plummeted to 3.5 million bushels.[12] In more recent years, oyster yields have dropped to such seriously low levels that many watermen have exchanged their work on the bay for jobs elsewhere with more consistent income.

As early as the turn of the century, the Maryland legislature had decided protectionist bills were needed if the state's valuable oyster industry was to survive. In 1906 the Haman Act was passed in an effort to establish leasing programs and to encourage the cultivation of seed oysters.[13] Introduced by B. Howard Haman, a Baltimore lawyer and state legislator, the act created the Board of Shellfish Commissioners to lease barren bay floor for the seeding of oysters.

The Haman Act also initiated a careful charting of Chesapeake Bay oyster beds. This arduous task was begun in June 1906 by an engineer from the United States Coast and Geodetic Survey, Charles C. Yates, who crisscrossed bay waters for the next six years. The *Yates Survey of the Oyster Bars of Maryland* still provides the most extensive information on Maryland's oyster resources.[14]

Concurrent with the decline of the oyster harvests was the expansion of commercial fishing ventures designed to exploit abundant supplies of bay fish and crab. Statistics for 1915 reveal the value of the peninsular "food fish" industry had reached $2.5 million. In that year Crisfield alone shipped 7.5 million dozen softshell crabs to distant markets.[15]

Industries other than food were also served by the bay. The inedible menhaden were widely caught and processed into fertilizer by L. E. P. Dennis offshore from Crisfield. The business was started on "Old Island" in 1871 and continued until the facilities burned in 1932.[16]

Even in prosperous times, beginning and maintaining

agricultural and industrial ventures was not accomplished without capital risk. To offset this, farmers, watermen, merchants, and businessmen alike turned to loan agencies for support. The Somerset Farm Loan Association was formed for farmers in 1917.[17] The rest of the population was served by the handful of county banks established during the late nineteenth and early twentieth centuries in Princess Anne, Crisfield, Marion, and Deal Island. In May 1914 a meeting of the Associated Banks of Somerset, Wicomico, and Worcester Counties included seven banks from Somerset: the Bank of Somerset, Peoples Bank of Somerset, Deal Island Bank, Bank of Crisfield, Marine Bank, Farmer's Bank of Marion, and the newly organized Bank of Marion.[18]

During the week of May 19, 1914, the *Marylander and Herald*, published in Princess Anne, printed a short description of the new Marion bank:

> *The Bank of Marion, Marion Station, MD., which was organized about January 1 of this year, opened its doors of their new building for business on Thursday, 14th instant.*
>
> *The new building is one of the most modern and best equipped bank buildings on the Eastern Shore.*
>
> *The building affords a good example of present day commercial architecture. The design is simple and dignified, but decidedly pleasing, and conveys at once the idea that the building was constructed for banking purposes. The size of the building is about forty feet long by twenty-four feet wide.*[19]

Along with improvements in the financial structure of Somerset County, the early twentieth century saw significant advances in public utilities and roads. However, the most revolutionary change in county life probably came from the introduction of electricity.

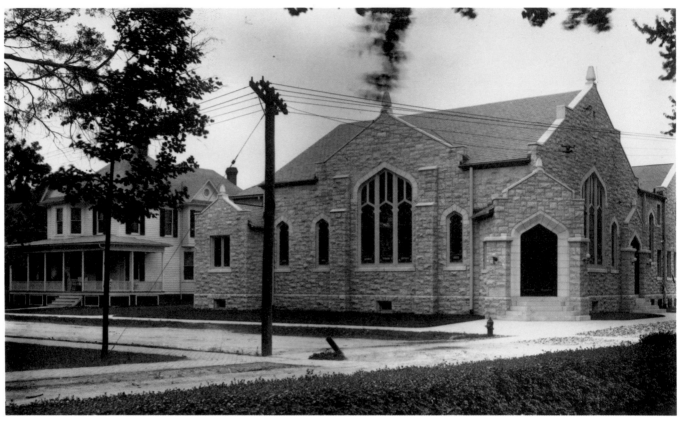

Antioch United Methodist Church, photograph c. 1920 (courtesy of William Marshall Scott).

Credit for establishing early electric service to Princess Anne is given to Everett C. Cannon, who purchased a gasoline-powered generator in 1914 and began supplying electricity as the Somerset Electric Company.[20] At the same time, the town commissioners solicited proposals for lighting Princess Anne streets, and Cannon's new company was chosen to provide this service.[21] Two years later the county commissioners appointed a special committee consisting of H. Fillmore Lankford, Thomas H. Bock, and Hampden P. Dashiell to supervise the wiring and lighting of the courthouse. The contract for this work was awarded to B. Horace Ford of Crisfield for $225.[22] Crisfield residents were able to purchase electric current from the Crisfield Ice Manufacturing Company after James B. Tawes purchased the business in 1912.[23]

Like electric service, the first telephone lines in Somerset County were erected early in the century by small, local companies competing for customers. The *Wicomico News*, published in Salisbury, announced on June 19, 1902, that "The Princess Anne Telephone Company is extending its line and will shortly reach Marion and Fairmount. The line at an early date will probably be run to Crisfield."[24] Only seven months later, in January 1903, the same paper reported that the Pocomoke Telephone Company, organized the year before, was ready to extend its lines to Crisfield and offer service within sixty days. The company also advertised that the rental of telephones would be $12 per year for both residences and businesses.[25] In 1904 the Manokin Telephone Company of Princess Anne was created by Ralph Hoyt, Albert Fitzgerald, George Bozman, Isaac Parks, and William Muir. The

company had twenty-one stations and eighteen telephones in service four years later.[26] At least one other venture, the Farmers' Telephone Company, also issued phone service in Somerset County. In January 1916 the principal officers were F. M. Widdowson, president; M. F. Hickmas, secretary; and Charles W. Long, treasurer.[27]

In step with national economic and business improvements was the introduction of the automobile. On the lower Eastern Shore, this event triggered desperately needed improvements to the county road system. In the late nineteenth and early twentieth centuries, a strong base of oyster shells was used to address the problem of perennially muddy roads. In 1916 a new shell road was laid between Princess Anne and Deal Island at a cost of $40,000, which included a new bridge over Law's Thoroughfare.[28]

Despite the hardening qualities of oyster shell roads, increasing automobile and truck traffic demanded a more durable surface. The first concrete road, laid in 1912, stretched between Princess Anne and the Wicomico County line.[29] Although principal roads eventually were paved in concrete, most of the secondary routes remained dirt until after World War II.

Alongside other modernizations in Somerset County was the development of a local hospital, carried out by a handful of county doctors. Although the idea of building a hospital originated in Crisfield around 1905, differing plans and problems stalled construction there, and the first Somerset County hospital was built at the main intersection of Marion in 1908.[30] Under the guidance of Dr. A. B. Allen, "Somerset Hospi-

Immanuel M.E. Church, Crisfield, southeast elevation.

tal" operated in this gable-roofed frame structure until the First World War.

In the meantime, efforts in Crisfield continued and by 1909 hospital officials had purchased and converted the old Gibson Store building on Main Street. On June 30, 1909, the "General and Marine Hospital" was dedicated and shortly afterwards offered medical care to town residents. The early hospital board of directors included Dr. Rastus R. Norris, Dr. Gordon T. Atkinson, and Dr. George Coulbourn.[31]

The new Crisfield hospital was praised by county and city residents as one of their finest achievements. Its presence meant they no longer had to hazard long steamboat trips to Baltimore for health care. As the years passed, fund-raising assistance from Crisfield civic groups and school children satisfied outstanding debts incurred when the hospital began, and its future on Main Street seemed secure for many decades to come. No Crisfielder could have predicted that an automobile accident in Westover would instigate the construction of a new facility within the next ten years.

In September 1919 Edward W. McCready, traveling with his daughter Susanne and her nurse, Henrietta Steinbeck, was involved in a fatal accident in Westover. Edward Mc-Cready and Henrietta Steinbeck died instantly, and it was reported that Susanne McCready died in the Crisfield hospital operating room. In memory of her husband, her daughter, and the nurse, and in recognition of the kindness the Crisfield hospital extended to her family, Caroline McCready contributed $200,000 to finance the construction of a new hospital facility on land that had formerly belonged to the McCready family on the Little Annemessex River. McCready Hospital opened its doors to patients in 1923.[32]

Also beginning in the early twentieth century, county educators pressed for modern schools that would compete with facilities elsewhere in the nation. In 1908 a new high school was built in Crisfield to accommodate a bulging city population, and fourteen years later this structure was replaced with a modern brick school.[33] In Princess Anne it was not until the late 1930s that the school commissioners decided to abandon the 1891 Victorian brick structure built in conjunction with the trustees of the Washington Academy. Then, instead of using the same site, the school was relocated on the north edge of town next to the Manokin Presbyterian Church. There, in 1938, a two-story brick structure was built on a generous, well-drained plot. This facility continued the Washington name on yet another school.

Two-story brick facilities improved the populous community of Marion as well. The old Marion Central School was assembled around 1912 and followed by the Marion High School in 1925.[34] Outside of Crisfield, Princess Anne, and Marion, older one and two-story frame schoolhouses served the population until the school system was consolidated into larger facilities after World War II.

The various religious denominations, some very old and some relatively new, used the prosperity of the early twentieth century to their best advantage by improving or erecting churches. Perhaps most aggressive were the Methodists. This group continued to expand its influence with yearly revivals throughout Somerset County, while many congregations undertook major building programs.

The Methodist congregation in Princess Anne grew steadily around the turn of the century, and by 1912 consideration was given to raising a new building.[35] With a significant contribution from Thomas H. Bock, part owner of the Cohn and Bock Milling Company, the congregation retained architect Leon Wilde Cranford of Wilmington, Delaware, to design a new church for their Main Street corner lot. On July 28, 1915, the cornerstone of the rusticated white marble church was set by contractors W. P. Pusey and Son.[36] Although the new church was dedicated close to a year later on July 2, the first worship service was not held until the following July after the pipe organ was installed.[37]

On a more ambitious scale were the two early twentieth century Methodist churches erected in Crisfield. After pur-

The Baptist Temple during construction, Crisfield, photograph c. 1920 (anonymous donor).

chasing a new lot on Main Street, the Immanuel Methodist Episcopal congregation financed the construction of an impressive Gothic Revival granite church. Two towers, one rising three full stories, flank the large, pointed arch windows of colored glass that pierce the street elevation. In 1930 the Asbury Methodist congregation initiated the construction of a cathedral-sized Gothic Revival structure southeast of Crisfield near the site where the congregation was formed in 1810.[38]

During the same period, a small group of Crisfield residents organized the first Baptist congregation in Somerset County in April 1889. Under the guidance of Reverend John S. Wharton, the early Baptist followers met in local homes before funds could be gathered to erect a church. By January 1890 a building committee had presented plans for a frame church sited on Maryland Avenue, and in October the new 36' x 70' church was finished at a cost of $2,940. Thirty years later, during the pastorate of Reverend Robert Killgore, the congregation embarked on the construction of a new brick church at

the corner of Somerset Avenue and East Main Street. Designed by Birmingham, Alabama, architect J. E. Green, the neoclassical Baptist Temple was erected by Crisfield builders Wilson & Co. in 1921 and dedicated on May 22, 1922.[39]

The Marion Baptist Church, organized in 1896, also planned the construction of an ambitious building in which to worship in the early 1920s. Perhaps inspired by the Crisfield building, the Marion church followed a neoclassical design with a colossal, square-columned portico and domed cupola dominating the principal elevation.

Meanwhile, in Princess Anne, a Baptist meeting was organized in 1916 and in that year the new congregation purchased part of Lot 19 facing Prince William Street. The history of the congregation recounts the tent meetings early members held on the property until money was raised for a building program. Construction began during the summer of 1920, and a special service in the new building was held the following July.[40]

Added to the religious community of Somerset County during the early twentieth century were Catholic and Mennonite congregations, which established churches in the Westover vicinity. The Mennonites began a church at Holly Grove, while the Catholics built St. Elizabeth's Church in the village of Westover.

In spite of the many achievements Somerset residents could stand behind during the first quarter of the twentieth century, much still needed to be done to alleviate inequitable conditions in terms of black education and employment. The prosperous 1920s, which may ultimately have led to long-term improvements for black residents, suddenly ended with the stock market crash in 1929. The ensuing economic and social problems, which lasted until World War II, preoccupied county, state, and national energies.

Depressed agricultural prices and the absence of a broad industrial base to provide jobs for local residents led many Somerset residents to leave the region during the Depression years. The economic problems of the 1930s were exacerbated in Somerset County by two bank closings and a devastating hurricane that ravaged county communities in 1933.

With the end of the 1930s and what must have seemed an interminable decade of difficulties, the 1940s brought war in Europe and the eventual revitalization of the Eastern Shore agricultural economy. Renewed interest and higher prices for Somerset County foodstuffs, livestock, and poultry marked the beginning of brighter economic prospects. In the decades following World War II, many farmers have successfully concentrated on corn and soybean crops while tending poultry houses for Perdue Farms, Inc.; Holly Farms Poultry Industries; and Mountaire Farms of Delmarva.

The late 1950s and 1960s also witnessed the election and reelection of J. Millard Tawes as the fifty-ninth governor of Maryland. The Crisfield native is well remembered for his great ambitions in many areas, including Chesapeake Bay conservation, increased funding for state education, improvements for the state highway system, and reforms in the municipal court system.

The past few decades have not been without painful problems in Somerset County. The lagging shellfish industry struggles with increasingly diminished harvests, the once superior rockfish population now must be protected by state law, and broad-based industrial investments have yet to materialize. Nevertheless, the late 1980s have witnessed increased interest in Somerset County, and the population has once again started to rise after a sixty-year decline. The open, uncongested nature of the landscape in Somerset County as well as its proximity to the Atlantic seashore make it attractive to many. With increased development pressures, the challenge to residents, county officials, and politicians will be to protect the irreplaceable historic and natural qualities that enrich life on the lower Eastern Shore. ❦

CHAPTER XI, 1900-1987
Twentieth Century Architecture

With the turn of the century, architectural traditions in Somerset County began to shift once again as national trends and innovations in building technologies increasingly influenced the region. Supplies of new building materials were easily acquired by county craftsmen, and nationally advertised house designs flooded current periodicals. Nevertheless, a strong conservatism continued to hold sway throughout the lower Eastern Shore and was strongly reflected in the inhabitants' widespread devotion to traditional vernacular house forms.

The largest share of early twentieth century construction in Somerset County is represented by the two-story, center hall, single-pile frame dwelling. With more than 150 years of continual use, this familiar vernacular house form was adopted by many rural and town residents for its straightforward sim-

plicity. As exhibited by the Bozman-Fitzgerald house near Monie, a wing was built to the rear of the main block to contain the kitchen and dining services. Turn-of-the-century decoration trims the eaves of the main house as well as the front porch for a stylish exterior. In addition, the three principal gables are covered with fish-scale shingles and topped by wooden finials. Inside, the central hall contains a turned baluster stair and paneled doors provide access to the rooms on each side. Internal brick chimneys, built against the interior partitions, served the stoves that heated the dwelling.

As reflected in the Bozman-Fitzgerald house, many early twentieth century dwellings were embellished with late Victorian decorative finishes popularized in former decades. Although stylish exterior trim was often limited to porches and eaves, the modest application did not hamper creative

Bozman-Fitzgerald house, south elevation.

Mabel Brittingham house, south elevation.

variety. The Mabel Brittingham house near Tulls Corner is a relatively plain, two-and-a-half story farmhouse erected around the turn of the century. Despite the undecorated nature of the first and second floors, the gable ends were sheathed with fish-scale shingles and the peaks were fitted with an ornate sawnwork screen of spindles and scrolls. Even less decorated is the exterior of the old Butler house near Cokesbury, and yet a five-point star was incorporated into the porch decoration there.

While many of these early twentieth century houses were stick-built in a traditional manner, other examples finished with similar details were shipped as prefabricated parts. Arriving at Somerset County railroad depots, they were loaded on trucks or wagons for delivery to the building site. The Carey farmhouse, erected around 1917-1919, was ordered

Carey farm, northeast elevation.

Coulbourn house, southeast elevation.

Happy Hollow farm, photograph c. 1920, W.T. Watson—photographer (courtesy of R. Patrick Hayman).

Lloyd Chamberlin house, northeast elevation.

from Sears, Roebuck and Company by Harry Sergent, a conductor for the New York, Philadelphia, and Norfolk Railroad. Many of the house parts still carry the stamped company name.

Sears, Roebuck offered prefabricated Queen Anne style dwellings in addition to a host of contemporary designs ranging from stately Colonial Revival houses to comfortable bungalows. In fact, a surprising number of houses standing in and around Marion and Westover were shipped in boxcars from Chicago and other distant cities.

The bungalow style became widely publicized and popularly built throughout America after the turn of the century. In Somerset County, the informal plans and practical living spaces of this style suited various needs as village or town residences, farmhouses, and tenant houses. The Lloyd Chamberlin house in Westover fits the definition of a bungalow, as expressed in the early twentieth century literature. The house was to contain "no more than the absolutely necessary number of rooms," with "no attic, or second story, and no cellar."[1] The traditional features of the bungalow style as seen in the Chamberlin house include the obvious horizontal nature of the structure, with low-pitched roofs and overhanging eaves incorporating a generous porch. In front, the projecting purlins that visually support the eaves are largely decorative features and suggest the oriental influence in the bungalow style's origins.

Less detailed but more typical of the examples of this style in Somerset County is the Milbert Shockley farmhouse, built during the early years of the century. The sweeping gable roof not only covers the principal living areas of the house but also the front and rear porches. Large gabled dormers expand the second floor space in a way compatible with the overall design.

Another pivotal architectural design source during the twentieth century stemmed from the Chicago World Columbian Exposition, held along the shore of Lake Michigan in 1893. Exposition architects and planners erected a "White City" of broad boulevards, sprawling parks, and neoclassical buildings.[2] The orderly and spotless nature of the idealized city was intentionally compared with the desperate living conditions of industrial America exemplified in adjacent Chicago.

Although sweeping social reforms were slow to materialize, the American public quickly embraced classical or colonial architectural aesthetics. Within a decade, colonial and classical revival designs had been disseminated throughout the nation in popular magazines and technical literature. The influence of the World Exposition soon appeared in Somerset County with the construction of Colonial Revival houses, neoclassical banks, and classical columned porches.

A straightforward interpretation of the Colonial Revival style is represented by the Coulbourn house near Hopewell, a two-and-a-half story frame house built in 1915. The symmetrical, five-bay elevation with a center entrance and dormered attic story recalls former Georgian and Federal style designs. More reflective of the twentieth century are details such as the six-over-one sash windows, the extended eaves, and the Colonial Revival interior woodwork.

Not all Colonial Revival designs followed rigid rules of symmetry. Architects and builders used various "colonial" features loosely in an effort to create original compositions. The Happy Hollow farmhouse at Polks Landing was not designed in imitation of any colonial dwelling, but a significant variety of classical elements was employed throughout the house. The river facade is dominated by a colossal Tuscan-columned portico, and the pediment is trimmed with a classical entablature, dentiled bed moldings, and a lunette window. Palladian-style windows pierce the gable end pediments, and the roof is marked by hip-roofed dormers. Stretching across the first floors on both the north and south sides are Tuscan-columned porches. The porch on the river side ends with an octagonal pavilion. Identical pavilions are found at Foggy Bottom and Brentwood.

Also at Brentwood is another version of Colonial Revival design. In 1916 an architect-designed addition was attached to the eighteenth century brick house. The two-story, T-shaped addition was planned with a gambrel roof, a popular feature of the style. The interior of the new addition was fitted with expertly crafted Colonial Revival woodwork, including a finely decorated stair. Instead of horizontal weatherboards, the exterior was sheathed with wooden shingles, a hallmark of yet another early twentieth century style uncommon on the Eastern Shore.

The Shingle style, as it became known, could be consid-

Octagonal pavilion at Foggy Bottom, north elevation.

Brentwood, photograph c. 1935 (courtesy of R. Patrick Hayman).

Melody Manor, south elevation.

United States Post Office at Crisfield, southwest elevation.

ered a subcategory of the Colonial Revival or perhaps the Queen Anne style since decorative interior and exterior finishes were often mixed. Designed by architect Stanford White, Melody Manor is the most elaborate example of the Shingle style on the lower Eastern Shore. Perched on a high knoll overlooking Wicomico Creek, the expansive two-story, T-shaped frame house is dominated by a round, three-story tower. The entire house is sheathed with round-butt shingles. Common to the style are the porches on the north side, which are incorporated under the main roof slope. The interiors are fitted with an eclectic mixture of Gothic and classically inspired woodwork.

Also developed on a national scale during the early twentieth century and repeatedly built in Somerset County on farm as well as town sites was a style of dwelling that originally had no distinctive name. Recently identified and placed by architectural historians in a category of its own is the four-square house. This term refers to the typical quartered plan of the dwellings, which generally have four principal rooms with squarish proportions on the first floor. The houses border on cubic shape, and steeply pitched pyramidal roofs enhance this form. Dormers often light third floor rooms. Inside, the house may be serviced by a central chimney stack and Colonial Revival woodwork generally finishes each of the rooms.

The commercial, public, and religious architecture of Somerset County provided further expression of neoclassical and Colonial Revival designs. Most notable is the collection of early twentieth century bank buildings that distinguishes the business districts of Princess Anne, Crisfield, and Marion.

Old Bank of Crisfield, southeast elevation.

The Peninsula Bank, formerly the Bank of Somerset, was built with walls of Roman-sized, iron-spot brick. Its prominent arched center entrance is flanked by corner pilasters with stone bases and capitals. The entablature and pediment are enriched with several rows of classical moldings. The old Peoples Bank of Somerset on Prince William Street, now the Somerset County Commissioners office, is noteworthy for its limestone Ionic columns, which flank the entrance and visually support the pediment. The old Bank of Crisfield, now the Eastern Shore National Bank, is a finely designed temple-front structure with Tuscan pilasters marking the street elevations and acanthus leaf consoles and a mid-level dentiled cornice highlighting the entrance.

The First Baptist Temple, Crisfield, northwest elevation.

Also in Crisfield is one of the most noteworthy Colonial Revival public buildings in Somerset County, the United States Post Office on Main Street. The Flemish bond brick building, erected in 1933, is distinguished by a molded water table, projecting quoins, and a bold modillioned cornice. The center entrance is framed by a classical surround and topped by a large, arched transom. The slate hip roof is highlighted by an octagonal Colonial Revival cupola that has a bell-curved roof and urn-shaped finials around its base.

Neoclassical buildings on a still grander and more monumental scale are classified under the Beaux Arts label, named after the Ecole des Beaux-Arts in Paris. Known for colossal-columned elevations and exuberant decorative finishes, the style is represented in Somerset County by the First Baptist Temple in Crisfield. Designed by Birmingham, Alabama, architect J. E. Green, the cross-shaped church boasts pedimented, Ionic-order porticos as well as an octagonal dome covered in red tile. Modillion block cornices enrich the perimeter of the roof, and acanthus-like decorations trim the octagonal

drum supporting the dome.

Architectural trends during the last fifty years have become even less regionalistic as national tastes and styles have dominated local construction. During the 1950s and 1960s, domestic building centered around the single story, ranch-style house, which in essence is a simplified and more conservative interpretation of the Prairie School architecture popularized by Frank Lloyd Wright and his students.

In the past thirty years, public fascination has been drawn consistently to the continuing research and restoration of Williamsburg, Virginia, begun in the early 1930s. As a result, national and local construction to a great degree has followed designs derived from America's colonial past. The restoration of Williamsburg and the preservation movement begun during the 1960s have fostered broad-based concern for saving historic structures that not only demonstrate former architectural tastes but also, and most significantly, give each region a specific sense of time, place, and historical development. 🌳

CHAPTER XII
Preserving Somerset

The restoration and preservation of historic houses in Somerset County appears at first to be a relatively modern issue developed during the past twenty years. However, investigation shows that Somerset history and architecture have drawn public as well as scholarly interest over the course of the last century. Since the 1880s, many county residents have expended a great deal of time and effort recording and preserving evidence of the past. As the twenty-first century approaches, however, much remains to be done to save buildings and archeological sites and the information they possess for future generations.

In the nineteenth century, historians directed considerable attention to the careful research of early Methodist, Presbyterian, and Episcopal congregations in Somerset County. David Wallace published his biography of Reverend Joshua Thomas, *The Parson of the Islands*, in 1861. This was followed by Doctor L. P. Bowen's *Days of Makemie* and Cassius M. Dashiell's "Manuscript History of Stepney Parish," both completed in 1885.

Following these early works, the Reverend Clayton Torrence, who arrived on the lower Eastern Shore in the fall of 1927, became entranced with the religious history of early Somerset County. Spurred on and supported by both Dashiell and Henry Fillmore Lankford, local clerk of the Somerset court, Torrence meticulously researched early county history as well as the events and people associated with the formation of the Quaker, Episcopal, and Presbyterian religions.[1] In addition, he spent innumerable hours completing partial genealogies on early Somerset families. His work, *Old Somerset on the Eastern Shore of Maryland*, first appeared in 1935 and was reprinted in 1966, 1973, and 1979. It has stood well the test of time.

Cassius Dashiell extended his interest in the Episcopal Church beyond research to direct and partially finance the stabilization of the Coventry Parish Church ruin at Rehoboth. The stabilization and capping of the three surviving walls was completed in 1928.

Interest in Somerset County and lower Eastern Shore history was manifested in other ways as well. John S. McMaster, a retired New Jersey attorney, resettled in the area and inspired the high school senior project known as the "Old Home Prize Essay." McMaster obviously intended the competition to increase awareness of the area's rich history in buildings, people, places, and events. Donating $100 to specific high schools, he hoped the interest bearing on these accounts would continually finance awards for the winning essays. Pocomoke City High School was the first to implement the idea in 1908, and the Onancock, Virginia, high school followed in 1909. By 1912 the senior project had been incorporated into the Princess Anne and Snow Hill high school curricula. In Crisfield Clarence Hodson donated $100 for the medals in 1913, and students there have competed for the Hodson Old Home Prize ever since.[2] Although this project has been interpreted in a number of ways at different schools through the years, it has challenged high school seniors across the region and undoubtedly increased sensitivity to regional architecture and history.

Perhaps one of the most ambitious undertakings in the county in the early twentieth century was Ralph P. Thompson's complete restoration of the Workington plantation house. Beginning in 1914 Thompson carefully restored the 1793 two-and-a-half story brick house, at the same time adding modern amenities. Tragically the impressive house burned in 1922, several years after he had sold the property.[3]

Other Somerset citizens with the foresight and fortitude to tackle unending restoration projects were Princess Anne residents John and Maude Wilson Jeffries, who purchased the forlorn story-and-a-half Boy Scout lodge on the corner of Church and Broad streets in 1943.[4] In time the mid-eighteenth century frame house was restored to modern standards, and today it stands out in Princess Anne as one of the few early town dwellings.

During the mid-1950s several important events ushered in an enthusiasm for historic buildings and Somerset history that has continued to the present time. In 1954-1955 the Rehoboth Presbyterian congregation retained the expert services of the Boston architectural firm of Perry, Shaw, Hepburn, and Dean for the partial restoration of their venerable brick church. Soon thereafter the regional interest in the past fostered by the continuing restoration of Williamsburg, Virginia, led to the formation of several local preservation groups. Intended to raise public awareness and appreciation for local history, these organizations have contributed greatly to the preservation effort in the county.

Olde Princess Anne Days, Inc. (OPAD) was established first. Inspired by Maude Wilson Jeffries, its members held a tour of Princess Anne in 1956 but did not formally organize until two years later. In the fall of 1958, the group held a

Workington parlor, photograph c. 1918, Robert Hughes & Company—photographer (courtesy of Mrs. Charles Wainwright).

county-wide historic house tour, which engendering support and attendance.[5] The Olde Princess Anne Days tour has been a fixture in the fall schedule of Somerset County ever since. The officers of OPAD during the first tour were Maude Wilson Jeffries, general chairman; John Deans, the Reverend Otho G. Brener, Jr., and John Bond, co-chairmen; W. Wilson Nelson, secretary; P. Morris Furniss, treasurer; and Clarence L. Byrd, publicity. Olde Princess Anne Days has been a leader in preservation-related activities since its founding. It has successfully raised money and applied those

Teackle Mansion, east elevation, Michael Harrison Day—photographer.

proceeds to the restoration of Teackle Mansion and several other local buildings.

As if that were not enough, Maude Jeffries continued her efforts to preserve Somerset County history with the purchase of the center section of the Teackle Mansion in 1960. With barely enough funds to acquire the structure, Mrs. Jeffries and her supporters at OPAD decided to remove the west side kitchen wing. Attached around 1900, this structure was in poor condition. Coincidentally, Upshur Evans, a great-great-nephew of Littleton Dennis Teackle, happened by and volunteered a check to pay for the demolition. The garden or river elevation of the center block was thus returned to its original appearance. Several years later, in 1968, Olde Princess Anne Days purchased the south wing of the mansion as well. An additional restoration project sponsored by the group was the story-and-a-half glebe house south of Princess Anne, once owned by the Somerset Episcopal Parish.[6]

It was also in 1960, on November 25, that Maude Jeffries organized the Somerset County Historical Society. In its first year she served as president, with Ballard Miles as first vice president, Harry C. Dashiell as second vice president, Mrs. Milbourne Muir as secretary, and Jesse Long as treasurer. Five years later, through a generous gift from Mrs. John Roberts, the society purchased the north wing of Teackle Mansion. The group has held an antique show and yearly candlelight tours in its efforts to maintain the north wing.[7]

The third and most recent organization, the Somerset

Princess Anne historic district, photograph c. 1903, E. I. Brown—photographer (courtesy of William Marshall Scott).

County Historical Trust, Inc., was founded during the early 1970s. Formed as the Somerset County committee of the Maryland Historical Trust (the state preservation agency), the group felt a need to address preservation-related issues that affected the county as a whole. Among its founders were Theodore T. Dorman, Elizabeth W. Hall, R. Patrick Hayman, Mary Value Dennis Clark, and Lida Mayo. The committee incorporated officially in 1973 as the Somerset County Historical Trust, Inc.[8]

The Somerset Trust holds monthly meetings to discuss preservation-related activities of concern to the county and the region. The group has sponsored research into local architecture and history, raising money and performing some primary source investigation. They have also held a number of educational events to introduce preservation programs and issues to residents of the county.

In February 1982 Gale H. Yerges accepted the chairmanship of the Somerset County Historical Trust. The following year the group voted to apply for matching funds through the Maryland Historical Trust in an effort to finance an intensive four-year survey of historic buildings in the county. More than any other single project the group has supported, this comprehensive survey and its publication will contribute vastly to the understanding and preservation of regional architecture.

At the same time this survey was initiated, the Somerset Trust commissioned a slide-tape presentation in an attempt to popularize historic local architecture. During the summer of 1983 a show was produced highlighting the sites in the county listed on the National Register of Historic Places. The county then had eighteen sites on the Register, a program of the National Park Service that recognizes the importance—whether local, state, or national—of historic buildings and structures and archeological sites that provide useful information about the past. With supportive grants from the Maryland Humanities and Somerset County Arts councils, the Somerset Trust circulated a forty-photograph exhibit throughout the lower Eastern Shore and southern Delaware. Titled "Somerset Images: Three Centuries of Building Traditions," the exhibit was intended to broaden awareness of Somerset County architecture and history throughout the region.

The Somerset County Historical Trust sponsored research of a different type in 1988 with a generous gift from Mrs. William Morsell, Jr. In an effort to establish a firm date for the construction of The Reward, one of Somerset's most unusual eighteenth century dwellings, Dr. Herman J. Heikkenen of Dendrochronology, Inc., Blacksburg, Virginia, applied his scientific tree-ring analysis to wood samples taken from the brick dwelling. By determining the last growth year of trees cut to build the house, he identified 1750 as the year it was constructed. A bark-edged sample allowed him to narrow the date even further, to the fall of that year.

Coventry Parish Church ruin, before 1988 stabilization, northwest elevation.

The Somerset County Historical Trust has also implemented day-long workshops addressing preservation issues relevant to Somerset County residents. These workshops have centered primarily on the National Register and the loan programs and tax benefits administered through the Maryland Historical Trust. Within the past few years the committee has made it a priority to help local residents benefit from state and federal monies through restoration projects funded by the Maryland Trust. Most successful was the restabilization of the Coventry Parish Church ruin at Rehobeth. The Salisbury firm of Becker/Morgan Architects was hired for the project, and Bruce J. Cantwell of Quantico supervised the repointing of the eighteenth century structure.

In addition to all these projects, the members of the Somerset County Historical Trust have kept as their primary goal the publication of this architectural history and inventory. The group hopes this book will be a permanent contribution to the understanding and preservation of local buildings. The information published here as well as the detailed study on which it is based will prove useful to planners, businesspeople, educators, students, and a broad cross-section of county residents and tourists.

The survey process began in the mid-1960s, before the Somerset County Historical Trust was founded. At that time, the Maryland Historical Trust along with local volunteers compiled the first list of significant historic sites in Somerset County. Paul A. Brinkman, an architecture student at Yale University, conducted a reconnaissance survey of the county in the summer of 1967. He produced Historic American Buildings Survey field forms, photographs, and slides for eighty-four sites. In June 1972 Michael Bourne undertook a more detailed survey that expanded the documentation for some previously located buildings and increased the inventory to about 100 sites. Selected buildings were targeted for nomination to the National Register of Historic Places, and between 1973 and 1976 a total of fifteen properties were added to the Register. Detailed forms were prepared by Maryland Trust staff members, survey interns, and local researchers.

Several historic sites surveys in Somerset County developed after the Maryland Board of Public Works adopted a policy in 1978 regarding the preservation of historic properties owned or to be acquired by the state. In 1979 a study of historic properties administered by the Department of Natural Resources investigated five wildlife management areas and one state park in the county. Surveys of the University of Maryland Eastern Shore campus and of state-owned railroad lines, including the now abandoned right-of-way from Westover to Crisfield, were also undertaken. Shortly afterwards, the Somerset Trust supported the listing of a Princess Anne historic district on the National Register of Historic Places, officially confirmed in October 1980.

In 1982 the Somerset County Historical Trust applied

for and received a matching Historic Preservation Fund grant from the Maryland Historical Trust to begin a detailed, comprehensive survey of the county. In contrast to the previous reconnaissance level surveys, this study, conducted between 1983 and 1987, focused on detailed architectural and historical research of over 400 individual properties, including those sites that had been previously identified. With detailed architectural information accompanied by chain-of-title research, complete histories were developed for the most significant sites. During the four-year study, nearly thirty individual properties along with a Crisfield historic district were nominated to the National Register. The vessels in the surviving Chesapeake skipjack fleet harbored in Somerset County were also listed as part of a statewide thematic nomination submitted by the Maryland Historical Society in 1985 and prepared with funding assistance from the Maryland Historical Trust.

Also critical to the understanding of Somerset County history is its rich store of archeological sites. These sites contain valuable and irreplaceable information concerning the prehistoric and historic periods of the region. This part of Somerset County history has attracted many devoted followers, chief among them Jean Messick and more recently Atwood Barwick. As members of the Lower Delmarva Chapter of the Archeological Society of Maryland, Inc. (a group of amateur archeologists who work under professional guidance), these volunteers have studied with many others the county's Indian occupation as well as its contact and settlement periods.

At this time 143 archeological sites have been identified as significant to Somerset County history. Contributing their professional expertise, Thomas Davidson and his wife, Ethel Eaton, traversed the lower Eastern Shore during the early 1980s in an effort to locate significant archeological remains. However, archeological knowledge of the region benefited most from the formation of the Lower Delmarva Regional Preservation Center and the Maryland Historical Trust/ Tidewater Administration intern program. Somerset County is addressed in detail in the Lower Delmarva Archeological Management Plan, produced by Davidson in 1981, as well as the intern study prepared by archeologist Richard Hughes the year before. In 1982 Tom Davidson produced a detailed study of Indian reservations in the region. Interest in free black communities resulted in another regional study, completed in 1983. Davidson's study of shorelines, conducted while he supervised the regional center, located sensitive historic and prehistoric sites. Surveys were carried out on Smith Island and in the county's interior to comply with federal and state laws requiring review of affected historic sites before government funds are released. These compliance surveys provided rudimentary information about once neglected areas.[9]

An intensive study by Tom Davidson and Ethel Eaton on the 605-acre site planned for the Eastern Correctional Institution identified ten archeological sites, two considered eligible for listing on the National Register. The site of the early Washington Academy was listed, but the second site was obliterated by the prison construction. Further research is needed to locate and identify other sensitive sites so future development will not obscure more clues to Somerset's distant past.

In the 1980s and 1990s, however, concerns in Somerset County revolve around the county's high unemployment rate and other economic problems caused by a decline in traditional local industries. The seafood industry is stagnant, suffering from the damage to local sea life caused by pollution, and farmers have largely switched from labor-intensive truck farming to more efficient grain agriculture. Local government has necessarily concentrated its efforts on pressing economic problems. Nonetheless, to ensure Somerset County maintains its sense of place and quality of life, short-term solutions that overlook these longer term issues must be replaced with solutions that show concern for the future. To this end, Somerset County can make preservation part of a strategy for achieving progress without detracting from the features that make the county a desirable place to live.

Maintaining Somerset's historic landscape can help address the county's financial problems in several ways. Tourism is presently the third largest industry in Maryland, and Somerset County has already taken the first step in profiting from it.[10] For more than thirty years the Olde Princess Anne Days tour has brought large numbers of people to the county. These visitors bring income into the area, spending money on food, lodging, and other necessities. They also go home as goodwill ambassadors from Somerset, impressed with its attractiveness and spreading the word about this place where life moves at a slower, more pleasant pace. Reinforcing visitors' positive impressions and preserving the atmosphere that has appealed to them will help bring more people through the county.

Particularly important are owners of light industry, who are also attracted by the slower-paced atmosphere and beauty

Skipjack Thomas W. Clyde, *Wenona, Maryland, photograph c.1950, A. Aubrey Bodine—photographer (courtesy of the Mariners' Museum, Newport News, Virginia).*

of a locale such as Somerset County. When starting up or relocating their companies, such entrepreneurs look for a place they want to live that will also draw steady, community-oriented workers. A community that respects its past and works to control its future is seen as a good place to do business.

In addition to attracting new residents, an area that has maintained its sense of place will keep its current residents. In our fast-moving modern world, people are looking for stability and strong communities where they can feel at home. Older buildings, with their more human scale, contribute to the feeling that a community is unique. In contrast, new construction often appears the same across the country, taking nothing from the region where it is built and contributing nothing to the local sense of place. Towns and counties that include preserving their history in the planning process often reap the benefits of increased local interest and investment. Nearby Berlin and Pocomoke City in Worcester County are good examples of the positive development that can come from planning with preservation in mind.

Rehabilitation—whether restoration or adaptive reuse—of older buildings can also create jobs in the building trades. Carpenters, painters, plumbers, and electricians, among others, are all in high demand. Rehabilitation and preservation projects create more jobs than new construction because they are more labor intensive. Specifically, 75 percent of the cost of most renovation or restoration jobs goes for labor as opposed to 50 percent in new construction. Thus, more money from preservation-related jobs enters the local economy.[11]

Many of the benefits of preservation efforts—both economic and social—can best be achieved by the partnership of local groups and local governments. To help such bodies organize their efforts, the Maryland Historical Trust published the *Maryland Comprehensive Historic Preservation Plan* in 1986 as a compendium of information, ideas, and strategies for local and state preservation efforts.[12] The plan provides a place to begin for local government officials and employees and members of local history and preservation groups who are looking for direction in their local preservation efforts. In particular, it recommends a broad approach to integrating preservation into the planning process, an approach anyone can apply to any locale in Maryland.

Five broad preservation goals are discussed in the *Comprehensive Plan*, outlining the interests and efforts of preservationists across Maryland. Assessing how working toward these goals would affect Somerset County will help local residents and county and town governments envision what they can achieve. Much has been started, but much remains to be done to preserve the county's past for future generations.

Boxwood garden, Princess Anne historic district, photograph c. 1930 (courtesy of Mrs. William Morsell, Jr.).

Glebe house and the Econo-Lodge, Princess Anne vicinity, September 1989, from the east.

The first goal calls for *increasing public knowledge and understanding of Maryland's history through identification, evaluation, protection, and interpretation of historic resources.*

Individuals and private non-profit preservation organizations in Somerset County have acted strongly in this area, beginning with the Olde Princess Anne Days tours and extending to the Somerset County Historical Trust's sponsorship of the historic sites survey that resulted in this book. More remains to be tackled, however, particularly surveying archeological sites and studying the historic twentieth century properties in the county's towns.

The second goal encourages citizens and governments to *preserve places of beauty and cultural importance in Maryland's communities and landscapes and to increase public aesthetic awareness by helping to manage changes in the environment.*

Beautiful surroundings enhance the quality of life for all who live in an area. Older buildings contribute their unique sense of time and place to a town or landscape, giving human scale and warmth often lacking in new construction. Streetscapes in Princess Anne, Crisfield, and small towns around Somerset County, with their porches, mature trees, and flourishing gardens offer a friendly, old-fashioned atmosphere. Farmhouses and outbuildings surrounded by fields provide serene settings for modern life. Historic landscapes are as appealing to those who travel through them—whether commuting, going shopping, or taking a walk after dinner—as to those who live in them.

If the surroundings of historic properties are not protected, however, much of the appeal of these sites is lost. The

glebe house on Route 13 outside Princess Anne is a good example of this problem. The house was restored in the 1970s by Olde Princess Anne Days, Inc., a dedicated group that took some trouble to return it to its eighteenth century appearance. Before the restoration took place, the State Highway Department constructed a maintenance depot next to the house. In 1989 a motel was built in front of it, and plans have been approved for a trailer park behind it. Formerly in a small stand of trees surrounded by fields, this remnant of the past is now literally surrounded by late twentieth century development. What the house has to tell about the past has been diminished. Perhaps with more awareness of the value of such structures and their surroundings, this remnant of earlier times could have been treated more sympathetically.

The third goal proposes using historic preservation to *strengthen community cohesion and pride and increase local revitalization activity.*

Residents interested in preservation can work on projects that address a broad range of community needs and interests, contributing to vital historic areas that meet the needs of today's citizens in comfortable, well-known settings. The idea is to stimulate property improvement, increase community pride, and encourage economic investment through renovation and other activities that emphasize the historic landscape.

In 1980 the Princess Anne Business Association expressed interest in using this approach to improve its business district. The group asked students at the University of Maryland School of Architecture to prepare a revitalization study of the downtown area. The resulting report discusses design consid-

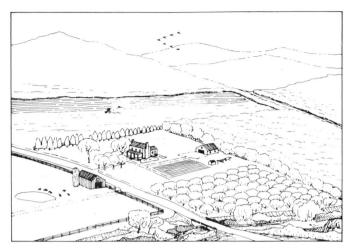

erations such as pedestrian and vehicular movement and de-sign elements including trees, lighting, signs, and the build-ings themselves.[13] Unfortunately, suggestions in the study were never followed up in any organized way.

Berlin and Pocomoke City both have had good experi-ences with preservation-initiated revitalization efforts. Per-haps the difference has been involved citizens who led the way by example. In Berlin a couple who owned a number of prop-erties began renovating them with an eye to historical accura-cy, showing other businesspeople what could be done. The town enacted a local historic preservation ordinance to gain control over its development. Berlin has emphasized its turn-of-the-century look and profited from doing so. The most dra-matic example of this is the Atlantic Hotel, which was recently returned at considerable cost from an eyesore to its previous position as a gathering place in the town. In Pocomoke City the mayor and business association initiated efforts to bring in new businesses to fill vacant shops and to improve the town's general appearance with plantings and other munici-pal projects.

Towns in Somerset County, particularly Crisfield and Princess Anne, could also benefit from using preservation tech-niques to spur revitalization efforts. Involved businesspeople and other local leaders can turn a town's economy around with a bold plan that includes preservation as an important plan-ning element.

The fourth goal calls for *maintaining, conserving, and pro-moting the efficient use of Maryland's natural and historic resources.*

In the light of new understandings about the impact of man's activities on the environment, it seems clear that preser-vation goals must be compatible with environmental goals. In addition to its aesthetic benefits, reuse of older structures is more energy efficient than demolition and new construc-tion.[14]

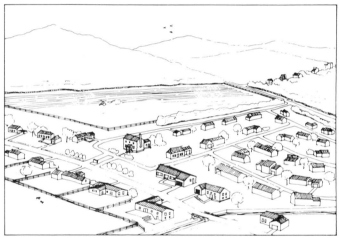

Protecting historic resources in their rural settings can protect open space and agricultural and forest land as well. In Somerset County most known prehistoric archeological sites are found along the county's waterways. These marshlands are also home to an amazing variety of wildlife and plants, whose place in the food chain has only recently been under-stood. Ducks and other waterfowl prized by hunters also make their home in these wetlands. Protecting these natural features from overdevelopment benefits a number of people, from the hunters and residents who cater to them, to the watermen

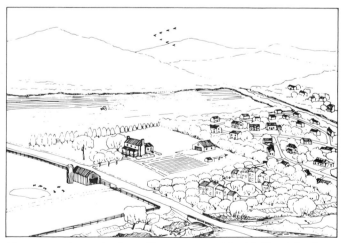

New construction can be planned in ways compatible with historic land-scapes. As shown here, a subdivision integrated into its surroundings does not disturb the landscape the way an insensitively planned development does. [Drawings by J. Timothy Keller from Samuel N. Stokes et al., Saving America's Countryside *(Baltimore: Johns Hopkins University Press, © 1989 National Trust for Historic Preservation), pp.144-145.]*

whose livelihood depends on the health of the area's ecosystems. Protecting the landscape is compatible with protecting the older buildings that populate it without stressing its resources.

The fifth goal recommends *expanding the role of preservation activity in the economic development of Maryland and its communities.*

Preservation efforts tend to improve a community in a number of ways. They can increase retail trade, attract new businesses and other investment, return vacant buildings to use, increase local tax revenue, add jobs, and generally stimulate pride and enthusiasm for a community on the part of its residents and businesspeople.[15] Such results are vital to the health of towns suffering from a decline in economic growth.

In addition to detailed discussions of these goals and their purposes, the *Comprehensive Historic Preservation Plan* suggests methods and techniques for achieving them on the local level. State and federal programs that local groups, governments, and individual property owners can use in their communities are also explained.

On the local level, the best way to make preservation effective is to include protection for historic properties and archeological sites in the land use planning process. Then, historic and prehistoric resources are no different than the other factors considered when development is planned. Like storm water management, soil type, and whether public facilities are adequate, effect on historic resources can be taken into consideration both by those making proposals and by the officials responsible for the approval process. The key is to encourage planning firms, architects, and government officials to address historic sites early, while a project is still in the planning stages.

The first step to incorporating preservation in the planning process is for county and municipal governments to map historic sites. Somerset County has incorporated National Register properties on its planning maps and has begun to develop additional maps that show the location of other sites on the Somerset County section of the Maryland Inventory of Historic Properties. Archeological sites also need to be included on these planning maps, a goal that could perhaps be achieved with matching funds from the Maryland Historical Trust and NOAA's Coastal Zone Management program. For example, in 1989 Anne Arundel County received a grant from the state's Coastal Zone Management program, which passed on federal National Oceanic and Atmospheric Administration

funds, to develop a computerized geographic information system. The Maryland Trust then provided a matching grant to include historic and archeological sites in this data base. Matching funds are also available for simpler projects, such as hiring a draftsman to help speed up the mapping of historic and archeological resources so this information may be used as part of larger planning processes.

Adopting a permit system for demolition is another simple way to consider the effect of new development or other changes on historic resources. Requiring such permits, with a waiting period, would allow for review by planners and concerned citizens. They would thus have the opportunity to seek solutions that would preserve important structures and archeological sites. Currently, demolition permits are required in Crisfield, but without a waiting period, and in Somerset County, but only if the building is to be demolished by fire. Princess Anne does not require such permits. Broadening the use of demolition permits in the county and its towns is an important goal for local preservation groups.

To go beyond mapping and demolition permits, the county government could incorporate preservation goals in its master plan and make concern for historic resources a county mandate. Help in designing such preservation efforts is available from a number of sources, including the Maryland Historical Trust and the Maryland Main Street Center at the state Department of Housing and Community Development. In addition, many counties and municipalities in Maryland have adopted state legislation to initiate local historic district zoning, forming their own historic preservation commissions to carry out this process. The legislation gives these jurisdictions more control over the appearance of their communities through the designation of individual sites and districts for special protection. Members of historic preservation commissions are appointed locally and review plans involving archeological and historic sites, recommending means by which they can function in twentieth century terms without losing their integrity.

Local governments that have effective zoning laws, including a preservation ordinance, have the option of participating in the Certified Local Government program. Created by the federal government in 1980 to recognize the important role of local governments in the preservation process, the CLG program gives local governments authority to review National Register nominations in their jurisdictions and gives them direct access to federal funds for local preservation projects.

Participation in the CLG program is approved by the Maryland Historical Trust and the National Park Service, but it is a local activity and could be initiated and carried out in Somerset County, Princess Anne, and Crisfield. Calvert County and the Town of Chestertown are two of eleven Maryland jurisdictions that currently participate in the program. Both have used matching funds available through the Maryland Trust to publish information about programs available to owners of historic properties and about the benefits of preservation in general. Calvert County has used CLG funds to sponsor a survey of buildings related to the tobacco culture there. Other Maryland counties and towns have also sponsored topical surveys, including studies of free black settlements. Development of local design guidelines, publication of a bimonthly newsletter, and sponsorship of day-long technical preservation seminars are other ways Certified Local Governments have spent funds received through the program.

Individuals, groups, and governments in Somerset County could also use several other programs administered by the Maryland Historical Trust to achieve local preservation goals. Both state and federal tax incentives are available to encourage the rehabilitation of historic structures. The state "Subtraction for Preservation of Historic Property" (known by its state income tax form number—the 502H program) allows owners of historic properties who also reside in them to deduct the cost of restoration activities from their state taxes. A number of Somerset County residents have taken advantage of this provision. Renovations at Caldicott, Hollyhurst, the Pauline Crockett house, and 205 Somerset Avenue in Princess Anne and a new roof at Waters River all qualified for participation in this program.

On the other hand, as of 1988 no Somerset County property owners had taken advantage of similar federal tax advantages available through the Tax Reform Act of 1986. This law applies to income-producing properties and would be useful to those renovating historic buildings for use as businesses or rental properties. In particular, Crisfield and Princess Anne could promote this program to encourage renovation of downtown commercial buildings.

Residents of Somerset County have taken advantage of state historic preservation grant and loan programs to preserve local buildings. These are the Maryland Historical Trust Historic Preservation Grant Program (formerly the state capital grant fund) and the Maryland Historical Trust Historic Preservation Loan Program (formerly the state revolving loan fund).[16] The brick walls of the Teackle Mansion north wing were repointed and some trim repaired and painted with a grant in the early 1980s. Masonry walls were stabilized and architectural fees provided during 1984-1989 for the Coventry Parish Church ruin. The owner of the skipjack *Thomas Clyde* is the recipient of both a grant and a loan for the preservation of that vessel. Most recently, a project to fund a new roof and new foundation for the Fairmount Academy and Knights of Pythias Hall in Upper Fairmount was approved for funds in 1989-1990.

In exchange for state grants and loans, property owners must donate an easement on the historic building to the Maryland Historical Trust. An easement is a document attached to the deed that requires any changes to the property to be approved by the Maryland Historical Trust and is designed to protect the state's investment in these buildings. Easements can also be donated to the Maryland Trust by owners who want to ensure the preservation of their historic properties. No one in Somerset County has yet availed themselves of this opportunity, although three property owners have donated easements to the Maryland Environmental Trust to protect more than 1,450 acres of county landscape.

Somerset County residents interested in preservation can work with a number of groups to further preservation goals in the county. In addition to the Somerset County Historical Trust, Inc. and the Maryland Historical Trust, the Maryland Environmental Trust and Preservation Maryland provide information and programs to help local citizens become active.[17]

In 1988 members of the Somerset County Historical Trust gathered to discuss the future of their group. Together they agreed on a list of goals they felt could realistically be achieved. The group plans to

• advocate increases in state and federal tax incentive programs and the creation of a county tax incentive that would emphasize the rehabilitation and reuse of the county's historic resources.

• support conferences, workshops, and special events and publicize information about preservation programs and accomplishments.

• participate in the development of a strong statewide network of preservation and historical organizations.

Boats on the marsh, Somerset County, July 1940, Farm Securities Administration, Jack Delano—photographer (courtesy of the Library of Congress).

• help governments in the county achieve Certified Local Government status.

• work with state agencies such as the Department of Economic and Employment Development's tourism and public affairs offices, *Maryland Magazine*, and state folklorist and the Department of Natural Resources to promote interest in Somerset County history.

• provide information on the benefits of using design standards and initiating compliance review at the earliest phases of project planning.

• provide information and work with local planning agencies and planning and design firms on the use of preservation tools and design standards in Somerset County.

• counterbalance any negative misconceptions of preservation as "elitist" through information and publicity about successful projects with community benefits.

The long-term preservation of Somerset County's past is critical to its future development. County residents and visitors have much to gain from the historic structures that define town streets and county landscapes, and the county has much to lose if these buildings and sites are left to uncertain fates. Together, local governments, local preservation groups, private property owners, and interested citizens can take steps to preserve the rich collection of eighteenth, nineteenth, and twentieth century buildings and the potentially rich mine of archeological information in Somerset County.

Preservation efforts in the county to date have achieved much: Somerset has the highest number of National Register sites per capita in Maryland and one of the most detailed historic sites inventories. Many private property owners have taken the initiative to preserve their historic houses. The county has begun to incorporate concern for historic sites in its planning process. Nonetheless, much remains to be done. It is time for the preservation effort to be carried more strongly into the public sector. To help local governments become active, individuals interested in preservation may have to delve into matters such as growth management, historic area zoning, farmland preservation, and other issues that come to the fore whenever a community wrestles with the problems of managing development. As it faces the future with its inevitable growth and change, Somerset County must decide how it wants to manage that development.

Residents concerned about the county's future can influence it in a number of ways. To ensure preservation is part of the planning process, join a group that advocates your views; let local officials know how you feel about protecting historic buildings and archeological sites; support efforts to protect these resources; and help educate others about the benefits of preservation. Active and interested citizens can protect the past and influence the future. 🌳

Notes

CHAPTER I

[1] D. G. Frey, "Regional aspects of the late glacial and post-glacial pollen succession of southeastern North Carolina," in *Ecological Monographs*, No. 23 (1953); Victor A. Carbonne, *Environment and Prehistory in the Shenandoah Valley*, PhD dissertation, Catholic University of America (Ann Arbor, Michigan: University Microfilm, 1976); and D. R. Whitehead, "Palynology and Pleistocene phytogeography of unglaciated eastern North America," in *The Quaternary of the United States*, ed. by H. E. Wright and D. G. Frey (1965).

[2] C. E. Ray, B. N. Cooper, and W. S. Benninghoff, "Fossil mammals and pollen in a late pleistocene deposit at Saltville, Virginia," *Journal of Paleontology*, No. 41 (1967); and J. E. Guilday, P. S. Martin, and A. D. McCrady, "New Paris No. 4: A pleistocene cave deposit in Bedford County, Pennsylvania," *Bulletin of the National Speleological Society*, No. 26 (1964).

[3] John C. Kraft and J. John Chacko, "Paleogeographic analysis of coastal archeological settings in Delaware," *Archeology of Eastern North America*, No. 6 (1978).

[4] William M. Gardner, "Paleo-Indian settlement patterns and site distributions in the Middle Atlantic" (preliminary version), paper presented at the January 1979 meeting of the Anthropological Society of Washington, Washington, D.C.; and Jay F. Custer, *A Management Plan for the Archaeological Resources of the Upper Delmarva Region of Maryland*, Maryland Historical Trust Manuscript Series No. 31 (Annapolis: MHT, 1983).

[5] Custer, *A Management Plan*.

[6] Richard B. Hughes, *A Preliminary Cultural and Environmental Overview of the Prehistory of Maryland's Lower Eastern Shore Based on a Study of Selected Artifact Collections from the Area*, Maryland Historical Trust Manuscript Series No. 26 (Annapolis: MHT, 1980).

[7] Custer, *A Management Plan*.

[8] Hughes, *A Preliminary Overview*.

[9] Custer, *A Management Plan*.

[10] Jay F. Custer, "The prehistoric archaeology of the Churchman's March vicinity: an introductory analysis," *Bulletin of the Archaeological Society of Delaware*, 13:1-41; Ronald A. Thomas, *Excavations at the Delaware Park Site (7NC-E-41)* (Dover: Delaware Department of Transportation, 1981); and Ronald A. Thomas, "Intensive archaeological excavations at the Hollingsworth Farm site, Elkton, Maryland," *Maryland Archaeology*, No. 18 (1), 1982.

[11] Cara L. Wise, *A Handbook for Delmarva Archaeology* (Wilmington: Delaware Department of State, Division of Historical and Cultural Affairs, Section of Archaeology, 1971).

[12] Custer, *A Management Plan*.

[13] Hughes, *A Preliminary Overview*.

[14] Cara L. Wise, "The Nassawango Adena Site," *Eastern States Archaeological Federation Bulletin*, No. 33 (Milford, Delaware: 1974).

[15] W. F. Kinsey and Jay F. Custer, "Excavations at the Lancaster County Park site (36LA96)," *Pennsylvania Archaeologist*, 52(3-4), 1982.

[16] Wayne E. Clark, "The Application of Regional Research Designs to Contract Archeology: The Northwest Transportation Corridor Archeological Survey Project," unpublished master's thesis, Department of Anthropology, The American University, Washington, D.C., 1976.

[17] Thomas E. Davidson and Richard B. Hughes, "Aerial Photography and the Search for Chicone," *Archaeology*, July/August 1986, pp. 58-76.

[18] Thomas E. Davidson, *A Cultural Resource Management Plan for the Lower Delmarva Region of Maryland*, Maryland Historical Trust Monograph Series No. 2 (Annapolis: MHT, 1981).

[19] Edward Arber, ed., *Travels and Works of Captain John Smith, President of Virginia and Admiral of New England, 1580-1631*, Vol. 1 (New York: Burt Franklin, 1910), p. 362.

[20] Thomas Harriot, *A briefe and true report of the new found land of Virginia*, with engravings by John White (1590; reprint ed., New York: Dover Publications, Inc., 1972).

[21] Arber.

[22] Arber.

[23] C. A. Weslager, "Indians of the Eastern Shore of Maryland and Virginia," in *The Eastern Shore of Maryland and Virginia*, ed. Charles B. Clark (New York: Lewis Historical Publishing Co., Inc., 1950).

[24] Raphael Semmes, *Captains and Mariners of Early Maryland* (Baltimore: 1937).

[25] Weslager.

[26] Thomas E. Davidson, "Historically attested Indian villages of the Lower Delmarva," *Maryland Archaeology*, 18(1):1-8.

[27] Weslager.

[28] Some small groups of native Americans remained in certain parts of Maryland. These people intermarried with non-Indians, but the memories of their culture never totally died and tales of their past were handed down from generation to generation. In 1988 the General Assembly of Maryland acknowledged the descendants of these early peoples of the Chesapeake when it passed the Indian Recognition Act, which gave official government recognition to the surviving inheritors of the native Marylanders' proud and honorable past. Frank W. Porter III, "Behind the Frontier: Indian Survivals in Maryland," *Maryland Historical Magazine*, 75 (1), pp. 42-54.

CHAPTER II

[1] Ralph T. Whitelaw, *Virginia's Eastern Shore, A History of Northampton and Accomack Counties*, Vol. 1 (1951; reprint ed., Gloucester, Massachusetts: Peter Smith, 1968), p. 21.

[2] Edward Arber, *Travels and Works of Captain John Smith, President of Virginia and Ad-*

miral of New England, 1580-1631, Vol. 1 (New York: Burt Franklin, 1910), p. 48. For clarity, abbreviations used in early documents have been spelled out. For the same reason, the use of "u" for "v" and vice versa has been dropped and modern usage adopted in quotations published in this book.

[3]Arber, Vol. 2, p. 415.

[4]Somerset County Judicial Records, Vol. DT 7, p. 12, Randall Revell vs. Richard Ackworth in a plea of trespass, 13 September 1670 (begins p. 6).

[5]Aubrey C. Land, *Colonial Maryland—A History* (Millwood, New York: KTO Press, 1981), p. 6.

[6]*Ibid.*, pp. 11-12.

[7]*Ibid.*, pp. 9-10.

[8]Edward B. Mathews, *The Counties of Maryland: Their Origin, Boundaries, and Election Districts* (Baltimore: Johns Hopkins Press, 1907), p. 421.

[9]Clayton Torrence, *Old Somerset on the Eastern Shore of Maryland, A Study of Foundations and Fathers* (1935; reprint ed., Baltimore: Regional Publishing Company, 1973), p. 12.

[10]*Archives of Maryland, Proceedings of the Council of Maryland, 1636-1667*, Vol. 3 (Baltimore: Maryland Historical Society, 1885), pp. 435-436.

[11]Torrence, pp. 26-27.

[12]*Archives of Maryland*, Vol. 3, p. 436.

[13]*Ibid.*, p. 452.

[14]Susie M. Ames, *Studies of the Virginia Eastern Shore in the Seventeenth Century* (New York: Russell and Russell, 1973), p. 7.

[15]Torrence, p. 30.

[16]*Ibid.*, pp. 30-33.

[17]*Archives of Maryland*, Vol. 3, pp. 473-474.

[18]Torrence, pp. 36-37.

[19]*Ibid.*, pp. 37-38.

[20]*Ibid.*, p. 388.

[21]*Ibid.*, pp. 39-42.

[22]Ames, p. 6.

[23]Torrence, pp. 49-50.

[24]*Ibid.*, p. 54.

[25]*Ibid.*, pp. 469-473.

[26]*Archives of Maryland*, Vol. 3, pp. 553-555.

[27]Torrence, pp. 72-73; and Somerset County Judicial Records, December 1665-December 1668, pp. 44-45, 17 January 1666.

[28]*The Oxford English Dictionary*, Vol. V (1933; reprint ed., London: Oxford University Press, 1961).

[29]Torrence, pp. 404-407; and Somerset County Judicial Records, November 1683-March 1683/4, Vol. L (prefix), p. 14, 28 November 1683.

[30]Torrence, p. 409; and Somerset County Judicial Records, 1687-1689, Vol. AW, p. 94, 14 November 1688.

[31]Torrence, pp. 409-410; and Somerset County Judicial Records, August 1693-November 1694, p. 90, 13 March 1693/4.

[32]Torrence, pp. 411-412.

[33]*Archives of Maryland, Proceedings and Acts of the General Assembly of Maryland, October 1678-November 1683*, Vol. 7 (Baltimore: Maryland Historical Society, 1889), pp. 609-610.

[34]Lois Green Carr and Russell R. Menard, "Immigration and Opportunity: The Freedman in Early Colonial Maryland," in *The Chesapeake in the Seventeenth Century, Essays on Anglo-American Society*, ed. Thad W. Tate and David L. Ammerman (Chapel Hill: University of North Carolina Press, 1979), p. 209.

[35]Somerset County Inventories, Vol. EB 14, p. 365, appraisal of the estate of Colonel Francis Jenckins, 27 June 1710.

[36]Torrence, pp. 373-375.

[37]*Ibid.*, p. 373.

[38]Somerset County Land Records, Vol. L, p. 560, deed from William Weedon to Francis Jenckins, 26 June 1700. In later years the Jenkins plantation was known as Hamp-ton (Torrence, p. 374).

[39]Somerset County Land Records, index, 1682-1710.

[40]Inventory EB 14/365.

[41]Somerset County Inventories, Vol. EB 14, p. 282, appraisal of the estate of Edward Day, 17 May 1699.

[42]Ruth T. Dryden, *Land Records of Somerset County* (n.p.: printed privately, n.d.), p. 107.

[43]Torrence, pp. 395, 397, and 414.

[44]T. H. Breen and Stephen Innes, *Myne Owne Ground, Race and Freedom on Virginia's Eastern Shore, 1640-1676* (New York and Oxford: Oxford University Press, 1980), p. 16.

[45]Dryden, p. 392.

[46]*Ibid.*

[47]Breen and Innes, p. 16.

[48]Somerset County Inventories, Vol. 14, p. 326, appraisal of the estate of Samuel Lennon, 10 October 1705.

[49]James Horn, "Servant Emigration to the Chesapeake in the Seventeenth Century," in *The Chesapeake in the Seventeenth Century, Essays on Anglo-American Society*, ed. Thad W. Tate and David L. Ammerman (Chapel Hill: University of North Carolina Press, 1979), p. 96.

[50]Ames, p. 233.

[51]Norman Penney, ed., *The Journal of George Fox*, Vol. 2 (Philadelphia: The John C. Winston Co., 1911), pp. 241-243, as quoted in Torrence, p. 497.

[52]Torrence, pp. 91-92, 101, and 108.

[53]*Ibid.*, p. 215.

[54]*Ibid.*, pp. 220-232.

[55]*Ibid.*, p. 245.

[56]Land, pp. 87-91.

[57]Torrence, pp. 150-158.

CHAPTER III

[1]Cary Carson, Norman F. Barka, William M. Kelso, Garry Wheeler Stone, and Dell Upton, "Impermanent Architecture in the Southern American Colonies," in *Win-*

terthur Portfolio (Chicago: University of Chicago Press, 1981), pp. 135-136.

[2]Somerset County Judicial Records, Vol. L (reverse), p. 105, Major John West against John Anderson [sawyer], 12 June 1677.

[3]Somerset County Judicial Records, Vol. L (prefix), p. 5, William Thomas against Richard Harris, 14 November 1683.

[4]Somerset County Judicial Records, Vol. L (reverse), p. 89, John Tyler [carpenter] against Coll. William Colebourne, 15 March 1676.

[5]Carson et al., p. 141.

[6]Somerset County Judicial Records, Vol. AW, p. 92, Captain William Whittington against John Swain, 14 November 1688.

[7]Carson et al., pp. 158-160.

[8]Torrence, pp. 409-410.

[9]Federal Assessment of 1798; and Ralph T. Whitelaw, Virginia's Eastern Shore, A History of Northampton and Accomack Counties, 2 vols. (1951; reprint ed., Gloucester, Massachusetts: Peter Smith, 1968).

[10]Whitelaw, p. 330.

[11]Phone conversation with Frank Horton, Museum of Early Southern Decorative Arts, 1983; and H. Chandlee Forman, Old Buildings, Gardens, and Furniture in Tidewater Maryland (Cambridge, Maryland: Tidewater Publishers, 1967), pp. 181-186.

[12]Somerset County Inventory Records, Vol. EB 14, p. 282, inventory of the estate of Edward Day, 17 May 1699.

[13]Somerset County Inventory Records, Vol. EB 14, p. 239, inventory of the estate of Andrew Jones, 22 December 1684.

[14]Somerset County Inventory Records: Vol. EB 14, p. 243, inventory of the estate of John Evans [planter] "praised at Wicomico," 12 July 1686; and Vol. EB 14, p.262, inventory of the estate of Colonel David Browne, 14 November 1697.

[15]Somerset County Inventory Records, Vol. EB 14, p. 365, inventory of the estate of Colonel Francis Jenckins, 27 June 1710.

[16]Somerset County Land Records, Vol. L, p. 30, John Lenham vs. Lawrence Gere, 10 November 1675.

CHAPTER IV

[1]Paul G. E. Clemens, The Atlantic Economy and Colonial Maryland's Eastern Shore, From Tobacco to Grain (Ithaca and London: Cornell University Press, 1980), pp. 38-39.

[2]Ibid., p. 39.

[3]Ibid., p. 111.

[4]Jacob M. Price, France and the Chesapeake: A History of the French Tobacco Monopoly, 1674-1791, and of its Relationship to the British and American Tobacco Trades (Ann Arbor: University of Michigan Press, 1973), pp. 666-667.

[5]Clemens, p. 111.

[6]Lois Green Carr, "The Economy of Colonial Somerset County, Maryland, in Comparative Perspective," unpublished manuscript prepared for the St. Mary's City Commission, pp. 12-14.

[7]Ibid., pp. 12-13.

[8]Ibid., p. 13.

[9]Ibid., pp. 13-14.

[10]Cary Carson et al., "Impermanent Architecture in the Southern American Colonies," in Winterthur Portfolio (Chicago: University of Chicago Press, 1981), pp. 173-174.

[11]Carr, "Appendix, Table 2: Percent of Estates with Craft Tools, Five Crafts, Somerset and Rural Anne Arundel Counties, 1658-1777."

[12]Archives of Maryland, Proceedings and Acts of the General Assembly of Maryland, 1733-1736, Vol. 39 (Baltimore: Maryland Historical Society, 1919), pp. 20 and 128.

[13]Philip Morris, The Wadeing Place (Princess Anne, Maryland: Marylander and Herald, Inc., 1974).

[14]Somerset County Land Records, Vol. N, p. 431, a plat of "Princess Anne Town As Located by the Commissioners April 1801."

[15]Archives of Maryland, Vol. 39, pp. 129 and 473-4.

[16]Archives of Maryland, Proceedings and Acts of the General Assembly of Maryland, May 1730-August 1732, Vol. 37 (Baltimore: Maryland Historical Society, 1917), p. 537.

[17]Archives of Maryland, Proceedings and Acts of the General Assembly of Maryland, 1740-1744, Vol. 42 (Baltimore: Maryland Historical Society, 1923), pp. 428-429.

[18]Somerset County Land Records, Vol. X, p. 72, warrant to determine ownership and value of lot in Princess Anne allotted for the courthouse and prison, 3 November 1743.

[19]Clayton Torrence, Old Somerset on the Eastern Shore of Maryland, A Study of Foundations and Fathers (1935; reprint ed., Baltimore: Regional Publishing Compapny, 1973), p. 4

[20]Raymond B. Clark, Jr., "Washington Academy, Somerset County, Maryland," Maryland Historical Magazine, XLIV (Baltimore: Maryland Historical Society, 1949), pp. 200-201.

[21]Clark, pp. 201 and 202; and Philip M. Marsh, Philip Freneau: Poet and Journalist (Minneapolis: Dillon Press, 1967), p. 28.

[22]Clark, p. 202.

[23]Torrence, p. 242.

[24]Ibid., p. 244 .

[25]Alethea Helen Whitney, A History of the Manokin Presbyterian Church, Princess Anne, Maryland, 1672-1980 (Denton, Maryland: Baker Printing Co., 1981), p. 28.

[26]In historic times this small Pocomoke River village was spelled Rehoboth. However, in the last few decades, the spelling has been changed to Rehobeth to distinguish the Maryland town from Rehoboth, Delaware.

[27]Torrence, p. 197.

[28]Somerset County Land Records, Vol. C, p. 196, deed from Stephen Horsey and Michael Holland to the vestry of Coventry Parish, 10 November 1760.

[29]Torrence, pp. 181-182.

[30]*Ibid.*, pp. 192-193.

[31]Somerset County Land Records, Vol. D, p. 68, Robert Geddes to Hamilton Bell, rector, et. al. 17 February 1767.

[32]Vestry Book of Somerset Parish, 1766-1825, entry dated 31 March 1767.

[33]*Ibid.*, entry dated 16 September 1773.

CHAPTER V

[1]Thirty-five Orphans Court evaluations from 1739-1759 extracted from Somerset County deed books by Thomas Davidson, Ph.d. copy at the library of the Maryland Historical Trust, Annapolis, Maryland.

[2]Marcus Whiffen, *The Eighteenth-Century Houses of Williamsburg, A Study of Architecture and Building in the Colonial Capital of Virginia* (Williamsburg, Virginia: The Colonial Williamsburg Foundation, 1960), p. 10.

[3]Discussion with John Fitzgerald, who was raised by the Sudler family, in April 1985.

[4]Somerset County Land Records, Vol. X, p. 104, Orphans Court evaluation for Revel Horsey, 24 March 1748.

[5]Somerset County Land Records, Vol. AZ, p. 168, Orphans Court evaluation for William Turpin, 19 July 1734.

[6]The restoration of Williams Green was accomplished in the early 1960s, at which time the mid-eighteenth century paneling was removed and then reinstalled. Discussion with Philip Stinchcomb, 1985.

[7]Somerset County Judicial Records, 1740-1742, p. 186, John McCuddy against Christopher Dominick Jackson, 3rd Tuesday of November 1740.

[8]Two contemporary examples of diamond stacks remain in Virginia. Bacon's Castle in Surry County on Virginia's western shore is the best known, but Wenona in Northampton County on Virginia's Eastern Shore stands only a few miles from The Reward.

[9]Somerset County Land Records, Vol.

A, p. 312, Orphans Court evaluation for Charles Woolford, 13 April 1753.

[10]Somerset County Land Records, Vol. B, p. 181, Orphans Court evaluation for Thomas Gibbons, 4 July 1757.

[11]Somerset County Land Records, Vol. A, p. 242, Orphans Court evaluation for Joseph Dashiell, 30 March 1752.

[12]Somerset County Land Records, Vol. A, p. 49, Orphans Court evaluation for George Dashiell, 12 April 1749.

[13]Somerset County Land Records, Vol. A, p. 51, Orphans Court evaluation for James Coventon, 27 March 1749.

[14]Somerset County Inventory Records, Vol. EB 14, p. 239, inventory of the estate of Andrew Jones, 22 December 1684; and Somerset County Land Records, Vol. AZ, p. 168, Orphans Court evaluation for William Turpin, 19 July 1734.

CHAPTER VI

[1]Charles S. Truitt, *Breadbasket of the Revolution, Delmarva's Eight Turbulent War Years* (Salisbury, Maryland: Historical Books, Inc., 1975), pp. 30-32.

[2]*Ibid.*, p. 2.

[3]*Ibid.*, p. 216.

[4]*Ibid.*, p. 2.

[5]*Ibid.*, p. 2.

[6]Typed copy of the Thomas S. Sudler diary in the possession of Mr. and Mrs. Joseph Eberly (original owned by Dr. Mervin Tubman Sudler), p. 3, entry dated 18 November 1803.

[7]Truitt, p. 159.

[8]Ernest McNeill Eller, ed., *Chesapeake Bay in the American Revolution* (Centreville, Maryland: Tidewater Publishers, 1981), pp. 241-244.

[9]*Ibid.*, p. 244.

[10]Truitt, p. 140.

[11]Alice E. Miller, *Cecil County, Maryland, A Study in Local History* (Port Deposit, Mary-

land: Port Deposit Heritage, Inc., 1976), p. 58.

[12]Letter book of Littleton Dennis Teackle, 1805-1807, pp. 22-23, p. 48, entry dated 2 February 1806, Quinby Family Papers, Accession #2338, Rare Books and Manuscripts, Alderman Library, University of Virginia, Charlottesville, Virginia.

[13]Sudler diary, pp. 2-3.

[14]1840 U.S. Census, Agricultural Schedule for Somerset County, Maryland.

[15]Letter from Levin Handy, clerk of the Somerset County Court, to David Ridgely, Princess Anne, 20 September 1841, Manuscript Collection, Maryland Historical Society, Baltimore, Maryland.

[16]Farm account books of James Wilson, 1773-1780s, MS 915, Maryland Historical Society, Baltimore, Maryland.

[17]Wilson farm account books, 5 July 1788.

[18]Somerset County Register of Wills (Annual Valuations, 1815-1827), Vol. GH 1, p. 295, Orphans Court valuation of the real estate of Levin and Arnold E. Waters, 23 September 1819.

[19]David Ridgely, "The General Outlines of the Geology of the State of Maryland; with the Local Geology of these Several Counties in the State...," manuscript in the collection of the Maryland Historical Society, Baltimore, Maryland (1841), p. 10.

[20]Federal Assessment of 1798, Dwelling Houses, Lands, Slave Schedules, Somerset County, Maryland. Orlando Ridout V, in his work "Re-editing the Past: A Comparison of Surviving Documentary and Physical Evidence" (22 April 1982), a paper from his research in Queen Anne's County, Maryland, has provided a precedent for using the federal assessment of 1798 as well as Orphans Court evaluations as indications of the late eighteenth century landscape.

[21]Federal Assessment of 1798, Lands As-

sessment, Somerset County, Maryland.

[22]David Ridgely, "The Geographical Description of the State of Maryland together with the outlines of its Geological Features; also of the Counties, Towns, Rivers, Bays, and Islands," a manuscript in the collection of the Maryland Historical Society, Baltimore, Maryland (1841), pp. 57-59.

[23]Federal Assessment of 1798, Slave Assessment, Manokin Hundred, Nehemiah King.

[24]Federal Assessment of 1798, Monie, Manokin, and Great Annemessex hundreds.

[25]Federal Assessment of 1798, Dwelling Houses, Wicomico, Monie, Manokin, Dividing Creek, Pocomoke, Great Annemessex, and Little Annemessex hundreds.

[26]Federal Assessment of 1798, Princess Anne, listings for Zadock Long and John Bloodsworth.

[27]Sudler diary, p. 1.

[28]*Ibid.*, p. 4.

[29]Federal Assessment of 1798, Princess Anne, listings for Captain Nehemiah King, Lot 13 (probably a rented house), William Done, and Dr. Arnold Elzey.

[30]Letter from Handy to Ridgely, 20 September 1841.

[31]Paired modillion blocks found on a group of contemporary buildings in Somerset County, Maryland; Northampton and Accomac Counties, Virginia; and New Bern and Edenton, North Carolina point to a common but undocumented design source.

[32]Somerset County Wills, Vol. EB 17, p. 105, Samuel Wilson, 29 April 1790 (25 May 1790).

[33]Somerset County Land Records, Vol. N, p. 530, George Wilson Jackson, merchant, to Littleton Dennis Teackle, 19 May 1802.

[34]Daniel J. Houlihan, *Teackle—The Mansion and the Man* (1976), p. 16.

[35]Somerset County Land Records, Vol. JP 1, p. 520, The Bank of Somerset from Henry James Carroll Trustee, 6 June 1814.

[36]Houlihan, p. 17.

[37]Somerset County Land Records, Vol. JD 1, p. 186, Lease to Robert J. Henry President Steam Co. from L. D. Teackle, 1 October 1815.

[38]Letter from Elizabeth Upshur Teackle to her sister, Anne Eyre of Northampton County, Virginia, dated 14 June 1818: "As ill news travels a pace, you have no doubt long since had information of the burning of the steam mill....," Quinby family papers, Alderman Library, University of Virginia, Charlottesville, Virginia; also Sudler diary, p. 15: "The great wonder Teackles Monument and Somerset Folly got burnt down on Wednesday night May 20, 1818 supposed loss to be nearly sixty thousand dollars or upwards. Folly, worse than mad folly."

[39]N. Niles, ed., *Niles' Weekly Register,* Vol. XVI, p. 282, entry dated 17 December 1831: "The court house of Somerset County, Maryland, at Princess Ann, was recently destroyed by fire—the books and papers all saved. The house has stood 87 years. Some of the other buildings in the village took fire, but were not materially injured."

[40]Letter from Handy to Ridgely, 20 September 1841.

[41]*The Village Herald,* 9 June 1835, Maryland Historical Society, Baltimore, Maryland.

[42]John C. Hayman, *Rails Along the Chesapeake, A History of Railroading on the Delmarva Peninsula, 1827-1978* (n.p.: Marvadel Publishers, 1979), p. 15.

[43]Letter from Littleton Dennis Teackle to Thomas R. Joynes, Esquire, Drummondtown, Accomack Co., Va., 1 February 1836, Quinby papers, Rare Books and Manuscripts, Alderman Library, University of Virginia.

[44]*The Herald,* 18 August 1838, Maryland Historical Society, Baltimore, Maryland.

[45]Hayman, pp. 16-18.

[46]Coventry Parish Vestry Minutes, 7 January 1793, p. 122: "Ordered by the Vestry that Thomas Bruff and Littleton Dennis Call on those who have had Bricks from the Old Church to pay 15/pM [15 pence per thousand] for them...."

[47]Coventry Parish Vestry Minutes, 12 August 1784, p. 54: "Advertisement[:] The Vestry of Coventry Parish intending to let out the Building of the New Church at Rehoboth the First Monday in September. Desire those Persons Who Would Wish to Undertake the Same or Any Part there of to Meet the Vestry at Rehoboth by Eleven O. Clock on that Day."; also vestry minutes from 7 March 1785, p. 60: "The Vestry Put the Building of the New Church to the Lowest Bidder and Was Struck as To Mr. Isaac Marshell at £700—that is To Say the Brick Work and Ruff Door frames and Window frames."

[48]Coventry Parish Vestry Minutes, 10 June 1786, p. 73: "& agreed with Elijah Braughton to Make 31 Window Frames at $^3/_9$ [£3.9] & With Robt. Lankford to make Bricks @ $^3/_6$pM [£3.6 per thousand]."

[49]Coventry Parish Vestry Minutes, 16 July 1787, p. 78: "The Vestry Proposed to the Parishoners who were There Assembled To fall on Some mode for Raising Money to pay of those who had claims For Work done & on the church & also to Make up Mr. Tingley's Salery & How the Said Church was to be finished."

[50]Clayton Torrence, *Old Somerset on the Eastern Shore of Maryland, A Study of Foundations and Fathers* (1935; reprint ed., Baltimore: Regional Publishing Company, 1973), p. 199.

[51]*Ibid.*, p. 199.

[52]Coventry Parish Vestry Minutes, 2 June 1846, pp. 46-47.

[53]Grace Protestant Episcopal Church Vestry Minutes, 12 April 1845, pp. 1-16.

[54]E. C. Hallman, *The Garden of Methodism* (n.p.: Peninsula Annual Conference of the

Methodist Church, [1948]), pp. 330, 331, and 334.

[55]Federal Assessment of 1798, Lands Assessment, Great Annemessex Hundred, John Gale.

[56]Hallman, pp. 330-334; Kenneth M. Dickey, *History of Antioch Charge* (Princess Anne, Maryland: n.d.), p. 1; and Woodrow T. Wilson, *Quindocqua, Maryland—Indian Country* (Baltimore: Gateway Press, Inc., 1980), p. 33.

[57]Adam Wallace, *Parson of the Islands* (Philadelphia: published by the author, 1861), p. 47.

[58]*Ibid.*, p. 330.

[59]*Ibid.*, pp. 403-408.

[60]Trustees minutes of the Washington Academy, 18 April 1797, p. 30, "In consequence of the burning of the Washington Academy the Trustees met for the special purpose of taking such measures as may be expedient for the welfare of the said institution." 14 January 1801, p. 41, "Resolved that Messrs. Thomas King, John Done, John C. Wilson, William Jones, and Henry J. Carroll be a committee to examine where and upon what terms a sufficient quantity of land not less than four acres can be procured for the purpose of erecting the academy." Maryland State Archives, Annapolis, Maryland.

[61]Trustees minutes of the Washington Academy, 28 January 1801, p. 42, "The Committee appointed to examine and determine on a fit and proper place for building of the Academy report that a piece of land belonging to Mr. Whittington King lying on the main road as the most eligible and for which Mr. King will take £10 per acres." Also, "Resolved that Captain John C. Wilson, Mr. James Wilson, Doctor Ker and Mr. J. Stewart be a committee to have the land so contracted for located and the same land laid off and ascertained by proper limits to the best advantage that they can obtain, not to be less

than 6 acres or more than 10 acres and that they contract for 150,000 bricks to be delivered on the premises."

[62]Trustees minutes of the Washington Academy, 28 January 1801, "The Committee appointed to contract for bricks report that they have executed a contract for the purpose with Mr. James Wilson." 7 October 1801, p. 45, "The board agreed with Isaac Gibbons to carry on the carpenters and joiners work on the Academy and executed a contract with him for that purpose. The board also agreed with Cyrus Sharp to execute the brick work of the Academy."

[63]*Eastern Shore Intelligencer,* 14 May 1805, Talbot County Library, Easton, Maryland.

[64]Somerset County Wills, Vol. JP 5, p. 117, Lazaraus Maddox, 26 March 1841.

[65]Somerset County Register of Wills (Annual Valuations, 1797-1805), Vol. EB 22, p. 292, Orphans Court valuation of the real estate of Major Nehemiah King, 14 August 1804.

CHAPTER VII

[1]Marcus Whiffen, *The Eighteenth-Century Houses of Williamsburg* (Williamsburg, Virginia: The Colonial Williamsburg Foundation, 1960), pp. 58-65.

[2]Helen Park, *A List of Architectural Books Available in America Before the Revolution* (Los Angeles: Hennessey & Ingalls, Inc., 1973).

[3]*Ibid.*

[4]1783 Federal Tax Assessment, Thomas King, Great Annemessex Hundred, "A new dwelling house with two rooms a hall and entry below, part of woodwork unfinished...."

[5]Mark R. Wenger, "The Central Passage in Virginia: Evolution of an Eighteenth Century Living Space," in *Perspectives in Vernacular Architecture* II, ed. Camille Wells (Columbia, Missouri: University of Missouri Press, 1986), p. 141.

[6]*Ibid.*, p. 139.

[7]Ralph T. Whitelaw, *Virginia's Eastern Shore, A History of Northampton and Accomack Counties*, Vol. II, ed. George Carmington Mason (Gloucester, Massachusetts: Peter Smith, 1968), pp. 1181-1183.

[8]Somerset County Land Records, Vol. N, p. 530, George Wilson Jackson, merchant, to Littleton Dennis Teackle, 19 May 1802.

[9]Distinct seams in the brickwork of each hyphen are located between the second and third bays, indicating different periods of construction.

[10]Letter of Elizabeth U. Teackle to her sister, Anne Eyre, 3 July 1819, "Our building is now under the plaistering discipline, and we hope to have it comfortable in a short time." Quinby Family Papers, Rare Books and Manuscripts, Alderman Library, University of Virginia, Charlottesville.

[11]Letter of Elizabeth U. Teackle to her sister, Anne Eyre, 14 June 1818, Quinby papers.

[12]Letter of Eleanor Gilliss Waters, undated, copy in collection of Old Princess Anne Days, Inc. Note: Eleanor Gilliss Waters was the daughter of William Gilliss Waters and Anne Glasgow Elzey, who married in 1799. Eleanor was evidently born a few years later. She died on 27 October 1822, therefore the letter is dated circa 1818.

[13]Somerset County Land Records, Vol. A, p. 51, Orphans Court valuation of two tracts of land belonging to Isaac Windsor, 15 April 1749.

[14]Federal Assessment of 1798, Heirs of Thomas Williams, Somerset County, Pocomoke Hundred.

[15]Federal Assessment of 1798, Somerset County, Maryland.

[16]Federal Assessment of 1798, Somerset County, Lands Assessment for Monie, Manokin, Dividing Creek, and Little Annemessex hundreds.

[17]Letter of Elizabeth U. Teackle to her

daughter, Elizabeth Anne Upshur Teackle, 10 August 1818, Quinby papers.

CHAPTER VIII

[1]1850 U.S. Census, Manufacturers Schedule.

[2]John C. Hayman, *Rails Along the Chesapeake, A History of Railroading on the Delmarva Peninsula, 1827-1978* (Marvadel Publishers, 1979), p. 22.

[3]*Ibid.*, p. 23.

[4]*Ibid.*, p. 66.

[5]Charles B. Clark, ed., *The Eastern Shore of Maryland and Virginia*, Vol. 1 (New York: Lewis Publishing Company, Inc., 1950), p. 539.

[6]*Ibid.*, pp. 543-546.

[7]Harry Wright Newman, *Maryland and the Confederacy* (Annapolis: published by the author, 1976), p. 225.

[8]Minute Book of the Board of Trustees of the Washington Academy, 1843-1910, Biography of Levin Lyttleton Waters by Cassius M. Dashiell.

[9]John R. Wennersten, "Tidewater Somerset, 1850-1970," unpublished manuscript, pp. 55-58.

[10]Clark, Vol. 1, p. 549.

[11]George H. Corddry, *Wicomico County History* (Salisbury, Maryland: Peninsula Press, 1981), pp. 23-25.

[12]Torrence, p. 429: "In 1867 (by Article 13, Section 2, of the Constitution of Maryland) Wicomico County was erected from parts of Somerset and Worcester Counties. The boundaries for Wicomico County were defined as 'beginning at the point where Mason and Dixon's line [Maryland-Delaware boundary line] crosses the channel of Pocomoke River, thence following the said line to the channel of Nanticoke River, thence with the channel of said river to Tangier Sound, or the intersection of Nanticoke and Wicomico Rivers, thence up the channels of the Wicomico River to the mouth of Wicomico Creek, thence with the channel of said Creek and Passedyke Creek to Dashield's or Disharoon's Mills [as located at that date], thence with the mill pond of said mills and branch, following the middle prong of said branch to Meadow Bridge on the road dividing the counties of Somerset and Worcester...thence due east to the Pocomoke River, thence with the channel of said river to the beginning... said parts of Worcester and Somerset Counties shall become and constitute a new County, to be called Wicomico County...'.

[13]*Smyrna [Delaware] Times*, 29 August 1866, citation transcribed by Kent Griffith.

[14]1860 U.S. Census, Agricultural Schedule, as cited in Clark, Vol. 1, p. 503.

[15]"A Peninsular Canaan," *Harper's Weekly*, 1879, p. 66.

[16]R. Lee Burton, Jr., *Canneries of the Eastern Shore* (Centreville, Maryland: Tidewater Publishers, 1986), p. 31.

[17]*The State Gazette and Merchants and Farmers Directory for Maryland and District of Columbia* (Baltimore: Sadler, Drysdale & Purnell, 1871), p. 698; copy at the Maryland Law Library, Annapolis.

[18]John L. Graham, ed., *The 1877 Atlases and Other Early Maps of the Eastern Shore of Maryland* (Peninsula Press, 1976), p. 30.

[19]Burton, p. 125.

[20]*Ibid.*, p. 126.

[21]Survey files of the Maryland Historical Trust, Annapolis, S-127, Crisfield Multiple Resource Area, prepared by Peter E. Kurtze and Peggy Bruns Weissman.

[22]Bayard Taylor, "Down on the Eastern Shore" in Harold D. Jopp, Jr., ed., *Rediscovery of the Eastern Shore: Delmarva Travelogues of the 1870s* (Wye Mills, Maryland: Chesapeake College Press, 1986), pp. 37-38.

[23]*The State Gazette.*

[24]Henry Hall, "Report on the Shipbuilding Industry," Government Printing Office, 1884, as cited in Frederick Tilp, *The Chesapeake Bay of Yore* (Annapolis and Richmond: The Chesapeake Bay Foundation, 1982), pp. 115-121.

[25]"A Peninsular Canaan," *Harper's Monthly Magazine*, May 1879, pp. 63-64.

[26]John R. Wennersten, *The Oyster Wars of Chesapeake Bay* (Centreville, Maryland: Tidewater Publishers, 1981), pp. 17-18.

[27]*Ibid.*, p. 38.

[28]*Ibid.*, p. 37.

[29]*Ibid.*, pp. 39-54.

[30]*Ibid.*, p. 43.

[31]*Ibid.*, p. 48.

[32]*The State Gazette*, p. 695.

[33]*Maryland and District of Columbia Gazetteer and Business Directory for 1891-92*, Vol II (Baltimore: R. L. Polk & Co., 1892).

[34]Deal Island was originally called Devil's Island and later "Deil's Island." The "v" was first dropped by Methodist ministers, and the spelling was then changed to "Deal's Island."

[35]Adam Wallace, *The Parson of the Islands: A Biography of the Late Rev. Joshua Thomas with Sketches of Many of His Contemporaries and an Account of the Origin of Methodism on the Islands of the Chesapeake and Eastern Shores of Maryland and Virginia* (Philadelphia: Office of the Methodist Home Journal,1872), pp.13-14.

[36]*Maryland Gazetteer*, p. 579.

[37]*Smyrna Times*, 28 March 1866, "The passenger trains on the Delaware Road now run to Princess Anne, Somerset county, Maryland, and the work of completing the line to Somer's Cove, on the Chesapeake Bay, is being pushed forward with considerable energy. Thirteen of Fourteen miles are yet to be finished. When finished, a line of steamers is to connect the Route direct with the Seaboard line of the South via Norfolk, a destination of 83 miles by water. This will make the Peninsular Railroad one of the Great thoroughfares of the North and the South." Citation

provided by Kent Griffith.

[38]Graham, p. 24.

[39]Somerset County Chancery Records, Case 912, Beckford plat division, drawn by William F. W. Miles, 10 April 1884.

[40]*Maryland Gazetteer*, p. 756.

[41]Graham, p. 29.

[42]*Ibid.*, p. 29.

[43]*Ibid.*, p. 30.

[44]*Ibid.*, p. 22.

[45]*Salisbury Advertiser*, 18 May 1872, citation provided by Kent Griffith.

[46]Hayman, p. 72.

[47]Coventry Parish Vestry Minutes, St. Mark's P. E. Church, Pocomoke City, Maryland, 25 July 1851.

[48]Torrence, p. 182.

[49]"Somerset Parish, A Compendium," no date, published during the tenure of the Reverend J. Randolph Field, Th.D., references transcribed by Anne Pettit.

[50]Vestry Minutes and Vestry Papers of St. Andrew's Church, M337, Maryland State Archives, Annapolis; transcribed by Anne Pettit.

[51]Alethea Helen Whitney, *A History of the Manokin Presbyterian Church, Princess Anne, Maryland, 1672-1980* (Denton, Maryland: Baker Publishing Co., 1981), pp. 31-32.

[52]John R. Wennersten, "Tidewater Somerset," p. 100.

[53]Clark, Vol. 1, p. 745.

[54]Ruth Ellen Wennersten, "The Historical Evolution of a Black Land Grant College: The University of Maryland, Eastern Shore, 1886-1970," unpublished thesis, 1976, University of Maryland, p. 1.

[55]Somerset County Land Records, Vol. HFL 4, p. 287, Richard C. Dale, executor, to John A. B. Wilson, 12 June 1886, and p. 309, John A. B. Wilson and Mary E. Wilson to Centenary Biblical Institute of the Methodist Episcopal Church of Baltimore City, 24 August 1886.

[56]Clark, Vol. 1, p. 751.

[57]"The Post-Land Grant University— The University of Maryland Report," 1981, p. 175.

[58]Clark, Vol. 1, p. 751.

[59]Ruth Ellen Wennersten, p. 12.

[60]Minutes of the Trustees of the Washington Academy, 1843-1910, entry dated 21 November 1890, no pagination, Maryland State Archives, Annapolis.

[61]*Ibid.*

[62]*Ibid.*, entry dated 26 May 1891.

[63]Woodrow T. Wilson, *History of Crisfield and Surrounding Areas on Maryland's Eastern Shore* (Baltimore: Gateway Press, Inc., 1973), pp. 81-86.

CHAPTER IX

[1]1850 U. S. Census, Somerset County, Maryland, listing for Seth Venables; transcribed by Ruth T. Dryden.

[2]Somerset County Commissioners Minute Book, 1856-1868, Maryland State Archives, Annapolis.

[3]Somerset County Land Records, Vol. LW 2, p. 21, deed of mortgage Francis Barnes from Seth D. Venables, 31 December 1852. The document reads, "Whereas Seth D. Venables has purchased a lot in Princess Anne from Francis Barnes...the said Francis Barnes has advanced and loaned to the said Seth D. Venables sundry sums of money to enable the said Seth D. Venables to improve the said lot by erecting buildings thereon...it being the lot where the said Seth D. Venables now resides."

[4]Antioch United Methodist Church Cemetery, gravestone of Seth D. Venables, born 12 July 1821, died 30 June 1897.

[5]Andrew Jackson Downing, *The Architecture of Country Houses; including Designs for Cottages, Farm-houses, and Villas, with Remarks on Interiors, Furniture, and the Best Modes of Warming and Ventilating* (1853; reprint ed., New York: Dover Publications, Inc., 1969), p. 285.

[6]Philadelphia architect Frank Furness (1839-1912) was well-known for his distinctive building designs, which were characterized by their solid massing and decorative masonry.

[7]Somerset County Land Records, Vol. OTB 22, p. 328, Robert W. Adams from James Teackle Dennis and Ida W. Dennis, 11 December 1897.

[8]Downing, p. 272.

CHAPTER X

[1]Thirteenth Census of the United States, Population Schedule for Somerset County, Maryland, 1910.

[2]*Maryland County Economic Data Book*, 4th revision (Baltimore: Maryland State Planning Department, 1962), p. 45.

[3]R. Lee Burton, Jr., *Canneries of the Eastern Shore* (Centreville, Maryland: Tidewater Publishers, 1986), pp. 132-135.

[4]John R. Wennersten, "Tidewater Somerset, 1850-1970," unpublished manuscript in possession of Wilmer O. Lankford, Princess Anne, Maryland, p. 255.

[5]*Marylander and Herald*, 8 May 1953 (office of the *Somerset Herald*, Princess Anne, Maryland).

[6]*Ibid.*, 16 May 1916.

[7]*Ibid.*, 8 May 1953.

[8]*Ibid.*, 4 January 1916.

[9]*Ibid.*, 8 May 1953.

[10]Wennersten, "Tidewater Somerset,' p. 265.

[11]*Marylander and Herald*, 8 May 1953.

[12]John R. Wennersten, *The Oyster Wars of Chesapeake Bay* (Centreville, Maryland: Tidewater Publishers, 1981), p. 137.

[13]Wennersten, "Tidewater Somerset," p. 97.

[14]*Ibid.*, p. 96.

[15]*Marylander and Herald*, 16 May 1916.

[16]Woodrow T. Wilson, *Crisfield, Maryland 1876-1976* (Baltimore: Gateway Press,

Inc., 1977), p. 5.

[17]*Marylander and Herald.*, 8 May 1953.

[18]*Ibid.*, 26 May 1914.

[19]*Ibid.*, 19 May 1914.

[20]Wennersten, "Tidewater Somerset," p. 276.

[21]*Ibid.*, p. 272.

[22]*Marylander and Herald*, 15 February 1916.

[23]Wennersten, "Tidewater Somerset," p. 274.

[24]*Wicomico News*, 19 June 1902 (microfilm at the Wicomico County Free Library, Salisbury, Maryland).

[25]*Ibid.*, 22 January 1903.

[26]Wennersten, "Tidewater Somerset," p. 274.

[27]*Marylander and Herald*, 11 January, 1916.

[29]Wennersten, "Tidewater Somerset," p. 281.

[30]Woodrow T. Wilson, *History of Crisfield and Surrounding Areas on Maryland's Eastern Shore* (Baltimore: Gateway Press, Inc., 1973), pp. 56-62.

[31]*Ibid.*, p. 56.

[32]*Ibid.*, p. 60.

[33]*Ibid.*, pp. 83-84.

[34]*Ibid.*, p. 205.

[35]Kenneth M. Dickey, *History of the Antioch Charge*, p. 2.

[36]*Marylander and Herald*, 23 June 1916.

[37]Dickey, p. 3.

[38]Wilson, *Crisfield, Maryland* , p. 101.

[39]Phone conversation with Ann Lawson, Crisfield, March 1989; and handwritten notes from Mary Goldsborough, 4 April 1989, compiled from original church minutes for church history to be published in celebration of the church's centennial.

[40]*Marylander and Herald*, 8 May 1953.

CHAPTER XI

[1]Clay Lancaster, "The American Bungalow," in *Common Places—Readings in American Vernacular Architecture*, ed. Dell Upton and John Michael Vlach (Athens and London: The University of Georgia Press, 1986), p. 82.

[2]David R. Goldfield, "North Carolina's Early Twentieth-Century Suburbs and the Urbanizing South," in *Early Twentieth-Century Suburbs in North Carolina*, ed. Catherine W. Bishir and Lawrence S. Earley (Lillington, North Carolina: Edwards Brothers, Inc., 1985), pp. 10-11.

CHAPTER XII

[1]Conversation with Elizabeth W. Hall, Catherine Ricketts, Evelyn Ruark, and Gale Yerges, Princess Anne, Maryland, August 1989.

[2]Conversation with William Cain, Somerset County Board of Education, Westover, and Pat Somers, teacher at Washington High School, Princess Anne, August 1989.

[3]Conversation with Mrs. Charles Wainwright, Baltimore, 2 December 1983.

[4]Conversation with Elizabeth W. Hall, et. al.

[5]*Ibid.*

[6]*Ibid.*

[7]*Ibid.*

[8]Conversation with Gale Yerges, Princess Anne, August 1989.

[9]Maryland Historical Trust, "Regional and County-by-County Assessment of Archeological Survey Coverage in Maryland," Preservation Policy White Paper #1 (Annapolis: Maryland Historical Trust, 1986), p. 14. Copies of Preservation Policy White Papers can be acquired for $2 each by writing or calling the Division of Historical and Cultural Programs, Attention: Preservation Planner, 45 Calvert Street, Annapolis, Maryland 21401; 301/ 974-3642.

[10]Maryland Historical Trust, "Economic Benefits of Historic Preservation in Maryland," Preservation Policy White Paper #6, p. 5, and "Historic Preservation in Maryland: An Analysis of Its Impact on the State's Tourism Industry," Preservation Policy White Paper #7, p. 1 (Annapolis: Maryland Historical Trust, 1987). Copies of Preservation Policy White Papers can be acquired for $2 each by writing or calling the Division of Historical and Cultural Programs, Attention: Preservation Planner, 45 Calvert Street, Annapolis, Maryland 21401; 301/974-3642.

[11]"Economic Benefits of Historic Preservation in Maryland," pp. 3-4.

[12]Maryland Historical Trust, *The Maryland Comprehensive Historic Preservation Plan: Planning the Future of Maryland's Past* (Annapolis: Maryland Historical Trust, 1986). The *Comprehensive Plan* has been formally adopted by the State of Maryland to direct its preservation activities. Copies are available for $10 from the Division of Historical and Cultural Programs, Department of Housing and Community Development, Attention: Preservation Planner, 45 Calvert Street, Annapolis, Maryland 21401; 301/974-3642.

[13]Ferdinand S. Johns, "A Revitalization Study of Downtown Princess Anne" (College Park, Maryland: University of Maryland Center for Architectural Design and Research, 1980).

[14]"Economic Benefits of Historic Preservation in Maryland," pp. 2-3.

[15]"Economic Benefits of Historic Preservation in Maryland," p. 4.

[16]These programs are administered by the Division of Historical and Cultural Programs, Office of Preservation Services (formerly the Technical Preservation Services section of the Maryland Historical Trust). For information, write or call OPS (as of September 1989) at 21 State Circle, Annapolis, Maryland 21401; 301/974-5007.

[17]Addresses and telephone numbers for these organizations (as of September 1989) follow: Somerset County Historical Trust, Inc., Route 3, Box 331 Princess Anne, Mary-

land 21853; Maryland Environmental Trust, 275 West Street, Suite 322, Annapolis, Maryland 21401, 301/974-5350; and Preservation Maryland, 24 West Saratoga Street, Baltimore, Maryland 21201, 301/685-2886. The Maryland Historical Trust is the state historic preservation agency. Part of the Division of Historical and Cultural Programs, Department of Housing and Community Development, it consists of a number of divisions: Office of Research, Survey, and Registration, 21 State Circle, 301/974-5000; Office of Preservation Services, 21 State Circle, 301/974-5007; Archeology Section, 21 State Circle, 301/974-5004; Office of Management and Planning, 45 Calvert Street, 301/974-3642; Office of Cultural and Educational Services, 45 Calvert Street, 301/974-5585; all in Annapolis, Maryland, 21401.

S-56, Sudler's Conclusion, southeast elevation.

SUDLER'S CONCLUSION (NR)
Circa 1700-1725, circa 1810
Manokin vicinity
Private

Sudler's Conclusion is well-known on the lower Eastern Shore as one of the most significant early houses to survive in the region. The age of the single story brick house is not known exactly, but architectural historians have generally agreed on the first quarter of the eighteenth century.

As with other early houses in the region, the brick walls were erected in carefully laid Flemish bond with decorative glazed header surfaces highlighting the checkerboard pattern. Similar to the Beauchamp house and Makepeace is the distinctive sawtooth belt course that marks the east gable end. The south side of the brick house, now pierced by a pair of twelve-over-twelve sash windows, once contained an arched doorway that opened into the principal room. The north side also has a bricked-up doorway.

The first floor is divided into two rooms, each distinguished by large, ovolo-molded floor joists. The original winder stair, part of which remains, rose in the southeast corner of the main room or "hall." Directly adjacent to the stair is a six-foot wide fireplace.

During the early years of the nineteenth century, a two-story, two-bay frame addition fitted with Federal-style woodwork was attached to the west gable end of the brick house. Also noteworthy on the property is the gable-front frame tobacco house, erected around the turn of the nineteenth century. This barn was one of the last structures of this type built on the lower Shore.

"Sudler's Conclusion" is the name Thomas Seon Sudler gave the 419 acres south of Back Creek that he had resurveyed under one name in 1789. His grandfather, Thomas Seon, had assembled extensive holdings between Back Creek and the Great Annemessex River, beginning with the purchase of a 100-acre part of "Barnaby's Lott" in 1747. It has been presumed the brick house was standing on the property when Seon acquired the land. In his will of 1781 Seon bequeathed all his property to his wife, Jane. After her decease, the lands were to pass to his grandson and namesake, Thomas Seon Sudler.

Sudler occupied the Back Creek plantation for over half a century, and he was taxed for "Sudler's Conclusion" as well as other lands in the federal direct tax assessment of 1798. His principal plantation was improved by the then single story brick house as well as a brick meat house, 12 feet square; a brick

milk house, 16 feet by 10 feet; and a brick kitchen, 20 feet by 16 feet. His other lands along the Great Annemessex were tenanted by a Richard Tull.

Thomas Seon Sudler died in 1832, and his large landholdings were partitioned between his two sons, William and Tubman, and his daughter, Eleanor Gilliss Sudler. The property remained in the Sudler family until the early twentieth century. The current owners purchased the house in 1971 and have proceeded through a carefully thought-out restoration of the early brick and frame dwelling.

POWELL-BENSTON HOUSE
Circa 1700-1725
Rehobeth vicinity (site)
Private

Considered one of the oldest houses to survive to modern times in Somerset County, the Powell-Benston house exhibited several features that suggested its early age. Construction evidence discovered when the house was dismantled suggests the brick-ended frame dwelling was erected in two principal stages: The original single story, one-room plan structure was later expanded with a two-room addition.

The early house was distinguished by a carefully laid Flemish bond brick end wall highlighted with glazed headers. Four small windows with alternating glazed rowlock arches pierced this wall, and judging by other construction features, the small openings were initially filled with casement windows. Inside the earlier section, the framing members remained exposed and had decorated corners. A large six-foot fireplace framed by a wide bolection molding provided the original source of heat and cooking service. Raised panel doors provided access to the corner stair as well as to closets on each side of the hearth.

Credit for the construction of this early brick-ended house is awarded to the Powell family. Occupation of this property is thought to have begun with Walter Powell, who acquired tracts of land on the north side of the Pocomoke River as early as 1670. Powell bequeathed parts of the tracts known as "Exchange," "Greenfield," and "Middle" to his son William in 1695. William, in turn, willed title to his property to his sons John, William, and Levin and to his daughter Margaret in 1715. Given the architectural features of the house, it could have been assembled by William, Sr. or his son William. In 1740 William Powell and his wife, Ellen, having relocated in Prince William County, Virginia, sold "Greenfield" and "Exchange" to Thomas Benston of Somerset County. Benston evidently remained on the Powell plantation until his death, when the property fell to his eldest son, William, who in 1757 transferred ownership of the plantation to his brother Thomas.

Thomas Benston was assessed for the plantation in 1783 and 1798. The description by the 1798 assessors reads as follows:

Situate about one Mile from Pocomoke River in Somerset County 1 Dwelling house 20 by 35 one story high with 4 windows 4 1/2 [feet] by 2 1/2 [feet] and 2 small windows 1 1/2 [feet] by 1/2 [foot] Ends Built of Brick rest wood, 1 Milk house 8 by 8, 1 Meat house 12 by 12 both of wood.

As indicated by the assessor's description, the

S-98, Powell-Benston house, photograph c. 1964 (courtesy of the Museum of Early Southern Decorative Arts).

S-62, Beauchamp house, northwest elevation.

one-room plan house had been enlarged by that time. In the 1798 assessment the plantation, referred to as "Greenfields," was further improved by a 30 by 20 foot barn probably used for tobacco, two corn houses, and a cider house.

Four years after the 1798 assessment, Thomas Benston was dead. The first item in his will directed, "I give and bequeath unto my grandson Thomas Benston all my lands which I now hold with the improvements and privileges thereunto belonging...I also give and bequeath unto the said Thomas Benston one bed and furniture, one yoke of oxen, all my ploughs and harrows, and cyder casks." The plantation did not remain in Benston hands much longer, however, for the "Greenfield" tract and adjacent lands were sold to Littleton Dennis in 1810 and then left to his heirs in 1833.

More recently, the farm has descended through the Tilghman family since James R. Tilghman purchased it in 1883. During the 1960s the curators of the Museum of Early Southern Decorative Arts, in search of historic fabric for period rooms, transported certain parts of the Powell-Benston house to the museum in Winston-Salem, North Carolina.

BEAUCHAMP HOUSE (NR)
Circa 1710-1730
Westover vicinity
Private

Sited along the north side of the head of the Annemessex River, the Beauchamp house is architecturally and historically significant for several prominent reasons. Building features suggest the initial one-and-a-half story, "hall" plan, brick-ended dwelling is one of the earliest small houses to survive on the Eastern Shore. The north gable end wall is laid in Flemish bond and exemplifies the most ambitious glazed brick patterns in Somerset County. The diaper pattern is found on only three other houses in the county (Makepeace, S-81; Waterloo, S-31; and Suffolk, S-227).

In addition to its noteworthy exterior, the house has retained a large percentage of its eighteenth century interior woodwork. The end wall of the "hall" is fitted with raised paneling that incorporates a built-in cupboard and an enclosed winder stair. From the bricked-up windows located in this wall, it appears the main room was upgraded with paneling in the middle of the eighteenth century. A series of exposed joists are finished with a cyma curve molded edge.

The southern half of the house was added later, perhaps during the third quarter of the eighteenth century. Originally divided into two rooms heated by corner hearths, the interior was consolidated into one room around the turn of the nineteenth century. Attached to the south gable end of the main block is an early nineteenth century service wing partially covered with beaded weatherboards.

Historically, the brick-ended frame house represents the first phase of permanent building in Somerset County. Settlement period dwellings built during the seventeenth century were eventually replaced by more permanent dwellings such as the Beauchamp house. The superior glazed brickwork and interior paneling suggest the house was erected for a prosperous planter.

Extensive research concerning the land

on which the Beauchamp house stands indicates the tract, known by the name "Puzzle," consisted of portions of three neighboring land surveys: "Johnston," "Contention," and "Discovery." The exact parcel on which the Beauchamp house was constructed is not known, but it is likely the early dwelling is located on "Discovery."

The initial survey for "Discovery" was patented to George Johnson in 1668. Johnson owned the 150-acre tract until William Planner, Sr. bought the property in 1695. It is thought that Planner lived on a tract known as "Cheap Price" at the mouth of the Annemessex. Joshua Kennerly of Dorchester County purchased "Discovery" from the Planner estate in 1711 and subsequently sold the tract to Edmund Beauchamp, Jr. in 1727. Beauchamp had inherited part of his father's plantation, and it seems likely he purchased the adjacent "Discovery" tract because of its proximity to the Beauchamp land known as "Contention." Edmund Beauchamp, Jr.'s son William evidently ended up living on the property. William Beauchamp purchased yet another part of the "Discovery" tract from his brother Robert on April 1, 1745. This parcel is described as "beginning at a marked Red Oak tree standing on the dam side at the upper end of the plantation where the said William Beauchamp now lives...." On the same day, April 1, 1745, William Beauchamp transferred the composite tract, then called "Puzzle," to William Jones (carpenter) for £25 and 2,000 pounds of tobacco.

William Jones sold "Puzzle" in 1753 to William Beauchamp's cousin and old neighbor, Isaac Beauchamp, a planter. Since Isaac Beauchamp had inherited part of the "Contention" property from his father, Thomas, it appears "Puzzle" was a subordinate tract given over to Isaac's son Thomas and his wife, Jane. Isaac Beauchamp's will of 1777 helps sort out at least two adjacent Beauchamp houses. To his wife, Sarah, Isaac left free use of his dwelling house and plantation, whereas to his son Thomas he bequeathed

the plantation where [Thomas] now lives and then to grandson Thomas...land divided from whereon I now live by a road leading from Thomas King's mill dam to Jesse Lister's and lying on the easternmost side of the said road....

Evidently, Thomas Beauchamp died between 1777 and 1783, for in the latter year his widow, Jean (Jane) Beauchamp, was assessed for a "middling good dwelling house, kitchen, barn, and other houses, a tract called 'Puzzle' and another parcel known as 'Remnant.'" With Jane Beauchamp's death shortly thereafter, the property passed to Thomas and Jane's son Thomas as directed by Isaac in 1777. Thomas Beauchamp of Great Annemessex Hundred was assessed in 1798 for

1 Dwelling House built of wood one story high 30 feet by 18 feet 5 windows 5 ½ feet by 2 ½ feet 4 Dormant windows 3 ½ feet by 2 ½ feet, 1 Kitchen 18 feet Square, 1 Milk House 8 feet Sqr.

Thomas Beauchamp's land assessment in 1798 included

4 Tracts of Land called Remnant, 13 acres; Puzzel, 90 acres; Flatland Marsh, 50 acres; pt Hartford Broad Oake and part of Catlins Venture, 41 acres; in the whole 194 acres on which are 1 Blk smith's shop 1 small Log House.

Interestingly, the blacksmith's shop listed in the land assessment suggests a strong connection with blacksmith William Beauchamp (Thomas's grandfather's cousin), who owned the property in the second quarter of the eighteenth century.

Thomas Beauchamp's will, which was proved on February 11, 1815, devised to his son Thomas G. Beauchamp "all the land whereon I now live...including all the lands lying to the westward side of the said road...." Included in the will was a clause that bequeathed to his five daughters

a priveledge in all lands lying on the west-most side of the road leading from the County road where the old blacksmith's shop formerly stood, up to the westmost corner of my old dwelling house where it joins the colonade which leads to my cook house and thence with a straight line through the colonade down to the branch....

The mention of a colonnade and cook house in this 1815 will indicates the colonnade was added after the 1798 tax assessment, but was replaced with the current kitchen by the mid-nineteenth century. Thomas G. Beauchamp occupied his father's house with his first wife, Maria Long, and his second wife, Leah A. W. King, until his death in 1837. Due to Thomas's insolvency, Isaac Beauchamp, Jr. was empowered to sell his brother's estate to Edwin M. Long through various land transfers dating between 1837 and 1847.

Edwin M. Long owned the old Beauchamp house until his death. At that time, the property could not be divided equitably among Long's heirs, so Robert F. Bratton was declared a trustee to sell it. On April 13, 1881, Bratton sold the 135-acre farm to William S. Long for $1,900. Twenty years later the farm entered Circuit Court once more to be sold by Robert F. Duer, trustee, to Edwin D. Long. The current owners purchased the house and seventy-three acres in 1985.

S-53, Salisbury, west elevation.

SALISBURY (NR)
Circa 1700, mid-18th century, circa 1882
Westover vicinity
Private

One of a handful of turn of the eighteenth century dwellings in Somerset County, Salisbury survives with several features that indicate its early date. The steeply pitched roof and formerly exposed eave construction, as well as a series of exposed, heavy pine floor joists in the back hall, suggest the earliest section was erected around 1700. This early brick house, which probably had one or two rooms on the first floor, was enlarged in the middle of the eighteenth century with a two-room Flemish bond brick addition to the south. A distinct seam in the brick walls indicates the two periods of construction. When the addition was attached, the story-and-a-half brick house measured approximately 39' across by 20' deep.

Aside from modifications such as the relocation of the stair around 1810-1830, the old brick house remained essentially unchanged until the last decades of the nineteenth century. For unknown reasons, it was decided around 1880-1890 to reduce the early brick house and erect a two-story, side hall/parlor frame section that reoriented the house to face north. From the jagged edges of the old brick walls at their juncture with the frame section, it is clear part of the early house was destroyed. In the process of rebuilding, two chamfered pine floor joists with lamb's-tongue stops were reused under the floor.

Although the date of the early house is inexact, credit for its construction has been assigned to Samuel Handy, who acquired the lower part of "Armstrong's Purchase" and "Armstrong's Lot" when his wife, Mary Sewell, inherited them in 1681. Handy occupied the plantation with his wife and large family until his death in 1721, when the property passed to his eldest son, Samuel. Samuel, Jr. bequeathed title to his son Thomas, who in turn devised ownership to his son Sewell Handy. Evidently, by the time Sewell acquired title to the property, questions surrounding the exact boundaries between adjacent Handy and Curtis lands required an official deed of partition to establish legal ownership.

Sewell Handy was dead by 1777, and his holdings were divided between his children. His son Thomas occupied the old brick house through the balance of the eighteenth century and was taxed for the property in 1798. The plantation was described then as

Two Tracts of Land called Armstrongs Purchase, Armstrongs Lott & Part Salisbury Lott, 348 acres, New Invention, 212 1/2 acres, in the whole 560 1/2 acres on which are 1 Barn, 1 Corn House, 1 old Lumber House.

By the time of this assessment, the old Handy house measured 39' across by 20' deep with five windows 5' by 2 1/2'. Accompanying the dwelling was a group of outbuildings that included a detached kitchen, a milk house, a smokehouse, and a cider house.

A more explicit description of the Handy plantation was entered in the records of the Somerset County Orphans Court at Thomas Handy's death around 1800. The appointed subscribers of the court provided the following description of the estate of Joseph, Harriet, Martha, and Mary Handy:

1 Dwelling House 42 feet by 21 one story high with brick walls covered one side with shingles and the other with plank, 1 barn 36 by 32 framed and weatherboarded with oak boards and covered with 3 feet oak shingles, 1 old barn, 1 corn house 28 by 9 covered with 3 feet shingles, 1 granary 18 by 18 covered with 3 feet shingles, 1 cyder house 12 by 16 covered with 3 feet shingles, 1 milk house 12 by 16 covered with 3 feet shingles, 1 out quarter 20 by 16 sawed logs covered with 3 feet shingles, 1 field at the west end of the farm containing 60 acres, 1 middle field containing about 50 acres, 1 field at the east end of the farm containing about 50 acres, 168 apple trees, 228 peach trees, 1 Lott Tobacco land lying on the west side of the dwelling containing 5 acres, 1 Lott of Tobacco land lying on the north end containing 1 1/2 acres, 1 Lott of Tobacco land lying on the east side of the dwelling house containing about 4 1/2 acres, 122 apple trees, 236 peach trees, 1 garden, 1 Lott heretofore occupied in Turnips containing 1/2 acre.

The river plantation remained largely in the Handy and related Sudler families until 1882. In that year, James N. Brumley purchased the farm, then reduced to 162 acres, for $1,500.

It is not known exactly when the property was first called "Salisbury," but life-long residents of the area knew it by that name around the turn of the century. The "Salisbury" name may have been used to differentiate the Handy plantation from the adjacent Curtis lands as both were taken from the same tracts.

Due to the late nineteenth century features of the front section of the house, it is generally believed the major reworking of the Handy house was carried out by James N. Brumley, who sold the property in 1919. More recently, the house was rescued from total ruin by Theodore and Virginia Dorman, who purchased the farm in 1963. From 1986 to 1988 the house was again extensively rebuilt when a full two-story, three-bay addition

was constructed to the east of the late nineteenth century section.

MAKEPEACE (NR)
Circa 1725-1750
Crisfield vicinity
Private

Perhaps the best known of the early dwellings of Somerset County, Makepeace belongs to the generation of plantation architecture dating from the first half of the eighteenth century. Several outstanding features contribute to the architectural and historical interest of this Flemish bond brick dwelling. The west gable end displays an elaborate glazed header diaper pattern, one of four examples in the county. A sawtooth belt course visually divides the first and second floors; this architectural feature is also found on the Beauchamp house (S-62) and Sudler's Conclusion (S-56).

The principal (south) elevation at Makepeace is a symmetrical four-bay facade highlighted by a checkerboard pattern of glazed bricks. Centered on the south elevation are two doors topped by segmental arches. The eastern door opens into a stair passage, and the western door opens into the principal living space, formerly known as the "hall." The house was initially finished with nicely molded floor joists, and large six-foot fireplaces heated the two principal rooms. Alterations to the woodwork were made during the late eighteenth and nineteenth centuries. Attached to the east gable end of the house is a single story colonnade and a story-and-a-half kitchen. Both frame structures probably date from the nineteenth century.

Although former attempts to estimate the age of Makepeace placed its construction in the seventeenth century, recent architectural and historical research has convincingly dated the brick house to the second quarter of the eighteenth century. Charles Roach, the third

S-81, Makepeace, southwest elevation.

generation to occupy and farm part of the Johnson's Creek land grant, is credited with constructing the house after he inherited his grandfather's plantation in 1727. John Roach, Jr. bequeathed to his son Charles "the plantation whereon my father dwelt being 200 acres, 150 called Makepeace and fifty of Exchange." To his other son, William, John, Jr. left "my now dwelling plantation."

John Roach, Sr. had patented "Makepeace" in 1663. Charles Roach occupied his grandfather's patent until 1747, when his estate, including seven slaves, was probated and assessed for £651.9.1. The early eighteenth century architectural features of the house combined with Charles Roach's substantial estate at the time of his death convincingly support the proposed date of construction.

Makepeace passed to Charles Roach's son William, who was assessed for the plantation in 1783. Included in the assessment were 297 acres on which stood "a brick wall dwelling house, two rooms below, kitchen and barn in midling repair...." William occupied the creek plantation until 1787, when the property passed to his son William.

In 1798 William Roach was assessed for "Makepeace" and tracts known as "Force Putt" and "Half Quarter." The Roach house was described as

> *1 Dwelling House built of Brick 30 feet by 20 feet One Story high, 4 windows 5 feet by 2¹/₂ feet, 4 Dormant windows 3 feet by 2 feet; 1 Kitchen 18 by 14 feet Fraim'd, 1 Milk House 8 feet Square, 1 Negro House 16 feet by 14 feet sawd logs, 1 Stable 16 feet by 14 feet saw'd logs, 1 Carriage House 16 feet by 8 feet Fraimed.*

After the deaths of William Roach and his second wife, Nancy Milburn Roach, in 1837 and 1839, respectively, ownership of the plantation entered a confusing period. The house was evidently occupied by Roach descendants and later by Sterlings, although the exact date when Elijah Sterling acquired the property has not been determined. In the 1870 estate division of Sterling's lands, Lot No. 1 with five acres was allotted to his son Luther. Luther died in 1890, and his wife, Mary, married William H. Chelton in 1904. Mary E. Sterling Chelton remained on the property until her death in 1936. Half interests in Makepeace passed to Mary Chelton's two sons, Elijah and Edmund William Sterling, and Elijah sold his half interest to his brother in November 1937. Edmund William Sterling owned Makepeace until 1978, and the following year the property passed to the current Sterling owners.

PANTHER'S DEN (NR)
Circa 1725-1750 and later
Venton vicinity
Private

Panther's Den is a story-and-a-half Flemish bond brick house located between the forks of Little Monie Creek. The building has a steeply pitched, wood-shingled roof with three dormers on each slope. The three-bay, center hall house, estimated to date from the second quarter of the eighteenth century, was enlarged later and remodeled inside around 1830-1850. Important exterior features include a plastered cove cornice and patterned brickwork incorporating glazed headers. Interior trim—including the stair, mantels, chair rails, and architraves—largely dates from the early nineteenth century remodeling. However,

eighteenth century fragments such as raised paneling, molded floor joists, tilted false-plate eave construction, and wrought-iron hardware remain in the house.

John Pantor (also spelled Panter and Panther) was an early settler (circa 1663-1666), as well as a prominent landowner and highway surveyor. The 200 acres called "Panther's Den" was granted to him on November 11, 1666. The sixth item in his will of 1714 states, "I give the plantation and land whereon I now live called as aforesaid 'Pantors Den,' after my wife Dorothy's decease unto my cousin Catherine Laws and the heirs of her body lawfully forever." It is not known when the brick house was begun, but in all likelihood it was the work of later owners.

As directed by Pantor's will, his property passed into the hands of Catherine and Pan-

tor Laws (also spelled Lawes). Pantor Laws's will of 1769 left the plantation to his children after his second wife's death. On May 1, 1792, John Laws, one of the heirs, conveyed to his brother Thomas 188 acres known as "Panther's Den." Six years later the federal assessment described the dwelling of Thomas Laws as

1 Dwelling house 45 by 20 feet brick one Story 4 windows 5 feet long 2 1/2 feet wide 4 windows 4 feet long 2 feet wide out of repair; 1 Cook house 16 by 20 feet, Colonnade 14 by 10 feet unfinished, 1 hen house 10 feet square.

The 45' by 20' measurements of the house indicate the initial 18' deep house had been enlarged by that time by Thomas, John, or their father, Pantor Laws. The entry "out of repair" suggests the improvements were relatively old.

The property did not remain in the family much longer for in May 1802 "Panther's Den" was sold to Robert Robertson for £1,000. Robertson died in the next year, willing the property to his wife, Anne Hack Robertson. The will specified that after her death, the property was to be equally divided among the children of George and James Robertson, Robert's brothers.

Thomas B. Robertson sold "Panther's Den" in March 1815 to Robert Leatherbury, who held onto the plantation until 1827, when he sold it to George B. Waller and his wife Maria. The Waller family kept the farm, known by the name "Lindenwood" in late nineteenth century land records, until 1903. At that time the 200 acres were sold to Mary M. Lloyd. The present owner acquired a 124-acre tract around the house in 1976.

S-84, Panther's Den, south elevation.

WILLIAMS GREEN (NR)
Circa 1733
Kingston vicinity
Private

Nowhere has the process of diligent historical research been more perplexing, but at the same time more rewarding, than in the history of Williams Green, known for most of the last fifty years as Williams Conquest. Past researchers accepted the "Williams Conquest" name largely because extensive research in the land records had not been completed for the property. Only recently have questions surfaced as to the authenticity of the early history of "Williams Conquest." Part of the confusion stemmed from the fact that one man, William Planner, owned most of the land on the south side of the Great Annemessex in the vicinity of Gales Creek (first known as Red Cap Creek) during the late seventeenth and early eighteenth centuries. Subsequently Thomas Williams and his descendants held the property through the balance of the eighteenth century and three-quarters of the nineteenth century. Vague descriptions, especially in early deeds, always make it difficult to sort out exact locations.

A closer analysis of the deeds, accompanied by the tract boundary maps drawn by Harry Benson in 1942, indicates the "Williams Conquest" tract patented to Michael Williams in 1663, was situated on the south side of the Great Annemessex River. The old Williams family house, on the other hand, was erected along the south shore of Gales Creek, a tributary of the Great Annemessex. The Gales Creek tract, known as "Double Purchase," was initially surveyed as 150 acres for William Stevens in 1679, but it was actually possessed by William Planner. (This should not be confused with Randall Revell's "Double Purchase" tract on Revell's Neck.) It is thought that Planner and his son William occupied the tract across the creek known as "Cheap Price." With the death of William Planner, Jr. in 1733, Thomas Williams inherited part of the extensive Annemessex River holdings that included the "Double Purchase" land on the south side of Gales Creek.

Considering the architectural features of the story-and-a-half Flemish bond brick house, it is reasonable to believe Thomas Williams financed its construction around the time of his inheritance and stretched the finishing of the interior over the following decades. Williams died in 1768 and left various parts of the creekside property to his grandsons, Planner, Thomas, David, and Levin. The inventory of Thomas Williams's estate taken in 1769 shows an extraordinary amount of finished linen and sundry items of cloth, suggesting he engaged in the manufacture and sale of woven goods. His total estate was valued at a tremendous £1,158.

In 1783 Thomas Williams's grandson Thomas was assessed for 285 acres of the nearby "Boston Town" tract as well as 415 acres known as "Williams Green." (Thomas Williams had resurveyed "Double Purchase" and another tract called "South Lot" in 1767 as "Williams Green.") The assessors found Thomas Williams's property improved by a "brick wall dwelling house, kitchen in good repair, other houses indifferent, young orchards, other improvements midling good." They also mentioned that the land, consisting of white clay, was "near the water." Fifteen years later Thomas Williams's creek plantation was visited once again by the federal assessors, who recorded a more explicit description of the improvements. On the property they found

1 Dwelling House built of Brick 45 feet by 23 [feet], 5 windows 5 1/2 feet by 2 1/2 feet, 6 Dormant windows 4 feet by 2 1/2 [feet] 1 Kitchen 20 feet by 16 feet, 1 Milk house 16 feet by 10 feet, 1 Smoake house 12 feet square, the above House out of repair, the above House is one story high.

Williams's land assessment in the same year included

S-64, Williams Green, northwest elevation.

S-30, Brentwood, east elevation.

2 Tracts of Land called Boston Town 285 acres, Williams Green 415 acres, in the whole 700 acres on which are 1 Barn 23 feet by 20 [feet] two 8 foot shades, 1 Tobacco House 32 feet by 20 feet, 1 Corn House 27 feet by 7 [feet]…on the above Lands is a Store House 22 feet by 20 feet.

Thomas Williams died in 1802 and devised to his wife Mary "one half part of all my lands whereon I now live (except the Store House and lot of ground at the head of the Creek field whereon my son William Williams now lives) and also my dwelling house and outhouses, garden and orchards…." A subsequent item in the will bequeathed to his son Thomas "all that part of my said lands whereon I now live which lie to the south of the above described lines and limits as mentioned in the clause to my son, William, reserving to my beloved wife the one half part hereof during her widowhood." Thomas Williams died in 1829 and in his will left his entire estate to his brother William who lived next door.

"Williams Green," as the plantation was referred to in the land records, remained in various family hands until 1871, when it was sold by Thomas J. Dixon, sheriff of Somerset County, to Daniel Middleton, Jr. of Washington, D.C. Middleton also acquired the adjacent Greenwood farm a few years later. The two Williams family houses were situated on the same 290-acre farm from the early twentieth century until 1963, when Philip and Alice Stinchcomb bought thirteen acres immediately surrounding the brick house. The Stinchcombs proceeded through an extensive restoration, but finally sold the property ten years later to Thomas S. George, Jr. and his wife, Sara. In the late 1980s the house was sold once again.

Architecturally, Williams Green stands out as one of the most significant early eighteenth century houses in Somerset County. The brick exterior is distinguished by glazed header checkerboard patterns, and segmental arches mark the principal window and door openings. Most notable, however, is the Georgian style woodwork that finishes each of the first floor rooms. Evidently, the interior remained unfinished until around 1740-1750 when the south end of the house was partitioned into two rooms and the elaborate raised panel woodwork was installed. The

expertly crafted interiors, some of the most ambitious work to remain on the Eastern Shore, resemble those at the Wicomico County house known as Bound's Lott. Both houses share raised diamond panels, sometimes referred to as hatchments, marking the overmantel in the "hall" as well as fluted pilasters and superior raised panel woodwork.

BRENTWOOD (NR)
1738, 1916
Allen vicinity
Private

The two-story Flemish bond brick house known as Brentwood for much of the last century stands on a prominent bank overlooking Wicomico Creek south of the small village of Allen. The house is recognized not only for its significant eighteenth century features, but also for the well-designed Shingle style addition attached in 1916 to enlarge the dining and service wings of the household.

Although the interiors of the eighteenth century house were modified when the dwelling was enlarged, the superior eighteenth century woodwork in the study was preserved.

S-69, The Reward, southeast elevation.

The half-pilasters of the overmantel are similar to the fluted pilasters of Bound's Lott (Wicomico County) and Williams Green (S-64).

The attributed builder of the brick house, Reverend Alexander Adams, had a significant role in early Somerset County history. Born around 1680, Adams was ordained as a deacon and a priest by the Bishop of London and arrived in Somerset County as the new rector of Stepney Parish in 1704. From about 1707 to 1711, he served as presbyter of the Church of England for the entire county of Somerset, which included four parishes, Stepney, Somerset, Coventry, and All Hallows. Adams served as rector of Stepney Parish for sixty-five years until his death in 1769.

The land on which Brentwood farm is situated was initially known as "Smith's Adventure," patented to Samuel Smith in April 1667. Five years later Smith conveyed half of "Smith's Adventure" to his daughter Sarah and son-in-law William Brereton. Following this transfer, parts of "Smith's Adventure" were resurveyed under new names: "Brereton's Chance" in 1675 and "Mile End" in 1680.

William Brereton and his wife died in 1690 and 1698, respectively, and the surveyed lands evidently passed to their son William. Beginning in the early eighteenth century, William Brereton and his wife Dianna began selling part of their inherited lands to Alexander Adams. The first transfer, a 165-acre tract,

occurred in March 1718, with a subsequent transfer in August of the same year. Also in 1718, Adams purchased "part of Smith's Adventure" from John and Hannah Waltham. During the following half-century, he added to his holdings and eventually created a large estate along Wicomico and Passerdyke creeks. The 1738 construction date for the Adams house was documented by an etched inscription on the back of an attic stair riser, but the stair was rebuilt during the early twentieth century. Before his death in 1769, Reverend Adams conveyed to his son Andrew a 160-acre parcel of "Smith's Adventure" and an eighteen-acre tract known as "Adams Purchase."

Andrew Adams's landholdings were recorded in the tax assessments of 1783 and 1798. The most complete description of the property now known as Brentwood was written in 1798:

Situated on Wicomico Creek near the Head thereof One Dwelling House of Brick Two Story High Thirty four feet by Twenty Eight feet with five Windows, five feet ten Inches by Twenty Eight Inches, Two [windows] four feet ten Inches by Twenty Eight Inches Eight [windows] forty four Inches by Twenty Eight Inches Four [windows] Thirty four Inches by Twenty four Inches, finished in plain Order and in good repair, Kitchen of wood Twenty

by Sixteen feet in very bad repair Meat House saw'd logs fifteen by fifteen in good order Milk House Ten by Eight feet, [milk house] five by Eight feet Including an Ice House.

Also located on the 320-acre plantation were two barns, a slave quarter, and a sawmill. Andrew Adams owned a total of twenty slaves, ten of whom were between the ages of twelve and fifty.

Andrew Adams, Sr. remained on the property for the next nineteen years. Then in November 1817 he bequeathed to his son Andrew Adams, Jr. "all my dwelling plantation whereon I now dwell called by the names of Smith's Adventure, Adams Purchase, and the End of Strife...." A little more than ten years later, Andrew Adams sold his grandfather's plantation out of the family.

The farm was sold many times during the second half of the nineteenth century, and much of the time the property appears to have been tenanted. On November 9, 1901, George Wallace Jarman of New York City purchased the 280-acre property in an effort to relocate his children to a more healthful climate on the Eastern Shore. From 1901 to 1964 the Jarman family owned the farm they renamed Brentwood. The current owners purchased the creek farm in 1964 from Shelby Hammond Jarman.

S-398, Glanville's Lot, photograph c. 1910 (courtesy of Kelvin Adkins).

THE REWARD (NR)
1750; April 18, 1794; 1826
Williams Point
Private

First among the houses on Maryland's Eastern Shore to be dated by the tree-ring analysis known as dendrochronology, the story-and-a-half brick house called The Reward was built during the fall of 1750 for planter Elias White. Unique in the collection of early houses in Somerset County, the squarish brick dwelling is the only extant structure in Maryland to display diamond stack chimneys. As originally constructed, the Flemish bond brick house was covered with a jerkinhead roof, another feature that distinguishes it from contemporary dwellings that have survived to modern times. Not as unusual, but also indicative of the age of the house are the three corner fireplaces and the exposed, beaded second floor joists. A second date, established by the tree-ring analysis—1826—documents a major reworking of the first floor structure under the house. At the same time the stair was rebuilt and Federal style mantels were installed.

Attached to the north side of the main block is a frame hyphen that connects the house and a story-and-a-half brick-ended kitchen. The construction date of the kitchen is established by date bricks in the chimney, which are inscribed April 18, 1794.

White family occupation of this property dates from as early as 1687, when Stephen White inherited the Pocomoke Sound property from William Stevens. White's grandson Elias eventually inherited the property, then totaling 626 acres, and had it resurveyed

under the name "White's Gift" on March 9, 1759. White mortgaged large portions of his plantation, however, and during the early 1770s his holdings were divided and sold. On November 22, 1773, David Williams purchased "White's Gift" for £1,065.

One year later the Pocomoke Sound plantation was resurveyed once again as "Williams Green." David Williams died in 1782, and his wife Martha was assessed for her land the next year. Described as situated "on the Mouth of the Pocomoke," "Williams Green" consisted of 488 acres and contained "A brick wall dwelling house, three rooms below in midling repair, kitchen, barn, and other improvements indifferent." Martha Williams's estate was valued in the 1783 assessment at the impressive sum of £1,245. Her husband's will directed that after her death the property would pass to their son Thomas.

By 1798 Thomas Williams had died and his heirs, Martha and Katherine Williams, are listed in the tax assessment of that year. Their plantation was described as

Situate on the mouth of the Pocomoke River adjoining a fast Landing on said River. 1 Dwelling house 30 by 30 one Story high with 3 windows 5 1/2 by 3, 2 windows 4 1/2 by 2 1/2, and 4 windows 3 1/2 by 2 1/2, Brick walls and wood Roof, 1 Kitchen 18 by 22 with a Covered way from said Kitchen to the Dwelling house of wood...

By 1809 Amelia Gale had inherited one-half interest in "Williams Green." With her husband, General John Gale, she sold her

share in the plantation to Ralph Milbourn, who in turn sold 300 acres to John Milbourn in 1817. The reworking of the first floor took place nine years later. The Milbourns retained ownership until 1847, when John Milbourn sold the plantation to William Adams. The Williams Point farm then passed through a half-dozen hands until the current owner acquired title to the property. The dendrochronological study was completed by H.J. Heikkenen during the spring of 1989.

GLANVILLE'S LOT
Early 18th century and later
Princess Anne vicinity (site)
Private

"Glanville's Lot" is the site of a highly significant early eighteenth century brick plantation house that survived until it burned in the early twentieth century. Photographs suggest the early house, following a hall/parlor plan, dated from the first half of the eighteenth century.

Documented in photographs of the dwelling are twelve-over-twelve sash windows flanking a center door. Six gabled dormers lighted the second floor rooms. A Civil War era addition fully covered the gable end of the old brick house. Built on a raised brick foundation, the two-story weatherboarded addition was lighted by large six-over-six sash windows and trimmed with eave brackets.

"Glanville's Lot" was surveyed initially on March 11, 1663, for William Glanville. The 500-acre tract appears also in reference to the establishment of ports and towns for the advancement of trade in Maryland. Along with Rehobeth, Snow Hill, and Green Hill, an additional site was considered "on a point of Land lying in the fork of Manokin River where Captain Henry Smith formerly lived sometimes called White House." By 1740 records indicate Captain John Tunstall was living on the plantation formerly occupied by

S-227, Suffolk farm, southwest elevation.

Captain Smith and that Tunstall was operating a shipyard on the site. At the same time, a court-appointed commission was established to determine the boundaries of "Glanville's Lot" for the Reverend James Robertson, an early Episcopal minister who was later buried on the property. His expensive, imported brownstone table marker has been relocated to the Coventry Parish churchyard at Rehobeth.

SUFFOLK FARM
Circa 1700-1750
Pocomoke City vicinity
Private

"Suffolk" is the name of a 1667 land patent of 1,000 acres located on Dividing Creek near the site of the second Somerset County courthouse, which was abandoned in 1742. The single story Flemish bond walls of the extant farmhouse suggest a date in the first half of the eighteenth century. A fading coat of white paint reveals a glazed checkerboard brick pattern on the front elevation and a diaper pattern on the south gable end.

In 1922 the early house was completely gutted by fire. Shortly afterwards, a frame second story was added and the interior of the brick house was remodeled. Aside from the eighteenth century walls, the property is primarily significant as an early archeological site.

ALMODINGTON (NR)
Circa 1750
Oriole vicinity
Private

Almodington stands out as one of the most elaborate plantation houses erected in Somerset County during the mid-eighteenth century. The four brick walls exhibit the finest in masonry craftsmanship. A carefully executed glazed header checkerboard pattern distinguishes the south side, which also has gauged brick jack arches over the first and second floor windows. The window and door openings on the north side are topped by an unusual segmental arch design of alternating glazed rowlocks and unglazed soldier bricks. The plastered cove cornices that finish the

front and rear eaves are only found on a handful of contemporary houses.

Inside, the first floor was originally fitted with the best carpentry available at the time. Because of the high quality of its design and execution, the west parlor raised paneling was removed from the house and installed in the Metropolitan Museum of Art as a backdrop for mid-eighteenth century furniture. A pair of shell-carved cupboards flanked a raised panel fireplace wall, and floor to ceiling raised paneling covered the other three walls.

Although the parlor woodwork was removed, the stair hall and east room survive with mid-eighteenth century finishes. A series of turned balusters and turned posts support a molded and ramped handrail; the elaborate railing encircles the stairwell on the second floor. A raised panel partition and raised panel window reveals distinguish the east room. The Federal style mantel was evidently added at a later date. Attached to the back of the house is a two-story, one-room plan, Flemish bond wing apparently added around 1790 to 1798.

S-40, Almodington, south elevation.

The original 1,000-acre "Almodington" tract, known to the Indians as "Portoback," was officially surveyed for John Elzey on November 10, 1663. Elzey lived in the area as early as 1661, when he was named one of three commissioners to grant warrants for land and to administer the oath of allegiance to the first settlers. Elzey did not live long after his arrival: Somerset Court records document that he died at Manokin and was buried on his plantation in 1664. "Almodington" passed to Elzey's two sons, Arnold and John, Jr., but John, Jr. was dead by 1667, so Arnold became the sole owner. Arnold Elzey's plantation was platted on June 8, 1720, as a result of judicial proceedings concerning the property. As drawn, the "Almodington" tract encompassed 1,083 acres and was bordered by the Manokin River on the south, Goose Creek on the east, and St. Peter's Creek to the west. Arnold Elzey lived until 1733, and he bequeathed to his daughters, Sarah and Elizabeth, the land south of his dwelling house on the Manokin. His son John Elzey received everything else.

Despite the established tradition that the Almodington house was erected by Arnold Elzey, architectural evidence suggests Arnold's son John financed the construction during the decades following his father's death in 1733. It is entirely likely that John built his ambitious two-story brick house on the site of his father's dwelling, which is designated on the 1720 plat.

When John Elzey died in 1777, his Manokin River plantation passed to his son Arnold. Oddly, Arnold Elzey died the same year as his father, and his heirs granted "Almodington" to his brother William with the understanding the plantation was for William's use, but that he did not have the right to sell any part of it. The 1783 tax assessment listed the "Almodington" plantation under Arnold Elzey's name in spite of his earlier death. Located on the property were "1 Brick Dwelling House, two stories high, midling good repair, kitchen barns and improvements, sorry." Containing 1,242 acres and nineteen slaves, "Almodington" was assessed at £3,513.

At the death of William Elzey, Sarah Elzey Jones inherited the plantation. She was the wife of Major William Jones, who was assessed for the 1,200-acre plantation in 1798. The description suggests changes had been made to the house since 1783:

1 Dwelling House 52 by 22 feet Brick two Storey high 6 windows 5 feet 6 Inches long 3 feet wide, 1 window 5 feet 8 Inches long 2 feet 4 Inches wide, 7 windows 5 feet 6 Inches long 3 feet wide, 1 window 6 feet long 2 feet 10 inches wide, Addition to [dwelling house] 26 by 20 feet Brick two Story 5 windows 5 feet 8 Inches long 2 feet 4 Inches wide, 6 windows 4 feet 10 Inches long 2 feet 4 Inches wide, 2 windows 2 feet long 22 Inches wide, 1 Cook House 24 by 22 feet wood, two Story, 4 windows 4 feet 10 Inches long 2 feet 4 Inches wide, 4 windows 3 feet 8 Inches long 2 feet 4 Inches wide, 1 window 2 feet long 22 Inches wide, Colonade 25 by 12, 4 windows 10 inches Long 2 feet 4 inches wide 1 Smoke House 12 feet square, 1 Milk House 12 feet square, 1 Lumber House, 22 by 20 feet, 1 Stable 28 by 24 feet 1 Carige house 20 by 16 feet, 1 Nessery [necessary] 8 feet square. Value $2,000.

Architectural evidence, along with the assessment descriptions, convincingly suggests the rear two-story ell was added between 1783 and 1798 and at the same time the colonnade was built between the house and the detached frame kitchen. Also included on the plantation were three additional houses (evidently for overseers or tenant farmers); one granary; four barns; two large corn houses (one measuring 40 by 10); and three quarters, built with larger than normal dimensions (averaging 30 by 20). The size of these quarters suggests a multiple family or dormitory arrangement for William Jones's eighty slaves.

Before his death, Major William Jones partitioned his vast holdings between three principal heirs. To Sally E. Jones he bequeathed his dwelling plantation; for Arnold Elzey Jones he confirmed inheritance of property Arnold had evidently occupied since 1818 (see Elmwood, S-41); and finally to Elizabeth A. W. Jones Waters he left a third tract, later known as "Homewood" (S-39).

As the wife of John C. Wilson, Jr. of Westover Plantation, Sally E. Jones Wilson sold Almodington to her stepsister Margaret Nichols, who sold it six years later to Isaac Atkinson. With the death of Anne W. Jones at Elmwood, Isaac Atkinson purchased original "Almodington" acreage from the Elmwood estate trustee, Levin L. Waters.

Waters was again appointed trustee sixteen years later when he dissolved the estate of Isaac S. Atkinson. On December 17, 1895, Waters sold "Almodington" to Elizabeth and Lena Woolford, who held the property for close to nine years. Lois Aldrich and others purchased the farm from Elizabeth E. Woolford, and the Aldriches owned the farm for the next quarter century. Several owners followed the Aldriches until John and Mary Honnecker purchased 222 acres and the house in April 1952. The current owner bought the farm in March 1980.

ARLINGTON
Circa 1750
Westover vicinity
Private

Arlington, erected around 1750 by Ephraim Wilson, is one of a small group of buildings that exemplify an extreme in architectural achievement. For this period, only four other houses in Somerset County (Almodington, S-40; Hayward's Lott, S-74; Waterloo, S-31; and Westover, S-50) equal the high building qualities expressed by Arlington.

Constructed in the best traditions of eighteenth century masonry craftsmanship, Arlington displays a glazed checkerboard brick pattern on each elevation as well as finely rubbed jack arches on the main facade. The front corners of the house and the edges around the front windows have rubbed brick borders. The windows and doors on the other three sides have segmental arches laid with alternating glazed rowlocks or soldier bricks. Stretching across the base of the roof is a rarely found plastered cove cornice. The interior has been significantly altered by the removal of the period woodwork in the first floor rooms, although the eighteenth century staircase remains partially intact.

David Wilson, in his will of November 1750, bequeathed to his son Ephraim "My plantation on the south side of Back Creek called Wilson's Lott." Considering the architectural features of this dwelling, it was built during the following decade but prior to Ephraim Wilson's death in 1777. To his daughter Peggy, Ephraim left "the plantation whereon I now live called Wilson's Lott." Peggy C. Wilson married her cousin, John C. Wilson, Sr., who had inherited neighboring "Great Hopes" plantation (commonly known as Westover) from his father, Samuel, in 1791. Peggy and John lived at "Great Hopes" and evidently tenanted out the "Wilson Lott" plantation to a John Ellis, who is listed in the 1798 tax assessment as the occupant of

1 Dwelling House built of Brick 50 feet by 24 feet two Story High 7 windows 4 feet by 3 [feet] 10 windows 3 feet by 5 [feet], 1 Kitchen 24 feet by 25 [feet] Built of Brick Two Story high, 1 Smoke House 12 feet by 14 feet 1 Stable 16 feet by 18 feet.

The land assessment mentions 600 acres as well as 1 barn, 1 negro house, and a corn house. The property appears to have been operated under the same arrangement until Peggy Wilson's death in the early 1830s. At that time, "Wilson's Lott" was to be divided between her three sons, John C. Wilson, Jr., Edward H. C. Wilson, and Henry P. C. Wilson. Edward H. C. Wilson had died by the time the will was proved, so the property was divided between the other two sons.

Through two deeds executed in the early 1830s, John Rider acquired "Wilson's Lott" and the adjacent tract known as "Totonias." Three years later the property was sold again to John Parsons. A short time later Littleton D. Handy bought the property from John Parsons and John Rider. In June 1860 John W. Crisfield, administrator of the estate of Littleton Handy, sold "Arlington," the singular name for the two tracts, to William S. Walker. "Arlington" was later the property of William and Anna Gale, who sold it in 1866 to Jesse and Catherine Cook. Jesse M. Cook is listed in the 1877 county atlas patron schedule as owner of a 612-acre farm, having moved to Somerset from Mercer County, New Jersey. The Ring family, the present owners, acquired the farm through several deeds beginning in 1912.

WESTOVER
Circa 1750-1760
Westover vicinity
Private

Westover farm, comprising tracts formerly known as "Great Hopes" and "Dear Purchase," contains the altered but nevertheless significant mid-eighteenth century plantation house of Samuel Wilson. Wilson was one of the most influential residents of Somerset County during the second half of the eighteenth century.

The two-story, five-bay center hall house was erected on Back Creek with an ambitious plan and careful attention to detail. A generous center stair passage divides the four-room first floor. Although now covered with stucco, the exterior masonry was distinguished by the best eighteenth century craftsmanship. Similar to neighboring Arlington, built by Samuel's older brother Ephraim, the Westover walls were laid in expensive glazed header Flemish bond brick with rubbed brick arches over the doors and windows.

Despite its architectural prominence, the house was subjected to varying degrees of maintenance through the second half of the nineteenth century. One description printed by *Harper's Weekly* in 1879 called it a

fine building, broad and roomy, with an air of vanished grandeur about it Decaying as the old Westover mansion now is, fallen into ruin here and there through years of neglect and ill usage, it still stands a monument of former Eastern Shore magnificence and hospitality…Such it might have been in the old times; but

S-51, Arlington, south elevation.

S-50, Westover, southeast elevation.

*alas! it is crumbling to ruin, and its glory
is rapidly departing. The ball-room is used
as a granary.*

By the last decade of the nineteenth century, the house was evidently in such poor repair that Frederick Baldt of Chester County, Pennsylvania, reworked it by adding a thick layer of stucco. Inside, the old woodwork was replaced with high-quality, quarter-sawn oak paneling. Although all of the domestic and agricultural outbuildings have been destroyed, a significant collection of aboveground burial vaults pertaining to the Wilson and Custis families remains behind the house.

In his will of January 5, 1732, Ephraim Wilson (1664-1733) bequeathed to his grandson Ephraim a 165-acre tract known as "Great Hopes," located on the north side of Back Creek. Ephraim also inherited title to "Wilson's Lott" in 1750 from his father, David Wilson (1704-1750). Since Ephraim owned "Wilson's Lott" on the south side of Back Creek, he transferred ownership of "Great Hopes" to his brother Samuel in June 1758.

David Wilson specifically states in his will that "Colonel George Gale, Ephraim King, Richard Waters, and my son Ephraim should take charge of my son Samuel and his estate until he arrives to the age of one and twenty." Throughout the following half century, Samuel Wilson amassed a tremendous agricultural and minor industrial complex at the head of Back Creek. In addition, he was a key figure in locating and building the Back Creek Academy (later known as the Washington Academy) in 1767.

The 1783 tax assessment of Samuel Wilson's property mentions "a brick dwelling house, two story high and kitchen, good, other improvements sorry." The value of his "Great Hopes" plantation house was set at £1,800, while his total worth was established at a tremendous £3,531. Seven years later Samuel Wilson's will was entered in the Somerset records. Most of his property was bequeathed to his son John Custis Wilson:

*I give the plantation whereon I live called
Great Hopes, except the small part which*

*runs from the new bridge to the north-
west corner of the academy land and so
with the line of the same up to a pine by a
ditch near the mill, to my son John.*

In 1798 the federal assessors once more described "Great Hopes," then containing 1,200 acres, along with 3,200 acres known as "Dear Purchase." John Wilson's dwelling plantation was described as

*1 Dwelling house 45 feet by 38 feet Brick,
two story…1 Kitchen 26 by 24 feet, two
stor[y] brick…Colonade 20 feet long 10
feet wide, 1 Smoke house 15 feet square,
1 Milk house 18 by 14 feet, 1 Stable 34
by 26 feet…1 Turkey house 14 by 12 feet,
1 Carige house 30 by 24 feet, 1 Lumber
house 20 by 16 feet, all in good repair.*

It is thought the house was enlarged with another colonnade and a ballroom during John Custis Wilson's ownership, making it one of the most impressive dwellings in the Somerset County of his day. Wilson and his

S-74, Hayward's Lott, east elevation.

wife Peggy lived at Great Hopes until their deaths in the early 1830s. John devised his property to his two sons, John Jr. and Henry P.C. Wilson. He stipulated in his will that his daughter Sally and her children, "the children of my son Edward and their heirs shall hold and enjoy the estate called and known by the name of 'Clifton.'"

Family ownership of "Great Hopes" and "Dear Purchase," by then known as Westover, did not continue long after John Wilson's death. John C. Wilson, Jr. and his wife Sally sold the plantation on May 23, 1832, to William Roach for $15,000. Roach turned around and sold the property four years later for the same price to George C. Jenkins, who then held on to it for thirteen years. Between 1849 and 1886, Westover was transferred three times. In November 1886 Frederick Baldt bought the estate from Edmund B. and Sarah Cook. It was during Baldt's twenty-one year occupation that the house was thoroughly reworked. The current owners' family purchased the farm in September 1917.

HAYWARD'S LOTT (NR)
Circa 1750-1760
Pocomoke City vicinity
Private

Hayward's Lott stands out as one of the largest and most expensive of Somerset County's mid-eighteenth century plantation houses to survive to modern times. In contrast to its contemporaries Almodington and Arlington, Hayward's Lott was built on a larger scale with all four walls executed in costly glazed brick checkerboard patterns. As at the other two houses, narrowly gauged rubbed brick arches top each of the front windows and segmental arches of alternating glazed bricks distinguish the other openings. The base of the house is defined by a bold molded water table, and rising through the gable ends are T-shaped chimneys.

The center hall floor plan of Hayward's Lott is defined by two rooms to the north and a large, single room to the south. Sadly, aside from a few doors, very little of the eighteenth century woodwork survived an exten-

sive renovation during the second quarter of the nineteenth century.

The original patent for "Hayward's Lott" dates to 1734, when Thomas Hayward had a 740-acre tract encompassing parts of "Williams Hope" and "Blake's Hope" resurveyed. The survey description mentions "ye now dwelling house of ye afsd Hayward," but the directional information outlining the metes and bounds indicates the first Hayward house was sited a short distance northwest of the present dwelling. Thomas Hayward, a longtime clerk of the Somerset court, died in April 1751. The plantation passed to his son Thomas, and it is reasonable to suggest he initiated the construction of this impressive house during the 1750s, at the same time the walls of Almodington and Arlington are thought to have been built. In 1753 Hayward married Sarah Elzey, daughter of John and Anne Elzey, linking two of the most powerful families in Somerset County. The Elzeys had Almodington built at about the same time, and it is not surprising that the two brick dwellings share so many similar features.

Thomas and Sarah Hayward maintained ownership of the impressive plantation through the Revolutionary War, and in 1783 the property was assessed with over 1,000 acres. At the time, the assessors found on the plantation a two-story brick dwelling as well as another brick house, "both in good repair." The total assessment, which included thirty-one slaves, was valued at £2,140.

When Thomas Hayward died in 1793, his will provided clear indications of his intentions. Hayward's Lott was to pass to his son John, and after John's decease to his grandson Thomas. With John's death in 1803, the plantation passed to the designated heir. However, Thomas Hayward died before his mother, Elizabeth, who devised the property in 1810 to another son, John Elzey Hayward.

It was during John Elzey Hayward's long ownership of the old plantation that the interiors of the house were heavily reworked. Family ownership of Hayward's Lott continued until the present owners purchased the house and eighty-six acres in 1948.

WATERLOO (NR)
Circa 1750-1760
Princess Anne vicinity
Private

Built around 1750 Waterloo is architecturally significant for several reasons. First, it is one of five prominent pre-Revolutionary War Somerset plantation houses. This collection of brick houses represents the height of architectural achievement on Maryland's Eastern Shore by the mid-eighteenth century. The brickwork of this two-story, Georgian style house displays carefully laid glazed brick checkerboard and diamond patterns in Flemish bond walls. Another distinction is that Waterloo is the only house on the lower Shore to have bold quoins on the three principal corners. The house is also pivotal in local design traditions, for it is the earliest example of a gable-front main elevation, an orientation not widely used until the following century. The four-room plan contains a mixture of Georgian and Federal period woodwork. The most dynamic feature is the triple-flight twisted baluster stair, one of only a few to survive in Maryland.

Henry Waggaman, the attributed builder, figures prominently in the history of Somerset County as well as of the state. He was one of the most distinguished landowners of his day and served as an elder of the Manokin Presbyterian Church. From 1750 until his death in 1760, he was a member of the Provincial Assembly of Maryland.

In the nineteenth century the property was owned by several prominent local families, including the Teackles, Rigginses, Handys, and Wainwrights, until 1864, when the county purchased the farm for an almshouse. The county retained ownership of the Monie Creek property until 1948.

Waterloo stands on a tract of land first known as "Carey's Purchase," patented to Richard Carey on November 20, 1666. Seventy-five years later Henry Waggaman, originally from the Eastern Shore of Virginia, purchased the Monie Creek land from Edward Chambers, "a collector of His Majesties Customs at Port Pocomoke." During the period from his initial purchase in 1741 until his death in 1760, Waggaman bought and sold numerous properties in central Somerset County. His wife, Mary Woolford Waggaman, also apparently inherited a sizable estate from her mother, Sarah Woolford.

It is thought the resources acquired from selling some of his wife's property combined with profits from his 1,000-acre plantation and merchant enterprises enabled Waggaman to finance the best in local craftsmanship for the construction of this ambitious dwelling. In 1751 he had his plantation consolidated under a resurvey known as "Waggaman's Purchase." Henry Waggaman's will was proved on June 25, 1761. To his eldest son, John Elliot Waggaman, he left

the whole of my lands lying on Great Mony being one tract of land called Waggaman's Purchase and part of two other tracts called Abbington, and the other called Carney Chance.

His wife, Mary, evidently remained on the property until her death in 1780. John Elliot Waggaman must have died before his mother, since her sons Henry and George are the only ones mentioned in her will.

Three years after Mary Waggaman's death, the federal assessors listed the Monie Hundred plantation on the 1783 tax assessment. Their description of the buildings reads

Brick Dwelling House, two-story high, good kitchen, barn and other improvements midling.

Henry Waggaman married Sarah Ennalls of Dorchester County and lived at Fairview near Cambridge. Since he lived outside Somerset, he sold his interests in his father's estate to his brother George in April 1793 for £3,000. Five years later the tax assessors recorded the plantation of George Waggaman as 1,726 acres and

1 Dwelling house 40 by 36 feet, Brick, two story high, 6 windows 7 feet long, 3 feet 4 Inches wide, 7 windows 4 feet 10 inches long, 2 feet 4 inches wide—out of repair—1 Cook house, 24 by 22 feet, brick, 1 Smoke house 10 feet square, 1 Milk house 8 by 6 feet, 1 Stable 20 by 18 feet with 10 foot Sheads on the side.

George Waggaman died intestate in the

S-31, Waterloo, south elevation.

following year, and because none of his heirs lived in Somerset County the family decided to sell the plantation. In 1803 Henry Waggaman advertised his father's estate in the *Eastern Shore Herald and Intelligencer*, an Easton-based paper:

> *I will sell about 1500 acres of land. Situated at the Head of Mani Creek about four miles from Princess Anne in Somerset County. There is on said lands a large brick dwelling house two stories high with an entry and three good rooms on a floor; the out houses are all good; the place has been for some years rented and of course out of repair as to the enclosures. It is among the handsomest situations in that county and it cannot be exceeded by any lands on the Eastern Shore for the finest timber. If the lands are not sold by the second Monday of January next, they will be laid off in lots of about 500 acres each to suit purchasers, and offered at public sale.*

Although the property was purchased the following August, the plantation was divided between buyers. Littleton Dennis Teackle acquired the house and 906 acres, while Levin Jones bought the balance of the estate. Neither purchaser held onto the property for long, though, and by 1815, after several transfers, George Riggin had purchased approximately half the acreage and the plantation buildings. Riggin occupied the plantation until his death around 1840, when his trustee, William Riggin, sold the property to Edmund Weatherly. Weatherly had lived on the farm for little more than a decade when he evidently died, and the property had to be divided equitably by the Somerset Court. The land was finally sold on September 4, 1855, "at half past two o'clock p.m. at the Court House door in Princess Anne." George E. Austin of Dorchester County purchased the property but soon afterwards transferred ownership to Dr. Littleton Handy. Handy lived on the farm only a few years, and at his death the property entered Chancery Court once more. In the settlement, John W. Crisfield, trustee, finally granted the property to Ware Wainwright on January 13, 1864. The plantation, for the first time, was referred to as "Waterloo, which formerly belonged to Littleton Handy." Six months later Wainwright sold the Waterloo property to the Trustees of the Poor of Somerset County for the county almshouse. Waterloo remained under county ownership until 1948 and was known at that time as the "Poor House Farm." H. Brittingham Roberts purchased the reduced acreage and the house in February 1948. The current owner acquired the farm in 1971.

WADDY HOUSE (NR)
Circa 1750
Princess Anne vicinity
Private

Built during the middle years of the eighteenth century (1740-1760), the Waddy house belongs to a small collection of early brick dwellings surviving in Somerset County. Contemporary with Williams Green (S-64) and Makepeace (S-81), the house displays similar features, such as glazed checkerboard brick wall patterns and segmental brick arches spanning the window and door openings. The story-and-a-half, three-bay brick house is a squarish structure with four rooms partitioned on the first floor. The interior retains a significant portion of its mid-eighteenth century woodwork with a raised panel overmantel in the parlor and a turned baluster stair in the hall.

Interestingly, the Waddy house repeats the fine glazed header Flemish bond wall construction and alternating glazed brick segmental arch pattern found at Almodington and Arlington. This similarity may be explained by historical associations that join the Elzey and Ballard families.

On November 26, 1754, Jarvis Ballard purchased from James and William Gray three tracts of land located near the head of the Manokin River for £181.5.0. John Gray had purchased the three parcels, known as "Derry," "Illchester" (or "Goldsmith's Delight"), and "Smith's Resolve," in the early part of the eighteenth century and bequeathed them in his will. Even though the three tracts are not mentioned specifically in the will of 1730, Gray did indicate that his "now dwelling plantation called Killmonum" would be inherited by his son William. With John Gray's dwelling located on the "Killmonum" tract, it is unlikely this prominent brick house was built before Jarvis Ballard's

purchase in 1754. The mid-eighteenth century date for the house is supported by its fine Georgian style finishes.

Jarvis Ballard evidently died in 1765, and the property passed to his son William, although no will has been found to confirm the inheritance. William Ballard is cited on the 1783 tax assessment with the same tracts of land his father had owned as well as a fourth parcel called "Ballard and King's Lot." The house description is vague: "One Dwelling House, good, Kitchen and other improvements, sorry." Ballard's property was assessed at £457.

The federal assessors in 1798, however, left no question as to the size and construction of William Ballard's house. They found the following structures on the plantation:

1 Dwelling house 32 by 32 feet one story Brick 4 windows 5 feet 8 Inches long, 2 feet 4 Inches wide, 3 [windows] 4 feet 10 Inches long 2 feet 4 Inches wide in midling repair, 1 Cook house 20 by 16 feet, wood, 1 Smoke house 10 feet square, 1 Stable 16 feet Sqr.

William Ballard held his father's plantation until 1803, when he sold it for £1,503 to Lambert Hyland. Although Hyland died intestate, it is presumed the property passed to Henry Hyland, for he sold the land to Marshall McDaniel for $2,000 in 1836. During the following thirty-six years, the composite property was sold three times. In 1872 William B. Williamson purchased the farm for $2,250. Williamson's name appears in the 1877 county atlas at this location, and he is listed in the atlas patron list as a former resident of Bucks County, Pennsylvania, who moved to Somerset in 1869. Subsequent owners include Amanda and Emma Lankford, who purchased the farm in 1893, and William E. Waddy, whose father bought the property in 1914.

S-87, Waddy house, southwest elevation.

S-83, Harrington, south elevation.

HARRINGTON (NR)
Circa 1750
Mount Vernon vicinity
Private

Located east of the Wicomico River and south of what is now called Stone Creek is the mid-eighteenth century house known as Harrington. Thomas Holbrook is credited with the construction of this four-room plan house following his acquisition of the family lands in 1741. The Holbrook plantation was assessed in 1798, and the property was described as follows:

Situated within One mile of Wiccomico River Near the Lower ferry, a Dwelling house of wood considerably Injured by worms Two Story 30 by 28 feet finish'd in plain order with five windows 64 Inches by 28 Inches, Two [windows] 64

Inches by 36 Inches, seven [windows] 54 Inches by 28 Inches, One [window] 44 Inches by 28 Inches, four windows 24 Inches by 20 Inches, Very Old Kitchen 47 by 20 feet, Smoke house, old 12 by 12 feet, Milk house 8 by 6 feet, Lumber House, Old, 24 by 12 feet...

The plantation lands included close to 1,000 acres, part of which was a tenant farm located near the "Witch Bridge" and improved with an old log dwelling, 16' by 14' with an end shed of 8', and a log barn measuring 20' by 20'. The tenant farm was operated by Samuel Covington.

Although the house was described as finished in "plain order," this phrase probably referred only to the exterior, for the interior of this two-story, three-bay frame house was fitted with finely crafted mid-eighteenth century Georgian paneling that has survived

largely unaltered. The first floor is divided into four rooms of unequal size with the stair hall in the southwest corner. East of the stair hall is the largest room, which was finished with exposed, beaded-edge floor joists; raised panel wainscoting; and a well-crafted chimney breast. Fluted pilasters flank the four raised panels over the fireplace. The other two rooms were fitted with fireplaces as well. Attached to the east gable end of the old house is a modern gambrel-roofed addition.

The initial patent for Harrington, dating to 1680, was assigned to Thomas Holbrook. Holbrook first surfaces in Somerset County records for his marriage to Alice Leverton in August 1676. He is also listed as a vestryman of Stepney Parish. In his will of 1717 he bequeathed his plantation to his son Thomas, and the property subsequently passed through four or five additional generations of Thomas Holbrooks.

S-400, Gunby-Lankford house, photograph c. 1885 (courtesy of Mrs. James L. Watts).

BANNISTER HOUSE
Circa 1770
Westover vicinity
Private

On the south side of the Manokin River on the eastern edge of Revells Neck is the Bannister house, a mid-eighteenth century, single story, three-bay Flemish bond brick structure on a raised brick foundation. The exterior and interior have been significantly altered, but the house retains a few original details. The north and east walls are laid in well-executed Flemish bond with a glazed header checkerboard pattern. A three-course belt course decorates the north gable end.

The Bannister house stands on land known as "Part of Double Purchase," which was occupied by the Bannister family through the late seventeenth and eighteenth centuries. In 1783 Charles Bannister's heirs were taxed for 160 acres that contained "One Dwelling

S-243, Bannister house, south elevation.

S-36, Cherry Grove, south elevation.

House and cellar, good, all other improvements sorry." Bannister's will provided that his wife Leah receive his entire estate, and after her death the property was inherited by Charles's sister, Ann Bannister Bowen, wife of Captain William Bowen. In 1798 the federal assessors found the following on the Bowens' part of "Double Purchase":

One Dwelling house 32 by 25 feet, one story Brick with 4 windows 4 feet 10 Inches long 2 feet 4 Inches wide, 4 windows 3 feet 8 Inches long 2 feet 4 Inches wide, in good repair.

The Rogers family purchased the farm in the 1960s.

GUNBY-LANKFORD HOUSE
Mid to late 18th century and later
Cash Corner vicinity (site)
Private

The Gunby-Lankford house formerly stood in southern Somerset County near Gunby Creek, a tributary of Pocomoke Sound. A photograph taken around 1885 captures not only the house but the contemporary Lankford occupants as well. The photograph indicates the house was erected in two distinct periods, the middle of the eighteenth century and the early part of the nineteenth century.

The far end, as depicted in the photograph, was a story-and-a-half, three-bay frame structure with a shed porch built across the front. The second floor rooms of this eighteenth century structure were lighted by traditional gabled dormers. Attached to the gable end of this house was an early nineteenth century two-story, four-bay frame addition with an exterior end chimney of brick. The asymmetrical front elevation had alternating doors and windows, while the second floor was lighted by four six-over-six sash windows.

Captured in the photograph were nine Lankford family members posing in front of the picket fence. From left to right were William Lankford, Cornelia Lankford (1849-1929), James Lankford, Sally Lankford, Julia Ann Lankford (1825-1898), Benjamin Lankford (1798-1886), Sarah Lankford Miles (1830-1898), Clara Miles Hodson, and Roman Lankford.

CHERRY GROVE
Circa 1750, circa 1825, circa 1900
Princess Anne vicinity
Private

The house that stands on Cherry Grove farm south of Princess Anne along Stewart Neck Road dates from three distinct periods. The westernmost section, a two-story, hall/parlor plan brick dwelling that has been stuccoed and converted to a kitchen wing, was probably built during the middle of the eighteenth century. Despite the modifications, this old brick house retains some early sash windows as well as raised panel wainscoting in the old "hall." The former parlor was divided to accommodate an early nineteenth century Federal style stair. Also added during the early nineteenth century was a single story brick section attached to the east gable end of the old house. After the turn of the twentieth century, the old house was enlarged once more with a frame addition that reoriented the dwelling from Jones Creek to the road. The only significant outbuilding is a one-room frame office due west of the house. Supported by a raised brick foundation, the beaded weatherboard structure is finished inside with plaster and lath as well as early nineteenth century woodwork.

Credit for the construction of the mid-eighteenth century brick house goes to Thomas Jones, who patented a resurvey called "Bridger's Lot" in 1748. The plantation, encompassing 370 acres on the north side of Jones Creek, passed to Thomas's only son, William, in 1766. William retained ownership of his father's creek plantation until 1807, when he transferred title to his son Thomas. The property remained in the Jones family until 1830, when William W. Handy purchased the 370-acre farm from Ephraim K. Wilson, the estate trustee.

In 1857 William W. Handy's executor, William C. Handy, sold the farm to Dr. Cadmus Dashiell. The front addition was built either by Sidney C. and S. Upshur Long, who owned the house at the turn of the century, or by Effie L. Kemp, who acquired title to Cherry Grove in 1907. In more recent times the farm has been held by the Croswell and Bailey families.

TURPIN'S PURCHASE
Mid to late 18th century
Manokin vicinity
Private

Located along the south shore of Back Creek facing an expansive cove is this two-story, stuccoed brick dwelling scored to imitate ashlar construction. Belt courses and glazed brick patterns visible under the flaking stucco as well as remnants of mid-eighteenth century woodwork suggest this house was heavily reworked during the early nineteenth century when the property was held by Whitty Turpin Fontaine.

Through the 1794 will of John Mason Fontaine, Whitty and his brothers and sisters inherited part of their uncle's land known as

"Turpin's Purchase." Four years later Whitty was listed on the federal tax assessment as owning a 446-acre tract of land called "Turpin's Purchase" and improved by

1 Dwelling House built of Brick, 30 feet Square, Two Storey high 6 windows 5 1/2 feet by 3 feet, 9 windows 5 1/2 feet by 2 1/2 feet, 1 Milk House 12 feet by 8 feet, 1 Smoake House 10 feet Square, 1 Kitchen 24 feet by 18 feet, The above Buildings out of repair.

After the turn of the century Whitty evidently reworked his uncle's old house by applying a coat of stucco and introducing a center stair.

Fontaine occupied the Back Creek plantation until the mid-nineteenth century, when he bequeathed "my dwelling house" to his daughter Margaret Hall. By 1877 the county atlas records William H. Ross as owner of the house and 800 acres. Mary A. Ross acquired full interest in the property in 1892 and passed it on to her son Charles A. Lankford in 1917.

BLOOMSBURY
Mid to late 18th century
Venton vicinity (site)
Private

"Bloomsbury Plantation" figures prominently in the history of Somerset County as the lands of Levin Winder, governor of Maryland during the War of 1812. Located on the south side of Little Monie Creek, the "Bloomsbury" tract was created in 1787 as a resurvey for Thomas Sloss. Sloss had acquired ownership of parts of several adjacent tracts, including "Bloyce's Hope," "Malborough," "Success," and "Pennywise," through his marriage to Mary Stoughton in October 1750. Mary was the daughter of William Stoughton, who had purchased these and other tracts early in the eighteenth century.

S-85, Turpin's Purchase, southwest elevation.

S-407, Levin and Mary Stoughton Winder, portraits c. 1793 by William Clarke (courtesy of Baltimore Museum of Art, Friends of the American Fund, BMA 1981.165).

Thomas and Mary Sloss probably began construction of the large brick house; however, it was listed as unfinished in the federal tax assessment of 1798, the year following Thomas's death. Thomas's will, proved in May 1797, divided the "Bloomsbury" lands between the couple's two daughters, Mary Stoughton Sloss Winder and Ann Stoughton Sloss Gantt. To Mary went half the land along with the dwelling house and outbuildings except for the barn. This plantation complex is apparently the one the federal assessors listed under the ownership of Levin Winder, Mary's husband, in 1798. The improvements were described as

1 Dwelling house 50 by 36 Brick two story high, 4 windows 7 feet 6 Inches long, 3 feet 9 Inches wide, 2 windows 6 feet long 1 foot 9 Inches wide, 8 windows 7 feet 6 Inches long 3 feet wide, 2 windows 5 feet long 21 Inches wide, 6 windows 6 feet 6 Inches long, 3 feet wide; 8 windows 6 feet 6 inches long, 3 feet wide; 4 windows 3 feet

long 21 inches wide, not finished and Brick work very Indifferent, 1 Cook house & Colonade 37 by 19 feet Brick one story, 3 windows, 3 feet 8 Inches long, 2 feet 4 Inches wide, 1 window 3 feet 3 Inches long 21 Inches wide, 1 Smoke house 12 feet square, 1 Stable 32 by 22 feet, 1 Carriage House 19 by 15, 1 Necessary 8 feet Sqr.

Levin Winder acquired the balance of the Bloomsbury plantation from his wife's sister and her husband in 1808, thereby controlling close to 1,000 acres along the Little Monie. Winder commissioned artist William Clarke to paint portraits of himself and his wife. The painting of Winder includes a partial rendering of a plantation complex, presumably Bloomsbury.

These portraits were executed in 1793 after Winder, who had reached the rank of lieutenant-colonel, had been retired from military duty for ten years. In 1806, at age fifty-nine, he entered public life once again to represent Somerset County in the Mary-

land House of Delegates. After he had served three one-year terms, the General Assembly elected him governor of Maryland in 1812. As a representative of the Federalist Party, Winder opposed a declaration of war against Great Britain in 1812. During the War of 1812 he sought federal and state aid to protect the Chesapeake from British warships. He was reelected governor in 1813 and 1814. Afterwards he served in the state Senate until his death in 1819.

Mary S. Winder evidently remained at Bloomsbury until her death in 1822. The family lands passed to William Sydney Winder and his wife, Araminta Rogers; however, William was forced to mortgage the creek plantation several times during the late 1820s and 1830s. In 1841 he finally sold the property to Samuel G. Holbrook, who resided on the plantation until his death in 1854. Two years later Samuel's widow, Mary L. Holbrook, transferred title to Bloomsbury to Nathan L. Langford (also spelled Lankford), in whose family the property has remained to this day.

Lankford family traditions relate that when Nathan purchased the farm in 1856, the old Winder house had been abandoned for several years and had reached a seriously deteriorated condition. The brick house was eventually replaced by a plain early twentieth century frame dwelling that now stands empty along the Little Monie.

WINDSOR (NR)
Circa 1767, 1797
Cokesbury vicinity
Private

Although it was known as the Burton Cannon farm during a large part of the nineteenth century, the construction of this house and early history of the property involves the Costen family, relatives of Burton Cannon. The main house dates from two distinct eighteenth century periods. The western half of the story-and-a-half house is a brick-ended structure evidently erected during the 1760s by Isaac Costen and his wife Sarah. A crudely etched date of 1762 or 1767 was found in this portion of the house during restoration in the 1950s and 60s. In 1797 Henry Costen enlarged the part brick, part frame hall plan house with the construction of a two-room addition that gave the dwelling an L shape. A 1797 dated brick and the initials "H. C." document date and owner. The interiors of the first floor rooms in both sections retain notable examples of eighteenth century woodwork. The parlor in the 1760s section is especially significant with a paneled fireplace wall and raised panel wainscoting.

Henry Costen's house is situated on a tract of land that was resurveyed in 1793 under the name "Windsor." Comprising parts of "Bear Point" and "Flatland," "Windsor" contained 482 1/4 acres west of Dividing Creek. "Flatland" was a tract surveyed and granted to Isaac Costen in 1764, while "Bear

S-77, *Windsor, southwest elevation.*

Point" had been owned by the Costen family since 1679, when the 500-acre survey was granted to Stephen Costen.

Isaac and Sarah Costen's son Henry inherited the "Windsor" tract after his mother's death in 1788. Henry financed the addition to his parent's house in 1797, and he was assessed the following year for this building:

about 9 miles from Princess anne Town, 1 Dwelling house 46 feet Long and thirty feet thereof 18 feet wide and the other 16 feet of its Length is 30 feet wide,…Built one End Brick Rest wood, one Story high.

Henry Costen died in 1807, and his widow, Anne, married John H. Cannon in 1813. As a result of a court settlement in 1828 involving Anne's dower rights in the property, the plantation house and acreage were sold to Burton Cannon, Jr., Anne's nephew. Cannon and Matilda C. Harris, married in January 1827, occupied Windsor plantation until the mid-nineteenth century.

In 1849 possession of the property was transferred to William M. N. B. Costen, who was developing one of the most impressive agricultural estates in the eastern portion of Somerset County. Costen probably used the property as a tenant farm, since he already lived a short distance south of it (see S-76). Costen's son and administrator sold the farm to Levin J. Butler in 1892, and Butler family ownership continued until 1914. Between 1914 and 1957 seven different owners held title to the property. In 1957 John Truden purchased the house and eighty-one acres and executed a carefully planned restoration that saved the dwelling from further decay. The present owners acquired the farm in 1974.

KINGSTON HALL (NR)
Circa 1780-1783
Kingston
Private

Extensive architectural and historical research has made the development of Kingston Hall much clearer than expected for an eighteenth century house. During the past half-century, historians who have tried to determine an exact date of construction have given estimates ranging throughout the first half of the eighteenth century. However, new information indicates Thomas King built Kingston Hall during the last two decades of the eighteenth century.

Similar to other "telescope" or stepped dwellings, this three-part brick house was built in stages. Construction was begun towards the end of the American Revolution, for Thomas King was assessed in 1783 for "A new dwelling house with two rooms, a hall and entry below, Part of woodwork unfinished." Fifteen years later King's plantation was described a second time by the federal assessors:

1 Dwelling House built of Brick 40 by 34 feet, Two Story high, 7 windows 5 1/2 feet by 3 1/2 feet, 10 windows 4 feet 8 inches by 2 1/2 feet, 4 garret windows 3 1/2 feet by 2 1/2 feet, 1 Kitchen built of Brick 24 feet Square, two Story high, 1 Dairy or Milk House 14 feet square, 1 Smoake House 11 feet 9 Inches Square, 1 Stable 35 feet by 26 feet, 1 Carriage house 20 feet by 16 feet, 1 very old Hen House 20 feet by 15 feet.

This second, more complete description specifies the surrounding outbuildings, most notably the two-story brick kitchen, which was built either at the same time as the house or between the two assessments. The single story colonnade, not mentioned in the assessment, was evidently erected after 1798 to connect the main house and domestic services.

Kingston Hall is architecturally significant for several reasons. In addition to being a prominent example of the colonnaded plantation house, it displays the earliest known local use of a Palladian-style projecting pavilion capped with a decorated pediment. Inside, the most important original woodwork is

S-63, Kingston Hall, south elevation.

located in the entry, and the hall is fitted with floor-to-ceiling raised paneling. The hall is the only fully paneled room to survive in Somerset County. Equally noteworthy features include the remnants of a wood-pin roof over the front pavilion and early finishes in the old kitchen. The conical-roofed brick icehouse is a rare outbuilding and one of a small collection of circular farm structures in Maryland.

Kingston Hall stands on a tract of land known as "Conclusion," which consisted of three separate tracts called "Straights," "Johnson's," and "Everden's Lot." These three tracts were consolidated under a resurvey initiated by Robert King II in 1728/29. Totalling 1,500 acres, the Annemessex River lands were specifically mentioned in King's will of 1755:

I give and devise unto my grandson Thomas King and to his heirs and assigns for ever, all my lands situate lying and being on the south side of Great Annemessex River and head thereof where his deceased father first settled.

Thomas King occupied the "Conclusion" tract through the remainder of the eighteenth century, and after his death around 1800 the property passed to his only child, Elizabeth Barnes King, who married Colonel Henry James Carroll. The Carrolls lived in the house through the early nineteenth century, and after Henry's death in 1818 their son Thomas King Carroll acquired control of the plantation. Thomas King Carroll held several prominent county and state offices, including a one-year term as governor of Maryland (1830-1831). Carroll began his political career as a state delegate (1816-1817), and then became a judge of the Somerset County Levy Court (1825-1826). Between 1826 and 1829 he presided over the Somerset Orphans Court. The Carrolls' daughter, Anna Ella Carroll (1815-

S-35, *Glebe house, east elevation.*

1894), was born at Kingston Hall.

The Annemessex River plantation did not remain in the Carroll family, however. A suit was filed in Somerset Court against Thomas King Carroll in an effort to retrieve accumulated debts, and a court-appointed sheriff, Samuel G. Holbrook, sold Kingston Hall to John Upshur Dennis in September 1837. With Dennis's death in 1851, the estate passed to his son George Robertson Dennis (1822-1882), a prominent politician who served in the Maryland House of Delegates, the state Senate, and finally the United States Senate.

Following the death of George R. Dennis, Kingston Hall was transferred in a court settlement to Alice J. Wood. Subsequent owners have included Harry T. and Vera B. Phoebus, Charlton and Virginia Gunter, and several others. The current owners purchased the house in 1975.

GLEBE HOUSE
1784
Princess Anne vicinity
Private

Specific dimensions recorded in the vestry minutes of Somerset Parish document the construction of this story-and-a-half brick and frame house south of Princess Anne. On March 5, 1784, the vestry considered the state of the house on the glebe and unanimously agreed,

it is necessary to build on the said Glebe a Dwelling House twenty eight feet long and

thirty feet wide, a meat house ten feet square, a stable eighteen by ten both of sawed logs, a framed milk house eight feet square, ordered that the advertisement be immediately set up in the most public places.

Thirteen days later a contract was struck with William Bowland for the sum of £368.7.6, with the house to be completed by December.

The vestry of Somerset Parish retained ownership of the glebe until December 1799, when the property was transferred to John Byrd for £300. Byrd sold it the following year to John and George Parker. John Parker's estate was settled in 1831, and his heirs sold "Davis's Choice," where the glebe house stood, as well as other tracts "on the main road from Princess Anne to Washington Academy" to Littleton Redden. Redden's son Littleton J. Redden died intestate, and John W. B. Parsons was appointed a trustee to sell the plantation. He did so on June 14, 1838, to Edward Long. The Long family retained possession until 1874, when the "Redden or Parker land," as it was known then, was conveyed to William J. Porter. The 140-acre farm was subsequently transferred to Milton F. Hickman and then to the Kings Creek Canning Company.

The old glebe house stands on land initially known as "Davis's Choice," a 600-acre tract patented to James and Margaret Davis on May 10, 1666. Three years later the Davises sold the land, situated along the

S-34, Beverly, east elevation.

upper fork of the Manokin River, to Henry and John Smith. In 1682 Henry Smith of Sussex County, Pennsylvania (later Delaware), sold 130 acres of "Davis's Choice" to Jacob Waring, who had the property resurveyed as "Turner's Purchase." Waring did not own the property for long but sold it to Reverend Thomas Wilson, minister of Manokin Presbyterian Church from 1685/6 to 1698. Reverend Wilson died circa 1702, and his granddaughter Margaret Lindow eventually inherited "Turner's Purchase." Margaret and her husband, James Lindow, occupied the property during the second quarter of the eighteenth century. Margaret Lindow continued to reside on the plantation until 1742, when she sold "Turner's Purchase" to the vestrymen of Somerset Parish for £280. A confirmatory deed executed in December 1747 by David Wilson of Ephraim states, "the land called Turner's Purchase, containing 130 acres formerly occupied by Reverend Thomas Wilson, deceased, grandfather of said David Wilson, whereon a certain Margaret Lindow formerly lived."

The nearly square (28'4" by 30'3") glebe house consists of three weatherboarded walls and a south gable end of Flemish bond brick with a projecting water table. The current appearance of the house is the result of an extensive restoration that included the removal of a full second floor added during the second quarter of the twentieth century. The

roof pitch as well as the roof construction were restored from evidence taken from the house as well as from a documentary photograph made before the second floor was added. Restoration was accomplished through the efforts of Old Princess Anne Days, Inc.

A large part of the late eighteenth century woodwork in the first floor remains intact, making the interior the most significant aspect of the dwelling. The first floor is divided into four rooms of unequal size, two heated by corner fireplaces and two (those on the north) unheated. The northeast corner room contains a quarter-turn closed stringer stair anchored by a bulbous turned newel post. The molded handrail is supported by a series of turned balusters. Raised panel fireplace walls distinguish the two south rooms.

BEVERLY (NR)
1785-1796
Princess Anne vicinity
Private

Often cited as one of the most impressive houses on the lower Eastern Shore of Maryland, Beverly is an architectural representation of the highest level of wealth achieved in the region during the post-Revolutionary era. Erected in a similar vein were nearby Workington (1793) and the Palladian style houses on the eastern and western shores of Virginia.

Measuring sixty feet across by forty feet deep, Beverly is distinguished by an impressive two-and-a half story, five-bay east elevation. Centered on the facade is a two-story, three-sided pavilion capped by a semi-octagonal roof. The steeply pitched hip roof has two gabled dormers, and twin brick chimneys rise from the core of the structure.

As were its aforementioned contemporaries, Beverly was planned on a generous scale with formal interiors enriched with Federal style woodwork. Common to many late eighteenth century houses is its broad center passage, which was often used for entertaining. To keep the passage space unobstructed, the stair was confined to its own room in the northwest corner.

The centerpiece to this King's Creek plantation was the brick dwelling, but estate and tax records describe an extensive complex of domestic and agricultural buildings that accompanied the house. In addition to the "elegant Brick dwelling house in good and compleat repair," assessors for the Somerset Orphans Court in August 1804 found another framed dwelling, an old kitchen, one large new quarter, one barn with two side sheds, "one elegant granary," one stable with two side sheds, one new corn house, one old corn house, one smokehouse, one milk house, one lumber house, one meat house, one schoolhouse, one necessary house, one blacksmith shop, one windmill, a poultry house, one

S-49, Workington, photograph c. 1918 (courtesy of Mrs. Charles Wainwright).

other stable, and an icehouse. Planted in the surrounding fields were 350 apple trees, 350 peach trees, and another 150 apple and peach trees. The assessors also stated in their report that one third of the land was to be cultivated in Indian corn annually and that they believed none of the tobacco lots should be cultivated in Indian corn.

Beverly was built by Nehemiah King II (1755-1802) on land that had been passed down through three generations since its original purchase in the late seventeenth century. Nehemiah's great-grandfather, Robert King I, developed a large plantation between King's and Back creeks before his death in 1696. In fact, Beverly stands on the tract of land originally known as "Beverly," purchased from Christopher Rousby in 1681. The "Beverly" name was dropped since Robert King's plantation was known as Kingsland. Robert King I died intestate, so his lands were devised to his only son and heir, Robert King II, who bequeathed his estate in 1755 to his son Nehemiah. Nehemiah King I occupied the old Kingsland plantation house until his death in 1767. He divided his estate between his children, leaving to Robert King the dwelling plantation and to Nehemiah II "lands on King's Branch." Between his inheritance in 1767 and his death in 1802, Nehemiah King II assembled the largest and most valuable plantation in Somerset County. By 1798 he controlled over 3,500 acres, and the federal assessors valued his estate at close to

$20,000, by far the largest value of any Somerset plantation assessed in that year. Included in the assessment records were seventy-four slaves.

After Nehemiah King II's death in 1802, his son Robert Jenkins Henry King inherited the plantation. In 1857 a commission was established to divide the lands of Robert J. H. King between his rightful heirs, Charlotte King Waters, Laura King Barnes, Anne Maria King (alias Aurelia W. White), Henry N. King, and George King. During their ownership, Isaac and Laura K. Barnes inherited part of the plantation on which they erected a second large house south of the brick dwelling. This structure evidently burned during the nineteenth century, but its site remains a potentially valuable mid-nineteenth century archeological site. In more recent years, Beverly was owned by Lynde Catlin, who restored the house in the 1930s after the interior had been gutted by fire.

WORKINGTON
1793
Westover vicinity (site)
Private

Built for Henry and Elizabeth Wilson Jackson in 1793, Workington stood on the south side of Back Creek within sight of Arlington (S-51) and Westover (S-50), two other Wilson family houses. Continuing a family preference for large and spacious dwellings,

Workington was planned on an elaborate scale with more attention to fine detail than most houses built in Somerset County during the last years of the eighteenth century.

The two-and-a-half story, five-bay brick house was highlighted by Palladian windows, a center projecting pavilion topped by a pediment, and a bold modillion block cornice. The pedimented entrance surround that framed the front door was added by Ralph P. Thompson during a restoration he initiated after purchasing the farm in 1914. From photographs taken before the house burned, it is evident the first floor had a very generous L-shaped stair hall. The decorated staircase ascended four flights to the third floor in the northeast corner, and raised panel arches supported by semicircular Ionic columns divided the passage. The parlor and dining room doorways were framed by the boldest architraves known to have been crafted for a Somerset County house. In addition, the walls of the hall were fitted with raised panel wainscoting and elaborate cornice moldings. The parlor, by far the most formal interior space, was richly decorated with a combination of Federal and Georgian period woodwork. Centered on the end wall was a Federal style mantel with intricate gougework decoration. The center tablet carried a basket of flowers design, and the flanking panels were intricately detailed as well. Framing the windows were unusually crossetted surrounds with a scrolled base molding. Paneled

S-55, Tudor Hall, southeast elevation.

interior shutters were hidden in the window jambs. The room was also finished with an elaborate modillioned cornice. Some of these interior features parallel the woodwork at Tudor Hall (S-55), Liberty Hall (S-52), and the Adams house (S-29). The superior finishes were not confined to the principal rooms, for the second floor passage was decorated with paneled arches, raised panel wainscoting, and dentiled cornice molding.

In addition to its superior architectural qualities, Workington was significant as the principal residence of Henry and Elizabeth Wilson Jackson, two influential landholders during the eighteenth and early nineteenth centuries. Henry Jackson owned the "Beckford" tract as well as other properties, and Elizabeth inherited the Back Creek lands where this house stood through her brother Levin's 1791 will. "Workington" was comprised of two tracts known as "Mount Ephraim" and "Mother's Care," which totaled 1,120 acres by the time of the 1798 tax assessment. In addition to a full complement of support buildings, the Jackson house and domestic outbuildings were described in the assessment:

1 Dwelling House built of Brick 54 by 38 [feet] Two Story high 12 windows 7 1/2 feet by 3 feet 8 Inches, 14 windows 6 1/2 feet by 3 feet 8 Inches 4 Garret windows 4 feet 5 Inches by 3 feet 9 Inches, 1 Kitchen built of Brick 28 feet by 21 [feet] two

story high 6 windows 4 feet 8 inches by 2 feet 4 Inches 7 windows 3 feet 8 inches by 2 feet 4 Inches, 1 Smoke House 12 feet Sqr—Logs, 1 Milk House 16 feet Long by 12 feet wide, 1 Stable 20 feet by 10 [feet]—saw'd logs, 1 Carriage House 26 feet by 20 feet not finished. Value $2500

The other plantation buildings included another dwelling house, 47 by 21; one negro house, 24 by 20; one lumber house, 30 by 20; one weaving house, 24 feet by 12; one blacksmith shop, 15 feet square; one corn house, 40 by 8; one barn, 44 by 32; and two other barns supposed to be 20 feet square. The assessed number of slaves totaled fifty-nine, with twenty-four between the ages of twelve and fifty.

As dictated by Levin Wilson's will, "Mount Ephraim" and "Mother's Care" were to pass to his nephew Robert after Elizabeth's death, and in the event of Robert's death to George Wilson Jackson, Robert's younger brother. In 1823 George Dashiell, sheriff of Somerset County, sold the 1,200-acre estate of the late George W. Jackson to John C. Wilson. After Wilson's death, Colonel John P. Gale purchased the "Workington" plantation in October 1837 but died within two months. His will devised "my real estate commonly called Workington to my children, William, Francis, George and Maria as joint tenants." The Gale children held onto the property for the following twenty-six years

and then sold it to Grantham Reynolds in March 1863. Between 1865 and 1911 Workington was bought and sold eleven times, until Ralph P. Thompson purchased the farm on April 6, 1914, from Augustus C. F. Wolfe. After his purchase, Thompson proceeded through a meticulous restoration of the brick house, but he sold the farm several years later. In 1922 the house burned to the ground.

TUDOR HALL (NR)
Circa 1785
Manokin vicinity
Private

Tudor Hall stands on land that was originally part of the 1,280-acre tract "Waters River" and descended to John Waters, who resurveyed a 490-acre tract named "Salem" in 1750. Waters bequeathed his plantation to his wife for her use and after her death to their son John. In 1783 John Waters was assessed for his "Salem" plantation, which contained a

Brick Dwelling house with two rooms and passage below in bad repair, kitchen, quarter, and barns also, good apple and peach orchards, other improvements midling good.

John Waters died the following year, and the Annemessex lands were inherited by Francis Hutchings Waters, the apparent builder of this ambitious frame house. It is highly likely that the dwelling was completed by the time Waters had "Salem" surveyed once more for 648 acres in 1789. The 1798 description identifies not only the new house, but the old dwelling as well:

1 Dwelling House of wood 38 by 34 feet two Story high, 10 windows 5 feet by 2 feet 8 Inches, 9 windows 5 feet by 2 feet,

4 windows 3 feet 4 Inches by 2 feet, 1 Kitchen built of Brick 20 feet by 18 feet two story high, 6 windows 3 feet 4 [inches] by 2 feet 3 Inches 3 windows 4 feet by 2 feet, 1 Smoake House—sawd logs 12 feet square, 1 stable 32 by 22 feet

The assessors described the earlier Waters family house as "1 Dwelling House built of Brick 48 by 20 feet, one story high...the above very old and in very bad repair." It is no wonder Francis Waters wanted a new house.

Tudor Hall, as it was later known, has survived as the most elaborately crafted late eighteenth century house in Somerset County. Furthermore, it is one of the few houses in the county to retain until modern times a colonnade connecting the main house with a two-story brick kitchen. Unfortunately, the colonnade no longer stands.

Architecturally, Tudor Hall is unsurpassed in Somerset County in its decorative treatment and amount of unusual exterior and interior fabric. The two-and-a-half story frame house is supported by a raised Flemish bond foundation, and expansive brick fire walls distinguish each gable end. Otherwise, the squarish house is sheathed with well-preserved beaded weatherboards. The modillioned cornice is an unparalleled design of blocks alternating with carved dogwood blossoms. Formerly attached to the east gable end was a single story, three-bay frame colonnade that joined the two-story brick kitchen to the main house. Family photographs of the house suggest the colonnade was added at a slightly later date (circa 1810-1830).

Inside, the first floor is divided into four rooms, three of which open off a large, squarish stair hall. Paneled wainscoting and a molded cornice trim the walls, and the quarter-turn stair has stringer decoration of carved flowers. Raised six-panel doors, framed by bold crossetted surrounds, open into the var-

ious rooms. By far the most elaborately finished space is the parlor, which occupies the northwest room. Centered on the west wall is a high Federal-style mantel covered with complex gougework patterns and unusual moldings. The center frieze tablet is decorated with a carved basket of flowers. The cornice is trimmed with modillion blocks and the lower edge is finished with a rope molding. The room is fitted with paneled wainscoting, and the doors and windows are framed by bold crossetted surrounds. The most dynamic feature of the second floor is the paneled soffit arch that divides the passage.

After Francis H. Waters's death in July 1826, his daughter Sarah Dennis Waters and Dr. Robert Ballard (married November 2, 1826) occupied the Annemessex River plantation. Dr. Ballard had an office built in the front yard, which is no longer standing. In June 1888 the Somerset Court partitioned "Tudor Hall" between the five Ballard children, and the house and 33 3/4 acres passed to their daughter Anne D. Lockerman and her husband, Francis S. Lockerman. The Lockermans sold adjacent Waters River and lived at Tudor Hall. In 1919 ownership passed to their daughter, Sallie W. Lockerman. The current owners purchased the farm in 1923.

LIBERTY HALL (NR)
1795
Westover vicinity
Private

Sited on the north branch of the Great Annemessex River, Liberty Hall displays the regional stepped house form common to the Eastern Shore of Maryland and, especially, of Virginia. Extensive historical and architectural research has developed a relatively clear picture of the changes made to Liberty Hall over a period of 200 years.

First mention of a specific dwelling house was recorded in 1783 during the ownership of James Curtis. The federal tax assessors found on his plantation a "Brick wall dwelling house, out of repair." Following Curtis's death in 1791, the 311-acre property was inherited by William Curtis, who began construction of a new house in 1795 near the old brick structure. Both buildings were identified in the 1798 tax assessment. William Curtis's dwelling and outbuildings were described as

1 Dwelling House built of wood 34 feet by 28 [feet] Two Story high 7 windows 5 1/2 feet long by 3 feet, 10 windows 4 1/2 feet by 2 feet 3 Inches 4 Garret windows 3 feet 8 I[nches] by 2 feet 3 I[nches], 1 Kitchen 18 feet by 16 [feet], 1 Milk House 8 feet Square, 1 Smoake House 12 feet Sqr, 2 Negro Houses 18 by 16 feet.

Also located on the property was "1 old Dwelling House 40 by 20 feet." The replacement of an earlier dwelling was common practice during the late eighteenth and early nineteenth centuries and was repeated on several nearby plantations, including Tudor Hall (S-55) and Waters River (S-54).

William Curtis's new house was fitted with raised panel wainscoting, dentiled cornice moldings, ovolo molded door and window surrounds, and elaborate mantels that combine Georgian and Federal period designs. The dining room mantel is very similar to mantels at Workington (1793) and the William Adams house (1790s). Unlike most houses in Somerset County, Liberty Hall has flush board wainscoting in the second floor bedrooms and passage.

The 1798 tax assessment indicates an 18' X 16' kitchen stood separate from the main house. At a slightly later date, the kitchen was joined to the house with a colonnade. By the second quarter of the nineteenth century,

S-52, Liberty Hall, northwest elevation.

this had been enclosed and raised to two stories. Around 1935 the old kitchen was shoved off into the marsh. In 1975 a two-story addition using old materials was erected on the site of the old kitchen.

The architectural history of Liberty Hall points clearly to the complex development of many stepped houses. At the same time, it helps dispel the often repeated argument that these houses were built strictly from the smallest section to the largest as the family grew or plantation income increased.

Liberty Hall stands on land known in the seventeenth century as "Armstrong's Lott" and "Armstrong's Purchase" (commonly

known as "Scipers Plantation"), which was patented to Matthew Armstrong, a Boston mariner, during the early to mid-1660s. His widow, Hannah, transferred ownership of a large part of "Armstrong's Lott" to Daniel Curtis on April 17, 1672. Curtis's will of 1680 bequeathed ownership of his plantation to his son James Curtis, who in turn willed the family land to his son Charles Curtis in 1721. Twenty years later Charles Curtis died and, like his father and grandfather, left "Armstrong's Lott" to his son, James. James Curtis, who had the land resurveyed for 311 acres in 1767, occupied the plantation for a full half-century. As directed by his will of 1791, "Arm-

strong's Lott" was to pass to his widow and after her death to their nephew William Curtis. Although Sinah Curtis did not die until 1799, William Curtis probably supervised the construction of the new frame house in 1795. Armstrong's Lott remained in Curtis family hands through the nineteenth century and acquired the name Liberty Hall around the time of the Civil War. The farm was not sold out of the Curtis family until 1938, when C. Foster Matthews acquired it. Theodore T. and Virginia C. Dorman purchased Liberty Hall in 1961.

GREENWOOD FARM
Circa 1790 and circa 1825-1850
Kingston vicinity (site)
Private

Perhaps the most intriguing of the stepped style houses of Somerset County was the five-part frame dwelling that formerly stood on Greenwood farm southwest of the Kingston crossroads. Since the house burned in 1970, its exact age and development are clouded. However, William Williams (1764-circa 1838) evidently built the oldest section on his father's creek side plantation during the fourth quarter of the eighteenth century. In 1798 he was assessed for

> *1 Dwelling House built of wood, 31 feet by 27 feet, Two Story high, 8 windows 5 1/2 feet by 3 feet, 10 windows 4 feet by 3 feet, 4 Garret windows 3 feet by 2 feet, 1 Kitchen 16 feet Square, 1 Smoake House 10 feet Square, 1 Milk House 16 feet by 12 feet, 1 Stable 8 feet square with a 8 foot shed to the same.*

Although Williams was only assessed for a 100-acre tract known as "Neighbors Conclusion," in 1802 he inherited the ground on which his house stood from his father, Thomas Williams. In 1829 he also inherited the adjacent lands of his brother Thomas.

By 1830 William Williams had amassed one of the most impressive estates in antebellum Somerset County. Encompassing more than 2,300 acres, his plantation was operated by sixty-eight slaves and contained eighty-three head of cattle, seventy hogs, and eight "yoke oxen." For transportation, Williams had two four-wheel carriages, one gig, one sulky, and two canoes. In the house were 491 ounces of silver plate. In 1830 the total county tax assessment of his property reached $26,610, an extremely high value for the period. It was probably during this prosperous time that the house was enlarged to its five-part size.

William Williams died around 1838, and his extensive plantation passed to his only son, William. He and his wife, Adeline Pechin, occupied the estate through the Civil War years. However, the destabilization of the Southern plantation economy at that time

spelled drastic losses for the Williamses, who eventually had to mortgage their land. In 1876 the property, then known as "Greenwood," was sold to Daniel W. Middleton, Sr. of Washington, D.C., as the result of a suit levied against Williams by Nathan J. Langford. From 1910 to 1938 the property was held by Charles T. Cannon.

CALDICOTT (NR)
Circa 1790
Rehobeth vicinity
Private

Historically known as Caldicott, this farm and orchard have been managed for two generations by the Vessey family, who acquired the property in December 1931. Situated on a high bank of the Pocomoke River, the prominent two-story, five-bay frame house faces dramatic views of indigenous cypress trees and tidal marsh as well as the surrounding orchard and farm.

Built between 1784 and 1798 for Littleton Dennis, Jr., this four-room plan frame house survives with over 90 percent of its original exterior and interior fabric. This gives the house a degree of integrity that distinguishes it among the Federal style houses of Somerset County. Divided into four unequal sized rooms, the first floor interior boasts fine examples of late Georgian and Federal style finishes that include a decorated, turned baluster stair; raised panel hearth walls and wainscoting; and enriched molded cornices. The Palladian windows in the center bay light the second floor passage. Several architectural features, such as the unusual transom over the front door, link Caldicott with Beverly, the builder's boyhood home located in neighboring Worcester County.

"Caldicott" was first patented to Colonel William Stevens on February 4, 1665. By 1783 the 500-acre tract had been divided into

S-65, Greenwood farm, northeast elevation.

S-72, Caldicott, north elevation.

three parcels owned by William White, Thomas Bruff, and Susannah Dennis, widow of Littleton Dennis (1728-1774) of Worcester County. Susannah Dennis's son, Littleton Dennis, Jr. (1765-1833) inherited the Somerset County property in December 1784 and constructed the house between this date and 1798, when he was assessed for the following buildings:

Situate on a Landing of Pocomoke River in Somerset County 1 Dwelling house 40 by 34 feet Two Story high with 8 windows 5 by 2 1/2 & 9 windows 2 by 5 feet & 10 windows 4 feet 1/2 by 2 1/2 feet..., with Brick Cellar, house Built of Wood, also one Kitchen 19 by 18 & 1 Milk house 9 by 9 & 1 Meat house 12 by 12 all wood, valued at $1,000.

Dennis was also assessed for another tract and farm buildings, as well as forty slaves.

Along with practicing law in Princess Anne and adjacent Virginia, Littleton Dennis served as county judge from 1801 to 1806. He also found time to manage an expanded farm, which totaled close to 5,000 acres at his death in 1833. Dennis's son Littleton Upshur Dennis (1804-1833) inherited the property, but his sudden death meant it passed almost immediately to his two children, Elizabeth and George. In 1867 George's daughter Elizabeth Murray Rush was forced to sell the property in a settlement of the Circuit Court of Somerset County, ending almost two centuries of ownership by the Dennis family. Through the following sixty years, the property changed hands more than a dozen times before Alice Vessey bought the farm in 1931.

WHITEHALL (NR)
Circa 1790
Loretto vicinity
Private

Whitehall, located in Wicomico Hundred on the south side of Wicomico Creek, is a large plantation house built partly of brick and partly of frame. The house, with its center stair hall and three well-finished first floor rooms, reflects the late eighteenth century trend toward more formal and spacious dwellings.

The two-and-a-half story, brick-ended frame dwelling follows an L-shaped plan with the center hall flanked by a large parlor to the west and two smaller rooms to the east. The parlor retains fine examples of late eighteenth century woodwork, including a Federal style mantel, raised panel wainscoting,

S-27, Whitehall, north elevation.

223

S-29, William Adams house, south elevation, photograph c. 1920, (courtesy of Charles Emery).

and a dentiled cornice. The eastern rooms retain period woodwork as well. Perhaps best remembered of Whitehall's notable features are the Civil War style murals in a second floor bedroom.

Whitehall stands on a tract of land initially called "Taunton Deane," which Benjamin Cottman purchased from Francis Roberts on June 25, 1671. Although Cottman is thought to have lived on the north side of Wicomico Creek, the property remained in the family for the next five generations. In 1798 Captain William Cottman was assessed for the following:

> *Situated on the South Side of Wiccomico Creek adjoining Mr. Thomas Hamilton, one Dwelling House of Wood, New, Two Story high with Brick Cellar and finished in good order, 46 feet by 20 feet with an Ell of 16 by 16 feet...Cook House 16 by 16 feet, Smoke House 12 by 12 feet, Milk House 8 by 10 feet, Stable 20 by 16...valued 700 Dollars.*

Additional property listed for Cottman mentions

> *a Parcel of Land Containing four Hundred Acres considerable part of which is flat clay ground and valued at Sixteen Hundred Dollars on which is Exclusive of*

> *the dwelling House and Houses appurtenant, a quarter old 24 by 16 feet, Corn house 28 by 8 feet, an Old dwelling house 24 by 20 feet, Kitchen 14 by 14 feet, Valued at forty Dollars.*

Captain William Cottman and his wife, Jane Dashiell, remained on the farm until 1815-1816, when both of them died. Jane Cottman outlived her husband by seven months and devised to her two daughters, Anna M. Bell and Araminta Maltilda Adams, "The Dwelling Plantation of their father's situated on the south side of Wicomico Creek." At this time the Cottmans' daughters directed that their holdings should be resurveyed, and on September 4, 1818, 617 acres was patented under the name "Bellville."

The farm passed out of the Cottman family in 1832, when William H. Bell sold it to James and Mary Kent. The property had nineteen subsequent owners, until the current owners bought the house and ten acres in 1962.

WILLIAM ADAMS HOUSE
Circa 1790
Allen vicinity (site)
Private

Formerly located on the south side of Wicomico Creek was the William Adams

house, one of the most anomalous eighteenth century dwellings in Somerset County. The two-story, four-bay Flemish bond brick house was built during the same period as Beverly and Workington, but with a completely different architectural focus. Instead of extravagant Palladian-inspired elevations, William Adams's house was designed with a more informal approach, which included a two-story porch across the entire front of the house. Not only was Adams uninterested in a pretentious formal entrance, but the principal elevation was asymmetrical. Unusual in the porch construction was a brick end wall that incorporated multipane sash windows on the first and second floors. As an extension of the gable end of the house, the porch wall included a molded water table and belt course as well as segmental arches over each window.

In contrast to the informal qualities of the exterior were elaborate interiors exhibiting high quality plaster decoration and raised panel woodwork. The few interior photographs that survive show intricate plaster cove cornices and ceiling medallions with trailing vine motifs as well as bold, Georgian-influenced mantels and crossetted surrounds.

William Adams, son of Reverend Alexander Adams, is credited with financing the construction of this late eighteenth century house on land he inherited through his father's will, probated in 1769. In 1783 William Adams's tax assessment listed tracts encompassing 571 acres. Between 1783 and his death in 1796, Adams improved the plantation with the brick house. In 1798 the federal assessors described the Wicomico Hundred plantation as

Situated on the Head of Wicomico Creek a Dwelling House (on a Valuable Farm) of Brick two Story (with a valuable cellar also a Portico the whole Length of the building) 40 feet by 20 feet with nine Windows 64 Inches by 36 Inches, Eight [windows] 44 Inches by 36 Inches, four [windows] 24 by 20 Inches, the whole finish'd in High Order and annext to it is a room of wood, One Story, 20 by 16 feet in

plain Order & Old with six Windows 44 Inches by 28 Inches, Cook Room adjoining 18 by 16 feet of wood with three windows 44 inches by 28 inches….

Standing near the house were several outbuildings, which included a 16' by 16' carriage house, a stable of equal size, a 20' by 16' meat house, a 12' by 12' dairy, and a 10' by 10' smokehouse. The plantation, then including 384 acres, was also improved by a 30' by 24' barn with 10' sheds, a 32' by 16' slave quarter, and two small dwellings. Situated alongside the road to Princess Anne was a "Store House with Cellar, 16' by 30'."

Since William Adams had died in 1796, the assessors listed the Adams heirs as the owners. William Cottman was designated as the occupant of the house. Two years later,

Adams family interests in the Wicomico Creek property were sold to Cottman, who lived in the house until his death in 1805. As a result of a clause in his will, the property was sold once again, and Cottman's executors transferred title of the farm to Andrew Adams, William's brother, for £3,910.

When Andrew Adams died in 1818, his large estate was divided between his grandnephew John Adams and his grandson George Adams Dashiell. John Adams inherited the "Smith's Adventure," "Adam's Purchase," and "End of Strife" tracts, while George A. Dashiell was bequeathed the balance of the property, mostly located on the south side of Wicomico Creek, which included the brick house. From George's hands, the property passed to his son James F. Dashiell, who maintained ownership until the middle of the Civil War. The old Adams farm was sold out of the family in 1863, and it was under other owners that the property was known as the "Mansion Farm" and later as "Cedar Lawn." During the early twentieth century, Dr. Edward E. Tull of New York began purchasing several tracts on the south side of Wicomico Creek. He acquired title to the old Adams farm, and regrettably the brick house was not maintained. The property remains under the ownership of the Tull estate.

MYRTLE GROVE
Circa 1800
Mt. Vernon vicinity (site)
Private

This house known as Myrtle Grove was one of the oldest houses to survive until modern times near Mount Vernon (another Myrtle Grove in the county is S-42). The two-story, three-bay main house exhibited features common to houses built around the turn of the nineteenth century. The side entrance, nine-

S-33, Myrtle Grove, west elevation.

over-nine sash windows, and steeply pitched roof suggest the estimated date of construction. The date is confirmed by the absence of the two-story frame dwelling listed on the 1798 federal tax assessment for Philip Jones, who owned the property at that time. A single story, 30' by 20' frame structure was assessed, but it is uncertain whether any part of this eighteenth century house survived in the early nineteenth century house.

Philip Jones acquired this part of "Mannings Resolution" through the will of his father, Daniel, in 1783 and occupied the tract through the turn of the century. Beginning in 1811 he transferred ownership of various "Mannings Resolution" lands to his son Alexander. In 1816 he left his entire estate to his wife, Margaret, and after her death to Alexander. Alexander established his plantation on the south side of what is now called Harper's Creek (see Millwood, S-32) and rented out his father's house. In 1849 he left his own plantation to his son Edward Augustus and the "lands where William Ballard lives to sons Denwood and Edgar." During the post-Civil War period the property was purchased by the Bounds family, in whose hands the farm remained until the 1960s.

ISAAC HARRIS HOUSE
Circa 1790, circa 1880
Wellington vicinity
Private

Historically known as the Isaac Harris house, this late eighteenth and late nineteenth century frame house stands on property more recently known as the Dryden farm or the Brittingham farm. The two-part dwelling combines a late eighteenth century, story-and-a-half hall/parlor dwelling, now a service wing, and a two-and-a-half story cross-gabled farmhouse built around 1880. As originally erected, the eighteenth century house had

brick gable ends. Evidently these were in such bad repair by the late nineteenth century that they were removed when the center hall, single-pile farmhouse was attached to the southwest gable end of the old house.

When the old hall/parlor house was converted to a service wing, an internal brick stove stack was inserted against the hall partition. The old parlor was made over into a kitchen, and the hall was apparently used as a dining room. Significant eighteenth century architectural features that survive include tilted false plates, interior vertical board walls on the first and second floors, and remnants of early beaded weatherboards. The late nineteenth century farmhouse has experienced only a few alterations and is representative of hundreds of its type built throughout the county.

The rear story-and-a-half hall/parlor house was evidently built by Isaac Harris during the fourth quarter of the eighteenth century. The 1798 federal assessment lists Isaac

Harris of John in Dividing Creek Hundred as owning

A Tract of Land called Tulls Addition with other adjacent Lands Lying in Somerset County about 7 miles from Princes Anne Town adjoining Steven Harris' Land with 1 Barn 20 by 30 & 1 Corn house 16 by 20 & 1 Stable 16 by 18 and 1 Dwelling where Betty Long Lives 16 by 18 one story of wood $550.00.

Also standing on Harris's land was his residence, which was described as

1 Dwelling house 20 by 32 one storey high with 4 windows 4 by 2 and 2 windows 3 by 2 with Ends Brick and sides and Roof wood & 1 Kitchen 32 by 16 & 1 Meat house 10 by 10 and 1 Milk house 8 by 10 all wood $450.00.

Harris's slave assessment included a total of

S-214, Isaac Harris house, south elevation.

S-195, Cedar Hill, southwest elevation.

eight, with four slaves between the ages of twelve and fifty.

In Isaac Harris's will, proved on March 21, 1816, he left interests in his estate to his wife, Sally, and their children. Sally lived another twenty-one years, and at her death her married daughters and one son sold her land by trustee to Samuel S. Costen on September 5, 1837. In 1845 Samuel Costen and his wife, Mary, sold the 221 acres to William M. N. B. Costen, who at that time was beginning to amass a tremendous agricultural complex, which totaled close to 4,000 acres by the fourth quarter of the nineteenth century. William Costen occupied his father's house about a mile to the southwest of this property (see S-76). In 1883 he transferred title of the old Harris farm to Marietta E. Clark, who in turn sold the property with her husband, Edward A. Clark, to Edward J. Brittingham in March 1886. The front addition was probably constructed either by the Clarks or the Brittinghams. The Brittinghams owned the property until 1909, when E. Florence Brittingham relinquished title to the 128-acre farm to Alton E. Dryden. The property remained in the Dryden family until 1972.

CEDAR HILL
1793
Westover vicinity
Private

Cedar Hill, more recently known as the Long farm, was the country residence of Dr. Matthias Jones and his wife, Milcah Gale Wilson Jones. Milcah Gale Wilson inherited the Back Creek mill property through her father Samuel's will, probated on May 25, 1790. Evidently she then financed the construction of this well-built, two-story frame house, dated to 1793 by an etched brick fixed in the west chimney.

As originally built, the first floor contained two rooms of unequal size, fitted with expertly crafted Federal style woodwork. Topping the front and back doors are rectangular transoms with diamond-shaped muntins. The 1798 tax assessment describes the residence as

1 Dwelling House 33 by 20 feet, wood, two story, 6 windows 5 feet 8 Inches long 2 feet 4 Inches wide, 10 [windows] 4 feet 10 Inches long 2 feet 4 Inches wide, 2 [windows] 3 feet long 21 Inches wide, New, 1 Cook house 18 by 14, Colonade, 12 by 10 feet, 1 Smok house 11 feet square, 1 Hen house, 14 feet sqr, wood.

Dr. Matthias Jones married Milcah Gale Wilson on August 5, 1797, and in 1803 the couple undertook construction of East Glen, a transverse hall house situated at the east end of Prince William Street in Princess Anne. Although their town dwelling was a more expensively erected and finished structure with a generous plan and fine details, the Joneses maintained their agricultural and commercial interests in this 465-acre Back Creek plantation.

Recorded on the Cedar Hill property in 1798 was the old Wilson mill, a twelve-foot square frame structure that, according to the land records, operated best during the winter and spring months. Also included in the assessment was a 22' by 8' storehouse and a 14' by 12' doctor's shop.

The property remained under the Joneses' control until Matthias Jones's death. As the result of an ensuing chancery court case, John W. Crisfield, trustee, sold the property to Nathaniel Dixon, Sr. in November 1838. At this time a few minor changes were made to the house, including new front and rear entrances and a center partition creating a formal hall. From local tradition and structural evidence found in the house while it was being restored, it appears a two-story porch was built across the front of the dwelling around 1840.

Various Dixon family members held title to the Back Creek property until 1851, when Nathaniel Dixon, Jr. sold Cedar Hill to Eleanor Tull, wife of Westover merchant William T. Tull. The Dixons reacquired the property in 1880. During either the Tulls' ownership or the Dixons' second ownership, the original colonnade and kitchen burned and a former slave house with a whitewashed interior was moved up to the east gable end of the house and converted into a new kitchen.

The last major changes to the house were accomplished around the turn of the century, after Edwin D. Long purchased the farm from N. Walter Dixon in 1900. The Longs pulled down the two-story porch and added projecting two-story pavilions to the front and back, giving the house its present asymmetrical appearance. In the spring of 1987 the house and three acres along the creek were sold from the adjacent farmland and a restoration was initiated by the new owners.

DAVID'S ADVENTURE
Circa 1790
Hudson's Corner vicinity
Private

This story-and-a-half frame house is a rare survival of the small 20' by 16' dwellings that once dotted the Somerset County landscape. Despite remodeling, the one-room plan dwelling retains an early shed-roofed addition and an extremely rare double clapboard roof. Exposed under the shed roof are two layers of oak clapboards that formerly protected the main house. The first layer has feathered edges and is laid parallel to the roof peak. The second layer is laid perpendicular to the roof ridge and survives with an outer layer of red paint. Another notable feature of the main house is the series of exposed beaded floor joists in the main room. Later alterations include aluminum siding, an enclosed front porch, and additions to the south and west.

The history of this property has been traced to an Evans Willing who, according to the 1798 tax assessment, owned several tracts of land. These included a 99-acre parcel called "David's Adventure," a 117-acre tract known as "Addition to Littleworth," a 70-acre piece named "New Virginia," and four smaller parcels. The residence and outbuildings surrounding it were valued at $110. The assessors described these buildings as

1 Dwelling House 20 by 16 feet, wood, one Story with an Addition of 10 feet on the side, 1 window 4 feet 10 Inches long 2 feet 4 Inches wide, 1 window 3 feet 8 Inches long 2 feet 4 Inches wide, out of repair, 1 Cook house 16 feet square wood, 1 Smoke house 10 feet square Brick, 1 Milk house 8 feet square, wood, 1 Stable 16 by 12, 1 hen house.

The survival of the Willing house is surely

remarkable when most dwellings of this type burned, rotted, or simply wore out.

MYRTLE GROVE
Late 18th century, circa 1820
Oriole vicinity
Private

Dr. Henry Hyland's Myrtle Grove is situated on the west side of St. Peter's Creek near Oriole. The two-story frame house has an irregular five-bay facade that alludes to the complicated nature of its building history. The eastern two bays of the dwelling, with original brick west wall, were clearly erected before the rest of the house. The brick wall was encased when the old house was re-worked during the first quarter of the nineteenth century with a west end addition that now includes the main entrance. Radical alterations to the interior of the original house included the relocation of the stair and chimney stack, as well as fully new interiors of Federal and Greek Revival woodwork. Frag-

ments of eighteenth century material remain on the second floor and in the cellar.

The exact age of the eighteenth century section has not been determined, but architectural evidence points to the last decades of the century. In 1798 Lambert Hyland was assessed for the Monie Hundred property, which involved two tracts—"St. Peter's Neck" and "Littleworth"—encompassing over 750 acres. Hyland's house was described as a two-story frame dwelling measuring 32' across by 20' deep. An unfinished colonnade and kitchen were included along with several domestic outbuildings.

Dr. Henry Hyland was evidently responsible for rebuilding his father's house about the time of his marriage to Harriet E. Aires on April 6, 1819. Henry and Harriet Hyland occupied the rebuilt house until Henry's death in 1856. Harriet E. Hyland married William R. Ballard in 1865, and the couple kept the property until 1881. Ballard was a prominent resident of the Dames Quarter Election District. The 1877 county atlas shows him at

S-251, David's Adventure, northeast elevation.

S-412, Old Washington Academy, photograph c.1900 (courtesy of William Marshall Scott).

this location on St. Peter's Creek, and in the list of atlas patrons he is designated as the owner of 400 acres. In 1881 Annie A. Hyland bought Myrtle Grove, but by 1913 the farm had passed out of her family.

The earliest owner of "Myrtle Grove," first known as "St. Peter's Neck," was Peter Elzey. He patented the 400-acre tract in 1663 and divided it between his daughters Eliza-

beth and Frances in 1716. Elizabeth Elzey married Lewis Rigby, who transferred the "St. Peter's Neck" lands to John Rigby. John's daughters, Elizabeth Rigby Hyland, Mary Rigby Glasgow, and Sarah Rigby Done, inherited undivided interests in their father's creek plantation. In 1785 Lambert Hyland purchased the interests of his sisters-in-law, and the property remained in the Hyland

family until the early twentieth century.

OLD WASHINGTON ACADEMY
1801
Princess Anne vicinity (site)
Private

The Old Washington Academy, the second building in a series of five Somerset County schools to honor President Washington, formerly stood two miles south of Princess Anne on the west side of the old Princess Anne-Westover Road. The two-and-a-half story, Flemish bond brick school was erected in 1801 to replace the initial academy buildings built along Back Creek before the Revolutionary War. Materials, including iron, brass, thirty pairs of hinges, and 7,895 nails, were salvaged from the first buildings after they burned in 1797 and evidently reused in the new building.

In January 1801 the trustees of the school decided to rebuild on a site closer to Princess Anne. They also appointed a committee, consisting of Major Wilson, Colonel Gale, Mr. Dennis, Mr. Robertson, and General Winder, "to prepare a plan of a house suited for an Academy together with the probable expense of erecting the same..." Although no aca-

S-42, Myrtle Grove, south elevation.

S-1, Beckford, southeast elevation.

demic source has surfaced for a design attribution, a professionally trained architect probably had a hand in the building's construction.

After the new location was chosen, construction of an ambitious 75' by 45' brick academy began in October 1801. During the building process, Littleton Dennis Teackle was asked to inquire about insurance for the new school, and in 1808 a policy was written with the Baltimore Fire Insurance Company with a yearly premium of $36. Classes in this building were discontinued after a new facility was built in Princess Anne in 1891. The 1801 building stood long enough to be captured in a photograph reproduced by E. I. Brown, a Princess Anne photographer, around the turn of the century.

Washington Academy, first known as Somerset Academy, was formed in 1767 by the prominent planter and lawyer Samuel Wilson. Recognized early as a rare type of institution for the region, the academy was formally incorporated by the trustees in 1779. The act of incorporation stated,

Whereas sundry of the inhabitants of Somerset County by their humble petition to this general assembly have set forth that

at their own cost and charge they have erected large and elegant and commodious buildings on Back Creek for a School sufficient for the comfortable accomodation of eighty students which has been already carried on to the great improvement of the youth of this and adjoining states, and to render it still more extensively useful and fix it upon a foundation which may have greater stability.

The trustees at the time included Jacob Kerr, Levin Gale, David Wilson, Samuel Wilson, John Winder, Henry Jackson, Thomas Maddux, William Polk, Isaac Henry, Henry Waggaman, and William Strawbridge. Also in 1779 the school was renamed Washington Academy to honor the Revolutionary War general.

BECKFORD (NR)
Circa 1803
Princess Anne
Private

Superbly built in the best craftsman traditions of the period, Beckford stands on the periphery of Princess Anne among mature shade trees and boxwood. The two-story,

five-bay Flemish bond brick house is considered a fine example of the stylistic mixture of Georgian and Federal designs distinctive in Somerset County. The large proportions of the 45' by 38'6" brick block recall mid-eighteenth century Georgian architectural formulas as does the expansive gable-on-hip roof. The window openings are highlighted with expertly crafted limestone jack arches with projecting keystones and the base of the house is finished with a molded water table, features commonly used in pre-Revolutionary War houses. By contrast, the entrance is framed with attenuated reeded pilasters topped by a decorative frieze and delicate cornice, features expressive of the Federal style. In addition, rather than a projecting belt course, the space between the first and second floor windows is marked by a series of inset plaster panels, a feature not employed until the turn of the nineteenth century in Somerset County.

The five-room plan house is finished on the highest order with elaborate Federal style woodwork and plaster decoration. The first floor is fitted with a delicate period stair, flat six-panel doors, classically inspired mantels, and molded plaster cornices in each room. The southwest drawing room is especially

S-48, Clifton, east elevation.

noteworthy for its large ceiling medallion and cornice of grape clusters and tobacco leaves. Also of interest are the marble fireplace surrounds, brass hinges, and brass box locks.

Credit for the construction of this ambitious house has been awarded to various eighteenth century owners of the Manokin River tract, but current research indicates the brick house was raised during the early years of the nineteenth century. Beginning in 1802 John Dennis, Esquire, began purchasing the "Beckford" lands from his in-laws, George Wilson Jackson and Leah Jackson Gale. The Jacksons had owned the "Beckford" tract for a quarter of a century, since Henry Jackson purchased the land in 1771 from John Anderson. In his will of 1795, Henry Jackson left the "plantation adjacent to Princess Anne Town" to his son George Wilson Jackson. As he was a minor in 1798, George Wilson Jackson's mother, Elizabeth Wilson Jackson, was listed on the federal tax assessment. At the time, the plantation, occupied by Dr. Ezekial Haney, was improved by

1 Dwelling House 45 by 24 feet, wood one story high; 13 windows, 3 feet 8 Inches long, 2 feet 4 Inches wide; 2 windows 4 feet 10 Inches long, 2 feet 4 Inches wide;

joining Princess Anne, 1 Cook house wood, 18 by 16 feet with 1 window 3 feet 3 Inches long, 21 Inches wide; Colonade, 18 feet by 16 feet with 2 windows 3 feet 2 Inches long, 2 feet 4 Inches wide; 1 Smoke house 12 feet Squr; 1 Stable 20 feet square.

After the turn of the century, John Dennis, one-time Maryland delegate and United States senator, assembled ownership of the "Beckford" lands through three purchases in 1802 and 1803. It is thought he directed the construction of his brick house shortly afterwards. Dennis did not get to enjoy his new house for long as he died in 1806. He devised lifetime estate rights to his wife, Elinor Jackson Dennis, and then the property was intended to pass to their son Littleton James Dennis. After the deaths of Littleton and his brother Henry in the late 1820s, residual family interests in the property were acquired by another brother, John Dennis, Jr., in November 1831. John Dennis, Jr. married Sallie E. Jones two years later, and the couple occupied the brick house until John's death in 1859. Sallie continued to reside on the property for the next twenty-eight years. As the result of a court settlement, the estate was

transferred to Henry Fillmore Lankford in December 1887. Beckford remained in the Lankford family until the early 1970s. In 1973 the current owner purchased the property.

CLIFTON (NR)
Circa 1805
Revells Neck
Private

The site where Clifton stands is best remembered as the plantation of Randall Revell and the location of Somerset Town (Somerton), an early port "for the unlading and selling of goods and merchandise brought into the province." In 1668 Randall and Katherine Revell devised a twenty-acre tract for the town on the south side of the Manokin River at "Deep Point." The extent of building at this site has not been determined, but the town lasted long enough to be included on Augustine Herrman's map of 1670.

In his will of 1686, Randall Revell devised his extensive property, known as "Double Purchase," to his wife Katherine, his son Randall, and his other children. In 1717 Randall Revell, Jr. bequeathed to his three sons, Charles, Randall, and William, "all my land equally divided amongst them and it is my desire that my three sons have an equal privedge of ye marsh, ye plantation I now live on...."

During the mid-eighteenth century the Revells sold large portions of their grandfather's "Double Purchase" tract. By 1783 Ballard Bozman had acquired 607 ½ acres on which the tax assessor in that year recorded "One Dwelling house, cellar kitchen, good barn with sundry other improvements." Valued at £1,823, the Manokin River plantation had thirty-four slaves, eleven horses, and forty-five head of black cattle. The property was divided between 250 acres of arable land and 357 ½ acres of woods. Also in 1783 Bozman willed his lands to his daughter Nelly Bozman Elzey, wife of James Elzey.

In June 1791 James and Nelly Elzey granted to Robert Elzey the "Double Purchase" land adjoining the Manokin River. However, Robert died shortly thereafter, and in the same year the property reverted to James Elzey, who then transferred it to his son James.

The 1798 tax assessment lists James Elzey with part of the "Double Purchase" tract on which stood "1 Dwelling house 30 by 24 feet wood, one story, out of repair" near the Manokin River. Although James Elzey was taxed for the property, the land was occupied by Gilliss McCommey, apparently a tenant. Elzey evidently moved to the property after the turn of the century, and the architectural details of the house suggest it is highly likely he financed construction of the two-story Flemish bond brick house during the first ten years of the nineteenth century. In 1819 Elzey transferred ownership of "all that tract of land on the Manokin River whereon the said James Elzey now resides" to Edward H. C. Wilson for $10,000. The large transfer price implies improvements on the scale of the transverse hall brick house.

As one of three heirs to John C. and

S-37, *Davis farm, southeast elevation.*

Peggy Wilson's extensive estates of Westover and Arlington, Edward H. C. Wilson assembled his own plantation at the end of Revells Neck by purchasing the Elzey house and much of the land surrounding it. Built with Flemish bond walls and generously sized rooms, the relatively new brick house provided him with domestic spaces of the size he had known as a child growing up at Westover and visiting relatives at Workington.

Edward H. C. Wilson only enjoyed his plantation for a few years, but before his death in 1823 he deeded the property to his brother John C. Wilson, Jr. in trust for his wife, Sarah, and their children. Sarah C. Wilson resided in the house until the late 1840s, when she conveyed the property then known as "Clifton" to Isaac S. Atkinson for $7,500.

During the middle years of the nineteenth century, the property was involved in a number of chancery court cases resulting from defaulted mortgages. In 1871 William H. Gale and Levin L. Waters, trustees, transferred the property back to Isaac Atkinson, who, in turn, sold it to Morris R. Stroud, Jr. of Philadelphia for $20,000. After Stroud sold the Manokin River property in 1884, Clifton was transferred five times until Mary Wooten Carpenter purchased 18.3 acres and the house in 1938.

By the time Mrs. Carpenter acquired the house, it had been abandoned as a dwelling and was used for hay storage. During her ownership, the interior of the house was

extensively reworked and the original center block was enlarged into a five-part dwelling with the addition of flanking hyphens and service wings. Also at this time the two principal first floor rooms were refitted with Georgian and Federal style woodwork. The original, decorated Federal style stair was preserved.

DAVIS FARM
1802
Princess Anne vicinity
Private

The Davis farm, currently known as Arbor Acres, occupies a prominent site along the Manokin River on Stewart Neck. On the property is a two-story, three-bay house built of Flemish bond brick and supported by a raised, common bond brick foundation. The expertly laid brick walls are pierced by segmental arched window and door openings on each elevation. Tall brick chimneys rise from the gable ends. The southwest end chimney is inscribed with the date "1802." Early twentieth century alterations include a completely new roof, two-story porches on both elevations, and a Colonial Revival interior. The two-story frame service wing appears to date from the late nineteenth century. Located between the house and the river are a pair of tablestones marking the burials of John Davis (1789-1835) and his wife Mary Elizabeth Ann (1787-1837).

SCHOOLRIDGE FARM (NR)
Circa 1800
Upper Fairmount vicinity
Private

Schoolridge farm derives its significance from its architecture as well as from its associations with Arthur R. Beverly-Giddings, who authored two novels while living on the farm. Architecturally, the two-story, side hall/double pile Flemish bond house is a fine example of the Federal period plantation houses in Somerset County. The well-built brick house stands on the first appreciable rise in terrain from the marshes of the Great Annemessex River. Both the exterior and interior retain 90 percent of the original circa 1800 architectural fabric. The mantels, doors, chair rail, and stair are well-executed Federal period forms.

With its location along the meandering Annemessex River, Schoolridge farm offered a romantic setting for two novels authored by the owner, Arthur R. Beverly-Giddings. *River of Rogues* was published in 1948; *The Rival Shores* followed in 1954.

The original survey of "School House Ridge" was drawn in 1753 for Richard Waters, who sold the ninety-eight acres two years later to shipwright Joshua Hall. Joshua Hall owned the property for thirty years and then sold the tract to Isaac Hall, eldest son of Charles Hall, on April 12, 1785. The following April brought a third transfer from Isaac Hall to Henry Miles. The deed identifies the property as "Halls Choice" in addition to "School House Ridge," part of a tract of marshland called "Hall's Hammock," and "Addition to Hall's Hammock."

In the 1798 tax records, Henry Miles of Great Annemessex was assessed for

Part of 3 tracts of Land called Halls Choice, pt of Schoolhouse Ridge, 165 acres;

pt. of Halls Hammock, 50 acres; addition to Halls Ham'k, addition to School House Ridge, 43 1/2 acres; in the whole 258 1/2 acres on which is 1 Dwelling House built of wood, 37 feet by 18 [feet] one Story high; 1 Kitchen, 20 feet by 18 [feet]; 1 Milk house, 12 feet by 9 [feet]; 1 Barn 32 by 20, the above House very old & Rotten.

The last line in the assessment suggests Miles occupied the old Hall family house until the turn of the century and then replaced the crumbling structure with a new two-story Flemish bond brick dwelling.

Henry Miles lived to enjoy his new house until his death around 1816. He died intestate, so his property entered Somerset County's circuit court. On June 2, 1819, "School House Ridge," then 176 1/2 acres, was sold to Daniel Ballard for $2,007. Ballard never lived on the farm, however, for his "home farm" was located on Back Creek near present-day

Manokin. In his will, proved April 10, 1847, he clearly stated that his son Thomas Emory Ballard was to inherit "all my farm lying on the eastward and southward side of the County road leading down Potato Neck and which formerly belonged to Henry Miles." Thomas E. Ballard and his first wife, Kitty, as well as their children, Elizabeth and Thomas, are listed in the 1850 Somerset County census. At that time, the farm was valued at $4,000. Kitty died in 1856, and Thomas married Rosina Turpin the following year.

At Thomas Ballard's death in 1879, "School House Ridge" passed to his son Robert T. Ballard. Twenty-four years later the property was transferred to S. Cooper Tyler, who held onto it until 1933. His daughters A. Louise Tyler and Rose E. Whittington inherited the property but sold their interests to Arthur and Doris Beverly-Giddings on February 8, 1946. The current owners bought the property in 1971.

S-60, Schoolridge farm, southwest elevation.

233

S-161, Daniel Ballard farm, west elevation.

DANIEL BALLARD FARM
Circa 1800
Manokin vicinity
Private

The most significant survival on the old Daniel Ballard farm near Manokin is the large, gable-front frame tobacco house, one of four in Somerset County. Built during the early nineteenth century as the last generation of its type, the tobacco house retains sections of beaded weatherboard fastened with wrought nails. The squarish center room was erected to hold most of the tobacco crop for curing, while the adjacent side sheds were used to hold tobacco or as a place to strip the crop. Another rare survival on this farm is the dairy, which was built around 1800 with a beaded internal frame and sheathed with wide beaded weatherboards.

The extant two-story frame house was reportedly built in 1909 by Herschel V. Maddox on the site of an eighteenth century dwelling, and scatters of brick rubble and potshards in the adjacent fields support the tradition. The 1798 federal tax assessment listed on the property, "1 Dwelling House built of Brick, 42 feet by 20 feet one Story high, 2 Dormant windows...." Also mentioned were several old buildings and an unusual array of brick outbuildings, including a 20' square brick kitchen, a 12' square brick "Cyder house" and a 12' by 12' smokehouse. The frame tobacco house, put together with wrought nails, was not included in the valuation, which suggests its early nineteenth century date.

Daniel Ballard (1763-1847) owned this property through the late eighteenth and early nineteenth centuries when the tobacco house and dairy were built. He died in 1847 and was buried on the farm. His will directed that "my farm on Back Creek whereon I now reside" would pass to his son Daniel J. Ballard (1808-1891). The latter remained on the family farm until his death and is also buried on the property.

PUNCHEON MILL HOUSE
Circa 1810
Puncheon Landing
Private

One of the rare early sites related to industry in Somerset County is the Puncheon Mill house, evidently erected during the early nineteenth century in association with the grist and saw mills that operated on the site during the eighteenth century. In 1806 Littleton Dennis, Jr. purchased parts of two

S-73, Puncheon Mill house, west elevation.

234

tracts—"Acquintica" and "New Town" — "standing at the Puncheon Landing being the Beginning Bounder of the aforesaid two Tracts & running from thence across the said Mill Race a little Below the said Saw Mill to an old ball Cypress stump standing by the side of the Grist Mill Race below the said Grist mill...."

Industrial activity continued at Puncheon Landing under the ownership of Littleton Dennis, Jr., who also financed the construction of the extant two-story, two-bay frame dwelling. Built on a raised common bond brick foundation, the house includes two rooms on each floor heated by corner fireplaces. The interior is fitted with Federal style woodwork, and a mixture of wrought and double-struck nails is found in the attic framing. Perhaps the most notable survival associated with the property is an eighteenth century frame hand mill formerly used to process various grains. The old mill house was restored in the 1960s, and a stepped addition was built to the north.

LITTLETON DORSEY HOUSE
Circa 1810
Upper Fairmount
Private

The Littleton Dorsey house is one of several houses on the Fairmount peninsula that date from the early years of the nineteenth century. In general form and date, it is similar to the brick farmhouse on Schoolridge farm (S-60). The use of a Flemish bond gable end wall in a frame house is a construction technique shared by nearby Tudor Hall (S-55). These parallels suggest an important link between these houses, which were built in the same two decades, from 1790 to 1810. Additional features worthy of note include large portions of beaded weatherboarding and well-executed Federal period woodwork.

The house stands on a tract of land known as "End of Strife," which was transferred from Levin Tull to Littleton Dorsey in October 1810. All indications suggest the house was erected in the early nineteenth century by Levin Tull or, more likely, Littleton Dorsey. A description in the 1798 federal direct tax assessment suggests a different structure: "one Dwelling House built of wood 25 feet by 20 [feet], 1 window 3½ feet by 2 [feet]." This does not describe the extant house; however, it is likely that materials from the old house were reused in the construction of the existing house.

Littleton Dorsey occupied the farm and is listed on the 1850 U. S. census as a farmer with an estate valued at $1,500. Shortly afterwards Dorsey died intestate, and his property entered circuit court. Under the auspices of the court, Wesley Tull bought the property in 1853. Eight months later Wesley S. Tull of Baltimore sold the farm to William J. H. Tull of Somerset County. The Tulls held onto the property until 1880, when Robert H. Jones bought the farm. For the next eighty-three years the Joneses owned the Tull farm, as it is referred to in early twentieth century land records. The present owners bought the property in 1963.

WATERS RIVER (NR)
Circa 1813
Manokin vicinity
Private

Waters River is significant as an exceptionally well-preserved and well-proportioned Federal period plantation house. Facing the Great Annemessex River, the house has several distinctive features that tie it to a prominent collection of its contemporaries. These include tall, narrow chimneys; recessed panels on the front and rear facades; and intricately carved woodwork. Inside, the dwelling has a

S-57, Littleton Dorsey house, southwest elevation.

S-54, Waters River, southeast elevation.

four-room plan with the stair rising in the southeast room. The stair features decorative scrollwork embellishing the stringer and diamond cross-sectioned balusters supporting a ramped handrail. A half-rail mirrors the main railing on the adjacent wall surface. The balance of the first and second floor rooms is finished with well-executed period woodwork.

This Flemish bond brick house was erected by a descendant of the original property owner, Major William Waters, who patented the 1,280-acre tract called "Waters River" on September 5, 1663. Major Waters resided in Northampton County, Virginia, and his Annemessex River property was divided along with his Virginia landholdings when he died. Members of the Waters family were prominent Quaker planters, and Quaker meetings were held on the Maryland lands of Richard Waters during the early eighteenth century.

By the time of the 1783 tax assessment, the wife of a later William Waters, Rose Harmanson, owned 352½ acres of "Waters River"; her husband had died two years before. Included on the premises was a "brick dwelling house with three rooms below—unfinished, kitchens, barns, and all in bad repair." Fifteen years later the house was described in the next federal tax assessment as the property of William Hayward Waters:

> 1 Dwelling House built of Brick 52 feet by 20 feet one Story high 7 windows 5 feet long by 2 feet 8 Inches, 3 windows 4 feet by 2 feet, 1 Kitchen 20 feet by 16 feet 1 Smoake House 12 feet square, 1 Milk House 12 feet by 10 feet 1 Carriage House 12 feet by 8 feet the above Houses are very old and out of repair.

It is clear the 1783 and 1798 descriptions refer to an earlier brick house, which family tradition relates was replaced around 1813 with the extant structure. This construction date is supported architecturally by the Federal period woodwork and the double-struck nails found in the attic framing. William H. Waters's will, proved in 1834, bequeathed to his son Thomas Littleton Waters "my Manor, or the Plantation whereon I now live."

Following the Waterses, the related Curtis and Lockerman families held title to the Annemessex River farm until 1888, when Margaret E. Robertson purchased the property. Various Robertsons, including Dr. Samuel H. Robertson, a local general practitioner, owned the farm from 1888 until 1943. The current owners bought the 312-acre farm in 1950.

JESSE H. WAINWRIGHT HOUSE
Circa 1815
Princess Anne vicinity
Private

Located on the periphery of Princess Anne is a two-story, three-bay frame dwelling historically known as the Jesse H. Wainwright house and in more recent years as the old Brittingham farm. The circa 1815 side hall/double-pile house has two towering exterior brick chimneys on the west end and original beaded weatherboards on three sides. The boxed cornice is finished with Federal style bed and crown moldings, and the front entrance is distinguished by a transom with comma-shaped corner moldings. The interior of the main house has been well-maintained and retains a large percentage of its original Federal style woodwork. The open-string staircase rises to the third floor in three flights; the stringer is fitted with a delicate scroll decoration typical of the period. The two large first floor rooms are fitted with Federal mantels. Attached to the west gable end is an early nineteenth century service wing that

S-11, Jesse Wainwright house, south elevation.

has been refitted as a modern kitchen and family room. The section nearest the house was formerly an open colonnade that connected the one-room kitchen to the house. Remaining in the kitchen are wide vertical boards and exposed floor joists. A ladder assembled with wrought nails formerly provided access to the loft.

Similarities in the Federal style finishes of the Wainwright house and the Colonel George Handy house in Princess Anne (S-7), built in 1806, suggest the same craftsmen worked on both dwellings. Identical comma-shaped moldings survive in both front door transoms, and the Federal mantels, chair rail, and doors follow the same patterns.

During the second half of the eighteenth century, the property on which this fine Federal period house stands was owned by Dr. Francis T. Cheney, whose father, Andrew Francis Cheney, had assembled several adjacent tracts into a large plantation during the 1760s and 1770s. Parts of "Hayward's Purchase," "Friendship," and "Newman's Last Conclusion" totaled 316 acres. The house is estimated to date from circa 1815, after Jesse H. Wainwright purchased 300 acres from John Teackle of Accomac County, Virginia. Wainwright occupied his plantation until his

death around 1822, when the property entered the Circuit Court of Somerset County. Settlement and sale of the farm were not accomplished until 1834, when it was transferred to Rosanna A. W. Wainwright, Jesse's widow, who later married James Brittingham. The property remained in the Brittingham

family until the turn of the century, when it was purchased by Marion S. Malone.

MILLWOOD
Circa 1815 and earlier
Mt. Vernon vicinity
Private

Tucked away along Harper Creek (formerly King's Creek) north of the Big Monie stands Millwood, a combination eighteenth and nineteenth century frame house consisting of four distinct sections. In the center of the structure is a story-and-a-half, late eighteenth century dwelling that was incorporated in a much larger Federal period plantation house. Around 1815 the main block and the hyphenated kitchen were attached to either side of the earlier frame house. Following the popular gable-front orientation, the two-story addition was planned with a transverse stair hall fronting two rooms. On

S-32, Millwood, south elevation.

S-217, Costen house, northwest elevation.

the other side, a single story hyphen or colonnade (now enclosed) led from the house to a story-and-a-half, one-room kitchen.

During the 1815 construction period, the principal sections of the house were fitted with fine examples of Federal period woodwork, much of which survives. The stair rises in the southwest corner of the hall to a second floor balcony. Although early nineteenth century woodwork was installed in the old house, remnants of a shiplapped board wall survive on the east gable end and a section of round-butt shingles dating to the eighteenth century was found under the shed dormer.

Also significant to the site is a large portion of the earthen dam that once impounded water for the gristmill referred to in tax records and deeds during the eighteenth and nineteenth centuries.

Rebuilding of the eighteenth century story-and-a-half house is estimated to date to 1815, after Alexander Jones began assembling an impressive plantation between Great Monie and King's creeks. Starting in 1811 and continuing to 1816, Jones and his wife Elizabeth purchased a handful of land parcels along the Great Monie. "Manning's Resolution," largest among the various tracts, was the site

of the plantation complex. This tract had been passed down in the Jones family since the late seventeenth century, and family ownership continued until the early 1970s. Alexander Jones was a prominent Somerset County planter, and he and his wife donated the land for nearby Grace Episcopal Church. Listed as an agriculturist in his 1849 will, Jones bequeathed ownership of this plantation to his son Edward Augustus.

COSTEN HOUSE
Circa 1805
Wellington vicinity (site)
Private

Architecturally, this small two-story, one-room plan house, which stood abandoned in an open field, was one of the most significant frame houses to survive in Somerset County. Despite its diminutive size, both the exterior and interior details surpassed the architectural sophistication found in many larger houses. The pedimented entrance was complemented by a delicate modillioned cornice. Inside, the first floor room had flat-panel wainscoting and a tight winder stair. The adjacent single story kitchen wing was also worthy of note with its interior horizontal board sheathing and exposed beaded joists.

Architectural features pointed to a circa 1800-1815 date for construction of the house, but little else is known about its early history and occupants. The house stood on part of "Costen's Care," a tract of land owned and farmed from the seventeenth through the nineteenth centuries by various generations

S-337, Samuel Miles house, north elevation.

S-336, Jones Choice, northwest elevation.

of the Costen family. The first mention of this specific house is located in the chancery court papers drawn up to settle William M. N. B. Costen's estate in 1892. In 1897 the land on which this house stood was apportioned to Marietta Costen Clarke, widow of Edward H. Clarke of Worcester County. It is not known whether Mrs. Clarke ever occupied the house, which was dismantled for salvage in the late 1980s.

SAMUEL MILES HOUSE
Circa 1820
Princess Anne vicinity
Private

The Samuel Miles house is an early nineteenth century four-room plan dwelling that was moved a short distance from its site and converted to a storage building in the 1960s. The two-story, three-bay frame house is distinguished by beaded weatherboards and a decorated cornice. The front cornice is embellished with bed and crown moldings as well as a drilled decoration of stylized classical swags under the soffit.

The four-room first floor is fitted with Federal period woodwork. The stair rises in two flights and each step-end is decorated with an applied scroll. Flush six-panel doors open from the hall into the adjacent first floor rooms, which are finished with flat-panel wainscoting. A layer of oak graining is visible under the gray paint in the parlor.

The land on which this house stands was assessed in 1798 for Samuel Miles. His dwelling house was described as

Situate in Somerset County about 5 Miles from Pokomoke River, 1 Dwelling house, 22 by 18, 1 story high with 3 windows 2 1/2 by 4 1/2 & 2 windows 3 1/2 by 2 1/2 & 1 window 1 1/2 by 2, Built with one End Brick, Rest wood & 1 wood Kitchen 12 by 12 & 1 Cook house 20 by 16 of wood & 1 Brick Smoke house 10 by 12.

The land assessment included

A Tract of Land Called Miles's Last Choice & other adjacent Tracts Lying in Somerset County Back in the woods about 5 Miles from Pokomoke River with 1 Barn 30 by 30 & 1 barn 24 by 40, & 1 Corn Stack 32 by 6 all wood at the place where he lives.

Evidently, Samuel Miles and his family occupied the single story house described in the tax assessment until the 1820s, when the extant house was probably built. The Federal period woodwork is similar to that at the nearby William Costen house (S-76), which is dated to 1829.

In Samuel Miles's will, proved on October 16, 1850, he stated that his wife, Sally, should have during her widowhood "all my lands whereon I now live...." After Sally Miles's death, the farm passed to William Miles and then to his son William F. W. Miles, who is shown at this site in the 1877 Somerset County atlas and included on the patron list. Samuel F. Miles, one of the last family members to own the property, was a long-time surveyor, whose career spanned a

large part of the twentieth century.

In its conversion for storage, the house received a new foundation, its chimneys were taken down, some mantels were removed, and a wing was taken off and demolished.

JONES CHOICE
Circa 1815, circa 1850
Venton vicinity
Private

Jones Choice is architecturally and historically significant for several reasons. The three-part stepped house is one of only a few still standing in the northern neck of Somerset County along Little Monie Creek. While the first floor of the old kitchen obviously dates to the early nineteenth century (circa 1815), the other two sections were built during the mid-nineteenth century. This pattern illustrates an important point in terms of the development of the stepped house form in Somerset County and the lower Eastern Shore—the large section of a stepped dwelling was not necessarily built first. The main house at Jones Choice follows the traditional side hall/parlor plan and is fitted with fine examples of mid-nineteenth century craftsmanship, especially the ramped mahogany handrail. The Federal period woodwork in the old kitchen is an important survival as well.

Historically, "Jones Choice" is associated with the Jones and Waller families. Patented to William Jones by 1663, portions of the Monie Creek lands were passed down through the family until the early nineteenth century.

S-38, Hollyhurst, south elevation.

William Jones occupied his plantation for close to three decades; during this period he was named a justice of the peace, an office he held between 1676 and 1689. After his death around 1690, the Monie Creek plantation passed to his second wife, Jane, and then to his sons John, Robert, and George. Through his father's will, John Jones (born in 1668) inherited the "Jones Choice" ground along the Little Monie on which this house stands. From him the property passed to a Robert Jones and then to John Jones of Robert (circa 1740-1799).

John Jones of Robert was listed on both the 1783 and 1798 tax assessments with over 300 acres of the "Jones Choice" patent. In 1798 his assessment included the following improvements:

> *1 Dwelling House 45 by 18 feet one Storey Brick, 4 windows 3 feet 6 Inches long, 3 feet wide, 2 [windows] 3 feet 8 Inches long, 2 feet 4 Inches wide, out of repair; 1 Kitchen 36 by 15 feet Brick, 1 Smok house 12 feet square, 1 Milk house 12 by 8 feet, 1 Cyder house 15 by 12 feet.*

After John Jones's death in 1799, his son Robert evidently began a building program to replace his father's house, which by the early nineteenth century had reached a state of disrepair. The current kitchen with its Federal style woodwork evidently dates from the

period of Robert Jones's ownership. Robert Jones occupied the Little Monie plantation until his death in the 1820s, and his administration account named his brothers James and John as well as his brother-in-law George Ormsby as the heirs.

After the estate settlement the "land which belonged to the late Robert Jones of John" was advertised in the *Village Herald* by his brother James Dashiell Jones of Baltimore. Portions of "Jones Choice" were sold through the late 1820s and 1830s. James Jones transferred a 150-acre tract containing the plantation buildings to George M. Willing on October 3, 1826. Ten years later Ballard Reid purchased the same tract. In the 1836 indenture the description of the land mentions "it being the next ditch to the westward of the house where Robert Jones formerly lived." Reid died the month after he bought the Monie Creek lands, and they passed to his daughter Nelly and her husband, George B. Waller. Six years later, on January 25, 1842, the 150-acre farm was transferred to Robert J. Waller for $500. Robert J. Waller improved the old plantation house by adding the two larger sections of the stepped dwelling and raising the roof of the old kitchen. The main house and middle section were fitted with Greek Revival style woodwork, including the finely crafted mahogany stair. Waller's initials, "B. W.," thought to stand for Bob Waller, were found on a rafter in the main section.

After Robert J. Waller's death in 1891, the property passed to his son Robert, who sold the farm in 1912 for $6,500. Since this transfer, the property has been sold nine times. The current owners bought 148 acres and the house in 1979.

HOLLYHURST (NR)
Circa 1816
Venton vicinity
Private

Facing a broad vista of the Manokin River, Hollyhurst stands on land originally surveyed for William Bozman on November 11, 1662, and known as "More and Case It." The derivation of the tract name is not known exactly, but it is thought to mean "to take root and hold." Bozman was one of the earliest settlers along the Manokin and was named to a commission on the Eastern Shore that granted land warrants and administered justice. Initially encompassing 1,200 acres, his land was divided between three sons, John, William, and George Bozman, in 1664.

The expansive Manokin River land grant was fragmented several times during the eighteenth century as it was divided among various Bozman descendants. At the close of the American Revolution, Isaac Bozman was assessed for a 130-acre tract of "More and Case It" on the Manokin. Isaac and George Bozman mortgaged the plantation to William

S-41, Elmwood, southeast elevation.

Williams, merchant, for £600 in 1790. Because they both died before the mortgage was satisfied, their plantation was offered at public sale, and in 1802 Ezekiel McClemmy Gilliss purchased the former property of George Bozman from Littleton Dennis. Fourteen years later, Gilliss mortgaged 700 acres of "More and Case It" to the Bank of Somerset for $10,000 in an apparent effort to finance construction of the extant two-story Flemish bond brick house.

Similar to many county plantation houses, Hollyhurst is supported by a raised foundation. But unlike most of its contemporaries, the two-story, three-bay house is covered by a parapet gable roof. Parapet gables were used on the wings of the Teackle Mansion (circa 1818). Regrettably, Hollyhurst burned in October 1915 and the original interior fabric was completely lost.

Although Ezekiel McClemmy Gilliss financed the construction of this brick house around 1816, he sold the property two years later to Dr. Levin Ballard for £1,065. Dr. Ballard retained ownership of the plantation until his death in 1843. His executor, Edward Long, sold "More and Case It" to Henry A. White in 1844 with a confirmatory deed executed in 1849. The 1850 census records 31-year-old Henry White, his wife Anne, and their children Fanny, William, and Wyatt on the farm. Fanny married Samuel S. Sudler on June 24, 1874, and she and her husband

lived on the farm. Sudler sold the property to Franklin Krips of Philadelphia on November 20, 1889. The Kripses called the property "Helena Park."

During the early twentieth century, the farm was the residence of Colonel E. Staunton Field, who named the farm "Hollyhurst." It was during the Fields ownership that a fire, which started in the attic above the kitchen, gutted the old brick house. The dwelling was rebuilt a few years later after Charles A. and Mercy Hover acquired the farm in 1917. Hollyhurst was nominated to the National Register of Historic Places in 1976 as part of the Manokin Historic District. The present owners bought the house in June 1981.

ELMWOOD (NR)
Circa 1820
Oriole vicinity
Private

Elmwood, one of the most distinctive Federal style plantation houses in Somerset County, stands prominently along the north bank of the Manokin River near Oriole. Structural evidence indicates the squarish, two-story brick main block was erected first, while the shorter brick and frame sections were built at the same time or later in the nineteenth century. Despite former estimates of an eighteenth century date, Elmwood was built in the first quarter of the nineteenth century and

combines Federal and Greek Revival stylistic features.

The principal elevation (east) is distinguished by a symmetrically placed door and windows topped by wooden jack arches with projecting keystones. The pedimented gable is pierced by unusual quarter-round attic window openings. The north and south elevations feature decorative cast-iron railings at each side door. Elmwood's interior has survived largely intact with important examples of Federal and Greek Revival style woodwork. Fixed in the northeast corner of the transverse hall is an open-string stair, which rises four flights to the third floor. Along with delicate stringer trim, a mason's divider and square were executed in wood and applied to the front of the first landing. The six principal rooms of the main house are fitted with period mantels, chair rail, molded baseboards, cornices, and fine door and window moldings. Surrounding the house is a rare collection of trees and shrubs planted in the mid-twentieth century.

Standing on part of the "Almodington" tract, the Elmwood estate is a result of the ambitions of Arnold Elzey Jones, a prominent farmer as well as a member of the Maryland Assembly from Somerset County. Jones's earliest ownership of the property is recorded in a deed executed on August 4, 1818, transferring the land to him from his father, Colonel William Jones, Sr. The transfer states "that for the consideration of one dollar current money and of the natural love and affection which he the said William Jones hath and beareth unto the said Arnold E. Jones," William Jones granted to his son "all that part of a tract called Almodington lying on the Manokin River...all that land lying south of the field called the graveyard field and known as the lower plantation." It is estimated that Arnold Elzey Jones built the extant brick plantation house within a few years of acquiring the property.

In 1825 the estate of William Jones, Sr. was formally partitioned between his son Arnold and his daughters Sally E. Jones and Elizabeth Ann Wilson Jones Waters. "Lot No. 1" was designated as the property of Arnold E. Jones, which he had evidently occupied since the transfer in 1818. Sally E. Jones received the old mansion house, while Elizabeth A.W. Jones was given the third lot, later known as "Homewood."

Arnold Elzey Jones continued to occupy

S-413, Pinto farm, west elevation.

the Manokin River plantation until his death in 1839. His will, proved on September 17 of that year, left to his wife Nancy (Anne W.) "his whole estate and at her death to be divided among the children." Anne W. Jones remained on the estate until the early 1860s, when the property was divided in settlement. On September 27, 1862, Elmwood was transferred to Thomas H. Fitzgerald for $11,500. For the next forty-nine years, the Fitzgerald family owned and occupied Elmwood. Albert

B. Fitzgerald et al. transferred ownership to John D. Page on September 11, 1911. Thirty-six years later Margaretta Stevenson Taylor purchased 315 acres and the brick house from Phillips and Suzanne Clark. Taylor and her husband, Norman, retired on the property and planted an exotic collection of trees and shrubs. The current owners purchased the property in 1983.

HOMEWOOD (NR)
Circa 1825
Oriole vicinity
Private

Popularly built in Somerset County until the mid-nineteenth century, gable-front houses such as Homewood were usually planned with a symmetrical, three-bay elevation topped by a Greek-inspired pediment, as is the case here. A central front door is framed by fluted pilasters, a four-light transom, and a simple entablature. Lighting the first floor are nine-over-six sash windows. A delicately crafted round window with radiating muntins is centered in the pediment.

In many cases, these transverse hall houses appear to have more than one principal elevation. At Homewood, the south hall door opens into a two-story porch, which covers the entire elevation. The first floor plan follows the same general scheme as other houses

S-39, Homewood, west elevation.

with a transverse stair hall and two large rooms behind. Homewood, in fact, repeats the floor plan of Elmwood (S-41) and a large collection of contemporary examples. Attached to the north side of the main house is a two-story service wing evidently erected at the same time as the main house.

Construction of this finely appointed frame house is attributed to William G. and Elizabeth A. W. Waters around 1825. After William Jones's death, the "Almodington" estate was divided into three principal parcels. Elizabeth A. W. Jones Waters received the section on which this house stands, and it was probably assembled shortly afterwards.

PINTO FARM
Circa 1805
Princess Anne vicinity
Private

Located north of Princess Anne and east of the old Pennsylvania Railroad line is the Pinto farm, which has remained in the same family since the early nineteenth century. Although Zadock Long purchased several tracts of land in 1803 and evidently financed the construction of the early, southern half of this two-story frame house, it is documented that he lived elsewhere (see Catalpa farm, S-408). The property was instead occupied by Long's daughter Leah Whittington Long and her husband, John V. Pinto. After Zadock Long's death in 1838, the farm was devised to Leah and her husband and in the event of their deaths to the grandchildren, Matilda W. and John E. L. Pinto. The farm was eventually partitioned in February 1869 between John V. Pinto and Matilda since John E. L. had sold his interests in the property. A month later John V. Pinto died, and the house, which he had received in the division, passed to the next generation of family owners.

Although the side hall/parlor house has been reworked recently, it retains an early nineteenth century stair, flush six-panel doors, and Federal style mantels and chair rail. A combination of wrought and double-struck cut nails suggests the early nineteenth century construction date.

EDGE HILL
Circa 1820, circa 1860
Princess Anne vicinity (site)
Private

Edge Hill was the country residence of John W. Crisfield, one of the most important residents of Somerset County during the mid-nineteenth century. As a prominent attorney, Crisfield helped establish the railroad connection with Somers Cove, later renamed Crisfield in his honor.

When Crisfield purchased this river property in 1839, a single story, brick-nogged frame house evidently stood on the site. During his ownership the house was enlarged in two ways: The front side hall/parlor section was attached and the earlier house, serving as a kitchen wing, was raised to two stories. These mid-nineteenth century additions were fitted with modest Victorian woodwork.

John W. Crisfield and his wife, Mary, acquired part of "Hayward's Purchase" situated along a bend in the Manokin River through a chancery case in Somerset Court dated November 1839. A covenant in the settlement stated that William Roach agreed to sell Crisfield the farm on which Charles Harding lived at the time. After Crisfield purchased the property he reworked the existing house. Mary W. Crisfield occupied Edge Hill after her husband's bankruptcy and death. In 1927 the Crisfield daughters sold twelve and a half acres and the house to Ralph and Martha Roush, who in turn sold the property to the First Baptist Church in 1960. Edge Hill was burned in 1984.

S-111, Edge Hill, southeast elevation.

S-408, Catalpa farm, west elevation.

CATALPA FARM (NR)
Circa 1825
Princess Anne vicinity
Private

Catalpa farm, located south of Princess Anne along the old Westover road, is most notable for the well-preserved nature of the farmhouse and outbuildings (including one of four known tobacco houses in Somerset County) and its associations with the Long family. Beginning with Zadock Long, who purchased "Law's Purchase," "Davis's Choice," and "Walton's Improvement" from John and Margaret Byrd and Mary Smith in 1804, the property remained in the Long family until the early 1970s.

Prior to Zadock Long's ownership, the plantation was apparently tenanted by Joseph Matthews, whose name is listed on the 1798 tax assessment as occupant of the land belonging to "John Bird." The improvements at the time included

1 Dwelling house 34 by 16 feet, wood one Story with 3 windows 4 feet 10 Inches long, 2 feet 4 Inches wide, 3 windows 3 feet 8 Inches long, 2 feet 4 Inches wide and in midling repair, 1 Cook house 20 by 16 feet.

Also on the property was another dwelling occupied by "Peggy Politte," which was described as

1 Dwelling house 30 by 18 feet wood, one story high, 4 windows 4 feet 10 Inches long, 2 feet 4 Inches wide with Addition of 15 by 10 feet with 1 window 3 feet 8 Inches long, 2 feet four Inches wide, 1 Cook house 16 by 15, 1 Milk house 8 feet square, 1 Lumber house 16 feet, 1 Stable 20 by 10 feet, 1 Nessery house 8 feet square, all in good repair.

Neither of these descriptions, however, fits the present building on the property. In any case, the late Federal design of the exterior and interior woodwork, as well as the use of mature cut nails throughout the house and outbuildings, suggests the house and early outbuildings were erected during the ownership of Zadock Long, which stretched from his purchase in September 1804 until his death in February 1838. Aside from his prominence as a substantial landholder, Long is well remembered as the owner of the Washington Hotel in Princess Anne.

Zadock Long's will, proved on February 13, 1838, stipulated that the "land purchased of John Byrd and wife and Mary Smith and the mill lot adjoining" would pass to Edward

H. C. Long. Edward Long occupied the farm until 1865, and at his death the "home farm and mill lot" passed to Charles Whittington Long, who held onto the property for fifty years. Charles W. Long sold the 335-acre farm, then known as Catalpa farm, to E. Walter Long in 1915. After the latter's death in 1971, the property passed to his personal representatives, Virginia L. Long and John W. Long. In 1974 Robert W. and Lois Long sold 5.94 acres surrounding the house and outbuildings to Donald L. and Elizabeth M. Henderson. The current owner purchased the same acreage from the Hendersons in 1984.

In addition to the well-preserved early nineteenth century farmhouse, Catalpa farm contains an unusual number of agricultural buildings no longer standing on most Somerset County farms. The rarest outbuilding is the tobacco house, one of four known to survive on the lower Eastern Shore. This tobacco house, built around 1825-1840, is smaller than the other three examples and was assembled with a broken roofline. The working elements of the barn are basically the same, however. The dairy, also dating from the second quarter of the nineteenth century, is a relatively infrequent survival as well, especially with its shelving and plastered interior still intact. The smokehouse, of the same date as the dairy and tobacco house; the late nineteenth century privy and corn crib; and the early twentieth century gambrel-roofed barn are more typical survivals from their periods.

Although the two-story, five-bay farmhouse is oriented on a center hall plan, the front block was assembled in stages, beginning with a side hall/parlor house. Attached to the rear was a single story hyphen that connected the house and the two-story kitchen. Shortly after initial construction, Zadock Long financed the addition of a two-story, one-room plan section on the north gable end. Later in the nineteenth century, the hyphen was raised another story.

DORMAN'S CONCLUSION
Circa 1820, circa 1860, circa 1900
Princess Anne vicinity (site)
Private

The construction history of this two-and-a-half story, three-bay frame house is more complicated than it appeared at first glance, although the uneven south fenestration pointed immediately to a shift in building periods. The oldest section, the western two bays of the main block, dated to around 1820. Erected during the ownership of William H. Dorman, the braced frame structure retained early nineteenth century features, including a corner stair and Federal style mantels, chair rail, and baseboard.

In 1857 John W. Crisfield purchased the part of the Dorman's Conclusion tract that included this house and incorporated it into his adjacent Edge Hill estate. At that time or

perhaps a few years later, when Crisfield transferred the property to his son Henry Page, the house was enlarged with a two-story, one-room plan addition that continued the roofline of the old Dorman house. The property is designated under the ownership of Col. Henry Page on the 1877 county atlas, and Page held title to the farm until 1884. Around 1900 the house was enlarged once more with a rear story-and-a half kitchen wing. Dorman's Conclusion was burned in 1989.

WILLIAM COSTEN HOUSE (NR)
1829
Wellington vicinity
Private

"Costin's Trouble" was patented to William Furniss in 1679, although the property evidently was occupied by his daughter Comfort and her husband, Stephen Costin. In his will of January 1697, Stephen Costin (later spelled Costen) devised portions of his plan-

tation to his sons Isaac and Stephen. Isaac's will of February 1743 assigned his portion to his son Isaac. Although Stephen Costin died intestate, his portion of "Costin's Trouble" fell to his son Stephen Costen, who subsequently sold the property to Matthias Costen, who is listed as a joiner in the land records. Although no will is recorded for Matthias Costen, the land apparently passed to his son Matthias, who had his portion of "Costin's Trouble" resurveyed as "Costen's Care" in 1794. In 1798 the tract was assessed in Dividing Creek Hundred. The valuation reads as follows:

Situate in Somerset County Near Dividing Creek about 5 Miles from Pocomoke River 1 Dwelling house 36 by 18 Two story high with 8 windows 2 1/2 feet by 3 1/2 feet Built with 2 Brick Chimneys Rest of Wood, 1 Kitchen 24 by 16 and 1 Milk house 12 by 10 and 1 Cook house 16 by 6 all wood.

Seven years after this assessment was made, Matthias Costen died and his plantation was willed to his son William. Born in 1779 William Costen was the fifth generation of Costens to farm the Dividing Creek property. In 1829 he replaced his father's house with the well-built, well-appointed transverse hall dwelling that stands today. A date brick of 1829 with the initials "W. C." is set into the upper portion of the chimney. William Costen died intestate on September 23, 1842. In all likelihood his wife, Mary M. Costen, occupied the plantation until her death in October 1854, although their son William M. N. B. Costen and his first wife, Henrietta Dickerson, apparently assumed full ownership of the family farm. Henrietta died in 1847, and William married Mary A. Costen.

In 1860, during William M. N. B.'s own-

S-416, Dorman's Conclusion, south elevation.

S-76, William Costen house, northeast elevation.

ership, the farm was assessed for $10,000. By 1877 Costen's total property neared 4,000 acres, making him one of the most prominent landowners in Somerset County.

The house William Costen built in 1829 displays a favorite architectural form in early nineteenth century Somerset County. Dominated by a bold gabled pediment with a modillioned cornice, the east elevation serves as the principal entrance with a center door and flanking nine-over-six sash windows. The cornice fascia is finished with an arched and drilled design repeated on the Henry Lankford house near Hudson's Corner (S-68), a construction parallel that suggests shared craftsmen. Inside, the transverse hall is distinguished by a delicate Federal style stair, which rises four flights to the third floor. The balance of the house has not been altered to any large degree and survives with 90 percent of its original woodwork. The common bond brick dairy immediately to the west of the kitchen wing dates from the early nineteenth century as well.

POMFRET PLANTATION (NR)
Circa 1820
Marion vicinity
Private

Widely recognized as one of the most significant sites in southern Somerset County,

Pomfret Plantation derives its historical importance from its architecture as well as from its associations with the prominent Coulbourne family. This early nineteenth century, two-story, four-room plan frame dwelling retains 95 percent of its Federal style interior woodwork and holds a notable place in the collection of Federal period plantation houses in Somerset County. A hyphen and kitchen addition date from about the same period as the house.

William Coulbourne, previously of Northampton County, Virginia, is thought to have settled on the lower Eastern Shore of Maryland between October 1663 and January 1664, when his son Solomon was born at Annemessex. Colonel Coulbourne, as he was later known, served in official positions in Maryland's late seventeenth century militia, in addition to holding the political office of high sheriff of Somerset County in 1673 and 1675. In 1670 he became a member of the Commission of the Peace, which drew up a treaty with the Nanticoke Indians in August 1687.

Coulbourne's plantation of 1,400 acres, which consisted of "a neck of land on the south side of the Annemessex River near the mouth of Coulbourne's Creek," was resurveyed in 1679. After Coulbourne's death in 1689, "Pomfret" passed to his eldest son, also William (1658-1701). William Coulbourne II married Anne Revell of Randall in 1678. In

1721 their two sons divided their father's Coulbourne Creek plantation equally. As expressed on a 1722 plat, William Coulbourne III (1682-1764) received the northern half of the tract along Coulbourne's Creek, while Solomon (1684-1749) received the southern half bordering Jones's Creek.

William Coulbourne III died in 1764 and devised his portion of "Pomfret" to his son William IV (1700?-1775). Eleven years later, William IV died, leaving his wife Sarah dower rights and his sons Robert and William V eventual claim to his property. Sarah Coulbourne was assessed in 1783 for 200 acres of the original survey of "Pomfret" "on the water," while her two sons, Robert and William, are listed with no land but with several slaves. Evidently William V inherited the plantation house after his mother's death, since he left it to his wife Mary in his 1789 will. Mary Coulbourne is found on the 1798 tax assessment with

1 Tract of Land called Pomfort containing 643 acres on which are erected the following Buildings, 1 Old Dwelling House 24 feet by 18; 1 Kitchen 18 feet by 14 feet; 1 Corn House 24 feet by 7 feet; 1 Smoake House 12 feet Square, 1 Barn 30 feet by 24 feet, 200 acres of the above land Marsh.

This land assessment mentions an "old dwell-

S-68, Lankford house, north elevation.

ing house," but Mary's house was described as

> *1 Dwelling House built of wood 20 feet long by 28 feet wide one Story high, 3 windows 3 feet 9 Inches long by 2 feet 9 Inches wide, 2 Dormant windows, 3 feet by 2 feet, 1 Kitchen, 18 feet long by 14 feet wide, S[awed] Logs; 1 Meat House, 12 feet square, saw'd Logs; 1 stable 18 feet by 14 feet, round Logs.*

These two house descriptions make it clear the eighteenth century "Pomfret" houses have not survived, and all aboveground traces of their support buildings have disappeared as well.

The extant three-part house is thought to have been built during the ownership of Mary Coulbourne's only son, William VI, who had the plantation resurveyed in September 1819. William VI died in 1830 but left no will. The property was inherited by Isaac H. Coulbourne (1808-1846), who executed a mortgage to Joshua P. Horsey on August 8, 1836. The deed of mortgage includes the statement "all that tract of land lying and being in Somerset County, and on Coulbourne's Creek, in Annemessex, called and known by the name 'Pomfret' being the same lands that the said Isaac H. Coulbourne inherited by the death of his father, William Coulbourne, containing six-hundred and forty acres."

In October 1841 Isaac sold "Pomfret," then containing 631 acres, to his second cousin once removed, also named Isaac (1777-1855), for $8,550. This Isaac and his wife, Leah (1788-1855), are buried in the fenced cemetery on the property, as are their eldest son, William (1811-1892), and his wife, Henrietta R. Coulbourne (1827-1906). William and Henrietta occupied the house during the fourth quarter of the nineteenth century, and he is designated in the 1877 county atlas as a shipbuilder and farmer of 250 acres. At the time of William's death in October 1892, his sons William R. and Isaac H. were appointed executors to sell their father's farm. On March 30, 1895, they transferred the farm to their sister, Addie M. Gunby, wife of Fred A. Gunby. After more than 250 years of Coulbourne family ownership, this portion of "Pomfret" was sold out of the family in 1921. Forty-six years and six transfers later, the present owners acquired "Pomfret" containing 421³/₈ acres in 1967.

LANKFORD HOUSE (NR)
Circa 1835 and earlier
Hudson's Corner vicinity
Private

The Lankford house stands on land that was surveyed in 1667 as "Hignett's Choice" and in 1683 as "Buck Lodge." Although "Hignett's Choice" was patented to Robert Hignett, 150 acres of the 300-acre tract belonged to Edward Dykes. Dykes (also spelled Dikes, Dickes, Doakes, Daax, Dakes, and Dokes) also owned a tract of 100 acres known as "Buck Lodge." These neighboring tracts are located at the head of Marumsco Creek.

S-82, Pomfret Plantation, southeast elevation.

Through various land transactions and inheritances, parcels of both "Hignett's Choice" and "Buck Lodge" passed to Edward Dykes's sons Edward Jr. and George and then to Edward Jr.'s son James Dykes. In 1783 James Dykes was assessed for 100 acres of "Hignett's Choice" as well as 150 acres of "Buck Lodge" on which stood "one framed dwelling house, two rooms below." In his 1791 will, Dykes left part of his Marumsco Creek property to his four sons. To his son Daniel (1763-1834), he left eighty-seven acres of "Hignett's Choice," and provisions in his will stated Daniel was to inherit the interests of his brothers James and Stephen if they died with no male heirs.

In 1798 Daniel Dykes was assessed for his Marumsco Creek plantation called "Hignett's Choice" as well as for adjacent tracts. The records show his dwelling measured 36' by 16' and had "Wood sides and Roof and Brick Ends, 1 story high." Also found on Daniel's property was "1 Kitchen 20 by 16, a Milk house 8 by 8 & 1 Meat house 10 by 10 of wood."

Thirty-six years after the tax assessment, Daniel Dykes died, leaving his son-in-law Henry Lankford as executor with authority to divide the farm between his five daughters and five grandchildren. On March 1, 1834, Lankford sold 163 acres of "Hignett's Choice" and "Buck Lodge" to Benjamin Lankford, who the same day sold the property back to Henry for $1,500. From architectural evidence, it is assumed Henry and his wife, Nancy Dykes, financed the construction of the extant two-story, four-bay frame dwelling. The single story hyphen was part of the Lankfords' building program since it connected the main house and the existing 20' by 16' frame kitchen mentioned in the 1798 tax assessment. When the hyphen was put up, the west gable end wall of the kitchen and the original kitchen stair apparently were rebuilt as well. The door to the stair appears to have been reoriented to open from the hyphen instead of from the kitchen. Henry Lankford occupied his new house for close to a decade until he died in the early 1840s. His estate was not settled until 1854, when John T. Lankford bought the 214 acres from the administrator of Henry's estate.

After 1859 the Marumsco Creek farm was sold out of the Lankford family and held by a half-dozen owners. In 1918 John T. Handy and George T. Corbin bought the farm; eight years later Corbin and his wife sold their interest to Handy. The farm is now owned by Handy's daughter Marian Sue Handy Anderson. Mrs. Anderson and her husband, John, restored the house in the 1950s.

The squarish two-story, four-bay frame house is trimmed with a significant mixture of Federal and Greek Revival details. The exterior cornice is distinguished by a decorative arched and drilled fascia below a row of modillion blocks. Inside, Greek Revival style mantels frame the two first floor fireplaces. The old story-and-a-half kitchen is used as a utility room, but a remnant of a rare board partition survives above the second floor ceiling.

Most important, this well-built farmhouse is clearly representative of the rebuilding process that transformed the county landscape during the late eighteenth and nineteenth centuries. While maintaining the familiar stepped house form, Henry and Nancy Lankford decided to erect a larger, more spacious dwelling than that of her parents.

BEECHWOOD
Circa 1830
Princess Anne vicinity
Private

The Beechwood estate was the long-time home of the Waters and Elzey families, who occupied the tracts known as "Manlove's Discovery" and "Gray's Adventure" from the

S-26, Beechwood, south elevation.

S-46, Severn Mister house, north elevation.

second quarter of the eighteenth century until the 1940s. The current two-story frame house was probably built during the ownership of Levin Littleton Waters after his marriage to Elizabeth R. W. Hyland on May 30, 1827. After Waters's death, a commission was established in 1850 to divide his landholdings, and Lot No. 1, consisting of the house and 110 acres, was apportioned to his son Levin L. Waters, Jr.

By the time the 1877 county atlas was produced, Levin L. Waters, Jr. was the Somerset County clerk of court and owned 315 acres. In his will, proved on April 12, 1912, the fourth item bequeaths the residue of his estate to his sisters Emily R. Waters and Eliza W. Waters. Eliza Waters Hart transferred the house to her husband through her will of January 1940, and he subsequently sold Beechwood to American Legion Post No. 94.

Since the American Legion post purchased the house, it has undergone several alterations, including the addition of a large meeting room on the west side and a thorough interior renovation. The south (front) elevation still retains its gable-front orientation. Unusual to Beechwood is its pedimented entrance, which echoes the gable front of the main facade.

SEVERN MISTER HOUSE
Circa 1815
Deal Island
Private

Built during the first decades of the nineteenth century, the Severn Mister house is perhaps the oldest dwelling to survive on Deal Island. The two-story, hall/parlor house retains distinctive Federal style details common to the early nineteenth century. The diamond-shaped muntin transom over the front door, exposed brick fire walls, and raised six-panel doors are features worthy of note. Attached during the middle years of the century, the rear service wing contains the stair and has a two-story side porch. The corn crib dates from the same period as the house.

Construction of this early Deal Island frame house is attributed to Severn Mister, who started purchasing land on Deal Island in 1814. In that year he acquired parts of "Purgatory," "Barbadoes," and "Self Preservation" from Thomas Rowe for $1,700. Eight years later Mister bought an additional tract called "Grave's End" from Charles Jones. In his biography of Reverend Joshua Thomas, Adam Wallace mentions Severn Mister as "a prominent and wealthy citizen of Deal's

Island for many years…on very intimate terms with Father Thomas. Their friendship continued after Captain M. removed to the western shore of Virginia, where he settled in Northumberland County."

In November 1839 Severn and Keziah Mister transferred ownership of the plantation to their son Bennett, who lived on the property with his family until mid-century. Thomas Bradshaw acquired title to the property in August 1861, and Bradshaw family members owned it until the 1930s. Addie W. and L. May Bradshaw repatented the farm under the name "Two Sisters" in 1929 before they sold the property.

WILLIAM PRICE HOUSE
Circa 1838
Wenona
Private

In November 1837 William Wallace sold parts of three tracts to William Price of Dorchester County. Included in the deed was part of a tract called "Graves End," part of "Barbadoes," and part of "Self Preservation." It is estimated from architectural evidence that William Price financed the construction of this two-story, three-bay frame dwelling during the next year. One of the oldest dwellings in the Wenona vicinity, the house with its transverse hall plan is a modest example of the Federal/Greek Revival style houses found throughout Somerset County. The Palladian window that pierces the gable front is an unusual feature not shared by other houses of the same form.

Adam Wallace, the biographer of Reverend Joshua Thomas, mentions Captain William Price in reference to Reverend David Wallace. He relates, "Most…marriages were solemnized at [Wallace's] own house on Deal's Island, which stood on the spot now occupied by the modern and elegant residence of

S-47, William Price house, northwest elevation.

Captain Wm. Price, the Custom house officer for that port." Price continued to reside in the house but in 1883 transferred title of the property to Addie W. and L. May Bradshaw, while retaining life tenancy. Price died around 1885, and the property passed from the Bradshaws to William Damerel in 1887. Barnie G. Shores owned the parcel from after the turn of the century until 1937. Afterwards Eddie and Edith Shores owned the house until 1972.

WEBLEY
Circa 1840, 1894
Princess Anne vicinity
Private

Supported by a minimal brick foundation, this two-story frame house dates from two principal periods. The initial Greek Revival dwelling, raised during the second quarter of the nineteenth century, followed the popular gable-front, transverse hall form. In 1894 the house was extensively reworked with a new two-story addition on the northeast corner and an entirely new roof. Protruding through the rebuilt roof is the original, unusually large brick chimney.

The interior has been partially reworked, once in the 1890s and again during the past few years. The transverse hall still contains the stair, which rises in the southeast corner. A Victorian newel post and turned balusters

support a molded handrail. Flat six-panel doors open into the two rooms west of the hall, and a shallow four-panel door opens into the late nineteenth century addition.

The tract of land known as "Webley" has been owned by the King and interrelated Miller families through the eighteenth and nineteenth centuries. The "Webley" tract was the site of an early Somerset County courthouse and later was the location of the two-story brick Washington Academy. The acad-

emy building formerly stood on the east side of US 13 across from this farmhouse.

W. J. SCHOCKLEY FARM
Early 19th century
Princess Anne vicinity
Private

The W. J. Shockley farm is a significant complex of early nineteenth century structures. The farmhouse was clearly built in two principal stages and was formerly extended to the south with a colonnade and kitchen. Exterior alterations have included a layer of asbestos shingles and the replacement of nine-over-six sash windows.

The outbuildings are relatively well-preserved examples from the mid to late nineteenth century. The stilted dairy is a rare type of structure, and the smokehouse, built of brick, is unusual for a Somerset County farm. It is apparent the mid-eighteenth cen-

S-343, Webley, east elevation.

S-28, Edinburgh, southwest elevation.

S-350, W. J. Shockley farm, southwest elevation.

tury paneling in the kitchen and the reused glazed bricks in the smokehouse were salvaged from a much older dwelling.

For more than a century, this farm has been owned by the Woolford or Shockley families. In 1885 W. J. Shockley rented the farm from William Woolford, and then in 1910 Shockley purchased the property. The farm passed to W. C. Shockley, who occupied the river-front property until the late 1970s.

EDINBURGH
Circa 1840
Polk Landing (site)
Private

Only a few plantation houses in Somerset County outwardly reflect what is traditionally thought to be the Greek Revival style. However, countless rural as well as town dwellings were trimmed with classically inspired features common to the second quarter of the nineteenth century. Although the Edinburgh plantation house has been lost, photographs taken before it was demolished reveal several exterior features that indicate its stylistic inspiration and date. The corners of the traditional two-story, five-bay frame house were accented with paneled pilasters, and the side-lighted center entrance was trimmed with a molded surround marked by plain corner blocks.

Construction of the house is attributed to Colonel Joseph S. Cottman, who purchased the "Edinburgh" tract for $2,948.74 at the trustees sale of the former lands of Littleton P. Dennis, held at the hotel of H. K. Long in Princess Anne on Tuesday, September 29, 1835. The terms of sale allowed twelve months credit for half the purchase price and two years credit for the balance. A final deed was executed in November 1837. The tract at that time included 652 acres. At the administration of Joseph S. Cottman's estate around 1863, the property passed to his second wife, Elizabeth Upshur Dennis Cottman. In more recent years the creek farm was owned by General William B. Cochran, who occupied the early twentieth century Colonial Revival house built on the same farm (see S-401) until his death in 1931. The old Cottman house was razed in the 1980s.

E. T. STEVENS FARM
Circa 1825, 1905
Pocomoke City vicinity
Private

Standing on a prominent ridge west of Courthouse Hill Road, this two-story, side hall/double-pile farmhouse appears to date from the second quarter of the nineteenth century. The exterior was reworked in 1905 at the same time the rear kitchen wing was attached. Accompanying the house is a gable-front frame barn and a small wood shed.

S-221, E. T. Stevens farm, southeast elevation.

Both outbuildings postdate the house.

A researched chain of title for this property has not been established, but it is shown on the 1877 atlas under the name of E. T. Stevens.

CAPTAIN WILLIAM VEASEY HOUSE
Circa 1800, circa 1850
Pocomoke City vicinity
Private

The Captain William Veasey house, standing on the north bank of the Pocomoke River, is a significant example of a stepped or "telescope" dwelling. The construction history of this house is interesting because the oldest portion of the three-part dwelling is the main block, in contrast to the popular notion that stepped houses developed in a strict pattern with the smallest section built first. The circa 1800 side hall/double-pile main block has a heavy mortise and tenon hewn frame and is the only section assembled with wrought nails and exposed framing members. The two shorter sections were added to this structure around 1850. Oddly, all the woodwork dates from the mid-nineteenth century, suggesting either that the house was unfinished for a long time or originally used for a different purpose. With its proximity to the river, it is not unlikely that the two-story frame served some sort of commercial function before its conversion into a house around 1860.

S-223, Captain William Veasey house, north elevation.

ADEN DAVIS HOUSE
Circa 1840
Marion vicinity (site)
Private

The old Aden Davis house was one of the few three-part stepped houses surviving in lower Somerset. From an analysis of the structure before it burned, it appeared the main two-story, three-bay block was erected first and the two shorter sections were either built at the same time or added later. The interior of the main house retained portions of its second quarter of the nineteenth century woodwork.

Due to the proximity of this tract of land to Coulbourn Creek, it has passed through the hands of several prominent Somerset families. Known in the land records as "Part of Pomfret" and "Ferry Bridge," the property is recorded in a transfer of land between William Williams and Hance Croswell in December 1814. The deed describes the land as

> lying and being in Somerset County in Little Annemessex and on the head of Coulbourns Creek...standing on the divisional line between said William Williams and William Miles and also on a road that formerly ran down from the county road to said Williams wind mill, thence running down towards Coulbourns Creek.

Hance (or Hans) Croswell lived on Jones Creek as a ship carpenter and apparently never lived on the Coulbourn Creek property. In December 1829 he transferred to his son Hope Croswell 135 acres "near the head of Coulbourns Creek" and "Part of Pomfret," "Ferry Bridge," and another tract known as "Horsey's Conclusion." Hope Croswell evidently lived on this property until his death circa 1841. The architectural details of the house suggest the extant dwelling dates from his ownership.

In 1841 a commission was established to settle Croswell's estate. The commissioners, Benjamin Lankford and William H. Curtis, transferred the Coulbourn Creek farm to Hance Croswell. By the late 1850s the property was in the hands of William Miles, Southey A. Miles, and Christina Miles. These three sold the 150-acre farm to Aden Davis, Sr. on September 22, 1859. Davis owned the property for the next fifty-eight years, and his name is designated on the 1877 Somerset County atlas. In 1927 the farm passed out of the Davis family; four transfers have occurred since that time.

NELSON HOMESTEAD (NR)
Circa 1836
Bedsworth vicinity
Private

The Nelson homestead, also known as the Elisha Riggin house, is an extremely important late Federal period plantation house. Several other stepped houses remain on the lower Eastern Shore of Maryland, but this house stands out as one of the least altered examples.

The three-part frame house, built circa 1836, is a finely crafted structure with intricate cornice details and distinctive endboards. The modillion block cornices are finished at each end with a decorative end board impressed with five-point stars. The first floor room of the largest section has raised panel wainscoting and a raised panel overmantel that survives with an early layer of tiger maple graining. Enriching the walls is a gougework chair rail and a dentiled cornice. The hearth is framed by a highly unusual early nineteenth century mantel with turned colonettes and applied decorations. The original stair, part of which remains, is

S-278, Aden Davis house.

S-245, Nelson homestead, south elevation.

fixed in the northeast corner of the room. The other two first floor rooms are finished with rare paneled walls and built-in cupboards that echo design traditions of the mid to late eighteenth century. Despite the early appearance of this woodwork, which may have been reused, construction evidence and cut nails found throughout the house indicate the three-part dwelling was built in one period.

Somerset County land records from 1790 show that Elisha Riggin purchased part of a land patent known as "Cork" from Jonathan Riggin. Eight years later the federal tax assessors listed Elisha Riggin in Little Annemessex Hundred as the owner of "one tract of land called Cork, 25 acres." The property was improved with a twelve-foot square log house. In 1804 Elisha Riggin, Jr., the attributed owner of the extant house, who is listed as a shipbuilder in the deed, sold his father's "Cork" lands to Captain Aaron Sterling for £26.16.5.

Riggin's whereabouts between 1804 and the 1830s are uncertain, but he is listed in Somerset County marriage records with three wives. He married Martha Mister on August 24, 1818; Amelia Cullen on January 13, 1820; and Hannah Miles on January 15, 1839. Amelia is mentioned in an 1837 deed with

Elisha, and Hannah is listed as his wife in his administration settlement.

Riggin evidently amassed a considerable estate in the shipbuilding industry or through inheritance, because in 1836 he purchased from William Roach, Sr. a 145 ½-acre tract,

being part of 'Makepeace,' 'Force Put,' 'Cabin Swamp,' and 'Exchange,' in Little Annemessex being the residue of land formerly belonging to the father of said William Roach, Sr.

After this transfer, Riggin made several transactions dated between 1837 and 1842, probably to pay off building debts incurred in the erection and finishing of this house.

In May 1842 Elisha Riggin, Jr. transferred legal ownership of his property to Eliza Roach for the sum of $775. The deed states,

all these lands in Little Annemessex upon which the said Elisha Riggin Junior now resides…and the said Elisha Riggin Junior doth hereby recognize the relation of Landlord and Tenant as to said land from this period and doth acknowledge himself as tenant to said Eliza Roach, her heirs, executors, and administrators.

Riggin evidently reneged on this agreement, and Eliza Roach sold the property in 1843 at a sheriff's sale to William Nelson. During the following year, Hannah Riggin sold Nelson her dower rights in the property.

William Nelson and his wife, Ellen Riggin, lived on the property until their deaths in 1881. The property passed to their son Edward L. Nelson in 1881 and to his only heir, Margaret E. Horsey, in 1925. No appreciable alterations were made to the house until 1933, when Margaret Horsey inserted a new stair in the middle section. Appointed trustees for Margaret Horsey sold the property in 1962. Four years later, the present owners acquired the house and 5.52 acres.

CULLEN HOUSE
Circa 1837
Hopewell
Private

The old Cullen house, in the center of the crossroads village of Hopewell, follows the regional vernacular stepped house form popularly referred to as "big house, little house, colonnade, and kitchen." The main two-story, three-bay block has a center entrance, diamond-shaped muntin transom, and flanking nine-over-six sash windows. Highlighting

S-80, Cullen house, northwest elevation.

the front and rear cornices are rows of modillion blocks that terminate at each end with an upside-down U-shaped end board. This distinctive decorative feature is repeated at the old Nelson homestead (S-245), which was built at the same time and probably by the same artisans. Attached to the north end of the main Cullen house is a shorter, story-and-a-half section that connects the colonnade and kitchen to the main house.

Construction of this four-part house is attributed to John Cullen, Sr., who purchased the 100-acre plantation from the estate of Lodowick Milbourn in December 1836. Identical finish features repeated at the William Nelson homestead tie these buildings to the same period of construction. Both dwellings exhibit a mixture of Federal and Greek Revival style elements. John Cullen transferred ownership of the property to his two sons, William T. and Jacob Hoke Cullen, in 1866. The Cullen family has maintained ownership of this farm to the present day.

Jacob Milbourn assembled the 100-acre plantation on which this house stands from two tracts in 1769. Composed of parts of "Hopewell" and "Upper Andua," Milbourn's plantation included 108 acres as well as a single story, 24' by 18' frame house; a 16' square kitchen; and several other outbuildings by the time of the 1798 tax assessment. Lodowick Milbourn inherited the Little Annemessex Hundred plantation through his father's will, proved in 1813.

NORFOLK
Circa 1837
Pocomoke City vicinity
Private

Standing prominently on its slightly elevated site, the Norfolk plantation house is a significant three-part frame dwelling supported by a raised foundation and covered with a steeply pitched gable roof. Despite proportions that suggest an eighteenth century date, architectural evidence and family tradition confirm that this large two-story, four-room plan dwelling was raised during the late 1830s for William T. Hargis. Large nine-over-six sash windows and delicate Federal style bed moldings under the cornice are

S-75, Norfolk, southeast elevation.

255

exterior features that support the nineteenth century date. The first floor is divided into four rooms with the stair rising in the southeast corner.

The plan and general appearance of the Hargis house are similar to Caldicott (S-72), Littleton Dennis's impressive plantation house on the Pocomoke River. However, in contrast to the late eighteenth century woodwork of Caldicott, a mixture of Federal and Greek Revival style finishes graces the Norfolk plantation house. The front two-panel Greek Revival style door is topped with a four-light transom and framed by a molded surround with plain corner blocks. Family tradition relates that the two-story kitchen formerly stood a distance away from the house and was joined to the dwelling by a colonnade around 1876.

William T. Hargis inherited title to the "Norfolk" plantation through the will of Levin Pollitt, probated in 1836. Also cited in Pollitt's will was an item that left his niece Mary D. Stevens "the place whereon I now live, it being part of land called Good Success and Dennis's Addition." Hargis married Sarah Costen, daughter of William Costen, who lived only a few miles away (S-76). The Hargises raised nine children in the large house. Carrie Hargis, the youngest child, married Samuel A. Evans, and the property remains in the Evans family.

JEPTHA HAYMAN FARM
1836, c. 1860
Kingston vicinity
Private

The Jeptha Hayman farmhouse is a significant two-story, center hall structure built in two principal stages and finished inside with Federal and some Greek Revival woodwork. The side hall/parlor south end of the frame house was built in 1836, dated by an inscribed

S-244, Jeptha Hayman farm, west elevation.

brick, while the north dining room was attached around 1860. The center stair survives with a square newel post topped by a ball finial and a decorated stringer. A flat six-panel door opens into the south parlor, which is fitted with a Greek Revival style mantel. Engaged columns flank the firebox and support a three-part paneled frieze.

The Somerset land records are not clear as to when Jeptha Hayman acquired this Marumsco Creek property, known as part of "Mitchell's Lott" and part of "Sword." Hayman's marriage to Mahala Fooks is recorded in the Somerset marriage records for January 30, 1838. Mahala Fooks evidently died, for

Hayman's marriage to Sally W. Benson is recorded for January 27, 1847.

It is not known when Jeptha Hayman purchased the property, but in all likelihood he had acquired it by the 1830s and may have been responsible for building the initial house in 1836. During the following half-century, he assembled a respectable farm on both sides of Marumsco Creek near St. Mark's Chapel. He was dead by 1876, and the Somerset Court appointed a commission to evaluate and sell his farmland. His widow, Sally Benson Hayman, retained rights to a widow's dower that included a portion of the dwelling house:

S-67, Watkins house, east elevation.

S-291, Clement Sterling house, southwest elevation.   *S-329, William R. Byrd house, northeast elevation.*

The property remains in Hayman family hands.

WATKINS HOUSE
Circa 1825 and later
Hudson's Corner vicinity
Private

Not much is known about the early nineteenth century history of this two-story frame house, which stands along the old Westover-Kingston Road near Hudson's Corner. Despite an overall layer of asphalt shingles, the uneven fenestration of the east elevation suggests the farmhouse was erected in at least two periods, beginning with the northern two bays and the story-and-a-half kitchen wing. The north gable end is notable for its exposed brick fire wall and its early nineteenth century corner stair and remnants of period woodwork. Evidently the main two-story structure was originally connected to the kitchen by a single story hyphen, which was raised to two stories during the third quarter of the nineteenth century. At the same time, or perhaps slightly later, the window sash were replaced and the roof was rebuilt with extended eaves.

A chain of title documents this farm as the "Old Watkins Place," named for Frank H. Watkins, who owned the property between 1912 and 1951. The property was held by the Davis family in 1877.

CLEMENT STERLING HOUSE
Circa 1830
Bedsworth vicinity
Private

Supported by a raised brick foundation, the two-story Clement Sterling house stands prominently against the low-lying land near Johnson's Creek in the vicinity of Bedsworth. The side hall/double-pile frame house was extensively remodeled around the turn of the century with the relocation of the chimney and the addition of narrow gable end windows. In spite of these exterior alterations, the early nineteenth century interior was left largely unchanged.

The generously proportioned side hall has flat panel wainscoting, molded chair rail, and a decorated staircase. Sawn scrolls embellish each step end. Five-panel doors open into the adjacent rooms, which are finished in a similar manner. The back room, or dining room, has a late Federal period mantel. The woodwork retains contrasting layers of mahogany and tiger maple graining. In addition, the kitchen survives with a paneled fireplace wall, enclosed winder stair, and flush panel wainscoting.

Older residents in the Bedsworth community identify this property with Clement Sterling, a former owner.

WILLIAM R. BYRD HOUSE
Circa 1840
Crisfield vicinity
Private

The William R. Byrd house is one of a handful of antebellum frame houses that survive southeast of Crisfield in an area referred to as "down the neck." The modest two-story, one-room plan main block and the story-and-a-half wing retain period features that include nine-over-six sash windows and an early nineteenth century stair. The house has retained its stepped form. A semi-detached summer kitchen formerly stood to the rear of the dwelling.

Historically, the parcel of ground on which the Byrd house stands was part of a larger tract known as "Hills Folly," which was occupied by the Byrd family during the eighteenth and nineteenth centuries. The house is named for William R. Byrd (1829-1887), who probably built it.

S-246, Watkins Point farm, north elevation.

JOHNSON HOUSE
Circa 1840
Crisfield vicinity
Private

The Geneva Cox house, also known as the old Johnson house, is a frame dwelling that stands on the old road connecting Hopewell and Bedsworth. The two-story, three-bay main house has a one-room plan. It is extended to the west by a single story section, while a hyphen and summer kitchen stretch to the north. The house is designated on the 1877 atlas under the name J. Johnson.

WATKINS POINT FARM
Late 18th century, circa 1850
Cash Corner vicinity
Private

Built on the first appreciable rise of land west of Gunby Creek, the Watkins Point farmhouse stands in distinct contrast to the expansive tidal marsh surrounding it. Also known as the James L. Horsey farmhouse, this stepped or "telescope" structure is one of the most significant architectural survivals in southern Somerset County. The Greek Revival dwelling is an important example of

a gable-front, transverse hall house. The attached one-room plan sawn log house with remnants of a raised panel interior end wall is the only known structure of its type standing in Somerset County. Presently used as a kitchen, the interior of the 18' by 15' log house is finished with beaded floor joists, finely molded window and door surrounds, molded chair rail, and wrought-iron hardware. Also significant is the rear shed of the log house, which has an exposed timber frame with beaded or chamfered plates and posts. The chamfered timbers appear to be reused materials from an older building.

A chain of title for this farm indicates the house stands on a tract of land known as "Watkins Point," a name that figures prominently in the early history of Somerset County as the geographical boundary separating Maryland and Virginia.

Earliest ownership of "Watkins Point" as recorded on the Maryland Rent Rolls shows a 150-acre tract surveyed in 1664 for John Horsey and possessed by Stephen Horsey. Stephen Horsey's will, proved on October 3, 1722, declared that the "Watkins Point" property would pass to his son Stephen, while his dwelling house and plantation, known as "Hannah's Delight," would be inherited by his other son, John.

Stephen Horsey II apparently established residence on the "Watkins Point" property because his will, proved on September 9, 1761, declared that his son Revill Horsey

S-260, Johnson house, south elevation.

would inherit "my Dwelling plantation whereon I now live after the death or marriage of my well beloved." To his grandson John Horsey, Stephen bequeathed "A parcell of land out of the Watkins Point patent."

Revill Horsey also occupied the Watkins Point tract and passed it to his son Stephen in 1781. Revill's will states, "to Stephen, a tract or parcel of land called Watkinses Point whereon I now live, one negro boy name George, etc."

Seventeen years after Stephen Horsey's inheritance, the federal assessors described the improvements on the Watkins Point plantation:

1 Dwelling House built of wood 24 feet by 20 [feet], an Addition 20 feet Square, One Story high, 3 windows 5 1/2 feet by 3 feet, 6 windows 3 feet 9 Inches by 2 1/2 feet, 1 Kitchen 15 feet square saw'd logs, 1 [kitchen] 18 feet by 15, Fraim'd, 1 Smoake House 10 feet Square, The above Houses very old & in bad repair. $130.

The sawn log kitchen described in the tax assessment is probably the extant log structure. Perhaps the decorated posts incorporated in the shed addition are materials reused from the other, "fraimed" kitchen.

In the nineteenth century Stephen Horsey and his wife, Peggy Marshall, (married May 13, 1817) lived at the Watkins Point farm and may have been responsible for replacing the single story house with the circa 1850-1860 Greek Revival dwelling. Stephen remained on the farm until his death. His sole heir, James Lambert Horsey, inherited the farm in 1856.

Horsey and his wife, Henrietta Watkins Horsey, owned the house until his bankruptcy in May 1870, when the property was conveyed to William H. Roach. According to the 1877 county atlas, Roach was a farmer and merchant who owned 700 acres in Lawson's Election District. In October 1889 Roach's executors, Julia F. Atkinson, William E. Roach, and Gordon T. Atkinson, inherited the property. During the past several generations, the property has been known as the John T. Adams farm, after the present owner.

BOWLAND FARM
Circa 1830 and later
Kingston vicinity
Private

Despite its remodeled and altered exterior, the Bowland farmhouse is a noteworthy example of a dwelling built in several stages beginning around 1830-1850. Structural evidence indicates the main house was built in two stages, one room at a time. The western two-story portion appears to have been built around 1830 and the second half added within the following two decades. Later in the nineteenth century, the house was extended again by a story-and-a-half addition to both the north (rear) and the east. The farm appears on the 1877 county atlas belonging to E. S. Broughton.

WILLIAM J. COULBOURN FARM
Circa 1850
Hopewell vicinity
Private

Dating to around 1850, the William J. Coulbourn farmhouse is a two-story, stepped style farm dwelling located near Jones Creek and the small crossroads of Hopewell. Architectural details and construction evidence suggest this long four-part house was built in one period. The main two-story, side hall/parlor house is framed by paneled pilasters and trimmed with bracketed eaves. A two-story porch (now enclosed) covers the front of the main block. Attached to the south gable end is a slightly shorter two-bay section also trimmed with brackets. The house extends farther south with a two-bay hyphen connected to the story-and-a-half, one-room

S-188, Bowland farm, south elevation.

kitchen, all dating from the mid-nineteenth century.

From the evidence accumulated so far, it appears that William Coulbourn erected this house during the third quarter of the nineteenth century. William C. Coulbourn, listed in the 1877 Somerset County atlas as a ship carpenter, is mentioned on the patron list as owning fifty-six acres on Jones Creek. After his death in 1883, the property passed to his wife, Sarah E. Coulbourn. In the event of her death, the farm was to be inherited by their son William J. Coulbourn. William J. and his wife, Mary Clayton Coulbourn, remained on the Jones Creek property until Mary sold it to Helen L. Bordwell in December 1941.

STEVENSON HOUSE
Circa 1840
Hopewell vicinity
Private

The Stevenson house is a modest, side hall/parlor frame farmhouse originally sheathed with beaded weatherboards. Exterior as well as interior remodelings have removed much of the original fabric. The nearby family cemetery is partially surrounded by a Victorian iron lattice fence. The house is named for Benjamin F. Stevenson (1809-1886), the probable builder, who is buried with his wife, Harriet, in the cemetery plot. Stevenson is designated on the 1877 county atlas patron list as a mariner who owned forty acres.

THOMAS WARD HOUSE
Circa 1864
Hopewell vicinity
Private

Standing within a short distance of Jones Creek near Hopewell is the Thomas Ward house, a two-story, transverse hall frame

S-281, *William J. Coulbourn farm, southeast elevation.*

dwelling built around 1864. The pedimented main block has a modillioned cornice and a small round window with pie-shaped panes. Extending to the north is a contemporary two-story, one-room plan section that connected the main house to the two-story kitchen. The kitchen has been torn down, but the brick chimney remains intact. Two twentieth century additions have enlarged the house to the southeast and west.

Period woodwork survives largely undisturbed in the main house. The stair rises in the southeast corner and has a heavily turned

newel post and turned balusters that support a ramped handrail. The pair of rooms behind the hall are fitted with mid-nineteenth century mantels that have widely fluted pilasters and friezes.

According to family tradition, the extant dwelling was erected around 1864 by Thomas and Susan Ward on the site of the Ward house that had burned the year before. The Jones Creek property had remained in Ward family hands since the original 200 acres were granted to Cornelius Ward and his wife, Margaret Franklin Ward, during the 1660s. The

S-282, *Stevenson house, northwest elevation.*

S-283, Thomas Ward house, southeast elevation.

land continued under Ward family ownership until 1922.

OLD BRADSHAW PLACE
Circa 1860
Marion vicinity
Private

Although the old Bradshaw house has been moved from its original creek-side location to a less prominent inland site, the circa 1860 stepped frame house has not been seriously compromised. A large portion of its interior fittings remains undisturbed.

The main two-story, two-bay block has a transverse stair hall with a large parlor behind. Boldly molded and crossetted door surrounds with shallow arched pediments frame six-panel doors on the first floor. The adjacent two-story, two-bay dining room appears to be contemporary with the main house; however, the single story kitchen was moved up to the dining room at a later date. Exterior weatherboards now covered by the dining room wall suggest this architectural change. The kitchen probably stood separate from the house and was attached later.

REHOBETH
18th and 19th centuries
Rehobeth
public and private

Rehobeth is an important riverside village due to its early formation and longstanding use as a local port or shipping point. The Rehoboth Presbyterian Church (1706) and the Coventry Parish ruins (1784-1788) are the most notable structures. The houses that define Rehobeth largely date from the mid to late nineteenth century and include two-story, two- and three-bay vernacular frame dwellings. One old nineteenth century store stands in the village group as well.

Rehobeth takes its name from the tract of land called "Rehoboth" patented to Colonel William Stevens in the third quarter of the seventeenth century. The name means "there is room." The village of Rehobeth was officially created by a 1683 act of the Maryland Assembly for the "encouragement of towns and points of entry for shipment of tobacco and other exports as well as the importation of goods from distant places."

S-279, Old Bradshaw place, northwest elevation.

With its deep channel, the Pocomoke River provided Rehobeth with an enviable deep-water port for larger draft ships. Boat traffic continued through the eighteenth, nineteenth, and early twentieth centuries until the steamboats discontinued service after World War I.

The town of Rehobeth was spelled "Rehoboth" until the 1950s, when the spelling was changed to avoid confusion with nearby Rehoboth, Delaware.

DR. THOMAS COSTEN HOUSE
Circa 1825
Rehobeth vicinity
Private

Standing just west of the village of Rehobeth is the Dr. Thomas Costen house, a two-story, four-bay center hall frame house. Supported by a raised brick foundation and sheathed with beaded weatherboards, the early nineteenth century house is distinguished by exposed brick fire walls on each gable end and a Victorian cross-gabled roof. Inside, a large portion of the Federal period woodwork, including a decorated stair, chair rails, and six-panel doors, remains intact. The mirrored mantel in the east room with detached Corinthian columns is a turn-of-the-century replacement.

Extending to the rear is a two-part stepped service wing. Construction details suggest the northern section, a single story kitchen, was joined to the main block with a single story hyphen. The hyphen was raised to two stories in the late nineteenth century.

Dr. Thomas Costen is identified as the owner of the property on the 1877 Lake, Griffing and Stevenson atlas of Somerset County.

FLEURY HOUSE
Circa 1830, circa 1860
Rehobeth vicinity
Private

Sited on high ground on the northwest side of the Pocomoke River, the Fleury house is a two-story, side hall/parlor frame structure that was enlarged during the third quarter of the nineteenth century with a two-story, two-bay gable end addition. Although the house has been moderately remodeled, some of the late Federal period woodwork survives intact. Stretching eastward from the house are expansive views of the tidal marsh of Worcester County dotted with cypress trees. The property was owned by a Charles C. Wetherill in 1877.

SHELLTOWN
19th and 20th centuries
Shelltown
Public and private

Shelltown is a small village located along the Pocomoke River approximately two miles south of Rehobeth. The houses face the main street, which connects Shelltown Road and the wharf. The small community is com-

S-253, Dr. Thomas Costen house, southeast elevation.

S-256, Fleury house, southwest elevation.

S-258, Shelltown.

S-200, Captain E. W. Milligan house, southwest elevation.

posed of approximately a dozen frame and recently built brick structures. The Cropper store is the only commercial structure. A few buildings date from the third quarter of the nineteenth century, but most were erected during the early twentieth century. Even though the extant dwellings in Shelltown date from relatively modern times, the existence of the village is documented as early as the late eighteenth century. The village was named for large shell deposits along the river banks.

SMITH FARM
Circa 1850
Shelltown vicinity
Private

The Tom Smith farm occupies a prominent site along the Pocomoke River near the small riverside village of Shelltown. Two stories high and five bays across, the main farm-house was built in two principal stages. The original house was a two-story, three-bay structure connected to the kitchen by a hyphen. During the 1930s the hyphen was raised to two-story height in line with the main house. The accompanying farm buildings date from the last fifty years.

SCHOOLHOUSE NO. 4
Circa 1860
Shelltown vicinity
Private

School No. 4 is on the north side of Shell-town Road a mile and a half south of Re-hobeth. The single story, gable-front frame building is supported by a brick pier founda-tion and trimmed with narrow corner pilas-ters. The southwest side has six large-scale windows that were added around 1920 in an effort to increase the amount of natural light-ing. This school is thought to have been the first to accomplish these lighting changes, which were imposed under state standards.

CAPTAIN E. W. MILLIGAN HOUSE
Circa 1840
Raccoon Point
Private

The Captain E. W. Milligan house, now known as Raccoon Lodge, is located at the end of an L-shaped dirt lane on Raccoon Point. This second quarter of the nineteenth century, side hall/parlor frame dwelling stands within ten yards of the Manokin River.

In the 1877 county atlas, Captain E. W. Milligan is shown as the owner of 225 acres on Revell's Neck. The house's proximity to the river suggests Milligan's associations with the water, as does his listing as an oysterman and a farmer in the list of atlas patrons. He was born in Somerset County around 1820.

S-257, Smith farm, west elevation.

S-272, School No. 4, southwest elevation.

S-216, William Costen tenant house, southeast elevation.

S-78, Stephen Costen farm, northeast elevation.

WILLIAM COSTEN TENANT HOUSE
Circa 1860
Wellington vicinity
Private

This two-story frame tenant house is a simple, third quarter of the nineteenth century dwelling located in the north central Dublin election district. It is one of the few tenant houses surviving from William M. N. B. Costen's agricultural estate, which totaled close to 4,000 acres by the 1870s. The unusually steep pitch of the kitchen roof gives the house an interesting appearance. All architectural details suggest the kitchen is contemporary with the front part of the house.

STEPHEN COSTEN FARM
Circa 1840
Wellington vicinity
Private

The Stephen Costen farmhouse is a plain two-story, five-bay, center hall frame dwelling flanked by exterior common bond brick chimneys. Extending to the rear is a single story hyphen, which connects the house and the one-room plan kitchen. Both the kitchen and the hyphen are finished inside with vertical beaded boards, while the front rooms are fitted with Greek Revival style woodwork.

Stephen Costen was the owner of this house according to the 1877 Somerset County atlas.

RICHARDSON FARM
Circa 1840
Princess Anne vicinity
Private

The Richardson farmhouse is one of the oldest houses standing along West Post Office Road immediately east of Princess Anne. The gable-front facade is the dominant architectural feature, and it repeats a building form common to the lower Eastern Shore. The house follows a transverse hall plan. During the late nineteenth century, a dining room/kitchen addition was attached to the north side of the main block. According to the 1877 Somerset County atlas the property was owned by a "Capt. Robinson."

S-345, Richardson farm, south elevation.

S-210, Carrigan farm, northwest elevation.

S-344, Covington house, west elevation.

CARRIGAN FARM
Circa 1850
Dublin vicinity
Private

The Carrigan farmhouse is a badly deteriorated, second quarter of the nineteenth century dwelling with Greek Revival interior woodwork. Circular sawn roof members, cut nails, and riven oak lath suggest a building date of circa 1850. The house previously had three sections, descending in height. The shortest section has been removed, and the center section has lost its roof.

This 100-acre farm, located on the north side of Mitchell Road, has been known in past years as the Carrigan farm or the Punch Johnson farm.

THORNTON
18th and 19th centuries
Princess Anne vicinity
Private

Thornton farm is situated on a high bank on the north side of the Manokin River west of Princess Anne. Patented in 1662 to William Thorne, the main tract encompassed 600 acres. The architectural survivals on the modern farm date to the fourth quarter of the nineteenth century, but located in the middle of a plowed field is a small cemetery that contains two of the oldest grave markers in Somerset County.

The large sandstone table marker in the cemetery was crafted for Alexander Brown, who inherited "Thornton" from Colonel David Brown around 1698. The tombstone bears the date 1712 and has an elaborately carved coat of arms. Also located in the cemetery is an anomalous marker for Captain John Blaney, who was born in Charlestown, Massachusetts, and died on January 5, 1715. The most remarkable aspect of this slate tombstone is the New England type carving that decorates the headstone and the footstone. A death skull flanked by wings tops the stone, and stars set in a circle head the

side panels. Down each side are breast motifs set between leaves.

COVINGTON HOUSE
Circa 1790, circa 1860
Princess Anne vicinity
Private

North of Princess Anne on the east side of the old Princess Anne-Upper Trappe road is the Covington house, a three-part stepped dwelling significant for its unusual form and late eighteenth century rear section. The other two parts of the house were built during the third quarter of the nineteenth century in two principal stages: The two-story main block was enlarged shortly after construction with a two-story, shed-roofed addition that contained the principal stair. Tilted false-plate construction and remnants of a wood-pinned roof distinguish the single story third section, which probably dates to the

S-348, Thornton.

265

S-399, Maple Grove, photograph c.1910 (courtesy of Clinton K. Lokey).

late eighteenth century.

The builder of the eighteenth century, one-room plan frame house has not been determined. Construction of the two larger sections probably took place around 1860, during Charles T. Marshall's ownership of the property. Marshall purchased eighty-six acres in August 1861 for $4,000 and sold fifty-six acres in 1865 for $5,000. The decreased acreage and increased sale price suggest capital improvements had been made on the farm, and the architectural features of the house agree with this estimated date of construction.

After a chancery court settlement, John E. Covington and his wife, Mary E. Covington, purchased the fifty-six acre property, referred to as "Pink Eye" in the 1874 deed. The farm remained in Covington hands for a large part of the next seventy-five years.

HOLLY GROVE
Circa 1853
Princess Anne vicinity
Private

Holly Grove is believed to have been part of the Adams family holdings south of Princess Anne in the late nineteenth century. Facing east, the front of this two-story, three-bay frame dwelling is oriented to the old Princess Anne/Westover road. Reported to date to 1853, the side hall/parlor house is trimmed with decorative eave brackets common to

antebellum houses. Attached to the back of the house is a two-story service wing. The chamfered post front porch was added around 1900.

MAPLE GROVE
1767 and mid-19th century
Westover vicinity (site)
Private

Maple Grove farm was located along Mennonite Church Road southeast of Westover.

The house, occupied by the Adams family during the nineteenth and twentieth centuries, was an interesting dwelling built in two principal stages. Clearly visible in historic photographs of the property is a mid-nineteenth century two-story, five-bay farmhouse trimmed with decorative brackets. A single story paneled post porch embellished with eave brackets stretched across the entire front of the center hall house.

Not clearly seen in photographs of the house is the earlier brick wing, dated to

S-339, Holly Grove, east elevation.

266

S-406, Arcadia, photograph c.1910 (courtesy of William Marshall Scott).

1767 by an etched brick. The date brick was found in the late 1970s when the house was dismantled and materials were sold for salvage. The full history of this property has not been established, but general information indicates the Adams family held it for much of the nineteenth century. Robert W. Adams, raised on the old family farm, decided to move closer to Princess Anne to educate his son at the Washington Academy. Adams purchased a farm on the southern edge of town, where his son Morris resided until the 1970s (see S-338).

ARCADIA
Circa 1850, circa 1920
Princess Anne vicinity
Private

The farm known as Arcadia is situated on the north side of the Manokin River a short distance west of Princess Anne. Improvements currently standing include a pair of early twentieth century frame dwellings and a large gambrel-roofed barn. The houses reflect the squarish, block-like proportions common to early twentieth century residential design. Gambrel-roofed barns are common for the twentieth century as well and were used to house dairy herds and large amounts of hay.

This Manokin River farm is also significant as the site of a prominent mid-nineteenth century house that burned around 1917. As depicted in an old photograph of the house, the two-story, three-bay frame dwelling was an unusual structure for Somerset County, having a four-room plan divided by a spacious cross hall that contained the stair. No other county house known to have stood at the time repeated such an elaborate plan. The bracketed eaves and porch, the Gothic-arched chimney flue covers, side-lighted entrances, and large six-over-six sash windows were popularly used during the third quarter of the nineteenth century. The house burned as the result of an explosion and fire caused by accumulated gas from a leaking light fixture.

WILLIAM MARTIN HOUSE
Circa 1860, circa 1900
Princess Anne vicinity
Private

The William Martin house is one of two nineteenth century houses at the end of Clarence Barnes Road. Facing west, this two-story, cross-gabled farmhouse is extended to the rear by a slightly older two-story service wing. Built around 1900 the center hall house is lighted by two-over-two sash windows. Entrance is provided through a partially glazed front door. The service wing is a shorter two-story structure, four bays long and one room deep with a two-room plan. A brick chimney rises through the roof to heat the wing, which has been remodeled to serve as a modern kitchen.

S-354, William Martin house, west elevation.

S-352, *LaVorgna house, northwest elevation.*

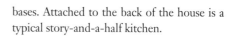

S-347, *Norman Pusey farm, south elevation.*

LAVORGNA HOUSE
Circa 1860
Princess Anne vicinity
Private

Standing on the north shore of the Manokin River is a two-story, five-bay center hall frame house that has been uniformly stuccoed. Corbeled brick chimneys rise from the single-pile front block as well as the two-story ell. Attached to the front of the house is a colossal columned portico added in the past few years. Immediately northwest of the house is a small family graveyard. The farm

was once part of the Anderson family's holdings along the Manokin.

NORMAN PUSEY FARM
Circa 1860
Princess Anne vicinity
Private

The Norman Pusey farm is one of a string of farms that borders West Post Office Road between Princess Anne and the Worcester County line. The standard two-story, three-bay farmhouse is distinguished by a pair of exterior brick chimneys with corbeled brick

bases. Attached to the back of the house is a typical story-and-a-half kitchen.

SANDUSKY FARM
Circa 1870
Princess Anne vicinity
Private

Surrounded by a group of nineteenth century outbuildings is an unusual late Victorian T-plan farmhouse covered with a combination mansard and gable roof. The mansard roof covers the north leg and directly abuts the cross gable roof. A turned post porch

S-342, *Sandusky farm, west elevation.*

S-340, *Cedar Lane farm, west elevation.*

S-108, Academy Grove historic district, southeast elevation.

with fan-shaped brackets skirts the perimeter of the north leg. The interior is fitted with unaltered period woodwork, including bull's-eye door and window surrounds, bracketed mantels, and a period stair with unusual features.

Within a short distance of the farmhouse is a collection of nineteenth century outbuildings that includes a full-dovetailed log smokehouse; a large, bilevel hay and dairy barn; a standard frame granary; and a wagon shed. Reused in the wagon shed framing are several beaded floor joists reportedly salvaged from an older building on the farm.

CEDAR LANE FARM
Circa 1870
Princess Anne vicinity
Private

Cedar Lane farm is located on the east side of the old Princess Anne-Westover Road south of Princess Anne. The nineteenth century cross-gabled farmhouse is accompanied by several contemporary outbuildings: A concrete-ribbed silo stands near a granary and two corn cribs. The winding entrance lane is bordered by a row of mature cedars.

ACADEMY GROVE
HISTORIC DISTRICT (NR)
Circa 1860
Upper Fairmount vicinity
Annual public fair

The Academy Grove historic district is composed of two well-known frame buildings—the Fairmount Academy and the Knights of Pythias Hall. Located between Upper and Lower Fairmount, these two Italianate-influenced structures are enhanced by their setting in a mature grove of cedar, oak, and pine trees. Notable features that tie the buildings together architecturally include bracketed eaves and corner pilasters. In addition to its architectural significance, the district is important for its association with the development of public education and civic organizations in the county during the second half of the nineteenth century.

Local tradition says a school was established on "Potato Neck" in 1839. However, the earliest known documented reference is found in the will of Lazarus Maddox, proved on March 26, 1841:

> *...I now establish and confirm the following to be the line between my home farm above described and my other lands here-after mentioned—commencing at the northwest corner of my field adjoining Edward T. Hall's store on the north side of the county road in Potato Neck, from thence running with a straight line to a marked pine tree standing near the School House down the neck on the same side of the County road aforesaid.*

The marked pine and schoolhouse are also referred to in an 1848 plat of a parcel of Daniel Ballard's land known as "School House Ridge."

With these two firm references, it appears a school was located on or near this site as early as 1839. However, a proper deed had not been executed for the schoolhouse ground by that time. In 1867 Thomas Emory Ballard granted to William Muir and others "one and one-half acres of land more or less to have and to hold the same in and for the use and purpose of a School House or Academy for the Education of Youth."

Despite an uncertain date of construction for the existing academy building, it seems most probable the trustees wanted a binding deed that would ensure ownership of a new academy. An early 1860s construction date is further strengthened by the fact that the Somerset County Board of Education min-

S-140, Rumbley.

utes begin in 1867 and no mention is made of erecting an academy in the Potato Neck District.

The name "Fairmount Academy" was evidently assigned to the building around the time of its construction, for early board of education references mention Fairmount Academy specifically. For instance, on April 17, 1867, the board ordered that "The Treasurer pay to the teacher of Fairmount Academy as Librarian the sum of twenty dollars provided by Chapter 7, Section 1, of the Public School Law."

The next building project at Academy Grove was the construction of the Knights of Pythias Hall circa 1872. Henry Rathbone founded the Society of the Knights of Pythias in 1864 in Washington, D.C. Fairmount Lodge No. 77 was established on May 5, 1872.

The similarity in architectural detail between the Fairmount Academy and the Knights of Pythias Hall suggests the hall was built soon after the lodge's inception. The first reference to the building is found in the board of education minute book of August 14, 1883, when a bill was submitted to the board for a $60 rental of the Knights of Pythias Hall at Fairmount. The Fairmount

Chapter of Knights of Pythias dissolved in 1911, but the building was still used for additional classroom space.

In 1888 the Fairmount Academy building was graced with a school bell ordered from the McShane Bell Foundry, McShane Company of Baltimore, Maryland, and probably delivered by steamboat. From the late nineteenth century until 1927, an academy staff

of five—one principal and four teachers—offered all twelve grades. Beginning in 1927 the grades were cut back to one through seven, and from 1944 to 1969 only the first six grades were taught at the school.

In 1972 the Somerset County commissioners decided to auction off all unused school buildings. This action galvanized a group of local residents to establish the Fair-

S-141, Thomas W. Blake house, southeast elevation.

S-142, Frenchtown.

mount Academy Historical Association. This group maintains the two buildings and holds an annual fair in the spring.

RUMBLEY
1860-1920
Upper Fairmount vicinity
Private

Small watermen's villages similar to Rumbley developed during the mid to late nineteenth century along the shoreline of Tangier Sound and the Chesapeake Bay, filling the need for modest housing close to the water. The two-story frame houses, which vary between two and three bays wide, face the water. In several instances, watermen's work sheds or shanties stand across from the dwellings, vividly reflecting the residents' close attachment to the bay.

THOMAS W. BLAKE HOUSE
Circa 1860
Rumbley (site)
Private

The Thomas W. Blake house, destroyed by fire in the 1980s, was the most ambitious nineteenth century house to survive in the small watermen's village of Rumbley. Standing within yards of Tangier Sound, the cross-gabled dwelling had a full two-story porch. A slightly older service wing extended to the rear. During renovation of this wing, sea oats (or grass) were found between the studs, evidently placed there to help insulate the structure. The oldest crab house standing in Rumbley is located in front of this house site. In the 1877 Somerset County atlas, the house on this point of land is designated as the dwelling of Thomas W. Blake, a local merchant.

FRENCHTOWN
1870-1930
Upper Fairmount vicinity
Private

Frenchtown is a small watermen's village located on a narrow ridge of land at the tip of the Fairmount peninsula bordered by Tangier Sound and the Jericho marshes. A string of a dozen houses and a few watermen's work sheds date from the late nineteenth and early twentieth centuries. Common to many water-oriented communities are the two-story, two- and three-bay frame dwellings with side or center hall, single-pile plans. In most cases, a shorter one- or two-room kitchen wing extends to the rear.

According to the 1877 county atlas, only three houses improved the narrow section of high ground at that time, while a handful of other dwellings were located on Hazards, an island to the southwest of Frenchtown. Older local residents relate that a few of the houses now in Frenchtown were floated across from Hazards and erected on new sites around 1900.

At the south end of the village is a small nineteenth century cemetery with tombstones belonging to the French family. In 1877 the houses were accompanied by a school and a Methodist church, both of which stood on the adjacent stretch of ground along the road that crossed the marsh.

MADDOX HOUSE
Circa 1870
Upper Fairmount vicinity
Private

The Maddox house stands at the end of Hall's Creek Road surrounded by tidal marsh. Dating from the third quarter of the nineteenth century, the side hall/parlor frame house rests on a brick pier foundation and is trimmed

S-143, Lower Fairmount.

with bracketed eaves. Similar to many houses of the period, the brick chimney rises against the hall partition and is finished with a corbeled cap.

The Maddox family appears in the chain of title from 1871 to 1874; John T. Parks purchased the creek property in 1874.

LOWER FAIRMOUNT
1860-1920
Upper Fairmount vicinity
Private

Lower Fairmount is a mid to late nineteenth century watermen's community situated on the low-lying, poorly drained soil of the western portion of the Fairmount peninsula. Several side streets extending at right angles from Maryland Route 361 allowed development off the main road. The two-story frame houses stand on generous lots and in one instance form a planned row. The communi-

ty boundaries are not well-defined and extend from the Fairmount Academy along Route 361 for approximately one mile. House types vary slightly, with two-story, two- or three-bay center hall structures with or without center cross gables. All the houses are of frame construction.

FORD HOUSE
Circa 1860
Lower Fairmount (site)
Private

In contrast to the modest houses in Lower Fairmount was this two-story, eight-bay frame house with bracketed eaves. It stood on the north side of the county road in that dispersed community. The long, single-pile frame dwelling was distinguished by a bracketed eave similar to that on the Hall house in Upper Fairmount (S-58). Also distinctive were the four brick chimneys with corbeled

caps that dominated the roofline. This house stood until 1987, when it was partially dismantled and eventually burned.

LOWER FAIRMOUNT POST OFFICE
Circa 1870
Lower Fairmount
Private

This small frame commercial building is located in Lower Fairmount amidst the dispersed group of two-story frame houses that comprise this watermen's community. A few changes have been made to this structure in an effort to turn it into a small house. The bracketed eaves and the six-over-six sash windows appear to be original to the post Civil War building. A store is located at this site on the map of the Fairmount Election District in the 1877 atlas, and according to local residents the building once doubled as a post office.

S-149, Maddox house, south elevation.

S-145, Ford house, south elevation.

S-164, Upper Fairmount.

UPPER FAIRMOUNT
1800-1920
Private

Upper Fairmount is one of the best-preserved rural villages in Somerset County. A variety of improved house lots, churches, stores, and small garden plots characterize the village. All buildings are of frame construction and reflect the middle class incomes of the village residents who built them. Small inland communities such as this one catered to the needs of local farmers and watermen during the nineteenth and early twentieth centuries.

Upper Fairmount's history is closely tied to the development of better inland roads, which reduced the need to travel by water. As a result of the improved transportation system, landlocked villages grew up along the major road that runs the length of the Fairmount peninsula. By the early 1820s

Maddox's Church had been formed in the village. The location of several important plantation seats within a short distance of Upper Fairmount undoubtedly helped maintain a relatively strong agricultural economy. The village apparently grew at a modest pace, with a flurry of building after the Civil War, which peaked around 1900. Since that time the village has experienced a slow decline and period of stagnation, which is the main reason its nineteenth century village character has been maintained.

HALL HOUSE
Circa 1825
Upper Fairmount
Private

The Hall house, located at the west end of Upper Fairmount, is one of the oldest houses to survive in the village. Notable architectural features include a side hall/parlor plan,

well-executed second quarter of the nineteenth century woodwork, and an exposed brick fire wall on the west gable end. During the third quarter of the nineteenth century, the frame house was extended with a two-story, two-bay frame addition trimmed with bracketed eaves. A small family burial plot is also on the property.

Exactly who built the original house is not clear, but the land was known as part of "End of Strife" and described in Lazarus Maddox's will of 1841, in which he left all his lands except his home farm to his two daughters, Sarah Hall and Kitty Ballard. Sarah and her husband, Tubman L. Hall, sold the tract where this house stands to Francis A. Hall in 1853. Francis Hall, his wife Mary, and three children are listed in the 1850 Somerset County census. Francis, described as a carpenter, may very well have built the east gable end addition.

S-147, Lower Fairmount post office, north elevation.

S-58, Hall house, south elevation.

S-59, Robert H. Jones house, northeast elevation.

ROBERT H. JONES HOUSE
Circa 1825, circa 1870
Upper Fairmount
Private

The Robert H. Jones house, standing in the center of Upper Fairmount, is the largest and most architecturally distinctive dwelling to survive in this small rural village. Despite its uniform three-bay elevation, the bracketed main house was erected in two principal sections; the circa 1825 west portion predates Robert H. Jones's ownership. The two-story frame service wing that extends to the rear is highlighted by a two-story porch on the west side and a butler's pantry on the east. An old photograph of the house shows a two-story porch stretched across the main facade.

Robert H. Jones purchased a fifty-four acre parcel "on the east side of the county road leading from James Town to Jericho" from Thomas E. Ballard in September 1862.

Presumably the property was improved by the two-story frame portion of the house that is finished with Federal style woodwork. From the architectural finish of the additions, it appears Jones financed extensive remodeling of the house around the time of his second marriage in 1875 to Elizabeth L. Tull, widow of Dr. J. Emory Tull. The "homeplace of Robert H. Jones" remained in the family through the lifetimes of his wife Elizabeth and son Robert H. Jones, Jr. and was not sold out of the family until 1973.

LEVIN B. HALL HOUSE
Circa 1820
Upper Fairmount vicinity
Private

The Levin B. Hall house is a significant early nineteenth century, side hall/double-pile dwelling with a mixture of late Federal, Greek Revival, and Victorian period trim.

The circa 1820 exterior details include an ovolo-molded backband surround that frames a flush, six-panel door. Located under the extended eave is a boxed cornice with bed molding. Around 1850-1860, the house was apparently remodeled with the addition of paneled pilasters and a turned post shed porch.

This farm, originally part of the holdings of Lazarus Maddox, was inherited by his two daughters, Kitty Ballard and Sarah Hall, through his will of 1841. His nearby "home farm" was bequeathed to another daughter, Milcah Ann, and her husband, Daniel Miles. Levin B. Hall and his wife, Sarah F. Hall, acquired legal title to a portion of the Lazarus Maddox holdings, including this house, from the heirs a few years later. The couple remained on the property until the late nineteenth century and were probably responsible for most of the exterior changes; however, it is not clear who erected the initial dwelling.

DR. J. E. TULL HOUSE
Circa 1865
Upper Fairmount
Private

The Dr. J. E. Tull house is one of the few houses in rural Somerset County that can be

S-157, Levin B. Hall house, east elevation.

S-150, Dr. J. E. Tull house, northeast elevation.

considered an interpretation of the Italianate style. The three-story main house is trimmed with paneled pilasters, and a bold bracketed eave highlights the hip roof. Paired four-over-four window sash light the first and second floors, and small paired windows illuminate the third floor. Attached to the back of the house is a two-story service wing. Accompanying this well-detailed dwelling is a group of contemporary outbuildings, including a pyramidal-roofed dairy, also trimmed with corner pilasters; a combination privy and workshop; a smokehouse; a corn crib; and a wagon house. A Tull family cemetery lies east of the dwelling.

Dr. J. E. Tull, a local physician of the mid-nineteenth century, is credited with constructing this center hall, single-pile frame house on a six-acre parcel of land he purchased from Robert H. Jones in 1864. The property description indicates the land was part of a tract known as "Hall's Adventure," situated on both sides of the county road leading from Jamestown to Jericho. Also mentioned in the deed is the lot's proximity to the Methodist Episcopal parsonage. Dr. Tull's grave marker is in the family burial plot next to the house and records his death on October 30, 1873. The village property remained

in his wife Lizzie's name and then his son Edward's hands until 1908, when the house was sold to W. Ernest Cox. The present owners purchased the property in 1972.

H. C. TULL HOUSE
Circa 1860
Upper Fairmount
Private

Supported by a raised common bond brick foundation, this two-story hip-roofed house stands out as one of the older and more distinctive houses in the village of Upper Fairmount. The center hall main house was heated by twin brick chimneys, which rise from the rear wall. Extending to the south is a two-story service wing. Also located on the property is a pyramidal-roofed dairy trimmed with paneled pilasters.

An exact year of construction has not been established, but architectural details comfortably date the Tull house to the third quarter of the nineteenth century. The dwelling is designated on the 1877 county atlas under the name H. C. Tull, who was the proprietor of the adjacent store, listed as H. C. Tull and Company.

PEARSON HOUSE
Circa 1870
Upper Fairmount
Private

The Pearson house stands at the east end of Upper Fairmount, where its well-preserved exterior is complemented by large shade trees. The two-story, L-shaped frame house follows the standard cross-gabled form, but the dwelling was turned to present an asymmetrical street elevation. Several features provide distinctive detail to this Victorian period house, including a chamfered-post porch, paneled corner pilasters, and arched attic windows.

WINDSOR HOUSE
Circa 1880-1900
Upper Fairmount
Private

The old Windsor house in the center of the village of Upper Fairmount is distinguished from other two-story, center hall houses by the wraparound porch that encircles the main block. Similar to many postbellum houses, the dwelling has front corners trimmed with simple pilasters with dentiled caps and a cen-

S-165, H. C. Tull house, north elevation.

S-166, Pearson house, northwest elevation.

ter cross-gable dominating the gable roof. The pair of brick chimneys piercing the roofline originally served iron stoves that heated the house.

CECIL FORD'S STORE
Circa 1880
Upper Fairmount
Public

In addition to being the only surviving nineteenth century store in the Fairmount area, Cecil Ford's store is the site of "Maddox's Church," home of the first Methodist congregation in Upper Fairmount. In 1874 the church trustees sold their early nineteenth century, gable-front frame church to Daniel W. Miles, Josiah Avery, and John T. Ford, trading as Miles, Avery, & Co. Converted to commercial use, the church was joined around 1880 by the extant two-story, shingled store building. A business letterhead from the turn of the century captures both structures. Although the church has been torn down, a few gravemarkers remain on the west side of the

S-154, Windsor house, south elevation.

store building as a reminder of the property's former use.

In January 1890 Daniel W. Miles sold this property to George A. Cox and Daniel T. Miles, who operated the business under the name of Miles and Cox. During the early twentieth century the store was officially known in the land records as the Fairmount Department Store. In addition to a general line of merchandise, a millinery shop was housed in a side shed on the 1880s store. The second floor occasionally served as a movie house for Fairmount residents. Cecil Ford and his wife, Bertha, have operated the business since 1954.

DANIEL MILES'S STORE
Circa 1890
Upper Fairmount (site)
Private

The store that belonged to Daniel Miles was a simple, single story frame structure standing in the center of Upper Fairmount across the road from Cecil Ford's store. In addition to a small merchandise business, Miles's building once housed the Fairmount post office. One of two store buildings in the village, the commercial building stood unused for many years until it was demolished in 1985.

S-155, Cecil Ford's store, south elevation.

S-156, Daniel Miles's store, north elevation.

S-159, John C. White house, southeast elevation.

S-150, Warwick house, south elevation.

JOHN C. WHITE HOUSE
Circa 1860
Upper Fairmount vicinity
Private

Standing a few yards from the Manokin River is this large two-story frame house, which dates to the mid-nineteenth century. The simply detailed square house rests on a high brick basement and is trimmed with corner pilasters.

Although this dwelling is dated circa 1860, the property was used for commerce for several decades before the house was built. In July 1821 Littleton D. Maddox and Henry Maddox sold a half acre of Maddox's Island, commonly known as the "warehouse lot." In 1865 John C. White and Tubman S. Parks bought the Maddox Island property from George and Sophronia A. Landon. John C. White is listed on the patron list of the county atlas as a sailor from Richmond, Virginia, who settled in Somerset County around 1859.

CAPTAIN WILLIAM T. FORD HOUSE
Circa 1860 and earlier
Upper Fairmount vicinity
Private

William T. Ford purchased this Maddox Island property in 1871 from Gustavos A. Maddox and his wife, Elizabeth, for $7,100. At the time of sale, the fifty-acre tract apparently contained at least part of this two-story, six-bay frame house. The center room contains interior woodwork from circa 1820-1840 as well as a single nine-over-six sash window. All other architectural fabric appears to date from late in the third quarter of the nineteenth century during the ownership of William T. Ford. The land records show Ford served as an oyster commissioner beginning on March 31, 1890.

WARWICK HOUSE
Circa 1880
Upper Hill vicinity
Private

The Warwick house stands on the northeast side of Fishing Island Road approximately a mile west of Upper Hill. The abandoned farmhouse dates to the 1870s or 1880s and is distinguished by a pair of front gables. The shorter two-story kitchen wing, which extends to the rear, is different from most, with a hip roof, dentiled eaves, and a brick chimney located on the side wall. This unusual chimney location is the result of a narrow stair hall, which is partitioned from the kitchen. The house is known locally as the birthplace and home of former county commissioner Earl Warwick.

S-160, Captain William T. Ford house, east elevation.

S-167, Upper Hill.

UPPER HILL
19th and 20th centuries
Upper Fairmount vicinity
Public

Centrally located on the Fairmount peninsula, Upper Hill is one of the few black communities in Somerset County that can trace its history to the early nineteenth century. By the time the Somerset County atlas was published in 1877, Upper Hill—originally known as Upper Freetown—included two dozen dwellings clustered around a Methodist church. The character of the community remains much the same today, with modest late nineteenth and twentieth century dwellings surrounding St. Andrew's M. E. Church.

Although a Methodist church was located near this site at least as early as 1877, the datestone on St. Andrew's reads, "St. Andrews M. E. Church, 1908, rebuilt July 30, 1923." The L-shaped frame church is supported by a rusticated concrete block foundation and is distinguished by a corner entrance tower. Pointed arch windows pierce each side.

SAM GREEN FARM
Circa 1857
Manokin vicinity
Private

The Sam Green farmhouse is a two-story, five-bay center hall frame house evidently built in at least two principal stages. Dis-

tinct shifts in construction between the third and fourth bays from the north indicate the different periods. Bracketed eaves and dentiled brick chimney caps distinguish this Manokin vicinity structure. The bracketed eave is identical to that on the addition to the Hall house in Upper Fairmount. Accompanying the house is a circa 1900 frame barn and a frame privy.

This 188-acre farm has remained a constant size since George R. Revell and John H. Ford purchased it from William S. Waters in 1857. It is believed the initial side hall/parlor section of the main block was built around 1857. Ford's interest in the farm was

sold to Revell (also spelled Revelle) two years later for $1,106.50. For the next sixty years the Revells owned the property. Captain George R. "Revel" is shown at this location in the 1877 county atlas. The farm remains in the Green family.

FURNISS TENANT HOUSE
Circa 1870
Manokin vicinity
Private

The Furniss tenant house is a simple two-story, three-bay frame house that stands on the south side of Back Creek. Its most dis-

S-168, Sam Green farm, west elevation.

278

S-171, Furniss tenant house, southeast elevation.

tinctive exterior feature is a single corbeled brick chimney with dentils. In the 1877 county atlas the structure appears under the name T. J. Furniss as an auxiliary building to the main Furniss homestead (now gone).

WILLIAM D. HOWETH FARM
Circa 1850
Manokin vicinity
Private

The William D. Howeth farm, also known in the land records as the Obadiah Clippinger farm, is located on the east side of River Road on the north shore of the Annemessex River.

S-172, William D. Howeth farm, southwest elevation of kitchen.

The farm is largely significant for the survival of an antebellum frame kitchen, which stands southeast of the farmhouse. Few detached kitchens have survived in Somerset County. Exposed on the south kitchen wall is a brick fire wall and a portion of brick nogging. Inside, the kitchen retains its period woodwork on both floors. The cross-gabled farmhouse appears to date from the third quarter of the nineteenth century but, unlike the kitchen, has been remodeled outside.

The full history of this farm has not been sorted out, but William D. Howeth bought two parcels of land from Thomas Sudler, the executor of the estate of Isaac Parks, in Jan-

uary 1860. The kitchen probably dates to the ownership of the Parks family, while the later farmhouse was evidently erected when Howeth owned the property. Obadiah Clippinger bought the farm from Albert Sudler, executor of Thomas Sudler's estate, on April 4, 1883.

COTTAGE HALL FARM (NR)
19th and 20th centuries
Manokin vicinity
Private

The Cottage Hall farm, more recently known as the George Maddox farm, is critically important as a complex of nineteenth century agricultural structures, perhaps the most complete collection surviving on the Eastern Shore. Farm buildings, in general, have an extremely high attrition rate due to changing agricultural practices. For this reason most Eastern Shore farms survive with only a few buildings from former times. The Cottage Hall farm, on the other hand, retains fifteen agricultural buildings dating from the early nineteenth through the twentieth centuries.

Centered in the group of buildings is a late nineteenth century Victorian farmhouse modestly trimmed with decorative brackets, fish-scale shingles, and colored glass windows. Attached to the back of the house is an early nineteenth century hyphen and kitchen. Directly behind the house is a pair of dairy buildings, a frame example built around 1800 and a brick structure erected around 1860. The latter is covered by a pyramidal roof trimmed with a wooden finial and a sawn fascia. Due west of the dairies is a dovetailed log smokehouse and a mid-nineteenth century frame kitchen. On the east side of the yard stand the principal agricultural buildings—a bi-level frame barn, an early nineteenth century granary, and a pair of corn cribs. Twentieth century structures include a frame tenant

S-86, Cottage Hall farm, southeast elevation.

house, two board-and-batten garages, and a latticed gazebo over the well.

Late eighteenth century records for the Cottage Hall farm indicate the property consisted of parts of several adjacent tracts, including "Salisbury," "Resurvey," "part of Wilson's Lott," and "part of Contention," which totaled 272 acres in 1798 and were owned by Thomas Seon Sudler. Sudler's principal property, however, was "Sudler's Conclusion," while the "Salisbury" tract was occupied by a tenant, Richard Tull. Assessed on the tenant farm in 1798 were the following buildings:

> *1 Dwelling House built of wood 24 feet by 18 [feet], 1 Kitchen 27 by 16 feet, 1 Smoake house 12 feet sqr., 1 Milk House 16 feet by 12 [feet], 1 Stable 16 feet by 14 [feet], 1 Corn House 24 feet by 8 [feet], Barn 32 feet by 20 feet, the above in bad repair.*

Except for the stable, which is now in ruinous condition, none of the buildings included in the assessment survives on the property. It appears Sudler financed the construction of a new generation of buildings

around 1800, and his descendants continued to maintain and improve the property until modern times.

Thomas S. Sudler's will of September 1832 is disappointingly vague, dividing his large estate between his two sons, William and Tubman, and his daughter, Eleanor. Although not specifically mentioned, the tenant farm on Sudler's Creek probably passed to William along with the other lands he then occupied. Ten years later William Sudler died, leaving as heirs his sons, William and Thomas C., and daughters, Ann G. and Mary E.

During the first forty years of the nineteenth century it is uncertain who occupied the Sudler's Creek farm, although it was clearly owned by the Sudlers. Not until Thomas C. Sudler's will of May 1881 is it evident that a Sudler lived there. Thomas stated in the third item of his will, "I give and devise to my son Albert Sudler the Cottage Hall farm where he resides…." Albert Sudler is shown on the 1877 Somerset County atlas and patron list with a 245-acre farm. In 1921 he transferred legal ownership of the farm to Amos C., Mervin T., and Oscar Sudler, all non-county residents. In 1940 the

property was purchased by members of another Sudler branch, George F. and Ruth L. Maddox, who owned the farm until the late 1970s.

THOMAS SUDLER FARM
Circa 1870 and earlier
Westover vicinity
Private

The Thomas Sudler farm (now known as the Bill Messick farm) is architecturally important due to the survival of two outbuildings constructed with wrought nails. The farmhouse was built in the third quarter of the nineteenth century on the site of an earlier house. A largely unaltered, full dovetailed sawn-log smokehouse with vertical shiplap siding stood behind the house until May 1984, when it was moved to Liberty Hall. Built circa 1800, the smokehouse has a loose board floor. Standing along the farm lane is a circa 1800, bi-level frame barn with a single flanking shed. Interior structural evidence indicates the barn was first used to air cure tobacco but was later converted for grain storage.

Until the mid-1940s, this farm was owned

S-338, Adams farm, west elevation.

and operated by the Sudler family, who acquired the property in the early nineteenth century through Martha Lester, first wife of William Sudler (married August 6, 1811). Thomas Sudler, son of William and Martha, purchased the farm after his father's death in 1842 and lived here until his death in May 1881. During his forty-year ownership, Sudler evidently built the present cross-gabled farmhouse on the site of his parent's dwelling and reused and refitted the old barn. In his will, Thomas Sudler devised the farm to John E.

Sudler and his wife Sallie, who occupied the property until 1947.

ADAMS FARM (NR)
Circa 1840, circa 1900
Princess Anne vicinity
Private

A distinctive architectural landmark south of Princess Anne, the double-galleried facade of the Adams farmhouse is as eye-catching as the neat complex of turn-of-the-century outbuildings that surrounds it. A thorough architectural analysis of the L-shaped farmhouse indicates the dwelling was erected in three principal stages dating from the second, third, and fourth quarters of the nineteenth century.

The oldest section, finished with late Federal and Greek Revival woodwork, comprises the southernmost section of the front block. In the few decades that followed construction of this section, the house was enlarged by a two-part service wing that extends eastward. The most radical alterations took place around 1900. The front portion was enlarged, the roof was raised, and a two-story gallery was built across the front. The interior reflects three separate periods, with woodwork in Federal,

S-173, Thomas Sudler farm, north elevation.

S-183, E. D. Long house and store, south elevation.

Greek Revival, and Victorian tastes.

Standing around the house are over a dozen outbuildings, a boxwood garden, and a grove of mature shade trees. The diverse group of agricultural and domestic outbuildings, considered the most complete collection of late nineteenth century support structures in Somerset County, include a frame wash house, a brick dairy with a pyra-midal roof, a frame smokehouse, a large frame barn, a potato house, corn cribs, a granary, and a privy.

For a large part of the past century, this property has been known as the "Adams Farm." Morris H. Adams inherited the property from his father, Robert W. Adams, in 1919 and occupied the farmhouse through the 1970s. Robert W. Adams had purchased the 100-acre property from James Teackle Dennis in December 1897; it was during his twenty-year occupation that the major alterations to the house took place.

Older land records refer to the property as including "Waggaman's Purchase," "Rowley's Ridge," "Addition," and "Waggaman's Lot" consolidated under one name, "Bellair." Construction of the oldest section of the house is attributed to John Woolford, who acquired the property in 1825 and subsequently willed it to Elizabeth G. Woolford Polk in 1836.

WESTOVER
19th and 20th centuries
Public and private

Westover, Maryland, is a small nineteenth and twentieth century village located in central Somerset County between Princess Anne and Crisfield. After the Eastern Shore Railroad reached Somers Cove in 1866, several railroad-oriented towns developed along its path, including Westover, which was the second stop south of Princess Anne. In 1877 the county atlas recorded the location of the depot as well as three stores, a post office, a steam

S-174, Westover, photograph c.1900 (courtesy of Mrs. Edwin D. Long).

S-175, Westover ticket office, northeast elevation.

sawmill, and a dozen houses. Many of the houses standing in Westover today date from 1877 to 1900 and are two-story frame structures.

The store operated by William T. Tull was located in part of his well-built frame house, which he had constructed around the time of the Civil War. Owned since the late nineteenth century by the Long family, the two-story, bracketed dwelling is perhaps the oldest structure to remain standing in Westover. The Long Brothers Cannery, located at the north end of the string of village houses, has processed locally grown tomatoes since the early twentieth century. Unlike most of the other fruit-packing concerns in the county, this one continues to operate. Another village landmark is the old Ruark-Ritzel flour mill, which stands at the south end of Westover (see S-176).

E. D. LONG HOUSE AND STORE
Circa 1860
Westover
Private

The E. D. Long house is the most prominent dwelling in Westover in size as well as architectural detail. Corner pilasters frame the large two-story, center hall house, and a bracketed eave stretches around the perimeter of the roof. Twin corbeled brick chimneys pierce the roof line and add further distinction to the well-built dwelling. The Tuscan-columned front porch as well as the two-story bay windows are sympathetic additions made during the early twentieth century.

William T. Tull is credited with the construction of the house around 1860. Tull is included on the patron list in the 1877 atlas as a merchant, which verifies a statement in the May 3, 1894, transfer of the property from Thomas J. and Sarah Dixon to E. D. Long:

This property being the homestead of the late William T. Tull with all the buildings thereon consisting of a dwelling and store house combined, store house and large barn and a priveledge of a waterway to drain said property.

The Long family has owned this property since 1894 and was known county-wide for the Long Brothers' store, which stood next to the house until recently. A large, late nineteenth century, board-and-batten frame barn, formerly used as a livery stable, and a small frame privy stand behind the store site.

WESTOVER TICKET OFFICE
Circa 1884
Westover vicinity
Private

The old Westover ticket office is now located along Maryland Route 361 near the house of the late Jennings Richards. Richards was the last ticket agent for the Pennsylvania Railroad, which discontinued passenger service to Westover during the summer of 1949. Within the next few years, the small station was moved to the yard of nearby St. Paul's M. E. Church, where it was used as a church hall and Sunday School room. When the Methodist congregation was dissolved, the ticket office was moved to Jennings Richards's backyard. There it stood until May 1987, when it was relocated along the north side of the Westover-Fairmount Road.

The simply detailed building, with its cruciform shape accented by a cross gable roof, follows a traditional form for village depots of the period. The extended eaves are underpinned with C-shaped brackets and small, colored glass windows pierce the gable ends. The beaded board interior was originally fitted with built-in seats and a central partition.

RUARK-RITZEL MILL
1876 and later
Westover
Private

The three-story core of the Ruark-Ritzel mill, erected by William Mahew Ruark in 1876, is the only mill of its kind to survive in Somerset County. In addition to its significance as the last of the steam-powered flour mills, the mill retains all its late nineteenth century machinery and equipment. Standing at the

S-176, Ruark-Ritzel mill, north elevation.

south end of Westover, the mill is an important visual and symbolic anchor to this railroad village.

In November 1875 S. Anne Britin sold William Mahew Ruark a 131-acre tract of land "on the south side of County road leading from Potato Neck to Westover and on the west side of the Eastern Shore Railroad...." During the following year, Ruark built the central core of this rambling flour mill and powered it by steam. By 1877 the mill was accompanied by a vast agricultural complex of close to 1,400 acres; these holdings made Ruark one of the most prominent men in the Fairmount/Westover area.

According to family history, as well as the 1877 county atlas, William Ruark settled in Somerset County around 1852, having moved south from Hooper's Island in Dorchester County. In later years, the mill was operated by the Ritzels, and the property remains in the Ritzel family.

RITZEL HOUSE
Circa 1890
Westover
Private

The Ritzel house is a circa 1890-1900 two-story, three-bay frame dwelling on the northwest corner of the intersection of Maryland routes 413 and 361 at the south end of Westover. It is one of two dozen late nineteenth century houses that comprise the village. The projecting front bay gives the

remodeled house a slightly different appearance; its associations with the neighboring flour mill add to the building's significance.

WILLIAM H. RUARK HOUSE
Circa 1880
Westover
Private

Built between 1880 and 1883 for William Henry Ruark, this cruciform plan house is one of the more substantial dwellings remaining in Westover and the only one with this formal plan. The corners of the house are trimmed with paneled pilasters and the eaves boast paired decorative brackets. Family tra-

dition relates that after building this house William H. Ruark left Somerset County for Norfolk, Virginia, and sold the house to his brother, Lafayette Ruark, around 1897.

MARY RITZEL HOUSE
Circa 1850
Westover
Private

The Mary Ritzel house is a mid-nineteenth century side hall/parlor frame house that stands at the lower end of the village of Westover. Exterior wall surfaces have been covered with aluminum siding, and the house has been divided into two apartments. The pe-

S-177, Ritzel house, southeast elevation.

S-178, William H. Ruark house, southeast elevation.

S-191, Mary Ritzel house, northeast elevation.

rimeter of the roof is trimmed with plain modillion blocks.

CHARLIE LONG FARM
Circa 1860
Westover vicinity
Private

The Charlie Long farm, located on the west side of the Old Westover/Princess Anne Road, contains a two-story, side hall/parlor farmhouse built circa 1860. The exterior decorative features are confined to bracketed eaves and the front porch, as is typical for this type of house. A large brick chimney with corbeled cap rises from the north gable end.

The major outbuilding on the property is a large weatherboarded frame barn with a gable-front orientation that dates from the late nineteenth century. A slightly projecting roof protects the hay rack apparatus.

JENNINGS RICHARDS HOUSE
Circa 1875
Westover vicinity
Private

The Jennings Richards house is a remodeled two-story, three-bay frame house that dates from the fourth quarter of the nineteenth century. The simple block cornice that trims the perimeter of the main roof is its most

distinctive feature.

The most significant aspect of this site was the Westover ticket office (S-175), which Richards moved behind his house in 1962. He was the last ticket agent at the Westover station, then operated by the Pennsylvania Railroad. The ticket office has since been moved off this property.

CLIPPINGER HOUSE
Circa 1870
Westover vicinity
Private

The Clippinger house is a moderately remodeled circa 1870, two-story, T-plan farmhouse

S-202, Charlie Long farm, east elevation.

S-192, Jennings Richards house, north elevation.

with simple decorative details confined mainly to the porch and the eaves. The leg of the T projects to the front and contains the side entrance hall. A corbeled brick chimney with dentils rises from the center of the structure. The house faces the old Westover-Kingston road south of Westover.

ALBERT PRICE TENANT HOUSE
Circa 1870
Westover vicinity
Private

The Albert Price tenant house is a relatively unaltered late nineteenth century Somerset County dwelling with simple but effective decorative details. As is common to many rural farmhouses, it has a bracketed eave, a turned post porch, and a dentiled chimney cap.

It is not known exactly when this house was built. A house appears on the 1877 county atlas map in this general area under the name

S-112, Barnes farmhouse, northeast elevation.

of W. S. Long, a local merchant. A blacksmith shop is also designated at the site.

BARNES FARMHOUSE
Circa 1820, circa 1850, circa 1900
Princess Anne vicinity (site)
Private

The Barnes farmhouse was a deceptively early frame house rebuilt with additions during the mid to late nineteenth century. The braced

mortise-and-tenon frame house with flush six-panel doors, chair rail, beaded board paneling, and beaded floor joists dated to the first quarter of the nineteenth century. The rear wing, on the other hand, was fitted with Greek Revival style woodwork common to the 1850s. This two-room plan service wing incorporated a large cooking fireplace in the south room. Around 1900 the side hall/parlor Federal style house was reworked in Victorian taste with an additional room to the west, an

S-185, Clippinger house, southeast elevation.

S-186, Albert Price tenant house, northeast elevation.

S-207, Francis Barnes farm, northeast elevation.

entirely new roof with a center cross gable, and a turned post front porch.

FRANCIS BARNES FARM
Circa 1880
Green Hill crossroads vicinity (site)
Private

Although they are now lost, a very significant Victorian period farmhouse and granary once stood on the Francis Barnes farm. Both struc-

tures evoked the decorative qualities of the period and were rare examples of rural Victorian architecture in Somerset County.

The farmhouse was a well-built, side hall/parlor frame structure with traditional L-shaped corner posts, heavier than normal framing members, and wall pockets for hiding window sash. The exterior was decorated with elaborate porches on three sides, Gothic-arched sash windows, and wooden pendants and spires at several major corners. Although

the original weatherboards were covered with asbestos, the wooden trim in several sections retained a faint suggestion of early paint schemes. The contemporary frame granary was decorated in the same manner with pierced bargeboards and pendants.

From the late 1860s through the 1880s, Francis Barnes, previously of Princess Anne, assembled a large agricultural and mercantile complex around the Green Hill crossroads. On the property known as the "Adams Farm," he erected this impressive T-plan Victorian farmhouse. Twenty years after his purchase of the property, Barnes defaulted on the mortgage and his property entered Chancery Court. It was sold in August 1890 to Clara R. and Tazwell Jones. The abandoned house and granary were demolished in the late 1980s.

ROSS FARM
Circa 1850
Princess Anne vicinity
Private

The Ross farmhouse is an important mid-nineteenth century dwelling in deteriorated but intact condition. The hip roof and twin chimneys combined with the untouched mid-nineteenth century interior woodwork distinguish this farmhouse from many others in this general area. The surrounding outbuildings postdate the house. Perhaps the most

S-212, Ross farm, southwest elevation.

S-203, Campoe farm, southwest elevation.

S-162, James E. Sudler house, southeast elevation.

significant object in the farmyard is the early twentieth century gas pump.

The 1877 county atlas shows Lafayette Ross, the probable builder of the house, at this site. He is designated in the patron list as the owner of a 900-acre farm.

CAMPOE FARM
Circa 1860
Westover vicinity
Private

Campoe farm is situated on the north side of US 13 approximately one-half mile west of the Green Hill crossroads. This two-story side hall/parlor frame house is a moderately significant example of a county farmhouse from the third quarter of the nineteenth century. It retains its unusual corbeled brick chimneys and some period mantels and woodwork although both the interior and exterior have been remodeled. The two-story tower that rises on the front corner was added circa 1890-1910.

JAMES E. SUDLER HOUSE
Circa 1860
Manokin vicinity
Private

The James E. Sudler house is a partially remodeled side hall/parlor frame dwelling apparently built by James E. Sudler around 1860. His father, Tubman W. Sudler, transferred the part of Sudler's Conclusion "where-

on the said Tubman W. Sudler lives" to his son on June 14, 1860. James Sudler farmed the property but eventually was forced to sell the land in the 1880s due to a defaulted mortgage. The farm was then sold to Maggie A. Green, who later married Francis S. Robertson.

GREEN HILL GRANARY AND WAGON SHED
Circa 1850
Green Hill crossroads
Private

Marking the southwest corner of the Green Hill crossroads is this joined mid-nineteenth century granary and wagon house. The main section, a bi-level, mortise-and-tenon frame structure that served as a granary, is partially sheathed with flush horizontal boards and covered by a tin roof. Wide board doors hung on long strap hinges are located on both levels. Extending to the north is a single story hyphen that connects the granary to a weatherboarded frame wagon house with a gable-front roof. The interior of the granary has an exposed mortise-and-tenon framing system. An open stair in the eastern corner of the building rises to the loft. The granary is featured with the store across the road (S-206) on an 1896 plat of Francis Barnes's holdings. Barnes owned most of the property at this crossroads in the late nineteenth century.

S-205, Green Hill granary and wagon shed, northeast elevation.

S-206, Green Hill store, southwest elevation.

GREEN HILL STORE
Circa 1870
Green Hill crossroads
Private

The Green Hill store is significant as one of only a few rural store buildings in Somerset County to survive until modern times. Although the building is deteriorating, its architectural elements are basically intact. The use of pocket windows on the second floor is noteworthy and establishes a construction parallel with two nearby structures (the Francis Barnes farmhouse and tenant house).

The Green Hill store is designated at this site on the 1877 county atlas and shows up in the mortgage settlement of Barnes's property in 1896. During the third quarter of the nineteenth century, Francis Barnes had assembled a large agricultural and mercantile complex surrounding this crossroads.

THOMAS J. DIXON HOUSE
Circa 1860
Marion vicinity
Private

The Thomas J. Dixon house is an interesting example of a nineteenth century farmhouse distinguished by a hip roof and bracketed eaves. The exterior and interior have been remodeled with the application of metal siding and board paneling.

This farm figures prominently in the early history of Somerset County as part of the Dixon family lands and as the site of Quaker meetings. It is an established local tradition that a former rear wing was an old Quaker meeting house, which had been moved up and attached to the house. This rear wing burned several years ago.

MARION
19th and 20th centuries
Marion
Private and public

Marion is the most complex rural crossroads located along the old Pennsylvania Railroad between Princess Anne and Crisfield. Located in the center of a large agricultural region, Marion became a significant loading and shipping center for agricultural products through the first half of the twentieth century. It has been called the "strawberry capital of the state" because of the volume of market strawberries shipped from Marion's strawberry block around the turn of the century.

The town was also the home of the first county hospital, situated in a two-story frame structure, currently vacant, on the southwest corner of the center crossroads. Standing on the northwest corner is one of the county's best-preserved rural bank buildings, with its neoclassical facade and pedimented front entrance.

When the Crisfield branch of the Eastern Shore Railroad (later absorbed into the Pennsylvania Railroad system) was constructed in 1866, several stations were erected along its path to service local rural communities. These included Westover, Kingston, Marion, and Hopewell. Marion was named for John C. Horsey's daughter Marion because he donated the right-of-way for the railroad.

Because of the size of the rural population surrounding Marion, the small depot village developed into a service-oriented vil-

S-261, Thomas J. Dixon house, southeast elevation.

S-270, *Marion.*

lage for the local agrarian economy. By 1877 the town boasted several craftsmen's workshops, including two carpenter shops, two blacksmiths, and two wagon shops. On each corner of the crossroads was a general store, and east of the intersection were two blacksmith shops as well as the Methodist Protestant church. The 1877 atlas suggests these structures were accompanied by at least ten dwellings. During the last decade of the nineteenth century and the first quarter of the twentieth, Marion witnessed its largest expansion. This period saw the rebuilding of the town center as well as the construction of several dozen houses along the two principal roads.

OLD MARION HOSPITAL
1905
Marion
Private

The old Marion Hospital, also known as Parson's Store, is a pivotal commercial building marking the southwest corner of the Marion crossroads. The two-story frame structure dates from the liveliest period of Marion's business history, the 1880s through the 1920s. The building served as the first Somerset County hospital from 1908 to 1917. An entry in the *Crisfield Times*, published on April 3, 1909, states,

> *The new hospital at Marion, to be known as the Somerset Hospital, is now complete and ready for patients. It is an up-to-date hospital, thoroughly equipped with all the latest improvements. The hospital is prepared to take care of thirty patients at a*

S-266, *Marion passenger station, southeast elevation.*

S-264, *Old Marion Hospital, east elevation.*

290

time. It has eight rooms besides four large wards. The operating room is worthy of special notice; it has been said by those who know, that it is one of the most thoroughly equipped rooms on the peninsula.

The building later became the Parson's Store, named for George Earl Parson, who bought the property in March 1940 and sold it thirty-seven years later.

MARION PASSENGER STATION
Circa 1900
Marion
Private

This turn-of-the-century passenger station stands along the abandoned bed of the Pennsylvania Railroad at Marion. The exterior has retained its basic shape, but both interior and exterior wall surfaces have lost all original details. The ticket booth is still located on the northwest side, and the hip roof has wide eaves that extend over the rectangular structure. The interior has been remodeled in recent years for retail space.

Although the building has lost most of its period detail, it is one of only two passenger stations in Somerset County to remain on its original site. The other stands in Princess Anne (see S-99).

MARION FREIGHT STATION
Circa 1880
Marion
Private

The Marion freight station is the last railroad freight station to survive on its original foundation in Somerset County. The single story board-and-batten structure is supported by concrete block piers, and the building is covered by a simple gabled roof. The southeast slope of the roof, which shelters three freight door openings, extends to a lower level than the northwest slope.

EASTERN SHORE NATIONAL BANK
Circa 1900
Marion
Public

The Eastern Shore National Bank stands on the northwest side of Maryland Route 667, which serves as the main north/south road through this small rural village. Three bays wide by two rooms deep, the brownish brick bank is distinguished by decorative corbeling and limestone jack arches with center keystones. Located between the first floor window arches and the cornice is a checkerboard brick pattern of light and dark brown bricks.

When the Eastern Shore National Bank and the Bank of Marion merged, it was decided the consolidated bank would occupy this building.

J. STANLEY ADAMS HARDWARE STORE
1911
Marion
Public

The J. Stanley Adams hardware store is one of the oldest continuing businesses in Marion, and the store building is one of the earliest commercial structures surviving in the village. Following a recent fire, the structure was covered with aluminum siding, but the period store front remains intact. This business began in 1911 as James Stanley Adams and Company,

S-267, Marion freight station, southeast elevation.

S-265, Eastern Shore National Bank, southeast elevation.

S-268, J. Stanley Adams hardware store, southwest elevation.

S-269, Whittington grain elevator.

and it continued under that name until 1935 when it became James Stanley Adams Hardware.

The store interior has been modified with the installation of new shelving and counters. A few fixtures, such as the store safe and a scale, date from the early twentieth century. Interestingly, the central brick stove stack does not descend to the first floor level but is supported by a small metal platform on a metal post. The brick begins approximately two feet from the ceiling, and the stack continues through the second floor. The stove has been removed.

OLD BANK OF MARION
1914
Marion
Public

The old Bank of Marion (formerly the Marion Pharmacy) is situated on the northwest corner of the Marion crossroads. The early

twentieth century, gable-front, polished brick bank building is one of the most architecturally distinguished structures to remain standing in this rural crossroads village. The two-bay principal elevation has a classical pedimented entrance with brick pilasters accented with limestone capitals and bases. The adjacent window as well as the small Palladian pediment window are highlighted with limestone arches. The west side elevation is marked by a cross gable.

When the two banks in Marion—Eastern Shore National and the Bank of Marion—merged, this structure was abandoned. More recently it served as a village pharmacy.

MARION BAPTIST CHURCH
1925
Marion
Public worship

The Marion Baptist Church, built in 1925, is the most imposing structure in this small

crossroads village. Standing on the northeastern edge of town, the massive brick church is supported by a raised brick foundation. The front (northwest) facade is dominated by a classically inspired gabled portico rising from a tiered platform of steps. The church serves as a prominent visual landmark due to its large size and domed bell tower. A date plaque records the 1925 construction date as well as the congregation's organization in 1896.

WHITTINGTON GRAIN ELEVATOR
Early twentieth century
Marion
Private

The Whittington grain elevator and storage silos are a visually dominant and once vital business located at the southwest end of Marion. These silos offered grain processing as well as safe storage of the crop before export on the railroad. Because the Crisfield branch of the railroad has not operated since

S-262, Old Bank of Marion, southeast elevation.

S-263, Marion Baptist Church, southwest elevation.

292

S-276, Whittington farm, northwest elevation.

the early 1970s, these massive silos are no longer used. Nevertheless, this agriculturally oriented industrial site is a significant visual landmark in this flat rural landscape. It also documents the important role of shipping grain by rail during the early twentieth century.

WHITTINGTON FARM
Circa 1825 and circa 1890
Marion vicinity (site)
Private

The Whittington farmhouse, burned in 1987, was a highly unusual late Victorian structure. Erected during the last decades of the nineteenth century, the front block was an addition to a modest one-room rear wing that predated the Civil War and served as the kitchen. The exterior of the main house retained a large portion of its period finish, including a two-story bay window, bracketed eaves, and paired window sash. The 1840s kitchen survived with some beaded weatherboards as well as exposed floor joists inside. Surrounding the farmhouse was a group of mid to late nineteenth century outbuildings that included two barns, a corn crib, and a privy.

JOHN T. LONG HOUSE
Circa 1900, circa 1840
Hopewell vicinity
Private

Under an exterior layer of aluminum is a house that dates from two periods. The main block was erected during the late nineteenth century, while the one-room kitchen predates the Civil War. Both sections survive with period woodwork, but the most signif-

icant features remain in the kitchen. This one-room interior has a series of exposed floor joists and a paneled hearth wall. A flat panel overmantel is flanked by a Federal style glazed cupboard and an enclosed winder stair. A portion of beaded weatherboards remains exposed on the southeast side of the kitchen, which is now covered by a shed-roofed porch.

DR. GEORGE COULBOURN FARM
Circa 1850
Tulls Corner vicinity
Private

The Dr. George Coulbourn house is a large mid nineteenth century dwelling built on a more generous scale than most farmhouses of the period. The two-story, five-bay frame house follows the center hall, double-pile form. The mantels and some doors have been removed, and the most significant interior feature is the open-string stair. Standing behind the house is an early twentieth century gambrel-roofed barn and a frame corn crib.

The property is associated with Dr. George Coulbourn. Thomas L. Coulbourn is designated on the 1877 county atlas.

S-290, John T. Long house, northeast elevation.

S-293, Dr. George Coulbourn farm, east elevation.

S-277, Samuel L. Tull house, east elevation.

S-248, R. H. Milbourne store, southeast elevation.

SAMUEL L. TULL HOUSE
1861
Tulls Corner vicinity
Private

The Samuel L. Tull house is a two-story, three-bay center hall dwelling that stands on the east side of East Creek near Tulls Corner. The hip-roofed frame house is trimmed with paneled pilasters and a bracketed eave. Interior brick stacks rise from the center of the structure to heat the house. The interior of the four-room plan house has remained essentially intact with bold mid-nineteenth century mantels, crossetted door surrounds, and a heavily turned newel post. The attic stair is enclosed, and scrawled on the rear face of the attic door is an inscription dated "May 14, 1881," which reads "all gone to the festival but me," signed Olive Tull. The 1861 construction date is recorded on the house as well.

Samuel L. Tull (1826-1906), the attributed owner and builder, was born and raised in the vicinity of Tulls Corner. By his mid-30s, he had acquired sufficient wealth to erect this fine two-story frame house near his crossroads store. The 1877 Somerset County atlas lists Tull as a "merchant" with a total property of 220 acres.

R. H. MILBOURNE STORE
Circa 1870
Kingston
Public

The R. H. Milbourne store is one of the few nineteenth century store buildings still in use in rural Somerset County. Similar to most in general form, the gable-front frame structure has been remodeled but retains its architectural integrity as a nineteenth century commercial building.

The single story frame building formerly stood on the northeast corner of the Kingston crossroads. When Maryland Route 413 was introduced to replace the old Princess Anne-Crisfield Road, the old store was moved to its present location on Route 413.

R. H. Milbourne is shown in the 1877 county atlas as owning several properties in the vicinity, including the store. A listing in the atlas business directory states,

R. H. Milbourne, Dealer in Dry Goods, Groceries, Notions, Boots, Shoes, Hats, and c. Kingston.

S-61, Francis Barnes tenant house, southwest elevation.

S-193, Old Chamberlin house, east elevation.

S-213, Leroy Mariner farm, southwest elevation.

FRANCIS BARNES TENANT HOUSE
Circa 1870
Green Hill vicinity
Private

The Francis Barnes tenant house is a dilapidated Gothic Revival farmhouse that shares common building features with two nearby structures, the Green Hill store (S-206) and the former dwelling of Francis Barnes (S-207). However, the most noteworthy structures on this property were the twin Victorian corn cribs that stood next to the house until they were moved to Talbot County in the 1970s. This farm is described in the estate survey of Francis Barnes's property conducted in 1898.

CECIL SCHROCK FARM
Circa 1870
Westover vicinity
Private

The Cecil Schrock farm is a group of third quarter of the nineteenth century farm structures. The farmhouse is a partially renovated, two-story, five-bay center hall dwelling with a T-plan service wing. The common bond brick dairy has been significantly reduced in size and capped with a twentieth century roof. Standing behind the dairy is a small frame smokehouse.

OLD CHAMBERLIN HOUSE
Circa 1800, circa 1880
Kingston vicinity
Private

The old Chamberlin house is situated on the north side of the Great Annemessex River between Kingston Hall and Liberty Hall. Dating to the first two decades of the nineteenth century is the collapsed rear wing, which contains wrought-iron flooring nails and a beaded board stair partition. The front portion is a two-story, cross-gabled addition erected around 1880-1900. Not much is known about this property aside from its early ownership by the Chamberlin family.

LEROY MARINER FARM
Circa 1870
Wellington vicinity
Private

The Leroy Mariner farmhouse is a standard two-story, three-bay structure from the third quarter of the nineteenth century with a two-story service ell to the rear. Three ordinary

S-189, Cecil Schrock farm, northwest elevation.

S-284, Fred Bradshaw house, northwest elevation.

S-286, John H. Miles house, southeast elevation.

outbuildings stand behind the kitchen wing. Like many rural farmhouses from this period, the exterior of this house is severely plain.

It appears this farm was part of landholdings belonging to Burton D. Gibbons during the third quarter of the nineteenth century. The farm is named after the current owner.

JOHN H. MILES HOUSE
Circa 1870
Hopewell vicinity
Private

A hip roof, bracketed eaves, and corner pilasters distinguish this two-story, three-bay farmhouse from other contemporary houses in the immediate vicinity of Hopewell. Interior brick chimneys finished with dentiled caps rise from the main block as well as the two-story rear wing.

For the past several generations this circa 1870 dwelling has been known as the Jesse Long house, but nineteenth century records show John H. Miles as the owner.

FRED BRADSHAW HOUSE
Circa 1870
Hopewell vicinity
Private

The Fred Bradshaw house is a two-story, five-bay center hall farmhouse standing along the old road from Marion to Crisfield. The symmetrical facade is very plain aside from the gabled entrance stoop and the bracketed eaves. Although this house type is relatively com-

mon in other portions of the state, the two-story, three-bay house is more usual in Somerset County, where countless examples dot the countryside.

JOHN LEWIS PORTER HOUSE
Circa 1870
Wellington vicinity
Private

With its gable-front elevation and bracketed eaves, the J. L. Porter farmhouse is a noteworthy variation of the two-story, three-bay house standard on Somerset County farms. Also uncommon are its overall size and the two-story engaged porch on the south side of the kitchen wing. The smallest section of

the house is reported to have been a slave quarter that was moved up to the house as a service wing. If this tradition is accurate, it is one of only a handful of quarters to remain in Somerset County.

Porter family occupation of this land dates back to a 1763 survey for a 319-acre tract known as "Porter's Purchase" near King's Creek. The exact location of the early house is unclear. This farmhouse was erected for John Lewis Porter (1829-1899) and his wife, Amanda T. Lankford Porter (1838-1905), around 1870. The property passed to Lynn Porter (1878-1976) after his father's death in 1899.

S-211, John Lewis Porter farm, northeast elevation.

S-187, R. H. Milbourne house, south elevation.

R. H. MILBOURNE HOUSE
Circa 1870
Kingston vicinity
Private

The R. H. Milbourne house is largely similar to standard T-plan Victorian period farmhouses with a decorative porch and eave brackets. The unusual treatment of the east end of the T provides an unexpected variation to the roof shape.

R. H. Milbourne apparently had this structure erected around 1870-1880 as an additional house on his property, which totaled 140 acres by 1877. His own house, marked "Residence" on the atlas map, was located a short distance away on what is now Charles Cannon Road. In addition to this waterfront property, Milbourne owned a third parcel farther down river and two lots at the Kingston crossroads. He is listed on the atlas patron schedule as a merchant.

JOHN D. EAST FARM
Circa 1870
Pocomoke City vicinity
Private

The East farm, situated on the northeast side of US 13 immediately south of the old Costen railroad station site, is a moderately significant agricultural complex. Following a fire, the circa 1870 farmhouse was remodeled. Accompanying the house are a few small agricultural buildings, including a potato house, a pump house, and a wagon shed. Perhaps the most noteworthy structure is the Quinton schoolhouse (below), which was moved to the farm after the school was abandoned.

Since 1916 this property has been owned by the East family. It was bought in that year by John D. East after he moved north from the Eastern Shore of Virginia.

QUINTON SCHOOLHOUSE
Circa 1870
Pocomoke City vicinity
Private

The old Quinton schoolhouse is a one-room plan structure that formerly stood along the Old Costen Road near the railroad crossing. Built circa 1870, it was also designated as School No. 3 in the Dublin Election District in the 1877 county atlas. Quinton Methodist Protestant Church stood next to the school. The church has been torn down and the school moved, but the cemetery remains to mark the site.

S-226, John D. East farm, northeast elevation.

S-225, Quinton schoolhouse, northwest elevation.

S-163, Cedar Point farm, north elevation.

After the school was abandoned, John East moved the building to his adjacent farm. This building is one of the few schoolhouses to remain standing in rural Somerset County. It is detailed with Gothic Revival features, and the interior has narrow beaded board wainscoting.

CEDAR POINT FARM
Circa 1881
Manokin vicinity
Private

Construction of the Cedar Point farmhouse is tied by tradition to the marriage of Mary (Mollie) E. Ballard to Charles A. Curtis on December 8, 1881. The initial house, a two-story, side hall/parlor dwelling, included a two-story rear dining room and kitchen wing as well as a semi-detached, board-and-batten summer kitchen. The east side of the rear wing included a two-story porch with a cross stick baluster railing. Distinguishing the side hall is a dogleg stair with a heavily turned newel post, a walnut handrail, and turned oak balusters. The second floor hall has unusual interior screened doors that provided a measure of protection from irritating pests.

The west side of the main block dates from the early twentieth century after Carlotta M. Cameron of Brooklyn, New York, purchased the old Ballard property from the heirs of Mollie E. Curtis. After the transfer in 1928, the Camerons enlarged the original house by adding the two-story west wing. At the same time, shed dormers were added to the south roof slope to increase light to finished portions of the attic.

The Waters family were the earliest owners of this Great Annemessex River farm, patenting a 1,280-acre tract called "Waters River" around 1663. By 1750 part of the original land had passed to John Waters, who had a 490-acre tract resurveyed under the name "Salem." The "Salem" plantation was held in the Waters family name until the death of Francis Hutchings Waters in 1826. His daughter Sarah Dennis Waters married Dr. Robert Ballard, and they occupied the family house,

S-196, Widdowson farm, southeast elevation.

S-201, *Samuel Barnes farm, east elevation.*

then known as "Tudor Hall." On the occasion of their daughter Mollie's marriage to Charles A. Curtis in 1881, a frame house was erected near Chamber's Cove west of the main house. Charles and Mollie Curtis remained on the property until their deaths, when the Camerons purchased the farm. In 1942 Henry L. and Elizabeth McIntire Gilliam bought the property, which they kept until the early 1960s. The present owners acquired the river property in 1970.

WIDDOWSON FARM
Circa 1882
Westover vicinity
Private

Widdowson farm is a collection of late nineteenth century buildings that has been significantly altered by the application of aluminum or metal sheathing. The most notable exterior feature of the two-story frame house is its pair of brick chimneys with heavy, corbeled caps. The pair of common bond brick silos behind the barn comprise the most significant aspect of the farm buildings. The two silos share the same roof.

SAMUEL BARNES FARM
Circa 1880
Westover vicinity
Private

The Samuel Barnes farm buildings postdate the 1877 county atlas. The farmhouse has been remodeled inside and out but retains some architectural significance. The barn has also been stripped of its Victorian trim but,

nevertheless, is a noteworthy late nineteenth century agricultural structure.

As reported by the owner, this farmland was once part of Beverly Plantation, owned in the third quarter of the nineteenth century by Isaac T. Barnes.

WILLIAM WHITTINGTON HOUSE
Circa 1880
Hopewell vicinity
Private

This Hopewell vicinity farm has been in the Whittington family since the third quarter of the nineteenth century, when George Edward Whittington, a local blacksmith, lived on the site. Although a portion of the house is thought to date from his ownership, major changes and additions were made by William L. Whittington, who farmed the property and also operated a local canning business in Hopewell around the turn of the century. The farm has passed to William's son Julian and his wife, Kathryn. The large house was enlarged and embellished with the addition

S-285, *William Whittington house, northwest elevation.*

S-271, Alfred Tull house, southwest elevation.

S-273, Alonza Tull house, north elevation.

of several porches. Dominating the front of the house is a two-story, colossal-columned portico. A single story Tuscan-columned porch wraps around the other three sides.

ALFRED TULL HOUSE
Circa 1880
Tulls Corner
Private

With cross gables on each side of a hip roof and chamfered post porches, the Alfred Tull house, built around 1880, is an interesting variation of the typical center hall county farmhouse. Double-leaf doors open into a center stair hall, which is flanked by a room on each side. A plain two-story service wing extends to the rear. Standing a short distance from the Tulls Corner crossroads, this Victorian farmhouse is one of four nineteenth century dwellings that distinguish the immediate vicinity.

ALONZA TULL HOUSE
Circa 1889
Tulls Corner
Private

The crossroads of Tulls Corner was an active intersection during the second half of the nineteenth century, when the agricultural economy thrived with the production of grains and various fruits. Located a mile south of Marion, Tulls Corner was dominated by Tull family holdings that had been maintained since the eighteenth century.

Born in 1854 Alonza Tull is credited with

the construction of this slightly unconventional farmhouse with clipped gable ends, a projecting front bay, and a decorative front porch. Adding interest to the yard are brick piers topped with ball finials that mark the old walkway.

LA VALLETTE HOUSE
Circa 1890
Crisfield vicinity
Private

Due to its isolated but prominent coastal site, the LaVallette house is a local landmark in Crisfield, especially for area watermen, who sight the chimneys of the house for their bearings. The single story, Queen Anne style frame house is covered by a combination of hip and gable roof shapes. The walls are cur-

rently sheathed with aluminum except for the gables, which retain fish-scale shingles and stick decoration.

Albert T. LaVallette, Jr., is documented in local records as a turn-of-the-century dealer in seafood from the Chesapeake Bay and Tangier Sound. He was known especially for hatching and raising diamondback terrapins for East Coast seafood markets. His house, named Ruth-Elie for his two children, was erected on a point southeast of Crisfield.

OLD MASON PROPERTY
Circa 1890
Pocomoke City vicinity
Private

The Mason farmhouse is a well-preserved Victorian period dwelling with simple late

S-292, LaVallette house, southwest elevation.

S-294, Berry house, southeast elevation.

nineteenth century detailing. The irregular main elevation includes a two-story, three-sided bay covered by a gabled roof. The single story rear wing is thought to be a few decades older than the main house. With its T-plan and minimal exterior elaboration, this two-story frame farmhouse is typical of Somerset County domestic architecture in the late nineteenth century. Property belonging to a William F. Stevens is designated on this site in 1877.

BERRY HOUSE
Circa 1900
Tulls Corner vicinity
Private

Standing on the north side of Whittington Road near Tulls Corner, the Berry house is distinguished by a profusion of decorative Victorian woodwork. The irregular plan front block has a single story, turned post porch with sawn brackets, spindles, and a gable front covered with fish scale shingles. The two-story bay window in the east bay is also topped with a gable front covered with fish-scale shingles.

RUMBLEY POINT ROAD HOUSE
Circa 1900
Tulls Corner vicinity
Private

Built at the turn of the century, this two-and-a-half story frame house stands on the east side of Rumbley Point Road north of Irish Grove. To keep the frame structure above the low-lying terrain, the house was built on a high brick foundation. This elevated foundation gives the structure additional height and prominence amid the broad horizontal stretches of tidal wetlands. It appears from the 1877 atlas that this structure is at least the second dwelling on the site. Scatters of pottery and brick fragments are located in an adjacent field.

One of the most significant aspects of this house is the beaded board interior finish of two rooms. The large kitchen is especially unusual with its built-in cupboards and enclosed stair. The interior trim retains its original paint scheme in an unusual variety of colors that includes red, blue, and yellow.

BOZMAN-FITZGERALD HOUSE
Circa 1900
Venton vicinity
Private

The Bozman-Fitzgerald house is a distinctive turn-of-the-century farmhouse with period Victorian trim. Common for the period is the two-and-a-half story, three-bay facade distinguished by a center cross gable. The

S-220, Old Mason property, southwest elevation.

S-259, Rumbley Point Road house, northwest elevation.

pointed arch sash windows and the modest decorative Victorian trim are typical of these center hall, single-pile farmhouses. The detached kitchen served the house as the principal cooking area in the hotter months of the year.

ORIOLE
Nineteenth and twentieth centuries
Private and public

The settlement history for the area surrounding St. Peter's Creek dates to the earliest period of Somerset County history; however, the village of St. Peter's, later renamed Oriole, did not develop until the nineteenth century. The organization of the Methodist church in 1810 appears to be the earliest date associated with a building on the county road that serves as the main street of this small watermen's community. By the time the 1877 county atlas was compiled, St. Peter's boasted a steam sawmill, a school, St. Peter's Church, and two dozen dwellings.

When it came time to establish a U.S. post office in the town, government officials

S-358, Bozman-Fitzgerald house, south elevation.

informed Thomas Smith, a local store proprietor and farmer, that the community had to distinguish itself from another Maryland town already designated St. Peter's. It is related that Smith submitted Oriole as the community name for the post office designation because of the large number of nesting Baltimore Orioles in the area. The name has remained the same since. The area continued to expand around the turn of the century, and the village as well as the county reached a peak in population around 1910. Since the Depression, Oriole and surrounding villages have dwindled in size and importance and remain quiet rural communities.

JOSEPH CROSWELL HOUSE
Circa 1900
Oriole
Private

The Joseph Croswell house, also called the Phoebus house, stands on the western edge of the watermen's village of Oriole north of St. Peter's Creek. Considered one of the most unusual Victorian houses in Somerset County because of its cruciform shape, this two-story frame dwelling boasts a pair of three-story towers covered with pyramidal roofs with slightly kicked eaves. Turned post porches extend to each side of the house and shelter the principal entrances. Adding contrast to the horizontal weatherboarding, now covered with asbestos, are gable ends sheathed with fish-scale shingles.

The Croswell family has long been known in the vicinity for operating a store at the west end of Oriole during the nineteenth and early twentieth centuries.

JOHN WILLIAM WEBSTER HOUSE
Circa 1885
Dames Quarter
Private

The John William Webster house is a modest two-story, two-bay frame house estimated to date to the late years of the nineteenth century. Construction of the side hall/parlor

S-364, Oriole.

S-331, *Thomas Bain Webster house, southwest elevation.*

S-332, *John William Webster house, southwest elevation.*

dwelling is credited to John William and Mary Ann Elizabeth Young Webster during their ownership of the lot. Mary Ann, called Annie in the land records, purchased the property in 1884, and the couple presumably erected the house during the next few years. The rear service wing follows the traditional stepped form with a short, single story hyphen and a slightly taller one-room kitchen. Standing next to the kitchen is a stilted dairy. In more recent years the house was occupied by the Websters' son Oliver O. and his wife, Minnie J. Webster, who purchased the property in 1912.

THOMAS BAIN WEBSTER HOUSE
Circa 1903
Dames Quarter
Private

Standing close to Tangier Sound is this two-and-a-half story, cross-gabled frame house built around 1903 by Thomas Bain Webster. According to family tradition, materials were purchased in Princess Anne and hauled to the building site, where Thomas erected the house himself. The original shape of the dwelling followed the traditional stepped profile with a hyphen and single story kitchen to the rear. Distinctive Victorian features include

the turned post front porch, the decorative eave brackets, and the period mantels inside.

DEAL ISLAND
Nineteenth and twentieth centuries
Public and private

Deal Island, first known as "Devil's Island" and later spelled "Deil's Island," was settled during the seventeenth century. Land patents were issued as early as 1673 for "Graves End" and 1675 for "North Foreland." Additional patents were executed through the eighteenth and nineteenth centuries and as recently as 1923 for a tract known as "Two Sisters."

During the eighteenth century the island tracts were owned by various individuals, including Captain Nehemiah King of "Beverly," who owned three tracts "all on Devil's Island." His resident tenants, John Webster and Isaac Gibson, occupied modest frame or sawed log houses measuring 20 feet by 16 feet. Sited on a tract called "Purgatory" in 1798 was the dwelling of Nicholas Roe, a single story, 20 foot by 18 foot brick house. Located near the Roe house were support buildings, including a 14 by 12 foot kitchen, a 9 foot square smokehouse, and a 10 foot by 6 foot corn house.

One of the most valuable properties on the island in 1798 was the plantation of Reverend David Wallace, assessed for $1,370. His dwelling was a single story frame house that

S-43, *Joseph Croswell house, north elevation.*

S-371, Deal Island, photograph c. 1910 (courtesy of Thurston's Studio).

measured 32 feet across by 20 feet deep. Along with the standard outbuildings, three tenant houses were also assessed on the 700-acre plantation. Reverend Wallace's dwelling is remembered as the location of many island weddings and religious meetings. The Wallace house site is presently improved by the Federal/Greek Revival style dwelling built by Captain William Price around 1840.

By the second half of the nineteenth century, "Deil's Island" (the v was dropped from Devil as a result of the strict Methodism that had spread throughout the island) had expanded into a bay-oriented community of 1,000 residents. The island was reached by a ferry that crossed Law's Thoroughfare until a wooden bridge was erected around 1870.

The fourth quarter of the nineteenth century witnessed additional growth, and by the turn of the century Deal Island was the second largest community in Somerset County. Boasting a population of 1,500 residents, the island was served by five general stores, two blacksmiths, a flour and grist mill, a sail loft, and a veterinary surgeon. By 1900 Captain Levin Anderson was operating a large hotel and store complex at the north end of the island near the quarter-mile long steamboat wharf. During the early twentieth century canning factories as well as an ice plant were

erected near the wharf, and by 1912 a branch of the Bank of Somerset had been established.

The first decades of the twentieth century also brought an increased population, which totaled 2,500 by the 1930s. After a devastating hurricane ravaged the region in 1933, the island entered a period of slow decline that lasted through the middle years of the century. Recently, increased interest in Deal Island as a retirement community has helped stabilize the island population.

The oldest house on the island is the old Bradshaw house, also known as the Severn Mister house, located on the southeastern periphery of the principal community of Deal Island. The two-story, two-room plan Federal style house dates to the first decades of the nineteenth century. The only commercial buildings to survive to modern times include the old Deal Island Bank and the Deal Island barber shop in the main village community.

Best known of the other buildings on the island are the Joshua Thomas Chapel and St. John's M. E. Church. The antebellum Greek Revival chapel housed the island's early Methodist congregation. Reverend Thomas, long called the "Parson of the Islands," served the Deal Island congregation as well as Somerset County in general, and at his death in 1853 he was buried at the corner of the chapel.

The main church is a large Gothic Revival frame structure with fine interior detail.

ISABELLA WHITE HOUSE
Circa 1875
Deal Island
Private

William T. Evans sold the lot on which this significant Deal Island house stands to Isabella White in 1871. The house is estimated to date from around 1875. Isabella White bequeathed the property—two acres bordering the public road—to her husband, Jacob, in 1895. After Jacob's death she indicated the property should be sold. According to the boundary descriptions the house stood next to Jacob White's shoe shop. In 1911 Wilbur C. Bozman purchased the house and lot, and the Bozmans retained title to the property until the mid-1960s.

The Isabella White house is one of the most distinctive nineteenth century dwellings to survive in the community of Deal Island. The two-story, side hall/parlor frame house survives with an unaltered weatherboarded exterior. Paneled pilasters highlight the four corners of the house and six-over-six sash windows with louvered shutters light both floors. The front door is sheltered by a Tus-

S-369, *Isabella White house, north elevation.*

can-columned, hip-roofed porch.

Attached to the back of the house is a hyphen and a two-story kitchen. This three-part dwelling is one of the better late examples of the hyphenated house type.

MARCELLUS T. WILSON HOUSE
Circa 1890
Deal Island
Private

The Marcellus T. Wilson house is an interesting late nineteenth century frame dwelling that has not been significantly altered. Its modest exterior finishes are complemented by intact Victorian interiors. Two mantels are especially unusual vernacular interpretations of Victorian designs. Also notable is the semidetached summer kitchen, which was originally sheathed with board-and-batten siding.

Construction of this center hall frame house is credited to Marcellus T. Wilson, who purchased a one-acre lot from William S. Thomas in 1888 for $200. Sixteen years later the same property sold for $500. The increase in lot value and the architectural features of the house suggest Wilson improved the property with the extant dwelling. Roland and Lorena Tankersly Webster purchased the house and lot in 1942 from Eddie and Louie Tankersly Collier.

NOAH WEBSTER HOUSE
Circa 1883
Deal Island
Private

Notably unusual for its large size and distinctive mansard roof, the Noah Webster house attracts the notice of travelers through Deal Island. A mature group of shade trees currently surround this late nineteenth century frame house. The principal elevation is a symmetrical five-bay facade with a center entrance and flanking sash windows. The unconventionally proportioned mansard roof is pierced by five pointed-arch dormers. Attached to the back of the house is a large service wing detailed in the same manner as the main block.

Commonly known as the "Noah Webster Homeplace," this impressive dwelling is thought to have been financed by Noah Webster after his purchase of part of the William

S-367, *Marcellus T. Wilson house, east elevation.*

S-45, *Noah Webster house, east elevation.*

Evans estate in 1883. Prior to Webster's purchase the property was owned by John Tignor and his wife, Mary Catherine, who had bought the land from the Evans trustee, John W. Crisfield, in 1870. The estate plat indicates a dwelling on the property, but the former house must have burned since architectural evidence indicates this structure dates from the fourth quarter of the century. Furthermore, local tradition credits Noah Webster with its construction.

DEAL ISLAND BARBER SHOP
Circa 1900
Deal Island
Private

The old Deal Island barber shop is a single story frame commercial building located in the center of Deal Island. One room in plan, the main block is extended by a shed addition that gives the building an asymmetrical appearance. Along with the Deal Island bank building, the old barber shop is one of only a few commercial buildings remaining in this island community.

S-370, Laura Bozman house, north elevation.

LAURA BOZMAN HOUSE
Circa 1913
Deal Island
Private

The Laura Bozman house is a standard two-story, three-bay frame dwelling commonly built around the turn of the century in watermen's communities such as Deal Island. The center hall frame house is severely plain aside from the decorative sawtooth edge that trims the eaves.

Construction of the dwelling dates to the second decade of the twentieth century,

S-366, Old Deal Island bank, northwest elevation.

S-368, Deal Island barber shop, northeast elevation.

306

S-375, Wenona, 1940, Jack Delano—photographer (courtesy of the Library of Congress).

following Laura F. Bozman's purchase of a half-acre lot from Wilbur C. Bozman in March 1913. The lot was carved from a larger property that Wilbur Bozman had purchased two years earlier from Alfonza Dix.

OLD DEAL ISLAND BANK
Circa 1912
Deal Island
Private

The old Deal Island Bank is one of three rurally sited, early twentieth century bank buildings remaining in Somerset County. The other two are located in Marion. This rectangular brick building with stretcher bond front and common bond sides has survived with its basic exterior features intact, including the double-door front entrance, marble window sills, and segmental-arched window openings. The interior has been refitted in the past few years for use as a machine shop. Prior to its adaptation, the building had reached a serious stage of deterioration following the collapse of the roof.

Construction of this bank building is estimated to date to 1912, when Julia Anne Shores and others sold this parcel of ground for $100. The parcel was part of the estate of Levin L. Shores, who in 1871 had purchased eight and a half acres from Amanda T. Rider for $500. The Deal Island bank remained in operation until the 1929 stock market failure. Six years after this catastrophe the property was included in a chancery settlement.

WENONA
Nineteenth and twentieth centuries
Deal Island
Public

Wenona is the smaller of the two communities on Deal Island, although the village is the site of the principal harbor. Separated from the main community on Deal Island by approximately a mile, Wenona is comprised of about fifty structures, a large majority of which were built during the fourth quarter of the nineteenth century and the first half of the twentieth century. By the time of the

1877 county atlas, fifty structures made up Wenona, and the community steadily grew until the turn of the century, when the population started to level off.

The dwellings that define Wenona are similar to those of other watermen's communities. Although they follow popular national styles, the houses tend towards smaller proportions than more standard examples found outside the water-oriented villages.

BROWN SAIL LOFT
Circa 1900
Wenona (site)
Private

The Brown sail loft stood at the southern tip of Deal Island in the waterfront community of Wenona. The warehouse-type frame structure combined a storage space and a large workroom for assembling various types of sails for work and pleasure boats. Situated on the edge of the Wenona waterfront, the loft provided watermen with a convenient source for cloth sails. Several generations of Brown

S-373, Brown sail loft, Wenona, November 1957, William T. Radcliffe—photographer (courtesy of the Mariners' Museum, Newport News, Virginia).

S-374, Vetra store, north elevation.

308

S-361, St. Stephens.

family members operated the business before its closing in the 1970s. The old loft had reached such a poor state of repair by 1988 that it was torn down.

VETRA STORE
Circa 1870
Wenona
Private

Centrally located in Wenona, the Vetra store is one of a few nineteenth century buildings standing near the island harbor. Although abandoned, the store building has not been altered aside from a layer of artificial siding. The two-story, cross-gabled frame store was also used as a boarding house.

J.S.C. Vetra is designated in the 1877 county atlas as a merchant and proprietor of the "Deil's Island" store. An advertisement in the business directory provides an idea of his stock:

Dealers in Dry Goods, Groceries, Hats, Caps, Boots, Shoes, Hardware, Queensware, Tinware, Ready-made Clothing, Drugs, Medicines, Patent Medicines, Toilet Soaps, Fancy Articles, Notions, & c. J.S.C. Vetra is also Proprietor of the Blacksmith shop. All kinds of work neatly and promptly done; also, Agent for the celebrated "Cucumber Pump."

ST. STEPHENS
Late 19th century
Venton vicinity
Public

The roadside village of St. Stephens is a late nineteenth century watermen's community located between Oriole and Dames Quarter on Maryland Route 363. Centrally located in the village is St. Stephen's Methodist Church, the best preserved of the town's late nineteenth century structures. The neighboring hous-

es have been renovated to varying degrees, but several houses retain period features such as original siding, decorative porches, and eave trim. Due to the low, poorly drained nature of the adjacent terrain, most village residents worked on the waters of Monie Bay and Tangier Sound rather than tending farms.

EWELL
19th and 20th centuries
Smith Island
Public

The initial patent for Smith Island dates to 1679, when 1,000 acres were surveyed as "Pitchcroft" for Captain Henry Smith, the island's namesake and a prominent figure in early Somerset County history. Henry Smith first appears in county records in 1669 as having relocated from Accomac County, where he was drawn into divorce proceedings by the Virginia court. Despite his marital problems in Accomac, Smith assumed prominent roles in Somerset as a justice of the peace, a captain of the militia, and a representative from the county in the Lower House of the Maryland General Assembly. Although he owned the large "Pitchcroft" tract, it is thought Smith actually occupied a tract patented as "Smith's Recovery," located on the south side of the Manokin River near the confluence of King's Creek.

Tax records indicate the island was occupied during the eighteenth century, and Dennis Griffith's map of Maryland, first drawn in 1794, indicates what was probably an earthen fort at the north end of the island. The presence of the fort as well as the island's strategic location at the bottom of the bay encouraged British occupation during the Revolution and later during the War of 1812.

During the first half of the nineteenth century, it is thought no more than 100 peo-

S-333, Ewell, Smith Island, January 1950, A. Aubrey Bodine—photographer (courtesy of the Mariners' Museum, Newport News, Virginia).

S-334, Tylerton, c. 1930, (courtesy of the Maryland State Archives: Special Collections, Robert G. Merrick Archive of Maryland Historical Photographs, MdHR G 1477-6721).

S-335, Rhodes Point, Smith Island, July 1945, A. Aubrey Bodine—photographer (courtesy of the Mariners' Museum, Newport News, Virginia).

ple occupied Smith Island, but as in most watermen's communities, the population expanded around the turn of the century. In 1861 Reverend J. A. Massey described the islanders:

> *The inhabitants of Smith's and Tangier's Islands may almost be called an amphibious race; for nearly all the men and boys spend fully half their time…on the water. Canoes, skilfully hollowed out of pine logs, and constructed with due regard to the purposes intended, are very numerous. They are rigged with two masts, with sails attached, which can be easily taken down or put up, and can outsail every vessel on these waters, that is not propelled by steam. When there is not sufficient wind for them to sail, the islanders are very dexterous in managing them with paddles.*

Methodist camp meetings have played an important part in the history of Smith Island. As early as 1808 religious gatherings were held at Tangier and probably shortly afterwards on Smith Island. At Ewell the same location has been continually used for such meetings since 1887 and has been incorporated formally as "The Wilson Butler Camp Ground." By the early twentieth century the Ewell meeting ground included thirty frame cottages and a 1,000-person auditorium. The camp increased in size until a fire destroyed the church, parsonage, and meeting ground complex in 1937. During the following years these buildings were rebuilt.

The buildings that comprise the small village of Ewell include many two-story, two- and three-bay frame dwellings, some of which date from before the Civil War. One of the oldest houses to stand until recent times was the house called Pitchcroft, located at the north end of the island.

TYLERTON
19th and 20th centuries
Smith Island
Public and private

Tylerton is a small watermen's village located on Smith Island in Tangier Sound. One of three villages on the island, Tylerton is geographically separated from Ewell and Rhodes Point by Tyler Creek, which runs between the island's two principal land masses. Merlin Gut runs east of the high ground on which Tylerton was built. During the nineteenth century a ferry operated between the two land masses, but now access is provided only by private boat travel.

Tylerton retains a more diverse collection of period dwellings than the other Smith Island villages. Two of the houses appear to date from the antebellum period. A group of "telescope" style houses with three distinct parts contrasts with the more standard two-story, two- or three-bay frame houses. A large percentage of the dwellings retain decorative exterior trim such as eaves brackets or intricately sawn bargeboards. The largest building in Tylerton is the Gothic Revival Methodist church in the center of the village. Quiet foot paths and large shade trees contribute to the continuing nineteenth century character of the community.

RHODES POINT
19th and 20th centuries
Smith Island
Public

Rhodes Point is the smallest of the three communities located on Smith Island. The watermen's village consists of approximately two dozen one- or two-story houses and the Calvary United Methodist Episcopal Church. Built in 1921 the L-shaped frame church has Gothic Revival style doors and windows. The houses largely consist of two basic types—the three-part "telescope" dwelling and the two-and-a-half story, cross-gabled frame house with a rear service wing. The largest structure standing in the village is a turn-of-the-

S-341, King's Creek Canning Company warehouse, northwest elevation.

S-228, Old Butler farm, west elevation.

century frame house on the north side of the bridge. Distinguished by a pyramidal roof with multiple gables, this squarish building is surrounded by a Tuscan-columned front porch. Located on the west side of the village road is a group of single story watermen's work shanties of board-and-batten construction.

KING'S CREEK CANNING COMPANY WAREHOUSE
Circa 1900
Princess Anne vicinity
Private

The King's Creek Canning Company warehouse stands on the east side of the old Pennsylvania Railroad bed immediately south of the fork in the rail line. The rectangular, utilitarian warehouse has three numbered sliding doors. Painted on the west side in white letters against a red background is "KINGS CREEK CANNING COMPANY." This warehouse is one of two key canning plants used by the Miller family through much of the twentieth century.

COKESBURY STORE
Circa 1900
Cokesbury
Private

The Cokesbury store is an unused building that still marks the crossroads at the intersection of Wallace Taylor Road and Cokesbury Road. Architectural features suggest a turn-of-the-century date, which is corroborated

by its absence from the 1877 atlas. The atlas shows a shop on the southwest corner, but the store site is unoccupied.

OLD BUTLER FARM
Circa 1900
Cokesbury vicinity
Private

The old Butler farmhouse occupies an elevated site on the east side of Cokesbury Road west of Dividing Creek. Family tradition dates this relatively plain Victorian house to the early years of the twentieth century. The

turned post front porch, which has a star motif in its sawnwork detail, is the most decorative feature of this gable-front structure. The farm contains the site of an eighteenth century house that belonged to the Costen family.

MABEL BRITTINGHAM HOUSE
Circa 1900
Tulls Corner
Private

The Mabel Brittingham house is one of the most accomplished Victorian dwellings in ru-

S-218, Cokesbury store, southeast elevation.

S-274, *Mabel Brittingham house, south elevation.*

S-353,

the pr
on the
mend
taled
1679.
aspect
geous
signifi
arche
Eaton
called

HERI
1906
Princ
Privat

Sited
River,
story,
by a ¡
this fa
less o
Some
rarely
bay w
clude
    T
Victo
serve
stair
trimn

ral southern Somerset County. Irregular in plan, the raised two-story frame house has upper gables embellished with elaborate decoration. The upper front gable is pierced by a tripartite, diamond pane sash window.

Stretching across the front is a Tuscan-columned porch with an off-center gable front.

MELODY MANOR
Circa 1904
Princess Anne vicinity
Private

Perhaps the most extravagant house to be erected along the Wicomico Creek during the twentieth century and one of only a few Shingle style houses in Somerset County,

Melody Manor has long been known for its unusual architectural features and exotic history. Most striking about the exterior of the T-shaped house is the round, three-story tower that dominates the southeast corner along the entrance drive. The tower roof is marked by a crenelated parapet. Encompassing more than twenty rooms, the expansive frame house is covered with round-butt shingles. Not uncommon for the period are the porch areas incorporated under a shed roof across the creek-side elevation. The interiors are finished in a traditionally eclectic fashion

S-402, *Melody Manor, north elevation.*

S-70, *Coventry Parish Church ruins, north elevation.*

COVENTRY PARISH CHURCH RUINS (NR)
1784-1792
Rehobeth
Public

The Coventry Parish Church ruins, architecturally significant for several reasons, are also an important reminder of the pivotal role the Anglican Church acquired as the official state religion during the seventeenth and eighteenth centuries.

The picturesque two-story Flemish bond walls with their ten brick jack arches make an impressive brick edifice. The three primary walls easily evoke the awe and inspiration often associated with abandoned structures. Measuring seventy-six feet across by fifty feet deep, this house of worship was the largest of its denomination on the Eastern Shore of Maryland. Its size and prominence are directly tied to the concentration of wealthy planters in Somerset County during the second half of the eighteenth century. In fact, similar construction techniques were repeated in several large plantation houses in the immediate vicinity.

Just as the building represents the eigh-

teenth century prominence of the Anglican Church, it reflects the later decline and loss of support for that church, especially among rural congregations such as this one. By the late nineteenth century, the static rural population combined with the competition from Presbyterian, Methodist, Baptist, and other denominations had severely curtailed vital growth for Coventry Parish. As a result, the ambitious eighteenth century brick church was abandoned for more modern structures in Pocomoke City, Crisfield, and nearby Marion.

The Church of England was made Maryland's official church in June 1692 by an act of first assembly under Governor Lionel Copley. Parishes were laid out in several counties, vestries were elected, and ministers were commissioned. In addition, a tax of forty pounds of tobacco was levied on every tithable person, regardless of religious belief, for the support and use of the church.

Somerset County, then comprising the entire lower Eastern Shore of Maryland, was divided into four parishes: Somerset, Coventry, Stepney, and Snow Hill. Early parish churches were located on navigable waterways with convenient access for their parish-

ioners. The Coventry Parish Church was situated in the early town of Rehoboth (now Rehobeth) on the Pocomoke River. The site of the first building is located directly behind the ruins of its replacement. From all indications, the first church was a single story brick structure of 28'2" by 59' erected in the late seventeenth or early eighteenth century. The parcel of ground where the church was built was not conveyed officially until 1735, when Robert Jenkins Henry sold the land to the Reverend James Robertson, John Dennis, Jr., Thomas Dixon, Thomas Hayward, Thomas Williams, William Lane, and Isaac Williams, vestrymen.

The first church, also a brick structure, was mentioned in the vestry minutes of January 7, 1793:

> Ordered by the vestry that Thomas Bruff and Littleton Dennis call on those who have had bricks from the Old Church to pay 15p. per hundred for them and to agree with Littleton Long to plant trees in the church yard under their direction and to put blocks at the church doors.

Ten years before the decision to disman-

S-66, St. Mark's Episcopal Church, southwest elevation.

tle the old church, the vestry had ordered and approved the construction of a new church at Rehoboth. Eighteen months later on Easter Monday, March 28, 1785, Isaac and Stephen Marshall were bound and obligated to build

A Brick House seventy-two feet long and forty-six feet wide from inside to inside, with a wall of twenty feet in height— beside a sufficient foundation in the ground with a wall as high as the Water Table of twenty-seven inches thick with a rest of three inches in the inside for sleepers.

Motions for completing additional work on the new church were entered from 1785 until late 1792. Bishop Clagett consecrated the building on July 17, 1803.

The Rehoboth church remained in use until the late nineteenth century, by which time the Episcopal congregations had dwindled, in size and no longer required the large rural church. The vestry decided to abandon the structure and merge with the congregation at the chapel of ease of St. Paul's near Marion, presently the governing body of Coventry Parish. As a result of stabilization efforts initiated by Cassius M. Dashiell of Princess

Anne, the ruins of the late eighteenth century church were commemorated at dedication services held on September 23, 1928. In 1988 work began once again to stabilize the walls with a grant from the Maryland Historical Trust.

ST. MARK'S EPISCOPAL CHURCH (NR)
1846
Kingston vicinity
Public worship

This unassuming single story frame church is typical of the modest meeting houses many rural congregations erected during the first half of the nineteenth century. The gable-front church has a single double door opening on the west end and three nine-over-nine sash windows on each side. A shorter single story apse partially covers the east gable end. The church and its interior have survived in relatively unaltered condition.

St. Mark's Church, Joshua Thomas Chapel, and Grace Protestant Episcopal Church are the only rural churches in Somerset County to exhibit a Greek Revival influence. St. Mark's has the gable-front orientation typical of the

style as well as characteristic Greek Revival woodwork.

A construction date of 1846 for St. Mark's is confirmed in the Coventry Parish vestry minute books:

This deed of donation for the house of worship recently erected at Kingston in Somerset County in Coventry Parish in the Counties of Somerset and Worcester under the name of St. Mark's Church was then signed by the rector, church wardens, and vestrymen present...June 2, 1846.

St. Mark's formerly stood approximately a quarter of a mile east of its present location. The building was moved to this site in the early twentieth century, after the Methodists abandoned the original church built at this intersection.

GRACE P. E. CHURCH (NR)
1847
Mount Vernon vicinity
Public worship

This Episcopal church was organized in 1845 in an effort to serve the Hungary Neck residents of Somerset County who lived too far from All Saints Church at Monie or St. Andrews in Princess Anne. Concurrent with the formation of the church was the designation of Wicomico Parish, which encompassed the tenth election district.

Vestry minutes from the period indicate the congregation's initial meetings were held at the "Witch Bridge School" beginning on April 12, 1845. At the first meeting, the preamble and resolutions were adopted and the first vestry was elected. Sitting on this vestry were Edmund Crosdale, Thomas W. Stone, Levin K. Leatherbury, Joseph B. Cottman, Isaac S. Atkinson, Alexander Jones, and Wil-

S-376, Grace P. E. Church, south elevation.

liam A. D. Bounds. The Reverend Meyer Lewin was approved as the church's first rector.

During the May vestry meeting, a building committee was established. This group included the rector, Alexander Jones, Levin K. Leatherbury, Isaac S. Atkinson, and Edmund Crosdale. In the fall of 1845, Alexander Jones and his wife, Elizabeth, donated the church ground to the trustees, and by February 1847 the vestry was meeting in the new church building. The records do not mention the craftsmen responsible for the work.

Grace Church is one of three Greek Revival style church buildings to survive in Somerset County. Unlike St. Mark's Church near Kingston and the Joshua Thomas Chapel, it has Gothic-arched windows and entrances. Inside, the simple square-topped pews, flush board wainscoting, and vaulted ceiling contrast with the decorative altar screen and the Gothic-arched door and window openings.

ST. PAUL'S P. E. CHURCH (NR)
1848
Tull's Corner vicinity
Public worship

St. Paul's Protestant Episcopal Church occupies an important place in the history of this denomination in Somerset County. Architec-turally, it is the earliest example of a pattern book Gothic Revival church. Evidently based on mid-nineteenth century design manuals, St. Paul's closely follows the type of building New York church architects such as Richard Upjohn and John Priest recommended for a country chapel. The tranquil site along Tulls Branch of East Creek with its tall loblolly pines and marsh grass complements the original exterior and interior finishes. The decorative cast-iron fence, added in 1908, remains in a remarkable state of preservation.

Historically, St. Paul's is the oldest congregation still active in Coventry Parish, one of four Anglican parishes laid out in 1692. The Coventry Parish church at Rehobeth was consolidated with the St. Paul's congregation around the end of the nineteenth century, when the main church was abandoned.

St. Paul's was originally formed as a chapel of ease known as Annemessex Chapel. The first building was begun by 1726 on a site near the head of Coulbourn's Creek. In 1818 the chapel was moved to a new location.

On Easter Monday 1848 the vestry of Coventry Parish considered a petition to relocate Annemessex Chapel once more. Several church members believed the 1818 site was no longer advantageous and that it would "retard the growth of the Church in that part of the parish and that its prosperity would be much increased by the erection of a chapel in the neighborhood of John H. Miles store."

That same day the petition was approved, and a building committee was established to superintend the rebuilding of the chapel. The 1818 church was dismantled, and according to church minutes the materials were reused in the construction of the 1848 structure. Despite this thriftiness, the new church was redesigned in a wholly new style—the popular Gothic Revival taste.

The simple rectangular chapel was covered in board-and-batten siding and topped with a steeply pitched roof. Two pointed arch doors provided access to the building; the front door originally was sheltered under a gabled entry. The vestry minutes record Isaac T. Marshall as the craftsman responsible for construction. On December 21, 1848, the new church was consecrated as St. Paul's.

The vestry minutes for the next fifty years do not mention any extensive changes. Not until 1894 was there a major effort to improve the church. On March 29 of that year the rector reported extensive improvements had been made to St. Paul's, including "renovation, painting, etc. at the cost of nine hundred dollars." The colored glass windows were probably installed at this time, along with the beaded board wainscoting and Gothic Revival church furniture.

Major changes after the turn of the century included the addition of a decorative iron fence around the property in 1908 and the 1960s construction of an attached church hall

S-79, St. Paul's P. E. Church, west elevation.

on the south side of the chapel. When the hall was added, the major alteration to the old church was covering the gabled entry.

ST. PETER'S M. E. CHURCH (NR)
1850, 1901
Hopewell vicinity
Public worship

Worshiping at the outset in a building known as Miles Meeting House, this Methodist Episcopal congregation dates to 1782. The first church was built two years later. In 1813 the congregation was renamed St. Peter's, and four years later a second church was finished. The second structure evidently lasted until 1850-1852, when the third edifice was raised. Thirty years later a new spire was erected and the Ladies Aid purchased a $1,000 bell from the McShane Foundry in Baltimore. Finally, in 1901 a Baltimore architect was hired to rework the 1850 building in Gothic Revival taste. The 1901 rebuilding included replacing the roof structure and relocating the front door in the tower. Aside from reconstruction of the tower spire after it was damaged by lightning, no further alterations have occurred since the turn of the century. The interior largely dates from the late Victorian remodeling, with angled pews and a beaded board ceiling with a coved cornice.

St. Peter's Methodist Episcopal Church is one of the best preserved rural Victorian church buildings in Somerset County. Unlike other contemporary examples, St. Peter's has not been compromised with artificial siding or disfigured with additions. The simply executed surface decoration, with layers of horizontal weatherboards and fish-scale shingles, distinguishes the main body of the church as well as the pyramidal-roofed tower. Also significant is the reuse of the circa 1850-1852 mortise-and-tenon frame in the 1901 remodeling. A Baltimore architect, remembered as Mr. Abdule, reworked the mid-nineteenth century frame by replacing the roof and removing all interior elements, including the slave gallery. A cemetery that reflects the span of worship at this site from the 1780s until the present day is located north and south of the building.

S-289, St. Peter's M. E. Church, northeast elevation.

S-254, Davis Chapel, northwest elevation.

S-219, Cokesbury United Methodist Church, northeast elevation.

JOSHUA THOMAS CHAPEL (NR)
1850
Deal Island
Public worship

The Joshua Thomas Chapel holds a critically prominent place in the history of Methodism on the lower Shore. Architecturally, the gable-front church is one of two surviving buildings erected in 1850 to house a Methodist congregation in Somerset County. Methodist gatherings were begun as early as 1781 on Deal Island, and tent meetings were held at "Evan's Hill," beginning on July 17, 1828. In 1849 the place of worship was relocated to "Park's Grove," the former name for the current church site. Father Joshua Thomas delivered his final sermon in this chapel in 1850, and after his death in 1853 he was buried at the south corner of the building.

Accompanying the church on the knoll during the second half of the nineteenth century were an academy, the post office, the campground, and a meeting hall for the Sons of Temperance. Surrounding the gable-front Greek Revival style chapel is an extensive nineteenth and twentieth century cemetery, and standing due west is the second church built by this congregation, St. John's Methodist Episcopal Church (see S-365).

DAVIS CHAPEL
1876
Rehobeth vicinity
Public worship

Davis Chapel, more commonly known as Rehobeth Methodist Episcopal Church, is a simple rectangular frame structure trimmed with bracketed eaves. At some point during the early twentieth century, a vestibule was attached to the front and a high, rusticated block foundation was substituted for the ear-

lier brick one. The additional space created under the building allowed for a church hall. Despite these changes, Davis Chapel is one of the least altered rural church buildings of the second half of the nineteenth century in Somerset County.

The original Rehobeth area Methodist congregation was organized in 1830 at Frogeye, and a church was evidently erected in the same year. However, in 1876 the congregation decided to move closer to Rehobeth and erected Davis Chapel within the year. The old

S-44, Joshua Thomas Chapel, southwest elevation.

S-355, All Saints Church at Monie, southwest elevation.

Frogeye property was sold to the local black Methodist congregation.

COKESBURY UNITED
METHODIST CHURCH
1876
Cokesbury
Public worship

The Cokesbury United Methodist Church is a simple, one-room frame structure erected in 1876 and enlarged twice. A small aluminum-sided foyer has been attached to the front, and an L-shaped concrete block wing extends to the rear. The nineteenth century church has been moderately remodeled inside but retains period pews and only slightly newer altar furniture.

ST. JOHN'S UNITED
M. E. CHURCH (NR)
1879
Deal Island
Public worship

St. John's United Methodist Episcopal Church is an elaborate Gothic Revival building that distinguishes the center of Deal Island along with the Joshua Thomas Chapel. Built when the congregation grew too large for the chapel, St. John's has a bi-level exterior with a three-story bell tower. The well-preserved

interior has decorative pressed tin ceilings and walls, turn-of-the-century furniture and fittings, and colored glass windows.

Around the church and chapel is a nineteenth and twentieth century cemetery with several cast-iron fences surrounding family plots. The two frame church buildings offer an interesting contrast between antebellum Greek Revival and postbellum Gothic Revival church architecture.

ALL SAINTS CHURCH
AT MONIE (NR)
1881
Venton
Private

All Saints Church is historically significant as the surviving representative of the Manokin River congregation established during the late seventeenth century on Arnold Elzey's plantation, "Almodington." Around 1710 the church site was moved from the edge of the

S-365, St. John's M. E. Church, southwest elevation.

Manokin River to its current location near the head of Little Monie Creek. A church erected by the congregation in the 1840s was consecrated as "All Saints' Church" by the Right Reverend William Rollinson Whittingham, bishop of Maryland, on November 10, 1845. This frame building was completely demolished on July 31, 1879, by a severe windstorm. Two years later, on May 5, 1881, the present Victorian structure was consecrated by the Right Reverend Henry Champlin Lay, bishop of Easton.

The single story rectangular church is a pristine survival of the small Victorian Episcopal churches common to rural areas. The plain weatherboarded exterior with its Gothic-arched windows is complemented by an untouched interior with a vaulted blue ceiling originally painted with small stars. Masterfully simple Victorian pews are finished with S-shaped ends topped by club finials. Wainscoted walls, Victorian altar furniture, and period lighting add to the historic qualities of the interior.

S-405, Mt. Zion Memorial Church, northwest elevation.

MT. ZION MEMORIAL CHURCH
1887, 1916
Princess Anne vicinity
Public worship

Mount Zion Memorial Church (now Mount Zion United Methodist Church) stands on the south side of Polks Road approximately three miles west of Allen Road. Following a T-shaped plan, the weatherboard frame church is highlighted with a three-story entrance and bell tower. Marking the gable ends are tri-

partite colored glass windows, and narrow lancet windows flank the gabled apse on the west side. Fixed in the northeast corner of the foundation is the datestone, which reads, "Mt. Zion Memorial Church, built by Rev. H. T. Rich, 1887, remodeled by Rev. R. C. Hughes, 1916." Along with a well-preserved exterior, the interior finishes have remained essentially unaltered, with a decorative matched board ceiling, Victorian church furniture, and arched openings that define the altar and choir stalls. The church cemetery, located on three sides of the building, has many aboveground burial vaults.

JOHN WESLEY METHODIST CHURCH
1887
Mount Vernon vicinity
Public worship

The John Wesley United Methodist Church, erected in 1887, is a prominent Gothic Revival frame church on the north side of Mount Vernon Road. In contrast to many other T- or L-plan churches, this building was designed with an axial plan and a corner bell tower. Also unusual is the use of round-arch window openings rather than the pointed arches typical of the Gothic Revival style. Surrounding the church on three sides is a nineteenth and twentieth century cemetery bor-

S-377, John Wesley Methodist Church, southwest elevation.

S-152, Upper Fairmount M. E. Church, photograph c. 1900 (courtesy of Thurston's Studio).

S-372, John Wesley M. E. Church, southwest elevation.

dered by a modern linked chain hung between brick piers. A church hall of later date stands on the south side of Mount Vernon Road.

JOHN WESLEY M. E. CHURCH
1889, 1914
Deal Island
Public worship

Located between the villages of Deal Island and Wenona, the Gothic Revival John Wesley Methodist Episcopal Church stands in sharp contrast to the low, marshy ground that surrounds it. The late Victorian T-plan church is similar to contemporary black churches in other parts of the county, where Gothic Revival finishes were used until after World War I. The surrounding aboveground cemetery is not unusual in Somerset County.

A black congregation has occupied this site as a place of worship since the third quarter of the nineteenth century. At this location in the 1877 atlas is the designation "Colored Church and School."

UPPER FAIRMOUNT M. E. CHURCH
1873
Upper Fairmount
Public worship

The first Methodist church in Upper Fairmount, known originally as Maddox's Church, was located on the east side of Cecil Ford's store on the northwest corner of Maryland Route 361 and Miles Road. The circa 1825 Greek Revival church was sold in 1874 and subsequently used by Daniel Miles, Josiah Avery, and John T. Ford as a store building. The Methodists erected their new church at the west end of town on the old parsonage lot in 1873. This acre-and-a-half parcel had been purchased from Lazarus Maddox in November 1844 to provide a residence for the ministers of the Methodist Episcopal church

S-153, Centennial M. E. Church, north elevation.

S-288, Hopewell M. E. Church, east elevation.

on the Annemessex circuit.

The upper Fairmount Methodist Episcopal Church is the largest and most architecturally elaborate structure in this rural village. Aside from capping the broach spire to protect it from lightning, this Gothic Revival board-and-batten church has not been significantly altered inside or out. The interior pressed metal walls and ceilings are especially noteworthy. Due to the prominent size and interesting detail of the building, it serves as a strong visual anchor at the west end of the village.

CENTENNIAL M. E. CHURCH
Circa 1884
Upper Fairmount
Public worship

The Centennial Methodist Episcopal Church, built in 1884 and remodeled in 1910, is an anomaly for rural black congregations in Somerset County. Its expansive two-story, three-bay by four-bay size is not matched by another rural black church. The molded pediments that top each of the first and some of the second floor openings are a simple but effective decorative treatment. The three-story bell tower that dominates the northwest corner is distinguished by circular and diamond-shaped openings.

BENNET'S MEMORIAL CHURCH
Circa 1898
Crisfield vicinity
Public worship

Bennet's Memorial Church is located southeast of Crisfield along William Maddox Road. The L-plan church is supported by a brick pier foundation, and it is lighted by narrow, colored glass lancet windows. Rising in the northwest corner is a multi-level bell tower that contains the double door entrance. Fixed in the northwest corner of the foundation is the church date plaque inscribed "Bennet's P. H. Church, 1898-1934."

HOPEWELL M. E. CHURCH
1891
Hopewell
Public worship

The Hopewell Methodist Episcopal Church is similar in date and architectural detail to Waters Chapel and Frogeye Church, two contemporary black Methodist churches in southern Somerset County. The L-shaped frame building was designed, like the other buildings, with a corner tower entrance topped by a belfry and spire. Although the spire and belfry have been removed, the tripartite windows are an especially noteworthy vernacular

S-330, Bennet's Memorial Church, west elevation.

S-121, Phoenix M. E. Church, northwest elevation.

interpretation of a formal Gothic Revival design feature. The north side of the church has an off-center, three-sided bay window lighted by four-over-four sash.

FROGEYE METHODIST EPISCOPAL CHURCH
Circa 1890
Rehobeth vicinity
Public worship

The Frogeye Methodist Episcopal Church stands at the intersection of Cornstack and Bryan Hall roads near Rehobeth. The T-shaped Gothic Revival church is similar to many in Somerset County with its corner entrance tower and tripartite colored-glass windows. Located north of the church is the cemetery. One graveyard plot is surrounded by a Victorian iron fence made by Stewart Iron Works of Cincinnati, Ohio.

Although the written history of many black churches is rather sketchy, the background of Frogeye Church is slightly more complete. The Frogeye congregation was organized by some white residents of the Rehobeth vicinity in 1830, and it continued as a white congregation until 1876. At that time the church was sold to a group of black residents of the area. Meanwhile, a new Methodist church, first known as Davis Chapel, was built in 1876 closer to Rehobeth on the Shelltown Road. The black congregation ap-

parently used the old church until the late nineteenth century when they erected the present building.

PHOENIX M. E. CHURCH
1897
Cash Corner vicinity
Public worship

The Phoenix Methodist Episcopal Church is located in the southern reaches of Somerset County on the west side of Gunby Creek near Cash Corner. Notable for its unaltered condition, the single story rectangular frame church stands on a brick pier foundation and is lighted by pointed arch colored glass windows. Unlike many of its nearby contemporaries, this congregation did not erect a large bell tower. Instead, the church entrance is marked by a gabled hood supported by stick brackets. The door is topped by a pointed arch transom filled with triangular panes of colored glass. The north gable end of the structure is marked by a simple five-sided apse also pierced by lancet windows of colored glass. Complementing the pristine exterior is the unaltered Victorian interior, which survives with beaded board wainscoting, a turned baluster altar rail, and late nineteenth century pews and sanctuary furniture.

QUINDOCQUA M. E. CHURCH
1913
Tulls Corner vicinity
Public worship

Significant among the prominent landmarks of southern Somerset County is Quindocqua Methodist Episcopal Church, which marks the intersection of three prominent roads in the vicinity of Tulls Corner. Built in 1913 on

S-252, Frogeye M. E. Church, west elevation.

a modified cruciform plan, the frame church commands visual attention with its tall, pyramidal-roofed bell tower. The well-preserved church exterior retains its original contrasting fabric of fish-scale shingles and weatherboard siding. Piercing the gabled elevations on three sides are large, tripartite colored glass windows.

The earliest history of Quindocqua Church is shaded with incomplete records, but tradition has held to a circa 1820 date for the organization of a Methodist Episcopal congregation independent of St. Peter's. The established church history relates that the congregation used a blacksmith's shop as a meeting house until 1847, when a new building was erected. That simple rectangular frame building served the group until 1913, when the third and present building was raised. The cornerstone was laid on September 23, 1913, and the recognized carpenters were Harold Maddox, "Sam" Maddox, Howard Hinman, Harold Taylor, "Jim" Dorsey, and Henry Evans. Aside from reusing the old bell, the new church was built at a cost of $4,500.

S-123, Quindocqua M. E. Church, southwest elevation.

ST. PAUL'S M. E. CHURCH
Circa 1883
Westover
Private

Largely due to its uncompromised appearance, St. Paul's Methodist Episcopal Church is one of the most architecturally significant buildings in Westover. A distinctive two-story entrance tower rises in the southeast corner of the church and is topped by a pyramidal roof. The roof flares at its base to cover the small belfry. Lighting the sanctuary are pairs of colored glass sash windows in each gable. This church is one of three in Westover, and although the congregation is inactive it is the best preserved of these buildings.

ST. JAMES UNITED METHODIST CHURCH
Circa 1886
Westover
Public worship

The rural black population living in the vicinity of Westover organized St. James United Methodist Church and erected this building in 1886. A few Victorian details survive, but for the most part this church has been extensively reworked. It is one of three churches still standing in Westover, and one of two that are still active.

S-182, St. Paul's M. E. Church, south elevation.

S-179, St. James United Methodist Church, southeast elevation.

ST. ELIZABETH CATHOLIC CHURCH
Circa 1900
Westover
Public worship

St. Elizabeth Catholic Church, standing on the west side of the old Westover-Kingston Road, is a turn-of-the-century frame structure dominated by a three-story bell tower that also contains the double-door entrance. Arched openings define the upper levels, and the tower is capped by a short pyramidal-roofed spire. The rectangular main block is lighted by colored glass windows. St. Elizabeth is one of three church buildings in Westover and serves the only Catholic congregation in Somerset County.

ST. STEPHEN'S CHURCH
Circa 1870
St. Stephens
Private

St. Stephen's Methodist Church is a well-preserved nineteenth century rural chapel located in the village of the same name. Surrounded by a modest collection of late nineteenth and early twentieth century houses, the church stands out as one of the best preserved structures in the village. The plain exterior is complemented by a largely unaltered interior, which features beaded board wainscoting and decorative pressed metal covering the walls and ceiling. Equally notable are the pine pews and Gothic Revival altar furniture.

ROCK CREEK M. E. CHURCH (NR)
1900
Chance
Public worship

The Rock Creek Methodist Episcopal Church is a prominent architectural landmark in this watermen's community east of Deal Island.

S-184, St. Elizabeth Catholic Church, east elevation.

S-362, St. Stephen's Church, south elevation.

S-363, Rock Creek M. E. Church, south elevation.

Similar to other contemporary churches, including St. John's on Deal Island, Rock Creek has retained most of its original exterior and interior finishes. The three-story bell tower with its arched belfry of wooden tracery is an especially distinctive Gothic Revival feature. The interior is equally distinctive with a semicircular sanctuary arrangement, beaded board wainscoting, and a beaded matched board ceiling. Construction of this church is specifically documented by a marble datestone reading 1900. The church was erected by W. J. Johnson, whose name is inscribed on the stone.

PERRYHAWKIN CHRISTIAN CHURCH
Circa 1910
Wellington vicinity
Public worship

The Perryhawkin Christian Church is a plain, single story, T-plan structure that stands on the west side of Petes Hill Road near Wellington. This rural frame structure, with its slight reference to the Gothic Revival style, is similar to several other churches from this period in the county. Rising in the southeast corner of the T-plan is a two-story tower with a pyramidal roof. The church cemetery is located on the east side of the road.

JOHN WESLEY M. E. CHURCH
1909
Green Hill vicinity
Public worship

The John Wesley Methodist Episcopal Church is a noteworthy Gothic Revival frame structure erected in 1909 and standing near the crossroads of Green Hill. The T-plan church is covered with asbestos siding and trimmed with sawn work in each gable. Several contemporary churches in the immediate vicinity share a similar entrance tower. The Gothic-arched entrance has a colored glass transom. A clover leaf design is worked into the gable end tracery. A twentieth century cemetery is located on the west side of the property.

WATERS CHAPEL CHURCH
Circa 1900
Kingston vicinity
Public worship

Distinguishing Maryland Route 413 at the intersection of Lover's Lane is Waters Chapel Church, a single story, L-plan, Gothic Revival structure dominated by a broach spire. The spire is topped with a small iron weathervane with a pair of intersecting hearts. Each principal gable of the church is pierced by a tripartite colored glass window, which lights the sanctuary. The sanctuary is one large room with the altar and choir stalls located under the west shed roof. To the back (east) of the sanctuary is additional seating space separated by folding paneled doors. The colorfully lighted interior is highlighted by a decorative wooden ceiling of diagonal and horizontal beaded boards divided into a grid pattern. This decorative treatment is similar to the ceiling of the John Wesley M. E. Church on Holland Crossing Road.

S-215, Perryhawkin Christian Church, east elevation.

S-204, John Wesley M. E. Church, south elevation.

S-250, Waters Chapel Church, southeast elevation.

ST. JAMES M. E. CHURCH
1885
Oriole vicinity
Private

Built in two stages, this two-part frame church marks the intersection of the Champ and Oriole roads. Set in the south pier of the main block is a marble plaque inscribed 1885. The front towers and multi-pane windows were added around the turn of the century. The old exterior double-door entrance is clearly visible in the vestibule. The heavy molded four-panel doors are topped with a four-light transom. Most notable is the unconventional pair of multi-level bell and entrance towers

separated by a single story gabled section pierced by a tripartite window. Directly west of the church is the accompanying cemetery with aboveground grave markers.

ST. JAMES CHURCH HALL
Circa 1885
Oriole vicinity
Private

The St. James Church hall helps define this important rural intersection along with the late nineteenth century church and graveyard. The church hall is a two-story, gable-front rectangular structure supported by brick piers and covered with narrow weatherboards.

The first floor room is finished with beaded board wainscoting and plaster walls. An enclosed stair rises against the north wall behind the meeting room.

SAMUEL WESLEY M. E. CHURCH
1903
Manokin
Public worship

The Samuel Wesley Methodist Episcopal Church in Manokin is dated 1903 by a foundation stone immediately to the right of the front steps. Its three-story bell tower and arched sash windows make it one of the most distinctive buildings along Maryland Route

S-359, St. James M. E. Church, northwest elevation.

S-360, St. James Church hall, south elevation.

333

361 between Westover and Upper Fairmount. Despite the date, a black congregation has occupied this site since the 1870s.

ST. MARK'S M. E. CHURCH
1915
Princess Anne vicinity
Public worship

St. Mark's Methodist Episcopal Church belongs to a large collection of rural black churches erected in the Gothic Revival style during the late nineteenth and early twentieth centuries. The T- and L-plans are most often distinguished by a corner entrance tower, and tripartite windows of colored glass are flanked by narrow lancet windows. St. Mark's follows this general description, with an L plan and a corner entrance tower capped by an unconventional pyramidal and octagonal spire. A modern Sunday school addition has been attached to the east side. Fixed in the corner of the foundation is a marble date plaque inscribed 1915.

JOHN WESLEY M. E. CHURCH
1897
Kingston vicinity
Public worship

Aside from a capping of the bell tower, this late nineteenth century frame structure is one of the best preserved rural black churches in southern Somerset County. It has several features in common with many contemporary church buildings, including a gable-front elevation, a corner entrance tower, and pointed arch colored glass windows. Like several churches in the Kingston/Hopewell vicinity, this building has distinctive tripartite sanctuary windows and a matched board ceiling inside. Located next to the church is the Odd Fellows hall, a two-story gable-front structure used as a church hall.

S-169, Samuel Wesley M. E. Church, north elevation.

S-346, St. Mark's M. E. Church, southeast elevation.

S-411, St. Paul's M. E. Church, south elevation.

S-124, Mt. Peer M. E. Church, west elevation.

ST. PAUL'S M. E. CHURCH
1906
Mt. Vernon vicinity
Public worship

St. Paul's Methodist Episcopal church is a simple, Gothic Revival frame structure that stands near Mount Vernon in the small community of Bobtown. The stylistic references for the building are limited to pointed arch window openings and a two-story bell tower topped with a pyramidal-roofed spire. As with other turn-of-the-century churches, the exterior walls are covered with a combination of horizontal weatherboards and decorative fish-scale shingles. Fixed in the southeast corner of the building is a datestone inscribed 1892, the year the congregation was formed, and 1906, the year the current building was erected.

MOUNT PEER M. E. CHURCH
1907
Marion vicinity
Public worship

The Mount Peer Methodist Episcopal Church stands southeast of Marion near Tulls Corner. Supported by a vented brick foundation, the L-shaped frame church is mainly lighted by colored glass lancet windows on three elevations. The west (principal) facade is also distinguished by a cloverleaf-shaped light in the upper gable. Fixed in the northwest corner of the brick foundation is a marble datestone with the inscription "Mount Peer M. E. Church 1889-1907." Standing southeast of the church is a two-story, asbestos-shingled frame church hall.

LIBERIA M. E. CHURCH
1912
Hudson's Corner vicinity
Public worship

According to the date plaque, the Liberia Methodist Episcopal congregation was formed two years after the close of the Civil War. The extant church, evidently the second building to house the congregation, was erected in 1912 in a simplified Gothic Revival design. Dominating the southeast corner is a three-story

S-120, John Wesley M. E. Church, northwest elevation.

bell tower, which also contains the double-door entrance. The rectangular sanctuary is lighted by pointed arch colored glass windows on the first floor; a small round window pierces the upper gable.

GRACE M. E. CHURCH
1924
Venton vicinity
Public worship

Grace Methodist Episcopal Church is one of the most recently built examples of a Gothic Revival church in Somerset County. Erected in 1924, this T-plan structure follows the same pattern as a dozen churches erected during the previous half century. Contrasting features include Palladian-type principal windows instead of Gothic-arched ones. Evidently this building was erected on the same foundation as the former church since the marble date plaque reads, "Grace M. E. Church, built 1893, rebuilt May 25, 1924, Pastor S. G. Dix." A cemetery of above-

S-119, Liberia M. E. Church, southeast elevation.

ground vaults surrounds the church on two sides, and a church hall sits on the north side of Fitzgerald Road.

MT. OLIVE METHODIST CHURCH
1873, 1905, 1947
Revells Neck
Public worship

Mt. Olive Methodist Church is located on the south side of Revells Neck Road approximately one-half mile west of Millard Long Road. Two datestones are found in the concrete block foundation; one has the dates 1873 and 1905, and the other is dated 1947. These dates reflect the different construction periods of the former buildings as well as the age of the current church, a single story, gable-roofed frame structure that is highlighted by a two-story tower topped by a pyramidal-roofed spire. The sides of the building are pierced by colored glass windows. The interior has been remodeled, but Victorian pews and altar furniture appear to have been handed down through the years. Interestingly, this church is identified on the 1877 atlas map at this site, but another Methodist Episcopal church is shown due east on the north side of Revells Neck Road. Not much is known about this second congregation.

S-356, Grace M. E. Church, north elevation.

S-198, Mt. Olive Methodist Church, northwest elevation.

Princess Anne

WILLIAM GEDDES HOUSE
(TUNSTALL COTTAGE)
Circa 1755
Princess Anne
Private

Much has been conjectured and written about this story-and-a-half frame house, which marks the southwest corner of Broad and Church streets in the center of Princess Anne. Most everyone has agreed the hall/parlor plan dwelling, which exhibits several features common to early domestic architecture, is among the oldest structures to remain standing within the town limits. The exposed framing members on the first floor and the finely executed raised panel end wall in the old "hall" convincingly suggest the house was built early in the town's history. Pinning down a more exact date proves much more complicated as well as more critical to the interpretation of the early development of Princess Anne.

Without any doubt the house was not built before Princess Anne was founded in 1733, for the L-shaped structure was clearly planned to stand on a town lot. Also, the partially excavated cellar shows no signs that the dwelling was ever moved. The question then comes to mind, was the house erected shortly after 1733 or, perhaps more reasonably, after 1742 when it was clear Princess Anne would be the seat of the county court and town investments and development would have justified financing a skillfully erected house with a finely paneled interior. As can be shown many times over in Maryland as well as in

Princess Anne, photograph c. 1900, E. I. Brown—photographer (courtesy of Robert Withey).

S-2, William Geddes house (Tunstall Cottage), east elevation.

Somerset County itself, much speculation surrounded seventeenth and eighteenth century town development. It was not uncommon for streets to be laid out, lots sold, and houses built, only for the town to fade away as trade and commerce moved elsewhere. The speculative ownership that characterized the early history of Princess Anne has confused latter-day researchers, who may have assumed the lots were improved, when in fact many remained unimproved or rented. Confusion on this matter has led some people to believe Captain John Tunstall may have erected this house, since he owned three lots in Princess Anne; however, it seems likely he purchased the lots on speculation. Rather than residing in Princess Anne, Tunstall chose to live by deeper water. In 1733 he purchased land

Situate on the South side of Manocan River in a place formerly laid out for a town called Somerset in the aforesaid County and Province, also a Schooner named the Providence of about fifty Tonns Burthen Together with her Sails, Riggen,

Anchors, Cables, Blocks, & all other appurtenances....

Keeping all this in mind, a reexamination of the chain of title for Lot 7 and adjacent lots helps to sort out the early history of this property. The first deed that specifically mentions Lot 7 was executed in November 1755 between Samuel Whittingham, son and heir of Heber Whittingham, and William Geddes, merchant. Although this may suggest that Heber Whittingham erected the house before his death in 1750, it is known through another deed, executed in 1774, that he occupied Lot 4, which passed down through the Whittingham family until the early twentieth century. Also, Samuel Whittingham sold Lot 7 for £1.17.6, a sum that does not suggest an improved property.

William Geddes, who is listed as a merchant in the land records, owned Lot 7 and adjacent Lot 8 until he sold them both in 1769 to Isaac Handy for £240, a price that definitely suggests substantial improvements. The 1769 transfer reads, "all that Lott and

Ground on which the said William Geddes heretofore lately Lived and on which the said Isaac Handy now lives...." Handy occupied the town lots for the remainder of his life, and although he left no will the property passed to his son Richard, who was taxed in 1798 for lots 7 and 8. Lot 7 was improved by

1 Dwelling House 28 by 15 feet with addition of 18 by 13 feet wood one story, 6 windows 4 feet 10 Inches long 2 feet 4 Inches wide 4 [windows] 3 feet 8 Inches long 2 feet 4 Inches wide, 2 [windows] 3 feet 3 Inches long 21 Inches wide, 1 Cook house 18 by 16 feet all out of repair.

Seven years later Richard Handy sold the lots, along with Lot 5 and Lot 6, to Littleton Dennis Teackle for $5,000. In 1807 Teackle transferred title of the old Geddes house to General John Gale, with whose family the house remained until 1819. After several transfers, lots 7 and 8 were purchased by George W. Dashiell in 1851, and the property was largely held by Dashiell descendants

S-96, Charles Jones house, southeast elevation.

until 1943, when John H. and Maude Jeffries purchased the town lot and restored the house, naming it Tunstall Cottage.

CHARLES JONES HOUSE
Circa 1780
Princess Anne
Private

Long thought to be one of the few dwellings to survive from the earliest years of Princess Anne's history is this three-bay, story-and-a-half house, located at the corner of Somerset Avenue and Broad Street, originally part of Lot 3. The fact that a house stood on this site as early as 1743 is documented in an early deed detailing the boundaries of the first lot for the county courthouse across the street. The deed reads, "on the south by a streight line drawn cross the main street from the south end of a house in the said Town belonging to Capt. Robert King and Capt. David Wilson...." From this reference it was reasonably assumed the extant house and the dwelling referred to in the deed were one

and the same. However, the few original architectural features to survive in the current story-and-a-half frame house suggest the 1740s building was destroyed sometime before the Revolution and replaced by the present house. Sections of eighteenth century feather-edged partitions reused as doors and beaded floor joists reused as studs indicate the extant structure was built with materials probably taken from the earlier house. Also, this later dwelling originally had a complicated plan with corner hearths heating three or four rooms, not unlike that of the Glebe house south of Princess Anne, which vestry minutes date to 1784.

Construction of this house is estimated to date to the 1780s, probably during the ownership of Charles Jones, who acquired title to the property in 1782. Jones is designated in the land records as an innholder and may have operated an ordinary or tavern on the site. He died intestate several years later, and in 1788 Lot 3 was sold to Dr. John Woolford. Three years later Woolford partitioned the lot and transferred ownership of the southern part to Parker Selby, who, according to

the deed, was living in the house. In 1798 Selby was assessed for Lot 3, which was then improved by

> 1 Dwelling House 36 by 30 feet wood one story 7 windows 3 feet 8 Ins long 2 feet 4 Ins wide 4 [windows] 3 feet 8 inches long 2 feet 4 Ins wide 1 Cook house 14 by 12 feet 1 Smoke house 12 by 10 feet 1 Milk house 14 by 12 feet 1 Cariage house 32 by 12 feet all in good repair.

The dimensions cited in 1798 agree with the size of the current building. After the turn of the nineteenth century the property changed hands several times. More recently, during the 1940s, the exterior and the first floor interiors were heavily reworked. Owner's Choice—a name often associated with the property—is taken from the earliest history of the lot. David and Rebecca Dent Brown, owners of the Beckford tract from which twenty-five acres were taken to lay out Princess Anne, were granted first choice of two lots, one of which was Lot 3.

MANOKIN PRESBYTERIAN CHURCH (NR)
1765, 1871-1872, 1888
Princess Anne
Public worship

The history of the Manokin Presbyterian Church occupies an important place in the development of Presbyterianism in Somerset County as well as colonial America. In 1672 a group of Presbyterians who had settled on the lower Eastern Shore petitioned the Grand Jury charged with overseeing public worship in Somerset County for a vigil permit to hold services of worship and to have their own minister. Permission was granted, and the Grand Jury called Robert Maddox to preach on the third Sunday of each month at the home of Christopher Nutter. Nutter

S-16, Manokin Presbyterian Church, south elevation.

lived at the head of the Manokin River, the current site of the church. In 1683 Reverend Francis Makemie arrived from Ireland at the request of Colonel William Stevens of Rehobeth. Under his leadership the congregations at Rehobeth, Manokin, Pitts Creek, Snow Hill, and Wicomico were organized.

The Reverend Thomas Wilson was the first ordained minister of the Manokin church. His name appears in the Somerset County land records as early as 1685, when he purchased 130 acres of "Turner's Purchase." Wilson served the Manokin congregation until his death in 1702.

By the mid-eighteenth century, the Manokin session deemed it necessary to replace the church. In 1764 the building was described as "decayed in almost every part and not worth repairing, and that it is too small to contain the people that often attend." As a result the congregation decided to "build a new one of Brick 50 by 40 in the clear, sixteen feet from the water table to the plate, to be covered with Cyprus shingles, to have a gallery at each end of Negroes with such windows, doors, and other matters as shall be convenient." In January 1765 Samuel Wilson submitted a bid for the construction of the new church at £790, but the sum proved too

costly and the structure was completed for £600. Originally, the south and east walls were laid in Flemish bond treated with glazed header highlights in a checkerboard pattern, and two arched doors were fixed in the south side on either side of the center window. An early photograph of the church, which was later altered, documents the former arrangement. In 1872 the eighteenth century church was heavily rebuilt by raising the roof and turning the orientation east/west. The two south doors were converted to windows, and an east end door was cut through. Inside, the old box pews and the galleries were removed. Finally, in 1888 a three-story bell tower with the main entrance was attached to the east gable end.

ST. ANDREW'S EPISCOPAL CHURCH
1767-1773, 1859, 1896
Princess Anne
Public worship

Central to the history of the Anglican Church in Somerset County is St. Andrew's Episcopal Church, contracted and built between 1767 and 1773. During the third quarter of the eighteenth century, the vestry decided to abandon King's Mill Chapel and relocate the

chapel of ease for Somerset Parish in Princess Anne. After petitioning the General Assembly of Maryland, lots 27 and 28 were purchased from Robert Geddes for £28 on February 17, 1767. Little more than a month later, the vestry advanced the plans for the new church. It was agreed the church would be

sixty feet in length and forty feet in width in the clear—exclusive of an arch or Simey Circle [semi-circle] for the Communion Table or Chancel, the walls to be twenty feet high between the surface of the Earth and the wall plates...four windows to be in each side, each window to contain forty eight panes of glass, the glass to be eight inches by ten inches, exclusive of an arch over each window...and also build a belfry to the said chapel provided two workmen can complete the same in twenty four hours—otherwise to be paid for the time over and above in preparation for the said work.

It was agreed the same day that Levin Ballard would build the chapel.

Construction of the Flemish bond brick church continued through the early 1770s. On August 7, 1770, the vestry ordered that adver-

S-3, St. Andrew's Episcopal Church, northwest elevation.

tisements be published in Princess Anne for persons "inclined to undertake to build a pulpit in the new chapel in Princess Anne Town of the same form of the Pulpit in the old chapel at King's Mill only the back of the Pulpit to be plastered." The pews were finally allotted on September 16, 1773.

Significant changes were not made to the eighteenth century church until 1859, when the northeast tower was erected. Through the following half century the entire interior was reworked in Gothic Revival taste with an exposed timber truss and Victorian church furniture. The broach spire was added in 1896. Both the exterior and interior have remained essentially unchanged since the turn of the century.

WASHINGTON HOTEL
1797, 1838, and later
Princess Anne
Public

Long-standing traditions in Princess Anne have held that an ordinary or tavern has operated at this location since early in the town's history. The oldest deed associated with this site, known as Lot 15, is dated October 2, 1751, when John Bell purchased both Lot 15 and Lot 16 for forty shillings. The following March, Bell sold Lot 15 to Henry Waggaman for £74. It is clear that Bell had improved the lot to some degree, for the 1752 deed states, "which the aforesaid John Bell now dwelleth and posseseth...." However, no

one can say what type of building was there or to what use he put it, other than its use as a dwelling.

Henry Waggaman did not own Lot 15 very long, for in 1755 he sold the property to John Done for £120. The Done family owned the property from 1755 until 1797. A tavern appears to have been operated on the site by 1780 under a lease to Zadock Long, who purchased Lot 15 and its improvements in June 1797. The federal assessment of 1798 details the appearance of the tavern property at that time:

> *1 Dwelling House 50 by 25 feet wood one story 8 windows 4 feet 10 Inches long 2 feet 4 Inches wide in good repair 1 Cook house 20 by 16 feet Study 18 by 12 feet 1 Bylard House 26 by 18 feet wood two stor[y] not finished 1 Stable 30 by 28 feet 1 Milk house 10 feet square.*

This description of Lot 15 offers several important insights about the building history of the site. The single story "Dwelling House" was undoubtedly the original structure on the lot, perhaps the improvement erected by John Bell at mid-century. Not uncommon for the period was the detached "Cook house" and the square milk house. Most important is the entry describing a two-story billiard house, which was still under construction at the time of the assessment. Evidently Zadock Long financed the construction of the northern portion of the current hotel shortly after he purchased the lot from John Done. The northern half of the hotel is appropriately finished with Federal style woodwork and assembled with wrought-iron nails. The stable was a common improvement for a tavern property, and the study must have stood independently as well.

Zadock Long owned the tavern until his death in 1838, when the property passed to

S-18, Washington Hotel, northeast elevation.

his son, Edward H.C. Long. After his father's death in February, Edward replaced the old Bell house. In place of the story-and-a-half eighteenth century dwelling, a two-and-a-half story addition was erected that followed the roofline established by the 1797 structure. When the new addition was attached to the billiard house, its gable end attic windows and exterior weatherboards were covered over, and they remain exposed in the attic.

Soon after the improvements were completed, Edward Long advertised the tavern in the *Somerset Herald*. The August 13, 1839, advertisement read:

> *The Subscriber offers for Lease...His Valuable TAVERN Establishment with its recent and extensive improvements, situated in the centre of Princess-Anne and adjacent to the Court House and Public Offices, in Somerset County. The main building and outhouses are in complete order, having been this past year rebuilt and repaired, and will be found equal, if not superior to any on the Eastern Shore.*
>
> *The site of the present buildings has been occupied and known as a Tavern Estab-*

lishment for more than seventy years and it is believed, that to an enterprising and efficient Innkeeper peculiar facilities are now presented to justify the investment of capital.

Edward Long

In February 1856 Edward and his wife Aurelia transferred the hotel to Henry E. L. Morris, whose ownership was short-lived. Although Morris owned the property for slightly less than two years, he and his wife Margaret made long-lasting changes. It appears from the records that they were the first to name the hotel after George Washington. They were also responsible for erecting the single story brick stable that remains behind the main building. In April 1869 the hotel property was purchased by William P. Rider, innkeeper, who managed the establishment for most of the following twenty-eight years. Most recently, the Washington Hotel has been managed by the Murphy family, who purchased it in 1956.

TEACKLE MANSION (NR)
Circa 1802, 1818-1819
Princess Anne
Open by appointment

Continuing the entrepreneurial tradition of early Somerset merchant-planters, Littleton Dennis Teackle capitalized on the resources available to him as a prominent merchant and statesman during the first half of the nineteenth century. Teackle established trade agreements with markets in England and the Caribbean as well as with the U. S. Navy Department for the timber and fittings used in America's early gunboat fleet. For instance, on April 14, 1806, 2,250 bushels of Indian corn were sent on his ship, the *Philanthropist*, to the Bahama island of New Providence. In return Teackle imported coffee, cocoa, and sugar to Baltimore. In 1806 he established contacts with the Liverpool firm of Barclay, Salkeld, and Company.

By the 1820s Littleton D. Teackle had shifted his focus to the Maryland House of Delegates, serving in office between 1824 and 1836. In addition to his extra-regional positions, Teackle influenced life in Princess Anne

S-10, Teackle Mansion, east elevation, Michael Harrison Day—photographer.

and Somerset County as president of the early Bank of Somerset and as a forerunner in the application of steam-generated power on the Eastern Shore with his Manokin River steam mill, built in 1815.

Along with his economic and political achievements, Teackle established an ambitious estate on the western edge of Princess Anne that rivaled the best Eastern Shore accommodations. Beginning in May 1802 he purchased several parcels of ground between the Manokin River and the western edge of the town. He centered his temple- or gable-front brick house on this site, deliberately building it in line with Prince William Street and oriented to face town. At the time the only other brick buildings in Princess Anne were the Episcopal and Presbyterian churches.

Not only is Teackle's house distinguished by its fine Flemish bond brickwork, but the main facade is highlighted with decorative plaster panels featuring fruit-laden urns and trailing grapevines. The center double-door entrance is accented with fine reeded pilasters, and the first and second floor windows are topped with rusticated wooden jack arches. The pediment is embellished with a finely

carved cornice, and the tympanum is pierced by a round window. Paralleling the strict balance of the exterior, the first floor interior was planned in forced symmetry, including an arched niche to match the stairway arch and false doorways in the parlor. Unusual for the period are two mirrored windows built into the hall partition; these reflect light into the otherwise dimly lighted parlor. The hall and parlor are further enhanced by plaster decoration including arch imposts, large ceiling medallions, and molded plaster cornices.

The first period of construction also included two bays of each adjacent hyphen. Small hearths in each hyphen room feed into flues built into the chimneys of the main block. The five-part brick house did not achieve its full size until 1818-1819, when Elizabeth Teackle supervised the construction of the service and bedroom wings while Littleton managed his affairs in Baltimore. In a letter to her daughter, Elizabeth Anne Upshur, Elizabeth Teackle wrote in August 1818, "Our buildings go on very well. The wings are shut in, and the roofs painted." Construction continued until the following summer. Not only did the Teackles' improved

house overshadow most of its contemporaries, but the gardens, as described by Elizabeth Teackle, must have added a blaze of color at the end of Prince William Street. On April 26, 1819, Elizabeth wrote to her sister, Anne Eyre of Northampton County:

I would give a thousand things if you would see this beautiful bash of mine, as it will soon be, covered with one vast shut of rose!...and my cowslip edging as it has been with its thousand golden eyes all looking upon my delighted grey ones at once!...and my scotch brooms as they are, perching themselves so saucily and laughing in my face...My hyasinths have been good, and the tulips gaudy...Your lemon tree is in bloom and looks remarkably well and hardy in the society of geraniums and roses which are assembled for the summer under a cherry tree in the garden. I have creeping cerus in bloom and will save you a cutting of that also, it is very pretty.

Located close to the main house was a score of outbuildings, including a large smokehouse, a combination brick wash house and

S-10A, *Teackle Gatehouse, southeast elevation.*

S-95, *Teackle tenement, northeast elevation.*

dairy, a brick ice house, a well, stables, granaries, poultry houses, and slave quarters. Before the construction of the south wing, a detached kitchen must have accompanied the outbuildings. A pair of two-story frame tenements flanked the entrance to the Teackle estate. Both structures were built with the gable-front orientation and were used to house servants (see S-10A and S-95).

In spite of these auspicious improvements, Littleton Dennis Teackle's finances were unstable at times, and twice he temporarily lost title to the property, first in 1812 and again in 1828. John Eyre, Elizabeth Teackle's brother-in-law, purchased the property in 1828 from the United States marshal Thomas Finely, after a suit was settled against the Teackle estate. Eyre transferred title to his niece Elizabeth Anne Upshur Teackle in 1831. Four years later, in September 1835, Elizabeth Teackle died at the age of fifty-two, after which the property entered yet another period of adjustment and refinancing. Finally, in 1839 Littleton advertised the town property in the *Somerset Herald*:

> The Estate of Beckford Mansion, the residence of the subscriber in Somerset County, Maryland may be purchased on reasonable and accomodating terms.
> The Mansion, as well as the Offices, including a Coach house and Stables, an Ice House, Wash House and Wood House with other necessary buildings of modern structure and the best material, are all on an extended scale and conveniently arranged.
> The situation is adjacent to the seat of justice in the county town, and near to the Manokin River. It is elevated and healthy.

> *The grounds, estimated at ten acres, have been highly improved and contain Orchards and Gardens of the choicest fruits, flowers and vines in qualities and varieties perhaps not excelled on this Peninsula.*
> *Littleton Dennis Teackle*
> *November 5, 1839*

Soon after, Teackle and his daughter, Elizabeth, and son-in-law, Aaron B. Quinby, sold the mansion with ten acres to Isaac Newman for $3,000. When Newman died a few years later in August 1841, the property passed to his two sons, Samuel Henry and Littleton Purnell Dennis Newman. Ten years later Samuel Henry Newman filed a suit in Somerset Court to have the property sold and the proceeds divided between him and his brother. At this time the estate was divided into eight lots, and the boundary line between Lot 7 and Lot 8 ran between the north wing and hyphen and the rest of the mansion. Francis Barnes, who had purchased Lot 2 for his own house, also purchased Lot 7 with the north wing and hyphen. After selling a northern portion of Lot 7 to Seth Venables, Barnes transferred the north wing and hyphen to Sarah D. Jones, who in turn sold this portion of Lot 7 to the trustees of the Female Academy. This school lasted only a few years, after which Lot 7 with the north wing and hyphen passed into the hands of Samuel and Sarah R. Jones and later the Dashiell and Woolford families. In 1965 the Somerset County Historical Society purchased the north wing. The center section and south wing, designated as Lot 8, was purchased in 1855 by Dr. John W. Dashiell, who occupied the mansion with his family until 1903. Dashiell descendant Olive

Dashiell Martin sold the center section of the mansion to Olde Princess Anne Days, Inc. in 1960. This sale was followed by the transfer of the south wing in 1968.

TEACKLE GATEHOUSE
Circa 1805
Princess Anne
Private

Marking the north and south sides of Prince William Street at the intersection of Beckford Avenue is a pair of two-story frame dwellings erected as tenements or servant quarters for Littleton Dennis Teackle's estate. The gable-front frame houses, built to mirror one another, marked the formal entrance to the most lavish property known to exist on the lower Eastern Shore. Ironically, the two "tenements" were the last buildings Teackle owned and occupied after his financial collapse during the late 1830s forced him to sell the main house. He shared these buildings with his servants, George Tilghman, Milchy Gray, Ann Handy, Sally Hyland, James Curtis, and others until 1848. In that year Teackle transferred "all those lots or parcels of land situated in the western precincts of Princess Anne including the two tenements lately occupied by the said Littleton Dennis Teackle and his servants... together with the ancient warehouse adjoining the public landing..." to John H. King and Edward M. Wise, merchants of Princess Anne. Not quite a year passed before King and Wise divided the property and sold the northern lot and tenement to Joseph F. Smith. The property remained in Smith family hands until 1897, when the title was acquired by Emma E. Dougherty, who occupied the house until

S-9, East Glen, west elevation, photograph c. 1967.

her death in 1922. Her daughter Elizabeth sold the house to W. Irving and Frances H. Galliher in 1953. (For the history of the southern lot, see S-95.)

TEACKLE TENEMENT
Circa 1805
Princess Anne
Private

Most recently known as Judge Tracey's house, this two-story, gable-front frame building has shared an intimate history tied to the Teackle estate with its across-the-street neighbor (S-10A). Although built of different materials and on a smaller scale, the side hall/parlor dwelling carries clear references to the brick mansion with its pedimented street facade (see S-10). The two frame houses were planned as servant quarters or tenements to mark the entrance to the Teackle property.

Construction of the tenements is estimated to date to the same general period as the mansion itself. In 1848 Teackle sold the two tenement buildings to John H. King and Edward M. Wise, trading partners under the name King and Wise. The following year the property was transferred to George W. Dashiell, who sold the house and lot to Wil-

liam Lecates the same day. It is thought Lecates occupied this house during the construction of his new house next door (S-6). For a large part of the nineteenth century, this Teackle tenement house was the residence of Thomas J. Dixon, a prominent county merchant who died in 1903.

EAST GLEN
1803
Princess Anne (site)

East Glen formerly stood at the east end of Prince William Street, and it is reasonably believed that the two-story, three-bay house was designed as an imitation of the center block of the Teackle Mansion. In fact, both houses shared a gable-front orientation, a transverse hall plan, and similar finish features. The paired modillion blocks that decorated the cornice were exact duplicates of the paired blocks that highlight the Teackle Mansion cornice. Differing features included a pedimented entrance with a finely crafted arched transom and another floor plan. Although both houses were built with a transverse hall, the stairs were located at the south end at East Glen, and the house had two rooms behind the hall instead of one.

The construction of this important Federal style house is documented by a rarely found statement in the 1803 deed for the property executed between George Wilson Jackson and Matthias Jones. Following the description of the metes and bounds of the three-and-a-half acre parcel is an additional comment: "being the Lott of ground whereon the said Matthias is now erecting a Dwelling House, with all and singular the privileges and appurtenances thereunto...." Dr. Matthias Jones and his wife, Milcah Gale Jones, owned the town property until their deaths in the late 1830s. Their heirs decided to sell their parents' house at public auction, and Isaac D. Jones was the highest bidder. He owned East Glen until mid-century, when he transferred the house to James U. Dennis. In 1865 John J. Dashiell bought East Glen, and following his death in April 1868 the property was held by his heirs. John's widow, Mary Ann Dashiell, evidently occupied the dwelling, for a Mrs. Dashiell is located on the 1877 atlas map of Princess Anne. At the turn of the century the property was conveyed to Lola V. Taylor. The deed specifically mentions that the land was the same ground on which J. Thomas Taylor, Jr. resided and conducted a carriage business. Over the past half century East Glen had a half dozen different owners until the town purchased the house and grounds in 1975. East Glen was demolished in the late 1970s and replaced with a parking lot until the new county library was erected on the site in 1988.

COLONEL GEORGE HANDY HOUSE
1805-1806
Princess Anne
Private

Standing at the east end of Washington Street on an axis with Beckford is Colonel George Handy's two-and-a-half story frame house, built in 1805 after he had purchased a six-acre lot adjoining the Town of Princess Anne. The land, located between Matthias Jones's lot and the lands of William Gilliss Waters, was sold by George Wilson Jackson in consideration of "one hundred and sixty pounds, twelve shillings and six pence."

It is thought Handy initiated construction of this fine Federal period house within a year of the transfer of property in June 1805. Uniform layers of beaded weatherboard siding, exposed brick fire walls, and superior Federal style woodwork support this building date. As originally built, the four-room plan main house was joined to the two-story frame kitchen by a single story hyphen or colonnade. During the late nineteenth century the colonnade as well as the roof of the main house and kitchen were completely rebuilt. Another story and a half were added to the colonnade, and a two-story bay was attached to the south side of the main block.

In spite of the exterior modifications, the interior of the main house has remained essentially unchanged. Similarities in woodwork found in this house and other Federal period dwellings, including the Teackle Mansion and the Jesse Wainwright house, suggest the same master craftsmen. The floor plan follows a four-room arrangement with a stair hall in

S-7, Colonel George Handy house, *northwest elevation.*

the northwest corner and the parlor directly behind. Two rooms, each heated by a corner hearth, divide the south end of the first floor. The two-story kitchen, built at the same time as the house, survives with a beaded joist ceiling and a large cooking hearth. Beaded weatherboard siding and an exposed common bond brick fire wall mirror the early nineteenth century features of the main block.

Also significant to the property is the only original log outbuilding to remain standing in Princess Anne. The square log structure has half-dovetailed corners and a pyramidal roof. Due to the tight nature of the well-chinked logs and the absence of any louvered openings, it seems likely the building was used as a smokehouse.

After Colonel Handy's death in 1820, his widow, Elizabeth, sold the property to Elizabeth A. W. Waters for $3,000. William E. Waters inherited the house and lot from his mother, and in 1866 William E. and Anna M. Waters conveyed the parcel to Hampden H. Dashiell and William T. G. Polk, partners trading under the name of H. H. Dashiell and Co.

After the Civil War, the house was purchased by Mary D. H. Langford, wife of Benjamin Langford. The Langfords owned the property for more than a half century and were probably responsible for the nineteenth

century reworking of the house. During the second half of the twentieth century the house has been occupied by the Wilsons, Cohns, and most recently the Dennises. Mary Value Dennis Clark purchased the property from the Cohns in 1970.

NUTTER'S PURCHASE
Circa 1800
Princess Anne
Private

Recent architectural and historical research on this single story side hall/parlor house suggests the dwelling was built during the ownership of Samuel Lippincott, who purchased a two-acre riverside property from William Lowber in 1800.

Listed as a currier in the Somerset County land records, William Lowber began leasing the property in 1788 with the intention of operating a tannery on the north side of the river. Although Lowber is documented as living on the property, architectural evidence indicates the extant house was not his. It was probably erected for the next owner of the tanyard, Samuel Lippincott. The dwelling is not listed in the 1798 federal tax assessment, but was constructed with wrought nails and finished with early nineteenth century style woodwork. The brick chimney was built to

S-15, Old Episcopal parsonage, southeast elevation.

serve two fireplaces, one in the parlor and a second in what is now the west end addition. Originally extending from the west side of the house was a one-room, shed-roofed section that served as the kitchen.

In 1804 Lippincott sold the tanyard lot to Littleton Dennis Teackle for "five hundred pounds Current money of Maryland," a sum that suggests substantial improvements for a two-acre property. After remaining in Teackle's hands for twelve years, the property was sold to John H. Bell in 1816, and then to Gideon Pearce in 1820.

The name of the house was taken from the earliest owner of the property, Christopher Nutter, who patented a 300-acre tract of land on the north side of the Manokin River in 1667. Nutter occupied this land, and his house was one of four sites where early Presbyterian meetings were held.

OLD EPISCOPAL PARSONAGE
Circa 1819
Princess Anne
Private

The old Episcopal parsonage is a prominent, early nineteenth century, Federal style dwelling that stands on a high knoll north of the Manokin River. The highly visible frame house retains its essential historic appearance with beaded weatherboards, original sash windows, and twin interior end chimneys. The most significant alteration to the early nineteenth century dwelling involved the raising of the colonnade to a two-and-a-half story elevation with a Gothic-arched dormer window. The early nineteenth century kitchen remains largely intact with a layer of beaded weatherboard siding and a well-preserved boxed cornice. The interior of the main house is fitted with sophisticated Federal woodwork, including paneled wainscoting; fancy mantels; a decorated stair; and original doors, chair rail, and baseboards.

Research indicates this part of "Hayward's Purchase" was improved by important dwellings throughout the eighteenth and nineteenth centuries. This elaborate Federal style house was evidently erected by Gideon Pearce around 1819 after he had assembled a plantation on the north side of the Manokin River beginning in 1816. In 1820 John McHenry of Baltimore bought the fifteen-acre parcel with the house for $3,000. In 1849 his heir, James Howard McHenry, sold the fifteen acres of "Hayward's Purchase" to the vestry of Somerset Parish for use as a parsonage. An entry in the vestry minutes from 1854 documents a few changes to the building at that time:

S-14, Nutter's Purchase, north elevation.

The Committee appointed by the vestry to make an examination and estimate of the repairs now required at the parsonage, 100 posts and railing—1500 plank for railing, 2000 shingles for stable, one sill for colonnade, material for two porches.

The vestry had the colonnade raised to two-and-a-half stories during the fourth quarter of the nineteenth century. In 1908 they sold the house to Henry Flurer, whose descendants still hold title to the Federal style house.

SARAH MARTIN DONE HOUSE
1823
Princess Anne
private

Relocated to a new site behind the Teackle Mansion, this two-story, three-bay frame house with a transverse hall plan formerly occupied the current site of the Princess Anne post office. Oscar E. Wilson sold the house to Milbourne T. Muir in 1947, and Muir subsequently moved it to its present location.

Sarah Martin Done's name is attached to the house because the land records show she had the dwelling built in 1823. For $275 Elinor and Littleton J. Dennis sold her "all that lot or parcel of ground in the precincts of Princess Anne Town on the west side of the county road leading from town to Washington Academy." The deed further states that the three-quarter acre parcel is the same lot "on which Mrs. Done hath lately built a dwelling house."

Less than a year later, Sarah Martin Done conveyed her new house on Main Street to Elizabeth Handy, who remained in the house until her death in 1837. Mrs. Handy's will of 1837 directs her daughters Martha and Anne to "sell the house and lot where I now live." But instead of doing so, Anne G. Handy

S-12, Sarah Martin Done house, southeast elevation.

conveyed full ownership to her sister Matilda Handy King and nephew George H. King. The Kings and Handys continued to reside in the house until 1860, when it was sold to Arthur Crisfield, who sold it nine years later to Henry and Virginia Page. In 1884 William Dale of Worcester County purchased the property, and the Dale family retained ownership until 1943. In that year Richard and Stella Dale sold the house to Catherine W. Ricketts, who transferred the dwelling to Oscar E. Wilson three years later. Wilson sold the house for $1,000 to Milbourne T. Muir, who moved it to the site behind the Teackle Mansion.

When this house was built in 1823 for Sarah Done, the gable-front orientation and transverse hall plan were architectural tradi-

S-24, Littleton Long house, northeast elevation.

S-105, Arnold H. Ballard house, north elevation.

tions two decades old in Princess Anne, popularized to a large degree by the Teackle Mansion and East Glen. The interior of Sarah Done's house is fitted with finely crafted period woodwork, including a decorated corner stair, six-panel doors, and Federal style mantels, one of which remains in the living room.

LITTLETON LONG HOUSE
Circa 1830
Princess Anne
Private

Marking the southwest corner of South Somerset Avenue and Washington Street is a two-story, gable-front frame dwelling erected for Littleton Long around 1830 and more recently known as the May house. Like other examples in town, the Littleton Long house follows the Federal style design precedents established by Littleton Dennis Teackle in the first years of the nineteenth century. Instead of the brick construction of the Teackle Mansion, the Long house was erected with a mortise-and-tenon frame skeleton sheathed with beaded weatherboards. The east or main elevation is a symmetrical three-bay facade capped with a simple pediment, which is pierced by a round window with radiating muntins. The floor plan follows in the same tradition with a transverse hall that fronts two rooms. The stair is fixed in the south end of

the hall and rises against the first and second floor windows.

Littleton Long, a town merchant, purchased a half-acre lot from Littleton J. Dennis, Henry J. Dennis, and Robert J. Dennis in November 1829 and presumably erected the house during the next few months. Long and his wife, Sarah, owned the house and lot for the next forty-seven years, finally transferring title to Ellen McMaster in 1876 for $2,500. McMaster's two daughters, A. Louise Duer and Ellen D. Fisher, and their husbands sold the property to Gulf Refining Company in 1927. Gulf divided the house from the unimproved yard and sold the house and lesser acreage to Ida L. Pusey two years later. On the southern portion of the lot, Gulf erected a Colonial Revival style gasoline station.

ARNOLD H. BALLARD HOUSE
Circa 1835
Princess Anne
Private

On September 14, 1835, Virgil Maxey, representing the Treasury of the United States, sold half of Lot 19 in Princess Anne to Arnold H. Ballard. The lot had been confiscated as part of the holdings of Littleton Dennis Teackle's estate. Ballard purchased the Prince William Street lot for $301, and then sold the property two years later to John H. King

for $600. The increase in transfer price suggests new improvements, and the early nineteenth century features of this two-story, side hall/parlor frame house agree with the estimated 1830s date of construction. The pedimented gable front is similar to that of other contemporary town dwellings.

As a merchant John H. King owned other property in Princess Anne, and he probably rented this house as he and his wife, Charlotte, are known to have occupied the dwelling they built on the northwest corner of Prince William and Church streets. In 1845 the Kings sold this property to Edward J. Wainwright, who occupied the house with his wife, Olive, until 1864. After the turn of the century, members of the Maryland Baptist Union Association purchased the adjoining corner lot and erected a church next to this early nineteenth century dwelling.

WILLIAM W. JOHNSTON HOUSE
1834-1835
Princess Anne
Private

Clearly one of the best detailed of the Federal style houses in Princess Anne, the William W. Johnston house occupies a prominent corner at the intersection of South Somerset and Antioch avenues. The two-story frame house, erected on a one-and-a-half acre parcel on what was the southern periphery of Princess Anne, was oriented with its fine gable front facing town, in the same manner as East Glen and the Teackle Mansion. The north facade is distinguished by an elaborate classical entrance with an arched fanlight, while the pedimented gable end is finished with rows of modillions. Centered within the pediment is an arched window. Identical moldings around the front door are found at Linden Hill (S-17). Inside, a generous transverse hall stretches across the front of the house, with two large rooms behind. The interior woodwork exhibits a mixture of late Federal and Greek Revival styles that reflects the 1830s construction date.

In November 1834 William Johnston and his wife, Rosina, purchased the corner lot from John and Sally E. Dennis of Beckford for $450, a sum that would not have included the house. Presumably, within the year, the Johnstons hired local carpenters to erect their finely detailed dwelling. Tradition relates that after the craftsmen were finished with the Johnston house, they started on Linden Hill.

In 1850 William W. Johnston was a prominent Somerset County merchant, as well as the owner of an important saw and grist mill. As a member of St. Andrew's Church he financed the construction of the bell tower in 1859. After Johnston's death in 1865 his wife inherited the property for her use, after which the house and grounds were to be devised to Ellen R. Dennis and Emily Upshur Johnston.

LINDEN HILL
1835-1836
Princess Anne
Private

On December 31, 1835, James Stewart paid Noah Rider $200 for a "parcel of land in the precincts of Princess Anne beginning on the county road leading from Princess Anne to the Poor House." On this tract he financed the construction of this fine late Federal style dwelling. Architectural evidence and Stewart family tradition agree that the three-part frame house was erected in one period. Interestingly, the design was conceived in the regional "telescope" or stepped form often accomplished in several stages.

The two-story, four-room plan main block is finished with Federal as well as some Greek Revival style woodwork. One of the most distinguishing features is the pedimented cen-

S-21, *William W. Johnston house, west elevation.*

ter entrance with its diamond-panel double doors and arched fanlight. This door is identical to the front door of the William Johnston house, built circa 1834. In fact, Stewart family tradition relates that the same craftsmen, after finishing the Johnston house, began construction of this house. Even though the two houses differ in plan and orientation, they share similar mixtures of Federal and Greek Revival features.

In the Stewart house, a delicate Federal period stair rises in four flights to the third floor, while the parlor and dining room are fitted with Greek Revival style mantels with half-round columns, paneled friezes, and stepped mantel shelves. The middle room and old kitchen are sheathed inside with wide pine paneling, and a large cooking fireplace survives in the kitchen.

James Stewart and his wife, Nelly Ker, resided at Linden Hill until their deaths, when the property passed to their son Dr. William M. Stewart and his wife, Henrietta Haynie. Henrietta outlived her husband by eleven years, and in 1896 the house passed to their children. In 1947 Stewart family ownership of the property ended with its sale to Ralph and Laura Powell. The current owners purchased the property from the Powells in 1970.

WOOLFORD-ELZEY HOUSE
Circa 1788, circa 1840
Princess Anne
Private

Extensive nineteenth century alterations and modern siding successfully disguise the true age of this two-and-a-half story frame dwelling situated on the south side of the Manokin River in Princess Anne. Buried under layers of later siding and behind additions is the late eighteenth century dwelling of Dr. John Woolford, who purchased Lot 3 in 1788 for £180. Seven years later he sold part of the lot to Dr. Arnold Elzey for £550, an increase in price that suggests an expensive improvement such as a well-built, two-story frame house. In 1798 the federal tax assessors described the improvements on Dr. Elzey's property as follows:

> 1 Dwelling House 36 by 32 feet wood two story 8 windows 5 feet 6 Ins long 3 feet wide 11 [windows] 3 feet 8 Ins long 2 feet 4 Ins wide 1 Milk house 12 by 8 feet 1 Cook house 21 by 14 feet 1 window 3 feet 8 Ins long 2 feet 4 Ins wide 1 Smoake house 10 feet square 1 Stable 30 feet by 16 feet with 10 feet shead on one side all in good repair.

S-17, Linden Hill, west elevation.

The assessors placed a $1,200 value on the house and outbuildings, an assessment that well exceeded any other property in town at the time. Dr. Elzey owned the property until 1805, when he sold it to John Stevens of Worcester County for $2,000. Seven years later Stevens transferred ownership of the old frame house and outbuildings to John Stewart, who left the property to his wife Jane and son James when he died in 1817. Stewart family interest in the property was sold to Dr. Samuel Ker in 1822 for $2,500. It is thought that Dr. Ker financed the major reworking that included a large addition to the south as well as a Victorian gable on the east roof slope during his thirty-year ownership of the house. During the same period a bracketed cornice was added to the perimeter of the main house and new window sash were introduced. Inside, the floor plan was reoriented to follow a side hall/double-pile arrangement. Later owners included John E. Fontaine, who bought the property shortly after the Civil War, and Joseph S. Colgan, who acquired title to the house from the Fontaines in 1875. Colgan family interests continued until the early twentieth century.

GENERAL GEORGE HANDY HOUSE
Circa 1845 and later
Princess Anne
Private

The General George Handy house carries an unusual degree of architectural and historical significance in Princess Anne. Built by George Handy around 1845, this town dwelling was initially only a single room deep and covered by a hip roof. Attached to the back of the original house was a colonnade and a two-story service wing. During the third quarter of the nineteenth century, the main house was extensively reworked. At that time the roof was rebuilt and the first floor interior was refitted.

S-19, Woolford-Elzey house, southeast elevation.

S-23, General George Handy house, photograph c.1870, E.I. Brown—photographer (courtesy of Robert Withey).

Despite these extensive Victorian alterations, the house retains large portions of its late Federal style woodwork on the second floor and in the service wing. As a result, it displays fine examples of craftsmanship from the two major architectural styles common to Princess Anne. Through much of the property's history the neighboring boxwood gardens, laid out when the house was constructed, belonged with the Handy house (see S-415).

BOXWOOD GARDEN
Circa 1850 and earlier
Princess Anne
Private

Long-standing tradition in Princess Anne has credited General George Handy with planting the well-known boxwood garden that has distinguished the center of town for the past century and a half. There is no doubt George Handy influenced the appearance of the garden during his ownership; however, a clause in the 1820 deed transferring the property from Elizabeth Handy to her son George suggests she may have started some kind of ornamental garden in the early nineteenth century. In the deed Elizabeth Handy stipulated that

"he the said George Handy will not erect on the said Lot and piece of ground any house or building during the lifetime of the said Elizabeth Handy or within the term of five years after her decease...." It seems reasonable to suspect from this protective clause that

Elizabeth Handy was guarding more than an unimproved lot and that she had created something on this property that she cherished. In addition to this half-acre lot, Mrs. Handy sold her son the main house where she had lived with her husband, Colonel Handy,

S-23, General George Handy house, c. 1890 (courtesy of Clinton K. Lokey).

S-415, Boxwood gardens, c.1930 (courtesy of Mrs. William Morsell, Jr.).

who had died that year. Three years later, in 1823, she purchased a house that Sarah Martin Done had erected across the street from her son, thereby maintaining residence close to her family and the property she loved. Elizabeth Handy died in 1837, and George

continued to maintain the garden north of his house until his death in 1856. To his wife, Mary Ellen, General George Handy left the "House and lot where he resides with adjacent lot or orchard or ornamental garden."

The garden remained under the care of

Mary Ellen Handy until she transferred ownership of the lot to her daughter, Elizabeth Handy Gale, in 1893. Around 1910 Elizabeth Gale financed the construction of the two-story frame house that stands at the east end of the lot bordering Beechwood Street. Three years before her death, Elizabeth Gale sold the property to Alfred P. Dennis. The garden was owned by the sons of Alfred P. Dennis, and then Mary Value Dennis Clark held title to it between 1947 and 1950. John B. and Helen W. Roberts bought the property in 1950.

THOMAS BRITTINGHAM HOUSE
Circa 1817
Princess Anne
Private

Located immediately south of the Colonel George Handy house on Beechwood Street is this two-story, three-bay frame dwelling currently sheathed with wood shingles and trimmed with an early twentieth century porch and dormers. Despite these later alterations, which disguise its age, the flush gable ends, nine-over-six sash windows, and large, brick interior end chimney stack indicate the house was erected during the first quarter of the nineteenth century. The interior retains some period features, but the centrally located stair has been removed.

A chain of title for this town lot indicates the house was erected for Thomas Brittingham around 1817. He had purchased the property the year before from Littleton Dennis Teackle for $300. In 1819 Brittingham sold the same lot to Jane Stewart for $1,200, an increase in price that documents construction of the extant dwelling during his ownership. In later years the property was the residence of John H. Stewart and his wife, Mary G. Jones, who married on April 15, 1839. John H. Stewart, a town merchant, purchased the old court-

S-8, Thomas Brittingham house, west elevation.

house lot from the county in April 1834 and proceeded to erect the extant store building (S-378). Stewart operated the store and lived at this Beechwood Street (formerly Back Alley) address through the middle years of the nineteenth century.

DOUGHERTY HOUSE
Circa 1835, circa 1867
Princess Anne
Private

Historically known as the Dougherty house, this two-story, T-shaped dwelling has stood on the northwest corner of Prince William and Church streets for over 150 years. The Prince William Street elevation offers an interesting contrast between antebellum and postbellum architectural styles common to Somerset County. The western half of the front block is thought to have been erected around 1835 under the ownership of John H. King, a prominent Princess Anne merchant, who purchased Lot 18 in January of that year for $895. The two-story, three-bay frame house followed the well-used vernacular side hall/parlor plan and was trimmed with late Federal style woodwork. Providing cooking services in a traditional manner was a two-story frame kitchen attached to the front block by a single story hyphen. Although some people have thought the kitchen of the Dougherty house dates to the eighteenth century, architectural features and tax records indicate it was erected at the same time as the house. The house evidently maintained this traditional stepped shape until the Civil War. In 1867 the house and lot were transferred to Zadoc Dougherty in the wake of a court settlement involving William J. Byrd, who had purchased the house from Charlotte King.

During Zadoc Dougherty's ownership of the house, which stretched from 1867 to 1910,

S-5, *Dougherty house, south elevation.*

he financed several changes. Most notable was the bracketed addition to the east gable end of the old King house. In an attempt to keep in step with prevailing Civil War era tastes, the extension was trimmed with eave brackets and fitted inside with bold mid-nineteenth century trim. Also during Dougherty ownership of the house, the hyphen was given a second floor, and a two-story section was added to the rear inside corner.

From Zadoc Dougherty, the house and lot passed by deed to Adelia Dougherty in 1910, and she willed the property to her daughter Ellen M. Dashiell in 1923. Ellen Dashiell transferred title in 1928 to Cassius M. Dashiell. The executors of his estate sold the Prince William Street house to Charles Edwin Hayman in 1936, and the corner house and lot remained in the Hayman family until 1969.

JOHN W. CRISFIELD HOUSE
Circa 1852 and earlier
Princess Anne
Private

The John W. Crisfield house is a significant town dwelling for many reasons. The main house is one of an important collection of gable-front dwellings built in Princess Anne during the early to mid nineteenth century. However, the Crisfield house was planned with a side hall, double-pile arrangement rather than the transverse hall tradition established by the Teackle Mansion. In addition, the

mid-eighteenth century rear section, formerly the Cheney house, is one of two Princess Anne dwellings that date from the colonial period. The fully paneled partition wall and the exposed framing members are its two most significant early features.

Significant to the main block is its association with U. S. Congressman John Woodland Crisfield. Prominent among the county attorneys of his day and president of the Eastern Shore Railroad Company, Crisfield encouraged the railroad's spur line to Somers Cove.

In contrast to its serene setting among planned gardens, brick walks, and old magnolias, the Crisfield house has had a rather confusing history that includes at least three major building periods. In 1927 the main house was relocated to its present site facing Washington Street.

The earliest portion of the Crisfield house is the present living room, a mid-eighteenth century frame structure thought to have been erected by Andrew Francis Cheney, who purchased Lot 30 in June 1755 from Thomas Jones of Worcester County for £45. Cheney then purchased what appears to be parts of adjacent Lot 25 from Benjamin Hobbs in 1758 and John Anderson in 1760. In both transfers the deed relates that the property is "All that parcel or Lott of Ground in Princess Ann Town which is contiguous and is the Lott next adjoining to and on the same side of the main Street that the Lott whereon the said Andrew Francis Cheney Now lives." Regret-

S-383, John W. Crisfield house, photograph c. 1915 (courtesy of Mrs. Clarence Leckey).

tably it cannot be said for certain if the living room section of the Crisfield house is Cheney's original house or another dwelling he erected after purchasing the sections of Lot 25. Before his death in February 1790, Cheney transferred Lot 25 to his son Francis Tubman

Cheney. Doctor Francis Cheney was assessed for the lot in 1798, at which time it was improved with "1 Dwelling House 30 by 24 wood one story."

A half-century later, in December 1851, John Woodland Crisfield purchased Lot 30

from William W. Johnston and financed the construction of a finely crafted two-and-a-half story frame house fronting Main Street. The Honorable John W. Crisfield occupied this house until his bankruptcy in 1876, when the property was sold to Anna L. Haines and Crisfield retired to his farm, Edge Hill.

Recent renovations to the former rear wing of the main house indicate it was built for Crisfield in 1858 by Princess Anne carpenter John Miller. In 1909 S. Frank Dashiell purchased the property from Anna L. Haines, and twenty years later the Dashiells moved the main section of the house to the lot behind this addition. It was at this time that the old Cheney house, by then converted to a storage building, was moved up to the relocated main house.

JUDGE LEVIN T. H. IRVING HOUSE
Circa 1850
Princess Anne
Private

Known by most Princess Anne residents as the St. Andrew's Episcopal Church rectory, this two-and-a-half story, side hall/double-pile frame house is the former home of Judge

S-420, Levin T. H. Irving House, southwest elevation.

Levin T. H. Irving, a prominent town attorney and judge who served in Somerset County court during the late nineteenth century. He is designated as the owner of this corner property on the Princess Anne map in the 1877 county atlas.

At the time of the atlas's publication, the house contained three distinct parts, two of which remain on the property today. The third part, a rear service wing, was moved a short distance and attached to another building on Beckford Avenue. The front section is distinctive for its gable-front elevation, Gothic pointed pilaster panels, and ashlar-style treatment in wood under the stair balustrade. As with a handful of other houses in Princess Anne, this peculiar stair construction points to the work of carpenter Seth D. Venables, who evidently erected this house around 1850.

FONTAINE-FITZGERALD HOUSE
Circa 1852
Princess Anne
Private

Upon division of Littleton Dennis Teackle's estate by the Newman family trustees, "Lot Number One" was sold to William Lecates. The deed, executed in July 1852, mentions that Lecates was residing at the time of the transfer in the neighboring estate tenement. Architectural evidence suggests Lecates engaged in a building program that financed the construction of this two-story, center hall frame house soon after he purchased the lot. He chose a well-known vernacular house form and had it trimmed with popular mid-nineteenth century Greek Revival features. Because of its traditional form, the house is often mistaken as an earlier dwelling.

The Lecates house is a remarkable survival from the mid-nineteenth century with close to 100 percent of its original finishes intact. Most notable on the exterior is the

S-6, Fontaine-Fitzgerald house, northeast elevation.

fine two-story pedimented porch supported by square paneled columns. The second floor porch survives with a cross-pattern stick handrail. Common to the Greek Revival period are the sidelighted entrances framed with a simple but bold paneled surround. The exterior is clad with consistent layers of beveled edge weatherboards, a type of siding found on the neighboring Francis Barnes house and other mid-nineteenth century structures.

The pristine exterior is complemented by an intact nineteenth century interior finished with Greek Revival style mantels and a highly unusual period stair. The triangular area below the stringer of the stair was rusticated in an effort to imitate large blocks, a trademark treatment of Princess Anne builder Seth Venables. The two-story service wing is as well-preserved as the main house. A large cooking fireplace remains in the kitchen, and period hardware survives on many of the four-panel doors.

The Lecates family owned the Prince William Street property until the 1880s, when William Lecates's heirs sold the house to Charles W. Fontaine. Fontaine occupied the house from his purchase on May 6, 1887, until his death in 1915. He willed the property to his cousin, Nannie C. Fontaine, for her lifetime. At her death the house and lot were transferred to Laura P. and George B. Fitzgerald in 1932.

SETH D. VENABLES HOUSE
1852
Princess Anne
Private

The history of the Seth D. Venables house (also known as the Maria L. Holbrook house) illustrates the often undocumented process of house financing and construction. Built in 1852 by house carpenter Seth D. Venables, this two-story, side hall/parlor dwelling follows a traditional vernacular house form and is trimmed with modest mid-nineteenth century woodwork. The frame house is covered with the same beveled edge weatherboards found on nearby houses, and the four-panel front door is topped with a bracketed lintel. The traditional finish of this vernacular house is similar to that of the slightly larger Fontaine-Fitzgerald house, which was built during the same decade. Attached to the back of the main dwelling is a two-story service wing.

The specific construction agreement for this house was written in a mortgage between Seth D. Venables and Francis Barnes on December 31, 1852. The mortgage states, "whereas the said Francis Barnes has advanced and loaned to the said Seth D. Venables sundry sums of money to enable the said Seth D. Venables to improve the said lot by erecting buildings thereon which said advances amount to the sum of one hundred and sixty five dollars and fifty cents...." In re-

S-94, Francis Barnes house, northwest elevation.

turn for the loan, Venables executed the mortgage to Barnes for the "lot where the said Seth D. Venables now resides." Four years later, in an effort to satisfy outstanding debts, Seth and Susan Venables sold this house and lot to Maria L. Holbrook for $1,100. Maria Hol-

brook remained in the house through the balance of the nineteenth century, and after her death it was sold to Annie L. Holbrook in 1911. Since 1925 the property has been owned by the Carey family. The current residents purchased the house in 1971.

FRANCIS BARNES HOUSE
1853-1854
Princess Anne
Private

Prominently sited on a corner of Prince William and Mansion streets, the Francis Barnes house also commands architectural distinction as a well-executed example of the Italianate style. The elevated height of the two-story, center hall house and the decorative bracketed cornices and paneled pilasters were combined by the builder, Seth D. Venables, in an effort to achieve a bold architectural statement then undeveloped in Princess Anne. Venables is credited with the construction of this house and several nearby dwellings that share identical period features.

The main house is divided in a traditional manner with a center hall and flanking parlor and dining room. The T-shaped service wing is believed to have been added after the Civil War during the ownership of Louis Morris. A service bell system was installed at the same time. Additional notable features include silver-plated hinge covers, china and silver-plated door knobs, and a marble mantel.

S-13, Seth D. Venables house, east elevation.

S-100, Levin Woolford house, southwest elevation.

Francis Barnes purchased "Lot No. 2" from the Newman estate trustee, John Done, for $330 in December 1853. Construction is presumed to have begun shortly afterwards, for Barnes transferred ownership of the house and lot to Albert E. Acworth four years later for $4,000. The property was described as "the same lot on which the said Barnes erected a dwelling house now occupied by the said Acworth." Francis Barnes bought the house back in April 1859, only to sell it seven months later to William H. Gale.

Dr. Louis W. Morris purchased the house in June 1863 and occupied it during the second half of the century. He had his office in the two-story frame house (now brick-sheathed) that stands west of the courthouse. Morris's heirs transferred ownership of the Francis Barnes house to Judge Henry L.D. Stanford in 1896.

LEVIN WOOLFORD HOUSE
Circa 1853
Princess Anne
Private

This two-and-a-half-story, side hall/double-pile frame house, located on the southeast corner of South Somerset Avenue and William Street, is distinguished from the other dwellings in Princess Anne by its steeply pitched mansard roof. This roof shape was popularized during the seventeenth century

by the French architect François Mansart and reused during the nineteenth century in what is referred to as the Second Empire style. Despite its distinctive roof shape, the floor plan of the Woolford house follows a traditional arrangement introduced in Somerset County in the eighteenth century. The front door opens into a generous stair hall, and the balance of the first floor is divided into two rooms to one side of the hall. Attached to the back of the main block is a two-story service wing.

The Woolford house is noteworthy for its significant mid-nineteenth century interior finishes, including a colored glass transom over the front door and the ashlar-style wall treatment under the stair. The latter feature appears to have been a trademark finish of carpenter Seth D. Venables and appears in a handful of contemporary Princess Anne houses.

Construction of the Woolford house is dated to 1853, the year after Washington Miles purchased the unimproved lot from

S-389, Joseph Brinkley house, southwest elevation.

S-89, Waters house, west elevation.

S-88, Rufus Parsons house (JOSH house) southwest elevation.

John and Sarah E. Dennis for $275. Washington and Caroline Miles owned the property for only two years, but within that time they financed the extant frame house. In December 1854 the couple sold their house for $3,075 to Henry King, who transferred the title to Levin Woolford four years later. Colonel Levin Woolford served as clerk of Somerset County Court through the second and third quarters of the nineteenth century. He and his wife, Anne E. Woolford, occupied the house until their deaths, and the property remained in the Woolford family until 1935. The present owners have held title to the house since 1957.

JOSEPH BRINKLEY HOUSE
Circa 1856-1857
Princess Anne
Private

Joseph Brinkley of Baltimore purchased a corner lot from Washington Miles in August 1856 and evidently engaged Seth B. Venables to erect a two-story, side hall/double-pile frame house. Venables is a well-documented carpenter who practiced house building in the middle years of the nineteenth century. With its pedimented front elevation, the Brinkley house followed in the gable-front tradition popular in Princess Anne. Interestingly, the service wing of the Brinkley house, built at the same time as the front block, is set off

axis with the main building to allow additional light into the dining room. Identical brick chimneys with dentiled caps rise from each section of the house, and the corners of the front block are trimmed with paneled pilasters. The interior is fitted with well-executed Greek Revival features.

Brinkley apparently owed Venables a balance of construction expenses and executed a deed to the property in lieu of actual payment. This debt was transferred three times, first to Venables then to Greenleaf Johnson, then to Charles T. Marshall, who sold the house and lot to William J. Porter on November 15, 1859, for $2,500. During the following month, William J. Porter exchanged this house and lot with Matilda F. and Martha A. Jones for property they had inherited from their father, Alexander. The Main Street property remained in the Jones family until the early twentieth century.

RUFUS PARSONS HOUSE
(JOSH HOUSE)
Circa 1858
Princess Anne
Private

In December 1857 Rufus M. and Charlotte Parsons purchased "Lot No. 4" of the old Teackle estate for $315. It is reasonable to assume that during the following year they financed the construction of this finely

appointed side hall/double-pile frame house. However, in March 1861 the couple sold "all that house and lot in the town of Princess Anne" for $3,300 to Hampden H. Dashiell, a prominent Somerset County merchant during the second half of the nineteenth century. The Dashiell family owned the corner property through the early twentieth century and were responsible for the few, sensitive alterations, including the bay window on the east side and the parquet floor in the downstairs hall. As originally planned, the kitchen was located in the cellar, but for modern convenience it has been moved to the rear wing. Most recently the site has been known as the JOSH house, an acronym of the current owners' names.

WATERS HOUSE
Circa 1859
Princess Anne
Private

Known for most of the last century as the Waters house, this two-story, center hall frame dwelling on South Somerset Avenue was evidently built on the eve of the Civil War by Sydney C. Long, who bought the lot from John and Henrietta Allen on February 4, 1859 for $200. Sydney and his wife, Mary, owned the property for a little over five years before they sold the house and lot, "now in the possession and occupancy of Sydney C. Long in or near Princess Anne," for $5,500. It appears the Longs acquired the inspiration for their bracketed house from Francis Barnes, who had finished construction of his bracketed, Italianate style town house a few years earlier.

Following the Civil War the property passed through a number of hands until John W. and Marianna Carroll acquired title to the house in November 1886. The Carrolls owned the frame dwelling for close to thirteen years, and then transferred the title to Henry J. Waters in 1899. When Waters died in 1942, his wife, Emily B. Waters, inherited the property. Emily W. Waters inherited it in 1960 and lived there until 1977.

DENNIS-DASHIELL HOUSE
Circa 1867
Princess Anne (site)

Perhaps the most elaborate example of the Italianate style in Somerset County was the Dennis-Dashiell house, which stood near the northwest corner of the intersection of South Somerset and Antioch avenues until the late

S-20, Dennis-Dashiell house, photograph c. 1967, northeast elevation.

1960s. The three-story, five-bay frame house was distinguished by an undulating roofline trimmed with large decorative brackets and over-sized modillion blocks. Rising through the roof were four brick chimneys topped with dentiled and corbeled caps. A three-bay front porch embellished with sawn balusters and sawn corner and eave brackets highlighted the first floor. The third floor was lighted by round arched windows, not uncommon for this revival style. Extending to the rear was a two-story service wing.

Credit for the construction of this impressive dwelling is given to James Upshur Dennis, who purchased the large corner lot by several deeds, beginning in December

1866. By 1900 James U. Dennis had died, and the house had passed to his daughters, Nellie H. Bratton, Maria R. Dennis, and Cecilia B. Dashiell. Nellie Bratton devised her interest in the property to the other two sisters. The house remained in the Dashiell family until the early 1960s.

THEODORE F. LANKFORD HOUSE
Circa 1875
Princess Anne
Private

On May 11, 1875, the trustees of the Antioch Methodist Episcopal Church sold Theodore F. Lankford part of the Main Street land the church had purchased from Sallie E. Dennis in 1867. The transfer price of $100 indicates the lot was unimproved at the time. Theodore F. Lankford is listed in the 1877 county atlas patron list as a carpenter and may have been responsible for the construction of his own house. His estate was settled in 1881, and the property passed back into the hands of the church, only to be sold again a few years later.

Stylistically, the Theodore F. Lankford house is a late example of the gable-front dwellings popularly erected in Princess Anne before the Civil War. Similar to the Joseph B. Brinkley house, is its two-bay street elevation topped with a pedimented gable. The Lankford house has pediments atop the two bays on the north and south sides as well. It

S-387, Theodore F. Lankford house, northeast elevation.

S-388, Beckford Avenue tenant houses, southwest elevation.

follows a modified side hall/double-pile plan, and most of its period woodwork is intact.

BECKFORD AVENUE TENANT HOUSES
Circa 1870
Princess Anne
Private

Built around 1870 the five tenant houses in this series follow the same basic form. A two-story, one-bay main block is extended to the south by a story-and-a-half frame section. The plain frame houses are lighted by a variety of six-over-six or two-over-two sash windows. This row of identical dwellings is an interesting contrast to the larger Victorian houses that line Beckford Avenue. Erected in the decade following the Civil War, these postbellum frame dwellings were built on "Beckford" land to house plantation slaves after Emancipation.

JOHN H. STEWART STORE
Circa 1836
Princess Anne
Private

Standing on the northeast corner of Somerset Avenue and Broad Street is the old Stewart store building, a two-story, three-bay commercial structure that retains its essential early nineteenth century form along with a few period finishes. The building has an intact boxed cornice with bed and crown moldings,

flush gable ends, and a few nine-over-six sash windows. It is one of the oldest commercial structures in Somerset County.

This corner lot was the location of the first county courthouse in Princess Anne. The purchase "for the erecting and building a Court House and prison upon in Somerset County" dates to 1743, after Worcester County was created from the partition of Somerset.

In December 1835 the Levy Court of Somerset County sold the lot to John H. Stewart, being

all that lot or parcel of ground on which the courthouse formerly stood in the Town of Princess Anne beginning at the northeast corner formed by the junction of Bridge and Broad streets in the said town and from the said corner running by and with Broad Street towards the public prison ninety-six feet....

Stewart, listed as a merchant in county records, erected the building shortly afterwards. He mortgaged the property several times, and an 1863 mortgage between him and Samuel W. Jones describes the property as "all that store house and lot of ground situate in Princess Anne in Somerset County and now occupied by the said John H. Stewart including the office and granary on said lot...."

S-378, John Stewart store house, south elevation.

S-382, *Election house, southeast elevation.*

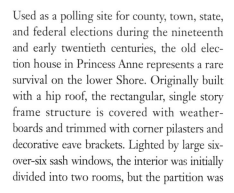

S-97, *John W. Crisfield law office, southwest elevation.*

JOHN W. CRISFIELD LAW OFFICE
Circa 1847-1848
Princess Anne
Private

This two-story, gable-front frame store is an important remnant of the antebellum commercial buildings that once defined Princess Anne. Echoing the pedimented facade of several prominent dwellings, this Federal/Greek Revival temple-front structure suited the narrow town lot and at the same time provided a handsome street elevation. Aside from an altered first floor, few changes have been made to the exterior. Flush board sheathing remains within the pediment and a pair of period shutters survives on the south wall window. Rising through the roof is a brick chimney finished with a dentiled cap.

Credit for construction of this commercial building is attributed to Littleton Long, who purchased the property in November 1847 for $300. The deed was executed between John W. Crisfield and Littleton Long. The description includes an exception that provided Crisfield access to his law office and the four-foot alley on the north side of the building. On first impression it seems this clause refers to the extant building; however, later deeds infer that the temple-front store replaced an earlier set of buildings. Eleven years later Sydney C. Long purchased the same lot for $1,200, an increase in value that suggests the construction of a substantial improvement. The deed mentions "the Store House and lot of ground thereto belonging situate in Princess Anne Town opposite the Washington Hotel." A year later John W. Crisfield purchased the same property from Sydney C. Long for an identical amount. Sub-

sequent deeds refer to this building as the law office occupied by John W. Crisfield.

ELECTION HOUSE
Circa 1870
Princess Anne
Public

Used as a polling site for county, town, state, and federal elections during the nineteenth and early twentieth centuries, the old election house in Princess Anne represents a rare survival on the lower Shore. Originally built with a hip roof, the rectangular, single story frame structure is covered with weatherboards and trimmed with corner pilasters and decorative eave brackets. Lighted by large six-over-six sash windows, the interior was initially divided into two rooms, but the partition was

removed long ago.

Although a brick pier foundation supported this building on its corner lot next to the old county jail, older residents relate that it had been moved to that site from another location. During 1986-1988 the election house was moved to its present site along the Manokin River and incorporated into a plan for a town park.

OLD PRESBYTERIAN
CHURCH LECTURE HALL
Circa 1860
Princess Anne
Public

Used by the Somerset County library from 1959 to 1988, this single story frame structure was initially erected as a "lecture room."

S-102, *Old Presbyterian Church lecture hall, southeast elevation.*

362

S-381, Old Somerset County jail, c.1903, E.I. Brown—photographer (courtesy of W. Marshall Scott).

In September 1862 a "Committee of the Presbyterian Church at Manokin" purchased the corner lot on which the lecture hall had recently been erected. The church owned the property until it was transferred to the Princess Anne Public Library, Inc. in 1959.

The gable-front frame building shares similar features with other mid nineteenth century structures in Princess Anne, with simple corner pilasters visually supporting a bracketed cornice. The classically inspired entrance with pilasters, entablature, and pediment is not an uncommon feature for buildings constructed in Princess Anne during this period.

SOMERSET COUNTY JAIL
1857, 1902
Princess Anne
Private

The Somerset County jail, once known as the "Gray Eagle," is the only nineteenth century structure with load-bearing stone walls in the county. Named for the color of the imported granite, this squarish two-story structure is the second jail to stand on this corner lot. The original jail, built on this site in 1857-1858, burned on Wednesday, March 19, 1902. An account printed by the *Wicomico News* on March 22 revealed that prisoners started the fire in the timber ceiling of their cell with a hot poker from the stove. Although the jail was heavily damaged, the fire was kept under control and did not spread to other parts of Princess Anne.

Three months after the fire, the Somerset County commissioners awarded a contract for rebuilding the jail to the B. F. Smith Fire Proof Construction Company of Washington, D.C. The specifications called for a two-story stone structure with a slate roof, steel girders, concrete floors, three "Bessemer steel cages," and one "Pauly tool proof cage for unruly prisoners." Evidently the old granite was not damaged, and the old stone was used in the construction of the new jail. The rebuilt facility served the county until 1987, when a new building was erected outside the city limits. Future plans for the old structure include renovation for town offices.

HENRY PAGE LAW OFFICE
Circa 1877
Princess Anne
Private

This single story, gable-front frame structure was originally the law office of Henry Page, son of John W. Crisfield, and a prominent Princess Anne attorney during the second half of the nineteenth century. Page acquired this small piece of the "Somerset Hotel Property" in March 1877 and apparently had the office constructed immediately as it is identified on the Princess Anne town map published in that year. Now covered with asbestos shingles, the rectangular frame structure was initially sheathed with weatherboards. The decorative brackets, which still remain, add a decorative period finish to an otherwise plain office building.

OLD BANK OF SOMERSET
Circa 1884
Princess Anne
Private

Distinctive among the nineteenth century commercial buildings of Princess Anne is the old Bank of Somerset, a two-story, three-bay brick structure highlighted with both round and pointed arch window openings. Match-

S-106, Henry Page law office, west elevation.

S-22, Old Bank of Somerset, west elevation.

S-379, Metropolitan United Methodist Church, south elevation.

ing paneled doors flank the centered, round-arched window opening, which is distinguished by a molded brick window head. The second floor follows a similar arrangement with two-over-two sash windows flanking a large center window. In contrast to the first floor, a pair of narrow lancet windows were designed under a modified version of the molded brick head. Additional embellish-

ments include a decorative, corbeled brick cornice and projecting corner pilasters. Attached to the back of the building is a pyramidal-roofed addition detailed in a similar manner.

Although this building housed the Bank of Somerset offices after the bank was organized in 1889, it was actually erected by the Mutual Fire Insurance Company of Somer-

set and Worcester Counties after the insurance company purchased the unimproved "Hotel Property" lot from Price J. Patton in 1884. Evidently the bank rented the office until a bank building was erected on the west side of Somerset Avenue in 1903. In 1955 the board of directors of the insurance company sold the brick office and lot to attorney Edgar A. Jones, and the structure has served as a law office since that time.

OLD MARYLANDER
AND HERALD OFFICE
Circa 1900
Princess Anne
Private

The old Marylander and Herald office is a turn-of-the-century brick building of straightforward commercial design. The rectangular brick block is capped by a slate hip roof, and slightly recessed bays define the front entrance and display window. Arched window openings on the north wall have simple Victorian decoration incised in the window headers. Without major alterations since construction, this simple commercial building contributes to the variety of period stores that remain standing along Somerset Avenue.

S-397, Old Marylander and Herald office, west elevation.

S-116, University of Maryland, Eastern Shore.

METROPOLITAN UNITED METHODIST CHURCH
1886
Princess Anne
Public worship

Purchased in the 1740s as part of the county court property, this lot was sold in the early nineteenth century when the courthouse was moved to its present site. The lot where the church stands was the location of the eighteenth century Somerset County jail.

In search of a site for a church in town, the trustees of John Wesley Methodist Episcopal Church purchased this lot from Thomas Dixon on June 2, 1884. Two years later the Gothic Revival brick church was ready for services. Facing Broad Street, the church is clearly visible from the center of town, and its spire is the second highest in Princess Anne. Dominated by the center entrance and bell tower, the main sanctuary is pierced with pointed arch, colored glass windows. A large round window marks the second floor of the tower, and the belfry is distinguished by period sawnwork. The original exterior fabric of the building has remained essentially unaltered with fading remnants of black accents around the principal window and door openings.

UNIVERSITY OF MARYLAND EASTERN SHORE
Founded 1886, 1939-1980
Princess Anne
Public

The University of Maryland Eastern Shore was founded in 1886 under the auspices of the Delaware Conference of the Methodist Episcopal Church and the Centenary Biblical Institute of Baltimore. Both organizations shared an interest in forming a black-oriented school for advanced learning on the Eastern Shore. In 1890 the federal government issued a mandate to the State of Maryland, along with other southern states, stipulating that federal support of its land-grant institutions would cease if adequate provisions were not made to accommodate Negroes. Rather than admit black students to the already established land-grant college at College Park, the state chose to negotiate with the Biblical Institute to provide a land-grant curriculum for members of the Negro race at Princess Anne. In the agreement, it was asserted that

The purpose and intent of this contract [is] to provide during its continuance for the youth of Maryland of the Colored Race like facilities for general education and espe-

cially for instruction in agriculture and mechanic arts—conducted in a separate school to those provided for the white youth of Maryland, and to thus conform in spirit and letter to the provisions of the act of congress approved August 30, 1890, for the more complete endowment and support of the college for the benefit of agriculture and the mechanic arts.

By this contract the academy was designated the Eastern Branch of the Maryland Agricultural College and thus was to receive federal funds under the Morrill Act of 1890. The institution continued as a private school, however, until 1926, when the state purchased the college outright. Even then, Princess Anne Academy, as it was popularly known, continued under the administrative control of Morgan State College for another ten years. During this ten-year period, the Princess Anne Academy moved from the junior college level it had achieved in 1925 to become a full-fledged four-year institution. In 1936 administrative control was finally transferred to the Board of Regents of the University of Maryland.

For the next twelve years the future of Princess Anne Academy was discussed extensively by various commissions, College Park officials, and government officers. The Marbury Commission (1947) in particular recommended that the institution be abandoned in favor of Morgan State inasmuch as the state had shown little effort toward developing it into a first-rate school. Nonetheless, in 1948 the president of the university, under extreme pressure to admit Negroes to College Park, changed the name of the Princess Anne institution to Maryland State College and maneuvered the legislature into quadrupling the state's investment in the campus. The Middle States Association established in 1954 that the viability of the Maryland State College was evident, and it was subsequently accredited as an autonomous institution of higher education.

By 1967 the president of Maryland State College had grown weary of the conditions and arrangements at the campus and requested that the school be designated a bona fide branch of the university system. After a long and exhaustive study, the petition was answered affirmatively and a bill was passed making Maryland State College the University of Maryland Eastern Shore effective July 1, 1970. This new status obligated the University of Maryland's board of regents to take the lead in upgrading the Eastern Shore campus to the level of the university's other branches.

Efforts were immediately undertaken to enrich the curriculum offerings and enhance physical plant facilities. The most obvious manifestations of this commitment in the physical plant are the Carver Hall Science Building, Ella Fitzgerald Center for the Performing Arts, Nutter Hall Dormitory, and the Student Cultural Development Center.

The core of the university campus is organized around a central quadrangle with the north-south axis created by Maryland Hall (1941) and Trigg Hall (1954). These buildings, representative of the typical Georgian

S-101, Joshua W. Miles house, west elevation.

Revival building style at UMES, have principal facades characterized by central projecting porticoes. Most of the other major buildings on campus are distributed around this quadrangle, including the oldest structures on campus: Kiah Hall (1940), Bird Hall (1940), and the student lounge (1939).

The first building to define the academy grounds was the former "Olney" plantation house, a two-story Federal style dwelling that stood on the property when the school opened in 1886. The old plantation house was razed in the 1970s.

HAMPDEN H. DASHIELL HOUSE
Circa 1870
Princess Anne
Private

The two-story, three-bay frame house standing on the corner of Broad and Church streets is the only board-and-batten dwelling in Princess Anne. Especially noteworthy are the Gothic points formed below the soffit by the converging battens. The asymmetrical elevation and the low-pitched hip roof are unusual architectural features in Princess Anne as well. In past years this house was the property of Hampden H. Dashiell.

JOSHUA W. MILES HOUSE
Circa 1890
Princess Anne
Private

Clearly one of the most ambitious houses erected in Somerset County after the Civil War, the Joshua W. Miles house stands out as the most elaborate Queen Anne style dwelling in Princess Anne. True to its stylistic label is the asymmetrical design, which incorporates a Tuscan-columned porch that wraps around the first floor, a three-story octagonal tower with a bell-curved roof, and a combination of gabled and hipped roof dormers lighting the attic. Distinguishing the large gabled dormer on the west (front) elevation is a Palladian-style window.

Joshua W. Miles, a prominent county attorney, is credited with financing the construction of this house around 1890. In addition to being one-time president of the Bank of Somerset, Miles was also a leading Democrat and was eventually appointed the federal collector of internal revenue for Maryland. Most recently the house has been used by the Hinman family as a funeral home.

S-4, C. H. Hayman house, northeast elevation.

C. H. HAYMAN HOUSE
1898
Princess Anne
Private

Hayman family tradition holds to an 1898 date of construction for this impressive Queen Anne style house on the southwest corner of Prince William and Church streets. In contrast to other Queen Anne style dwellings in Somerset County, such as the Joshua W. Miles house, also in Princess Anne, and the Pauline Crockett house in Crisfield, the Hayman house was designed with stronger references to the Colonial Revival style. Encircling the basically symmetrical north facade is a Tuscan-columned porch trimmed with a balustrade of urn-topped posts. With similar classical inspiration, the recessed center entrance is framed with slender colonnettes. Paralleling the porch is a rooftop balustrade with classical urns finishing each post. The only truly asymmetrical exterior feature is the two-story bay that extends from the east side of the house. Lighting the third floor is a combination of hip-roofed and gabled dormers. Inside, the first floor rooms are fitted with neoclassical mirrored mantels, colored tile hearths, and original turn-of-the-century hardware.

Charles Harrison Hayman erected this finely built dwelling four years after he purchased the corner lot from Hampden P. Dashiell for $1,000. Hayman is better known for starting the C. H. Hayman and Sons hardware store on Lot 4, which he also purchased in 1894.

THOMAS H. BOCK HOUSE
Circa 1890
Princess Anne
Private

Clearly an expensively built dwelling for its period, the Thomas H. Bock house exhibits many features not often found on Queen Anne style houses in Princess Anne. The large, irregular plan frame residence is dis-

S-380, Hampden H. Dashiell house, northwest elevation.

S-392, Thomas H. Bock house, southeast elevation.

S-417, Julia A. Humphreys house, east elevation.

S-391, Banes Layfield house, southeast elevation.

tinguished by multiple gables sheathed with fish-scale shingles and a two-story, semi-octagonal tower on the southeast corner. The tower roof is finished with a flame-shaped finial, and narrow brick stove stacks rise to each side. Colored glass windows and a wraparound porch are additional Victorian features that provide interest.

Thomas H. Bock, part owner of the Cohn and Bock Milling Company, which operated in Princess Anne through the nineteenth and early twentieth centuries, financed the construction of this Victorian house on Somerset Avenue. More recently the property was the site of the Levin Wilson funeral home, but within the past few years the house has been converted into apartments.

OLD WASHINGTON HIGH SCHOOL
1891-1892
Princess Anne (site)
Private

During a November 1890 meeting of the board of trustees for the Washington Academy, President John W. Crisfield submitted his opinion on the condition of the old academy building erected in 1801 (see S-412). He believed the structure, located on a rural site, had reached such a poor state of repair that it would be prohibitively expensive to rework the aging building. A few months later Daniel Collins, a local brick manufacturer, was asked to assess the academy, and in April 1891 he reported

To the Trustees of the Washington Academy, building probably contains 250,000 [bricks]….to be worked into a new wall 200,000 could be obtained, brick good quality, very few salmon or soft bricks; large quantity of timber, The gable above the front door outside seems to have for many years leaked fearfully, and all the timber to this extent and below it is rotten; all the rest seems to be in good preservation. We counted 31 pannel doors; sound and in good condition and may be used again.

Later that month the academy trustees conferred with the School Board of Somerset County and agreed to join together in the construction of a "new school building in which can be accomodated, with comfort and convenience both the high school and the primary schools of the said town."

With materials from the 1801 Washington Academy building, masons and carpenters began work during the summer of 1891 on a stylish new brick school west of the Beechwood estate. More than any other building known to stand in Somerset County at the time, the new Washington High School

S-414, Old Washington High School, c. 1900, E.I. Brown—photographer (courtesy of W. Marshall Scott).

reflected the massive proportions and decorative exuberance of Romanesque Revival architecture as borrowed from the architect Henry Hobson Richardson. E. I. Brown's turn-of-the-century photograph of the building captures the highly decorative brick patterns and molded brick courses that highlighted the arched entrance and window openings. Dominating the structure was a pair of three-story stair towers marked by an assortment of window openings and capped by slate pyramidal roofs. This expressive Victorian building stood a relatively short period of time, for it was razed during the late 1930s when plans were advanced to build a new high school on the northern edge of town.

JULIA A. HUMPHREYS HOUSE
Circa 1893
Princess Anne
Private

Located at 212 South Somerset Avenue is the Julia A. Humphreys house, erected around 1893. Humphreys purchased the unimproved lot from Thomas H. Bock in August of that year, and it is reasonable to assume she financed the construction of the house shortly afterwards. The eaves of the two-and-a-half story, center hall frame house are trimmed with decorative Victorian brackets and bargeboards. Most noteworthy is the hip-roofed front porch, which is supported by turned posts and embellished with sawnwork. Similar to contemporary houses located south of

it, this house has dentiled brick chimneys piercing the roofline.

BANES LAYFIELD HOUSE
Circa 1885
Princess Anne
Private

The Banes Layfield house is a standard two-and-a-half-story, three-bay, center hall frame house erected during the late nineteenth century. Although not recognized for any unusual exterior features, the cross-gabled residence adds to the turn-of-the-century atmosphere of South Somerset Avenue. Subtle details that contribute interest to the dwelling are the dentiled brick chimneys and the round-arched windows in each gable.

HENRY L. BRITTINGHAM HOUSE
Circa 1890
Princess Anne
Private

The Henry L. Brittingham house is a large, T-shaped, late nineteenth century frame dwelling that stands in a line of contemporary buildings on the west side of South Somerset Avenue. Although the house has been moderately remodeled and converted to a dentist's office, the two-and-a-half story dwelling retains a mixture of Victorian and Colonial Revival features. The eclectic residence contributes to the uninterrupted row of period houses that characterize south Princess Anne.

Henry L. Brittingham purchased this lot in July 1887, when this section of the "Beckford" tract was being subdivided into building lots. The house was apparently erected within the next few years. Brittingham occupied the house until the early twentieth century, and his heirs, H. Lawrence and James Francis Brittingham, sold the house and lot in 1921. In later years the property was the home of William B. and Ethel M. Long. More recently Dr. Richard Arnold and Martha Louise Bevan used the house as a residence and office.

EDMUND D. YOUNG HOUSE
Circa 1900
Princess Anne
Private

Located in the southernmost residential block facing South Somerset Avenue, the Edmund D. Young house is a less elaborate example of the Queen Anne style than its nearby neighbor the Thomas H. Bock house. More conservative in decorative finishes, this irregularly shaped frame house has a two-story, five-sided corner tower and a wrap-around porch supported by Tuscan columns.

The house was erected for Edmund D. Young, who purchased an unimproved lot from Thomas H. and Angie L. Bock, who lived next door. Edmund D. and Bessie B. Young occupied this house until their deaths in 1927 and 1929, respectively. The property remained in their daughters' hands until 1950.

S-394, Emma A. Lankford house, east elevation.

EMMA A. LANKFORD HOUSE
Circa 1900
Princess Anne
Private

Unlike its immediate neighbors, the Emma A. Lankford house is a two-story, gable-front frame dwelling. The rectangular shaped residence is sheathed with a combination of plain weatherboards and fish-scale shingles. The north and south side walls are interrupted by one- or two-story bays trimmed with Victorian sawnwork. Lighting both main floors are two-over-two sash windows, while the attic is illuminated with pointed arch windows.

Emma A. Lankford purchased this South Somerset Avenue house and lot from Thomas H. Bock in 1910 for $2,800.

ALBERT E. KRAUSE HOUSE
Circa 1903
Princess Anne
Private

Similar to many turn-of-the-century houses in south Princess Anne, the Albert E. Krause house is characterized by a mixture of Victorian and Colonial Revival features. This eclectic mix of design elements is common to the Queen Anne style, which was popular during the years surrounding the turn of the century. The irregular or asymmetrical elevations and plan, with multiple projecting bays or gables, are common to the style as are the wrap-around porch and colored glass windows. Inside, the house is fitted with the original oak woodwork, which ranges from intricate Victorian spindles to the classical treatment of egg-and-dart molding around the doors. The mirrored mantel in the parlor is an especially rare period element.

On March 25, 1903, Albert E. Krause acquired this Somerset Avenue (then Main Street) lot for $458 and proceeded to finance

the construction of this impressive frame dwelling. More recently the house was the residence of John and Kathy Groutt.

DANIEL COLLINS HOUSE
Circa 1910
Princess Anne
Private

Dominating the south end of Princess Anne is the Daniel Collins house, a well-built early twentieth century brick dwelling

that remains largely intact with well-preserved pressed brick walls, a slate roof, and a modillioned cornice. Additional references to the Colonial Revival style include the Palladian windows that light the dormers. With its strong architectural presence, the Collins house is a prominent visual anchor to the south end of the Princess Anne Historic District. Also on the property is one of only a few brick outbuildings remaining in town. The rectangular common bond brick structure predates the house. It is similar to the

S-395, Albert E. Krause house, east elevation.

S-384, Harry C. Dashiell house, southeast elevation.

S-385, Anna L. Haines house, south elevation.

stable behind the Washington Hotel and was evidently used as a carriage house and stable.

Daniel Collins, remembered as Princess Anne's brick manufacturer during the late nineteenth and early twentieth centuries, financed the construction of this house on land he had acquired in 1895.

HARRY C. DASHIELL HOUSE
Circa 1905
Princess Anne
Private

The Harry C. Dashiell house is a well-preserved turn-of-the-century, T-plan frame dwelling trimmed with modest Victorian features limited mainly to the turned post front porch. The house contributes to the mixture of late Federal and Victorian dwellings that mark this residential district in the east end of town.

Harry C. Dashiell purchased this Beechwood Street lot in 1919 from Anna L. Haines, and the associated plat of the property designates the frame house. Dashiell and his wife Emily occupied the house for the next fifteen years and in 1934 sold the property to Gordon Tull. Item eight in Tull's will of 1944 transferred ownership of the house and lot to his nieces, Eva Tull Mills and Doris Tull.

ANNA L. HAINES HOUSE
1909
Princess Anne
Private

The Anna L. Haines house is an important early twentieth century brick house in Princess Anne. Not only is it one of the few brick houses in town, but it is a prominent dwelling that marks the northwest corner of Beechwood and East Washington streets. It is obvious this T-plan house was constructed in the

best traditions of early twentieth century craftsmanship. It is a simple Victorian style structure with Colonial Revival details patterned after dwellings Anna Haines knew in Philadelphia. Two-story bay windows distinguish both street elevations, and the roof is covered with slate shingles.

Construction of the house dates to the months after Anna L. Haines sold the majority of the old Crisfield property she and her husband had purchased in 1876. On the first day of March 1909, she sold "all that house

S-396, Daniel Collins house, northeast elevation.

S-91, Somerset County Courthouse, photograph c. 1915 (courtesy of Robert Withey).

and lot on Main Street…whereon she now resides, except so much of said lot as lies or is situated east of a straight line…." The reserved lot of ground Anna L. Haines did not convey was the site of her new brick house. Upon her death in 1925, the Washington Street house and its furnishings were devised to her daughter, Emily H. Fitzgerald.

JOHN HOLLAND HOUSE
Circa 1902
Princess Anne
Private

The John Holland house, more recently known as the Muir house, is a two-and-a-half story Queen Anne style dwelling built during the early twentieth century. John Holland, a local businessman who is remembered as operating a cannery in east Princess Anne, financed the construction of this Somerset Avenue dwelling. The well-built frame house retains its slate roof as well as a Tuscan-columned porch that stretches across the east and south elevations. A projecting gabled pavilion highlights the entrance. The interior survives largely undisturbed with a decorated oak stair and tiled hearths. Classical Corinthian columns flank the mirrored overmantels as well as the fireplaces. Hidden pocket doors also distinguish the first floor rooms.

The property has been held by the Muir family since the late 1920s.

SOMERSET COUNTY COURTHOUSE
1904-1905
Princess Anne
Public

Standing prominently in the center of Princess Anne is the Somerset County Courthouse, a two-and-a-half story red brick, Georgian Revival structure nine bays across by five bays deep. The principal elevation, facing Prince William Street, is distinguished by a portico of fluted Ionic sandstone columns with classical entablature and balustrade. The windows are highlighted by limestone arches with projecting keystones on the first floor and round arches on the second. Distinguishing the perimeter of the roof is a modillion cornice of molded metal, and small lunette windows pierce each pediment. The first floor is divided by a generous cross hall that separates corner offices, while the courtroom is located on the second floor.

Architects Frank E. and Henry R. Davis are credited with the Georgian Revival design, and the construction firm of W. P. Pusey and Son of Snow Hill was awarded the project in 1904 at the cost of $28,451. Before construction began, the 1833 courthouse and

S-418, John Holland house, northeast elevation.

S-104, Peoples Bank of Somerset, northeast elevation.

the old Teackle Bank building, which had been converted to county offices, were torn down. An account written at the time of demolition reported that brick and other materials were salvaged from the old buildings and incorporated in the new courthouse.

County ownership of this corner property, known as Lot 16, began in April 1827 when the Levy Court purchased the former location of the Bank of Somerset from the District Court of the United States for $3,000. At the time, the lot was improved by a two-story, five-bay brick structure erected around 1815. When the eighteenth century courthouse burned in 1831, the Levy Court decided to relocate the county buildings on this Prince William Street site. On April 4, 1832, the court appointed George A. Dashiell and Alexander Jones to contract for the erection of new accommodations that could be used by the next May term. The design of the 1833 courthouse followed the Federal gable-front design established thirty years earlier by Littleton Dennis Teackle.

BANK OF SOMERSET
1903
Princess Anne
Public

The Bank of Somerset, known since 1975 as the Peninsula Bank, has occupied this neoclassical brick structure on Somerset Avenue since its construction in 1903. The street ele-

vation of the original single story, three-bay bank, erected in yellow-brown Roman-sized brick, is dominated by an arched double-door entrance capped by an elaborate classical pediment. In addition to an intricate decorative tympanum, the cornice is composed of rows of modillions, egg-and-dart moldings, and dentils. When the bank was originally built, a fenced-in yard flanked the building to the south, while the house and store of Wilmer O. Lankford stood to the north. More recently, the original bank building has been extended to the north, south, and west with sympathetically designed additions executed

in polished yellowish brown brick; stone tablets have been engraved with the bank's name. Before construction of this impressive neoclassical brick structure, the Bank of Somerset occupied the first floor office of the Mutual Fire Insurance Company of Somerset and Worcester Counties across the street.

PEOPLES BANK OF SOMERSET
Circa 1907
Princess Anne
Public

The single story, neoclassical brick and stone building on the south side of Prince William Street across from the courthouse was built for the Peoples Bank of Somerset about 1907. Similar to the courthouse, the bank is constructed of dark red brick that contrasts with the sandstone columns and trim highlighting the window and door openings. The temple-front bank rests on a granite foundation.

Established in 1895 the Peoples Bank of Somerset was organized by Oliver T. Beau-

S-103, Bank of Somerset, east elevation.

S-99, Princess Anne railroad station, west elevation.

champ, Hampden P. Dashiell, and Robert F. Duer. In the same year B. Frank Lankford sold the Peoples Bank a building and lot on Prince William Street for $500. This structure was used until the present neoclassical building was erected. Since the bank closed in 1933, the structure has been used as the Somerset County Department of Health and, more recently, as the Somerset County commissioners' office.

PRINCESS ANNE
PHARMACY BUILDING
Circa 1907-1908
Princess Anne
Public

The Princess Anne pharmacy, formerly known as the Cohn store building, marks the southwest corner of the intersection of Prince William Street and Somerset Avenue in the center of Princess Anne. This prominent corner lot has been improved by a store since Lambert Hyland owned the property during the late eighteenth and early nineteenth centuries. The two-story commercial block that houses the pharmacy on the first floor and apartments on the second is distinctive for its decorative brick cornice and series of arched second floor windows.

Rudolph S. and Edward Herrman Cohn purchased the corner lot from Mary A. Ross in November 1907, and it is reasonable to believe the two-story brick structure was raised within the year. The store property, improved by a two-story frame building, had formerly been under the proprietorship of

Benjamin F. Lankford, John L. Lankford, and William H. Ross.

PRINCESS ANNE
RAILROAD STATION
1913
Princess Anne
Private

As profits reached superior levels during the first decades of the twentieth century, the New York, Philadelphia, and Norfolk Railroad financed the replacement of their Eastern Shore stations with new brick facilities. The Princess Anne station, built in 1913, was similar to the others, with a broad hip roof that sheltered the rectangular brick structure. As originally designed, round-arched louvered vents marked the roof. When passenger service was discontinued, the Princess Anne sta-

tion was sensitively reworked as a day care center in the mid-1980s. The building currently houses a real estate firm.

ANTIOCH UNITED
METHODIST CHURCH
1915-1917
Princess Anne
Public worship

The Antioch United Methodist Church is a prominent building distinguishing south Princess Anne. Built of semi-coursed white marble with smooth as well as rusticated finishes, the Gothic Revival church was designed by architect Leon Wilde Cranford of Wilmington, Delaware. The single story building is detailed with tripartite Gothic Revival windows, pointed arch double doors, and parapet gables.

S-107, Princess Anne pharmacy building, photograph c. 1967 northeast elevation.

S-419, Old Gulf station, east elevation.

S-386, Princess Anne volunteer fire station, southeast elevation.

Records indicate Methodist meetings were begun in Princess Anne around 1817, and the minutes of the Somerset County Bible Society document meetings held in the Princess Anne church in 1828. The first deed for Antioch church is dated June 1, 1832, when John Dennis transferred ownership of the church property to John Waters, Levin Ballard, James Phoebus, Stephen Drura, Richard Waters, Daniel Ballard, Lewis Phoebus, Arnold Ballard, and William Sudler as trustees. The former Methodist church was a single story brick building with a three-story entrance and bell tower probably erected during the second quarter of the nineteenth century. After a large increase in membership, plans to replace the brick building were advanced in 1915. The cornerstone of the new marble church was laid on July 28, 1915, and dedication services were held on July 2, 1916.

OLD GULF STATION
1927
Princess Anne
Private

In the major oil companies' push to rehabilitate their service stations across the country, distinctive early twentieth century structures are quickly torn down or converted to other uses. One of the few to remain relatively intact in Somerset County is the old Gulf station in the heart of Princess Anne. The building was erected around 1927, when the old Littleton Long or McMaster property (see S-24) was divided after its sale to the Gulf Refining Company. The building still boasts several features that point to its Colonial Revival style origins. Most distinctive is the pedimented front topped with a cupola.

PRINCESS ANNE VOLUNTEER FIRE STATION
1947
Princess Anne
Public

The Princess Anne fire station is a well-designed neo-Federal brick structure built in 1947. The two-story brick station, built of stretcher bond, has parapet gable ends, brick jack arches, a stone belt course, and a decorated cornice. The modillion blocks are especially well detailed for a utilitarian type building. Sited next to the Washington Hotel, the firehouse with its attractive revival design contributes to the historic appearance of Somerset Avenue.

S-410, Antioch Methodist Church and parsonage, c. 1910,
E. I. Brown—photographer (courtesy of William Marshall Scott).

S-410, Antioch Methodist Church, northeast elevation.

Crisfield

Crisfield harbor with the "Ethelyn Dryden," 1947, A. Aubrey Bodine—photographer (courtesy of the Mariners' Museum, Newport News, Virginia).

CAPTAIN LEONARD S. TAWES HOUSE (NR)

Circa 1840, circa 1880
Crisfield
Private

The Captain Leonard S. Tawes house is a noteworthy nineteenth century survival in Crisfield. The original house, a two-story, two-bay frame dwelling dating from the 1840s, is one of the oldest frame houses in the bay-side town. After Captain Tawes purchased the property in 1880, he reworked the extant house, substantially enlarging it to a two-and-a-half story, three-bay, center hall dwelling. Reusing some of the old woodwork, including the Greek Revival mantels and four-panel doors, the carpenters introduced a center stair in popular Victorian taste. The exterior, on the other hand, was reworked to achieve a uniform late nineteenth century appearance with a decorated porch stretching across the full front of the building. This architectural contrast is not unusual in conservative Somerset County where materials were often reused.

Captain Tawes's house is also notable for the survival of the winter and summer kitchens to the rear. The well-ventilated, semi-detached summer kitchen, originally connected to the main house by an open breezeway, was used during the hot months of the year in an effort to reduce accumulated

S-327, Captain Leonard S. Tawes house, east elevation.

S-316, Dr. Somers house, north elevation.

heat. By contrast, the winter kitchen, used during the colder months, helped to increase the warmth of the main block. The stilted dairy in the side yard is one of a few in Somerset County, and the property still retains a rare picket fence.

The house is also important as the home of Captain Leonard S. Tawes, who commanded trade ships that sailed between Baltimore, Boston, and as far south as Rio de Janeiro. Captain Tawes owned part interest in the schooner *City of Baltimore*. In 1967 the Mariners' Museum of Newport News, Virginia, published Robert H. Burgess's edited version of Captain Tawes's journals in a volume entitled *Coasting Captain, Journals of Captain Leonard S. Tawes, Relating His Career in Atlantic Coastwise Sailing Craft from 1868 to 1922.*

McCREADY HOUSE
Circa 1870
Crisfield
Private

One of a handful of dwellings to survive from the first decade of Crisfield history, the McCready house has distinguished the northwest corner of Main Street and Somerset Avenue since it was erected around 1870. The two-story, T-shaped frame house, common for the third quarter of the nineteenth century, was built with the leg of the 'T' facing Main Street. This orientation provided a bold gable-front elevation as well as a convenient space for a wraparound porch. The snake-curved porch brackets are an especially unusual decorative feature. In addition to the well-preserved nature of the house, the yard is surrounded by one of the few surviving picket fences in Crisfield. A group of outbuildings accompanies the dwelling.

DR. SOMERS HOUSE
Circa 1870
Crisfield
Private

The Dr. Somers house is located at 313 West Main Street next to the Whittington-Long house. Unlike its neighbor, the three-bay frame dwelling is a more standard house type for the mid to late nineteenth century with its two-story height, symmetrical fenestration, and centered cross gable. Identical corbeled brick chimneys rise from each gable end. Attached to the back of the house is a two-story, one-room plan kitchen wing. The interior of the house is finished in a straightforward manner with simple Victorian woodwork.

Although a complete title search has not been completed on this house, the lot had been improved by the time the 1877 county

S-325, McCready house, southwest elevation.

S-318, Crockett house, north elevation.

atlas was published. The map makers designated a J. Holland as the owner. The house was the residence of Dr. Somers in more recent times.

WHITTINGTON-LONG HOUSE
Circa 1870
Crisfield
Private

Standing on the south side of Main Street in uptown Crisfield, the Whittington-Long house is one of the earliest and most prominent houses to remain standing in the central business district. The two-story, L-shaped frame house is dominated by a colossal Tuscan-columned portico. Marking the center bay of the second floor is a sidelighted entrance that evidently opened onto a second floor porch at one time. The enclosed shed porch and brick flower shop were added around 1924.

The name of the original owner is not clear, but this house appears to have been built around 1870. An improvement is referred to on "Lot No. 9" in a transfer of land from William Roach, Thomas J. Dixon,

and William F. Veasey to Harriet A. Whittington. The half-acre lot,

purchased by the said Veasey of said Roach and Dixon, but not heretofore conveyed, which said lot is shown as Lot No. 9 upon the plat of said Roach and Dixon, together with all the improvements thereon,

was sold in May 1872 to Harriet Whittington for $1,500. Such a large sum for a half-acre lot suggests the property had been

S-315, Whittington-Long house, north elevation.

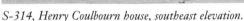
S-314, Henry Coulbourn house, southeast elevation.

S-323, Orrie Lee Tawes, Sr. house, north elevation.

improved at the time of transfer. Harriet and her husband, Isaac T. Whittington, lived in the house until 1899, when the property was sold to George W. Long. Long occupied the property until 1911, when his court-appointed heirs sold the house and lot to Alida Woodland. The current owners, the Corbins, purchased the property from Alida Woodland in March 1938.

HENRY COULBOURN HOUSE
Circa 1870
Crisfield
Private

Historically known as the Henry Coulbourn house, this squarish, two-and-a-half story frame dwelling is distinguished by an undulating bracketed eave and a fanciful front porch. Unlike other porches in Crisfield, this one has standard corner and eave brackets that are accompanied by rectangular eave panels incised with trailing tendril motifs. The east end of the house is marked by two bay windows also trimmed with brackets. Along with all the Victorian detail, the front door is framed by a classically inspired door

surround with pilasters and a simple entablature.

While current residents know this house as Dr. Sterling's office, older residents in Crisfield identify the property as the former home of Henry Coulbourn. An I. H. Coulbourn is designated on this lot on the 1877 Crisfield map.

CROCKETT HOUSE
Circa 1890
Crisfield
Private

One of the clearest indications of the success of the oyster packing industry in Crisfield is the Crockett house. It is the most elaborate Queen Anne style dwelling to remain standing in this bay-side town. The exterior alone carries a wider variety of decorative wall and window treatments than any other house. Also notable is the elaborate Frank Furness style paneled brick chimney on the east side of the frame house. Inside, the rooms are fitted with quarter-sawn oak or heart pine woodwork that retains its natural finish.

Family tradition and research has indicat-

ed the present dwelling stands on the site of the Crockett house that burned in the 1890s. Ananias R. Crockett is designated on this town lot in the 1877 atlas, and he is listed in the book's patron list as an oyster packer. Ananias Crockett's son Abednego Riggin Crockett is credited with the construction of the extant house. According to tradition, after a business trip to Denver, he ordered the plans of a house he had seen there and financed the construction of the same structure on the site of his father's house.

ORRIE LEE TAWES, SR. HOUSE
Circa 1895
Crisfield
Private

Family tradition says Orrie Lee Tawes, Sr. built this Queen Anne style frame house around 1895, and the property remains in the hands of his daughter. In contrast to nearby houses of the same style and date, this dwelling has a two-story circular tower and a wraparound Victorian porch. The entrance bay is topped by a three-sided bay window surmounted by a gable-front roof. The lower corners of the gabled roof are trimmed with Victorian brackets with paired corner pendants. The interior rooms have not been significantly altered, and the front hall ceiling survives with elaborate plasterwork.

WHITTINGTON HOUSE
Circa 1900
Crisfield
Private

Standing prominently on the corner of West Main and Third streets in the center of Crisfield, the Whittington house is another one of the important Queen Anne style frame houses that marks the financial success of oyster packers around the turn of the century. Similar in form to the nearby L. E. P. Dennis house, this elaborate example is distinguished by a fully lighted, three-story octagonal tower and a wraparound porch supported by slender Tuscan columns.

This dwelling is known by older Crisfield residents as the Whittington house.

S-324, Albert Sterling house, north elevation.

ALBERT STERLING HOUSE
Circa 1900
Crisfield
Private

The most eye-catching feature of this turn-of-the-century house is its rare Eastlake style front porch with arched wood screens dominating each bay. The turned post porch railing has equally unusual rectangular panels with a series of five or six round cutouts. In comparison, the two-story, two-bay, side hall/parlor frame house is relatively plain. A few gabled dormers and a bay window on the east side add interesting shapes to the L-shaped dwelling. The interior retains most of its period oak woodwork.

L. E. P. DENNIS HOUSE
Circa 1900
Crisfield
Private

The L. E. P. Dennis house, currently housing the Bradshaw Funeral Home, is one of a collection of turn-of-the-century Queen Anne style houses standing in Crisfield. The nearby Whittington and Crockett houses are two contemporary dwellings that have similar architectural lines. The Queen Anne style is characterized by an irregular floor plan and a complex roof shape often highlighted by a corner tower. The contrasting weatherboard siding and fish-scale shingles are common for the period. Covering the first floor is a Tuscan-

S-321, Whittington house, southwest elevation.

S-317, L. E. P. Dennis house, southwest elevation.

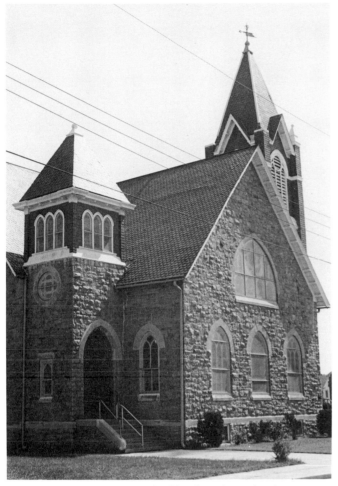

S-319, Immanuel United Methodist Church, southwest elevation.

S-92, Mount Pleasant M. P. Church, north elevation.

columned front porch, a classical element that exemplifies the eclectic nature of the style.

L. E. P. Dennis is best remembered as the owner of the menhaden fish factory located on nearby "Old Island." The factory site is still marked by a tall brick chimney stack. The Dennis family occupied this prominent house until the second quarter of the twentieth century. In later years the Covington family established a funeral home on the property.

MOUNT PLEASANT M. P. CHURCH
1892
Crisfield
Public worship

Distinguished as the most elaborate Victorian Gothic church in Somerset County, Mount Pleasant Methodist Protestant Church stands on the south side of West Main Street in the heart of Crisfield. Highlighted with granite belt courses, water tables, and buttress caps, the stretcher bond brick facade is flanked

by a four-story bell tower on the west and a two-story octagonal tower on the east. Centered on the north (front) wall is a large tripartite colored glass window flanked by two colored glass lancet windows. The northeast corner tower is also lighted by lancet windows, and equally notable are the round terracotta decorative panels that mark the second floor. The tapered octagonal spire is finished with a dentiled cornice and capped with a ball finial.

The west tower is the architectural focus of the building. Rising four stories, the combination entrance and bell tower dominates the brick church as well as the Crisfield skyline. Fixed in the northwest corner of the base are two datestones. The most obvious stone commemorates the 1892 construction of the current church, while an additional stone on the back of the tower was evidently salvaged from the congregation's former 1876 building.

IMMANUEL UNITED METHODIST CHURCH
1909
Crisfield
Public worship

The Gothic Revival design of the Immanuel United Methodist Church is one of the most ambitious interpretations of the style in Somerset County. The T-plan of the main church is elaborated by two corner towers, the southeast tower rising three full stories and distinguishing the Crisfield skyline. The polished stone used for the Gothic-arched windows and doors is set off by the building's rusticated granite walls.

Organized in 1869, Immanuel M. E. Church began as a branch congregation of St. Peter's Church near Hopewell. In 1873 the foundation of the first building was raised on the northwest corner of Church and Horsey streets in Crisfield, although the completed church was not dedicated until December

S-320, Samuel Maddrix toy shop, north elevation.

S-313, J. W. Riggin furniture store, south elevation.

1880. According to the *Garden of Methodism*, by E. C. Hallman, the building caught fire in 1887 during the visit of Bishop Warren. Fortunately, the fire was extinguished before it had caused extensive damage. An addition was attached to the church in 1889. After the turn of the century, the Immanuel congregation bought a new lot facing Main Street and erected the present structure at a cost of $50,000 in 1909.

SAMUEL MADDRIX TOY SHOP
1887
Crisfield
Private

Perhaps the oldest store building in Crisfield, this two-story, three-bay commercial structure is conveniently dated by an embossed year of construction in the upper portion of the parapet roof. Not only is the building's Victorian brickwork well preserved, but the first floor storefront has not been significantly altered either. The recessed double-door entrance is flanked by large plate glass display windows, and a mid-level bracketed cornice tops the storefront.

Although the earliest history of this building has not been determined, the structure is remembered distinctly as the former toy shop operated by Samuel Maddrix during the early twentieth century. Somewhat later the structure served as the Justice grocery store.

J. W. RIGGIN FURNITURE STORE
Circa 1900
Crisfield
Private

This large, two-story, brick commercial building on the north side of Main Street shares the same historic distinction as the Peyton Pharmacy building across the street. Both structures mark the easternmost advance of the devastating 1928 fire, which started in the old opera house and spread through much of uptown. Although the first floor shopfront has been reworked, the second floor and upper wall surface decorative Victorian brickwork survives. Five windows are topped

S-304, Jersey Island packing houses, northwest elevation.

S-312, W. E. Ward & Bro. store, north elevation.

with elaborate arched and corbeled hoods interrupted by keystones. Running across the wall surface above the windows is an enriched brick cornice.

Older residents in Crisfield recall this building as the location of the J. W. Riggin furniture store, which operated during the second quarter of the twentieth century. More recently it housed the Saltz furniture store.

W. E. WARD & BRO. STORE
Circa 1900
Crisfield
Private

Until recently, this two-story, three-bay brick building on the south side of Main Street was the site of the Tull and Price Insurance Company. Similar to many commercial structures in town, the exterior decoration is minimal

and limited to brick arches over the second floor windows.

W. E. Ward & Brother operated a wholesale candy store in this structure during the early to mid twentieth century.

JERSEY ISLAND PACKING HOUSES
Circa 1900
Crisfield
Public

Jersey Island has been occupied throughout Crisfield's history by seafood packing houses. For many years the small peninsula was connected to Crisfield's downtown by a lift bridge. The two principal warehouses, owned by L. R. Carson and the Milbourne Oyster Company, are two early twentieth century structures built of common bond brick and highlighted by single-pane or two-over-two sash windows. Each building is bordered by wharf bulkheads on at least one side for unloading fresh seafood. The crabs or oysters, in season, are processed in these waterfront buildings and then shipped by truck from Crisfield.

SEA ISLE FURNITURE STORE
Circa 1900
Crisfield (site)
Public

The two-story, four-bay commercial building occupied by the Sea Isle furniture store was a standard common bond brick structure with four segmental arched window openings on the second floor. The first floor storefront had been altered; however, the rear elevation was largely intact on both floors with segmental arches of corbeled brick. The gable parapet roof was trimmed with decorative brick cornices. This structure burned in 1987 along with several nearby buildings.

S-303, Sea Isle furniture store, southeast elevation.

S-302, Old Customs house and post office, southeast elevation.

S-301, Old Cochran Lumber Company office, southeast elevation.

OLD CUSTOMS HOUSE & POST OFFICE
Circa 1910
Crisfield
Public

The old Crisfield customs house and post office (now used as a hardware store under the name of Clarence Sterling and Son) is a two-story, combination beige and red brick commercial building located in the center of downtown. The simply executed classical facade is divided by four plain brick pilasters highlighted with limestone capitals. Due to the similarity in detail between this building and the Marine Bank of Crisfield, it is thought the customs house was erected during the first decade of the twentieth century. Crisfield's earlier customs house was a large Victorian brick building located along the wharf near Dock Street.

OLD COCHRAN LUMBER COMPANY OFFICE
Circa 1900
Crisfield (site)
Private

The old Cochran Lumber Company office, now known as J. P. Tawes lumberyard, was located on Broad Street in downtown Crisfield. The lumberyard occupies an entire block and consists of a large frame warehouse and shed. The old company office stood on the property until 1988. A single story, hip-roofed frame structure, it was covered with a combination of weatherboards and fish-scale shingles. The patterned slate roof had slightly kicked eaves and broad soffits. The office interior was equally notable with its beaded board sheathing and an original vault.

EASTERN SHORE NATIONAL BANK
Circa 1900
Crisfield
Public

Sited prominently in downtown Crisfield, the Eastern Shore National Bank (formerly the Bank of Crisfield) is one of the town's most architecturally distinguished commercial structures. The diminutive Beaux-Arts design is a classically inspired temple-front with corner pilasters topped by an entablature and dentiled pediment. Doric pilasters frame the center door opening, which is elevated and flanked by paneled columns with acanthus leaf capitals. Engraved just below the entablature is the former bank name. The southwest street elevation is marked by four Doric pilasters that separate three bays.

HORSEY BROTHERS DEPARTMENT STORE
Circa 1900
Crisfield
Private

The Horsey Brothers department store is a large, squarish commercial building on the northeast corner of the intersection of Maryland Avenue and the alley that leads to the J. Millard Tawes Museum. The turn-of-the-century structure is a plain brick warehouse-type building with a parapet roof and simple brickwork finishes. The arched and dentiled window headers as well as corbeled brick cornices add interest to an otherwise utilitarian commercial building. During the early twentieth century, the Horsey Brothers department store was one of the largest retail merchandise businesses in Crisfield.

S-300, Eastern Shore National Bank, southeast elevation.

S-298, *Marine Bank of Crisfield, southeast elevation.*

S-297, *Ward and Briddell insurance office, southeast elevation.*

WARD AND BRIDDELL INSURANCE COMPANY OFFICE
Circa 1900
Crisfield
Public

The Ward and Briddell Insurance Company office is one of a collection of turn-of-the-century masonry buildings that line Maryland Avenue between Main Street and the wharf. In contrast to the others, this building has been altered to a large degree with an exterior layer of stucco and a remodeled interior. The old insurance office safe remains in the building.

MARINE BANK OF CRISFIELD
1905
Crisfield
Public

Standing on the northwest side of Maryland Avenue, the Marine Bank of Crisfield is an early twentieth century bank building designed with simple but clear references to classical orders and symmetry. Four Ionic pilasters, which rise from simply molded granite bases, divide the southeast elevation into three bays. The pilaster shafts are of a brownish brick, while the capitals are made of carved limestone. Between each pair of pilasters is a large door or window opening with a finely tooled keystone arch. Dating to 1905, this bank represents a prime period in Crisfield history, when the earlier frame buildings were replaced with more permanent brick struc-

S-296, *Horsey Brothers department store, northwest elevation.*

S-93, The Baptist Temple, northwest elevation.

tures. The building has served as a community museum.

JACK JONES HOUSE
Circa 1890
Crisfield
Private

Located within a short distance of the seafood packing houses, this small two-story, two-bay frame dwelling is one of the oldest surviving row houses erected for seafood workers. Its very modest proportions and minimum attention to decorative detail characterize most worker housing in Crisfield. This row house was formerly accompanied by several others.

ST. PAUL'S A. M. E. CHURCH
1906
Crisfield
Public worship

St. Paul's African Methodist Episcopal Church stands on the southwest corner of Broadway and Fourth Street, one block south of Main

Street in the center of uptown Crisfield. Built in 1906 the seven-course common bond brick church has a T-plan and is covered by a steeply pitched, patterned slate roof. A three-story tower in the northeast corner of the plan contains two Gothic-arched entrances at the top of a five-step flight of stairs. The bell tower has been removed, but the bell was preserved and placed in front of the church. The maker's inscription reads,

Buckeye Bell Foundry, 1892, Vanduzen and Tift, Cincinnati, Presented by the Cheerful Workers, April 1, 1892.

The bell was salvaged from the church that previously stood on this site. The marble cornerstone, located in the northeast corner of the existing church, states the first church was erected in 1886, burned on May 20, 1906, and rebuilt the same year.

THE BAPTIST TEMPLE
1921
Crisfield
Public worship

Dominating the neighboring dwellings on Somerset Avenue and Main Street, the Baptist Temple stands out as the most impressive neoclassical building in Somerset County. An Ionic-columned portico with a decorated pediment dominates the Somerset Avenue elevation, and an octagonal drum supports the red-tile dome. The sides of the drum are pierced by round-arched windows and trimmed with acroteria. The dome is topped with a rounded finial. Gabled side elevations give the impression of a Greek-cross plan.

Designed by Birmingham, Alabama, architect J. E. Green, this impressive brick church was erected by Crisfield builders Wilson & Co. in 1921. In contrast to other religious

S-305, St. Paul's A. M. E. Church, northeast elevation.

S-299, Jack Jones house, northwest elevation.

S-306, Crisfield Arcade, north elevation.

S-307, United States post office, southwest elevation.

groups in Somerset County, the Crisfield Baptist congregation is a relatively new one, having formed in April 1889. Their first church, in 1890, served the congregation for thirty years until it was decided to finance the construction of this Somerset Avenue building.

CRISFIELD ARMORY (NR)
1927
Crisfield
Public (restricted)

The Crisfield Armory, built in 1927, stands on the eastern edge of Crisfield along East Main Street. Designed to emulate a medieval fortification, the two-story, seven-bay red-brick structure is trimmed with limestone accents that highlight the water table, buttresses, string course, and entrance bay. The center bay is distinguished by a stone arch that marks the entrance and identifies the

structure. The Maryland state seal is carved in stone in the uppermost section of the crenelated wall. Twin towers, which flank the entrance, rise above the main block and are trimmed with similar stone finishes.

The armory was built after a commission of local residents and the American Legion joined in an effort to establish a permanent facility to honor young men returning home from World War I. The armory has served in various ways from a skating rink to a meeting hall. Recently, the building has undergone extensive interior and exterior renovations.

CRISFIELD ARCADE
Circa 1930
Crisfield
Private

The Crisfield Arcade is a large, prominent building located in the center of uptown Cris-

field. In 1928 the old opera house, a Victorian brick structure, burned in a town fire that started there during an 8:30 P.M. showing of "Love," starring John Gilbert and Greta Garbo. In place of the opera house, the Crisfield Arcade was erected in yellowish brick with slight references to the Art Deco style. The north elevation is divided by four plain pilasters topped with stone ball finials. The double or tripartite windows are bordered with dark, liver-colored brick.

UNITED STATES POST OFFICE
1933
Crisfield
Public

The United States post office stands on the northwest corner of West Main Street and Fourth Street in the center of uptown. The prominent Colonial Revival public building has a central three-bay block flanked by three-bay wings. Built in Flemish bond brick, the single story structure is covered in slate and topped by a distinctive, bell-shaped cupola. The front door is situated on a raised platform with access provided by a twin stair of marble steps surrounded by iron railings. The double-door entrance is framed by a classical entablature with an arched fanlight. The decorated, ovolo-molded door surround is flanked by fluted pilasters, which support a cushion frieze and broken cornice. The cushion frieze is inscribed "Post Office." The wall surface to each side of the entrance is decorated with a round medallion containing a relief sculpture of a classical profile.

S-118, Crisfield Armory, northwest elevation.

S-309, *Nora S. Davis Shoppe, south elevation.*

S-311, *Bank of Crisfield, south elevation.*

S-310, *Peyton pharmacy building, north elevation.*

GIBSON COMMERCIAL BLOCK
Circa 1930
Crisfield
Public

The Gibson commercial block, which includes three storefronts, was erected at the same time as the nearby Crisfield Arcade, during the few years after the 1928 uptown fire. Similar to the arcade, the two-story yellow-brick structure is highlighted with liver-colored brick in the decorative cornice and window surrounds. The center bay is slightly taller than the adjacent bays. The Gibson name is embossed in reddish brick in the center above the storefronts.

NORA S. DAVIS SHOPPE
Circa 1929
Crisfield
Public

The Nora S. Davis Shoppe, operating since the early 1960s as Scher's Clothing Store, stands on the north side of West Main Street in the center of uptown Crisfield. The circa 1929, two-story commercial front was erected in a yellowish brown brick, while the side elevations are of red brick laid in common bond. Unlike many store buildings in Crisfield, the first floor front has not been significantly altered. The recessed entrance has a vaulted ceiling and flanking display windows. Piercing the second floor are four six-over-one sash windows, and the upper portion of the wall is finished with a decorative rectangular panel of basketweave brick. Slightly pro-

jecting corner pilasters frame the building and support a cornice of diagonally set bricks.

Known during much of the twentieth century as the Nora S. Davis Shoppe, the business was named after its original proprietor, Nora Stephens Davis, who started a women's clothing and yard goods store in Crisfield around 1918. After the 1928 fire destroyed a large portion of the central business district, Nora Davis financed the construction of this brick building on a new site. After her death in 1952, the business was operated by her daughters, Nellie Huntley Davis and Marie Stephens Davis, until the early 1960s.

PEYTON PHARMACY BUILDING
Circa 1920
Crisfield
Public

The Peyton pharmacy building, standing on the south side of Crisfield's main street, is a three-story brick commercial structure laid in Flemish and common bond. It marks the easternmost point to which the 1928 fire advanced on the south side of Main Street. The five-bay front elevation, with its well-laid glazed header checkerboard pattern and decorative brick cornice, is a prominent building architecturally.

The building is named for Dr. Sarah M.

S-308, *Gibson Commercial Block, north elevation.*

S-117, Island Belle.

Peyton, a prominent local physician who served Crisfield through a large part of the twentieth century.

CHESAPEAKE MASONIC LODGE
1926
Crisfield
Private

Marking the southwest corner of West Main Street and Somerset Avenue is the neoclassical Masonic lodge, a well-built Flemish bond brick structure with a commanding temple-front portico. Four Tuscan columns support a cushion frieze and a modillioned pediment. The four corners of the building are highlighted with concrete quoins, and a modillioned cornice stretches around the rectangular structure.

BANK OF CRISFIELD
1937
Crisfield
Private

The uptown branch of the Bank of Crisfield (later renamed the Eastern Shore National Bank) formerly occupied this simplified Art Deco style building. Erected in 1937 in the central business district, which had been destroyed by fire nine years earlier, the bank front is a very plain Art Deco design with only basic references to the often elaborate linear style. The vertical emphasis expressed in the tall brick panels and the recessed entrance bay along with the decorative door handles are the clear architectural references that pinpoint the building's design inspiration.

ISLAND BELLE (NR)
1916
Ewell

Built on Smith Island in 1916, the *Island Belle* was used for sixty-one years as the principal means of public transportation between the island and Crisfield. The vessel, 48 feet long with a beam of 14 feet and a capacity of 20 tons, has a round stern, deadrise wooden hull and forward pilot house. Its top speed was 8 knots.

Like its successors, the *Island Belle* provided the islanders with a dependable link to doctors, schools, and stores in Crisfield and delivered mail, food, and other necessities on a daily schedule. The boat lies on the bottom of the harbor at Ewell.

S-326, Chesapeake Masonic lodge, north elevation.

Traditional Bay Work Boats

Skipjack races on Tangier Sound, 1929, Ida Mae *at lower left and* Robert L. Webster *in the center (courtesy of the Mariners' Museum, Newport News, Virginia).*

Chesapeake oyster fishery dates to the early nineteenth century, when vessels from Delaware, New Jersey, New York, and New England came to the area to dredge for oysters. Depletion of the bay's oyster population appeared inevitable, and in 1820 the first conservation laws were passed. This legislation prohibited dredging in Maryland waters and restricted the harvesting of oysters to hand tongers. Such laws proved unenforceable, however, especially when Thomas Kensett established Baltimore's first oyster cannery in 1828.

Kensett received the first American patent for his process to "preserve animal, vegetable, and other perishable goods." Oysters were

an extremely perishable product and one for which there was a wide demand, making them an ideal test for mass marketing commercially canned goods. Kensett's process allowed for national distribution of Maryland's oysters and markedly increased demand for the product.

In 1865 the earlier conservation laws were amended to allow licensed Maryland vessels to dredge under sail in specific deep water areas. During this era the Chesapeake Bay bugeye was developed from the log canoe to serve as an oyster dredge boat. Other traditional bay vessels—sloops, schooners, pungies—also entered the dredging fleet, and by the peak years of the early 1880s over 700

licensed Maryland vessels were engaged in dredging for oysters. In 1884-1885 a record l5 million bushels were marketed from the bay.

By the 1890s, however, the oyster catch had diminished and shipbuilding costs were escalating, largely because the supplies of large timber were depleted and labor costs were rising. The old log-bottom bugeyes—the preferred oyster boats—were no longer built because the large logs needed for the hulls were in short supply. A framed bugeye, more expensive and harder to build, replaced the log bugeye as the dredge boat available to watermen. The more traditionally designed pungies, schooners, and sloops were even more expensive to assemble than the new bugeye. The need clearly existed for an easily and cheaply constructed vessel.

The skipjack type evolved at this time from the traditional, unframed, generally flat-bottomed bay crabbing skiffs. The skiff was enlarged in size and given a deadrise, or V-bottom, hull. The resulting box-built skipjacks were inexpensive to build and easy to repair. Without bottom frames and with short cross-planks that did not have to be curved to fit the shape of the hull, these centerboard sloops could be built by a trained house carpenter or by the watermen themselves. The first recorded vessel of this type, with a cross-planked V-bottom, is the *Ruby G. Ford*, built in 1891 at Fairmount, Maryland, and still sailing in the oyster fleet. The typical rig for a skipjack consists of a jib-headed mainsail and a single large jib with a club on the foot.

The peak production period for Maryland's skipjacks extended from the early 1890s to the years just before World War I. By the 1930s a fleet that had numbered close to a thousand had dwindled dramatically as old vessels were abandoned in the face of low oyster prices and an almost non-existent market. The post World War II era saw a revival of the oyster industry and a group of new skipjacks was added to the fleet, bringing the numbers back into the seventies. By 1971, however, the fleet had dropped to forty-three vessels, with a more or less steady decline ever since.

The Chesapeake Bay skipjack has survived because of the Maryland dredging law that still allows only sail-powered vessels to dredge for oysters. Past amendments in the law now enable watermen to use motorized "push" boats, or yawl boats, to propel the skipjacks over the oyster beds two days a week. The largest catch is usually harvested on these "push" days. If current state laws are repealed in favor of private ownership of oyster beds and power dredgings (as is now the case in New York and New Jersey), the traditional Chesapeake Bay skipjack will vanish as a working vessel.

(A large part of the information in this section was taken from the thematic National Register nomination prepared in 1985 by Mary Ellen Hayward, PhD, in conjunction with the Maryland Historical Trust and the Maryland Historical Society.)

SKIPJACK *SUSAN MAY* (NR)
S-241
1901, Wenona

Fore-and-aft planked sloop built in Pocomoke City, Maryland; length—46 feet, depth 1.6 feet, beam 15.9 feet, tonnage—10.

SKIPJACK *FANNY L. DAUGHERTY* (NR)
S-233
1904, Wenona

Two-sail bateau built in Crisfield, Maryland; length—41.3 feet, depth 1.6 feet, beam 15.9 feet, tonnage—10.

SKIPJACK *IDA MAY* (NR)
S-238
1906, Chance

Two-sail bateau built in Deep Creek, Virginia; length—42.2 feet, depth 3.3 feet, beam 14.4 feet, tonnage—/.

SKIPJACK *F. C. LEWIS JR.* (NR)
S-234
1907, Wenona

Two-sail bateau built in Hopkins, Virginia; length—39 feet, depth 3 feet, beam 14.6 feet, tonnage—6.

SKIPJACK *CLARENCE CROCKETT* (NR)
S-232
1908, Wenona

Two-sail bateau built in Deep Creek, Virginia; length—44.6 feet, depth 3 feet, beam 14.7 feet, tonnage—7.

SKIPJACK *HOWARD* (NR)
S-237
1909, Wenona

Two-sail bateau built in Deep Creek, Virginia; length—45 feet, depth 3.1 feet, beam 15.3 feet, tonnage—8.

SKIPJACK *THOMAS W. CLYDE* (NR)
S-242
1911, Wenona

Two-sail bateau built in Oriole, Maryland; length—54.4 feet, depth 5.3 feet, beam 18.2 feet, tonnage—21.

SKIPJACK *ROBERT L. WEBSTER* (NR)
S-114
1915, Janes Island

Two-sail bateau built in Oriole, Maryland; length—60 feet, beam 20.4 feet, tonnage—34.

SKIPJACK *SEA GULL* (NR)
S-239
1924, Deal Island

Two-sail bateau built in Crisfield, Maryland; length—46.6 feet, depth 4.3 feet, beam 15.9 feet, tonnage—10.

SKIPJACK *CITY OF CRISFIELD* (NR)
S-231
1948, Wenona

Two-sail bateau built in Reedville, Virginia; length—44.7 feet, depth 1.7 feet, beam 15.8 feet, tonnage—10.

SKIPJACK *HELEN VIRGINIA* (NR)
S-235
1948, Wenona

Two-sail bateau built in Crisfield, Maryland; length—43.2 feet, tonnage—10.25.

SKIPJACK *SOMERSET* (NR)
S-240
1949, Wenona

Two-sail bateau built in Reedville, Virginia; length 44.9 feet, depth 1.5 feet, beam 15.7 feet, tonnage—9.

SKIPJACK *CALEB W. JONES* (NR)
S-230
1953, Wenona

Two-sail bateau built in Reedville, Virginia; length—44.1 feet, depth 1.5 feet, beam 16.5 feet, tonnage—10.

SKIPJACK *H. M. KRENTZ* (NR)
S-236
1955, Wenona

Two-sail bateau built in Harryhogan, Virginia; length—44.3 feet, depth 4.9 feet, beam 15.6 feet, tonnage—8.

Bibliography

PRIMARY SOURCES

Archives of Maryland, Proceedings of the Council of Maryland, 1636-1667, Vol. 3 (Baltimore: Maryland Historical Society, 1885).

Archives of Maryland, Proceedings of the Council of Maryland, 1667-1687/8, Vol. 5 (Baltimore: Maryland Historical Society, 1887).

Archives of Maryland, Proceedings and Acts of the General Assembly of Maryland, October 1678-November 1683, Vol. 7 (Baltimore: Maryland Historical Society, 1889).

Archives of Maryland, Proceedings and Acts of the General Assembly of Maryland, May 1730-August 1732, Vol. 37 (Baltimore: Maryland Historical Society, 1917).

Archives of Maryland, Proceedings and Acts of the General Assembly of Maryland, 1733-1736, Vol. 39 (Baltimore: Maryland Historical Society, 1919).

Archives of Maryland, Proceedings and Acts of the General Assembly of Maryland, 1740-1744, Vol. 42 (Baltimore: Maryland Historical Society, 1923).

Coventry Parish vestry minutes, various volumes, Maryland State Archives, Annapolis, St. Mary's Protestant Episcopal Church, Pocomoke City, Maryland and St. Paul's Church, Marion, Maryland.

Crisfield Index, Crisfield Leader, Crisfield Post, and Crisfield Times, various issues, Enoch Pratt Free Library, Baltimore.

Diary of Thomas Seon Sudler, typescript, 1799-1818 with transcribed entries from earlier period. Original owned by Dr. Mervin Tubman Sudler.

Eastern Shore Intelligencer, 14 May 1805, Talbot County Free Library, Easton, Maryland. Farm account books of James Wilson, 1773-1780s, MS 915, Maryland Historical Society, Baltimore.

Federal Direct Tax Assessment of 1798, microfilm, Somerset County Library, Princess Anne, and Wicomico County Free Library, Salisbury, Maryland.

Grace Protestant Episcopal Church vestry minutes, various volumes, Grace Protestant Episcopal Church, Mt. Vernon, Maryland.

Heads of Families at the First Census of the United States taken in the year 1790. Baltimore: Baltimore Publishing Company, 1965.

Graham, John L. ed. *The 1877 Atlases and Other Early Maps of the Eastern Shore of Maryland* (Peninsula Press, 1976).

Letter of Eleanor Gilliss Waters, c. 1818, copy located in collection of Old Princess Anne Days, Inc., Teackle Mansion, Princess Anne, Maryland.

Letter of Levin Handy, Clerk of Somerset Court, to David Ridgely, 20 September 1841, Maryland Historical Society, Baltimore.

Letter book of Littleton Dennis Teackle, 1805-1807, Accession #2338, Quinby family papers, Rare Books and Manuscripts, Alderman Library, University of Virginia, Charlottesville.

Marylander and Herald, various issues, Office of the *Somerset Herald*, Princess Anne, Maryland.

Minutes of the Somerset County Board of Education, "Agreement entered into by the Trustees of the Washington Academy and the School Commissioners of Somerset County, Maryland," as filed with the Minutes of the Trustees of the Washington Academy, 26 May 1891, Maryland State Archives, Annapolis.

Niles' Register, various volumes, Enoch Pratt Free Library, Baltimore.

Quinby family papers, Accession #2338, Rare Books and Manuscripts, Alderman Library, University of Virginia, Charlottesville.

Salisbury Advertiser, various issues, Wicomico County Free Library, Salisbury, Maryland.

Sixth Census of the United States, 1840, Mines, Agriculture, Commerce, and Manufacturers Schedule, microfilm, Maryland State Law Library, Annapolis

Seventh Census of the United States, 1850, Manufacturers Schedule, Maryland State Law Library, Annapolis.

Smyrna Times, various issues, citations provided by Kent Griffith, Salisbury, Maryland.

Somerset County Commissioners Minutes, 1856-1868, Maryland State Archives, Annapolis.

Somerset County Equity Records, various volumes, Office of the Clerk of Somerset Court, Somerset County Courthouse, Princess Anne, Maryland.

Somerset County Inventories, various volumes, Maryland State Archives, Annapolis.

Somerset County Judicial Records, various volumes, Maryland State Archives, Annapolis.

Somerset County Land Records, various volumes, Office of the Clerk of the Court, Somerset County Courthouse, Princess Anne, Maryland, and Maryland State Archives, Annapolis.

Somerset County, Maryland, maps showing the counties, names, etc. of land surveys and resurveys compiled by Harry L. Benson, Baltimore, 1942, microfilm, Wicomico County Free Library, Salisbury, Maryland.

Somerset County Marriage Records, Office of the Clerk of Somerset Court, Somerset County Courthouse, Princess Anne, Maryland.

Somerset County Orphans Court Valuations, various volumes, Maryland State Archives, Annapolis, and Register of Wills, Somerset County, Maryland.

Somerset County Proceedings of the Levy Court 1827-1840, Maryland State Archives, Annapolis.

Somerset County Tax Records, various volumes, Maryland State Archives, Annapolis.

Somerset County Wills, various volumes, Register of Wills, Somerset County Courthouse, Princess Anne, Maryland.

Somerset Herald, various issues dating 1827-1846, Maryland Historical Society, Baltimore.

Somerset Iris and Messenger of Truth, issues dating 1828-1829, Enoch Pratt Free Library, and Maryland Historical Society, Baltimore.

"Somerset Parish, A Compendium," no date (published during the tenure of the Reverend J. Randolph Field, Th.D.), source provided by Anne Pettit.

Somerset Parish vestry minutes, various volumes, Maryland State Archives, Annapolis.

Somerset Union, issues dating 1856-1861, Enoch Pratt Free Library, Baltimore.

State Gazette and Merchants and Farmers Directory for Maryland, 1871, Maryland Law Library, Annapolis, Maryland.

Statistical Gazetteer of the State of Maryland. Baltimore: J. S. Waters, 1856.

Tax Assessment of 1783, microfilm, Wicomico County Free Library, Salisbury, Maryland.

The Herald, various issues, Maryland Historical Society, Baltimore.

Trustees Minutes of the Washington Academy, Maryland State Archives, Annapolis.

Village Herald, issues dating 1827-1838, Maryland Historical Society, Baltimore.

Wicomico News, various issues, Wicomico County Free Library, Salisbury, Maryland.

SECONDARY SOURCES

Alsop, George A. *A Character of the Province of Maryland.* 1902; reprint ed., Freeport, New York: Books for Libraries Press, 1972.

Ames, Susie M. *Studies of the Virginia Eastern Shore in the Seventeenth Century.* Reprint ed., New York: Russell and Russell, 1973.

Andrews, Matthew Page. *History of Maryland: Province and State.* Hatboro, Pennsylvania: Tradition Press, 1965.

Arber, Edward, ed. *Travels and Works of Captain John Smith, President of Virginia and Admiral of New England, 1580-1631* 2 vols. New York: Burt Franklin, 1910.

Baer, Elizabeth. *Seventeenth Century Maryland: A Bibliography.* Baltimore: John Work Garret Library, 1949.

Barley, M.W. *The English Farmhouse and Cottage.* London: Henley and Boston: Routledge and Kegan Paul, 1961.

Bozman, John Leeds. *The History of Maryland, from Its First Settlement in 1633 to the Restoration in 1660, with a Copious Introduction, and Notes and Illustrations.* 2 vols. Baltimore: J. Lucas and E. K. Deaver, 1837.

Breen, T. H. and Innes, Stephen. *Myne Owne Ground, Race and Freedom on Virginia's Eastern Shore, 1640-1676.* New York and Oxford: Oxford University Press, 1980.

Brunskill, R.W. *Illustrated Handbook of Vernacular Architecture.* London: Faber and Faber, 1971.

Burgess, Robert H. *Coasting Captain, Journals of Captain Leonard S. Tawes, Relating His Career in Atlantic Coastwise Sailing Craft from 1868 to 1922.* Newport News, Virginia: The Mariners Museum, 1967.

Burgess, Robert H. and Wood, H. Graham. *Steamboats Out of Baltimore.* Cambridge, Maryland: Tidewater Publishers, 1968.

Burton, R. Lee, Jr. *Canneries of the Eastern Shore.* Centreville, Maryland: Tidewater Publishers, 1986.

Carr, Lois Green. "The Economy of Colonial Somerset County, Maryland, In Comparative Perspective." Unpublished manuscript prepared for the St. Mary's City Commission, St. Mary's City, Maryland.

Carr, Lois Green and Menard, Russell R. "Immigration and Opportunity: The Freedman in Early Colonial Maryland." In *The Chesapeake in the Seventeenth Century, Essays on Anglo-American Society.* Edited by Thad W. Tate and David L. Ammerman. Chapel Hill: University of North Carolina Press, 1979.

Carson, Cary; Barka, Norman F.; Kelso, William M.; Stone, Garry Wheeler, and Upton, Dell. "Impermanent Architecture in the Southern Colonies." *Winterthur Portfolio.* Chicago: University of Chicago Press, 1981.

Clark, Charles Branch. *The Eastern Shore of Maryland and Virginia.* New York: Lewis Historical Publishing Company, 1950.

Clark, Raymond B., Jr. "Washington Academy, Somerset County, Maryland." *Maryland Historical Magazine*, XLIV (1949).

Clemens, Paul G. E. *The Atlantic Economy and Colonial Maryland's Eastern Shore, From Tobacco to Grain.* Ithaca and London: Cornell University Press, 1980.

Coffin, Lewis A. and Holden, Arthur C. *Brick Architecture of the Colonial Period in Maryland and Virginia.* New York: Architectural Book Publishing Company, 1919.

Corddry, William H. *Wicomico County History.* Salisbury, Maryland: Peninsula Press, 1981.

Cumming, William P.; Hillier, S. E.; Quinn, David B., and Williams, G.; *The Exploration of North America, 1630-1776.* New York: G. P. Putnam's Sons, 1974.

Dalrymple, E. A., ed. *Narrative of a Voyage to Maryland, by Father Andrew White, S. J. An Account of the Colony of the Lord Baron of Baltimore. Extracts from Different Letters of Missionaries, from the Year 1635 to the Year 1677.* Fund Publication 7. Baltimore: Maryland Historical Society, 1874.

Davis, Ralph. *The Industrial Revolution and British Overseas Trade.* Leicester, England: University Press, 1979.

Davis, Ralph. *The Rise of the Atlantic Economies.* Ithaca, New York: Cornell University Press, 1973.

Dickey, Kenneth M. *History of Antioch Charge.* Princess Anne, Maryland: no date.

Downing, Andrew Jackson. *The Architecture of Country Houses; including Designs for Cottages, Farm-houses, and Villas, with Remarks on Interiors, Furniture, and the Best Modes of Warming and Ventilating.* 1853; reprint ed., New York: Dover Publications, Inc., 1969.

Eller, Ernest McNeill, ed. *Chesapeake Bay in the American Revolution.* Centreville, Maryland: Tidewater Publishers, 1981.

Fletcher, Stevenson Whitcomb. *Pennsylvania Architecture and Country Life, 1640-1840.* Harrisburg: Pennsylvania Historical and Museum Commission, 1971.

Forman, Henry Chandlee. *Early Manor and Plantation Houses.* 2nd ed. Baltimore: Bodine and Associates, Inc., 1982.

Forman, Henry Chandlee. *Old Buildings, Gardens, and Furniture in Tidewater Maryland.* Cambridge, Maryland: Tidewater Publishers, 1967.

Forman, Henry Chandlee. *Tidewater Maryland Architecture and Gardens, A Sequel to Early Manor and Plantation Houses of Maryland.* New York: Bonanza Books, 1956.

Goldfield, David R. "North Carolina's Early Twentieth-Century Suburbs and the Urbanizing South." In *Early Twentieth-Century Suburbs in North Carolina.* Edited by Catherine W. Bishir and Lawrence S. Early. Lillington, N.C.: Edwards Brothers, Inc., 1985.

Graham, John L., ed. *The 1877 Atlases and other Early Maps of the Eastern Shore of Maryland.* Peninsula Press, 1976.

Hall, Clayton C., ed. *Narratives of Early Maryland, 1633-1684.* Narratives of Early American History Series. Edited by John F. Jameson. New York: Scribners. Reprint ed., New York: Barnes and Noble, 1946.

Hallman, E. C. *The Garden of Methodism.* Peninsula Annual Conference of the Methodist Church, 1948.

Hayman, John C. *Rails Along the Chesapeake, A History of Railroading on the Delmarva Peninsula, 1827-1978.* Marvadel Publishers, 1979.

Houlihan, Daniel J. *Teackle—The Mansion and the Man.* 1976.

Jopp, Harold E., ed. *Rediscovery of the Eastern Shore: Delmarva Travelogues of the 1870s.* Wye Mills, Maryland: Chesapeake College Press, 1986.

Lancaster, Clay. "*The American Bungalow.*" In *Common Places—Readings in American Vernacular Architecture.* Edited by Dell Upton and John Michael Vlach. Athens and London: The University of Georgia Press, 1986.

Land, Aubrey C. *Colonial Maryland—A History.* Millwood, New York: KTO Press, 1981.

Land, Aubrey C.; Carr, Lois Green; Papenfuse, Edward C., ed. *Law, Society, and Politics in Early Maryland.* Baltimore and London: Johns Hopkins University Press, 1981.

Miller, Alice E. *Cecil County, Maryland, A Study in Local History.* Port Deposit, Maryland: Port Deposit Heritage, Inc., 1976.

Morris, Philip. *The Wadeing Place.* Princess Anne, Maryland: Marylander and Herald, Inc., 1974.

Newman, Harry Wright. *Maryland and the Confederacy.* Annapolis: published by the author, 1976.

Papenfuse, Edward C. *A New Guide to the Old Line State.* Baltimore: Johns Hopkins University Press, 1976.

Park, Helen. *A List of Architectural Books Available in America Before the Revolution.* Los Angeles: Hennessey & Ingalls, Inc., 1973.

Porter, Frank W. *Indians in Maryland and Delaware, A Critical Bibliography.* Bloomington and London: Indiana University Press, 1979.

Price, Jacob M. *France and the Chesapeake—A History of the French Tobacco Monopoly, 1674-1791, and of Its Relationship to the British and American Tobacco Trades.* Ann Arbor: The University of Michigan Press, 1973.

Ridout, Orlando V. "Re-Editing the Past: A Comparison of Surviving Documentary and Physical Evidence." Unpublished manuscript, 1982.

Scharf, John T. *History of Maryland, from the Earliest Period to the Present Day.* Hatboro, Pennsylvania: Tradition Press, 1967.

Scisco, Louis D. "Discovery of the Chesapeake Bay, 1525-1573." *Maryland Historical Magazine,* 40:277-86.

Shomette, Donald G. *Pirates on the Chesapeake: Being a True History of Pirates, Picaroons, and Raiders on the Chesapeake Bay 1610-1807.* Centreville, Maryland: Tidewater Publishers, 1985.

Smith, Daniel Blake. *Inside the Great House, Planter Life in Eighteenth Century Chesapeake Society.* Ithaca and London: Cornell University Press, 1980.

Steiner, Bernard C. *Descriptions of Maryland.* Johns Hopkins University Studies in Historical and Political Science 11-12. 1904; reprint ed., New York: Johnson Report, 1973.

Stiverson, Gregory. *A History of Deal Island, 1607-1877.* Annapolis: Hall of Records, Department of General Services, 1977.

Tate, Thad W., and Ammerman, David L. *The Chesapeake in the Seventeenth Century, Essays on Anglo-American Society.* Chapel Hill: University of North Carolina Press, 1979.

Tatham, William. *An Historical and Practical Essay of the Culture and Commerce of Tobacco,* 1799.

Taylor, Bayard. "Down on the Eastern Shore." *Harper's New Monthly Magazine*, Volume 43, Number 257 (October 1871) as cited in Harold D. Jopp, Jr. ed. *Rediscovery of the Eastern Shore: Delmarva Travelogues of the 1870s*. Wye Mills: Chesapeake College Press, 1986.

Tenth Census of the United States, 1880, Manufacturers Schedule, Maryland State Law Library, Annapolis.

Thirteenth Census of the United States, 1910, Population Schedule for Somerset County, Maryland. Wicomico County Free Library, Salisbury, Maryland.

Tilp, Frederick. *The Chesapeake Bay of Yore, Mainly about the Rowing and Sailing Craft*. Annapolis and Richmond: The Chesapeake Bay Foundation, Inc., 1982.

Torrence, Clayton. *Old Somerset on the Eastern Shore of Maryland, A Study of Foundations and Fathers*. 1935; reprint ed., Baltimore: Regional Publishing Company, 1973.

Truitt, Charles S. *Breadbasket of the Revolution, Delmarva's Eight Turbulent War Years*. Salisbury, Maryland: Historical Books, Inc., 1975.

The Voyages of Giovanni da Verrazano, 1524-1528. New Haven: Yale University Press, 1970.

Wallace, Adam. *The Parson of the Islands: A Biography of the Late Rev. Joshua Thomas with Sketches of Many of His Contemporaries and an Account of the Origin of Methodism on the Islands of the Chesapeake and Eastern Shores of Maryland and Virginia*. Philadelphia: Office of the Methodist Home Journal, 1872.

Walsh, Richard, and Fox, William Lloyd, ed. *Maryland—A History*. Baltimore: Maryland Historical Society, 1974.

Wenger, Mark R. "The Central Passage in Virginia: Evolution of an Eighteenth-Century Living Space." In *Perspectives in Vernacular Architecture, II*. Edited by Camille Wells Columbia, Missouri: University of Missouri Press, 1986.

Wennersten, John R. *The Oyster Wars of Chesapeake Bay*. Centreville, Maryland. Tidewater Publishers, 1981.

Wennersten, Ruth Ellen. "The Historical Evolution of a Black Land Grant College: The University of Maryland, Eastern Shore 1886-1970." Unpublished master's thesis, University of Maryland, 1976.

Whiffen, Marcus. *The Eighteenth-Century Houses of Williamsburg, A Study of Architecture and Building in the Colonial Capital of Virginia*. Williamsburg, Virginia: The Colonial Williamsburg Foundation, 1960.

Whitelaw, Ralph T. *Virginia's Eastern Shore, A History of Northampton and Accomack Counties*. 2 vols. 1951; reprint ed., Gloucester, Massachusettes: Peter Smith, 1968.

Whitney, Alethea Helen. *A History of the Manokin Presbyterian Church, Princess Anne, Maryland, 1672-1980*. Denton, Maryland: Baker Publishing Company, 1981.

Williams, William Henry. *The Garden of American Methodism, The Delmarva Peninsula, 1769-1820*. Wilmington, Delaware: Scholarly Resources, Inc., 1984.

Wilson, Woodrow T. *Crisfield, Maryland, 1876-1976*. Baltimore: Gateway Press, 1977.

Wilson, Woodrow T. *History of Crisfield and Surrounding Areas on Maryland's Eastern Shore*. Baltimore: Gateway Press, 1973.

Wilson, Woodrow T. *Quindocqua, Maryland —Indian Country*. Baltimore: Gateway Press, Inc., 1980.

Wise, Jennings Cropper, *Ye Kingdome of Accawmacke on the Eastern Shore of Virginia in the Seventeenth Century*. Richmond, Virginia: The Bell Book and Stationery Company, 1911.

Young, Ruth H. *Campus in Transition—University of Maryland Eastern Shore*. New York: Office of University Publications, 1981.

Glossary

ABACUS—the slab that forms the topmost part of the capital of a column, shaft, or chimney.

ACANTHUS—a plant with thick, fleshy scalloped leaves used on carved ornament, often found on Corinthian capitals.

APRON—a piece of exterior finished trim used under a windowsill that serves both as decoration and protection from the weather.

ARCADE—a line of arches and their supporting columns; also a covered walkway with a series of arched openings along one or both sides.

ARCHITRAVE—the lowest of the three main parts of the entablature; also, more loosely, the molded frame surrounding a door or window.

ASHLAR—hewn blocks of masonry wrought to even faces and square edges and laid in horizontal courses with vertical joints, in contrast to rubble or unhewn stone straight from the quarry. Ashlar construction was sometimes imitated in wood.

ASTRAGAL—a small molding circular in section, often decorated with a bead and reel enrichment.

BACKBAND—an outer molding used to enrich a window or door surround.

BALUSTER—a short post or pillar in a series supporting a rail or coping and thus forming a balustrade.

BALUSTRADE—the railing of a stair or porch that includes the balusters and the handrail.

BARGEBOARDS—projecting boards that are placed against the incline of the gable of a building and hide the ends of the horizontal roof timbers, sometimes decorated.

BAROQUE—of, pertaining to, or characteristic of a style in art and architecture developed in Europe from about 1550 to 1700 and typified by ornate scrolls, curves, and other symmetrical ornamentation.

BAT—a portion of a brick.

BATTEN—a wood strip placed over a flush seam between two adjacent boards.

BAY—a vertical division of the exterior or interior of a building marked not by walls but by fenestration, buttresses, units of vaulting, etc.; also, a projection of a room usually pierced with many windows.

BEAD—the convex, rounded end of a decorative member.

BED MOLDING—a small molding located directly under the cornice.

BELL CURVED ROOF—a roof that assumes the S-curve of a bell.

BELTCOURSE—a convention in masonry construction used to define floor levels; usually consisting of a horizontal line of projecting bricks, which are sometimes finished in a decorative manner.

BOARD-AND-BATTEN—a type of wooden siding composed of vertical boards nailed to the house frame with a narrow strip placed over each joint. The battens were sometimes molded.

BOLECTION MOLDING—a molding used to cover the joint between two adjacent surfaces with different levels.

BRACKETS—small supporting pieces of wood or stone often formed of scrolls or volutes to carry projecting weight.

BROACH SPIRE—a spire that is octagonal in plan, placed on a square tower and rising without an intermediate parapet.

BUNGALOW—a general term used to identify a popular late nineteenth and early twentieth century style of single story or story-and-a-half houses usually characterized by simple horizontal lines, wide projecting roofs, numerous windows and porches incorporated under the roof slopes.

CANTILEVERED JOISTS—beams that support a second floor and extend beyond the plane of the first floor wall.

CASEMENT WINDOW—a metal or timber window with the sash hung on the side of the jamb and opening outwards or inwards.

CHAIR RAIL—a wall molding fitted around a room to prevent chairs, when pushed back against the walls, from damaging the surface.

CHAMFER—the surface made when the sharp edge of a piece of wood, brick, or stone is cut away, usually at an angle of 45 degrees to the other two surfaces. It is called a hollow chamfer when the surface made is concave.

CHIMNEY BREAST—the brick or stone structure projecting in or out of a room and containing the flue.

CLAPBOARDS—narrow, hand-split boards usually measuring four to five feet; commonly used in the seventeenth and eighteenth centuries for sheathing walls and roofs as well as interior partitions.

COLLAR BEAM—a horizontal tension member in a pitched roof connecting paired rafters, generally found midway up the rafter. Its function is to keep the rafters from spreading due to the weight of the roof.

COLONIAL REVIVAL—a style of American architecture that generally dates between 1870 and 1920 and reflects a renewed interest in pre-Revolutionary designs.

COLONNADE—a series of columns placed at regular intervals. On the Eastern Shore of Maryland this term is often used to identify an open or enclosed passage that connected the main house with the kitchen.

COLONETTE—a small or slender column.

COMMON BOND—a method of laying brick courses whereby a single row of headers is alternated with three or more rows of stretchers.

CONSOLE—an ornamental bracket with a compound curved outline usually of greater height than projecting.

CORBEL—a projecting block, usually of brick or stone, supporting a beam or other horizontal member.

CORINTHIAN ORDER—an Athenian invention of the fifth century B.C. that accented the capital with two ranks of acanthus leaves. However, in later Roman practice the Corinthian entablature achieved a distinct identity. The Corinthian order, as employed from the sixteenth century onwards is based on Roman examples, notably the temples of Vespasian and Castor and Pollux in the Forum.

CORNICE—a horizontal, molded projection that crowns or completes a building or wall. Also, the uppermost part of the entablature.

COVE—a concave molding nearly a quarter circle in section.

CRESTING—an ornamental ridge on a wall or roof.

CROSSETTED SURROUND—window or door frames that have a stepped molding at the header level; Sometimes referred to as dog-eared surrounds.

CROWN MOLDING—the uppermost part of the cornice.

CUPOLA—a dome, especially a small dome on a circular, square, or polygonal base crowning a roof or turret.

CUSHION FRIEZE—a convex band below the cornice in the entablature.

CYMA—an S-shaped curve often used in molding profiles.

DAIRY—a small domestic outbuilding where milk was processed and stored.

DENTIL—a small square block used in rows to decorate cornices.

DIAMOND STACK CHIMNEYS—chimneys that are set diagonally on a base and when drawn in cross-section render a diamond shape.

DIAPER PATTERN—a surface decoration in brickwork, sometimes executed in glazed bricks, in the shape of repeating lozenges or squares.

DOG-LEG STAIR— a series of steps that consist of two flights at right angles with a half landing between them.

DORIC ORDER—separated into two distinct types, the Greek and Roman, which have a similar treatment of the frieze. The most distinguishing feature is that the Roman Doric order was set on a base while the Greek Doric order was not.

DORMER WINDOW—a window with vertical sides and front that has been introduced into the slope of a roof; Sometimes referred to in eighteenth century records as a dormant window.

DOUBLE PILE—a term used to refer to a house two rooms deep.

DRIP MOLDING—a projecting member of a cornice from which rain water drips and is thus prevented from running down the face of the wall below.

EGG-AND-DART MOLDING—an ovolo molding enriched with a pattern based on alternating egg shapes and arrow-heads.

ELL—a wing of a building at right angles to the main structure.

ENGLISH BOND—a method of laying brick courses whereby one course of headers is alternated with a single row of stretchers.

ENTABLATURE—the upper section of a classical order resting on the capital and including the architrave, frieze, and cornice.

FACADE—a face of a building; especially, a face that is given distinguishing treatment.

FANLIGHT—a window, sometimes semi-circular, over a door in Georgian and Federal style buildings, with radiating muntins to suggest a fan.

FASCIA—a flat horizontal band or member in a classical entablature.

FEDERAL STYLE—a style of American architecture that followed the Revolutionary War and generally dates from the early 1780s to the 1820s. Paralleling the neoclassical designs popularized in England by the Adam brothers, the American version of neoclassicism often included patriotic symbols that reflected the birth of a new nation.

FENESTRATION—the design and placement of windows in a building.

FINIAL—an ornament fixed to the peak of an arch or an arched structure.

FISH-SCALE SHINGLES—wooden shingles of varying shapes (rounded, pointed, etc.) used to sheath late nineteenth and early twentieth century houses in various patterns.

FLEMISH BOND—a method of laying brick whereby headers and stretchers alternate in each course horizontially as well as vertically. Sometimes the header bricks have a bluish-green glazing that renders an elaborate checkerboard pattern.

FLUTING—a series of parallel concave gouges used as a decorative technique. This type of decoration contrasts with reeding.

FOREBAY—the projecting section of a barn that extends beyond a lower level.

FRIEZE—a plain or decorated horizontal part of an entablature between the architrave and the cornice.

GABLE—the triangular wall section at the ends of a pitched roof.

GABLE-ON-HIP-ROOF—a complex roof shape whereby the four sloping sides of a hip roof are surmounted by a shallower pitched gable roof.

GAMBREL—a ridged roof with two slopes on the front and back, the lower with a steeper pitch.

GAUGING—brick selected for color and rubbed to a smooth surface on all faces; used for decorative purposes.

GEORGIAN—a general term used to identify the prevailing style of eighteenth century architecture in Great Britain and the North American colonies. The style, named after George I, George II, and George III, rulers of England from 1714 to 1820, was derived from classical, Renaissance, and Baroque stylistic forms.

GLAZED CLOSET—a cupboard or closet that has doors partially made of glass panes.

GLAZED HEADER BRICK—the butt end of a brick that has received a glossy bluish-green finish used in decorative masonry patterns.

GOTHIC ARCH—the pointed arch popularly used in late medieval and Gothic Revival architecture.

GOTHIC REVIVAL—one of the imitative styles of medieval architecture popularized during the mid-nineteenth century.

GRAINING—a painterly technique of imitating more expensive woods on inferior surfaces; often carried out to the point of abstraction.

GRANARY—a farm building in which various grains are stored.

GREEK KEY—a geometric ornament of horizontal and vertical straight lines repeated to form a band in the stylized shape of a key.

GREEK REVIVAL—a mid-nineteenth century style that closely followed architectural forms and details common to buildings of ancient Greece.

GUANO—a substance composed chiefly of the dung of sea birds or bats, accumulated along certain coastal areas or in caves and used as fertilizer.

GUILLOCHE—a pattern of interlacing bands forming a plait and used as an enrichment on a molding.

HAMMERBEAM ROOF TRUSS—a horizontal bracket usually supported by braces and projecting at the wall plate level to carry arched braces and struts.

HATCHMENT—a panel bearing the coat of arms of a family.

HEADER—a brick laid across rather than parallel with the wall and sometimes glazed for a decorative pattern.

HIPPED ROOF—a roof that has four sloping sides usually of equal angle.

HYPHEN—the intermediate section of a house that connects the main block with an adjacent wing.

IONIC ORDER—originating in Asia Minor about the middle of the sixth century, B.C., the order is distinguished in Roman examples by the voluted capital and dentils in the cornice.

JACK ARCH—a masonry arch of brick or stone where the individual bricks or stones are set at an angle.

JERKINHEAD ROOF—a gable roof marked by clipped outer ends; also known as a clipped gable roof.

JOISTS—equally dimensioned timbers ranged parallel wall to wall or resting on girders to support the floor above.

KEYSTONE—the wedge-shaped stone in the center of an arch.

KICKED EAVES—a feature often associated with seventeenth and early eighteenth century gable roofs where the pitch of the roof just above the eaves is slightly shallower than that of the main slope.

LAMB'S-TONGUE STOP—a decorative terminus to a chamfer in the shape of an S-curve.

LANCET WINDOW—a slender pointed arch window popularly used in Gothic Revival buildings.

LANTERN—a cupola or small structure on a roof, with glazed openings or windows.

LATH—a thin strip of wood usually nailed horizontally in narrowly spaced rows to receive an application of plaster.

LINTEL—the horizontal top piece of a window or door opening.

LOUVERS—boards or slats—sometimes movable—set at an angle in an opening that allow air circulation and prevent water penetration.

LUNETTE—a crescent-shaped or semi-circular space, usually over a door or window, that may contain another window, a sculpture, or a mural.

MANSARD ROOF—a roof with two slopes on all sides, the lower one being very steep and the upper one nearly flat.

MANTEL—an ornamental facing around a fireplace.

MARBLEIZING—a painterly technique of imitating more expensive materials such as marble on inferior surfaces.

MASONRY—a form of construction involving the joining of stone, brick, or block and resulting in finished paving, walls, veneer, or vaulting.

MAULED RAILS—long riven timbers that have been split with a maul and wedge.

MEDALLION—a piece of ornamental trim, usually oval or square, which is carved or molded, often representing an object in relief.

MITRE—to bevel ends of a molding or timber to meet at an angle.

MODILLION—a small console or bracket applied to the soffit of a cornice.

MOLDED BRICK—a decorative, specially shaped brick.

MOLDING—a piece of decorative trim used to cover joints and introduce varieties of contour into edges or surfaces.

MORTISE-AND-TENON JOINT—a tightly crafted joint consisting of a cavity that is prepared to receive a similarly shaped projection (tenon) of another piece with an intersecting pin to hold the two members together.

MUNTIN—a light vertical or horizontal framing member to hold panes in a door or window.

NECESSARY—a privy.

NECKING—the horizontal molding that separates the shaft of a column from the capital. In chimney construction, it is the plaster or stuccoed band that separates the chimney shaft from the corbelled cap.

NEOCLASSICAL—a revival of classical aesthetics and forms in art, architecture, music, and literature.

NEWEL POST—an ornamental post that supports the railing at the head or foot of a staircase.

NOSING—that part of the tread of a stair that projects over the riser.

OGEE—a double curve with the shape of an elongated S.

OPEN-STRING—in stair construction, when the end carriage or stringer has its upper edge cut out to fit the steps.

ORDER—In classical architecture, a column with base (usually), shaft, capital, and entablature, decorated and proportioned according to one of the accepted modes—Doric, Tuscan, Ionic, Corinthian, or Composite.

OVOLO—a rounded convex molding, often a quarter section of a circle.

PALED GARDENS—usually a small garden plot surrounded by a short fence of pointed stakes or boards.

PALLADIAN—in reference to the mid-nineteenth century architectural style derived from the designs of the Renaissance architect Andrea Palladio (1518-1580).

PANEL—1. a flat surface recessed below the surrounding area, set off by molding and held in place by rails and stiles. 2. a sheet material used as a wall covering.

PARAPET—a low wall, sometimes battlemented, placed to protect any spot where there is a sudden drop, for example, at the edge of a bridge, quay, or house top.

PARTY WALL—a common wall that separates two adjoining buildings.

PAVER—a tile, stone, or brick used as a floor, deck, or ground surfacing material.

PAVILION—a projecting surface on a facade to provide architectural emphasis.

PEDIMENT—a crowning feature of porticos, pavilions, doorways, or other architectural features, usually of low triangular form, sometimes broken in the center to receive an ornament.

PENT ROOF—a small, shed-like roof without upright supports that usually butts the house above the first floor windows.

PIER—a squarish supporting member usually of wood, brick, or concrete block.

PILASTER—a flat, rectangular column with a capital and base set into a wall as an ornamental motif.

PLATE—in frame construction, a horizontal member capping the exterior wall studs upon which the roof rafters rest.

PLINTH—the lowest part of a base under the column or door frame.

PORTE-COCHERE—a covered entryway or porch large enough to accommodate vehicles.

PORTICO—a roofed space, open or partially enclosed, forming the entrance and centerpiece of the facade of a temple, house, or church, often with columns and a pediment.

PURLIN—a horizontal timber laid parallel with the wall plate and the ridge beam approximately halfway up the slope of the roof, resting on the principal rafters and forming an intermediate support for the common rafters.

PYRAMIDAL ROOF—a roof that takes the form of a pyramid.

QUEEN ANNE STYLE—an eclectic late nineteenth century style characterized by irregularity of plan and massing and a wide variety of surface textures.

QUOINS—the dressed stones at the corners of buildings, usually laid so their faces are alternately large and small.

RAFTERS—structural timbers rising from the eaves to the ridge and supporting the roof covering.

RAISED PANELING—wooden panels set within a joined framework for doors or a wall finish.

RAKE—the slope or pitch of a roof.

RANCH STYLE—popular mid-twentieth century style of domestic housing that stemmed from the single story, horizontal designs of Prairie School architecture introduced by Frank Lloyd Wright.

REEDING—an ornamental style of finish characterized by carved or molded half-round shapes that have the appearance of reeds lying side by side. This type of decoration contrasts with fluting.

RETURN—a piece of trim that finishes the side projection for a stair tread, mantel, or cornice.

REVEAL—the inside face of a doorway often treated with raised or flush panels.

RIDGEPOLE—the uppermost structural member of a roof where the rafter ends meet; also called a ridgeboard, ridge piece, ridge plate, ridge beam, or ridge rafter.

RISER—the upright surface of a stair between two treads.

ROCOCO—an ornate architectural style marking the closing years of the Baroque period of the late seventeenth century. Particularly popular in France and Austria, the exuberant style was known for its light colors and finely detailed features.

ROMAN BRICK—a specialized brick size normally longer and thinner than standard brick.

ROMANESQUE REVIVAL—a late nineteenth century revival of pre-Gothic architecture featuring heavy, rock-faced stone or brick walls and round-arched windows and doors.

ROPE MOLDING—a carved molding that assumed the shape of a stylized rope; usually incorporated into elaborate cornice profiles.

ROUND-BUTT SHINGLES—wooden shingles that were cut with a circular bottom edge that created a distinctive pattern when applied.

ROWLOCK ROW—a row of bricks laid on the narrow, long edge with the butt end exposed.

RUBBED BRICK—a sanded finish of red brick that rendered a brighter color whereby door and window openings or other features could be highlighted against the regular wall surface.

RUSTICATION—masonry finish where the joints between the blocks are deliberately emphasized or where the outer surface of the block is left rough or worked in such a way as to give a textural effect.

SASH—any framework of a window; may be movable or fixed; may slide in a vertical plane or be fixed.

SEGMENTAL ARCH—an arch formed of a segment of a circle or ellipse.

SHED ROOF—a single pitched roof often used for dormers and simple kitchen additions.

SHINGLE STYLE—the American term for the Domestic Revival of the 1870s and 1880s, influenced initially by Norman Shaw.

SHIPLAP SIDING—closely fit flush weatherboard siding. When installed, the angled edge of one board is nestled next to the angled edge of the adjacent board.

SHOULDER—the sloping shelf created on the side of a masonry chimney where the width of the stack abruptly changes.

SIDELIGHT—a framed area of fixed glass alongside a door or window opening.

SILL—1. a horizontal timber that rests on the foundation at the bottom of the frame of a wood structure. 2. the horizontal bottom member of a window or door frame.

SMOKEHOUSE—a dependency where meat was cured by means of dense smoke and then sometimes stored.

SOFFIT—the surface of the underside of an architectural feature.

SOLDIER ROW—a row of bricks set on end with the narrow face exposed.

SPANDREL—the triangular space between the curves of two arches.

SPINDLE—a turned baluster or short turned decorative member in architectural ornament.

SPLINE—a thin piece of material set in a notch or groove in the edge of adjacent members to form a stronger joint, sometimes seen in floor construction.

STANDING SEAM—a type of metal roof construction where the seams of the metal sheets are folded up and then over on themselves for a waterproof joint. The joints remain perpendicular to the plane of the roof slope.

STICK-BUILT—long-standing tradition in frame construction where the house is erected by individually nailed framing members.

STOOP—a small porch, usually with several steps, at the entry of a building.

STRETCHER—the long face of a brick when laid horizontally.

STRING COURSE—a horizontal band or molding set in the face of a building as a design element; also beltcourse.

STRINGER—a long, heavy horizontal timber used for any of several connective or supportive purposes; in stair construction, the outside diagonal timber that supports the stair. The outside face of the stringer is a surface that is often decorated.

SUMMER KITCHEN—an outbuilding used in the hotter months of the year for the principal cooking services of a household; sometimes attached to the main house by a colonnade or breezeway.

SURROUND—the border or casing that frames a window or door; also architrave.

SWAG—a molding in the form of a garland or festoon representing flowers, fruit, or fabric.

TABLE MARKER—a large flat engraved stone marking a grave, usually of marble and supported by a brick foundation.

TANNERY—the site where rawhides are transformed into leather.

TANYARD—the section in a tannery where the tanning vats are located.

T-SHAPED CHIMNEYS—a chimney stack that contains three flues and follows the shape of a T in cross-section.

TELESCOPE HOUSE—a regional term used on the Eastern Shore of Maryland and Virginia to identify houses that were built with a stepped profile, usually, but not in all cases, decreasing in height from the main block to the kitchen.

TENON—a narrow extension on a wood member that is inserted in a cavity or mortise to form a secure joint.

TIE BEAM—a horizontal beam that joins the front and rear walls.

TILTED FALSE PLATE—a beam that is rectangular or square in section set diagonally into the outer edge of the tie beams to serve as a rest for a series of notched rafter feet that are secured by nail or peg; largely used during the seventeenth and eighteenth centuries and infrequently after 1800.

TRANSOM—a narrow, horizontal window over a door.

TREAD—the horizontal surface of a step.

TRIPLE-RUN-STAIR—a stair with three flights of steps.

TRUNNEL—a wooden peg that swells when wet; used to fasten timbers.

TURRET—a small ornamented tower or tower-shaped projection on a building.

TUSCAN ORDER—the simplest order, supposedly derived from Etruscan temples; recognized easily by a smooth column surface and largely undecorated entablature.

TYMPANUM—the recessed, ornamental space or panel enclosed by cornices of a triangular pediment.

VALLEY—the trough formed when two sloping, non-parallel planes of a roof meet.

VERNACULAR ARCHITECTURE—a broad multidisciplinary field of study centering around regional every day environments and their components. Vernacular buildings are viewed as those structures built in response to the everyday needs of a certain populace without the professional assistance of trained architects. Personal priorities and technologies change with time, and as a result, vernacular buildings are not just limited to historic periods.

VICTORIAN—a general term used to identify buildings pertaining to or dating from the period of Queen Victoria's reign over Great Britain and Ireland (1837-1901).

VOLUTE—an ornamental spiral found on Ionic, Corinthian, or Composite capitals.

VOUSSOIR—one of the wedge-like stones that form an arch; the middle one is called a keystone.

WAINSCOT—a facing or paneling, usually of wood, applied to the lower portion of a wall.

WATER TABLE—a projecting ledge, or molded base, along the side of a building designed to throw off rain water.

WEATHERBOARDS—overlapping horizontal boards covering a timber frame wall. These sawn boards are wedge-shaped in section, and the upper edge is thinner. It was a standard practice to finish the lower edge of the board with a decorative bead.

WEATHERING—the sloping portion of a chimney stack that carries the larger dimension of the base to the smaller dimension above. The surface is usually covered with brick, though in some cases it is covered with clay, tile, or stone.

WINDER STAIR—a series of triangular pie-shaped steps that provide access to an upper level in a confined space.

WROUGHT NAIL—an iron nail made by a blacksmith with a shaft that tapers on four sides and a hand-hammered head; also called a rosehead. These nails date primarily from before 1810.

YEOMAN—an independent farmer, especially a member of a former class of small free-holding farmers in England.

Donors

The Somerset County Historical Trust, Inc., wishes to acknowledge its appreciation to the following people, organizations, and businesses for their financial assistance of its preservation-related activities in Somerset County. In addition to this list the Trust recognizes also the countless others who have shown continued interest and support by attending various special events.

Mark Adams
E. Stanton Adkins
Mr. and Mrs. Freedom H. Ainsworth
Mrs. John C. Anderson
Clara Lankford Annan
Mrs. Joseph F. Baugher
Mrs. L. Creston Beauchamp
Becker/Morgan Architects
Beitzel Cabinet & Millwork Co.
Mr. and Mrs. Rudolph Beitzel
Dr. and Mrs. Gregorio M. Belloso
Mr. and Mrs. Thomas M. Bennett
Mr. and Mrs. George B. Benson
Stanley F. Benson
Mr. and Mrs. John L. Bond
Miss Briget Bradshaw
Mr. and Mrs. Robert Brightman
Mr. and Mrs. James Britton
Mr. and Mrs. Howard S. Buhl
C &P Telephone Company
Mr. and Mrs. Omar Carey
Mr. and Mrs. Robert Chamberlin
Mr. and Mrs. Robert Chamberlin, Sr.
Charles C. Chervenie
Mr. and Mrs. Richard M. Cooley
Mrs. Mark Cooper
Mr. and Mrs. Richard Cooper
Joseph W. Coulbourn
Mr. and Mrs. Wilbert J. Coulbourn
Dr. and Mrs. Frank Craig
Mr. and Mrs. Robert F. Creed
Richard Crumbacker
Mrs. Reginald Cullen
Mr. and Mrs. Leo Dahlmanns
Dr. and Mrs. Basil Darwent
Mr. and Mrs. Michael Harrison Day
Mrs. Eugene Delgass
Theodore T. Dorman
Virginia Corbin Dorman
The Honorable and Mrs. E. McMaster Duer
Mr. and Mrs. Joseph Eberly
Mr. and Mrs. Robert Erickson
Fairmount Academy Historical Association
William Tarun Fehsenfeld
George B. Fitzgerald
Mr. and Mrs. William B. Fontaine
Mr. and Mrs. Fred T. Ford, Jr.
Mrs. Ralph French
Dr. and Mrs. James P. Gallaher
Mrs. W. Irving Galliher
Mr. and Mrs. Thomas S. George, Jr.
David Germanowski

Dr. William Gill
Grace Episcopal Church
Mr. and Mrs. David Graham
Mr. and Mrs. Wilson O. Green
Kent Griffith
Mrs. B. K. Haffner
Mr. and Mrs. John S. Haffner
Dr. and Mrs. John Haines
Miss Elizabeth W. Hall
Richard Hall
Mr. and Mrs. John Handy, Jr.
Happy Jack Pancake House
Mr. and Mrs. Edison Hawkins
Mr. and Mrs. R. Patrick Hayman
Joe Hayman and Sons
Mr. and Mrs. Sidney W. Hayman
Henderson-Elliot & Pryor Insurance Agency, Inc.
Hinman Funeral Home
Mr. and Mrs. James L. Hinman, Sr.
Elizabeth R. Holland
Stanley Alan Hurwitz
John H. Jeffries
Meredith Johnson
Robert Johnson
Ruth K. Keeler
Wilmer O. Lankford
Mr. and Mrs. Thomas Larsen
Mr. and Mrs. Francis P. Lawrence
Mr. and Mrs. Banes Layfield
Mr. and Mrs. Clinton Lokey
Mr. and Mrs. Edwin Long
Mr. and Mrs. William B. Long
Lexine Davis Lowe
Mr. and Mrs. Donald Mabe
Martin Fish Company, Inc.
Maryland Heritage Committee
Maryland Historical Trust, Department of Housing and Community Development
Maryland House and Garden Pilgrimage
Maryland Humanities Council
Maryland Office of Tourism
Maryland State Archives
Maryland State Arts Council
Maryland State Bank
Charles Massey
Mrs. Harry Miller
King Miller, Jr.
Mr. and Mrs. Stephen F. Monick
Olsen's Furniture & Antiques
Oliver Morrell
Mrs. William Morsell, Jr.
Mrs. William Moton
Mr. and Mrs. Thomas Nicholson
Mr. and Mrs. Charles Nittel
James Gorham Oglesby
Mr. and Mrs. Harry Palmer
Peninsula Bank
Ida S. Phillips
I. Theodore Phoebus
Mr. and Mrs. Charles B. Pinto
Mr. and Mrs. Elmo Powell, Jr.
William E. Powell

Princess Anne Business & Professional Women's Club
Princess Anne Lioness Club
Rehobeth Ruritan Club
Mrs. Charles Richards
Peter E. Richardson
Mr. and Mrs. Hollis Riggin
Mr. and Mrs. Gary Rinker
Mrs. William Ruark
Mr. and Mrs. Gene Russell
St. Andrews Episcopal Church Women
Miss Dorothy Scott
Mr. and Mrs. W. Marshall Scott
Mr. and Mrs. Robert F. Sharpe, Jr.
Dr. and Mrs. Ritchie Shoemaker
Shoreland Club
Joseph F. Shores
The Honorable Lloyd L. Simpkins
Ms. Mildred Skirven
Mr. and Mrs. Harrell Smith
Mrs. Marcella W. Smith
Mr. and Mrs. Richard P. Smith
Somerset County Arts Council
Somerset County Bicentennial Constitution Committee
Somerset County Commissioners
Somerset County Historical Society
Somerset Landscape Company
Somerset Ruritan Club
Mr. and Mrs. Randolph Stadler
Rebecca Stadler
Stewart, Poe & Oglesby
Mr. and Mrs. Robert Street
Tawes Insurance
J. Edwin Tawes
Mr. and Mrs. Phillip W. Tawes
Mr. and Mrs. Reed Taylor
Jerry E. Tiller
Mr. and Mrs. Edward Todd
Paul B. Touart
Mr. and Mrs. Robert L. Touart
Town of Princess Anne
Mrs. Paul Towson
Mr. and Mrs. Paul V. Twining, Jr.
Captain Alan Tyler
Mr. and Mrs. William Vessey
Mrs. Charles Wainwright
Dr. and Mrs. J. Richard Warbasse
Mr. and Mrs. E. Wallace Warwick
Dr. and Mrs. Wilcomb Washburn
Mr. and Mrs. Frederick Waters
Levin L. Waters
Mr. and Mrs. James Watts
Mr. and Mrs. W. Miller White
Dr. Alethea Whitney
Mrs. Anne T. Whittington
Wicomico Garden Club
Logan C. Widdowson
Mr. and Mrs. Guy Windsor
Mr. and Mrs. Steven G. Woodward
Mr. and Mrs. Merton S. Yerger
Mr. and Mrs. Howard F. Yerges

Historic Sites Inventory Index

S-304 Jersey Island packing house, Crisfield
S-305 St. Paul's M. E. Church, Crisfield
S-306 Crisfield Arcade, Crisfield
S-307 U. S. Post Office, Crisfield
S-308 Gibson Commercial Block, Crisfield
S-309 Nora S. Davis Shoppe, Crisfield
S-310 Peyton pharmacy building, Crisfield
S-311 Bank of Crisfield, Crisfield
S-312 W. E. Ward & Bro. Store, Crisfield
S-313 J. W. Riggin Furniture Store, Crisfield
S-314 Henry Coulbourn house, Crisfield
S-315 Whittington-Long house, Crisfield
S-316 Dr. Somers house, Crisfield
S-317 L. E. P. Dennis house, Crisfield
S-318 Pauline Crockett house, Crisfield
S-319 Immanuel United Methodist Church Crisfield
S-320 Samuel Maddrix Toy Shop, Crisfield
S-321 Whittington house, Crisfield
S-322 House, Crisfield
S-323 Orrie Lee Tawes, Sr. house, Crisfield
S-324 Albert Sterling house, Crisfield
S-325 McCready house, Crisfield
S-326 Chesapeake Masonic Lodge 147, Crisfield
S-327 Captain Leonard S. Tawes house, Crisfield
S-328 Sterling house and cemetery
S-329 Byrd homestead
S-330 Bennet's Memorial Church
S-331 House, Crisfield vicinity
S-332 House, Crisfield vicinity
S-333 Ewell Survey District
S-334 Tylerton Survey District
S-335 Rhodes Point Survey District
S-336 Jones Choice
S-337 Samuel Miles house
S-338 Adams farm
S-339 Holly Grove farmhouse
S-340 Cedar Lane farm
S-341 King's Creek Canning Company
S-342 Sandusky farm
S-343 Webley
S-344 Covington house
S-345 Richardson farm
S-346 St. Mark's M. E. Church

S-347 Norman Pusey farm
S-348 Thornton
S-349 John Myers house
S-350 W. J. Shockley farm
S-351 Milbert Shockley farm
S-352 LaVorgna house
S-353 Malchow house
S-354 William Martin house
S-355 All Saints Church at Monie
S-356 Grace M. E. Church
S-357 James Phillips house
S-358 Bozman-Fitzgerald house
S-359 St. James M. E. Church
S-360 St. James Church Hall
S-361 St. Stephens Survey District
S-362 St. Stephens Church
S-363 Rock Creek M. E. Church
S-364 Oriole Survey District
S-365 St. John's M. E. Church, Deal Island
S-366 Deal Island Bank, Deal Island
S-367 Lorena Webster house, Deal Island
S-368 Deal Island Barber Shop, Deal Island
S-369 Isabella White house, Deal Island
S-370 Laura Bozman house, Deal Island
S-371 Deal Island Survey District
S-372 John Wesley M. E. Church, Deal Island
S-373 Brown sail loft, Wenona
S-374 Vetra store, Wenona
S-375 Wenona Survey District
S-376 Grace Protestant Episcopal Church
S-377 John Wesley Methodist Church, Mt. Vernon
S-378 John Stewart store, Princess Anne
S-379 Metropolitan Church, Princess Anne
S-380 Hampden Dashiell house, Princess Anne
S-381 Somerset County Jail, Princess Anne
S-382 Election House, Princess Anne
S-383 John W. Crisfield house, Princess Anne
S-384 Gordon Tull house, Princess Anne
S-385 Anna L. Haines house, Princess Anne
S-386 Princess Anne Fire Department, Princess Anne
S-387 Theodore F. Lankford house, Princess Anne

S-388 Beckford Avenue tenant houses, Princess Anne
S-389 Joseph Brinkley house, Princess Anne
S-390 Henry L. Brittingham house, Princess Anne
S-391 Banes Layfield house, Princess Anne
S-392 Thomas H. Bock house, Princess Anne
S-393 Edmund D. Young house, Princess Anne
S-394 Emma A. Lankford house, Princess Anne
S-395 Albert E. Krause house, Princess Anne
S-396 Daniel Collins house, Princess Anne
S-397 Old Marylander and Herald office, Princess Anne
S-398 Glanville's Lott
S-399 Maplegrove
S-400 Gunby-Lankford house
S-401 Happy Hollow farmhouse
S-402 Melody Manor
S-403 Tull farm
S-404 Foggy Bottom
S-405 Mt. Zion Memorial Church
S-406 Arcadia
S-407 Bloomsbury
S-408 Catalpa farm
S-409 Historic Churches of Somerset County
S-410 Antioch United Methodist Church, Princess Anne
S-411 St. Paul's M. E. Church, Mt. Vernon
S-412 Old Washington Academy
S-413 Pinto farm
S-414 Old Washington High School, Princess Anne
S-415 Boxwood Garden, Princess Anne
S-416 Dorman's Conclusion
S-417 Julia Humphreys house, Princess Anne
S-418 John Holland house, Princess Anne
S-419 Old Gulf station, Princess Anne
S-420 Levin T. H. Irving house, Princess Anne

Index